THE OXFORD HANDBOOK

SONDHEIM STUDIES

THE OXFORD HANDBOOK OF

SONDHEIM STUDIES

Edited by
ROBERT GORDON

OXFORD
UNIVERSITY PRESS

OXFORD
UNIVERSITY PRESS

Oxford University Press is a department of the University of Oxford.
It furthers the University's objective of excellence in research, scholarship,
and education by publishing worldwide.

Oxford   New York
Auckland   Cape Town   Dar es Salaam   Hong Kong   Karachi
Kuala Lumpur   Madrid   Melbourne   Mexico City   Nairobi
New Delhi   Shanghai   Taipei   Toronto

With offices in
Argentina   Austria   Brazil   Chile   Czech Republic   France   Greece
Guatemala   Hungary   Italy   Japan   Poland   Portugal   Singapore
South Korea   Switzerland   Thailand   Turkey   Ukraine   Vietnam

Oxford is a registered trade mark of Oxford University Press
in the UK and certain other countries.

Published in the United States of America by
Oxford University Press
198 Madison Avenue, New York, NY 10016

© Oxford University Press 2014

First issued as an Oxford University Press paperback, 2015.

Library of Congress Cataloging-in-Publication Data
The Oxford handbook of Sondheim studies/edited by Robert Gordon.
pages ; cm
Includes bibliographical references and index.
ISBN 978-0-19-539137-4 (hardcover : alk. paper); 978-0-19-025819-1 (paperback : alk. paper)
1. Sondheim, Stephen—Criticism and interpretation.
I. Gordon, Robert, 1951 November 28- editor
ML410.S6872O94 2014
782.1'4092—dc23
2013036906

For my Dad,
Whose love of jazz
First ignited my life-long interest in Broadway musicals

CONTENTS

PART III SONDHEIM IN PERFORMANCE

PART IV SONDHEIM ACROSS THE MEDIA

LIST OF ILLUSTRATIONS

ACKNOWLEDGMENTS

I wish to thank my Commissioning Editor, Norm Hirschy, for his warm and enthusiastic support of this volume and his patience throughout the long period of its gestation. My gratitude is also due to the Production Editor at OUP, Lisbeth Redfield, and the Copy Editor, Michael Durnin, for their generous and painstaking efforts in guiding me through the technical phase of the book's production. My thanks also to the staff at Photofest who were extremely helpful in my search for appropriate photographic images.

The initial impetus to produce this handbook came as a result of the conference, Sondheim: Collaborator and Auteur, which I organized at the suggestion of Olaf Jubin at Goldsmiths, University of London, in November 2005; Dr Jubin's advice and help throughout the editorial process have been invaluable.

My grateful acknowledgment goes to the following copyright holders for permission to use photographs:

Photofest: 1.1, 1.2, 4.1, 5.1, 7.1, 8.1, 8.2, 15.1, 16.1, 16.2, 16.3, 17.1, 17.2, 18.1. 18.2, 23.1, 24.2, 25.1, 26.1, 27.1

UK TIPS Images: 4.2

Joan Marcus: 2.1, 6.2, 16.4, 19.1

Tristram Kenton: 1.3, 7.2, 13.3,

Richard Hein: 10.1

Catherine Ashmore: 10.2, 13.1, 21.1, 22.1, 26.2

New York Public Library, Martha Swope Collection: 6.1, 11.1, 11.2

Michael Le Poer Trench: 13.2

Arenapal: 13.3, 13.4, 14.1

Paul Kolnik: 20.1

Eliot Elisofon, Getty Images: 24.1

Kip Poliakoff: 12.1

Notes on Contributors

Stephen Banfield is a musicologist and Emeritus Professor at the University of Bristol. His books include *Sondheim's Broadway Musicals*, winner of the Kurt Weill and Lowens awards; *Jerome Kern*, and several on British art music of the earlier twentieth century. Future publications will include social histories of music in an English region (the West Country) and in the British Empire, and a study of classical music's propensity to depict soundscapes.

Geoffrey Block Distinguished Professor of Music History at the University of Puget Sound, is the author of *Enchanted Evenings: The Broadway Musical from Show Boat to Sondheim and Lloyd Webber, Richard Rodgers*, and *Ives: A Concordat Sonata*, the editor of *The Richard Rodgers Reader*, and coeditor (with J. Peter Burkholder) of *Charles Ives and the Classical Tradition*. He is also General Editor of Yale Broadway Masters and Series Editor for Oxford's Broadway Legacies.

Andrew Buchman is a composer, who teaches in interdisciplinary curricula at the Evergreen State College in Olympia, Washington. As a scholar of American musical theatre, he has contributed to the *Oxford Dictionary of American Biography* and written a number of papers for regional and national conferences on works by Stephen Sondheim, including an exploration of the musical sources for "Please Hello" from *Pacific Overtures*, and a comparison of stage and screen versions of *Sweeney Todd*.

Bud Coleman is a Professor at the University of Colorado Boulder and Chair of the Department of Theatre and Dance. A former dancer with Les Ballets Trockadero de Monte Carlo, Fort Worth Ballet, Kinesis, and Ballet Austin, he has directed and choreographed over three dozen musicals, including *Company* in Vladivostok, Russia, under the auspices of the US State Department Cultural Envoy program. He was a Fulbright Lecturer at Waseda University and Kyoritsu Women's University in Tokyo. Bud's essays have been published by Cambridge University Press, St. James Press, Theatre History Studies: Choreography and Dance. With Judith Sebesta he edited *Women in American Musical Theatre*.

Garrett Eisler is Assistant Professor of Theatre Studies at Ithaca College. He earned a PhD in Theatre at the City University of New York Graduate Center, as well as an MA in English from NYU and an MFA in Directing from Boston University. In addition to essays for several academic journals (including *Studies in Musical Theatre*) he has contributed chapters to the *Best Plays Theatre Yearbook* series (Limelight Editions) and written on contemporary theatre for the *Village Voice, Time Out New York*, and *American Theatre* magazine.

Paul Filmer is Honorary Research Fellow in Sociology at Goldsmiths College, University of London. He has published work in sociological theory, methods of sociological research, and sociology of culture, including specific studies in sociology of art, literature, music, dance and popular culture. His work on sociology of the musical includes studies of both musical theatre and film musicals.

Ben Francis has written book and lyrics for two musicals: *Letter From An Unknown Woman* and *The Dancing Chef*. He has provided sketches for the long-running BBC radio comedy programme *The News Huddlines*, and his book *Christopher Hampton: Dramatic Ironist* was published by Amber Lane Press. He is currently completing a PhD on Stephen Sondheim at Goldsmiths, University of London.

Joanne Gordon Artistic Director of California Repertory Company and Chair of the Department of Theatre Arts at California State University Long Beach, is an award-winning director whose accolades include five Drama-Logue Awards, a Los Angeles Critics Choice Award and being named "Best of the Year" by the *Los Angeles Times*. As an internationally renowned Sondheim scholar, she has directed a number of this extraordinary artist's works worldwide, including the first Chinese-language production of *West Side Story* in Beijing. Published work includes *Stephen Sondheim: A Casebook*; frequent contributions to *The Sondheim Review* and *Art Isn't Easy: The Theater of Stephen Sondheim*.

Robert Gordon is Professor of Theatre and Performance and Director of the Pinter Centre for Performance and Creative Writing at Goldsmiths, University of London. Publications include essays on postwar British theater, South African theater, Shakespeare, Wilde, Pirandello, and *Stoppard: Text and Performance*. His xperience as actor and director informs the survey of modern acting theory in *The Purpose of Playing*. *Harold Pinter: The Theatre of Power* was published in 2012 and his production *Pinter: In Other Rooms* toured to Berlin, Prague, Budapest, and Thessaloniki in 2011. He recently directed Kander and Ebb's *Steel Pier* in Brno, Czech Republic, and he is coediting the *Oxford Handbook of the British Musical*.

Daniel Gundlach is a counter tenor who has performed internationally with L'Opera de Paris, the Théâtre du Châtelet, the International Bach-Akademie Stuttgart, Les Musiciens du Louvre Grenoble, and throughout the United States and Canada. Currently based in Berlin where he maintains an active performing schedule, he studied musicology at the University of Illinois Urbana, where he received his master's degree in vocal accompanying under John Wustman (www.danielgundlach.com).

Roger Hickman is the Director of Musicology at the Cole Conservatory of Music at CSU Long Beach. Among his publications are the textbook *Reel Music: Exploring 100 Years of Film Music*, the monograph *Miklós Rózsa's Ben-Hur: A Film Score Guide*, the commentaries for the *Norton Scores*, and several articles for *The New Grove Dictionary of*

Music. Active as a performer, he is the music director of the Long Beach Ballet Company and the Four Seasons Youth Orchestras, and he has guest conducted a number of symphonies, including those from San Diego, Indianapolis, and Dallas.

Olaf Jubin is Reader in Media Studies and Musical Theatre at Regent's University London and a Visiting Lecturer on the MA in Musical Theatre at Goldsmiths, University of London. He obtained his PhD from the Ruhr-Universität Bochum, Germany and has written and coedited several books, among them a study of the German dubbing and subtitling of Hollywood musicals and a comparative analysis of reviews of the musicals of Sondheim and Lloyd Webber. He has published essays on the reception of Sondheim in Germany and on the London version of *Follies*, and is coediting the *Oxford Handbook of the British Musical*.

Raymond Knapp Professor of Musicology at UCLA, has authored *The American Musical and the Formation of National Identity* (winner of the George Jean Nathan Award for Dramatic Criticism) and *The American Musical and the Performance of Personal Identity*, along with many articles on related subjects, and has coedited *The Oxford Handbook of the American Musical*. His other books include *Symphonic Metamorphoses: Subjectivity and Alienation in Mahler's Re-Cycled Songs*, and he is currently working on a book titled *Surviving Absolute Music: Haydn, German Idealism, and the Persistent Dualities of Music in the New World*.

Robert Lawson-Peebles worked at the Universities of Oxford, Princeton, Aberdeen, and Exeter. Among other positions, he has been a Fellow of the Salzburg Seminar and a Leverhulme Emeritus Fellow. He has published three books on the cultural history of the American environment, a history of earlier American Literature, and over ninety articles on subjects ranging from Sir Walter Ralegh to the relationship of ideology and the arts. He has a lifelong interest in American music. He edited *Approaches to the American Musical*, and is currently working on a two-volume history of the cultural impact of jazz in Britain.

Miranda Lundskaer-Nielsen is a Senior Lecturer in Drama at Bath Spa University where she teaches American Drama and Musical Theatre. She has an MA in Text and Performance Studies from Kings College, London/RADA, and a PhD in Theatre from Columbia University. Dr. Lundskaer-Nielsen was an Associate Producer of the New York Musical Theatre Festival and worked for two years for the British writers' organization Mercury Musical Developments. She is the author of *Directors and the New Musical Drama: British and American Musical Theatre in the 1980s and 90s*.

Nathan R. Matthews is a music director and conductor, director, composer, pianist, and educator. Matthews has composed a music theater work, *The Count of Monte Cristo*. He conceived, orchestrated, and arranged *It Goes Like It Goes, The Music of David Shire*. Matthews has worked on Broadway: *Children and Art, A Tribute to Stephen Sondheim on the Eve of his 75th Birthday; Amadeus*; off-Broadway; at the Santa Fe Opera; and on concert tours for Columbia Artists. He is producing Artistic Director of the Riverside

Opera Ensemble, New York City and Associate Professor and Director of Music Theatre at the State University of New York at Buffalo.

Marianne McDonald, PhD, MRIA, Professor of Classics and Theatre, University of California, San Diego, has over 250 publications. She is the author of *The Living Art of Greek Tragedy*, coeditor of *Amid Our Troubles: Irish Versions of Greek Tragedy*, and her latest book is *Space, Time, and Silence: The Craft of Athol Fugard*. Her translations (all of Greek Tragedy) and her own award-winning plays are performed nationally and around the world. Her latest plays are *A Taste for Blood*, a vampire play set in Dublin, and *Peace*, about a dysfunctional Irish alcoholic family, with a ghost as commentator.

Robert L. McLaughlin is Professor of English at Illinois State University. He has published widely on postmodern literature and culture, particularly on the work of Thomas Pynchon. His articles on Stephen Sondheim have been published in the *Journal of American Drama and Theatre* and the *Sondheim Review*. He is currently completing a book on Sondheim and postmodernism. He is the author, with Sally E. Parry, of *We'll Always Have the Movies: American Cinema during World War II* and the editor of *Innovations: An Anthology of Modern and Contemporary Fiction*.

David Savran is a specialist in American theater, music theater, popular culture, and social theory. He is the author of eight books, most recently *Highbrow/Lowdown: Theater, Jazz, and the Making of the New Middle Class*, winner of the Joe A. Callaway Prize. He has served as a judge for both the Obie and the Lucille Lortel awards and was a juror for the 2011 and 2012 Pulitzer Prize in Drama. He is Distinguished Professor of Theatre and holds the Vera Mowry Roberts Chair in American Theatre at the Graduate Center of the City University of New York.

Robynn J. Stilwell teaches at Georgetown University. Her research interests center on the meaning of music as cultural work, including the interaction of music and movement in such media as film, video, television, dance, and sport. Publications include work on Beethoven and cinematic violence, musical form in Jane Austen, whiteness and rockabilly, French film musicals, psychoanalytic film theory and its implications for music and for female subjects, and the boundaries between sound and music in the cinematic soundscape. The current project is a study of modality in television, drawn from its precedents in film, theater, radio, and concert performance.

Scott F. Stoddart is the Dean of the School of Liberal Arts at the Fashion Institute of Technology, SUNY. He has published on the fiction of Henry James, E. M. Forster, and F. Scott Fitzgerald; the musical plays of Stephen Sondheim; and the films of the Coen Brothers, Jane Campion, Jack Clayton, John Ford, Oliver Stone, and Martin Scorsese, and on the image of the president in Hollywood film and television, including *The Adams Chronicles* (1976). He is author of *The 1980s: American Popular Culture through History* and editor of *Mad Men: Critical Essays on the Television Series* (2010). He is currently writing *"Queer Eye" for a "Straight Dick": Contextualizing the Queer Villain in Film Noir*.

Joseph Swain is author of *The Broadway Musical: A Critical and Musical Survey*, which won ASCAP's Deems Taylor Award in 1991. Other books include *Musical Languages, Harmonic Rhythm: Analysis and Interpretation*, and *Sacred Treasure: Understanding Catholic Liturgical Music* (published by Liturgical Press).

Dominic Symonds is Reader in Drama at the University of Lincoln. His research focuses on poststructuralist approaches to the musical. He is joint editor of *Studies in Musical Theatre* (Intellect) and founded the international conference Song, Stage and Screen. He is also coconvenor of the music theater working group of the International Federation for Theatre Research. He has recently coedited two collections of essays for the IFTR, *The Legacy of Opera: Reading Music Theatre as Experience and Performance* and *Gestures of Music Theatre: The Performativity of Song and Dance*. His monographs *We'll Have Manhattan: The Early Work of Rodgers and Hart* and *Broadway Rhythm: Imaging the City in Song*, will appear in 2014.

Millie Taylor is Professor of Musical Theatre at the University of Winchester. Before becoming an academic she worked as a freelance musical director for almost twenty years, which included two productions of *Sweeney Todd*. Recent publications are *British Pantomime Performance, Musical Theatre, Realism and Entertainment*. In January 2012, she was guest editor of a special issue of *Studies in Musical Theatre* on "Voice and Excess." Forthcoming publications (both with Dominic Symonds) are an edited collection, *Gestures of Music Theatre: The Performativity of Song and Dance,* and a text book, *Studying Musical Theatre*.

David Thomson is film critic for the *New Republic* and he has written for both *The Independent* and *The Guardian* in London. His books include *The Biographical Dictionary of Film* (now in its fifth edition), *Have You Seen…? A Personal Introduction to 1,000 Films*, and, most recently, *The Big Screen: The Story of the Movies and What They Did to Us*. He lives in San Francisco, where he saw a concert performance of *Sweeney Todd* as important to him as seeing *Into the Woods* on Broadway.

Keith Warner is an internationally renowned theater and opera director. In the last thirty years he has directed over 150 operas, plays, and musicals in fourteen countries worldwide. He is celebrated for his productions of Wagner, including *Lohengrin* in Bayreuth and *Ring Cycles* in Tokyo and London (Covent Garden). He championed subsidized companies taking on the Sondheim canon in the early 1980s and directed *Pacific Overtures* at English National Opera, and *Being Alive*, a gala for Aids Charities at the Theatre Royal, Drury Lane, London. He will direct a new production of *Sweeney Todd* at opera houses in Copenhagen, Houston, and San Francisco.

Matt Wolf is London theater critic of the *International Herald Tribune*. He spent thirteen years as London drama critic for *Variety* and more than twenty years as arts and theater correspondent out of London for the Associated Press. His first, and formative, Sondheim production was the original Broadway version of *Sweeney Todd*, which he saw during his freshman year at Yale and returned to many times. He has lived in London his entire professional life.

Stacy Ellen Wolf is Professor in the Program in Theater and Director of the Princeton Atelier in the Lewis Center for the Arts at Princeton University. She is the author of *Changed for Good: A Feminist History of the Broadway Musical* and *A Problem Like Maria: Gender and Sexuality in the American Musical*, and coeditor, with Raymond Knapp and Mitchell Morris, of *The Oxford Handbook of the American Musical*.

THE OXFORD HANDBOOK OF

SONDHEIM
STUDIES

INTRODUCTION

LIKE Frank Loesser's *Guys and Dolls* (1950), the musicals of Rodgers and Hammerstein, Cole Porter's *Kiss Me Kate* (1948), Kander and Ebb's *Cabaret* (1966) and *Chicago* (1975), virtually all of Sondheim's musicals are classics of American musical theater. Within a decade of their first performances, each show had attracted a cult following that led to major revivals in more or less continuous cycles. Since its 1970 premiere on Broadway, *Company* has been revived twice in New York and twice in London. In addition to large-scale regional productions and a legendary concert staging in 1985, *Follies* (1971) received its third Broadway revival in 2011, while it has been fully staged three times and been given a number of concert stagings in London. In the past decade, *Sweeney Todd* (1979) has been revived three times to great acclaim in the West End, and once on Broadway. Highly successful revivals of *Sunday in the Park with George* (1984) and *A Little Night Music* (1973) transferred from the West End to Broadway in 2008 and 2009 respectively, and in 2012 a revelatory London production of *Merrily We Roll Along* (1981) garnered what must surely be the most universal praise ever accorded the production of a Sondheim musical.

Like Arthur Miller, Tennessee Williams, George Gershwin, and Rodgers and Hammerstein before him, Stephen Sondheim has achieved iconic status in American culture. What makes his work so important in a genre that has most often been viewed as commercial entertainment rather than art? Since 1970 the shows to which he has contributed have been the most widely debated, most artistically ambitious, and most experimental in approach to form in the musical theater. They have achieved the status of modern classics because, although they are not among the longest running on Broadway or in London, they have been more frequently revived On- and Off-Broadway, in opera houses and in regional and amateur theaters around the United States, in Britain, and occasionally elsewhere than those of any artists in the field since Rodgers and Hammerstein. *Company* represents a new paradigm of nonlinear musical structure, utilising elements of musical comedy[1] and the musical play[2] to create a postmodern form commonly—although unsatisfactorily in Sondheim's view—labelled the "concept" musical.[3] In sharp contrast to the work of his mentor, Oscar Hammerstein, the musicals to which Sondheim has contributed are commonly regarded by scholars in the field of popular entertainment as the most consciously and consistently critical of American society and values.[4] The fact that they are studied in music, theater, literature, and cultural studies courses at many universities is a further indicator of their cultural status.

More than forty years after Roland Barthes proclaimed "the death of the author,"[5] and notwithstanding Sondheim's own insistence on the importance of his collaboration with talented directors like Harold Prince and James Lapine, as well as respected librettists such as Arthur Laurents, Burt Shevelove, Larry Gelbart, George Furth, James Goldman, Hugh Wheeler, and Jerome Weidman,[6] it is Sondheim alone who has achieved the status of *auteur*.[7] In various ways, the chapters in this volume explore the paradox of a highly original auteur operating so willingly as a collaborator—a paradox that becomes unavoidable when art is created in an industrial context.

The analysis of a musical is a complex and often risky business. Given its hybrid form, there is no consensus among musical theater scholars with regard to an appropriate discipline-specific terminology or methodology for the analysis of musico-dramaturgical structure. It may well be the case that a single analytical approach is untenable or even undesirable. Whatever the case, the scope and ambition of Sondheim's work as composer–lyricist—no matter with whom he collaborates as librettist—constitute a peculiar problem for scholar and critic, in part as a consequence of his dramaturgical ambitions as songwriter and composer of sung scenes:

> When I'm writing dramatic stuff, I'm a playwright. This is a worked-out scene, and I can tell the actress how to play this scene, and the music is part of the dialogue. I can tell her why the music gets quick *here*, why it gets slow here, why there's a ritard *there*, why there's a so-called key-change *here*...because I have reasons.[8]

Conceptually, the hybrid mixture of component parts in any musical—dialogue, action, music, lyrics, dance, and scenography—poses a problem for analysis. Ideally the complex conjunction of elements that constitutes each moment of a musical should be comprehended as a musico-dramaturgical gestalt, whose separate elements interact in performance to create a hybrid, which is neither song nor dance nor spoken drama nor mime nor music, but a new ensemble generated from a synthesis of their various possible permutations. Even a relatively straightforward song-and-dance number like "All I Need Is the Girl," from *Gypsy* (1959), is conceived as a complicated game of acting, singing, dancing, and instrumental musical accompaniment, employing the different combinations of acting-music, acting-singing-music, acting-singing-dancing-music, acting-dancing-music, situated in a particular scenic location that indicates both place and time period, and is lit in a particular way. While the number may be fully realized only when music and lyrics are staged by a director and a choreographer, the elements of scenography and dance must, in schematic form, be imagined as an aspect of its composition.[9]

In response to the extraordinary heterogeneity of the musical as a genre and in recognition of the limitations of their own specialist expertise, critics understandably tend when writing about individual examples to focus on the element they are best qualified to comprehend. In order to exploit the full range of complementary methodological and competing critical perspectives available, this *Handbook* adopts a multidisciplinary and occasionally an interdisciplinary approach to the analysis of Sondheim's musicals. Musicological and dramaturgical scholars, literary and film critics, and musical theater practitioners are invited to explain his radical reinvention of the artistic form of the Broadway musical as a series of creative responses to various traditions of artistic innovation and popular entertainment, while cultural critics, historians, and sociologists reflect on the meaning of these musicals as reactions to the changing sociocultural contexts in which Sondheim and his collaborators have been living and working.

Chapters in the first section ("Intertextuality and Authorship: Toward Nonlinear Forms") explore problematic questions of authorship peculiar to the cultural milieu of Broadway musical theater, tracing the play of intertextuality, direct influence, and original innovation from a number of complementary perspectives in order to identify authorial strategies as responses to the traditions of art and commercial theater that confront Sondheim and his collaborators with competing creative possibilities. In demonstrating how an artist as ambitious as Sondheim brings into play intertexts as wide-ranging as Anthony Shaffer's *Sleuth* (1970), three stage melodramas about Sweeney Todd from 1847, 1968, and 1971, the film *Hangover Square* (1945), the sonata form of the classical symphony, Bach's *St Matthew Passion*, César Franck, and the Dickensian musical, Stephen Banfield (Chapter 1) identifies Sondheim's genius as his extraordinary ability to integrate the commercial values of the Broadway musical with the aesthetic ideals of a highly cultivated auteur. Banfield's multisensory analysis of "God, that's Good," as a sung scene in act 2 of *Sweeney Todd*, serves as a model analysis of the interplay of multiple sign systems operating in the performance of a single musical number.

Robert McLaughlin (Chapter 2) demonstrates how the postmodern sensibility informing Sondheim's musicals from *Company* to *Road Show* (2010) manifests itself through the fracturing of the typically linear narrative of the Rodgers and Hammerstein book musical and through the experimentation with self-reflexive forms that subvert realist modes of representation to expose the uncertainties of the contemporary moment and to subject modern American life to interrogation from radically altered perspectives. Dominic Symonds (Chapter 3) further explores the formative influence of Oscar Hammerstein II as mentor to the young Sondheim, tracing Sondheim's elaboration of Kern and Hammerstein's innovations in the use of the "sung scene" as a dramaturgical unit through a detailed analysis of *A Little Night Music*, and illustrating how Sondheim deploys the palindrome—a structural pattern modeled on Rodgers and Hammerstein's formal experiment in their groundbreaking *Allegro* (1947) *South Pacific*—as a compositional principle in *Anyone Can Whistle* (1964) and *Sunday in the Park with George*.

Chapter 4 interrogates Sondheim's response to the mentorship of Hammerstein from a different angle. By highlighting the placement of songs as self-standing "turns" within what in performance recalls a series of items on a burlesque or vaudeville bill, I analyze the dramaturgical technique of songs that empower comic performers to act out the logic of character and plot in a metatheatrical style that pays knowing homage to the simple clichés of early musical comedy. The chapter demonstrates how, by avoiding the pseudonaturalistic conventions of the musical play Sondheim frees himself and his later collaborators to experiment with postmodern forms of nonlinear narrative. David

Savran (Chapter 5) elaborates on the topic of intertextuality by interrogating *Anyone Can Whistle*'s relationship to the theater of the sixties. His incisive analysis of Sondheim and Laurents's absurdist satire on conformism contextualizes the musical as a response to the changing sociocultural and aesthetic values of the Off-Off-Broadway theater scene in the early sixties, explaining the show's ambivalent and unsatisfactory resolution as a result of its anomalous positioning on Broadway as an avant-garde musical aiming for commercial success in a highly conservative environment.

The industrial context of production reinforces the truism that musicals are not written but rewritten. The second section ("The Art of Making Art") concentrates on aspects of craft and the aesthetic and technical concerns motivating the process of collaboration with producers, directors, scenographers, orchestrators, actors, and musicians under the material and economic circumstances of the Broadway industry. Miranda Lundskaer-Nielsen (Chapter 6) examines the seminal role of producer and director Harold (Hal) Prince in the fashioning of musicals from *Company* to *Merrily We Roll Along*, identifying the formative nature of his contribution to the initial conception, visual realization, and thematic coherence of the shows and arguing that his work with Sondheim offered a new approach to production processes in the industry. Andrew Buchman (Chapter 7) complements these reflections on the problems and possibilities inherent in such a collaborative working process to provide a detailed outline of the many revisions by Sondheim and George Furth of *Merrily We Roll Along*, from its initial failure on Broadway in 1981 through a series of revivals, culminating in a more or less definitive version in 2002. Bud Coleman (Chapter 8) focuses on the function of scenic design and dance in accomplishing the full expression of each musical's visual conception, highlighting in particular the crucial contributions of scenographer Boris Aronson, director and choreographer Michael Bennett, and director, playwright and visual artist James Lapine to the development of *Company, Follies*, and *Sunday in the Park with George*, and illustrating the collaborative nature of musical theater creation. Nathan Matthews (Chapter 9) collects first-hand accounts of the artistic aims of a number of celebrated orchestrators of Sondheim musicals and collates their commentaries to build up a picture of a recurring phenomenon in Sondheim performance over the last decade—the reorchestration of these shows for different (and smaller) groups of musicians. The impact on musical performance of John Doyle's surprising use of "actor-musicians" in *Sweeney Todd, Company*, and *Merrily We Roll Along* in small theater spaces is explored by several orchestrators. Garrett Eisler's chapter on the various incarnations of *Road Show* (*Wise Guys* and *Bounce*) (Chapter 10) takes up the topic of revision to examine Sondheim and Weidman's relentless search to develop an appropriate musico-dramatic form for a subject that had originally attracted Sondheim as long ago as 1954, further illuminating the intricately interrelated processes of writing and staging entailed in the construction of a musical.

Chapters in the third section of the book ("Sondheim in Performance") engage with the notion of the musical as a performance event, exploring different aspects of the meaning of the works as performances, as well as taking some preliminary steps toward constructing a production history of the Sondheim canon. Olaf Jubin's in-depth explication

(Chapter 11) of the way patterns of doubling in the casting of James Lapine's production of *Sunday in the Park with George* generates new insights into the way meaning can be inherent in performance and production as much as in the forms of written composition. Through careful comparison of the attitudes towards art in act 1 (1884) and act 2 (1984), his reading of the acting and staging offers a concrete exemplification of the self-reflexive quality so typical of Sondheim's work. Joanne Gordon's personal account (Chapter 12) of the reception of her own production of *Assassins* (1990) in Los Angeles (2007) analyzes the significance of a performance of this controversial piece within the sociocultural moment of the Iraq War, offering a provocative view of the politics of Sondheim performance in the United States. Matt Wolf employs his extensive experience of the production and reception of Sondheim's musicals in the United Kingdom (Chapter 13) as an American theater reviewer based in London to identify the wide range of interpretive approaches by British directors in both subsidized and commercial theaters to a number of Sondheim's works whose repeated revival soon gave them the status of modern classics. As an international opera director whose 1987 production of *Pacific Overtures* (1976) for the English National Opera introduced Sondheim to the British opera house, Keith Warner reflects on both the pleasures and challenges of performing these musicals in international opera houses (Chapter 14), locating Sondheim's artistic achievement at the point of intersection between popular and high culture and investigating the impact of increasing commercialization on art produced within the subsidized sector.

The fourth section of the *Handbook* ("Sondheim across the Media") addresses Sondheim's interest in and sensitivity to the range of audiovisual media, with chapters exploring his work for cinema and television, his adaptations of two films into stage musicals and the screen version of *Sweeney Todd* (2007). Sondheim's love of cinema is well documented, but his collaboration with James Goldman in the creation of a rare original television musical and his songs and soundtrack music for films have seldom been subjects of sustained critical commentary. Robynn Stilwell (Chapter 15) offers a detailed, interdisciplinary explication of the absurdist musical dramaturgy of *Evening Primrose* (1966), illustrating the writers' skilful integration of television studio drama techniques with songs to shape a unique piece that is commonly regarded as the earliest manifestation of Sondheim's distinctive voice as a mature composer. Geoffrey Block (Chapter 16) examines in some detail the step-by-step process through which two films, Ingmar Bergman's *Smiles of a Summer Night* (1955) and Ettore Scola's *Passion d'Amore* (1981), were transformed by Sondheim–Wheeler and Sondheim–Lapine into the stage musicals *A Little Night Music* and *Passion* (1994), while Roger Hickman (Chapter 17) broadens the scope of the volume by taking into consideration individual songs written by Sondheim for several films, and focusing in some detail on the placement and meaning of the five songs he wrote for Warren Beatty's *Dick Tracy* (1990) within the film's narrative scheme. His notion of Sondheim's "cinematic" approach to musical theater paradoxically informs the musicological analysis of the scores for Beatty's *Reds* (1981) and Alain Resnais's *Stavisky...* (1974). In direct contrast with Sondheim's own opinion that Tim Burton's commercially successful film version of *Sweeney Todd* is the most effective transfer of a stage musical to the screen, David Thomson employs his compendious knowledge as a commentator and reviewer of cinema to offer an incisive critique of the film's failure to translate the unique qualities of the stage musical into a potent cinematic language (Chapter 18).

In the fifth section of the collection ("Sondheim across Genres"), writers reflect on Sondheim's subtle and often ironic exploitation of genre conventions. Questions are raised concerning the exploitation of pastiche and parody, framing strategies, and the manipulation of audience expectation by the composer-lyricist and his collaborators, as audience responses to individual works are affected by the sophisticated deployment of recognizable conventions and styles of operetta, melodrama, kabuki theater, tragedy, musical comedy, opera, revue, vaudeville, burlesque, and the musical play. Four chapters explore the transformation of conventional subject matter by Sondheim and his collaborators through a process in which a wide range of preexisting musical and theatrical genres are reinvented through the play of modern sensibilities on older forms. Joseph Swain's chapter on *A Little Night Music* (Chapter 19) identifies its musical and dramaturgical debt to the tradition of Viennese operetta in order to demonstrate the ways in which Wheeler and Sondheim subvert the most recognizable conventions of the genre to create a more cynical piece— "whipped cream with knives" in Harold Prince's words.[10] Marianne McDonald's comparison (Chapter 20) of Sondheim's first adaptation of Aristophanes' *The Frogs* (written with Burt Shevelove in 1974) with the expanded version (in collaboration with Nathan Lane in 2004) reveals two contrasting responses to ancient Greek comedy, the first of which is sensitive to the mystical and poetic strands of Aristophanes' original whereas the latter highlights the crudely sexual innuendo that animates the biting political satire of a society at war. Millie Taylor's chapter on *Sweeney Todd* (Chapter 21) reveals how Sondheim's deployment of music and song to evoke depths of feeling and intimations of psychological complexity produces tragedy from the stock melodrama of an urban myth whose various manifestations haunt popular nineteenth- and twentieth-century theater and film. Ben Francis (Chapter 22) responds to Sondheim and Lapine's post-Bettelheim use of fairy stories by undertaking a close reading of their multiplicity of intertwined narrative structures to identify a thematic motif of disenchantment in *Into the Woods* (1987), showing the quest for mature psychological and moral insight in the musical to be not only an underlying aim of Sondheim's alternative versions of popular entertainment archetypes but also a subversion of Bettelheim's notion of the psychological function of fairy tales.

Chapters in the final section ("Sondheim, Identity, and Society") engage with questions of cultural, political, and personal identity posed by Sondheim's musicals within the context of contemporary American society. Stacy Wolf's judicious analysis of the representation of women in Furth and Sondheim's *Company* (Chapter 23) problematizes gender as an issue in the Sondheim canon that has until now received little serious attention. By pointing to the contradiction between the quirky intelligence and emotional energy of a range of female roles that have proved gifts for actors, and the restrictions placed on these characters by the play's prefeminist assumptions concerning their socioeconomic status, Wolf reveals a significant "blind spot" within Sondheim's neoliberal political construction and opens up a potentially fertile field for future critics.

Robert Lawson-Peebles' examination (Chapter 24) of the artistic aims of *Follies* in the context of a parallel consideration of Ravel's *La Valse* enables a process of reflection on Goldman and Sondheim's Proustian retrieval of the vanished interwar culture exemplified by the Ziegfield—and equivalent— "Follies" shows. Explication of the musical's multiple layers of allusion to both popular culture and high art of the period reveals the complex ambivalence generated in subjecting the mid-century myths of American society to the harsh light of the post-Vietnam moment, not merely indicating the astonishing variety of Sondheim's musical sources but also exposing his critique of their ideology. As a sociologist, Paul Filmer is concerned to identify how *Pacific Overtures* maps the tension between the national and global conditions of late twentieth-century American cultural identity and their relation to the Enlightenment ideals of American society (Chapter 25). By scrutinizing the modes of representation of the principal characters and the processes of transition between traditional and modern societies his chapter explicates the meaning of the binary division of *Pacific Overtures* into sequential parts as it tracks the inevitable inversion of progress into tragedy. Scott Stoddart's queer reading of the Sondheim canon (Chapter 26) concentrates chiefly on *Company, Merrily We Roll Along, The Last of Sheila* (1973), and *Road Show* in order to interrogate the relationship between Sondheim's iconic status as a representative of the gay sensibility and his ambivalence towards his own homosexuality. From his discussion of Sondheim's first characterization of an overtly homosexual character in the comic lyrics of "The Boy from..." to his interpretation of "The Best Thing that Ever Has Happened to Me," Addison Mizner's and Hollis Bessemer's gay love duet in *Road Show*, as an artistic coming-out for Sondheim, Stoddart identifies the strategies through which Sondheim has challenged and remade the heteronormative paradigm of the twentieth-century Broadway musical. Raymond Knapp's chapter (Chapter 27) concludes the volume by assessing Sondheim's attitude and position as a progressive American artist. By identifying the complex attitudes to American society implicit in his work as, in Knapp's words, "primary author" of musicals, the chapter at the same time analyzes his ambiguous status within the society as cultural icon. Viewing Sondheim's aesthetic approach to the form as a sustained critique of what he calls the "Hammerstein compromise"—a celebration of "the American Dream" in its liberal, antiracist, and humane version—Knapp reads *Anyone Can Whistle* as a darkly parodic version of Meredith Willson's celebration of small-town America in *The Music Man* (1957) before analyzing the complex nature of Sondheim's reputation as American legend.

The twenty-seven chapters in this volume can surely leave little room for doubt that Stephen Sondheim's work with several collaborators has radically transformed the history of American musical theater. If the first era in the development of the American musical as art form saw the triumph of musical comedy (1916–43) and the second witnessed the preeminence of the musical play (1943–64), the epoch of the postmodern nonlinear musical inaugurated in 1970 by *Company* must be regarded as the age of Sondheim. This volume aims to provide a comprehensive survey of Sondheim's achievements and to indicate why they continue to exert a profound influence on generations of musical theater writers who have made his innovations their starting point.

NOTES

1. Some critics have regarded the aesthetic principles of musical comedy with their unashamedly presentational approach to performance, as "Brechtian."

2. Although the development of the integrated musical play by Hammerstein and Kern in *Show Boat* (1927) and Hammerstein and Rodgers in *Oklahoma!* (1943), *Carousel* (1945), and later works involves the convergence of the Wagnerian principle of musical integration with the dialogue-and-song dramaturgy of musical comedy, Hammerstein's musical play format attempts to conceal the break between dialogue and song through the deployment of various devices that merge conversational dialogue with "sung scenes," arias that function as soliloquies and group song-and-dance numbers that dramatize in pseudo-naturalistic terms the social ceremonies of the community. Thus the disparate musical and dramatic segments are integrated in a motivic principle borrowed from the Wagnerian *Gesamtkunstwerk*, with songs being reprised and sections of musical material from these numbers being motivically deployed as underscoring at various points throughout the piece.

3. See Chapter 4, note 14, and Chapter 6, page 104, for further explanation of this term.

4. Popular entertainment forms are generally thought by cultural analysts to deliberately or unconsciously reinforce the social and political status quo.

5. See "The Death of the Author," in Roland Barthes, *Image–Music–Text*, translated and edited by Stephen Heath (London: Harper Collins, 1977), 142–9.

6. Sondheim himself is always quick to point out the importance of the librettists as coauthors of the musicals; in the dedication of *Finishing a Hat* (2010) he listed every "unsung" playwright with whom he has collaborated.

7. The notion of the "auteur" derives from French film theory of the fifties, which regarded certain directors (rather than screenplay writers) as contributing the artistic signature that guaranteed the uniquely coherent authorial identity of their films, as opposed to the majority of films that were merely the products of skilful technicians servicing the industrial demands of the studios. In Chapter 27, Raymond Knapp uses the term "primary author" to indicate the preeminent status among his collaborators ascribed to Sondheim.

8. Mark Eden Horowitz, *Sondheim on Music: Minor Details and Major Decisions* (Lanham, MD, and Oxford: Scarecrow, 2003), 25.

9. Wagner was the first to identify explicitly the heterogeneity of art forms that comprised the manifold form of musical drama, regarding music as the unifying structural principle capable of integrating all the other art forms—poetry, painting, sculpture, dance and drama—to create a *Gesamtkunstwerk*. The paradigmatic example of Wagner's "total art work," while it may be useful in comprehending certain kinds of opera, is misleading when applied to the modern musical, whose various elements are not fully subsumed within the musical structure of the work but are interrelated in complicated combinations of performance modes that may at one point appear as separate components and at another be subsumed in the formation of a compound.

10. Craig Zadan, *Sondheim and Co.* (New York: Harper and Row, 1986), 182.

PART I

INTERTEXUALITY
AND AUTHORSHIP:
TOWARD
NONLINEAR FORMS

CHAPTER 1

SONDHEIM'S GENIUS

STEPHEN BANFIELD

THROUGHOUT a working life of six decades in the musical theater, Stephen Sondheim has by virtue of this medium been both collaborator and auteur.[1] Yet the name of Sondheim has far outweighed those of his colleagues and his milieu in academic discussion. There is, it seems, something uniquely fascinating and compelling about the force, individuality, and consistency of Sondheim's creative will. That force is sensed in his reception at least as far back as *Sleuth*, Anthony Shaffer's play of 1970 (filmed in 1972, with Laurence Olivier and Michael Caine, and in 2007, with Michael Caine and Jude Law), which was originally to have been called *Who's Afraid of Stephen Sondheim?*[2] It needs to be asked, and has not been asked nearly enough, how or why such a dominating, control-hungry artist should have sustained such a single-minded career in a medium so bound by collaboration, not to mention expediency. The career is deeply paradoxical and at the same time strangely moving, as though the pretensions of the single aspiring artist had not after all entirely lost touch with a paying mainstream audience by the start of the twenty-first century.

A partial explanation perhaps lies in the highly technical, limited-choice media of music and lyrics. Music's very notation is far more prescriptive than any other element in a stage musical. But a great deal in a Sondheim show (let us still call it this for the time being) works by being amenable to opening out from the connoisseur's world of technique to the lifeblood of amateur appreciation. By amateur is meant here not just the "ordinary" paying member of a theater audience, but all those from neighboring disciplines and crafts who have come up against his work, *starting with his original collaborators*. Right from the beginning, one senses, he found himself writing as someone who could somehow do more than, and stay one step ahead of, everyone else involved with the show. This will not have been the case with *West Side Story* (1957) and perhaps not with *Gypsy* (1959); indeed, Leonard Bernstein and (to argue against myself, since he was not a musician) Jerome Robbins must have been his role models in this respect. But from the moment one of Sondheim's own songs first hit the rehearsal piano, as often as not with Sondheim himself at the keys, there was a manifest cleverness involved, and therefore an auteurship, that no one else present could match, either in principle or in practice. The proof of creation, the emotional pearl, the thing to hold onto when the show seemed to be getting nowhere in its development, was already there in the manuscript (or very soon would be, once a song was written), and did not need experimentation on the stage with actors and costumiers and directors to generate a lifeblood for the entire enterprise. And Sondheim knew full well that no one else around him in the rehearsal room ever had such magic powers. At bottom everyone was relying on him.

Collaborative his medium was, however, and one might see Sondheim coming to terms with this by setting himself two agendas—a self-imposed challenge, conscious or inevitable, to discharge a debt to two traditions. Those two traditions were, first, the trade of Broadway, bound to vaudeville values and essentially collaborative, and second, the intellectual sanction of liberal arts America, essentially individualistic and *auteuriste*. Sondheim, it seems, has spent a lifetime paying off this debt, and doing so with genius, a word which I shall take not entirely at face value. One could argue that the trade of Broadway was an inheritance from his father, who worked at the parallel and overlapping trade of the garment industry, while the liberal arts background was a legacy from his parents' divorce: doing well at an expensive school and college would see him through the divorce while incurring a debt that was not just liberal but literal.[3]

He was far from the first musical theater practitioner to bring these two sides together, but he did nevertheless respond to a unique moment in a unique way. Swayne, in *How Sondheim Found his Sound*, serves to remind us of the opportunities and expertise with which Sondheim was surrounded at Williams College in the late 1940s.[4] The United States had won the war and the peace, was entering its great period of affluence, and could sport the best teachers for the best students anywhere, not least because of the influx of European immigrants available as faculty, coming as they did from what was seen as a more consciously intellectual tradition. A four-year undergraduate program, a modern curriculum, well-funded facilities, and a devoted staff all too happy to have been demobbed put the higher-education system on an enviable plane, as yet without any serious challenge from alternative agendas. No wonder that Sondheim's lyrics would in due course seem to echo *The Waste Land* or Emily Dickinson, his music Stravinsky, Milhaud, or Hindemith, his comments a knowledge of nonmusical theater stemming from academic study of it as well as attendance and participation.[5] His teachers had made serious art rewarding for him to study; he went on to reward us similarly. Those who dislike this side of him find themselves reacting to one who has always been the clever student, from his senior thesis to his earnest, competitively self-justificatory comments in interviews and exchanges. Those happier with the product prize his scholar's devotion to detail, accuracy, context, and technique.

At the same time something else was going on. Little of this description would have applied to Oscar Hammerstein in his younger days, though it needs to be remembered that Hammerstein first met Rodgers at Columbia University.[6] Yet Hammerstein remained Sondheim's single most important mentor. The famous afternoon session with Hammerstein when Sondheim was fifteen, in which Hammerstein picked apart *By George* and taught him everything he knew about musical theater, probably occurred only a month or two after the sudden death of Jerome Kern, perhaps in the Christmas vacation of 1945–6, perhaps a little later. Kern, though from a comfortable middle-class family, had not been to college, and *his* genius in popular musical theater was much more a distillation of business training and experience than of liberal arts aspirations, however much he tried to impress Robert Russell Bennett. One imagines Hammerstein in his bereavement—it was nothing less—wanting to pass on all he had learnt from Kern before he began to forget. Thus the vaudeville and liberal arts traditions were in a position, over a concentrated period of little more than four years, to provide a precise mixture of fuel for Sondheim to combust.

But especially since Kern and Hammerstein's *Show Boat* of 1927, to remain with these two figures for a moment, popular musical theater has itself learned to negotiate between collaboration and authorship on a different axis from the one just proposed for Sondheim: it started collaborating with the auteurs of the past. Musicals can be touched by long shadows in this respect. *Hello, Dolly!*, for example, traces its lineage all the way back to John Oxenford's *A Day Well Spent*, a one-act London "operetta" of 1836 with music from unknown sources, via two plays by Thornton Wilder and an Austrian farce by Johann Nestroy.[7] *Cabaret* likewise represents a complex chain of incarnations.[8] If we look at *Sweeney Todd* from this standpoint, it will lead us back to the notion of both collaboration and authorial genius but with a different spin on them. The *Sweeney Todd* plays need considering briefly prior to penetrating another type of shadow, that of genre and the spirit of place as it settles on London. Both these topics will show Sondheim's genius collaborating with the past and *negotiating the authorship of ideas* through the appropriation of sources. We shall remain with *Sweeney Todd* for the remainder of this chapter.

George Dibdin Pitt's *The String of Pearls*, the first dramatic source for *Sweeney Todd*, played at the Britannia, Hoxton, a London "bloodbath" theater, in 1847.[9] The general idea of British melodrama in Pitt's day seems to have been that of the modern pornographic novel: you had to have an orgasm, or in this case a murder, on every page. In the first act of Pitt's *The String of Pearls*, almost every scene (which means every couple of pages) ends with someone being "polished off," as Todd puts it in his stereotypical asides, or at least going down the chute from the chair. Here is one such episode from act 1 scene 1:

> *Enter Jean Parmine*
> JEAN: Good evening, neighbour; I would have you shave me.
> SWEENEY: Your servant, Mr Parmine—you deal in precious stones.
> JEAN: Yes, I do; but it's rather late for a bargain. Do you want to buy or sell?
> SWEENEY: To sell.
> *Produces a casket and gives it to Jean*
> JEAN: (*examining pearls*) Real, by heaven, all real.
> SWEENEY: I know they are real. Will you deal with me or not?
> JEAN: I'm not quite sure that they are real; let me look at them again? Oh, I see, counterfeit; but so well done that really for the curiosity of the thing I will give you £50.
> SWEENEY: £50? Who is joking now, I wonder? We cannot deal to-night.
> JEAN: Stay—I will give you a hundred.

SWEENEY: Hark ye, friend, I know the value of pearls.

JEAN: Well, since you know more than I gave you credit for I think I can find a customer who will pay £11,000 for them; if so, I have no objection to advance the sum of £8,000.

SWEENEY: I am content—let me have the money early to-morrow.

JEAN: Stop a bit; there are some rather important things to consider—you must know that a string of pearls is not to be bought like a few ounces of old silver, and the vendor must give every satisfaction as to how he came by them.

SWEENEY: (aside) I am afraid I shall have to polish him off. (Aloud) In other words, you don't care how I possess the property, provided I sell it to you at a thief's price; but if, on the contrary, I want their real value, you mean to be particular.

JEAN: I suspect you have no right to dispose of the pearls, and to satisfy myself I shall insist upon your accompanying me to a magistrate.

SWEENEY: And what road shall you take?

JEAN: The *right* path.

As Jean turns, Sweeney springs upon him. A fierce struggle ensues. Sweeney succeeds in forcing Jean into the chair. Sweeney touches a spring, and the chair sinks with a dreadful crash. Sweeney laughs and exclaims, "I've polished him off!" as scene closes.[10]

It is money, not revenge, that makes the world go round in this old version: Todd has no sooner purloined a string of pearls from his previous victim than, after an inconvenient interruption from the shop boy Tobias, his next arrives.

Austin Rosser's play of *Sweeney Todd*, published by Samuel French in 1971 following a Dundee premiere, is not only much more recent but also much more daringly in tune with modern sensibilities. Sweeney's victim in the scene given below is Lupin, an unctuous and villainous clergyman very much in the position of Pirelli in the Wheeler and Sondheim version; and what is being acted out is a classic sadomasochism game. The Wheeler and Sondheim S and M elements seem rather undeveloped by comparison, for Rosser has Todd clever and daring enough—playing for real risks—to get *himself* into the chair first, at the mercy of Lupin's hold on the razor. That cunning, insidious reciprocity with reversal of roles is the point of the near-anagrammatic play on Lupin's name with the "Tulip" references—Freudian touches followed up in Todd's final speech before the act 1 curtain about cutting flowers:

SWEENEY: Here! Take these! (*He tosses the bag of jewels to Lupin*)
    . . .
    Between us we would gain enough wealth in two years to live as lords in golden palaces. Here! Look at 'em! (*He pushes the ropes of pearls, etc, at Lupin*) Go on! Touch 'em!

LUPIN: (*almost choking with delight as he examines them*) Oooh, oh, ah, aah! But now tell me, how do you manage?

SWEENEY: To polish them off?

LUPIN: (*nodding*) To polish them off!

SWEENEY: Ha! Ha! (*He takes the black bag from Lupin, picks up the jewel box and deposits them on a chair*) Now you watch! I say, "Good day, sir!" (*He walks to the door pretending a customer has entered the shop*)
Lupin follows behind Sweeney, enjoying the "entertainment"
"Certainly, sir. No, not that chair, sir, this one. The light is better, sir, and it's more comfortable!" And they sit like this. (*He sits in the barber's chair, still pretending*)
Lupin gets caught up in the fun
Get the brush!
Lupin does so and starts to lather Sweeney
Don't you tickle! Oh, ha! Ha! Ha! Ha! It tickles! Now the razor! Get it quick!
Lupin goes for the razor
Then when you're sitting comfortably, somethin' horrible happens. You'd never think anything was. Have you ever shaved anyone? Get the razor, man! It's sharp! Now slide it gently down my skin.
Lupin does so
Ah, yes. One would never think anything was going to happen. Tell me, would you suspect?

LUPIN: (*handing Sweeney the razor*) Let me try.

SWEENEY: (*handing Lupin the sheet*) Put this round you! (*He swiftly takes a noosed rope from under the wash-stand and throws it over Lupin from behind. As he binds Lupin to the chair*) Aha, my little bird—caught!

LUPIN: But I'm your partner.

SWEENEY: (*behind the chair*) But you are, my dear Tulip—I mean Lupin—you still are, for ten seconds. (*He gets the brush and lather mug*) Now I'll lather you. Oh, you've a very good skin. (*He returns the mug and brush and picks up the razor*) A very good skin. The razor is going over it like a slender skater. You know, when I go near the neck I want to draw my razor across it—like a violin. Isn't it strange—and there are no musicians in the family. (*He starts to sing*) "Oh, tis a tulip stem I draw my blade across—blade across!"

LUPIN: Please, please! (*Hoping to humour Sweeney*) Ha, ha, don't joke.

SWEENEY: I'm not. I usually slit 'em in the cellar. There are a number there now; some of 'em dead, some of 'em almost dead—it's a terrible long drop to the cellar, you know—waiting to go to the lovely Lovett. For your next stop, mate, is the pie factory!

LUPIN: (*imploring*) No, no, Todd, please.
The LIGHTS begin to dim

SWEENEY: (*quietly*) So now, partner, you know everything—(*slowly*)—everything you were snooping to find out from Lovett. I was listening you know.
The LIGHTS are now so low that only the outlines of the figures can be seen
So this is where our partnership ends. (*He cuts Lupin's throat*)
The LIGHTS come up to half full. Lupin is seen dead in the chair, his head dropping forward. Sweeney, with the open razor in his hand, comes down and speaks to the audience
As a little child I used to cut the flowers with Granny's scissors in her sunlit garden. Oh, oh, I wish the whole world were a throat so that I could cut it!
Curtain[11]

Now, was Christopher Bond, his play the source of the Sondheim–Wheeler *Sweeney Todd*, influenced by Rosser? It is unlikely, unless he changed his script a good deal between the 1968 Stoke-on-Trent version and the 1973 Stratford East one, Rosser's coming in between the two. But although no one ever mentions Rosser, the possibility that Sondheim or Wheeler may have drawn on it is intriguing. Sondheim's own sensibility as refracted in *Sleuth* and developed in his screenplay for *The Last of Sheila*, all within a few years of his seeing Bond's play in London, would surely have been attracted to it. Most striking is a reference from Sweeney in Rosser's play to "find[ing] out the men who carry a lot of wealth—who have few prying relatives—men who won't be missed much": this is in Sondheim and Wheeler, of course, but not in Bond. The play-within-a-play element in the extract above is also highly suggestive. Todd's "Certainly, sir" speech seems echoed in his "Epiphany" in the musical, while the following episode reminds us that live theater, especially in a piece such as *Sweeney Todd*, is in any case a kind of S and M contract, actors and technicians having to submit to, command, and trust each other in deadly earnest if a performance is to come off without lethal mishap. The mattresses beneath the chute must be securely in place, the barber's victims unable to ascertain their own safety; the apron must not get caught up in the chair, to avoid genuine risk of hanging. (Having the chair tip Sweeney's victims backwards, head first down the chute, was a brilliant touch in Tim Burton's film, not least because unfeasible in the theater.)

As suggested earlier, dramatic precursors are only one set of coordinates for assessing the company genius keeps. Another takes the generic aspects of location, and London is the best source of all for *Sweeney Todd*. The public fascination with the dirty, wicked metropolis, this fascination a draw for entertainment as early as *The Beggar's Opera* of 1728, was most famously and enduringly encapsulated by Dickens. His tropes, all of them enjoying a long afterlife, include those of darkness, fog, and obscurity; of lamplight and fire; of Bedlam—iron bars and prison; of basements and attics and all kinds of domiciliary extremes; of jostling and beggars and Cockney quick-talkers; of the sounds of bells; of Jews, Aladdin's caves, and thieves' kitchens; of urchins and innocent observers (including Sykes's dog); and of much more.

What one might for convenient shorthand term the Dickensian musical is a definite subgenre — recall *Oliver!*, *Pickwick*, *Scrooge*, *My Fair Lady*, or *Mary Poppins*, with its chimney pots. So is the Dickensian film, and *Hangover Square* of 1945 provides a perfect example of it, though set rather later, at the beginning of the twentieth century. The film's title already denotes staginess, for a London square is inherently theatrical, as George Bernard Shaw realized when at the conclusion of one of his music criticisms he described a policeman's ballet occurring in his own, Fitzroy Square, at one o'clock in the morning.[12] And if *Hangover Square*'s opening sequence collaborates knowingly with Dickens, unconsciously with Shaw, it demonstrates Wheeler and Sondheim collaborating no less purposively with *Hangover Square*, which Sondheim has always stressed as a major influence on *Sweeney Todd*.

In the film's opening scene, a street piano with a curious flame coming out of its side is playing a shrieking, discordant waltz. From a lamplighter, the camera moves further up to where an intruder murders an ancient, bearded, and bespectacled antique dealer and sets fire to his shop by throwing the kerosene lamp to the floor. The dazed but respectable-looking murderer is then seen wandering the streets, bumping into other pedestrians. Here, then, we have the jostling, hostile passer-by, with "Look where you're going" as equivalent of "Off with you, I say" to the Beggar-Woman in *Sweeney Todd*; the Jewish Aladdin's cave (though the antique dealer is called Ogilby); the ever-present flame or pyromaniac motif of the lamplighter (and a lamplighter appears in the very first stage direction in Bond's play); the nasty deed happening "above" (with an important camera viewpoint); and, most obviously, "City on fire," which, not being in Bond or the other play sources for *Sweeney Todd*, provides one of the many examples that link Wheeler and Sondheim directly with this particular inspirational source. The very first thing seen in the film, along with the flame, is the turning handle of the barrel piano, enough to remind anyone of the meat grinder in *Sweeney Todd*.

A later expository scene in *Hangover Square*, about twenty minutes in, may be taken as a further compendium of intertextual collaboration. The protagonist George Bone has met his female nemesis, the music-hall singer Netta, and is walking home with her and her accompanist. Here, the idea of taking a turn—another concordance with Shaw and his Fitzroy Square ballet—contributes to the trinitarian symbolism of the film when Mickey tells George that he will cure his hangover in the morning by walking three times round the square. He and Mickey have just composed a popular ballad called "All for you"; that title too has a Sondheim resonance.[13] On the walk home from the pub, the "dirty London" motifs include the ever-present flaming lamps and the play made with the roadworks, another Dickensian motif, symbolizing the "great black pit" of London, Cobbett's "great wen." George, though drunk, must avoid the hole in the road (though, later, a pile of lead pipes fails to do so, which sets off another murder), the hole being a plausible corollary to dungeons and the cellars in *Sweeney Todd*. Finally, consider the cat, a kind of artful dodger—though, unlike those that evade Mrs. Lovett's chopper, not artful or quick enough, as the film later demonstrates—or an (initially) innocent observer of the relations of others, like Tobias. Passing from one patron to another, it functions as an extension of the idea of the urchin (who, like Tobias, gets "taken in," in a double sense).

Later in the film there is a third obvious "turning" reference (just as Bone commits three murders, one attempted, two successful). A character says, "Turn the handle like this, three times" to crank a telephone for ringing off. Again, this is not in Christopher Bond's play, a further demonstration that Wheeler and Sondheim reach directly back to *Hangover Square*.

Genius is by nature selfish and ambitious. Even when shy, it exacts accomplishment on its own terms, appropriates everything in its way, emulates only in order to surpass, and collaborates, if not as auteur, at least, to excuse a pun, *avec hauteur*. It is overreaching and overweening, driven by the motoric engine of creativity. All-consuming, like George the pyromaniac, it is, in short, demonic. But it has to be accountable. George, the genius composer in *Hangover Square* (Figure 1.1), is more than a melodramatic character driven by some kind of machinery (his blank moods), for before he tries to murder Netta's fiancé he touches the back of his neck, as he does when his trances are coming on.

FIGURE 1.1   Laird Cregar as George Harvey Bone in *Hangover Square*, directed by John Brahm (1941).

At this point he is beginning to act out *real* murderous tensions that inhabit his psyche, and like a tragic hero is responsible for his actions, all the more so as his musical career becomes increasingly obsessive.

There is a price to pay. The idea is, of course, Faustian. Bone, like Todd, has excessive ambition based on a formidable, professional artisanal technique, which is seen as demonically unnatural and brings about his downfall. The barber, the "proper artist with a knife," is a composer, and a high-class one at that. Like Todd, Bone practices the "execution" of his creations on "less honourable throats," and it is the social grubbing that he gets entangled with—the lower-class *id* battling with his "classical" *ego*—that dramatizes the schizophrenia. He doesn't exactly sell his noble soul for commercial gain, but is caught up in a dichotomy of love and duty in which his sexual and artistic demons are at destructive loggerheads. This theme is an important one in Sondheim: Frank in *Merrily We Roll Along*, another George in *Sunday*, and most importantly Neil in *All That Glitters* (like *Merrily*, based on a George Kaufman play about an artist) represent a theme to which Sondheim seems to have returned constantly.

Here *we* must return to the question of collaboration, for several times in the preceding paragraphs the phrase "Wheeler and Sondheim" has had to be used. Most of the Dickensian concordances must have been written into *Sweeney Todd* by Wheeler, not Sondheim. We do not yet know exactly what role Sondheim's persuasive genius will have played in that process. We probably never shall unless his collaborators, those still alive, speak for themselves. If that fails to happen, where does it leave the over-reaching auteur genius among them?

To ask a different question, what is it about music itself that makes it so susceptible to this theme of overweening genius? The film scholar Claudia Gorbman gets to the heart of the matter when she discusses how music's "anempathy" means that once its machine is set going it is oblivious of, indifferent to the human events played out against its turning, rolling continuation. "A street organ plays while a murder is taking place," she says of the opening of *Hangover Square*, while the point and the climax of the film, of course, are that "a concerto plays while a symphony hall is burning down."[14] Indeed, Bernard Herrmann's musical score for *Hangover Square* has the same aspirations, against the cinematic odds, toward the "perfect machine 'e planned" as do some of Sondheim's scores against the even greater theatrical odds. The summation of its musical materials in the piano concerto heard apparently complete in the final ten minutes of the film, in which for example the opening barrel piano waltz becomes a scherzo motif, deserves a musicological study of its own, no less than the musical structures of, say, *Passion* or *Sunday in the Park with George*.[15]

Genius is heartless; Sondheim's music has been accused of being heartless; indeed, he has used the word himself.[16] My own view of the matter is that if Sondheim has saved his soul it is through *subjecting* his genius, and his music as it actually features in Broadway musicals, to collaboration. *Sweeney Todd* shows a musical score that in its intense, intricate, and sometimes savage beauty seems to condone or glory in the very devastation its protagonists cause; and shows lyrics that couch the most dreadful serial murders in the most hilarious, irresistible wit. Perhaps no other work could get us so close to being the gleeful accomplices of Fred and Rosemary West, to actually *feeling* the demonic joy they took in playing with their victims as though murder were a fine art—and this is not something to be said lightly.

What, then, pulls him, and us, back from the brink of immoral collusion? It is a question posed in many of his musicals, including *Assassins, Passion*, and *Road Show*. The man who can wield such dangerous tools of musical and lyric delight, putting them apparently at the emotional service of John Wilkes Booth's white supremacism, of the arguably murderous Fosca, and the callous, amoral Mizner brothers, has been frequently resisted for his demonic craft. But Todd does get his comeuppance, and music fades into silence as he himself is murdered. Sondheim too gets his, one might argue, in the multidisciplinary hurly-burly of the theater, where almost never does one have the opportunity to follow his musical and lyric train of thought in all its intricacy or with the right degree of clarity and balance, simply because there is too much going on—too much to look at, too much else being heard. They too get murdered.

The best way to demonstrate this point is to experience a complex musical number twice, in two different ways: once as the perfected, liberal arts exercise in the controlling intellect of Sondheim the auteur, then as the vaudeville number we actually see in the theater. If the ungiving machinery of analysis somehow implicates the former, is Sondheim the collaborator redeemed by the latter? We can decide, though only the former experience can be demonstrated here on paper, by examining "God, that's Good!" from *Sweeney Todd*.

This number is the opening scene of act 2. First, a reminder of its overall symmetrical position in the musical. It is a variation on certain aspects and numbers of act 1, perhaps functioning like the sonata-form recapitulation within a classical symphony. The curtain rises on a transformed Mrs. Lovett and her shop, which now has not the worst but, as Sondheim's sketches for the song show, "the best pies in London."

The London mob had appeared in the act 1 scene in St. Dunstan's marketplace, the other parallel to this number. There Toby was drumming up a crowd for Pirelli's wares and services. By act 2 he has changed his master (the old one is now a pie) but not his tune. He opens the number with his sales-pitch prelude or verse section to the song, which, appropriately enough to his drumming and strutting, is cast overall as a march and trio. And along with the mob go the sounds of London, especially the bells. The Westminster chimes, a four-note sequence as opposed to the three thumps of the crowd, similarly open both scenes.

In act 1, Toby's sales of Pirelli's Miracle Elixir were scoffed at by the superior barber Todd, and as the crowd got restive and began to ask for their money back he turned his march into double-quick time to keep control of them. Here, in the act 2 number, Mrs. Lovett, a woman "of limited wind," as she described herself in act 1, does the same for the opposite reason, in order to keep pace with the satisfaction of her customers who are demanding more. And as she does so, her sidekick Todd is waiting impatiently upstairs for his fancy new chair to arrive, just as in act 1 he was pacing up and down waiting for the Beadle to come and have his hair cut.

As for the symmetries within the song itself, despite the number's complexity they are really quite simple, but best explained with the help of a diagram (Figure 1.2). This needs to be read as a single journey from left to right as the song progresses. At first, as already stated, it sounds as though it is going to be a short verse–refrain popular song for Toby; this structural implication is indicated with the italic x and y within its square bracket. But since the y part turns out to be the first limb of a march and trio, it is necessary to read the whole number according to the top row of algebra: that is, the march is the big A section, the trio is the contrasting B section, and then a shortened version of the march returns, making a symmetrical ABA structure, what musicians call ternary form. The very title of the song seems to reflect this shape, with its transformation of "God" into "good." With the music, however, there is a slight complication in that the trio section, B, also returns overlaid onto part of A. Marches since the later nineteenth century have often recapitulated the lyrical B section, making an ABAB form overall. Sondheim merges the two forms with his contrapuntal overlay, literally a matter of hearing the two tunes simultaneously. (There is nothing new in this; Sullivan did it continually.)

But cast the eye down to the lower reaches of the diagram and it can be seen that this upper-case algebraic representation of the song's form is a way of making sense of what are actually a far greater number of short sections, seventeen in all. These are like little separate scenes within a complex action, or like the stage blockings of a director, or like the camera shots in a film, constantly intercutting. Each of these seventeen short sections, with the exception of the opening two, is based on a sixteen-bar musical paragraph, though some are curtailed, some longer; and ignoring toppings and tailings,

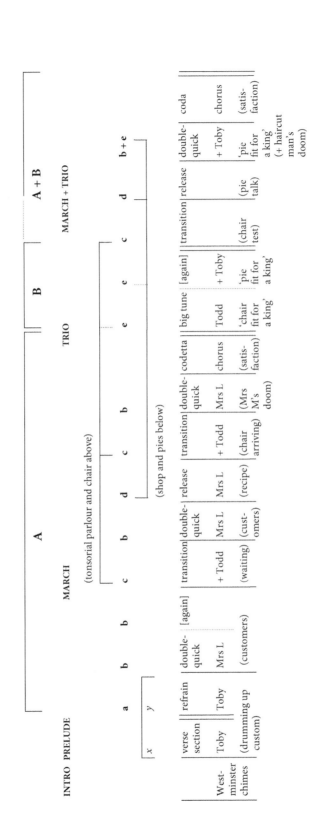

Figure 1.2 "God, that's Good," formal diagram.

there are five different modules of music, **a**, **b**, **c**, **d**, and **e** (the lower-case algebra), distributed repeatedly among the sections. The one labelled **a** never recurs, because it is Toby's sales pitch from act 1. The real body of the song is Mrs. Lovett's ceaseless chatter, the **b** music of the double-quick march, plus Todd's fixing up of his special barber's chair, sung to the gorgeous big tune of the trio, **e**. So the march and the trio correspond roughly to the two alternating focuses of action in this complex scene, what is going on downstairs in and around Mrs. Lovett's pie shop, and what is going on in Todd's tonsorial parlor up above, a binary opposition exploited throughout the show.

The casual audience member, CD listener, or DVD viewer will have noticed a few extra things. Anyone who has directed the piece will have noticed hundreds more. Sondheim keeps musical and lyric ideas yoked in various ways. Everything we hear to the music of **b** is Mrs. Lovett talking to her customers or shouting to Toby about them, and that holds the whole scene together. Note, however, how many different minuscule pieces of action she has to deal with in her virtuoso act of overall control, surely an analog for the composer's own role as overall puppeteer. We hear her attending in some way or another to no fewer than eight characters: the waiting man, the drunkard, the beggar-woman, dim Toby, impatient Todd, her cronies (whom she updates on her rival Mrs. Mooney's nemesis), nonpaying customers, and the man who arrives providentially for a haircut just as she's sold out. And a third strand in these threads of signification, linking her doings with Todd's, is the eulogy to the pies themselves. In the "release" section of the music (**d**) she releases her recipe (not the real one, of course) and talks about the content of the pies; Toby takes up this description when he sings about "a pie fit for a king" to the repeat of the trio tune, **e**. All three sections (**b**, **d**, and **e**) are obsessed with gravy (appropriate enough to the flowing tune, and a subtextual preparation for the blood flowing so freely in the following number). The melody of **e** is a marvelous tune, fit for a king indeed, with the wonderful irony that it is first sung to a chair, secondly to a meat pie. In fact its first three notes are a relaxing transformation of the "excuse me" musical motif of module **c**, signifying impatience for action, that marks time throughout the "waiting" transition sections—Todd waiting for the chair to arrive, waiting for it to come up the stairs, and waiting to see whether it will work properly when he tests it. Here again, in this motif, the idea of one, two, three asserts itself, spelled out for all to hear when Todd arranges the "knock on wood" signal with Mrs. Lovett and given a wonderfully Stravinskian touch of rhythmic dislocation when she forgets the third knock. This dislocation is analogous to what happens in the music when the ostinato of three quarter notes that we keep hearing—for instance, in the chorus codetta and coda—straddles the duple meter (as can be seen in the thumbed right-hand notes of the piano part on the last page of the piano–vocal score, which duplicate those of the sopranos in the chorus). No one but Sondheim could have made such a simple stage action, that of three strokes, work for him at so many different levels, right down to the stylistic fabric of the musical continuum.

He puts in far more than a listener can grasp, of course. Does anybody consciously hear all of these words from Toby as he sings the trio tune? "Is that a pie fit for a king / A wondrous sweet and most particular thing? / You see, ma'am, why there is no meat / Pie can compete / With this delectable pie! / The crust all velvety and wavy, / That glaze, those crimps… / And then the thick succulent gravy… / One whiff, one glimpse… / So tender / That you surrender."[17] Nor does one have time to take in the full effect of Sondheim's counterpoint, rich harmony, and general finesse of voice-leading in that trio section, which can be sampled at slow, detached leisure by playing Figure 1.3 on the piano at whatever speed the fingers and ears demand for the full sonorities to register. (This is the second time around. The first time, at the point marked x, there are no F♮s but an F♯. Try it.)

The chorus interjections, represented by the lowest voice on the upper stave, in three and sometimes four parts, are particularly delicious (like the pies). They enrich the harmonic effect, counteract any staidness in the rhythm, and help build a climax. Their unpredictably cross-rhythmic "Yum!"'s somehow remind me of the second choir's questions in the opening chorus of J. S. Bach's *St. Matthew Passion*, just as the canon at the unison in Figure 1.3 reminds me of the last movement of César Franck's Violin Sonata. Intertextuality can lead the listener (I cannot speak for the composer) to unexpected places.

The conscientious musical theater composer in such circumstances is like the mediaeval stained-glass artist or roof sculptor, lavishing infinite care on things the viewer never sees; if one never hears everything in actual performance, inevitably one loses yet more when the primary focus is visual. In fact there is so much going on visually in "God, that's Good!" that one's eyes cannot take it all in either, which leaves the ears at a double disadvantage. In conclusion, then, if genius is the infinite capacity for taking pains even when the artist's work will eventually serve somebody else's star turn and much of its detail will be lost, then the vaudeville tradition has perhaps preserved this particular genius in a state of grace, just as it hallowed many earlier ones only within the unmarked graves of theatrical collaboration. Let us not begrudge Sondheim his following or deplore his self-justificatory obsessiveness so long as he continues to inhabit and be buffeted around by the dirty, messy, imperfectly collaborative world, not of Dickensian London, but of the modern musical theater. It has kept him sane, unlike the murderous Bone and the wicked Todd, and it will assure him audiences for a long time to come.

FIGURE 1.3 "God that's Good," bars 183–91 (musical reduction).

Notes

1. Elements of this essay were first presented at a Stephen Sondheim Society study day on *Sweeney Todd* at the Haymarket Theatre, Leicester, on November 23, 1996; the session included readings from the Rosser and Dibdin Pitt versions of *Sweeney Todd* performed by my MA students Fran Birch, Tim Harding, and Helen Smith (née Wrigley). I am grateful to Tim Harding for having drawn my attention to Rosser's play in the first place. Nine years later, a more fully developed text incorporating this material and entitled "Sondheim's Genius" was presented on November 25, 2005, at Goldsmiths' College, University of London, in the conference Stephen Sondheim: Collaborator and Auteur.

2. Anthony Shaffer, *Sleuth* (London: Samuel French, 1970); Craig Zadan: *Sondheim & Co.*, 2nd ed. (London: Pavilion, 1987), 167.

3. For Sondheim's biography through college, see Secrest: *Stephen Sondheim: A Life* (New York: Alfred A. Knopf, 1998), 1–83.

4. Swayne, *How Sondheim Found his Sound* (Ann Arbor: University of Michigan Press, 2005), 139–42.

5. See Banfield, *Sondheim's Broadway Musicals* (Ann Arbor: University of Michigan Press, 1993), 19, 106, 150–51, 394; J. D. McClatchy: "Laughter in the soul," *The Poetry of Song: Five Tributes to Stephen Sondheim*, ed. George Robert Minkoff and J. D. McClatchy (New York: Poetry Society of America, 1992), 5; Steve Swayne: "Sondheim's Piano Sonata," *Journal of the Royal Musical Association 127*, no. 2 (2002), 258–304.

6. Hugh Fordin, *Getting to Know Him: Oscar Hammerstein II* (New York: Ungar, 1977), 29.

7. John Oxenford, music unknown, *A Day Well Spent*, one-act operetta (English Opera House, Lyceum Theatre, London, April 4, 1836); Johann Nestroy, music by Adolf Müller: *Einen Jux will er sich machen*, Posse mit Gesang (Theater an der Wien, Vienna, March 10, 1842); Thornton Wilder: *The Merchant of Yonkers* (Guild Theatre, New York, December 28, 1938) and *The Matchmaker* (Royal Lyceum Theatre, Edinburgh, August 23, 1954); Michael Stewart and Jerry Herman: *Hello, Dolly!* (St. James Theatre, New York, January 16, 1964). The chain of collaborations did not stop there: Tom Stoppard reworked Nestroy's farce in English as *On the Razzle* (Lyttelton Theatre, London, September 18, 1981).

8. See James Leve, *Kander and Ebb* (New Haven: Yale University Press, 2009), 36–9.

9. Kilgarriff gives the date of the first performance as March 1, 1847. See Michael Kilgarriff, ed., *The Golden Age of Melodrama: Twelve 19th Century Melodramas* (London: Wolfe, 1974), 241. A "penny dreadful" version for reading in serialized prose marginally preceded it in the same season.

10. Kilgarriff, *Golden Age*, 248–9.

11. Austin Rosser, *Sweeney Todd: A Victorian Melodrama* (London: Samuel French, 1971), 21–2.

12. Dan H. Laurence, ed., *Shaw's Music* (London: Bodley Head, 1981), vol. 1, 932–3.

13. He composed a song of that title for *Saturday Night* (1954).

14. Both statements are somewhat inaccurate: the instrument at the opening of the film is a barrel piano, the venue at its end a private mansion. See Claudia Gorbman, *Unheard Melodies: Narrative Film Music* (London: BFI, 1987), 151–161.

15. Further, the structural ramifications of the fashionable confluence of film and piano concerto in the early 1940s deserve an essay. It would encompass *Brief Encounter*.

16. Banfield, *Sondheim's Broadway Musicals*, 182.

17. Stephen Sondheim and Hugh Wheeler, *Sweeney Todd: The Demon Barber of Fleet Street*, libretto (New York: Dodd, Mead), 119.

CHAPTER 2

....

SONDHEIM AND POSTMODERNISM

....

ROBERT L. MCLAUGHLIN

About midway through *Follies*, Stephen Sondheim and James Goldman's 1971 musical about the reunion of the casts of a Ziegfeldesque Follies, one character says to no
one in particular, "Wasn't that a blast? I love life, you know that? I've got my troubles
and I take my lumps, we've got no kids, we never made much money, and a lot of folks
I love are dead, but on the whole and everything considered...(*She loses the thread*)
Where was I?"(53)[1]. This attempt to sum up one's life into a grand statement and derive
meaning from it and then to lose the thread, the narrative glue that holds it together, is
paradigmatic of the play as a whole and suggestive in general of the skepticism many of
Sondheim's plays hold toward narrative as a means of structuring and containing meaning. This skepticism, which is shared by much of the drama and fiction of the postmodern era, functions in many of the plays Sondheim and his collaborators presented from
the 1970s into the twenty-first century to challenge the dominance of narrative as an
aesthetic, epistemological, and ontological structure.

I place Sondheim's career in the context of two overlapping cultural moments. The
first is the exhaustion of the Rodgers and Hammerstein aesthetic of the Broadway musical. With *Oklahoma!* in 1943, Richard Rodgers and Oscar Hammerstein II remade the
Broadway musical by insisting on the integration of all its elements—story, character,
song, dance, comedy, design. Each element had to be justified in terms of the story and
characters, with extraneous material, no matter how entertaining, removed. One result
was a musical theater capable of treating serious topics in a thoughtful manner. Another
result was an aesthetic of realism—the introduction of a suspension of disbelief or the
construction of a fourth wall—that had never previously been a part of the musical theater. Because of the success of *Oklahoma!* and the series of musicals that Rodgers and
Hammerstein subsequently produced, the integrated-musical aesthetic dominated
Broadway for the next twenty years. By the mid-1960s, however, the possibilities for
the Rodgers and Hammerstein–style musical were beginning to run dry. A number of
new musicals—*Man of La Mancha, Cabaret*, and *Hair*, for example—in various ways
eschewed Rodgers and Hammerstein–style realism, calling attention to their own artificiality as a way of developing their themes.

The second context for Sondheim's musicals is the growing cultural presence of post-modernism, which by the late 1960s was evidenced in all the arts.[2] *Postmodernism* is a slippery and sometimes contentious term to define, not least because the postmodern enterprise resists definitive definitions. For me, postmodernism is marked by overlapping aesthetic, epistemological, and ontological concerns. Briefly, postmodernism dismisses the primacy of individual experience by suggesting that all experience—lived experience, spoken experience, written experience—is mediated through language that preexists our immersion into it. Thus postmodern art does not seek to make the process of representation invisible, as realism seeks to do so as to foster a suspension of disbelief, but rather makes it opaque or at least translucent. This self-referentiality, the awareness of the discourse that is expressing the art, the fogging of the mirror art holds up to nature, the refusal to let the audience suspend its disbelief, the self-awareness of art pointing, not to the world, but to itself pointing to the world, is the seminal feature of postmodernism. Connected to this is a skepticism about narrative as a meaning-conveying vehicle. Similarly, our immersion in language suggests an idea of the self at odds with the humanist model of the individually created, autonomous identity. Rather, our possibility for being arises from the societal discourses—about gender, race, class, ethnicity, religion, and so on—that we inherit; the self is socially constructed. By drawing attention to the discourse- and narrative-driven construction of the self, postmodernism calls into question the concept of a coherent, inherently purposeful identity. Finally, following from the rest is an epistemological and ideological critique of totalizing systems, any system that seeks to account for, make understandable, and control all knowledge.[3]

Although Sondheim's first shows as lyricist, *West Side Story* (1957) and *Gypsy* (1959), and composer–lyricist, *A Funny Thing Happened on the Way to the Forum* (1962) and *Anyone Can Whistle* (1964), all exhibit some postmodern themes, especially regarding identity construction and the reproduction of ideology, and although the last two flirt with a humorous critique of narrative structure, in form they all generally work within the Rodgers and Hammerstein aesthetic. *Company*, which premiered on Broadway in 1970 with music and lyrics by Sondheim, book by George Furth, direction by Harold Prince, and choreography by Michael Bennett, marks the postmodern break with the integrated musical play. The play focuses on Robert, a Manhattan bachelor, and five married couples who gather to celebrate his thirty-fifth birthday. There is no plot as such. Rather, a series of scenes follows in which Robert interacts with the couples and with three girlfriends and through which the play explores marriage and personal relationships—their virtues, their eccentricities, their disadvantages. In form the play dispenses with the realism of the Rodgers and Hammerstein aesthetic, violating the fourth wall. The songs, rather than arising from the dramatic situation or the characters' emotions, tend to comment on the action and are often performed by characters observing, not participating, in a scene (as in "It's the Little Things You Do Together"). Although Sondheim has frequently expressed his dislike of Brecht, the result is nevertheless an alienation, wherein the audience is encouraged not to identify with the characters but to consider the ideas about relationships the play is developing. Further, *Company* eschews classic narrative form. The structure recalls a revue or vaudeville (an impression reinforced by the pastiche number "What Would We Do without You?") in that generally there is no chronological or causal necessity ordering or linking the scenes. Instead, the structure is cyclical, the main event being Robert's birthday party, which plays out differently each time it recurs, and the main musical motif being the "Bobby, Baby" theme, in which the couples implore Robert to spend time with them and which recurs, vocally or instrumentally, at those moments when Robert's sense of self becomes confused.

This cyclical structure functions thematically as well. The play challenges our cultural reliance on narrative as a knowledge-constructing, meaning-providing vehicle. In a scene where Robert smokes marijuana with one of the couples, Jenny argues that Robert should be married because, "a person's not complete until he's married"[4] (39). A stoned David agrees, "Your life has a—what? What am I trying to say? A point to it—a bottom" (39). The implication here is that marriage gives one's life story a structure: a goal to aim at, the achievement of which provides closure. In the broadest of terms, we meet someone, fall in love, marry, and enter the nonnarrative timelessness of happily ever after. It is this narrative structure, basic to so much of our cultural experience, from fairy tales to Hollywood cinema, and absorbed by us into the epistemological framing of our life stories, that *Company* seeks to challenge through its own eschewal of conventional narrative. The play's dramatic tension is achieved by juxtaposing this traditional narrative structure and its association in the play with marriage with the cyclical form and its association with constant pleasurable activities. In the "Bobby, Baby" theme the characters call out to Robert to join them at a concert, at the opera, on an outing to the beach or the zoo, to play Scrabble, and most insistently to "come on over for dinner!" (19). Throughout the play we see and hear about Robert engaging in these kinds of activities plus drug use, drinking, casual sex, and homosexual curiosity. As he says at the beginning of the play, in response to the many messages on his answering machine, "whatever you're calling about my answer is yes" (4). This is the lifestyle he embraces while resisting the individuality and narrative restrictions of marriage. Robert neatly sums this all up when discussing his apartment with a girlfriend: "I've always liked my apartment but I'm never really in it. I just seem to pass through the living room on my way to the bedroom to go to the bathroom to get ready to go out again" (85).

The tension between these two structures and their associated themes is developed throughout the play. The narrative structure of marriage fails because the couples as far as we can see do not find the security of a clear meaning in or purpose for their lives. There is no happily ever after. Their fascination with Robert is in many ways based on their jealousy of his life of pleasurable activities. However, the life of pleasure is undercut as well, not least because in its repeatability it lacks a point, a narrative goal, and so seems like so much pointless, meaningless action. Further, as we hear in "Another Hundred People," the never-ending activity of Manhattan drives people apart, interdicting communication and connection, resulting in "a city of strangers" (50). So where does this leave Robert? In pre-Broadway versions of the play, the authors rejected endings where, on the one hand, Robert ended up proposing to a woman ("Multitudes of Amy") and, on the other hand, he ended up embracing the world of constant, near-hedonistic activity ("Happily Ever After"). The song Sondheim finally settled on, "Being Alive," significantly chooses neither the narrative of marriage nor the pointlessness of the cycle. Rather, as the participle *being* suggests, Robert expresses here his realization that meaning is made in the process of living, not in an imagined goal that provides an unreliable anchor for a life story, nor in the disconnection and aloneness of pointless activity. He sings,

> Somebody crowd me with love,
> Somebody force me to care,
> Somebody let me come through,
> I'll always be there
> As frightened as you,
> To help us survive
> Being alive, being alive, being alive. (116)

Life is frightening because it is unfinished, in-process. Life stories are necessary not because they provide factitious protection against an in-process life but because they can be shared with another person and, more important, because, in engaging another person's life story, we emerge from the confines of our own.

Follies, a 1971 musical with music and lyrics by Sondheim, book by James Goldman, and codirection by Harold Prince and Michael Bennett, is, like *Company*, a plotless musical.[5] Set in a dilapidated, about-to-be-torn-down theater, the play represents a reunion of the performers who appeared in a series of Weismann Follies, one every year between the world wars. In short scenes not bound by chronology or space, we hear snatches of conversation among the partygoers, we see numbers from the Follies, some apparently actually performed, some apparently surreal, and we see, upstage and in the wings, observing and assessing, the ghosts of the partygoers' past selves, the young people they once were who still inhabit the theater. The ghosts function as memories in some scenes, but in others they are actually present as characters, and in the London version they eventually interact with their older selves. The main characters are two couples who, back in 1941, were the best of friends. Benjamin Stone and his wife, the former Phyllis Rogers, have risen from humble beginnings to Kennedy-esque political power and social standing. Buddy Plummer and his wife, the former Sally Durant, are securely middle class; he is an oil equipment salesman, and she is a desperate housewife, not so secretly pining over the lost love of her life, Ben Stone. Not too long into the party, the four of them gather and in "The Girls Upstairs" gradually remember their shared past. When their younger selves appear and act out a scene before their eyes, they are unnerved, and they try to dismiss the importance of the past, singing, "Everything was possible and nothing made sense" (31). This is an important idea for the musical. The four principals are dependent on imagined life stories with beginnings and anticipated ends as a means of organizing disparate life events into a structure—a narrative structure—that can support meaning. In this song while they dismiss the naïveté of their younger selves, they are attracted to their optimism. They recognize both the liberation of not having a narrative governing one's life—the feeling that everything is

FIGURE **2.1** Ron Raines and Bernadette Peters as Ben and Sally in *Follies*, Kennedy Center, Washington, DC (2011).

possible—and the fear of not having a narrative structure to support meaning—the feeling that without one, nothing will make sense. In a scene a little later, Ben, while trying to convince Sally that he has no regrets about his life, unintentionally reveals that he is lying but also, more important, that connecting one's identity to the structure of a life story creates a prison. He sings,

> You take one road,
> You try one door,
> There isn't time for any more.
> One's life consists of either/or. (37)

He concludes, "The Ben I'll never be, / Who remembers him?" (40). The imagery here, linking the life narrative to the metaphor of a journey, suggests something of a Borgesian garden of forking paths, where an infinite number of journeys, of life stories, exist simultaneously but become reduced, via stubborn insistence on narrative necessity, to one. The musical, in its form and presentation, explodes this necessity as the possibilities for other lives are palpably present (Figure 2.1).

On the night of the reunion the principals have all reached positions of crisis in the ways they find meaning in their lives and how they know themselves. Each has chosen a destination for his or her life, an imagined narrative endpoint that governs the organization of life events into a cause-and-effect-based sequence leading necessarily to itself. A point of crisis has been reached because, for each character, life events have failed the imagined life narrative and the meaning it seeks to support. Sally's case is the clearest. Her goal was marriage to Ben and an imagined happily ever after with him. After he dumps her for Phyllis, Sally marries Buddy, but becomes clinically depressed as the life she leads becomes separated from the life story she had imagined. The reunion is a last desperate chance for her to go back, recover the narrative she lost, and restore meaning and purpose to her life. The others' cases are similar. Buddy's anticipated endpoint is the American Dream of home and family, a dream that fails because of his nomadic career as a salesman and because he knows that he has never won his wife's love. Phyllis has achieved her goal, transforming herself into a consort appropriate to the great man, Benjamin Stone, but in the process, has lost a sense of her starting point and so cannot imagine the narrative that connects her youth to her present. Ben has achieved his American Dream—wealth, fame, and influence—but he has done so in a way that has warped his relationships with others, dehumanizing them and, in the process, himself.

While the musical frames the characters' identity crises in terms of their failed life narratives, it also calls into question narrative itself. We have already seen how the play rejects linear narrative in its form. By presenting the past and present simultaneously, it also fragments the characters' life stories and the drama we are watching. We see snippets of the characters' pasts, we see the characters as they are on this evening in 1971, and we hear some of their memories of their pasts, but none of this is presented linearly. Rather, we are left to arrange the fragments and imaginatively fill in the gaps, leaving much that is indeterminate and uncertain. In so doing, we see the limitations of our own narrative-making, limitations the characters share in their life-narrative-making. The model for the show as a whole is Carlotta's song "I'm Still Here." In it, Carlotta, a survivor—Weismann Follies performer, movie star, TV actress—reviews her life, but does so in terms of incidents, not narrative:

> I've been through Reno,
> I've been through Beverly Hills,
> And I'm here.
> Reefers and vino,
> Rest cures, religion and pills,
> But I'm here.
> Been called a pinko
> Commie tool,
> Got through it stinko
> By my pool.
> I should have gone to an acting school,
> That seems clear.
> Still, someone said, "She's sincere,"
> So I'm here. (59)

This stanza is typical, with its slew of incidents and apparently scrambled chronology. Like the rest of the show, it offers incidents disconnected from narrative: we can work to infer the implied narrative, but we know that the result will never be complete or definitive. We might also start to think of means of knowing that are not narrative-based.

At the moment when the principals reach the highest pitch of narrative crisis, fighting with each other and directly addressing and fighting with their younger selves, when all is chaos and violence seems inevitable, the dusty and crumbling theater becomes a beautiful, stunningly artificial world of bright colors and sunshine, and the play makes the transition into Loveland. Chorus boys and girls and showgirls enter, singing of the joys of love, while the principals stare in understandable disbelief. This is not, however, a musical comedy *deus ex machina* come to resolve the characters' problems. Rather, it is a smiling nightmare world, where the futility of the characters' desire to make meaning for their lives is exposed. The Loveland sequence is emphatically self-referential; in its sets and costumes, pastiche songs, and high-powered, showbusiness performances, it calls attention to its own theatricality and artificiality. It ups the ante on something the play has been doing all night: fogging up the usually transparent relation between life and art, the process of representation. Here, the play and the characters are delivered out of narrative: Loveland's revue form is essentially nonnarrative; but more important, Loveland is removed from time's arrow, on which narrative is dependent. The first words sung as we move into Loveland are, "Time stops..." (83). Loveland is a different kind of representation, in a way pure representation, because, in its celebration of its own form and style, no attempt is made to make it seem to be actual life. The characters, struggling with their own failed narrative representations, are folded into pure representation, where they are simultaneously audience, performers, and subjects of their own performances. The distinction—and distance—between narrating subject and narrated character is broken down entirely. Narration, along with the personal pronoun *I* as a means of holding that narration together, collapses. In its place, we have the distinctly nonnarrative form of the Follies—sketches, songs, and dances, presented one after the other in no chronologically or causally determined sequence. Randomness governs the organizational scheme. This form works against what the characters—and probably the audience—want: a coherent, linear, meaning-providing narrative. The form also, in its very name, mocks the characters' follies, both the folly of their life choices that have led to the dilemmas they are in and the folly of trying to find the meaning and purpose of their lives in narratizing them. After Ben's breakdown precipitates the collapse of Loveland, the couples take different approaches to dealing with their identity crises. Buddy and Sally retreat hopelessly into their failed life narratives, but Phyllis and Ben cautiously resolve to seek meaning for their lives in the process of living rather than in the structure provided by an imagined end.

The subsequent musicals of the 1970s explored the limits of narrative structure in different ways. *A Little Night Music* (1973), a romantic farce, is more heavily plotted than *Company* and *Follies*, but its narratives are set within various levels of artifice, from the theatricality of the Liebeslieder to the self-conjured life narratives of the principals. *Pacific Overtures* (1976), focusing on the United States' forced opening of Japan to international trade in 1853, imagines the conflict in terms of competing historical narratives in which dominant and subaltern positions are reversed. *Sweeney Todd* (1979), a tale of commerce and revenge, features characters who are each acting in different narratives from the one he or she imagines.

Sondheim, Prince, and librettist George Furth, returned to the themes of narrative, identity, and meaning in their 1981 musical *Merrily We Roll Along*. Based on a 1934 play by George S. Kaufman and Moss Hart, the musical tells the story of three friends, Franklin Shepherd, a composer, Charley Kringas, a playwright and lyricist, and Mary Flynn, a novelist, who meet in the enthusiasm of youth, when everything is possible. The play traces what happens to their dreams and goals as time passes and they are faced with life's surprises, travails, successes, and disappointments. The trick here is that the play moves chronologically backward. It begins on an evening in 1976 at a party for the opening of a movie Frank has produced.[6] The movie is apparently a hit, but Frank's personal life is a mess. His second wife, Gussie, formerly a Broadway star, was supposed to have starred in the movie but was deemed too old; she resents being in the shadows and suspects, correctly, that Frank is having an affair with the young actress who took over her part. Frank is estranged from Charley, his former writing partner, so estranged, in fact, that the very mention of his name brings the party to an uncomfortable standstill. Mary, unable to re-create the success of her one and only novel and suffering from a longtime unreciprocated love for Frank, has become a critic and a drunk; the disturbance she causes at the party results in a permanent break with Frank. The scene reaches its climax when Gussie throws iodine in the eyes of Frank's mistress. The ensemble, commenting on the action, reprises the title song, asking, "How did you get to be here? / What was the moment?" (29). The play then moves backward in time as it looks for the turning points, the places where multiple possibilities morphed into narrative necessity.

As in *Follies*, the play's structure serves to fragment the characters' claims to a coherent self and points out the identity crisis that results from the disjunction between an anticipated narrative endpoint and the path a life actually takes. It also, in its defamiliarizing, antichronological movement, implies the forward movement of time, time's arrow. By divorcing its narrative structure from time's arrow, *Merrily We Roll Along* calls into question and frees itself from the expectation that narrative be progressive, that when we reach the endpoint, the point of narrative closure, conditions will have improved or new knowledge will have been gained or a lesson will have been learned. Instead, *Merrily We Roll Along* presents an entropic version of time: as time goes on, instead of getting better, things fall apart; instead of narrative closure providing an ordered and potentially meaningful structure, events tend toward chaos. Over and over, the play's score offers songs that begin with the promise of a better future only to fall victim to the entropic movement of time: "Not a Day Goes By," "Now You Know," "Bobby and Jackie and Jack," and the play's central song, "Good Thing Going." The last song's first two verses establish the promise of a love relationship, the good thing that is "going" in the sense of moving forward. By the final verse, however, entropy has set in:

> And while it's going along,
> You take for granted some love
> Will wear away.

> We took for granted a lot,
> But still I say:
> It could have kept on growing,
> Instead of just kept on.
> We had a good thing going,
> Going,
> Gone. (114)

Over time, love wears away, forward movement gives way to stasis, stasis gives way to loss. "Going" now implies a running-out, and the vocal score indicates that the last word, "Gone," is to be sung pianissimo, a soft falling away rather than a more definite closure. After Frank and Charley sing the song at a producer's party, Gussie leads the guests' applause and says, "Wouldn't you all just like to live your entire life to that music?" (115). The irony, of course, is that they do.

Another structural paradigm at work here is based on repetition and variation. The other two paradigms—the backward-moving narrative and the forward-moving time's arrow—though in tension, are both nevertheless linear. This other aspect of the show's structure, which operates principally in the score, makes connections between past and present through repeating melodies, harmonies, lyrics, and dialogue or by presenting variations on them. The result is a layering effect wherein incidents disconnected in time are brought into resonating proximity. Sondheim says, "The idea of the score was that it was built in modular blocks, and the blocks were shifted around.... You take a release from one song and you make that a verse for a different song, and then you take a chorus from a song and make that a release for another song.... It's like modular furniture that you rearrange in a room: two chairs become a couch, two couches at an angle become a banquette."[7] This modular technique is the basis for the cyclical connections across time, which creates possibilities for meaning beyond the other, linear structures. For example, the melody line for a passage from the title song,

> Dreams don't die,
> So keep an eye on your dream...
> Time goes by
> And hopes go dry,
> But you still can try for your dream (2)

becomes the accompaniment figure for "That Frank," the song for Frank's party in the opening scene, thus underscoring the disjunction between Frank's initial narrative goal and his actual life events. Later, the melody we first hear in "Franklin Shepard, Inc.," where Charley is complaining about Frank's moving away from his music to become a businessman ("And the telephones blink / And the stocks get sold," etc. [43]), is used again as the verse to "Now You Know" ("So you've made a mistake, / So you're singing the blues..." etc. [79]), where Charley and the others are convincing Frank to drop his contestation of his scandalous divorce and go on a cruise. The connection is important because, while on the cruise, Frank develops his desire to have the privilege, wealth, and power of the truly rich, contributing to the transformation Charley deplores in the first song. Repeating the melody reveals Charley's implication in Frank's transformation: as much as he hates it, he is one of the ones responsible for it. The position of judgmental purity from which Charley continually accuses Frank of selling out is undercut.

The first sung words in *Merrily We Roll Along* are "Yesterday is done" (2) and they are echoed in the opening stanza of the final song in the show, "Our Time" (155), but everything else in the play works to demonstrate that yesterday is not done, the past is never over. The tension created by the three structural paradigms the play employs reveals an increasingly complex relationship between the past and the present and an increasingly complex awareness of how we perceive the past, how we make sense of it, how we relate to it, and how we use it to govern our sense of our lives.

In the plays of the 1980s, 1990s, and the first decade of the twenty-first century, Sondheim and his collaborators continued to explore the limitations of conventional narrative and to find new possibilities for meaning in unconventional structures. *Sunday in the Park with George* (1984) examines artistic creation, taking us inside Georges Seurat's great painting *Sunday Afternoon on the Island of La Grande Jatte* and conflating art and the world. *Into the Woods* (1987), in its first act, intertwines the ineluctable forward-moving structure of fairy tales with a backward-looking desire to restore fragmented families. In its second act, narrative structure is lost altogether, and the characters try to find meaning by taking responsibility for their actions and by forming ad hoc relationships. *Assassins* (1991) undercuts the complacent narratives of the American Dream by putting them in the mouths of the men and women who have tried to kill US presidents. *Passion* (1994), by taking an epistolary form, presents characters who are trapped in discourse, their own letters and the larger societal discourses that have shaped their expectations for love, gender roles, and physical beauty. They pursue love as a means of escaping representation and entering into an extralinguistic real. *The Frogs* (2004)[8] uses a classical Greek play to depict a contemporary world immobilized by overused and meaning-depleted language. It calls for a revitalized language as a step toward meaningful political action.

Sondheim's newest musical, *Road Show*, written with John Weidman and directed by John Doyle, premiered Off-Broadway in 2008. It extends the examination of narrative from the area of personal identity to national identity. *Road Show* is the story of Wilson and Addison Mizner, colorful brothers who cut a swath through the United States in the first third of the twentieth century. Wilson was what Mizner-chronicler Alva Johnston calls a "conversational artist,"[9] reportedly the wittiest man of his time and something of a shady Renaissance man. He was involved in numerous pursuits—prospecting in the Yukon, running a New York hotel of ill repute, playwriting, managing prizefighters, marrying a wealthy widow, hawking real estate, screenwriting—and he almost always managed to turn them into some kind of con game. Addison was the respectable brother. After some years traveling and living as a hanger-on in New York's high society, Addison discovered a calling as an architect. His style, which was an amalgamation of other styles from around the world, especially Spain, became for a time the latest thing in Florida, where many of the buildings he designed in Palm Beach and Boca Raton still stand. Both brothers became involved in the 1920s Florida land boom, and when the bubble burst, so did their fortunes.

Road Show brings together themes from many of Sondheim's previous shows. Like *Follies* and *Merrily We Roll Along*, it critiques the connection of life stories and journey metaphors as a means of finding meaning. Like *Assassins*, it explores the dark side of the American Dream. Like *Gypsy*, it depicts an entropic America, looping back onto itself and slowly running down. Like *Passion* and *The Frogs*, it shows a society drowning in exhausted and referentless language and the desperate need to break out of the consequent hyperreality. These themes are put in motion in its opening number, "Waste." The play begins with Addison on his deathbed. He has reached the final narrative standpoint of his life, the point where the life story moves out of time and stands as a completed, supposedly meaning-providing structure. What he finds, however, in an office-furniture-junk-pile of an afterlife, are the various people he knew all pronouncing judgment on his life story, summing it up as "a waste." This kind of summative judgment, however, this interpretation of a finished narrative, is undercut in the play, as, after the first scene in the afterlife, Addison and Wilson revert to young men, and we see their adventures played out chronologically until we wind up with them again after their deaths. Their lives are packed with incidents, but the incidents don't cohere into a neat, well-made narrative, and cause and effect are supplanted by chance, surprise, and capriciousness. As the brothers contemplate eternity, the set a junk pile and the stage littered with the $100 bills characters have thrown around all evening, their father announces, "I expected you'd make history, boys. Instead, you made a mess" (98).[10] History is a neat, well-structured narrative; life is frequently a mess, too big to fit neatly inside a single story.

Implied in the foregoing is another significance of the title "Waste": the movement from order to chaos—entropy. One of the ways the tension between order and chaos, progress and devolution, is established is through the metaphor of the journey. On his deathbed, Papa Mizner, as he sings of America as "a land of opportunity and more," seems, in his waistcoat and top hat, to represent the class of men who, following Manifest Destiny and enacting the frontier thesis, moved west, helped settle and define the territory that became the United States, and grew prosperous. Papa asks his sons to imagine "a road straight ahead," that will allow them to achieve "the very best / That you can be," and will be the vehicle for a "quest / For something better, just around the corner". (16, 17). His philosophy clearly envisions history as linear and progressive: it moves in a straight line and continually improves upon the past. His faith is in an infinitely improvable world. However, Papa's song contains the contradictions at the heart of Manifest Destiny. As a philosophy, its goal was the conquering, settling, and civilizing of the continent for European-descended Americans. As a practice, its movement was a clear line from east to west. As a myth of America and Americans, however, it has no end. Papa Mizner's generation reached the westernmost point of the continent and in that sense closed the frontier, but they did not close the myth-generated desire for progress, achievement, and wealth. His bequest to his sons is this myth. The boys' response to this bequest makes up the main dramatic tension of the play. In a country with no remaining frontiers, where language is used-up, and where hype takes precedence over reality, how does one escape from the closed system of the dying, entropic world and find what is beyond, the new?

The Mizner brothers, in their search for a new frontier in the new century, are forced by the dead end of the Pacific Ocean to abandon the progressive, vector-like movement west and instead circle back around the points of the compass. They go north to the Yukon, east to New York City, and south to Florida, a circular movement suggesting a lack of direction, goal, and purpose and a gradual but inevitable loss of energy and the loss of meaning from the American mythos. The myth of purpose, opportunity, and success that the boys inherited from their father is now an empty story. Addison's architectural and design style is an amalgamation of styles borrowed piecemeal from other cultures and combined. He tells one client that every house should have a history, and then he creates one for the house he is designing for her: he imagines a castle in Spain, hundreds of years old, beset first by Saracens, then by Goths, and finally by the Moors, "raping and pillaging and putting in cabanas and a tennis court" (61). Of course, this is an imagined, ready-made history, not an actual one. His combinations of architectural styles do not represent actual history so much as Baudrillardian hyperreal history, a history made into image. Seen in this way, Addison's designs arise from and participate in the exhaustion of discourse, referentless styles combining and recombining endlessly with other referentless styles. In one sense, then, *Road Show* establishes as its setting an America suffering from the exhaustion of its national narratives, an exhaustion of its artistic discourses, an exhaustion of its language. It is an America with its frontiers closed and its boundaries rigid, a closed system entropically losing energy and meaning, a totalized system in which the possibilities for knowledge, truths, and ways of being are inexorably slipping away.

In another sense, however, *Road Show* shows us the Mizner brothers, particularly Wilson, offering a response to the hopelessly determinate, meaning-deprived, and totalized twentieth-century American system. Wilson is adept at engendering narratives as a means of conjuring possibilities for the new in a system that tends to close down possibilities. Like Robert in *Company*, and unlike the characters in *Follies*, Wilson finds the meaning of a narrative in the process of its being narrated, not in the finished structure of the completed narrative. The completed narrative is equivalent to death, the ultimate closure of the system. A narrative in process offers, not determinate, inevitable death, but, like *Sunday in the Park with George*'s blank page or canvas, so many possibilities. Wilson tries to make Addison see this in "The Game," singing, "Every card you're dealt opens new frontiers—" (32).

After marrying wealthy widow Mrs. Myra Yerkes, Wilson acts out his philosophy in "That Was a Year." Finally financially independent, Wilson manages prizefighter Stanley Ketchel, writes a play with Paul Armstrong, and fixes horse races with a jockey, all the while engaging in New York nightlife. He is like a vaudeville performer keeping an astounding number of plates spinning on the top of poles. He sings of New York,

> Every place you look
> Is an open book,
> Every street a new frontier!
> If you sizzle, swell.
> If you fizzle—well,

> Nothing fails for long.
> If it doesn't fly, it doesn't,
> And it's time to sing another song! (47, 48)

When, at the end of the song, his wife tosses him out, it is partly because of the rate at which he is spending her money, but also partly from sheer exhaustion: she cannot keep up with his many narratives. In his Boca Raton sales pitch Wilson puts his own spin on his father's vision of a progressive, constantly improving movement through time when he says that as we go along the journey we are constantly "reinventing ourselves" (91). Rather than follow one road or one life story through time to the inevitable closure of death, Wilson takes multiple roads and lives multiple life stories at the same time, taking a quantum leap from one story to another or, when necessary, creating a brand new story. His philosophy of reinvention, using exhausted language to create something temporarily new and then moving on to something else, allows him to resist closure and entropy. Wilson is irresponsible, selfish, and maddening, but the narratives he generates and acts on at least temporarily resist the entropic, deathward movement of the American myth in the twentieth century.

Road Show's treatment of the theme of transcending closed systems ends ambiguously. On the one hand, Wilson's multiple, enlivening narratives are only temporary. In the Yukon, in New York, and in Florida, he can keep things bouncing only so long. The sound effect of the giant crash that signals the end of the land boom also marks the falling and smashing of Wilson's many spinning plates. On the other hand, in the return to the show's frame, the brothers find themselves in some kind of heavenly afterlife—they have beaten death. Death, it turns out, is not an end—narrative closure, the stoppage of time, the completion of structure—but a beginning, another chance for reinvention. When Wilson asks, "where do you think guys like us go after they die?" Addison responds, "I don't think they go anywhere. They just keep going…" (99). At this point, the road to eternity appears before them, and Wilson proclaims that it is "The greatest opportunity of all!" (99). It is a road that never ends, toward a frontier that never closes, offering infinite possibilities for reinvention and spinning narratives. This is the opposite of the entropy of a closed system. *Road Show* suggests that postmodernism as an alternative to the totalized narratives of the American mythos may not be as exhausted as it appears. In its insistence on multifarious narratives putting multiple worldviews in dialogue, it still offers the possibility for surprise and a way out of a closed system.

It might be tempting to see a narrative pattern in Sondheim's career, an evolution from the Rodgers and Hammerstein–style aesthetic in which he was trained through the postmodernism of the 1970s and 1980s to the later plays' desire to break out of the closed circle of self-referential representation. However, constructing such a pattern would be antithetical to the critique of narrative and narrative knowledge that so many of his plays explore and would indeed be a project Sondheim himself resists. In an interview, asked about the evolution of his career, he says, "I'm unable to take any kind of bird's-eye view of what I do. I don't even like the word *career*. When your whole body of work is done and you're dead, then someone can look back."[11] Instead, we might imagine his career as a number of roads, pointing in different directions, all being traveled simultaneously: the advancing of the Rodgers and Hammerstein aesthetic; the return to the revue and musical comedy forms; the embracing of the postmodern; the look forward to an aesthetic beyond postmodernism. If there is a common goal among these roads, it is to revise aesthetic structures in such a way as to give us new ways of understanding art, our world, and ourselves.

NOTES

1. Page references to *Follies* are drawn from James Goldman and Stephen Sondheim, *Follies* (New York: Random House, 1971).
2. While scholars have not explored this context in depth, others have noted its importance. In his introduction, Banfield calls for studies of Sondheim's postmodernism (Stephen Banfield, *Sondheim's Broadway Musicals* [Ann Arbor: University of Michigan Press, 1993], 7–8). Although she doesn't use the term *postmodernism*, Gordon connects Sondheim's work to avant-garde, nonmusical theater (Joanne Gordon, *Art Isn't Easy: The Achievement of Stephen Sondheim*, Carbondale: Southern Illinois University Press, 1990, 8, 34, 36).
3. The main theorists I'm drawing on for this overview of postmodernism are Michel Foucault (*The Order of Things: An Archaeology of the Human Sciences* [New York: Vintage, 1994]), Jean-François Lyotard (*The Postmodern Condition: A Report on Knowledge*, trans. Geoff Bennington and Brian Massumi [Minneapolis: University of Minnesota Press, 1984]), John Barth ("The Literature of Exhaustion," *Atlantic Monthly*, August 1967, 29–34), Charles Russell ("The Context of the Concept," *Bucknell Review: Romanticism, Modernism, Postmodernism*, ed., Harry R. Garvin, 181–93, [Lewisburg: Bucknell University Press, 1980]), Linda Hutcheon (*A Poetics of Postmodernism: History, Theory, Fiction*, New York: Routledge, 1988), Louis Althusser ("Ideology and Ideological State Apparatuses [Notes towards an Investigation]," in *Lenin and Philosophy and Other Essays*, trans. Ben Brewster [London: New Left, 1971], 121–73), Zygmunt Bauman (*Modernity and Ambivalence* [Ithaca: Cornell University Press, 1991]), Mikhail Bakhtin (*The Dialogic Imagination: Four Essays*, ed. Michael Holquist, trans. Caryl Emerson and Michael Holquist. [Austin: University of Texas Press, 1981]), and Catherine Belsey ("Constructing the Subject: Deconstructing the Text," in *Feminist Criticism and Social Change: Sex, Class, and Race in Literature and Culture*, ed. Judith Newton and Deborah Rosenfelt, 45–64 [New York: Methuen, 1985]).
4. References to *Company* are drawn from Stephen Sondheim and George Furth, *Company* (New York: Theatre Communications Group, 1996).
5. Note that I will be working from the 1971 script, not the radically rewritten 1987 London version, nor the more modestly but still, in my opinion, unhappily revised 2001 version.
6. References to Stephen Sondheim and George Furth, *Merrily We Roll Along* (New York: Music Theatre International, 1994). Note that this version which I analyze is different in many respects to the 1981 original—see Andrew Buchman, this volume, Chapter 7.
7. Craig Zadan, *Sondheim & Co.*, 2nd rev. ed. (New York: Perennial, 1989), 270.
8. The reference here is to the second version as written by Nathan Lane and Sondheim for performance at the Lincoln Center in 2004.
9. Alva Johnston, *The Legendary Mizners* (New York: Farrar, Straus, and Giroux, 1986), 3.
10. References to *Road Show* are drawn from Stephen Sondheim and James Weidman, *Road Show* (New York: Theatre Communications Group, 2009).
11. Jackson R. Bryer and Richard A. Davison, eds., *The Art of the American Musical: Conversations with the Creators* (New Brunswick: Rutgers University Press, 2005), 196.

CHAPTER 3

"YOU'VE GOT TO BE CAREFULLY TAUGHT": OSCAR HAMMERSTEIN'S INFLUENCE ON SONDHEIM

DOMINIC SYMONDS

THE relationship between Stephen Sondheim and Oscar Hammerstein II has been warmly profiled,[1] and its central moment mythologized. It is 1946. "Ockie" is basking in the afterglow of *Oklahoma!* and *Carousel* when fifteen-year-old Stevie presents him with the treatment of his show, *By George!*, asking for it to be critiqued as if it were a professional piece. Hammerstein condemns the show, but offers a packed tutorial in which he dissects his protégé's work. "I learned more in that afternoon than most people learn about song-writing in a lifetime,"[2] reports Sondheim. Under his mentor's watchful eye he wrote four more apprentice pieces: one from a play he admired, one from a play he thought he could improve, one from a story rather than a play, and one an original. Then Ockie introduced the young man to Artie, Jerry, and Lennie,[3] and *West Side Story* was born.

Despite their closeness, the pastoral, roseate, and earnest romanticism of Hammerstein's lyrics seems a far cry from the sly, urban cynicism of Sondheim's;[4] still, to consider either as no more than a lyricist is to underestimate their contributions to the musical stage. This chapter will explore some of the influence that Hammerstein has had on Sondheim, focusing particularly on structure: the way that each has developed song structure beyond the thirty-two-bar AABA model, scene structure using montages of modular blocks, and show structure through trajectories of desire and resolution.[5]

RODGERS AND HAMMERSTEIN: THE INTEGRATED MUSICAL

Rodgers and Hammerstein have long been credited with the development of the integrated musical, and although no formal "Integration Theory" exists, the main principles of integration can be defined:[6] song comes at moments of emotional intensity and flows seamlessly out of the scene with the aid of heightened dialogue, underscoring, recitative, and a preliminary verse. In this arrangement, the formal structure of a thirty-two-bar song (typically in AABA form) is accepted as a stylized expression of the protagonist's emotion.

This understanding of integration is useful, though it has been challenged,[7] and its central tenet—that song comes at a moment of heightened emotional intensity—is for Sondheim somewhat simplistic:

> There's an old cliché that when a character reaches a peak of emotion, and it's too great for speech, he has to sing. There's some truth to that, but not a lot, because characters don't often reach that peak of emotion.... For most of the songs in most shows, it's not the peak of emotion, it's where does music explode the emotion? Where does the music change, or even sometimes, I suppose, diminish and make crystalline, whatever the notion [sic: emotion?] is, at the same time it carries the story forwards?[8]

The fact that Sondheim questions such a common assumption suggests that his work might challenge that of his predecessors. But that is to assume that Rodgers and Hammerstein's development of integration technique was itself as simplistic as integration theory suggests. In fact, a more sophisticated understanding of integration had been central to their work even before their collaboration began: Rodgers's earlier writing with Lorenz Hart on *Dearest Enemy* (1925) and *Chee Chee* (1928), and Hammerstein's collaboration with Jerome Kern on *Show Boat* (1927) and *Music in the Air* (1932) intended that "the whole score ... be viewed as something analogous to a suite or a symphony."[9] Indeed, Kern has been integral to the integration project, and may even be said to have influenced Hammerstein through their early collaborations.[10]

In this there is the real sense of a lineage from Kern and Hammerstein through Rodgers and Hammerstein to Sondheim, all of whom have developed techniques for structuring dramatic narrative in the idiom of extended song form. It is this aesthetic that defines the integrated musical as distinct from the integration of opera: in the integrated musical, the popular song form—structured in lyric stanzas, based around short musical phrases—remains a staple building block; it is a different approach to the classical aesthetic, and one that has often suffered from comparison.[11] Sondheim, however, is passionate about defending this approach, rather than adopting what he calls an "arioso" style:

> Everybody writes so-called "sung-through" pieces, and it's because anybody can write sung-through pieces. It's all recitative, and they don't develop anything, and it just repeats and repeats and repeats.... Whereas a show like *Merrily* ... tells the story in thirty-two bar songs. I mean some of the songs are 108 bars, but they're sections of thirty-two bars—and by thirty-two bars I mean the whole thing is based on modules of four-bar and eight-bar phrases.... I see why opera composers had a good time: it's much easier.[12]

In order to see how Hammerstein contributed to this aesthetic, it is instructive to consider three ways in which he carefully built upon existing practice: by extending the thirty-two-bar conventions of song form, by developing scenes using modular reprises, and by constructing tight dramatic trajectories that bind shows together.

WORKING IN THIRTY-TWO-BAR SONG FORM

The majority of Golden Age musical theater songs are constructed in either AABA or ABAC patterns. In a typical AABA song, the first eight bars establish a melodic and harmonic pattern, the second eight vary that pattern, the third eight present a response with a second subject, and then the main pattern is reprised in a final eight-bar section resolving to the tonic.[13] Typical collaborative practice was for the composer to initiate the process by writing a thirty-two-bar song, and for the lyricist to then write lyrics. This sort of practice operated on Broadway for many years, and spawned many of the show-tune standards that are classics today.

However, this working practice creates an interesting problem for a medium that purports to be creating dramatic pieces, because these songs are built on *musical* principles, and based around structures defined by eight-bar musical phrases. The consequence of this is that, no matter how "bewitched, bothered and bewildered" a character might be (as Vera claims to be in "Bewitched" from Rodgers and Hart's *Pal Joey*), she expresses these dynamic, dramatic states in a very resolute and measured way, and in regular eight-bar thoughts:

> I'm wild again,
> Beguiled again,
> A simpering, whimpering child again—
> Bewitched, bothered and bewildered am I.
> Couldn't sleep
> And wouldn't sleep
> Until I could sleep where I shouldn't sleep—
> Bewitched, bothered and bewildered am I.[14]

Vera's emotional state has not changed or developed; and more than this, it is not even defined as being specifically *her* emotional state—anyone can sing this song. Indeed, its nonspecificity can be seen in the seemingly endless stanzas of lyrics that Hart supplied, both for this show and for subsequent occasions.[15]

The Rodgers and Hammerstein approach was very different: it was Hammerstein who made initial choices about the composition of the song, supplying Rodgers with lyrics already structured into their metrical pattern. Even early on in their collaboration we can see this makes a difference, when a character who is also bewitched, bothered, and bewildered expresses himself in a far less measured way than Vera does in *Pal Joey*. Jud's "Lonely Room" (from *Oklahoma!*), to be sure, is structured in metered stanzas, but the song itself progresses through different patterns of structure, to express Jud's own erratic mood swings. As can be seen in Figure 3.1, the structure is built around eight-bar blocks, but in a less conventional, ABBCA[1] pattern.

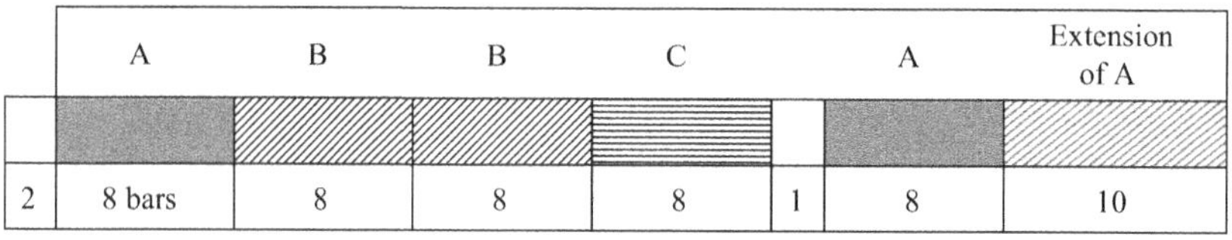

	A	B	B	C		A	Extension of A
2	8 bars	8	8	8	1	8	10

FIGURE 3.1 The musical structure of "Lonely Room" from *Oklahoma!* (1943) by Richard Rodgers and Oscar Hammerstein II.

When material does recur in "Lonely Room," as it does toward the end of the song, it is not simply repeated, but is instead a variation of the A section, extended and developed to reveal Jud's dramatic journey through the song, and evidenced in (the meter of) Hammerstein's lyrics:

> The floor creaks,
> The door squeaks,
> And the mouse starts a-nibblin' on a broom,
> And the sun flicks my eyes—
> It was all a pack o' lies!
> I'm awake in a lonely room...
> [Extension:] I ain't gonna dream 'bout her arms no more!
> I ain't gonna leave her alone!
> Goin' outside,
> Git myself a bride,
> Git me a womern to call my own.[16]

Jud's dynamic, dramatic state is expressed in dynamic and dramatic form, revealing Hammerstein's experimentation with structural form in the musical, adapting the rigidity of the song form in pursuit of greater *dramatic* possibilities. In this, Hammerstein challenges what Joseph Swain has called "the inherent anti-dramatic nature of [song] form."[17]

Indeed, as Scott McMillin's expert analysis suggests, the innovation of the so-called "integrated" musical was in using song form as a dramatic structural device that characterizes the protagonist's particular situation by hesitating, repeating, stumbling through or eventually achieving the thirty-two-bar song as a point of fulfilment:

> The drama is about finding that structure.... Musical time is being called away from the tight structures of the popular song formats and arranged into a kind of avenue that leads to song or that connects one song to another. The avenues are made of song elements, eight-, twelve-, or sixteen-measure segments that may have been heard earlier.... One could say that characterization and plot are being advanced by the song, as integration theory would have it, but that is not exact enough. The song *is* characterization and plot.[18]

Carousel

Both Hammerstein's understanding of eight-bar phrasing *and* his experimentation with it are evident in the lyrics to "Soliloquy," from *Carousel*, a song that was specifically written to reveal the main character Billy Bigelow's "varied feelings about impending fatherhood."[19]

The song begins with a fairly conventional stanza whose rhyme scheme links the first and second halves ("man / can"). The first three lines have eight syllables each (with a beat missing in line 3), a conventional structure that is easy to musicalize. However, line 4 breaks the meter significantly. In terms of the drama, this is appropriate: the chaotic surge in syllables during line 4 reflects Billy's sudden burst of machismo in the lyrics. But this line presents interesting problems to Rodgers if he is going to wed the rhyming couplet "man / can" in the meter of the music (needless to say, it is a problem Rodgers overcomes) (Figure 3.2a).

The next stanza continues in the same format (another A section), anticipating a change in material for the next eight-bar phrase (the B section). However, rather than returning to original A material for the final section, as a conventional AABA song would, the song is disrupted. Billy has become fired up, and his thought process does not suggest a return to the same mood. Instead, Hammerstein offers Rodgers lyrics that are not metered in an eight-bar phrase and which defy conventional musicalization (Figure 3.2b).

(a)

∪	—	∪	—	∪	—	∪	—				
I	won-	der	what	he'll	Think	of	me!				
∪	—	∪	—	∪	—	∪	—				
I	guess	he'll	call	Me	"The	old	man."				
∪	—	∪	—	(∪)	—	∪	—				
I	guess	he'll	think		I	can	lick				
	—	∪	—	∪	—	∪	—	∪	—	∪	—
	Ev'	Ry	oth-	Er	fel-	ler's	Fa-	ther—	Well	I	can![i]

FIGURE 3.2A Scansion in the first stanza of "Soliloquy" from *Carousel*.[52]

(b)

—		—
Not		him!
—	∪	—
Not	my	boy!
—		—
Not		Bill...

(The name, coming to his lips involuntarily, pleases him very much)

—
Bill! [i]

FIGURE 3.2B Scansion at the end of the first stanza of "Soliloquy" from *Carousel*.

Moreover, the thought process here even goes through a sudden shift *within* the line—Billy is bristling and hot-headed for the first two utterances, and then suddenly (as Hammerstein writes in the script), struck by the name "Bill" that "com[es] to his lips involuntarily."[20] It is writing that wholly matches the dramatic situation of the character.

To be sure, this section of the song works very much as a preliminary verse (as opposed to the main verse or chorus of the refrain), which—as Citron reports—had developed as an integration device used to transport the ear from speech to song and to allow collaborators to effect the seamless emergence of song from dialogue.[21] The song proper, we could argue, perhaps begins with the refrain, "My boy, Bill."

Nevertheless, the same disruption of song form occurs even when the main refrain is reached—disruptions guided by the jumpy thought process Billy has and his emotional response to those thoughts. The result is an extended composition in which the heightened expression of song is not just an emotional outpouring (as we see in "Bewitched,") but a combination of thinking, responding to events, working through issues, fighting emotion, questioning convictions, and so on; a *sophisticated* expression of dramatic character[22] (see Figure 3.5) shows how this complex, long-form song is constructed.

SONG FORM FOR SONDHEIM

The distinction between the collaboration of Rodgers and Hart and that of Rodgers and Hammerstein rests on whether music or lyrics came first.[23] Sondheim's work is interesting, because as both lyricist and composer, the words and music effectively spring up already integrated: "Once the lyric starts to take shape, I don't want it to get too far ahead of the music, and vice versa. Then it's a matter of developing both simultaneously."[24]

As his career has progressed, Sondheim has also experimented beyond the traditional thirty-two-bar form—with a good degree of influence not only from Hammerstein but also from Harold Arlen and Milton Babbitt, as Steve Swayne confirms. Sondheim's thought about song, Swayne reports, "encompasses more than the popular notion of a discrete musical composition with a relatively fixed set of measures containing a limited vocabulary of musical gestures and a concomitant fixed set of words."[25] Song for Sondheim—as it was for Hammerstein—becomes a form whose structure itself offers a dramatic dynamic.

The trilogy of songs, "Now," "Later," and "Soon" in *A Little Night Music*, shows strong evidence of this.

Fredrik's "Now" (Figure 3.3a) is established in an extended structure of fifty-two bars, comprising an initial thirty-bar AA¹BB¹ section followed by a second section of twenty-two bars that modulates and extends three occurrences of one motif (CC¹C²). The AA¹BB¹ section returns twice, while further modulations and extensions expand the C section between these repeats. Finally, a coda concludes the song. The fast-paced material reflects Fredrik's plotting, each thought process a development of the last as he reasons his way logically through a series of possible courses of action. The developing

(a)

A	A¹	B	B¹	C	C¹	C²
4	4+4	4+4	4+4	6	4+2	4+2	6

A	A¹	B	B¹	C	C¹	C²	C³	C⁴	C⁵	C⁶
4	4+4	4+4	4+4	6	4+2	4+2	6	4+1	8+1	9+2	1

A	A¹	B	B¹	End
4	4+4	4+4	4+4	8	16

FIGURE 3.3A The structure of "Now" from *A Little Night Music.*

and increasingly complicated thought is therefore matched by an increasingly complicated development (of the C section material); at the end of each verse, when his thoughts come full circle, he starts his ruminations again and it therefore makes sense for the musical material to begin again, wittily paralleled by the lyrics ("Which eliminates B and which leaves us with A.")

If "Now" is constructed around the thought process of the character, it is the emotional journey of a bothered and bewildered (if not bewitched) Henrik that is explored in "Later." "Later" is carefully crafted into a complicated verse with two main motifs, ABB¹A¹ (Figure 3.3b). The initial motifs are introduced as four-bar sections, but then as they reappear, each is extended to six bars, in a deliberate interplay of words and music: Henrik's moody muttering is expressed through broken musical and lyric phrases during the first A section ("Later... When is later?"); the use of incessant rhymes on repeated notes in the B section magnifies his petulant griping ("What's your rush, Henrik? Hush, Henrik! / Goodness how you gush, Henrik! Shush, Henrik!"); his exasperated frustration finally bursts out in a sustained top B over two bars ("For God's sake!") at the end of the B¹ section before he simmers down and returns to his previous muttering, reprising and developing previous material in A¹. The extensions of both the A and B material reflect his increasing frustration, and the fiery cello accompaniment to the song (purportedly played by Henrik himself) serves as a passionate counterpoint to the vocal melody, expressing Henrik's pent-up *ennui*. Within the B section itself, two distinct motifs can be heard, the second a kind of cadenza that lengthens and develops each time the material returns, reflecting Henrik's increasing exasperation.

Finally, Anne's song "Soon" offers a more conventional song structure in AA¹BC form, with A and C sections of twelve bars and an extended B section of thirty-two bars, which again consists of two distinct motifs of four bars, each repeated four times (Figure 3.3c). Here a hemiola figure pits the rhythm of the melody against the gentle rise and fall of the accompaniment. The dreamy tone of the scene—with Fredrik napping beside her as she muses—is captured in both the rising long notes of the melody and the modulation of keys between each section. Anne's reverie is suddenly interrupted by a frantic cello solo

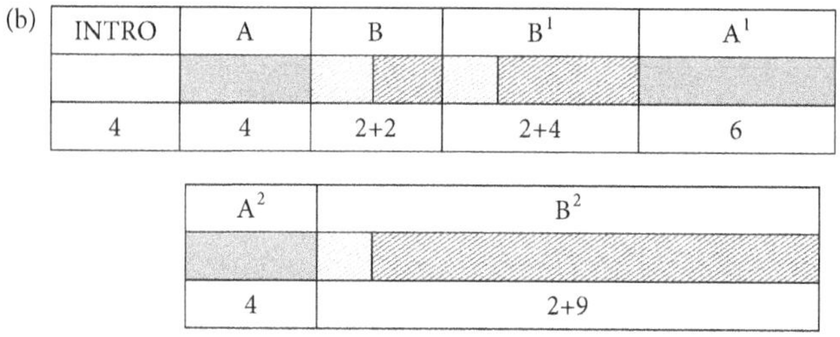

(b)

INTRO	A	B	B^1	A^1
4	4	2+2	2+4	6

A^2	B^2
4	2+9

FIGURE 3.3B The structure of "Later" from *A Little Night Music*.

(c)

INT	A	A1	B	C
4	12	12	32 (4+4+4+4, 4+4+4+4)	12

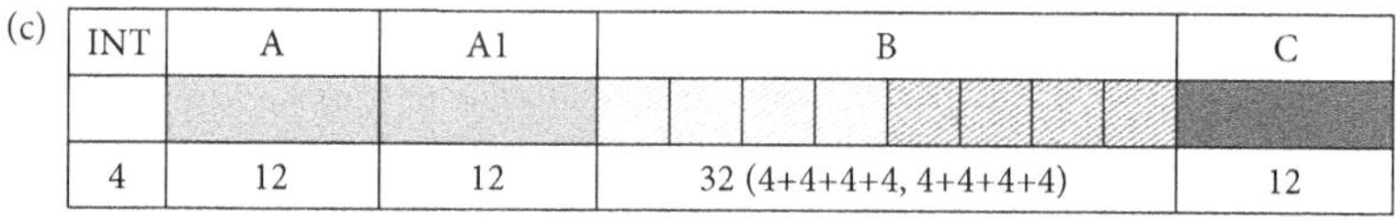

FIGURE 3.3C The structure of "Soon" from *A Little Night Music*, prior to the Trio.

that she hears from the next room, which reminds us of Henrik's presence and wakes Fredrik. The song begins again, though this time with Fredrik's "Now" and Henrik's "Later" layered over it in a clever trio of the three characters' thoughts and feelings.

Although three individual songs, the trilogy very much works as a compound structure. This is quintessential Sondheim, introducing techniques that recur throughout his mature shows, and notably in *Sunday in the Park with George* and *Into the Woods*, whose respective characters' inner journeys are dramatized through the integration of words and music, and—importantly—in the idiom and developed structure of song form.

Allegro and the Modular System

Sondheim was an impressionable teenager, reduced to tears when he saw *Carousel* in its opening season on Broadway.[26] However, it is Hammerstein's next show, *Allegro*, that he acknowledges as the more influential. At seventeen, this was his first experience working in professional musical theater (as "glorified office boy"[27]), and his fond attachment to the show is hardly surprising given the similarities between its act-one narrative and his own life experiences starting at college, becoming sexually mature, and gaining distance from his home life.

Sondheim has recognized in *Allegro* the "experimentalism of its form,"[28] and several of its experimental elements can be seen in later Sondheim shows: a Greek chorus commentating on a protagonist's life (*Company*), the appearance of grandmother-figure "ghosts ('presences,' as Oscar called them)"[29] (*Follies, Sunday in the Park with George*), and a theme of youthful ambition and integrity turning to corruption (*Climb High, All that Glitters, Merrily We Roll Along*). This was a musical based around a concept, and that fact alone signals its influence on Sondheim's writing.[30] However, it is perhaps its fluid form—its "trying to figure out a fresh way to move from song to story without encores or a break"[31]—that has most influenced Sondheim's ability to tell stories: "Right away I accepted the idea of telling stories in space, of skipping time and using gimmicks like the Greek chorus."[32]

In part this was achieved in the staging, which dispensed with the former front-of-tabs scenes that hid cumbersome scene changes on the main stage. The resulting quickening of pace meant that complex stories could be told, which moved beyond the narrative confines of Aristotelian time or place. In *Allegro*, this allows for (almost) a whole life story to be told in one play; subsequently it would allow Sondheim to tell stories across great distances in time (*Follies, Sunday in the Park with George*), weaving multiple character narratives in and among one another (*Into the Woods*), or focusing several protagonists' individual trajectories on a central theme (*Assassins*). Where *Allegro* (and afterwards *South Pacific*) created technical gadgetry like the "serpentine curtain"[33] or the "lap dissolve"[34] to aid transition between scenes, Sondheim's shows would subsequently benefit, through the vision of directors such as Harold Prince, from their own technical effects, like the working elevators of *Company*, which allowed smooth but dynamic transitions between character chapters.

In *Allegro*, Hammerstein developed the idea of the musical scene as a montage, a composite of material encountered elsewhere in the show, or short recurring snippets, some of only four or eight bars in length[35]. This was a development of the structuring McMillin observes in *Carousel* ("eight-, twelve-, or sixteen-measure segments that may have been heard earlier"[36]). The most obvious example of this occurs through a fifteen-minute section of act 1, incorporating vocal numbers 1–8 and covering forty pages of the vocal score, as Joseph Taylor Jr. grows up. The main number forming the backbone of this material is song no. 2, "I Know it Can Happen Again," composed in a strophic lyric and sung by Joseph's grandmother. The simplicity of this compositional form (an A section that can be used repeatedly or with variations) both dramatizes the character Joe as childlike and lends itself to the sort of composite writing that Hammerstein was attempting. The strophe is musicalized in twelve bars by Rodgers, formed according to the suggestion of the lyrics into a main root of eight bars and an auxiliary of four bars; the twelve bars are simply repeated and conclude with a short coda to comprise the whole number. The first eight bars are then used directly as the full extent of song no. 3, "Pudgy Feet," and the final eight bars of no. 5, following an extended dance sequence; no. 6, "Winters Go By" uses two repeats of the eight-bar section followed by a single rendition of the four-bar section.

Around this, material from no. 1, the "Joseph Taylor Jr." motif, recurs in No. 8, and the entirety of no. 7, "Poor Joe," is used as an ongoing motif throughout the show (Figure 3.4).

Song no. 4, "One Foot, Other Foot," also uses an eight-bar sequence constituted as a march and structured into another strophic sequence, which Rodgers musicalizes AA[1]BBBA[1]CCA[2]B. This is material also encountered in the subsequent dance instrumental (no. 5), and in the finale of the show, where Joe metaphorically starts out again. When the songs in full appear, they represent the most complete expressions of the characters' thoughts and feelings, and these "precursors" or "remembrances" of the material

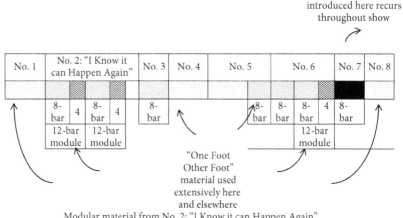

"Poor Joe" material
introduced here recurs
throughout show

Modular material from No. 2: "I Know it can Happen Again"
reprised in No. 3, No. 5, No. 6, etc.
"Joseph Taylor Jr." material from opening number reprised at end of growing up section in
No. 8

FIGURE 3.4 Graphic plan of extract from act 1 of *Allegro*, showing repeated modules (not to scale).

offer ways of anticipating or sustaining dramatic and character development before and beyond the central moment of expression.

In truth, the capacity for complex musical composition in this sort of segmented writing is limited, and much of Rodgers's music is built around derivative chord sequences so that many of the sections remain simplistic and interchangeable. However, this is long-form composition guided by a dramatic impetus, a technique that Sondheim explicitly captured from the start of his professional career.

SONDHEIM'S "MODULAR FURNITURE"

At the end of act 1 of *Anyone Can Whistle* is an extended Interrogation Scene, "Simple," whose 639 bars are a composite of several short motifs: an eight-bar section, "Grass is green..." (first heard in bars 8–15); the cross-rhythmic refrain of the five-bar "Simple" motif (bars 16–20); "I am the master of my fate and the captain of my soul" (bars 90–93); and three syncopated eight -bar sections, "A woman's place..." (bars 214–21), "You can't judge a book by its cover..." (bars 281–8), and "The opposite of dark is bright..." (bars 298–305). Using this material (almost exclusively), Sondheim builds the entire scene, often layering the different motifs on top of one another, sometimes in an *ad lib.* arrangement, sometimes in formal counterpoint (see Figure 3.6). Like the layered sections of *Allegro*, this musical material is rather simplistic and formed in small harmonic sections, making its jigsaw-like composition manageable.

Elsewhere, he would develop this technique: for *Merrily We Roll Along* he used a system he described as "modular furniture":

> You take a release from one song and you make that a verse for a different song, and then you take a chorus from a song and make that a release for another song, and then you take an accompaniment from yet a different song and make that a verse in another song.[37]

Banfield considers this further in *Sondheim's Broadway Musicals*, and his analysis is worth referring to here.[38] As he also notes, Sondheim complements this modular score structure with "verbal motifs" that are reprised, "preprised," and varied throughout the show.[39] He continued to use this approach, particularly in the "Putting it Together" sequence of *Sunday in the Park with George*[40] and throughout the entire score of *Into the Woods*.

Sondheim's use of reprises needs some explanation, since his discomfort with repeating material has been well documented.[41] The reprise has typically featured prominently in musical theater, partly as a leitmotif device, but perhaps more commonly as a way of promoting the "take-home tunes" within the show, thereby ensuring the sale of sheet music to capitalize on profitability. Sondheim recalls pressure from Richard Rodgers to include a reprise when they worked together on *Do I Hear a Waltz*. (Like many of his contemporaries, Rodgers had no qualms about commercializing his product, and even his work with Hammerstein includes reprises such as the finale material of "Oh What a Beautiful Mornin'" in *Oklahoma!*) However, for Sondheim, whose commitment is to the drama, there can be little valid reason to repeat song material, particularly lyrics:

> It's very difficult to find a way that is honest for the evening and therefore doesn't break the audience's concentration and doesn't remind them that they are in a Broadway theatre listening to a reprise.[42]

Despite this, the modular use of thematic material offers a reprise of sorts, with recurring melodies and harmonic blocks consolidating a character's dramatic journey. Indeed, one trend in Sondheim's work is to structure shows in a sort of "reprise with variations" form: the original conception of *Night Music* involved a story that kept restarting at the whim of Mme. Armfeldt; in *Follies*, the ghosts of one existence reenact a counterpoint to the real lives of a later existence; and the second acts of both *Sunday in the Park* and *Into the Woods* contain much material revisited from the first act. In act 2 of *Sunday in the Park*, "It's Hot up Here" uses material from "Sunday in the Park with George"; "Putting it Together" reworks "Finishing the Hat"; "Move On" echoes "We Do Not Belong Together"; and "Sunday" closes the end of both acts; Sondheim has further suggested[43] that the cut-out models of George in "Putting it Together" echo those of the act 1 soldier, and that the song's blocking in the original production echoes the pattern of "The Day Off," inspired by another Seurat painting, in act 1.

Crucially, these are not dramatically pointless reprises: the revisited material develops the dramatic trajectory of the show and in part utilizes its sense of *déjà vu* to contribute to the anticipation of the drama's denouement. In McMillin's terms, the careful structuring of song material constructs a dramatic trajectory against which narrative and characterization can be layered. "Refrain seeks to become its own signifier through repetition.... Refrain bears a memory of its own repetition."[44]

South Pacific and the Trajectory of Desire

A very obvious example of this can be seen in *Oklahoma!*, where Curley and Laurey's act 1 "People Will Say We're In Love" is revisited as "Let People Say We're in Love" in the second act, using our memory of the music (melody, rhythm, lyrics) of the first dramatic encounter to carry over into the subsequent scene. This is the dramatic use of what Banfield has called "creative correspondences,"[45] mirroring or paralleling moments between one act and the next.

This use of correspondence initiates and resolves a part of the "trajectory of desire," a dynamic idiomatic of any romance genre. The principal protagonists are introduced, complications block their happiness, but they overcome adversity and become united in the end. This is a simple dynamic which easily responds to structural analysis, paralleling the conventions of musical form (sonata form), wherein two themes (protagonists) are introduced in the exposition, undergo a development in which complexities and variations are added and worked through, and finally return to an anticipated resolution. The "trajectory of desire" in musical theater is typically introduced in the "I Want" number near the beginning of the show,[46] and concludes in the "Resolution Number" close to the end, thus forming a neat structure that binds the whole dramatic narrative around character and emotion. Such a linear trajectory—desire, complications, resolution (or exposition, development, recapitulation)—is endemic of integrated structure, allowing musical reprises to bind together narrative arcs.

South Pacific expands this technique significantly: its story involves two blossoming relationships (see Figure 3.7,) one between French plantation owner Emile de Becque and American military nurse Nellie Forbush, and one between Lieutenant Cable of the US Marines and the exotic islander Liat. The trajectory of the first relationship begins when we first meet Emile and Nellie.[47] It is clear that a relationship will form, and their own hopes for this (the "I Want" that launches the trajectory) are expressed in the "Twin Soliloquies": "This is what I need / This is what I've longed for / Someone young and smiling / Climbing up my hill," sings Emile. Nellie's feelings are slightly more cautious: "Wonder how I'd feel / Living on a hillside"... "We are not alike / probably I'd bore him"... "Wonder why I feel / Jittery and jumpy."[48] Still, we expect that by the end of the show they will be brought together, and our desires are fulfilled by the end of the narrative. When she fears he may have been killed, she reprises *his* central musical material, "Some Enchanted Evening." This is standard integrated technique, the exposition and recapitulation of one major theme, shared or passed between characters to reflect their emotional connection. "Some Enchanted Evening" is heard four times through the course of the drama, each time offering a slight nuance to the ongoing relationship.

Of course, we expect obstacles to arise as part of the narrative development. The first occurs when Nellie is ordered to spy on Emile in act 1 scene 5. The suspicion this arouses causes her to rethink her hasty involvement with Emile whom she then "washes right out of her hair." The trajectory of this dynamic might be seen to conclude with Emile's much later reflection of loss, "This Nearly Was Mine," and thus a second circular unit can be isolated within the first (D). Finally, a third unit (F) can be highlighted when the lovers' reunification in scene 12 is thwarted by a second obstacle, the issue of prejudice just as the act 1 curtain falls. Nellie finds out that the charming Polynesian kids are in fact Emile's own children by his previous wife, and the act culminates with reprise material reminding us of the impact this will have on their relationship.

Likewise, the secondary relationship between Cable and Liat can be illustrated in a trajectory born in their initial encounter and dashed in Cable's refusal to marry her in act 2 scene 1 (E)—a decision based in racial politics. Beyond this the storyline is reinforced by a dramatic arc (C) that introduces the prospect of a handsome lover in Cable's initial entrance, and literally dies with Cable's death in action. There are further dramatic trajectories, such as those of Billis and Bloody Mary; and the use of the same song material—"Dîtes-Moi" (A), representing the unwitting role of Emile's children in the drama—to bookend the show.

This careful construction of the dramatic narrative, using song material to consolidate emotional, narrative or thematic arcs, can be considered "palindromic," with "events leading up to and away from the central point of the action…which…mirror each other in reverse."[49]

Sunday in the Park with George

Early shows such as *Saturday Night* operate around a "trajectory of desire"; a structure that *West Side Story* and *Forum* also map onto. By the mid-80s, Sondheim clearly adopts a "palindromic" approach, crafting his two most experimental shows, *Sunday in the Park* and *Into the Woods*, in tight, Hammersteinian structures. The palindrome is key, since it requires a central point toward and away from which the dynamic of the drama moves, and it is not difficult to see in this deliberate patterning of form the delight of the game-player Sondheim, famous for enjoying puzzles, crosswords, and other abstractions of form.

Sunday in the Park maps very closely to the conventional Hammersteinian structuring. A series of concentric dramatic trajectories can be superimposed over the spine of the show (Figure 3.8). Seurat's desire for "Order…" that bookends the show establishes its thematic discussion of Art;[50] the relationship between Dot and George through different time periods and even characters (young George / Marie); the theme of children and parents, addressed in "Beautiful" and "Children and Art."

A further circle can be seen in the "red book" dynamic—Dot's "Lesson Number 8: Pronouns"—and its resolution in George's song, "Lesson 8." Here we see several thematic links: the "Order" and "Precision" that guide Seurat's artistry are reflected in the rules of grammar that Dot attempts to learn; the discussion of artistic value that spans 100 years is closely tied to cultural assumptions about the value of learning and knowledge; and the documentation of facts, events, and personalities is refracted through comparisons between the painting's "recorded truths" and Marie's reading of those as disputed in the little red book.

Most obviously, the stunning creation of Seurat's painting, which is the climactic highlight of act 1 (and itself a resolution), acts as an enunciation of artistic completion, reflected in the beautiful chorale-like "Sunday" and later revisited to acerbic effect at the launch night of the Chromolume #7 (the "Art" circle).

Figure 3.8, which views these dramatic dynamics as patterns of concentric circles, reveals the drama to focus on a central point. The core of this whole composition—the central pivot of the palindrome—is the death of its main character, which affects every other character and finds its expression in the "Eulogies" early in act 2.[51] Indeed, this pivotal point in the drama is itself reinforced by its careful anticipation in the earlier "death" of Dot and George's relationship, and its (palindromic) echo in the death of Marie some time later.

It is a further example of how the dramatic dynamic of musical theater can be put together with careful structural precision, following ideas initiated in Hammerstein's work. Undoubtedly, this is a formal "game" that appealed to Sondheim as early as *Allegro*, and it is therefore not surprising that similar palindromic circles of desire and resolution can be seen in the structure of that show (see Figure 3.9).

CONCLUSION

My consideration of Hammerstein's influence on Sondheim has concentrated on the ways in which the dramatic dynamic can be structured through song, through a modular montaging of scenes, and through creating palindromic trajectories within a whole show. To be sure, this is not an exhaustive analysis of Hammerstein in Sondheim. As Steve Swayne's book articulately demonstrates, the nature of "influence" is far more complex, multivalent, and viral than the simple inheritance of one man's "tricks of the trade" by another. Very often, individuals themselves remain unaware of their own influences, tendencies, and processes, and it is certainly fair to say that Sondheim has moved a long way beyond simply writing derivative shows in the style of Oscar Hammerstein. If there is a single, accepted influence that Sondheim has inherited, it is to experiment: to explore, to develop, and to push the limits of a form that is still growing half a century after the death of his mentor.

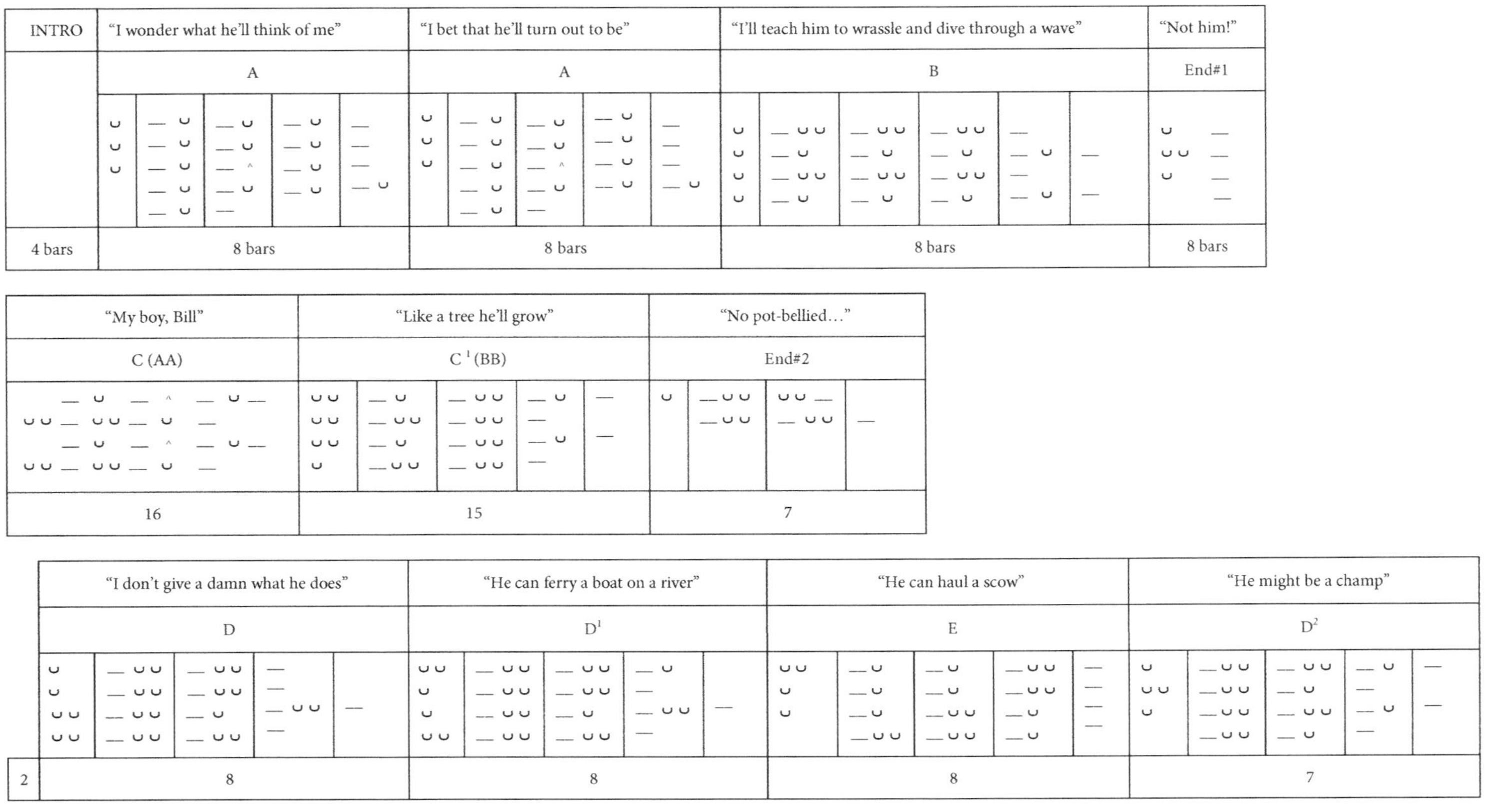

INTRO	"I wonder what he'll think of me"	"I bet that he'll turn out to be"	"I'll teach him to wrassle and dive through a wave"	"Not him!"
	A	A	B	End#1
4 bars	8 bars	8 bars	8 bars	8 bars

"My boy, Bill"	"Like a tree he'll grow"	"No pot-bellied…"
C (AA)	C¹ (BB)	End#2
16	15	7

"I don't give a damn what he does"	"He can ferry a boat on a river"	"He can haul a scow"	"He might be a champ"
D	D¹	E	D²
8	8	8	8
2			7

Spoken: "His mother would like that. But he wouldn't be President unless he wanted to be. Not Bill!"

FIGURE 3.5 Oscar Hammerstein II's extended (lyric) structure of "Soliloquy" from *Carousel*.[53]

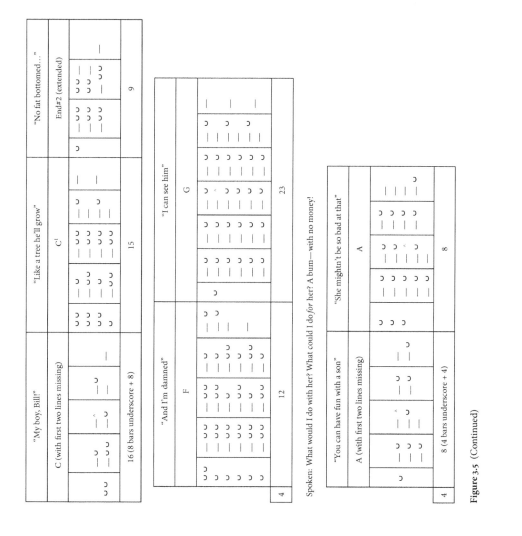

Spoken: What would I do with her? What could I do *for* her? A bum—with no money!

Figure 3.5 (Continued)

"My little girl" | "Dozens of boys" | "She has a few"

C² | H | C²

8 | 8 | 8

"I got to get ready before she comes!" | "She's got to be sheltered" | "I'll go out and make it"

C³ | C¹ | End#2

8 | 8 | 8 | 6

4

Figure 3.5 (Continued)

No. 13: "Interrogation – Part 1 (Simple)"

7	8	12	2	8	10	9	9	4	5	8	4	17
	"Grass is green"	"Simple"										Sprechstimme section

No. 13A: "Interrogation – Part 2"

7	21
	"Grass is green" material in canon

No. 13B: "Interrogation – Part 3"

8	29	9	2	8
"A Woman's Place…"				Ad lib

No. 13C: "Interrogation – Part 4"

6	8	8	8	8	10	23	16	8	42
	"You can't judge a book…"		"The opposite of…"						

No. 13D: "Interrogation – Part 5"

6	6	3	9	3	28	4	4	4	10	4	16
		Ad lib		Ad lib							"Watch-cry" sprechstimme

No. 13E: "Interrogation – Part 6"

3	3	13	3	45	47
			Ad lib		Canon / Ad lib

KEY:		
Introductory material	"A Woman's Place…"
"Grass is Green"	"You can't judge a book…"
"Simple"	Ad lib of all material
"I am the master of my fate"	

FIGURE **3.6** Graphic plan of the "Interrogation Scene (Simple)" from *Anyone Can Whistle*, showing repeated modules (approximately to scale).

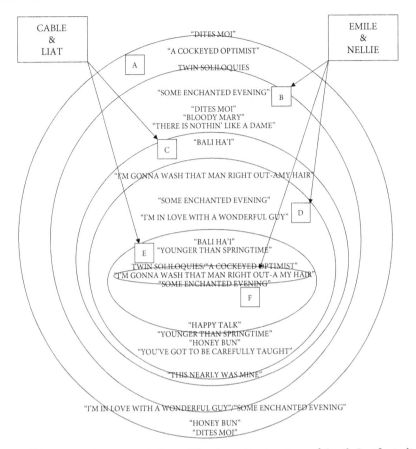

FIGURE **3.7** Diagrammatic representation of the dramatic structure of *South Pacific*, indicating dramatic trajectories in the relationships of Emile and Nellie and Cable and Liat.

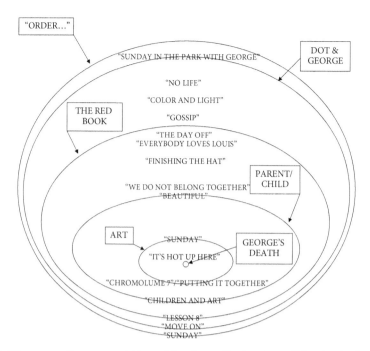

FIGURE 3.8 Diagrammatic representation of the dramatic structure of *Sunday in the Park with George*, indicating thematic trajectories that determine the "concept" of the show.

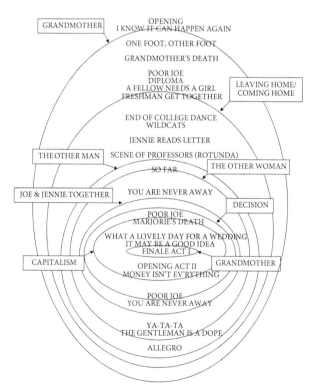

FIGURE 3.9 Diagrammatic representation of the dramatic structure of *Allegro*, indicating thematic trajectories that determine the "concept" of the show.[54]

NOTES

1. Not least in Sondheim's own words: see "Theater Lyrics," in *Playwrights, Lyricists, Composers on Theater: The Inside Story of a Decade of Theater in Articles and Comments by its Authors, Selected from their Own Publication*, ed. Otis L. Guernsey Jr., 61–97 (New York: Dodd, Mead, 1974), 62–3; Hugh Fordin, *Getting to Know Him: A Biography of Oscar Hammerstein II* (New York: Da Capo, 1995), xi–xiv.

2. Sondheim, "Theater Lyrics," 63.

3. Arthur Laurents, Jerome Robbins, and Leonard Bernstein were the other collaborators on *West Side Story*, all more established than Sondheim.

4. Andrew Milner, "Let the Pupil Show the Master: Stephen Sondheim and Oscar Hammerstein II," in *Stephen Sondheim: A Casebook*, ed. Joanne Gordon (New York and London: Garland, 1997), 156.

5. For more thorough considerations of Sondheim's influences see Stephen Banfield, *Sondheim's Broadway Musicals* (Ann Arbor: University of Michigan Press, 1993) and, in particular, Steve Swayne, *How Sondheim Found his Sound* (Ann Arbor: University of Michigan Press, 2005).

6. Broadway conductor Lehman Engel has written several books detailing typical integration features. He champions a number of shows, among which Rodgers and Hammerstein are well represented: *Pal Joey* (1940), *Oklahoma!* (1943), *Carousel* (1945), *Annie Get Your Gun* (1946), *Brigadoon* (1947), *Kiss Me, Kate* (1948), *South Pacific* (1949), *Guys and Dolls* (1950), *The King and I* (1951), *My Fair Lady* (1956), and *West Side Story* (1957). Lehman Engel, *The American Musical Theatre: A Consideration* (New York: Macmillan, 1967), 75. For the 1987 reprint of the book he added *Gypsy* (1959), *Fiddler on the Roof* (1964), *Company* (1970), and *A Little Night Music* (1973), three of which involve Sondheim's input.

7. Among others who have challenged the preconceptions of integration is Scott McMillin, *The Musical as Drama* (Princeton and Oxford: Princeton University Press, 2006).

8. Mark Eden Horowitz, *Sondheim on Music: Minor Details and Major Decisions* (Lanham, MD, and Oxford: Scarecrow, 2003), 71.

9. Stephen Banfield, *Jerome Kern* (New Haven and London: Yale University Press, 2006), 212.

10. See Banfield, *Jerome Kern*, and Joseph P. Swain, *The Broadway Musical: A Critical and Musical Survey*, 2nd rev. ed. (Lanham, MD, and Oxford: Scarecrow, 2002).

11. Stephen Banfield eloquently—if dismissively—describes this as a "quasi-symphonic fabric" made up of "concatenations and reprises of song forms" (*Jerome Kern*, 218, 212). McMillin and others question claims of integration in the "integrated" musical; see, for example, Dan Rebellato, "'No Theatre Guild Attraction Are We': *Kiss Me Kate* and the Politics of the Integrated Musical," *Contemporary Theatre Review* 19, no. 1 (2009): 61–73.

12. Sondheim in Horowitz, *Sondheim on Music*, 20.

13. For a deft explanation of both AABA and ABAC forms see Gerald Mast, *Can't Help Singin': The American Musical on Stage and Screen* (Woodstock, NY: Overlook, 1987), 27–9.

14. Dorothy Hart, ed., *Thou Swell, Thou Witty: The Life and Lyrics of Lorenz Hart* (New York: Harper and Row, 1976), 154.

15. Sondheim has been disparaging about this approach: "My guess is that he had this amount of music to fill out," he comments about another Hart lyric; Sondheim, "Theater Lyrics," 85.

16. Richard Rodgers and Oscar Hammerstein II, *Six Plays by Rodgers and Hammerstein* (New York: Random House, n.d.), 47–8. These are the published lyrics to "Lonely Room,"

though as Tim Carter reveals in *Oklahoma! The Making of an American Musical* (New Haven and London: Yale University Press, 2007), 109, Hammerstein "managed to preserve the accentual patterns" of previous drafts as he developed the song. Amy Asch reveals that the extended lyric stanza is not included in Hammerstein's own edited collection of his lyrics, which, given their dramatic significance, is an interesting omission. Amy Asch, ed., *The Complete Lyrics of Oscar Hammerstein II* (New York: Alfred A. Knopf, 2008), 284.

17. Swain, *Broadway Musical*, 50.

18. McMillin, *Musical as Drama*, 137–8. McMillin's discussion is worth reading in its entirety (pp. 130–39), particularly in relation to the use of song structure as dramatizing device.

19. Richard Rodgers, *Musical Stages: An Autobiography*, 2nd ed. (New York: Da Capo, 2002), 138.

20. Ibid., 138.

21. Stephen Citron, *The Musical from the Inside Out* (London: Hodder and Stoughton, 1991), 55n. Examples of preliminary verse are commonplace before this period, and are not simply a device used by Hammerstein.

22. We should be careful not to undervalue Richard Rodgers's role in this: although I have argued that it was Hammerstein's initial structuring of the lyrics that established the dramatic form of their songs, it was Rodgers's idea that Billy might suddenly realize his child could be a girl (see Frederick Nolan, *The Sound of their Music: The Story of Rodgers & Hammerstein* [New York: Applause, 2002], 161); Rodgers also suggests that he had given Hammerstein early indications of what the music might be like for this section—"not the actual melody but the general tone, colour and emotion I thought would be appropriate," *Musical Stages*, 240.

23. This is a question posed in a delightfully ironic interview to Charlie Kringas, lyricist to Franklin Shepard in *Merrily We Roll Along*.

24. Swayne, *How Sondheim*, 197.

25. Ibid., 231.

26. Ibid., 64.

27. Meryle Secrest, *Stephen Sondheim: A Life* (London: Bloomsbury, 1998), 53.

28. Nolan, *The Sound of their Music*, 173.

29. Ibid., 171.

30. Sondheim explicitly rejects the term "concept musical," and by implication his involvement in any development of such a form, see Joanne Gordon, *Art Isn't Easy: The Theater of Stephen Sondheim*, rev. ed. (New York: Da Capo, 1992), 7.

31. Fordin, *Getting to Know Him*, 277.

32. Secrest, *Sondheim*, 56.

33. Sondheim, "Stephen Sondheim recalls *Allegro*," in *Rodgers and Hammerstein's Allegro: First Complete Recording* (Masterworks Broadway CD 88697-41738-2), liner notes, 15–17 (16).

34. Fordin, *Getting to Know Him*, 278.

35. Several accounts attribute the experimentation of *Allegro* to Hammerstein including Fordin, *Getting to Know Him*, 256–8, and Agnes de Mille in Geoffrey Block, ed. *The Richard Rodgers Reader* (Oxford and New York: Oxford University Press, 2002), 129; this notwithstanding, the modular structure of *Allegro* bears similarities to the structure of the Rodgers and Hart show *Chee-Chee*, as Rodgers explains: "To avoid the eternal problem of the story coming to a halt as the songs take over, we decided to use a number of short pieces of from four to sixteen bars each, with no more than six songs of traditional form and length in the

entire score. In this way the music would be an essential part of the structure of the story rather than an appendage to the action," in Rodgers, *Musical Stages*, 118.

36. McMillin, *Musical as Drama*, 138.

37. See Craig Zadan, *Sondheim & Co.*, 2nd rev. ed. (New York: Harper and Row, 1989), 270.

38. Banfield, *Sondheim's Broadway Musicals*, 327–35.

39. Ibid., 334.

40. Swayne compares this to a "composite cinematic scene" (*How Sondheim Found*, 202) picking up on the modular montage, but also on the impression that one scene is viewed from a variety of different camera angles.

41. See Swayne, *How Sondheim Found*, 228–31.

42. Ibid., 228.

43. Stephen Sondheim and James Lapine, *Sunday in the Park with George*, DVD audio commentary (Image Entertainment ID4586MBDVD, 1986, 1999).

44. McMillin, *Musical as Drama*, 109–10.

45. Banfield, *Sondheim's Broadway Musicals*, 364–5.

46. In Elizabeth Bell, Lynda Haas, and Laura Sells, *From Mouse to Mermaid: The Politics of Film, Gender and Culture* (Bloomington: Indiana University Press, 1995) 178.

47. Figure 3.7 illustrates how dramatic trajectories are launched and resolved in *South Pacific*. The main musical numbers are indicated, and I have used circles to demonstrate how each trajectory binds a section of the show together. Of course, this diagrammatic illustration is not "to scale" in the sense of measuring temporal, diegetic, or even musical structure; however, it does offer a useful indication of how Hammerstein's structure orders the show through these dramatic arcs.

48. Rodgers and Hammerstein, *Six Plays*, 277.

49. Banfield, *Sondheim's Broadway Musicals*, 322. I borrow this term deliberately from Stephen Banfield, who has discussed Sondheim's later technique using this metaphor, and who recognizes its use in modernist and serialist composition, and some late twentieth-century dramatic form.

50. Discussed in detail on the original production's DVD audio commentary (Image Entertainment ID4586MBDVD, 1986, 1999).

51. Banfield observes the contribution of music to the play's tight sense of structure, which introduces here the twelve tones that form the musical palette of the piece and which represent the twelve groups of characters in the painting and the twelve shades of color on Seurat's canvas. Banfield, *Sondheim's Broadway Musicals*, 356.

52. Of course, there are other ways of scanning this stanza, and Rodgers in the end chose to musicalize the whole verse around a dactylic meter. By doing this, almost all the lyrics of lines 3 and 4 trip through a short four-bar phrase.

53. As Asch has observed (*Lyrics of Hammerstein*, 315), the original cast recording of the show includes an additional stanza immediately before "My little girl." Interestingly, this stanza introduces a different metrical pattern again.

54. The outermost circle reflects the influence of Joe's grandmother who returns as a ghostly figure accompanied by her musical motif. The innermost circle also reflects grandmother, and comes at the crucial denouement of act 1. The second circle represents Joe leaving home for college in act 1, and then returning to his roots in the song "Come Home." Both Joe and his sweetheart Jennie meet other love interests in parallel moments of each act: Jennie meets Bertram in act 1, then has an affair with Mr. Lansdale in act 2; Joe falls for

Beulah in act 1, then Emily in act 2—notably, each of these minor characters is given an important musical number at these points ("So Far" and "The Gentleman is a Dope"). An important decision occurs in each act, first when Joe decides not to accept Jennie's father's lucrative job opportunity, and later when he turns down the chairmanship of the hospital to concentrate on his vocation. Finally, a Hammersteinian comment on capitalism (for which Hammerstein received some criticism) has Jennie's parents flaunting their wealth at the end of act 1 and then losing it all at the beginning of act 2.

CHAPTER 4

"OLD SITUATIONS, NEW COMPLICATIONS": TRADITION AND EXPERIMENT IN *A FUNNY THING HAPPENED ON THE WAY TO THE FORUM*

ROBERT GORDON

ALTHOUGH *A Funny Thing Happened on the Way to the Forum* (1962) won the Tony Award for Best Musical in 1963, Stephen Sondheim's own significant contribution to its quality went almost entirely unrecognized.[1] The attitude of New York reviewers toward the songs ranged from indifferent to negative and Sondheim was not even nominated in the category of best music and lyrics.[2] With hindsight, one might ask whether it is not *Forum*'s score that is the key to its artistic originality, as well as the matrix from which a new form of postmodern musical would emerge. As lyricist for *Gypsy*,[3] Sondheim had already helped to achieve the apotheosis of the musical play while simultaneously exposing its limits. In following *Gypsy* with *Forum*, it was logical for him to reject Oscar Hammerstein II's model of "integrated" musical dramaturgy, yet in returning to play variations on the "boy meets girl" intrigues of twenties' and thirties' musical comedy, collaborators Burt Shevelove, Larry Gelbart, and Sondheim did not revert to the dramatic values of Cole Porter or Rodgers and Hart but attempted something more ambitious. In Sondheim's words, "*Forum* is not generally recognized as being experimental, but I find it very experimental. *Forum* is a direct antithesis of the Rodgers and Hammerstein school. The songs could be removed from the show and it wouldn't make any difference."[4] But the repeated success of *Forum* in numerous revivals since its premiere, belies Sondheim's often-quoted opinion that its songs are dramaturgically irrelevant. Reviewing a London revival of the show by the National Theatre in 2004, Michael Billington claimed that "although Sondheim once said that 'about three-quarters of the score is wrong,' here a dozen wrongs add up to a right."[5]

Sondheim's own opinion concerning the mismatch between libretto and score may have been reinforced by his friend and soon-to-be-collaborator James Goldman, who admired both the script and score but thought they were written in different styles: "The book is written in a kind of low-comedy vaudeville style with elegant language, and you have written a witty score, a salon score."[6] Ironically, Goldman's observation may draw attention to a major reason for the show's enduring success. It is remarkable that, in spite of the constraints imposed on Sondheim by the terms of this particular collaboration, the songs in *Forum* are a crucially significant aspect of its dramaturgy.

One of the reasons why the comedies of Plautus, Terence, and their Greek forebear, Menander, are never revived professionally today is that, notwithstanding the skill of their plotting, the social reality that made the types of the wily slave, the lecherous old man, domineering wife, and pretty-but-brainless lovers recognizable and funny, is so alien that these stock characters are now just theatrical stereotypes without the specificity that animates satirical comedy.[7] If an audience cannot laugh *at* the recognizable perversity of the comic dupes or identify *with* the good nature, and innocence of the romantic heroes, the comedy becomes merely a mechanical collection of contrived coincidences and slapstick gags, lacking the motivation of living personalities to breathe histrionic life into it.[8]

The songs in *Forum* supply that histrionic life, enabling audiences to hear the characters' thinking. They thus prompt critical judgments on the characters' interactions that enhance the pleasure of observing how the mechanism of comic justice fits the manner of each individual's comeuppance to the particular nature of his or her perverse, stupid, or antisocial behavior. Far from being superfluous to the farcical plotting, the songs actually complicate the action by "melopoetically"[9] elaborating the thought processes of the agents who motivate its causal logic: the music evokes feelings, while the lyrics reflect thoughts and emotional attitudes, economically supplying what conventional action and dialogue cannot. The complex play of music and lyrics in the songs allows for intricate and infinite variations in harmonious, counterpointed, contradictory, or ironic relationships between the musical and the verbal components.[10] Their placement and form are likewise ingenious, varying the mood and pace of the performance and establishing a style whose self-conscious cleverness not only matches but enhances the metatheatricality of Shevelove and Gelbart's book.[11]

Forum's early working title, *A Roman Comedy*, implied from the outset the collaborators' distance from the type of Plautine farce they meant to deconstruct. While celebrating the stock mechanism of Roman comedy from which it borrows a number of plot motifs, the libretto at the same time exposes the vulgarity of that form by translating Latin wisecracks into the archetypal gags of American burlesque and performing a *reductio* on the absurdity of a plot that, while perfectly constructed for performance, is replete with as many hackneyed situations and second-hand jokes as the television sitcoms Shevelove and Gelbart had in fact spent much of the 1950s writing. In *Forum*, form mocks content in a way that anticipates *Follies*.[12] The pastiche of the form renders Roman comedy as camp, inviting the spectator to revel in a ritualized rehash of the oldest comic clichés in Western theater.[13]

Within the arc of Sondheim's own artistic development, *A Funny Thing Happened on the Way to the Forum* (1962) represents an idiosyncratic attempt to reconcile the musical comedy format imposed by the farce material with his own preference for writ-ing integrated musical drama. In the event, *Forum*'s deconstruction of outdated modes of musical theater performance constitutes a key to understanding Sondheim's later experimental exploration of the nonlinear approaches that constitute the postmodern "concept" musical:[14]

> I had begun to feel, way back during *Gypsy*, that the whole notion of Broadway musi-cals depending on "integrated" songs—numbers that spring from the dialogue and further the plot—ought to be re-examined, and perhaps changed. Though the tone of *Anyone Can Whistle* was off, the songs did break with tradition: they commented on the action instead of advancing it, and I think their relation to the book was excellent. In *Forum* I'd already tried another break: songs that were respites from the action. In *Company* the songs were respites and comments.[15]

Although his lyrics for *Gypsy* reveal a complete mastery of the conventions of the "golden age" musical play, throughout the time Sondheim was working on *Gypsy*[16] he was dissat-isfied with its spuriously naturalistic melding of action with song. His desire to move toward a more abstract form of nonlinear musical dramaturgy is overtly signaled in the self-consciously experimental nature of *Anyone Can Whistle* (1964), conceived immedi-ately after *Forum*. The experience of working with Burt Shevelove and Larry Gelbart on *Forum* no doubt enhanced his sense of detachment from *Gypsy*'s saturated conventions; nonetheless it was *Gypsy* that fortuitously afforded Sondheim his first opportunity to explore a new approach to the craft of musical dramaturgy within an individual song.[17]

By mixing fragments of songs and bits of music associated earlier in the show with Madame Rose, Sondheim assembled in "Rose's Turn" a stylized sequence whose fractur-ing of the nondiegetic form of song in a musical play mimics the collision of fantasies and memories symptomatic of Rose's mental disintegration.[18] "Rose's Turn" effects a decon-struction of the linear narrative of conventional action and song: it fuses the nondiegetic technique of representing the process of introspection typified by Billy Bigelow's sung "Soliloquy" in *Carousel* with the expressionistic means of evoking Laurey's conflicted unconscious in the fragmented form of a dream in *Oklahoma!*[19] Whereas Rodgers and Hammerstein's "Dream Ballet" is accompanied by a medley of contrasting musical themes drawn from songs in act 1, and arranged as an aural mosaic that connotes the shifts in Laurey's ambivalent feelings toward the various characters who have already sung these tunes, "Rose's Turn," in addition to deploying a recognizable motivic pattern by repeating and varying previously used musical material, quotes from several of the show's key lyrics, occasionally altering them in significant ways.

Thus the brazen defiance of "Everything's Coming up Roses" at the close of act 1 is subject to a set of ironic variations near the end of the show that sonically enacts Rose's nightmare of thwarted ambition.[20] The screamed repeats of "For ME! / For ME!" that precede the final sung notes of the number horribly distort the clamorous celebration of indomitable willpower that concludes act 1, subverting the conventions of the musical play the character has thus far inhabited, by inserting an expressionistic representation of the mental disorder of a woman whose life is falling apart. "Rose's Turn" does not forward the narrative through song: Rose stops the show in order to *perform* her number directly to the audience in the vaudeville act of her own imagining. ("HERE SHE IS, BOYS! HERE SHE IS WORLD! HERE'S ROSE!!"[21]) (Figure 4.1). Rose's transformation of her own life into the triumphant performance she has always dreamed about constitutes a self-contained drama that deploys the brash vernacular of vaudeville and burlesque to enable the audience to *experience* her trauma for the first time in the show. It is a *coup de thé âtre* that anticipates the monodrama of Joanne's "The Ladies Who Lunch" in *Company*, exploiting the diegetic form of a vaudeville act or "turn" (in Rose's imagination) as the vehicle for the nondiegetic sung scene portraying her inner conflicts. The pun on the word "turn" calls attention to the paradoxical overlapping of nondiegetic representation with bravura diegetic performance that invariably provokes both a chilling recognition of the character's mental disturbance and a "show-stopping" ovation for the triumph of the acting-singing performer.

Gypsy startles its audience by proffering not one eleven o'clock number but two. A conventional showbusiness musical would present the climactic striptease montage of Gypsy/Louise's "Let Me Entertain You" as a ritualistic celebration of her Cinderella-like ascent to stardom. *Gypsy* deliberately risks anticlimax by including "Rose's Turn" as a dysfunctional alternative to the traditional happy ending: here Rose stops the show with a stark enactment of the tragedy of showbusiness failure. Louise takes her clothes off only to conceal the nothing which the spectator imagines to lie underneath. In her rage

FIGURE 4.1 Angela Lansbury in "Rose's Turn" from *Gypsy* (1974)

against reality Rose performs a grotesque parody of Louise's act that unintentionally exposes the outmoded entertainment forms of vaudeville and burlesque for the shabby clichés they have become. As she struggles to face the emptiness of a present without illusions,[22] Rose performs a psychological striptease that unwittingly destroys the very possibility of the showbiz dreams she believed her children would realize. The naturalistic reconciliation scene with Louise that follows provides closure of a muted and emotionally ambivalent kind, the cathartic force of the preceding number keeping its potential sentimentality in check.

"Rose's Turn" afforded Sondheim his first professional experience as a playwright in song,[23] proving he could deploy the theatrical language of vaudeville to create a metaphorical portrayal of the thought processes of a person whose mental landscape is confined to showbusiness. The ironically apt misappropriation of vaudeville and burlesque allusions to create the soundtrack of Rose's emotional crisis prepared Sondheim for the oblique and playful depiction of minds at work in the songs he wrote for *Forum*. Unlike Hammerstein's naturalistically integrated "sung scenes," the numbers in *Forum* are not surreptitiously woven into the fabric of the dialogue to maintain the uninterrupted flow of nondiegetic illusion. Instead, they exploit the direct audience address of vaudeville or burlesque in the complex manner of "Rose's Turn." By enabling the overt *acting-out* of both the rational and the emotional logic that shapes each character's intentions before these come into collision with changing circumstances, the songs function as vital building blocks in *Forum*'s cause–effect architecture of plot and character. As the songs prompt the audience to savor the subjective wishes and fantasies of respective characters while laughing at the perverse nature of their foibles, they transmute stock agents of farce into recognizable personality types, adding the piquancy and complexity of human emotions and ideas to a plot constantly threatening to descend into a fast and furious dance of puppets.

An analysis of the precise placement and function of each individual number reveals the intricate mesh of song with action in *Forum*. From the moment the actor playing Pseudolus buttonholes the audience in the guise of Prologus (drawing attention to the distinction between actor and character), he advertises the ironic and self-reflexive quality of both book and score:

> Something familiar
> Something peculiar
> Something for everyone—a comedy tonight!
> Something appealing
> Something appalling
> Something for everyone—a comedy tonight! (20)[24]

If music and lyrics here invoke the convention of such "showbiz" anthems as Berlin's "There's No Business Like Show Business" and Porter's "Another Openin' Another Show," they also subvert it. The inspired rhyming contrast of "familiar" with "peculiar" signals from the start how perversely clichéd the show will be, while the bathos in the clever conjunction of "appealing" and "appalling" teasingly casts the spectators as philistines in their eager anticipation of the lowbrow humor and voyeuristic spectacle being promised. It may have been Jerome Robbins who during the Washington try-out attributed the show's failure to elicit laughter to the lack of an opening number which cues the farce to come,[25] but it was Sondheim who inventively solved the problem by writing the wittily appropriate "Comedy Tonight." The rueful self-deprecation of this unique version of the traditional paean to show business undermines the conventional celebration in the knowing and ribald style of the burlesque clown. By establishing an immediate rapport between comedian and audience, the song privileges their supe-rior intelligence and knowledge above the stupidity or ignorance of the rest of the cast, ironically advertising the pleasure of "slumming it" in the company of the world-weary sophisticate playing Prologus/Pseudolus.

Sondheim's opening use of direct address establishes a convention that will be exploited in every double-take or aside to come, justifying the convention of singing directly to the audience as much as to the other characters—and thereby revivifying a style of musical comedy performance rendered obsolete by the musical play of the 1940s and 1950s.[26] Unlike the putative naturalism of nineteenth- and twentieth-century farces by Georges Feydeau, Arthur Wing Pinero, and Ben Travers, Plautine farce is not math-ematically plotted to construct a smooth flow of realistic action that contrives to place the right person in the wrong situation at the right time—or the wrong person in the right situation at the wrong time, depending on whose perspective one adopts. It would disrupt the form and logic of such farce if the characters were to interrupt the flow of events in order to turn to the audience and comment on the action. Yet this is pre-cisely what Pseudolus and all other "wily slaves" in Roman comedy do: they behave like stand-up comedians in a vaudeville or burlesque show.[27] Like a harassed stage manager, Pseudolus attempts to control the outcome of a plot that continuously threatens to spiral chaotically out of control by means of a virtuoso sequence of impromptu inventions—a classic emblem of free will in combat with the indifference of chance.

As "a scenario for vaudevillians"[28] Forum privileges performance over plot, exhuming past performance forms only to reveal that there is still as much life in the ancient gags of Roman comedy as there is in the more recent clichés of burlesque, vaudeville, and television comedy (Figure 4.2). In taking the audience into his confidence, Pseudolus bridges the 2000-year gap between Roman times and the present, leeringly insinuat-ing the continuous persistence of lust and greed as motives. The numerous allusions to American showbusiness in Forum reinforce the metadramatic construction of its nar-rative as a virtual montage of comic sketches. Burt Shevelove commented on the way these sketches are strung together by noting: "Although... [the plot is] really a series of interconnected incidents, one incident has to start before the incident before it can be solved."[29] Songs in themselves may represent incidents or may function to motivate inci-dents or even to comment on incidents performed as equivalent items on the bill of a variety show, thereby enabling Sondheim to structure each as a self-contained "turn."[30] As a consequence, the songs do not merely help advance the drama, they are the drama!

In accordance with Rodgers and Hammerstein's structural model, the first act of Forum is almost twice the length of the second, the preponderance of songs being placed

FIGURE 4.2 Frankie Howerd as Pseudolus in *A Funny Thing Happened on the Way to the Forum*, London (1963).

in act 1. This dramaturgical scheme fully immerses the audience in the mental universe of the dramatis personae by the end of the first act, obviating the need for further exposition or motivation and preparing the ground to ensure that the reversals and slapstick confrontations of act 2 have maximum impact.

Sondheim's deployment of the widest possible range of appropriate song types ensures a varied diet of entertainment whose artfulness both sustains and complicates the burlesque style of the show.[31] The arresting of action for each song not only enhances tension by challenging the audience to anticipate what might happen next but also enables the extended development of a character's reflections in a rhetorical mode that functions like Elizabethan soliloquy—or indeed the direct audience address inherited by Shakespeare from Plautus and Terence. Sondheim's comments on the logic of song placement and the dramaturgical purpose of the songs reveal his particular understanding of this rhetorical convention:

> in all of the shows I write, the songs are plotted based on where they are necessary to tell the story and where the story can be told better by song. There's an old cliché that when a character reaches a peak of emotion, and if it's too great for speech, he has to sing. There's some truth in that, but not a lot, because characters don't often reach that peak of emotion…in most shows, it's not the peak of emotion, it's where does the music explode the emotion? Where does the music enlarge, or even sometimes,

I suppose, diminish and make crystalline, whatever the notion is, at the same time it carries the story forward?[32]

In Roman comedy, a stock ingénue such as Hero would be unlikely to indulge in direct address to the audience, yet the second number starts by playfully emphasizing his "turn to the audience" to sing:

> Now that we're alone
> May I tell you
> I've been feeling very strange?
> Either something's in the air
> Or else a change is happening in me. (28)

"Love, I Hear" offers a complete contrast to "Comedy Tonight." Sensitive and hesitant, it perfectly characterizes both Hero's innocence and his instinct as a young lover. Hero has knowledge of love only through what he has been told or has voyeuristically observed, however his academic knowledge of the subject is being forcefully put to the test by his attraction to Philia. It is not a big ballad, but it calls to mind a "charm song" of musical comedy convention. Musically it conveys Hero's feelings but its lyrics delineate the contrastingly rational self-analysis of a naïve adolescent in the process of making discoveries about the meaning of his experiences. At the same time the song has a significant expository function, revealing how Hero's romantic feelings could provide a mechanism to advance Pseudolus's own self-interest. The song establishes a relaxed and carefree rhythm of action, at this point without a hint of the frenetic pace that the plot complications will engender.

The rhythm of the next song, "Free," is more urgent, its subject entirely germane to the dramaturgical scheme. Sung by Pseudolus with some assistance from Hero, "Free" illustrates the impulse that fuels the slave's subsequent plotting. The number builds Pseudolus's main objective of liberation from slavery upon the foundation of Hero's infatuation with Philia. The authors translate the conventional wish of Plautus's slave characters to become free citizens into an assertion of a fundamental democratic right. Although both motives are comically treated, the linking of Hero's wish for romance with Pseudolus's desire for freedom, is a way of emphasizing Pseudolus's expectation as both properly civilized and instinctively right. While it may not at first appear complex, the song is both musically and dramaturgically sophisticated, appealing to the audience's most basic belief in human rights. The song melopoetically enacts the springing and racing rhythm of Pseudolous's process of thinking out loud, portraying his debate with himself in the guise of a conversation with Hero. The transition from speech to song is effortless, the word "free" first being spoken by Hero and then sung by Pseudolus. Although written to be sung and not spoken, the spareness of the song, with its many short lines and the continual reiteration of the word "free" as a sung exclamation, imitates the movement from thought to speech, emphasized by the way singing repeatedly appears to descend to speaking and vice versa. The song's sequence of images presents a dialectical progression of thought from the sheer pleasure of freedom as a fantasy to a more concrete image of Pseudolus as a citizen exercising civic rights in a manner that

momentarily leads him to doubt the advantages of their concomitant personal responsibilities, before he finally synthesizes the notions of rights and responsibilities in a more
complex concept of democracy:

> Be you anything from king to baker of cakes
> You're a vegetable unless you're free!
> It's a little word, but oh, the difference it makes:
> It's the necessary essence of democracy,
> It's the thing that every slave should have the right to be,
> And I soon will have the right to buy a slave for me!
> Can you see him?
> Well, I'll free him! (35)

Music and lyrics cleverly represent the oscillation between the slave's enlightened rationalism and his selfish instincts, but the tension is resolved in the joke about
Pseudolus as citizen, free to buy a slave merely to experience the pleasure of freely choosing to grant him freedom. Pseudolus's humanity and mental agility are demonstrated
in the swift sequence of associated and opposed ideas, and while prompted to laugh at
Pseudolus's cupidity and cynicism the audience is tacitly made his accomplice in the plot
to help himself by helping Hero. The alliance of Hero's and Pseudolus's needs motors the
plot, initiating a series of incidents that becomes so complicated it necessitates a succession of fast-paced improvisations by Pseudolus, involving deception, disguise, mistaken
identity, and lucky chance. Sondheim deploys the songs for a double purpose: whereas
music enables the spectator's subjective identification with both Hero's and Pseudolus's
motives (and links these), lyrics characterize the two figures in a more critical light as
respectively hopelessly infatuated and shrewdly self-interested.

The decision before the Broadway opening to replace all but the first verse of "The
House of Marcus Lycus" by a dance-mime in which the courtesans advertise their wares
to Pseudolus (and the audience) [33] in a burlesque bump-and-grind reveals the confidence of the collaborators, who knew they could afford to lose most of the extremely
funny original lyrics because performance of the stylized action underscored by musical
material from the song would make the point in a less repetitive way. Dance and mime
are indeed so completely integrated into the fabric of *Forum*'s action at two points, that
they can hardly be perceived as separate components.

The music and lyrics for "Lovely" are yet another example of the show's dramaturgical economy. At the point when in a typical musical comedy one expects a traditional
love duet for the young leads, Sondheim manages to create a love song that, while it
is charming, nevertheless knowingly exploits the audience's assumption that conventional young lovers must inevitably be as vacant as they are pretty. The lyrics demonstrate that Philia is cute rather than dumb, endowing her with enough intelligence
to perceive that loveliness is a performance ("Lovely is the one thing I can do"). Such
self-awareness is not only a comic reversal of the normal expectation of the type but also
renders the naïvety of Hero's slight variation of the refrain hilarious. This number usually elicits much laughter, demonstrating how music and lyrics enhance and complicate

the libretto's self-consciously parodic style through the comic inversions of stock types and situations. Again, the tempo of the song determines the rhythm of the performance, slowing Pseudolus down and prompting him to persuade Philia and Hero in song to follow his plan.

On the surface "Pretty Little Picture" seems merely to interrupt the increasingly frenetic stage action, but although it might be a respite from physical action, there is a subtextual urgency in performance as Pseudolus once more performs an improvisation on the theme of his "brilliant idea" to lure the perversely hesitant lovers into an elopement in order that he may secure his freedom. The song's exponentially more appealing narrative of escape highlights Pseudolus' inventiveness, employing the linguistic conceit of a painter who must add one detail after another to progress from a blank canvas to the final image of liberation which constitutes a masterpiece. The sound of the sea and the rhythm of rowing are charmingly conveyed by the music, while the repeated alliteration and occasional assonance of the lyrics combine to paint the imaginary picture in aural terms. Pseudolus's performance of the song is in itself an act of the creative imagination intended to stimulate Hero and Philia to visualize the future happiness that elopement would bring. He paints them a romantic picture of connubial bliss in imagery that reminds us of his own anticipated liberation from slavery ("Have a little freedom on me"). It is so convincing that Philia and Hero are caught up in the fantasy for a moment.

> HERO and PHILIA:
> No worries
> No bothers
> No captains,
> No fathers! (51)

The metaphoric image of total freedom is quite unexpectedly negated by Philia's literal-minded assertion of her moral duty as a courtesan. (PHILIA: "As long as the captain has a contract I must go with him. That is the way of a courtesan." [52]) Her perversely moralistic response destroys the complicated pattern of Pseudolus's plot obliging him to invent a new plan to deal with yet another unexpected obstacle.

Forum's one guaranteed showstopper follows "Pretty Little Picture" and exploits its motif of fantasizing about love at a much more literal level. "Everybody Ought to Have a Maid" parallels Pseudolus's attempt to stoke up the young lovers' ardor with his cunning manipulation of an old man's lust. Sondheim's scintillatingly comic exploitation of multiple rhymes and other linguistic devices is a regular audience pleaser but, strictly speaking, it is extraneous to the accelerating action. In my view the song is a virtuoso demonstration of the way wit can be used to slow the accelerating pace of the farce and heighten the suspenseful anticipation of impending comic disaster. At just such an apparently arbitrary respite during the dénouement of Oscar Wilde's thoroughly self-reflexive comedy *The Importance of Being Earnest*, Gwendolen paradoxically remarks, "The suspense is terrible; I hope it will last."[34] The audience of *Forum* is given time to savor the thought of plot reversals to come and to enjoy Pseudolus's extreme resourcefulness as he is once again forced to think on his feet—quite literally in the case of the soft-shoe shuffle that usually accompanies the song. Where Pseudolus was previously obliged to fill in the detailed picture of a romantic adventure for the dull and unimaginative young lovers, here he merely has to channel the libidinous overflow of Senex's voyeuristic fantasies.

Senex's version of the song is followed by an extended repeat with variations involving Senex, Hysterium, and Pseudolus, and in turn by a second repeat with further variations involving these characters plus Lycus. The accumulating number of performers during the repetitions constitutes a highly effective structural device. The piling up of soft-core pornographic images stimulates at least the heterosexual men in the audience to fantasize along with the old lechers, at the same time as they laugh knowingly at the age-old comic truism concerning the mechanism of masculine desire. It is a beautifully crafted song, but the delight it regularly provides audiences derives as much from the cleverness of its placement to create a deliberate diversion from the characters' immediate gratification of their desires, as from its intrinsic wit as a musical-lyrical composition.

Up to this point, the songs have determined a pattern of dramatic tension that positions the audience on the side of Pseudolus and Hero in plotting to resolve their interrelated desires for freedom and romantic fulfilment. Hysterium's outbreak of hysteria in "I'm Calm" is an instance in which music and lyrics onomatopoeically imitate the accelerating pace of the plot, prompting the audience to share the morbid anticipation that is provoking Hysterium's panic while laughing at his failed attempts to repress it. "Impossible" is written as a musical scene that employs a series of asides by Senex and his son Hero to dramatize a stock motif in comedy from Menander to Molière of father and son as rivals for the attention of the same girl. Yet again, there is no distinction between dramaturgy and score as the song exploits every nuance of the comic situation to elicit laughter at both characters' expense.

The climax of the first act is the entrance of Miles Gloriosus, dramatic tension being created by the music's echo of a portentous Hollywood epic and undercut by the bombast of the lyrics which ironically expose Miles as a stupid, brutal, and self-important narcissist:

> My bride! My bride!
> Inform my lucky bride:
> The fabled arms of Miles are open wide!
> Make haste! Make haste!
> I have no time to waste!
> There are shrines I should be sacking,
> Ribs I should be cracking,
> Eyes to gouge and booty to divide! (81)

The intermission arbitrarily freezes the show at the point of maximum plot complication, Pseudolus's bathetic interruption being yet another reminder of the theatrical artifice initially advertised in "Comedy Tonight."

There are not only fewer songs in the second act of *Forum* but, with the exception of the reprise of "Lovely," they function straightforwardly to propel the manic acceleration of the plot. Domina's accidental meeting with Hysterium when she returns home to confirm her suspicion that Senex is "up to something low" (108), leads her to confess her connubial misery ("The moment I am gone, / I wonder where he'll go"[108]) to her slave in the artfully conceived "That Dirty Old Man," a blues-inflected number whose melismatic wailing, set to a whirling dance rhythm with "Arabian" orchestral coloring, evokes the exaggerated sensuality of the harem numbers in *Kismet* (1953).[35] The song wittily counterpoises Domina's tender yearning for love ("I'll hold him, / Enfold him, / Where is he?" [108–9]) against the violence of her anger and frustrated libido ("Abusing me (if he only would!) [109]").

Like the two other new numbers in act 2, it is comparatively brief, providing an excellent opportunity for the actress to make comic play with the contradictory extremes of Domina's emotions while at the same time allowing her visually to illustrate the advancement of action by stalking the stage in pursuit of her husband, only to accidentally discover Miles Gloriosus, with whom she flirts rather coyly before her exit to the town. The growing fury of her singing expresses in aural terms her increasingly desperate desire—echoing that of all the protagonists—to achieve satisfaction: the growing insistence of its rhythm mimics the spiraling of the plot towards its moment of maximum confusion before the dénouement.

Philia's "That'll Show Him" is the least distinctive and also the shortest song in the score. While Banfield has pointed out that it is the only song whose joke is external to its musical-lyrical composition,[36] it does function effectively as a direct translation of spoken dialogue into song, ironically revealing how the conjunction of character and situation makes fools of the young lovers:

> When I kiss him,
> I'll be kissing you,
> So I'll kiss him morning and night,
> That'll show him! (114)

It allows the actors to make comic capital of the contrast between Philia's sexual curiosity about being wooed by the Captain and Hero's jealous torment as his beloved fantasizes about the perverse pleasures of being a concubine.

The suspense continues to mount when Pseudolus hides the lovers in the garden, at which moment the shock of Hysterium's entrance in "virginal gown and wig" is bound to provoke laughter. Prompted by Hysterium's fear of discovery ("HYSTERIUM: He'll never believe I'm a girl. Look at me. Just look at me. / PSEUDOLUS: I can't take my eyes off you"), the two slaves sing a reprise[37] of "Lovely" with Hysterium in drag pretending to be the beautiful young Cretan courtesan promised to Miles Gloriosus. Maximum comic effect is secured by placing this drag travesty of a love ballad shortly after "That'll Show Him," while the pile-up of plot complications at this juncture permits Sondheim to demonstrate his skill in creating a subtext[38] of competing motivations that endows the sung scene with its comic urgency. The song is a gift for two low comics. The juxtaposition of the slightly arch simplicity of the lyrics against the comic action in the song never fails to generate huge laughs. The lyrics vary the young lovers' original version for added comic effect (e.g., "Frighteningly lovely" [117] in place of "Absolutely lovely"). The spectacle of

Pseudolus's desperate attempts to reassure the fearful and skeptical Hysterium that he makes a convincing young bride, while the panicking Hysterium seeks to escape before singing in an effort to persuade himself that the disguise will be credible, is quintessential American burlesque. This reprise brilliantly illustrates the technique of building up a song as a burlesque or vaudeville skit, one item in the series of routines that structures the stage action of *Forum*.

Whereas some songs elaborate the kinds of comic action comparable to the arbitrary contrivances and intricate webs of misunderstanding in dialogue scenes, certain silent set-piece routines of pantomimic comedy conversely exploit conventions of clowning as formalized as dance or song that in themselves become discrete "turns." The most complex example occurs ten minutes before the end of the show, fully exploiting the possibilities of Roman comedy's scenic convention of three houses with doors and two outdoor exits to stretch farcical confusion to its limit:

> HYSTERIUM *exits into* SENEX's *house.* SENEX *exits into* ERRONIUS's *house, singing* "Everybody Ought to Have a Maid." HYSTERIUM *pokes his head out of door and ducks back into house as he sees* EUNUCH *enter with* VIBRATA. EUNUCH *pushes her into* LYCUS's *house, exits, chattering.* HYSTERIUM *starts out of house once more as* PSEUDOLUS *runs on, kicks him from behind.* (124)

The mock funeral service, with its chanting and wailing soldiers and skimpily clad courtesans as mourners following at the insistence of Miles Gloriosus, becomes another comic set piece. The ironic tension of music and lyrics produces bathos: the solemn atmosphere evoked by the exaggerated archaism of the music accompanying a repeated lyrical reminder of the bride-to-be's profession ("All Crete was at her feet" [120]), and emphasizing the grotesque incongruity of Hysterium's appearance as the dead courtesan, climaxed by the archetypal slapstick gag in which the terrified Hysterium falls off the bench and is forced to scramble back on it. All the loose ends are tied up in the time-honored manner of farce from Plautus to George Abbot, and the ending serves to remind the audience one more time that the absurdly arbitrary plot resolution is the equivalent of all the other items in the vaudeville or burlesque show that has given Plautine farce its Broadway showbiz rationale—it is yet another piece of *schtick* on a bill that ends with a reprise of "Comedy Tonight."

A slight but significant variation in the final chorus is introduced by Senex: "Something for everyone— / A tragedy tonight" (133). This inverts Prologus's lyric "Tragedy tomorrow / Comedy tonight," which opens the show by introducing the various dramatic genres as equivalent items in the theatrical repertoire, in order to extend the Bakhtinian notion that the solemn genre of tragedy and its anarchic obverse, comedy, are mutually interdependent, carnival (as articulated in comedy) being a necessary subversion of the restrictive social order.[39] Hero's happiness in love frustrates his father's libidinous desires, illustrating the truism that "one person's joy is another's unhappiness." Not only does the lyrical variant give the reprise added piquancy in view of what the audience have witnessed since they heard the song at the show's opening, it heightens the metatheatricality of the reflections provoked by this musical-comedy-a bout-Plautine-musical farce in the deadpan style to which the audience has become accustomed.

As an exercise in musical theatre writing, *Forum* may have been a peculiarly difficult experience for Sondheim,[40] but it provided the opportunity to test the viability of exploiting a more "abstract"[41] form of farcical plotting to connect and motivate a series of set-piece routines, each of which played witty variations on the core narrative motifs. The tension between his mastery of Hammerstein's principles and the more self-consciously contrived dramaturgy of early musical comedy tested Sondheim's ingenuity to its limits. Clever pastiche and affectionate parody of the archaic entertainment forms of vaudeville, burlesque, and revue, which formed the matrix of early American musical comedy, freed Sondheim from the restrictions of the musical play and resulted in a unique masterpiece whose critical reputation and popular appeal have grown steadily in the five decades since its Broadway premiere.

The experiment of *Forum* prepared Sondheim for a series of unconventional projects in the 1960s. Each of these represents a different form of alternative to the "golden age" book musical[42] and they culminated in Sondheim and George Furth's ground-breaking *Company*. The commercial failure of *Anyone Can Whistle* did not persuade Sondheim to attempt a more "operatic" form,[43] in which music contours the dramatic experience. Despite his regularly professed aversion to Brecht's didacticism,[44] Sondheim's close acquaintance with Brecht and Weill's *The Rise and Fall of the City of Mahagonny*[45] and his problematic but serious attempt to write English lyrics for *A Pray by Blecht*[46] at Jerome Robbins's behest provided him with a sound knowledge of Brechtian theater techniques,[47] reinforcing his own personal discovery in *Forum* of the redundancy of non-diegetic songs that arise "spontaneously" from the fiction of dialogue scenes. The new method of exploiting musical comedy conventions as the basis for a more abstract type of dramaturgy motivated his subsequent experiments. In *Company*, the Brechtian use of songs as commentaries allowed Sondheim to overcome his earlier doubts about the function of songs in *Forum*. But it was *Forum* that provided Sondheim with the opportunity to free himself from the constrictions of the musical play and create an experimental show that tested the possibilities of postmodern musical theater.

NOTES

1. Reviewing the show for *The Village Voice* on May 17, 1962, Jerry Tallmer expressed a popular contemporary notion of the reasons for *Forum*'s success: "Brilliance ... doesn't much come out of the book ... yet less out of the narrow-band-spread melodies and semi-cleverish lyrics by Stephen Sondheim. No, it comes out of Mr Abbott's extraordinary talent for hoking and heightening every line, every situation, every occasion placed within his hand ... his talent for timing, and his talent for talent." (Reprinted in the *Sondheim Review* 16, no. 1 [fall 2009]: 27) Paradoxically, this view involves a complete misunderstanding of the relationship between written text and performance: it is only because book, music and lyrics are so brilliantly conceived and interrelated to create a scenario for performance that Abbot's timing of gags had any chance of success. Implicit in Tallmer's misconception is the very comprehension of a musical as a form of performance.

2. See Craig Zadan, *Sondheim & Co.*, 2nd rev. ed. (New York: Harper and Row, 1989), 72, and Meryle Secrest, *Stephen Sondheim: A Life* (New York: Alfred A. Knopf, 1998), 157.

3. Some critics, e.g., Mark Steyn, *Broadway Babies Say Goodnight* (London: Faber, 1997), regard Sondheim's lyrics for *Gypsy* (1959) as the finest in the history of the integrated book musical, perfectly exemplifying the imaginative fidelity to the idiolect of characters within a coherently observed social milieu that Hammerstein's poetics demand. *Gypsy* and *West Side Story* (1957) are themselves regularly rated as among the ten most fully accomplished examples of the "golden age" book musical—see Lehman Engel, *The American Musical Theatre: A Consideration* (New York: Macmillan, 1967).

4. Quoted in Zadan, *Sondheim and Co.*, 68. Sondheim's typically self-deprecatory assessment of his own contribution to the show is complemented by his admiration of its libretto: "I think that the book is vastly underrated. It's brilliantly constructed...the plotting is intricate, the dialogue is never anachronistic...It's almost like a senior thesis on two thousand years of comedy with an intricate, Swiss watch-like farce plot...It's almost a foolproof piece" (Zadan, *Sondheim & Co.*, 69–70).

5. *The Guardian,* July 12, 2004.

6. "We were about to go into production when I got a funny feeling in the pit of my stomach that something was dreadfully wrong with the score...I had James Goldman...read the script. He said, 'It's delightful and it's brilliantly put together and it's very elegant.' And then I had him listen to the score, and he said: 'It's a terrific score.' I said, 'Why do I feel peculiar?...' And he said, 'No, it's just that the score and the book have nothing to do with each other. The book is written on a kind of low comedy vaudeville level with elegant language, and you have written a witty score, a salon score. Either the score should be lower or the book should be more of a salon piece.'" *Sondheim Review* 17, no. 1 (fall 2010), reprinted from the *Dramatists Guild Quarterly*, 15, Autumn, 1978.

7. Although the characters and the situations they confront are still understandable, changes in both social conditions and social values over a period of two thousand years mean that the original social satire embodied in the comic typology of the stock characters has lost its immediacy so that the idea behind each characterization may be discernible, but it may no longer provoke laughter. Without a speaking knowledge of Latin the world of the plays is even more remote, Plautus's virtuoso and ribald wordplay being mostly lost in translation.

8. Audiences still respond spontaneously to the comic situations of Molière, Shakespeare, Congreve, Sheridan, and Wilde in performance because the characters, although not always complex, are still vivid and identifiable as types, who think and feel in ways we can understand or criticize.

9. See Stephen Banfield, *Sondheim's Broadway Musicals* (Ann Arbor: University of Michigan Press, 1993), 7

10. For a masterful analysis of Sondheim's brilliant exploitation of the form of the Broadway song, see Banfield, *Sondheim's Broadway Musicals*, 98–121

11. Sondheim expresses the difficulty he initially experienced in exploiting musical comedy conventions as follows: "[P]lotting the score...[is] a question of how the dramatic arc of a show progresses and where the music is required. And it's a matter of where music is necessary to the show...You can sing about anything. We could sing this conversation, but does music enhance it? Is music necessary to it? In *Forum,* for example, I had a terrible time writing that score...because I had been brought up by Oscar Hammerstein to think of songs as being little scenes and necessary to telling the story. And Burt Shevelove said: 'But there's a whole other way to write songs—the way the Greeks did it, and the way the Romans did it and the way Shakespeare did it—which is to savor the moment.' And

that, in fact—up until Rodgers and Hammerstein—was precisely the way all songs in the musical theater were written, except for Oscar's … songs had a different function in those days … I used to complain to Burt …: 'The script is so brilliant, these songs are just going to hold things up.' He said: 'No, this script will be relentless without the relief and respite of songs that just take little moments and play with them and give them air.' And so I gradually got to accept that." Horowitz, *Sondheim on Music*, 71.

12. The self-reflexive effect produced by means of a complex play of pastiche and parody is allied to the tendency that Stephen Banfield considers to be "dissociation" of the songs from the flow of action in *Forum*." See Banfield, *Sondheim's Broadway Musicals*, 92–3

13. The great British stand-up comic Frankie Howerd, as a consequence of his personal triumph in the role of Pseudolus in the London premiere of *Forum*, had a long-running comedy series called *Up Pompeii!* written for him, based on the exploits of a Roman slave like Pseudolus and making use of all the comic clichés of this tradition.

14. The term "concept musical" was first used by the reviewer Martin Gottfried in respect of Kander and Ebb's *Zorba* (1968) directed by Harold Prince; although the term is ubiquitous it is now regarded by many scholars and practitioners as misleading, and is not favoured by Sondheim.

15. Quoted in Joanne Gordon, *Art Isn't Easy: The Achievement of Stephen Sondheim* (Carbondale: Southern Illinois University Press, 1990), 9.

16. He had begun working with Gelbart and Shevelove on *Forum* even before he commenced work on *Gypsy*; see Meryle Secrest, *Stephen Sondheim: A Life* (New York: Alfred A. Knopf, 1998), 149.

17. Director and choreographer Jerome Robbins had conceived the climactic moment just before the show ends as an expressionistic ballet. By using fragments of dance as nightmare images of Rose's remembered past, the ballet would have revealed how the triumph of Madame Rose's daughter Louise, in her new incarnation as the great striptease star Gypsy Rose Lee, forces Rose to confront her own failure to satisfy her desperate hunger for showbusiness success. When Robbins was unable to choreograph this dramatic climax as a dance, he invited Sondheim to talk with him about the number one evening. Sondheim already had an idea that he was able to sketch out with Robbins's assistance (Secrest, *Sondheim*, 138–9).

18. Sondheim wrote no new music for the number but, since the composer, Jule Styne, was unavailable on the evening in question, Sondheim himself constructed the whole song from musical material already written for the show by Styne. Although Sondheim had great admiration for Styne as a prolific melodist, he was more than a decade Styne's junior and was far more radical in his approach to the function of songs in *Gypsy* as a continuation and intensification of the drama.

19. In the development of the musical as genre, Sondheim's invention might be seen as an innovation of the same order as De Mille's "Dream Ballet" in *Oklahoma!* (1943), or the three through-composed dream sequences in Weill, Gershwin, and Moss Hart's *Lady in the Dark* (1941), which convey the progress of Liza Elliot's psychoanalysis in song, dance, and music.

20. The act 1 finale, "Everything's coming up roses and daffodils, / Everything's coming up sunshine and Santa Claus, / Everything's coming up bright lights and lollipops, / Everything's coming up roses for me and for you!" is transformed at the end of "Rose's Turn" into "Everything's coming up Rose— / Everything's coming up roses— / Everything's coming up roses / This time for me! / For me— / For me— / For me— / For ME!" Stanley Richards, ed., *Ten Great Musicals of the American Theatre* (Radnor, PA: Chilton, 1973), 365, 389.

21. Arthur Laurents, Jule Styne, and Stephen Sondheim, *Gypsy*, in Richards, *Ten Great Musicals*, 387

22. Structurally, the transformation of Louise and Baby June's cute kiddie number "May We Entertain You?" into Gypsy Rose Lee's (Louise's) striptease routine, "Let Me Entertain You," sexualizes the innocent clichés of the little girls' vaudeville song and dance to become the typically risqué lyric accompanying the bump and grind of a burlesque act, while at the same time emphasizing the irony of Louise's ascent from failed vaudeville performer to burlesque star, as Rose is reduced from aspiring manager of a headline vaudeville act to the neglected mother of a stripper. The grotesque spectacle of Rose attempting to prove that she is more talented than both of her daughters by quoting bits of the old vaudeville act and the bump-and-grind routine in "Rose's Turn" finally accomplishes the demythologizing of old entertainment forms that was initiated as affectionate parody in the opening of act 1.

23. Sondheim has said that he "treat[s] lyrics as short plays whenever I can...I'm by nature a playwright, but without the necessary basic skill: the ability to tell a story that holds an audience's attention for more than a few minutes." In Stephen Sondheim, *Finishing the Hat: Collected Lyrics (1954–1981) with Attendant Comments, Principles, Heresies, Grudges, Whines, and Anecdotes* (New York: Virgin, 2010), xxii. See also note 30.

24. Quotations are drawn from the libretto: Burt Shevelove, Larry Gelbart, Stephen Sondheim, *A Funny Thing Happened on the Way to the Forum* (New York: Applause, 1991).

25. See Zadan, *Sondheim & Co.*, 71.

26. Given the classical erudition of Shevelove and Sondheim, one can assume that this deployment of what were the original conventions of Roman comic performance is deliberate; it was Sondheim, Shevelove, and Gelbart who exploited its late nineteenth-century parallels in American burlesque and vaudeville.

27. This is comparable to English Restoration comedy, which advertises the intelligence of its characters by displaying the wit of its principal players.

28. Author's note, *A Funny Thing Happened on the Way to the Forum*, 18.

29. Zadan, *Sondheim & Co.*, 67–8.

30. The revue format has been the structural principle of most American entertainment forms from the eighteenth century to the present day—minstrel show, vaudeville, burlesque, the spectacular "Follies" of Ziegfield and his many rivals, the radio and television variety show, and the contemporary pop concert. Theater historians generally regard early American musical theater as an amalgamation of the vaudeville or revue format with the narrative structure of melodrama and/or stage comedy.

31. "When I'm writing dramatic stuff, I'm a playwright. This is a worked-out scene, and I can tell the actress how to play this scene, and the music is part of the dialogue. I can tell her why the music gets quick *here*, why it gets slow here, why there's a ritard *there*, why there's a so-called key-change *here*...because I have reasons." In Horowitz, *Sondheim on Music*, 25

32. English comedies from Wycherley to Tom Stoppard have traditionally exploited the fast-paced and complicated plotting of farce while at intervals suspending the flow of action to foreground the characters' witty set-piece conversations that demonstrate the intelligence that determines the translation of motive into method.

33. Revivals of the show usually restore the whole of Sondheim's original song, which invariably generates enormous laughter.

34. Oscar Wilde, *Complete Plays* (Harmondsworth: Penguin, 1981), 310.

35. Wright and Forrest's *Kismet* (1953) was itself based on musical themes from Borodin's *Prince Igor*.

36. Banfield, *Sondheim's Broadway Musicals*, 97.

37. In "Theatre Lyrics," in *Playwrights, Lyricists, Composers on Theater: The Inside Story of a Decade of Theater in Articles and Comments by its Authors, Selected from their Own Publication*, ed. Otis L. Guernsey Jr. (New York: Dodd, Mead, 1974), Sondheim stated his aversion to the use of reprise in "golden age" musicals: "I find the notion that the same lyric can apply to the first act and the second act *very* suspect.... In the case of *Forum,* we did a reprise for comic intent. That is to say, you heard the song again, but in an entirely different context, and in fact with a different lyric."

38. See "Theatre Lyrics" for Sondheim's discussion of the principle of subtext in the dramaturgical construction of a song.

39. See Mikhail Bakhtin on the carnivalesque in *Rabelais and his World* (Bloomington: Indiana University Press, 1941).

40. "In *Forum,* for example, I had a terrible time writing that score (Next to *Merrily,* it was the hardest score I ever had to write.)" Horowitz, *Sondheim on Music,* 71. Larry Gelbart: "[Collaborating] was not always smooth sailing. We were forever asking Steve ... to write songs not for Lenny Bernstein ... but for the audience. I remember Steve snapping back once, 'You want those kinds of songs, call Jule Styne.' ... Steve wanted his score to be more than musical relief." Interview with Michael J. Bandler, *Sondheim Review* 16, no. 1 (fall 2009): 25–6.

41. "[T]he critics and audiences were startled originally that a play following Rodgers and Hammerstein and all their descendants could be written so abstractly as *Forum.*" (Burt Shevelove, in Zadan, *Sondheim & Co.,* 76).

42. These include *Evening Primrose,* a one-act television musical with a book by James Goldman that first manifests his unique voice as a composer. See Banfield, *Sondheim's Broadway Musicals,* 45–6, Stephen Citron, *The Musical: From the Inside Out* (London: Hodder and Stoughton, 1991), 140–42 and Chapter 15 in this volume for discussion of *Evening Primrose.*

43. Sondheim has often confessed to disliking opera: "I don't like opera, but I have a feeling that I wish I did. Because ... it's much more satisfying and easier to write something like *Passion* than it is to write something like *Merrily We Roll Along.* To write a thirty-two bar song that has freshness and style to it and tells the story is really hard. And nobody does it anymore. Everybody writes so-called 'sung-through' pieces, and it's because anybody can write sung-through pieces. It's all recitative, and they don't develop anything, and it just repeats and repeats and repeats." Horowitz, *Sondheim on Music,* 19–20.

44. He also claims not to have been influenced musically by Kurt Weill, an assertion easier to justify (see, for example, Banfield, *Sondheim's Broadway Musicals,* 305).

45. I am indebted to Lara Hausez for pointing out to me that Sondheim considered an offer to adapt the lyrics of *The Rise and Fall of the City of Mahagonny* after *Gypsy* opened on Broadway. Indeed, the conception of *Road Show* (2009) may be seen to echo *Mahagonny* in a number of respects.

46. This involved collaborating with Jerome Robbins, Leonard Bernstein, and John Guare to musicalize Brecht's *The Exception and the Rule* as *A Pray by Blecht.*

47. See Zadan, *Sondheim & Co.,* 115–16.

CHAPTER 5

ANYONE CAN WHISTLE AS EXPERIMENTAL THEATER

DAVID SAVRAN AND DANIEL GUNDLACH

STEPHEN Sondheim has an aversion to playing it safe. *Company* dispenses with a linear plot in favor of loosely connected vignettes. *Follies* freely mixes present and past, literally bringing back not only his protagonists' younger selves but also the musical conventions of the 1920s and 1930s on which they cut their teeth. *Pacific Overtures* borrows from kabuki to critique US imperialism, while *Sweeney Todd* remains the only musical that uses cannibalism as a metaphor for capitalist modes of production and consumption. *Sunday in the Park with George* reworks the musical style of Steve Reich and interposes one hundred years between acts 1 and 2, while *Assassins* chooses for its heroes the most unlikely set of villains. Yet even in the Sondheim canon, *Anyone Can Whistle* remains an anomaly. His most revered flop, it opened in April 1964 to mostly negative reviews, including a pan in the *New York Times*, and eked out nine performances despite the proven track records of its creators (music and lyrics by Sondheim, book and direction by Arthur Laurents, and choreography by Herbert Ross) and its Hollywood stars (Lee Remick and Angela Lansbury, in her Broadway debut). Having over the years become a cult musical, it has inspired many critics to reflect on its failure.[1] They often focus, however, less on the show's content than its context: the still recent Kennedy assassination, the Birmingham race riots, the intensification of the Vietnam War, the burgeoning student protest movement, and the musical revolution sparked by the British Invasion, John Coltrane, and the radicalization of former folksingers like Bob Dylan and Joan Baez.

But the theatrical context for *Anyone Can Whistle* was even more volatile than its social context. Unquestionably, the most important development in early 1960s theater in New York was the eruption of a socially and politically engaged Off-Off-Broadway that defied the conventions of the psychologically realist, commercial theater. Joe Cino's Caffe Cino and Ellen Stewart's Cafe La Mama introduced a succession of innovative young playwrights (including Sam Shepard and Lanford Wilson), while groups like the Living Theatre and the Open Theatre opted for a politically radical, performance-based theater founded upon improvisation and ensemble work. The preceding decade had been the principal growth years for Off-Broadway, during which time it "found its niche primarily as the rescuer of those shows overlooked or mishandled by Broadway or those to which Broadway closed its doors."[2] But by 1964, Off-Broadway had become primarily "a spawning ground for Broadway," while Off-Off was still an experimental theater, "an alternative to the established theatre rather than a way into it," peopled by unpaid artists.[3] Given the restlessness of United States culture in the 1960s, this experimental theater was beginning to have an impact even on Broadway, in plays such as Edward Albee's *Who's Afraid of Virginia Woolf?* (1962), Arthur Kopit's *Oh Dad, Poor Dad, Mama's Hung You in the Closet and I'm Feelin' So Sad* (1962), and Dale Wasserman's *One Flew Over the Cuckoo's Nest* (1963). But it was ignored by Broadway musicals, most of which continued to recycle the conventions of Rodgers and Hammerstein and their predecessors, and preferred that radical politics be left at the stage door.

When *Anyone Can Whistle* debuted, *Hello, Dolly!, Funny Girl*, and *Oliver!* were the biggest hits on a Broadway that catered to a liberal, upper-middle-class, middle-aged, urban clientele. Most younger men and women preferred the Rolling Stones, François Truffaut, Jean-Paul Sartre, and Lenny Bruce to Neil Simon and Jerry Herman, and were forsaking the theater for rock concerts and foreign films. When the cultural ferment of the mid-1960s slowly began to affect the Broadway musical, it signaled the beginning of the end for the Rodgers and Hammerstein formula, which would soon be challenged, if never completely supplanted, by concept musicals and rock musicals. Yet *Anyone Can Whistle* was clearly a transitional piece, premiering just as US culture—and the commercial theater—was beginning to undergo a seismic shift, and even the pedigree of its makers could not save it from audiences that did not fully understand or appreciate its audacity. The musical's portrait of a washed-up, bankrupt, drought-stricken town and its corrupt elected officials exposed the economic and psychological underside of the post–Second World War boom and was unlikely to win it many champions among the Broadway theater-going classes. In defense of the piece, Sondheim and his critics have unanimously repeated the claim, "It was way ahead of its time."[4] I would argue, on the contrary, that it was very much a product of its time. In fact, no other musical of the period epitomizes the social and cultural contradictions as vividly as *Whistle*.

An Experimental Musical

Anyone Can Whistle attempted to bring the kind of theatrical and political provocation that was flourishing Off-Off-Broadway to Broadway audiences who were quite unfamiliar with experimental idioms. The show uses and exploits a crazy, over-the-top theatricality that made it far more flamboyant and audacious than most other musicals of the period. And although Sondheim did, at least for the Mayoress's songs, use "the vernacular of the musical theater," he did so "in an ironic way" ("empt[ied] of content") that would have been novel and disquieting to theatergoers expecting the Rodgers and

Hammerstein vernacular.[5] And despite the presence of two "highly romantic" ballads (the title song and "With So Little to Be Sure Of"), the musical language of *Whistle* is far more ambitious and has far more "gingery dissonance" than *Hello, Dolly!*'s.[6] At the same time, the musical's book is a curious hybrid: part satire, part romance, part Broadway razzle-dazzle, part political polemic. It has two convoluted plot lines, the stories of a tourist-attracting, fake miracle and of escaped inmates from the local asylum, the Cookie Jar. The corrupt Mayoress, Cora Hoover Hooper (originally played by Angela Lansbury), along with her posse of crooks, appear primarily in the former. The latter plot features an unlikely pair of romantic leads, the hyperrational Cookie Jar Nurse Fay Apple (Lee Remick) and J. Bowden Hapgood (Harry Guardino), a willful, idealistic nonconformist shipped off to the Cookie Jar who turns the tables on the authorities by masquerading as its new doctor (Figure 5.1). The two plots intertwine in the second and third acts when Nurse Apple disguises herself as the much less sensible Lady of Lourdes to investigate the so-called miracle. Nurse Apple and Hapgood have a brief love affair and he persuades her to try to liberate herself from the tyranny of her own intellect.

At the end, a new miracle is discovered in a neighboring town and the still-gullible pilgrims rush off to pay homage, just as Nurse Apple and Hapgood decide to take on the corrupt world and its deluded inhabitants together rather than apart. Despite its simple

FIGURE **5.1** Lee Remick and Harry Guardino as Nurse Apple and Hapgood in *Anyone Can Whistle* (1964).

outline, the plot becomes insanely over-complicated, almost as if it set out to verify *Whistle*'s moral: "the best hope for the world's sanity lies in madness."[7]

The conceit that the sane are truly mad and the mad truly sane is ancient, but it had been given new life during the Cold War by Existentialism, the publication of Antonin Artaud's *The Theatre and Its Double* (1938; English translation 1958) and R. D. Laing's *The Divided Self* (1960), plays like Jean Genet's *The Balcony* (1957; New York premiere 1960) and Friedrich Dürrenmatt's *The Physicists* (1962; English translation 1963), and countless other cultural productions that denounced instrumental rationality as oppressive and authoritarian. This conceit was reinforced by popular sociological works that condemned conformity, including David Riesman's *The Lonely Crowd* (1950), William H. Whyte's *The Organization Man* (1956), and Herbert Marcuse's *One-dimensional Man* (1964). On the critical front, the 1961 publication of Martin Esslin's *The Theatre of the Absurd* helped popularize the work of Ionesco, Beckett, and Genet in the United States and spread the gospel of absurdism.[8] And although these books and plays were highly regarded in intellectual circles, Laurents and Sondheim were the first to mine them for a Broadway musical. They did so, moreover, during a period when Broadway was undergoing an acute identity crisis caused, the press maintained, by the dwindling number of new productions, the "deterioration of the New York climate for theatrical production," the failure of new plays by established playwrights, the proliferation of British imports, and "huge financial losses."[9] To try to offset these losses, some commercial producers and writers set their sights on attracting the young, well-educated, hip audiences that frequented Off- and Off-Off-Broadway.

Sondheim and Laurents responded to the theatrical crisis by writing what in 1964 was almost an oxymoron, an "experimental" musical whose theme, Sondheim claims, "was very daring" for its time.[10] And while its theme may have been daring for Broadway, it was well-worn in intellectual circles. Nonetheless, *Whistle* was much more ambitious musically and dramatically than most musicals of the period, including Sondheim's previous hit, *A Funny Thing Happened on the Way to the Forum* (1962), which, he claims, represents "a reversion to pre-Rodgers and Hammerstein principles of American songwriting," using songs as "respites" from the action.[11] *Whistle*, on the other hand, has a cohesive if eclectic score built on the first four notes of the overture, a second resolving to a fourth, and all the songs are "based on seconds and fourths."[12] Yet it also uses the diversity of song types that had become the stock in trade of musical comedy: foxtrots, marches, ballads, charm songs, waltzes, and so forth. Orchestrated by Don Walker, one of the deans of American orchestrators (who had orchestrated *Carousel* [1945], *Finian's Rainbow* [1947], and *The Music Man* [1957]), it has a harmonic and contrapuntal richness, texture, and adventurousness that set it apart from other shows of the early 1960s. The absence of violins and violas in the pit, moreover, lends some of the songs an atypical astringency and brassiness, and mitigates the sweetness of the ballads. And while about half the songs are traditionally structured thirty-two-bar songs, Sondheim regularly modifies the form by unexpected modulations, changes of meter, and lengthening of both refrains and releases (as eight-bar phrases are often extended elaborately). Despite these novelties (and a three-act rather than two-act structure), *Whistle* remains a big, splashy Broadway musical, complete with a large singing and dancing chorus.

Anyone Can Whistle is unique, and for some, uniquely problematic, because of the shotgun marriage it engineers between its absurdist plot and the conventions of musical comedy, between its portrait of a conformist society gone mad and its raucous silliness. Yet conformity and logic are not its only satirical targets. It also casts a jaundiced eye on consumerism, tourism, advertising, political corruption, the hunger for miracles and heroes, nuclear weapons, and sexual repression. Its bleak moral seems contradicted by Laurents's brittle, vaudevillian comedy that borrows much from farce, including mistaken identities, shabby disguises, and characters with funny names. Although it is clear what *Whistle* critiques, it is much less clear what it is advocating. Yet this very imprecision is symptomatic of the contradictions inherent in the dominant political philosophy of the early 1960s, liberal individualism, which was both redemptive, because it opposed standardization and conformism, and egocentric, because of its tendency toward an arrogant and selfish solipsism. And while *Whistle* might seem to be advocating for a more communal approach to personal and social problems, it is even more suspicious (as Raymond Knapp points out in Chapter 27 in this volume) of political philosophies that champion the collective, believing the mob too easily seduced by demagogues and too prone to believing consumerism the supplier of miracles. In the musical, Hapgood and Nurse Apple exemplify a positive, emancipatory individualism and Cora a negative, rapacious one. The collective, meanwhile, is more ambivalently portrayed, disdained for its conformism yet at the end of act 1 and in act 2, a reservoir of revolutionary energy.

The difference between *Whistle*'s two individualisms is so deep-seated that, as Stephen Banfield points out, the two plot lines and their affiliated characters cannot be integrated.[13] Almost all the Mayoress's songs are flashy, musical-comedy pastiche numbers that hearken back to the 1940s and telegraph the message that the Broadway musical vernacular is glitzy and superficial, a commodity designed to divert tired businessmen and their wives. (Banfield describes Cora as "a negative version of Dolly Levi in *Hello, Dolly!*"[14]) Nurse Apple and Hapgood, on the other hand, are given what Banfield calls "symphonic (or romantic) music" that alternates between tender ballads and angry anthems that have an undeniably revolutionary fervor.[15] But I would like to suggest that the inability to integrate these plots, characters, and musical styles is less an artistic or personal failing on the part of Sondheim and Laurents than a product of the conceptual limits placed on these disaffected, liberal, upper-middle-class men choosing to work in a commercial theater on whose munificence they depended yet whose ideologies and conventions they distrusted.

A MUSICAL AT WAR WITH ITSELF

The social, musical, and theatrical contradictions of Broadway in the early 1960s are most clearly and brilliantly played out in *Anyone Can Whistle*'s act 1 finale, a fifteen-minute scene, "Simple," which is anything but simple and which represents a theatrical tour de force that no subsequent piece in *Whistle* even tries to match. Passionately and inventively setting forth the musical's message about madness and conformity, it was Sondheim's then most structurally complex song and weaves together two of the period's fixations, absurdism and radical politics, while both exploiting and subverting Broadway vernaculars. Its antecedents are not Rodgers and Hammerstein but opera and operetta, as well as musicals with through-composed scenes like *Of Thee I Sing* (1931) or *Lady in the Dark* (1941). It is structured as a sequence of six interrogations during which Hapgood, pretending to be the new psychiatrist, is charged with distinguishing between pilgrims and Cookies. However, over the course of the scene it becomes clear that his mission, in fact, is not to separate the mad from the sane but to demonstrate the futility of said operation. "Simple," which alternates solo, chorus, *Sprechgesang*, and spoken dialogue over underscoring, is a steadily intensifying and exceptionally dramatic scene whose structure is closer to free association than deductive logic. Musically, it is made up of discrete modules (including, centrally, an A–B–A song) that are repeated, varied, and finally overlaid contrapuntally to bring the act to a frenzied, chaotic close. Beginning in E♭, the song goes through dozens of modulations until it finally ends in F major, a key quite unrelated to its opening.

Hapgood introduces the interrogation by announcing he will proceed "according to the principles of logic" and then goes on (not unlike the Professor in Ionesco's *The Lesson*, 1951) to ridicule and demolish rational modes of inquiry.[16] The number begins with a mid-range, two-chord ostinato that echoes the major second resolving to a fourth that begins the overture. This ostinato constantly resurfaces throughout the song, becoming increasingly irregular and chromatic as the scene unfolds. Above the ostinato, in 2/2, Hapgood sings his nursery-rhyme-like, A–B–A refrain, which has a nearly tautological lyric:

> Grass is green,
> Sky is blue,
> False is false and
> True is true.
> Who is who?
> You are you,
> I'm me! (53)

This first diatonic, duple-meter eight-bar phrase is followed by an eight-bar release (whose lyric is little more than repetitions of the word "simple"), which at first seems as uncomplicated as the song's title. What makes the release remarkable, however, and so dramatically apt, is a three-measure hiccup—its initial measures are in 3/4. Listening to it, one is momentarily disoriented, unable to determine the underlying rhythmic pulse. Is it in duple or triple time? And although it returns to duple time in the repeat of the A section, the dramatic meaning of "Simple" is represented precisely in and by the rhythmic equivocation of the release. After all, the ostensible purpose of the scene is to separate the mad from the sane yet in this deceptively straightforward ditty, the impossibility of knowing the difference between two and three demonstrates the hopelessness of the task. "Simple," moreover, gains added resonance when one recognizes that the two time signatures between which it equivocates are also called simple and compound meters. The remainder of the scene magnifies this rhythmic undecidability by using hemiolas and other 3/4 gestures and oscillating back and forth between simple and compound meters, sometimes almost imperceptibly, and including sections in which the two meters become entangled or overlaid. It is thus nearly impossible not to see these two meters as an analogue to Hapgood's Group One and Group A, the units into which he separates the townspeople.

Throughout *Anyone Can Whistle*, duple and triple time battle each other, the simple meter associated with jingles, marches, nursery rhyme-like songs, foxtrots, and ballads, and the triple rhythms with a nostalgic, romantic, operetta-like fantasy world in which things really are simple, pure, and good. At the same time, however, the complex meter sabotages these romantic fantasies insofar as it is prone to falling into a kind of *moto perpetuo* that sometimes threatens to career out of control. It is as if *Whistle* were demonstrating that the Broadway musical was at war with itself—which in a way it was in the early 1960s—as a new social and theatrical world was colliding head on with old-fashioned conventions. And each section of "Simple" represents a battle in that war, a quasi-Existentialist struggle between existence and essence, reality and theatricality, authenticity and cliché, played out through a succession of stereotypical characters and situations.

The first interrogation that follows Hapgood's simple refrain is performed in a kind of sing-song *Sprechgesang* (with frequent changes of meter) and features an absolutely average, married man, George, with "Two children," "Two TV sets," "Two martinis," "Bank on Friday," "Church on Sunday," and so on (55–6). Hapgood tests George, as he does everyone else, by soliciting from him a watchcry, "a saying you learned that you have used ever since to govern your life." However, George's watchcry, "I am the master of my fate and the captain of my soul," is belied by the utterly conformist creature he has become (55). And conformity lurches into the metaphysical when Hapgood finally asks, "do you ever wonder whether you're real?" to which George replies, "No, sir. I know I'm not" (58). Existential crisis or social fact? Because George, of course, is not real but a character in a musical who is himself merely an abstraction: the idea of the average man.

After a second refrain of "Grass is green" and the interpolation of various clichéd watchcries from the townsfolk, comes the third part of the interrogation, the saga of June and John: the war of the sexes meets the theater of the absurd.[17] Sung over a heavily syncopated, Latin jazz-like ostinato, June and John, who have serious pronoun problems, mindlessly parrot their watchcry, "A woman's place is in the home," while telling the story of their gender-reversed relationship in which June supports John because "his corporation went bust" (62). Bespeaking both the farce and tragedy of compulsory heterosexuality during the post–Second World War domestic revival, the interrogation ends with a minor-key, bluesy lament, marked *molto rubato*: "And home is where he hangs her hat, / And that is where she hangs himself" (63).

The transition to the fourth part of the interrogation is an eight-measure, twelve-part, polytonal quasi-fugato (sung *ad libitum*), that is the musical equivalent of a pile-up, a multivehicle collision, as the townspeople robotically declaim their banal watchcries: "If at first you don't succeed, try, try again"; "Never look a gift horse in the mouth"; "Seeing is believing."[18] The fourth part brings to the fore Martin, a Negro, who changes key and sings a short, eight-bar blues refrain with a flatted third: "You can't judge a book by its cover" (65). Martin's occupation, moreover, "Going to schools, riding in buses, eating in restaurants," nonchalantly announces the three most politically charged activities in the still segregated South during the Civil Rights era. It also inspires a vaudevillian joke as Hapgood asks, "Isn't that line of work getting rather easy?" to which Martin replies, "Not for me. I'm Jewish." (65) Martin's very presence, moreover, inspires Hapgood's next ditty (and a modulation from E♭ to G), a sing-song version of a classic syllogism (which Banfield labels a "trite jingle") that yet again reveals the fallibility of logic: "The opposite of dark is bright, / The opposite of bright is dumb. / So anything that's dark is dumb" (66).[19] Although Martin gets the last word, the stage directions indicate that he "*shuffles over to* [Group] *One, Uncle Tom style*" (67). What is most remarkable about this scene, which chooses not to condemn racism but to parrot racist clichés, is that it ends up in effect interrogating the liberal Broadway audience, putting them in the position of having to choose whether or not to read Hapgood's discourse ironically. And while this confrontational strategy may have been common Off-Broadway, it was novel in a Broadway musical. Nonetheless, this brief and breezy reference to segregation represents a rather watered-down antiracism in contrast to the angrily antiracist plays that opened Off-Broadway during the 1963–4 season, *Dutchman* by Amiri Baraka [LeRoi Jones] and *Funnyhouse of a Negro* by Adrienne Kennedy.

Following a brief dialogue over a Stravinskian, polytonal ostinato in complex meter (although notated in 2/2), Cora takes stage and turns "Grass is green" into "*a gay waltz,*" eliminating the irregularities, as is her wont, in an attempt to seduce Hapgood (68). The waltz is picked up by the chorus of pilgrims and Cookies singing "one-two-three" repeatedly (and maddeningly) over an accompaniment that, superimposing simple and complex meters, sounds like it is tripping over itself. All the while, the members of the chorus are yelling out, demanding to be put into Group One or Group A (69). In the next section, Sondheim alternates between two modules: the pile-up of watchcries and spoken dialogue, modulating up a diminished third when it repeats. He then adds the "Simple" refrain to the mix as Hapgood interrogates the almost interchangeable town functionaries over the continuing ostinato that becomes more and more out of sync harmonically with the vocal line. Some sections are introduced by sudden key changes that produce the impression that a character or group is hijacking the tonality of the song, trying to establish its own home key. All the while, Hapgood reasserts his authority, spitting orders at the two Groups, "Rub your stomachs!" "Pat your heads," turning his patients into the crazed automata that so terrified both liberals and conservatives during the 1960s (70). Comptroller Schub interrupts the chaos when he yells out to Hapgood, "Communist!" (Arthur Laurents had been called before the House Committee on Un-American Activities and although he was cleared, his "scripts had to be vetted in Washington" and he was subsequently blacklisted.[20]) Hapgood dismisses Schub with another "trite jingle" in the form of another illogical syllogism (about the politics of left and right) before being confronted by Chief of Police Magruder, whom he turns into a marching martinet and whose words he twists so that he, too, seems officious and absurd.

The war between existence and essence continues to escalate in the sixth interrogation, which represents the climax of act 1, and begins as Hapgood sings his refrain again,
but now reharmonized bitonally (melody in A minor, accompaniment in E major), its
lyric discombobulated, tautology become oxymoron: "Grass is blue, / Sky is green" (74).
After sparring verbally with Treasurer Cooley over a Stravinskian chorale for winds
(marked *religioso*) and another pile-up of watchcries, Schub stops the proceedings in
what becomes the final showdown with Hapgood: "We are going to end all this right
here and now" (77). Over a slow, "*single spaced*," rumbling beat in the deepest bass,
Hapgood asks his last two questions, "Where does most of your money go?" and "What
do you think of someone who makes a product and doesn't use it" (76–7). Schub's replies
lead Hapgood to his final peroration, as the beat changes into a menacingly dissonant
version of the scene's opening ostinato (that keeps slowly modulating up and is marked
crescendo e accelerando poco a poco):

> Most of your money goes to the government in taxes. What does the government do
> with most of the money? Make bombs.... But you say to make a product and not to use
> it is crazy.... And doesn't that make you crazy for letting them waste your money...?
> But perhaps the government is making bombs because it means to use the product.
> Which means everyone will be killed.... Which means you are paying most of your
> money to have yourself killed. Which means,... you are the maddest of all (78)!

Hapgood's proof of general insanity is followed by a mad recapitulation of the "Simple"
refrain as both Groups intone a riotous mixture of fragments of dialogue (which even
includes *Sprechgesang* glissandos). Although notated in 4/4, this recapitulation also mixes
simple and complex meters, all the while gradually modulating up from D to G and then
dropping back to C. During the chant, both Groups close in on Cora, a screwball, sequined
Stalin, whom they toss "*in the air like a broken puppet.*" Then all of a sudden, "*The light
goes almost black except for a weird glow from the footlights. The two Groups run down to
the footlights and, in a straight line…, chant*[*ing*] *fast and shrill, with mounting intensity*,"
ask their final desperate question over and over, in C major, the key of triumph: "Who is
what? Which is who?" His case proven, Hapgood points out the obvious: "You are all mad."
His line is followed by "*a burst of gay, wild circus music*" while a light bar, "*resembling the
balcony rail of a theatre*," is lowered from the flies and floods the audience with light. "*At
the same time, the real balcony rail lights*" come up and "*we see the company sitting in theatre
seats and laughing and applauding louder and louder as / The Curtain Falls*" (79–80).

"ANY PARADE IN TOWN WITHOUT ME
MUST BE A SECOND CLASS PARADE!"

The act 1 finale of *Anyone Can Whistle*, with the theater audience confronted by its
crazed doppelgänger, announces that all the world's a stage and that characters differ

from spectators as Group One differs from Group A; in other words, not at all. This provocative gesture brings the musical's moral home with a flourish that recalls the era's obsession with questions of authenticity, theatricality, and role playing, an obsession exemplified by the popularity of Erving Goffman's *The Presentation of Self in Everyday Life* (1959) and Eric Berne's *Games People Play* (1964). This bold ending also evokes the much more subdued close of Genet's *The Balcony*, when Madame Irma, the proprietor and stage manager of a House of Illusions, addresses the audience: "You must now go home, where everything—you can be quite sure—will be falser than here."[21] A second radical play *Whistle* calls to mind is Peter Weiss's *Marat/Sade* (1964), as directed by Peter Brook for the Royal Shakespeare Company, which is set in an asylum and ends with rioting inmates threatening to assault both the onstage spectators and the theater audience. *Marat/Sade*, however, opened in London four months after *Whistle* closed.

Anyone Can Whistle also clearly plays off countless social and political anxieties of the era, not least the dread of nuclear holocaust—some three years after President Kennedy promoted a national bomb shelter program, two years after the Cuban Missile Crisis, and one year after the Partial Test Ban Treaty. Despite the treaty, "[n]uclear fear was a shaping cultural force" as the United States and the Soviet Union continued to stockpile nuclear weapons by the thousands.[22] Countless bestsellers, television shows, and films like *On the Beach* (1959), *Fail-Safe*, and *Dr. Strangelove* (both 1964) attracted large audiences, although denounced by the government for being "very harmful because [they] produced a sense of utter hopelessness."[23] But nuclear fear, like madness and consumerism, were not traditional subjects for Broadway musicals and Sondheim and Laurents's experiment doubtlessly unnerved more theatergoers than it enthused.

Anyone Can Whistle did, however, take up one theme that reverberates through almost every Broadway musical, even if its development of the theme was quite untraditional: the individual versus the collective.[24] As I argue above, *Whistle*'s treatment of this theme was keyed to contemporary debates and, in 1964, was overdetermined by US anti-Communist propaganda; fears of conformity, totalitarian societies, and mass-produced human beings; and the burgeoning of a mass-movement politics aimed at mobilizing the disaffected and producing radical change. And while these issues were historically contingent, there is another dimension to the opposition between individual and collective that has a much longer history. For the Broadway musical has, since its earliest days, been a showcase for star and chorus, the surpassing individual and those nearly anonymous singers and dancers who back up the star and serve as her foil. (The Broadway musical is one of the few cultural forms that almost always place women front and center.) In *Whistle*, the predatory Cora is constructed as the fabulous individual, the antiheroic star who, Joanne Gordon notes, exudes a "dazzling surface splendor" yet "whose performance [i]s all style and no content."[25] And although in 1964, Lee Remick's and Harry Guardino's names were placed above the title along with Angela Lansbury's, Nurse Apple and Hapgood are part of the nonconformist collective, two Cookies who have lost their way and who lack the narcissistic temperament (and the extroverted, brash, pastiche songs) of the star. Yet at the same time, they also represent (as Raymond Knapp observes) a redemptive individualism that, in *Anyone Can Whistle*, seems the best antidote to an insane world.

Anyone Can Whistle is unable to solve the puzzle of individual and collective. Rather, it is one of those musicals that symptomatize the plight of the human subject during a historical moment when it did not take a Herbert Marcuse to see that human beings are less free agents than preprogrammed citizens and consumers. Significantly, musicals are often the best place to look for disturbances in subjectivity because of the opposition they almost inevitably stage between individual and collective, star and chorus. Consider the irony, after all, in Hapgood's first interrogation of the robot named George, who emerges from the chorus and announces his watchcry: "I am the master of my fate and the captain of my soul" (55). Thinking himself a free agent, George is utterly unaware that he is no more nor less than a social calculus, a stereotype, a rubber stamp. Or the fact that Hapgood insists on addressing Cookies, pilgrims, and elected officials alike by his own name, further eradicating social and psychological differences. It is little wonder that several of the most celebrated musicals that followed *Whistle* are similarly obsessed with the relationship between the one and the many and the problematic of human agency, including *Hair* (1968), *1776* (1969), *Company* (1970), and *A Chorus Line* (1975), the *locus classicus* of this subgenre. These shows struck a nerve because, by any measure, the 1960s and early 1970s described a period of political and social crisis during which the status of liberal individualism was highly contentious. How can the individual subject be really free when consumerism functions as a form of social control?

As an innovator working in a theatrical form that is a barometer of changing circumstances and conventions, Sondheim has long been preoccupied with the problem of the collective. Although *Anyone Can Whistle* questions the relationship between individual and society, it does so less completely or confidently than several of his later musicals that use collective heroes. *Pacific Overtures* may give the leading role to the Narrator, *Into the Woods* to the Witch, and *Assassins* may be bookended by the stories of John Wilkes Booth and Lee Harvey Oswald, but all three produce the group as protagonist. All three carefully interweave their several plots and ensure that their eleven o'clock numbers— "Next," "No One Is Alone," and "Another National Anthem"—are performed by all, or many, of the dramatis personae. Moreover, each of these songs is precisely about the making (and potential unmaking) of the collective, whether it be modern Japanese society, fairytale heroes, or a fellowship of presidential assassins.

Anyone Can Whistle, however, dates from an earlier period when liberal artists and intellectuals of Sondheim's and Laurents's generation were genuinely torn. On the one hand, they still believed the collective to be a conformist herd. On the other, they had become increasingly sympathetic to the Civil Rights movement and the quickly growing, mass opposition to the military-industrial complex. This ambivalence plays itself out on many levels in *Whistle*, not least of all in the contradiction between its theatrical and musical experimentation and its formulaic, musical-comedy conclusion that romantic love is the best hope for the world. Although there are countless songs and scenes I could single out as examples of this contradiction, I want to conclude by looking at "A Parade in Town," Cora's big act 2 number and one of the show's most conventional and oft-recorded songs. This vigorous march, however, is less a solo than a kind of unplanned dialogue in the town square between collective and individual, between the chorus, for whom Hapgood is the new savior, and the star, the abandoned Mayoress. At its opening, Groups One and A march on, bearing identical placards, chanting "Hooray for Hapgood" and mechanically singing his praises in what is, in fact, the song's verse. Cora tries unsuccessfully to get their attention and after they pass her by, sings a thirty-two-bar, A–B–A–C refrain that expresses both her delight and dejection. In the first half of the refrain, she envisions the quintessential American public spectacle, one long mined by composers for the theatrical thrills it generates as a celebration of national identity: "I see flags, I hear bells, / There's a parade in town." But in the second half, to nearly identical music, her excitement turns to disappointment when she realizes she has been snubbed. Before she can begin her reprise, the choruses "*storm on again,*" robotically reiterating their watchcry: "As long as we're told where to go, / There isn't a thing we need to know." Cora then repeats her refrain, interrupted by the choruses' cheers, only to realize her own belatedness: "Tell me, while I was getting ready / Did a parade go by?" (110–12).

It is tempting to see Cora's disorientation in "A Parade in Town" as an allegory for the disorientation of musical comedy in the early 1960s, when it was being outflanked by a host of more popular and radical musical and theatrical forms and becoming increasingly a kind of middlebrow coterie art.[26] For the Broadway musical was unquestionably suffering a kind of identity crisis in those years caused in part by the eruption of one of the most explosive social and cultural revolutions in US history. Yet this particular crisis is, I believe, more properly seen as one among many to which the musical has responded since the 1920s, when its conventions and its position became consolidated as light middle-class entertainment.[27] So many writers of canonical musicals, from the Gershwins and Kurt Weill to Rodgers and Hammerstein and Leonard Bernstein, deliberately set out to challenge formulas that, in their view, had become stale or ossified. Yet at the same time, because the Broadway musical is arguably the most formulaic and commercial of theatrical genres, all found themselves ineluctably beholden to those conventions that would guarantee at least a measure of popular success.

Stephen Sondheim is unquestionably the rightful heir to these writers and, like them, has both abided by and broken the rules. If Sondheim has been the most consistently daring of them all, that fact is in part a response to the extremely volatile social and cultural climate in which he has lived as well as to his own desire to restore a measure of high cultural legitimacy to a genre that has always been a bastard art. For most of his career, Sondheim has been receptive to innovations practiced by contemporary playwrights, composers, directors, and designers. At the same time, he is an extremely well-educated composer and lyricist who knows the history of the form so intimately that his plays always reference and revise the tradition of which he is a part. He has collaborated frequently with men (most notably, Harold Prince and James Lapine) who have encouraged him to defy conventional wisdom and he has enjoyed, if not popular acclaim, then an unparalleled *succès d'estime*. His first experimental musical, *Anyone Can Whistle*, was a bold step in revolutionizing Broadway. That it had to wait years to find an audience is a tribute less to Sondheim's prescience than to his ascendency since the 1970s as his generation's preeminent transformer of the entire field of Anglophone music theater, a category that includes the Broadway musical and opera, to be sure, but that also embraces many new, hybrid theater forms that his musical and theatrical experiments have inspired.

NOTES

1. *Anyone Can Whistle* has been periodically revived in theaters in the United States and the United Kingdom, and was performed with all-star casts at Carnegie Hall in 1995 (as a benefit for Gay Men's Health Crisis) and in 2010 as part of the City Center Encores! season celebrating Sondheim's eightieth birthday.
2. Arnold Aronson, *American Avant-garde Theatre: A History* (London: Routledge, 2000), 44.
3. Jack Poggi, *Theater in America: The Impact of Economic Forces, 1870–1967* (Ithaca, NY: Cornell University Press, 1968), 172; Michael Smith, quoted in Poggi, *Theater in America*, 196.
4. Stephen Sondheim quoted in Craig Zadan, *Sondheim & Co.*, 2nd edition (New York: Harper and Row, 1986), 82.
5. Stephen Sondheim, in David Savran, *In Their Own Words: Contemporary American Playwrights* (New York: Theatre Communications Group, 1988), 227–8.
6. Stephen Sondheim, quoted in Meryle Secrest, *Stephen Sondheim: A Life* (New York: Alfred A. Knopf, 1998), 162.
7. Howard Taubman, "The Theater: 'Anyone Can Whistle,' " *New York Times*, April 6, 1964, 36.
8. The book's publication is even noted in Henry Hewes, "The Season in New York," in *The Best Plays of 1961–1962*, ed. Henry Hewes (New York: Dodd, Mead, 1962), 7.
9. Henry Hewes, "The Season in New York," in *The Best Plays of 1962–1963*, ed. Henry Hewes (New York: Dodd, Mead, 1963), 3.
10. Sondheim, quoted in Secrest, *Sondheim*, 161.
11. Sondheim, in Savran, *In Their Own Words*, 227.
12. Stephen Sondheim, quoted in Stephen Banfield, *Sondheim's Broadway Musicals* (Ann Arbor: University of Michigan Press, 1993), 123.
13. See Banfield, *Sondheim's Broadway Musicals*, 141–5.
14. Ibid., 143.
15. Ibid., 138.
16. Arthur Laurents and Stephen Sondheim, *Anyone Can Whistle: A Musical Fable* (New York: Random House, 1965), 52. Further references will be noted parenthetically in the text.
17. The published text differs from the vocal score and I am, as a rule, following the published text, which, unlike the score, includes the watchcries.
18. Music and lyrics by Stephen Sondheim, book by Arthur Laurents, *Anyone Can Whistle* (piano score) (New York: Chappell, 1968), 69–70.
19. Banfield, *Sondheim's Broadway Musicals*, 136.
20. Arthur Laurents, *Original Story By: A Memoir of Broadway and Hollywood* (New York: Alfred A. Knopf, 2000), 29.
21. Jean Genet, *The Balcony*, trans. Bernard Frechtman (London: Faber, 1966), 96.
22. Paul Boyer, "From Activism to Apathy: The American People and Nuclear Weapons, 1963–1980," *Journal of American History* 70, no. 4 (March 1984), 823.
23. Civil defense director Leo Hoegh, quoted in Boyer, "From Activism to Apathy," 824.

24. See Raymond Knapp, *The American Musical and the Formation of National Identity* (Princeton: Princeton University Press, 2005).

25. Joanne Gordon, *Art Isn't Easy: The Theater of Stephen Sondheim* (Carbondale: Southern Illinois University Press, 1990), 29.

26. See David Savran, "Middlebrow Anxiety," *A Queer Sort of Materialism: Recontextualizing American Theater* (Ann Arbor: University of Michigan Press, 2003), 3–55.

27. See David Savran, *Highbrow/Lowdown: Theater, Jazz, and the Making of the New Middle Class* (Ann Arbor: University of Michigan Press, 2009).

PART II

THE ART OF MAKING ART

CHAPTER 6

··

THE PRINCE–SONDHEIM LEGACY

··

MIRANDA LUNDSKAER-NIELSEN

Reviewing the first London production of *Sweeney Todd*, Martyn Sutton reflected that "the show is easier to appreciate than to define."[1] This evaluation neatly sums up the common reaction to the six Broadway musicals that Harold Prince and Stephen Sondheim created as director-producer and composer-lyricist: *Company* (1970), *Follies* (1971), *A Little Night Music* (1973), *Pacific Overtures* (1976), *Sweeney Todd* (1979), and *Merrily We Roll Along* (1981). With their eclectic range of influences, the Prince–Sondheim musicals defy easy positioning on the cultural barometer and like other maverick musicals, such as *Porgy and Bess* (1935), *Pal Joey* (1940), *Lady in the Dark* (1941), and *Candide* (1956), they have helped to challenge preconceptions about the parameters of musical theater in relation to other performance arts.

In its broadest sense, musical theater runs the full cultural spectrum from lowbrow (vaudeville or music hall) through middlebrow (musical comedy, musical plays, operetta) to highbrow (music theater, including opera). What is so interesting about the Prince–Sondheim shows is that they repeatedly transgress these traditional boundaries between different musical and dramatic traditions, combining ambitious and uncomfortable themes, formal experimentation and musical sophistication with the humor, wit, visceral excitement, and emotive power of the Broadway musical theater. But while the shows vary widely in tone, form, and content—and notwithstanding the significant contributions of the different librettists, orchestrators, choreographers, and designers who worked with them—there are certain recurring factors that characterize the Prince–Sondheim partnership. First, both artists had a sophisticated and practical understanding of American musical theater. Second, they were both interested in cultural forms beyond musical theater, including theatrical and musical developments abroad. Finally, they aspired to create musicals that were intelligent, probing, and disturbing, as well as entertaining—all within the commercial arena of Broadway. None of these are exclusive to Prince and Sondheim; it is the combination of all three that gives their body of work a distinctive quality and position within the musical theater canon.

A Creative Partnership

In considering the Prince–Sondheim musicals, it is important to acknowledge the central role of Prince in the creative process, given the exalted position that Sondheim has acquired—sometimes to the point of viewing him as an auteur. For while there are certainly common threads that run through Sondheim's work, there is also a very clear demarcation between the Prince shows and the later collaborations with librettist-director James Lapine (*Sunday in the Park with George, Into the Woods, Passion*) that reflect the profound role that each director played not just in the staging but also in the conceptual and developmental stages of the shows.

As numerous interviews have testified, Prince's work with Sondheim was very much a creative partnership and the shows themselves are the result of a close collaboration between the two. One reason why Prince's authorial contribution has been relatively sidelined in some discussions may be that he has been billed simply as a director and producer, unlike his contemporaries Jerome Robbins, Bob Fosse, and Michael Bennett, who started to be billed as "conceivers" as well as directors and choreographers.[2] Subsequently, it has become increasingly commonplace for the original director and other members of the creative team of a new Broadway musical to receive a share of the show's royalties along with the writers where they have been substantially involved in the development of the show. While it can be argued that this practice has blurred the distinction between authorial and interpretive roles, and might in some cases be con-strued as stretching the definition of authorship, the absence of a dramaturgical credit in Prince's case masks his enormous influence on the development of his shows from concept to production in terms of theme, plot, tone, structure, and characters.

Fundamental to the Prince–Sondheim partnership was a shared vision of musical theater as a vehicle for complex and sometimes uncomfortable ideas as well as enter-tainment, and an approach that combined respect for their Broadway predecessors with a desire to push the genre forward. While Sondheim and Prince worked within the com-mercial Broadway marketplace, these ambitious goals inevitably impacted on the shows' reception by both critics and audiences. In a joint 1975 interview, Sondheim noted that critics alone cannot explain the modest runs of shows like *Company* and *Follies;* unlike long-running musical comedies like *Hello, Dolly!*, he points out, the Prince–Sondheim shows "tell the audience something that they don't want to hear."[3] During the interview, Sondheim and Prince revealed some of the mechanisms of their working relationship, from the purely pragmatic (Prince works best in the first half of the day, while Sondheim prefers the latter half) to Sondheim's admission that in a collaboration he always drags his feet a lot and the joint reflection that they tend to agree on the largest and tiniest aspects of a work, but to disagree on the area in between.[4] The differences between them also extend to outlook and temperament: Sondheim will point out all the pitfalls, whereas Prince sees how things will work.

What seems clear from this and other interviews—and from detailed accounts of the development processes in Hirsch, Ilson, and Zadan[5]—is that Prince and Sondheim are both committed to a creative and mutually respectful collaborative process. There is no question that as creative producer and director Prince was ultimately what Goldman calls the "muscle" behind the shows, whether in the conceptual stages or making final changes out of town.[6] However, Prince has characterized himself as an enthusiast of the collaborative approach, reflecting that "I do like to oversee a whole lot, but I don't think I'm a control freak at all . . . I would say that I'm as open as anyone I've ever known who does this. Collaboration is regenerative; when I hit a stone wall, the answer is out there, and not necessarily with me."[7] In addition, he notes in his autobiography that whereas choreographer-directors like Jerome Robbins could be abrasive and heavy-handed with actors (reflecting the "elements of sadomasochism" in the dancer-choreographer relationship), "that process doesn't work for me. I need to have fun in rehearsal. I need the laughter, no matter how emotional things get. I shy away from contention. Contrary to my peers, the show is not for me the most important thing in the world."[8] This inclusive attitude extends also to their other collaborators, not least librettists and designers. In particular, Prince has spoken of the key role of designers such as Boris Aronson, who was brought in almost at the moment of conception, often discussing the show in terms of its sound, smells, the food the characters ate, and the feel of the place, for six months before the actual designs started to materialize.[9] This collaborative approach was evident as early as *Company*. It was originally a play by George Furth, but the planned production fell through and Sondheim suggested to Furth that he should show it to Prince—who in turn suggested that they turn it into a musical using a vignette structure.[10] Designer Boris Aronson was brought in early on and became an integral part of the planning process, with Sondheim's opening number "Company" being written after seeing the model of Aronson's set of glass and metal with elevators and slides (Figure 6.1).[11]

FIGURE **6.1** Boris Aronson's set design for *Company* (1970).

One of the most important aspects of the Prince–Sondheim partnership is that both artists had strong dramaturgical skills and interests. In Prince, Sondheim found a producer and director able to think like a playwright in terms of the overall tone and structure of the show. In Sondheim, Prince found a composer and songwriter who combined musical sophistication with the ability to think practically in terms of character development and staging. Librettist John Weidman's recollection of the development process of *Pacific Overtures* highlights Prince's key dramaturgical role: "Hal had a stronger vision than anyone else in the room of what he wanted—how he thought the piece should work. He would sit with me and Steve and talk about it. Eventually we reached a point where I went away and did the first half of the first act and everybody was happy with that. Then I went away and did the second half of the first act. Hal didn't like that at all and so I did a rewrite which he was much happier with."[12] Once some of the libretto was in place, Sondheim started work on the score.

Sondheim has described his own approach to songwriting as deeply character- and actor-based. Thus for Frederik's songs in *Night Music* "I used heavy rhyming because he is a character who rationalizes everything and does a lot of thinking."[13] Conversely, he has often dismissed his celebrated lyrics for "I Feel Pretty" in *West Side Story* on the grounds that the clever internal rhymes are completely out of character for a simple Puerto Rican girl. There is also a pragmatic understanding of acting and staging in the structure of his songs: "I always stage a number within an inch of its life when I'm writing. As I write a number, I always explain in great detail what I intend. The director is free to change it or not but he has a blueprint...I time things, I time beats out. If you want the character to cross from here to there, or has to pick up a coffee cup and drink it or whatever it is, I time those things here in my studio."[14] He typically doesn't start work on a score until at least part of the libretto is in place and has often ended up writing songs with particular actors in mind. The role of Joanne in *Company* was essentially written for Elaine Stritch and, referring to *Night Music*, Sondheim reflected that "some of my best ideas come after I get to see the actors rehearsing the material. For example, one day after seeing Glynis [Johns] perform her second act scene with Len [Cariou] in a different way, I got an idea, went home, and that night wrote 'Send in the Clowns'...which is pretty good for me as it usually takes me a week to write a song."[15] The ensuing level of dramatic richness and complexity—both at thematic and character level—may explain the enduring appeal of the Prince–Sondheim shows to leading theater directors and the tendency to cast many of the lead performers primarily from an acting rather than a singing background, such as Judi Dench as Desirée in the 1995 Royal National Theatre production of *A Little Night Music*.

"BROADWAY BABIES"

One of the most remarkable things about these innovative musicals is that they were created within the Broadway marketplace of the 1970s. While the rise of Off-Broadway and nonprofit theaters had created a new home for experimental plays from the 1950s onward, musicals remained a resolutely commercial art form and Broadway was not only the main but also essentially the only place for first-class musical theater. Prince recalls that when he was starting out, "there was not a lot of regional theatre; there was summer stock…All the experience you got was essentially confined to the New York area, from which the road companies went across the country."[16] Both Prince and Sondheim came of age in this world. Sondheim was introduced to the inner workings of writing for Broadway at a young age through his unofficial apprenticeship with Oscar Hammerstein II, who functioned as his mentor and surrogate father. Starting his career as a gofer on Rodgers and Hammerstein's *Allegro*, he gained recognition as the lyricist of hit shows *Gypsy* and *West Side Story* and composer-lyricist of *A Funny Thing Happened on the Way to the Forum*, which demonstrated his remarkable facility for subtle word-play and musical dramaturgy.

Prince, too, grew up professionally on Broadway. His career began in the production office of George Abbott, a Broadway playwright, director, and producer whose work spans from the 1920s to the 1980s, and who is particularly associated with Broadway musical comedies of the 1940s and 50s. Prince's Broadway work as coproducer of *West Side Story* (1957), producer of *Fiddler on the Roof* (1964), and later as producer and direc-tor of the groundbreaking *Cabaret* (1966) gave him valuable experience of selling serious musicals to Broadway backers and audiences, and an early awareness of the balancing act between artistic integrity and commercial pragmatism that was required. As a direc-tor, Prince is the first to acknowledge the huge influence of Abbott on his approach to rehearsals and staging: "the respect, soundheadedness of Abbott's organization, lack of emotionalism, lack of patience with theatricality offstage—this sanity influenced Robbins, influenced me, has influenced others."[17] In addition, he learned the importance of truth—"how absolutely necessary it is to be truthful in whatever style you're working in…That if the actor responds honestly, whether it's slamming a door, there had better be a good reason. And if it's appropriate and honest, the audience will respond. When the audience heard the noise of the door slamming at the end of *Sweeney Todd*, I knew they'd shiver. They had every reason to."[18] Equally, he has emphasized the crucial impact of choreographer-directors, and Robbins in particular, on the use of musical staging. In a 1989 interview, he noted that whereas traditionally characters moved from left to right across a stage, leaving sets to give depth, Robbins used the full space and had actors moving from upstage to downstage.[19]

The fact that the Prince–Sondheim shows were developed within the Broadway eco-system had a discernible impact on the work, for while their musicals were far more innovative and less obviously commercial than traditional musical comedies, they shared the same financial restrictions, including high production costs and a responsi-bility to investors. In particular, Prince's dual role as producer and director required him to think pragmatically about the work, such as his insistence that the original, bleak finale of *Company* ("Happily Ever After") was replaced by the more affirmative if still rather ambivalent "Being Alive." The influence of the commercial environment on the cre-ative process became very apparent when, after the dissolution of the Prince–Sondheim partnership in 1981, Sondheim collaborated with James Lapine within the very different context of Playwrights Horizons, a small nonprofit Off-Broadway theater. The different approaches are reflected in the underlying subject matter, themes, and aesthetic tone of the original staging and the published scripts. Broadly speaking, the Prince shows tend to be driven by social themes (modern marriage in 1960s America, the effects of Western imperialism) and by the resources and demands of a Broadway theater; conversely, the Lapine–Sondheim musical *Sunday in the Park with George*, created for a small stage and budget, is much more introspective and psychologically driven. In a 2002 interview, Sondheim explained the differences between the two aesthetics and by implication their crucial role on the creative process:

> Hal and I grew up in the commercial theatre—we're Broadway babies. One of the joys of creating with Jim Lapine is that he comes from a different generation—he grew up in Off-Broadway. Off-Broadway has a very different sensibility; it's a much looser way of putting on a show—although James is a meticulous writer and plots very carefully. But his approach to a show, even his approach to writing, is not necessarily traditional—for example, the notion of starting at the beginning. Sometimes he starts in the middle. Working with Lapine was startling to me because of the different approach not only to the actual writing but to the producing. James said, "Come on, I have friends at Playwrights Horizons, we'll put it on there." With Hal it was, "Okay, I think we can get the Majestic Theatre next fall, so we'll do it then." It gears your mind differently.[20]

WIDER INFLUENCES

But while the Broadway traditions of writing, producing, and staging were clearly part of their creative DNA, Prince and Sondheim were also strongly influenced by wider dramatic and musical styles. After the 1950s, the Broadway musical was increasingly divorced from new developments in both popular music (rock 'n' roll, the Beatles, Elvis Presley, Motown) and the new American and European drama in terms of tone, subject matter, theatrical style, and relationship to the audience. Notwithstanding one-off attempts to bring the Broadway musical up to date (most notably *Hair*, which tellingly transferred to Broadway from the nonprofit New York Public Theatre), the tendency was firmly toward old-fashioned nostalgia, epitomized by Jerry Herman's *Hello, Dolly!* and *Mame*, and toward the visceral excitement of work by choreographer-directors like Fosse and Bennett.

In effect, Prince and Sondheim were both perpetuating and breaking with tradition in their approach to musical theater. Their shows follow in the tradition of American musicals as cultural indicators reflecting the national mood. Scholars like Raymond Knapp[21] and John Bush Jones[22] have highlighted the key role of musicals in reflecting and shaping the American sense of national identity in the twentieth century, whether through the early flag-waving George M. Cohan shows, the patriotic nostalgia of

Oklahoma! during the Second World War, or the pro-American cultural politics of *Silk Stockings* during the Cold War. However, the rather different tone and themes of the Prince–Sondheim works can be attributed to the shift in the national mood and self-image of America from the optimism and patriotic pride of the first half of the century to one of self-doubt, confusion, and disillusionment. The late sixties and seventies were a time of great social changes in America and the same cultural shifts that spawned events as diverse as the Vietnam War protests, the legalization of divorce, and major social movements (civil rights, women's liberation, gay rights) created a generation of Americans who actively questioned the social institutions that underpinned the often self-satisfied and homogeneous American sense of identity as portrayed in most Golden Age musicals. While Off-Broadway was quick to respond to this shift in mood, the Broadway musical (with notable exceptions like *Chicago* and the Prince-directed *Cabaret*) largely ignored the seismic cultural shifts and continued to emulate the feel-good mood of earlier times. By contrast, Prince and Sondheim both subscribed to the idea of theater as a social force whose primary aim was not necessarily to please and entertain the audience, but to challenge and even provoke them with unsettling subject matter and characters. In addition, both artists have a strong awareness of their work as part of an attempt to push the boundaries of Broadway musical theater. Prince points out in his autobiography:

> There is a deliciously unmotivated musical, a cherished memory of yesteryear, which some of our critics lament the loss of. Not I. I think that shows in which songs are utterly unmotivated, in which characters react inconsistently for laughs, mindless and pleasantly entertaining though they may be, through overpraise dangerously inhibit the future of the musical theatre.[23]

While Sondheim's songs are often moving and entertaining, and while Prince's staging is often technically thrilling, their craft is always a means to an end, with their shows harnessing the visceral power of musicals to make audiences confront the world around them and their own place within it. In this sense, the Prince–Sondheim musicals have more in common with the American and European drama of the time than with most Broadway musicals in terms of tone, content, and relationship with the audience. Working within the framework of the Broadway musical theater, their shows draw on a broad palate of theatrical and musical influences that include European directors like Erwin Piscator, the Brecht-influenced British director Joan Littlewood, Russian expressionism, British music hall and melodrama, European operetta,[24] and film composer Bernard Herrmann. In addition, the tone, subject matter, and formal experimentation of the shows are more aligned with American playwrights of the times, adopting the kind of questioning approach to middle-class complacency that can be found in different ways in the 1960s and 70s in Neil Simon's tragicomic Broadway plays *Plaza Suite* (1968), *Last of the Red-hot Lovers* (1969), and *California Suite* (1976), in Edward Albee's psychologically lacerating *Who's Afraid of Virginia Woolf?* (1962) and in Sam Shepard's deconstruction of the idealized American family in plays like *Curse of the Starving Class* (1964) and *Buried Child* (1978).[25]

THE SHOWS

All these influences can be seen in their body of work, which exhibits an interesting and sophisticated relationship between form and content, with the ambitious and complex themes and topics realized through innovative scores, librettos, and approaches to staging. In this section, I will be illustrating how collaborative choices about form and content shaped the now canonical Prince–Sondheim shows. Both Prince and Sondheim are often associated with the "concept musical," of which *Company* is commonly regarded as the first example,[26] which was subsequently used to denote a show that is theme- rather than plot-driven. Both artists have dismissed this term, but it is certainly true that all the Prince–Sondheim musicals are built around thematic ideas that are reflected in the structure of the shows themselves—a clear example of content dictating form.

This was evident from their first, groundbreaking collaboration as director and writer on *Company*—a modern musical that captured very precisely the sense of confusion and possibility of an era in which the institution of marriage and the rules of sexual relationships were being challenged in the courts and in the everyday lives of the respectable middle classes who constituted both the characters of musicals and the bulk of their audiences. *Company* is a musical about the complexities of modern relationships, based around the central character of Bobby, a thirty-five-year-old New Yorker struggling with an ambivalent attitude to exchanging his bachelor lifestyle for the benefits and compromises of marriage. It is structured as a series of thematically related scenes, each one exploring a different aspect of the tension between the opposing desires for freedom and emotional closeness. As Banfield points out, this structure of "sketches, episodes, or separate stories held together by some common element or character" can also be found in the experimental Weill–Lerner musical *Love Life* (1948), in Offenbach's *Tales of Hoffmann* (1880), and subsequently in Neil Simon's *California Suite* (1976).[27] However, there is no question that in 1970 *Company* seemed startlingly fresh within a Broadway musical theater canon that had been overwhelmingly plot- and character-driven since the Rodgers and Hammerstein era.

Sondheim's score for *Company* undoubtedly forms the heart of the show, including songs like "Sorry-Grateful," in which Bobby's male friends explain the compromises of married life; "The Ladies Who Lunch," in which the thrice-married Joanne paints a witty but acerbic portrait of society wives; and the finale, "Being Alive," in which Bobby tentatively opens himself up to the idea of long-term commitment with another person. While Sondheim crafted a musically distinctive and dramatically rich score, the overall structure and thematic focus of the show draw on a number of different influences, including Prince's interest in social politics and different kinds of theatrical storytelling. The use of montage and a nonlinear approach to time were previously seen in *Cabaret* four years before, and were drawn from Prince's exposure to Russian Expressionism at the Taganka Theatre in Moscow, which he has described as "a turning point in my thinking as a director."[28] Similarly, Prince has noted how the structure and tone of

Company were influenced by his and Sondheim's admiration for the British director Joan Littlewood, whose production of *The Hostage* they had seen at the Theatre Royal Stratford East in London:

> I was crazy about it. The sure, yet impulsive way she maneuvered currents of reality and fantasy compatibly in one play was something. And I admired how she cued in fragments of songs—the show had many—and how they erupted from rather than grew out of moments. They had the abrasive effect of attacking when you least expected, creating such life. Sondheim and I talked about that play then and for years, and a decade later the songs in *Company* were cued out of a conscious debt to *The Hostage*.[29]

This influence can be seen not only in the spoken dialogue and in the overall structure and staging but also in Sondheim's music and lyrics, such as the abrupt juxtapositions of tone in "Not Getting Married Today," where the serene sounds of a choir are interspersed with the prospective bride's frenzied emotional outbursts.[30]

Follies, their second collaboration, went even further in the symbiotic relationship between theme and form. Prince had read—and disliked—early drafts of the show that Sondheim was writing with James Goldman under the title *The Girls Upstairs*. When he eventually agreed to come on board he instigated significant changes, transforming the show from a fairly literal and prosaic piece to a poetic and thematically driven piece that included flashbacks and actors playing the characters' younger selves. At his request, the script was written as a screenplay so as to facilitate a fluid, cinematic staging to complement the poetic and dreamlike quality of the piece itself.[31] *Follies* is set in a derelict theater about to be torn down and is ostensibly a musical about two ex-showgirls and their husbands who are made to confront the disparity between their youthful dreams and present lives at a final reunion before the bulldozers close in. Thematically, though, this is a musical about nostalgia, about the disillusionment of the Vietnam generation, and arguably also about the end of the Golden Age of American musical theater. The themes are realized through the structure, with the lead characters played by two actors representing their present-day and younger selves. The idea of nostalgia is also explored through the score, with contemporary numbers (the cynical "Could I Leave You?") offset by lavish pastiche numbers that emulate earlier musical theater styles ("Beautiful Girls," "One More Kiss") and draw the audience into the characters' nostalgia for the past. In "Who's That Woman?" (often referred to as "the mirror number") the past and present merge as the present-day middle-aged women's impromptu performance is shadowed by the ghosts of their beautiful younger selves who move gracefully among them. These structural and musical devices come to a dramatic climax in the final "Loveland," sequence where the four lead characters' present-day crises are played out allegorically in their performance of pastiche vaudeville numbers; for example, Sally's marital unhappiness is transposed into the romantic ballad "Losing My Mind," and the mental and emotional cost of Ben's professional success becomes "Live, Laugh, Love," in which his debonair performance of a sophisticated top-hat-and-tails number breaks down as he descends into self-doubt.

A Little Night Music, based on Bergman's film *Smiles of a Summer Night*, again explores the complex emotional demands of adult relationships. On one hand, the show evokes the romanticism and escapism of operetta with its elegant European setting, recurring use of the 3/4 waltz time signature and its urbane, witty humour. On the other hand, the underlying themes of the show and the intellectual and emotional demands on the audience are far more complex and sombre than those of either operetta like *The Merry Widow* or American musical comedy. Sondheim's later comments on the development of *Night Music* are a prime illustration of his and Prince's dramaturgical, thematic approach and also of the differences between them:

> I saw it as a darker Chekhovian musical...I had already written six songs that were much bleaker, more reflective, almost out of Strindberg, and Hal finally persuaded me that instead of it being as dark as Bergman, we should go entirely in reverse. And of course he was right. I usually love to write in dark colors about basic gut feelings, but Hal has a sense of audience that I sometimes lose when I'm writing. He wanted the darkness to peep through a whipped-cream surface.[32]

Pacific Overtures is arguably the most thematically ambitious Prince–Sondheim musical. Originally, John Weidman wrote to Prince with an idea for a play about the opening up of Japan and at Prince's suggestion he developed it into a play told from the Japanese viewpoint and using Japanese theater to tell the story.[33] The play was in the late stages of casting when Prince decided it would work better as a musical and brought in an initially reluctant Sondheim. Completed in 1976, the musical *Pacific Overtures* was an unusual response to the bicentennial celebrations of the Declaration of Independence and American freedom from its colonial powers. Rather than creating a patriotic celebration of American independence, Prince and Sondheim chose to focus on the way in which America, once the subject of European colonial rule, subsequently played an aggressive role in the Western trade invasion of Japan. *Pacific Overtures* tells the story of the 1853 arrival of Commodore Matthew Perry to Japan and the rapid transformation of Japan into a capitalist and consumer-based society after 200 years of seclusion, with all the cultural sacrifices and compromises that this entailed. The show uses a combination of Broadway and Kabuki theater traditions and, unusually, tells the story from a Japanese perspective. This marked a departure from Rodgers and Hammerstein's earlier "oriental" musicals, *South Pacific* and *The King and I*, which retain a very Western perspective and sound despite their foreign setting, to the extent that Bruce McConachie has argued that these shows are in fact a form of cultural imperialism.[34] Musically, Sondheim has pointed out that "There isn't much Oriental music in *The King and I*. It's actually mostly Broadway music with Oriental orchestrations."[35] By contrast, his aim with *Pacific Overtures* was to use the difference between Japanese and American musical styles for dramaturgical purposes: "I was trying to start with kind of faux Japanese-scale music and, as the country gets westernized, to gradually make the music more Western. The last number is really a Westernization of the opening number."[36] Perhaps understandably given the ambitious subject matter and formal experimentation, *Pacific Overtures* received a lukewarm critical reception when it opened on Broadway.

Sweeney Todd, based on the British urban legend about a murderous barber in nineteenth-century London, appealed to Sondheim and Prince for different reasons. The story was originally a penny-dreadful serial, a ballet, and a popular Victorian melodrama, but it was Christopher Bond's 1973 play version that attracted Sondheim to its musical potential and to the idea of creating a musical thriller. While the final show was indeed subtitled "A Musical Thriller," Sondheim's original ideas for the show as an intimate piece were strongly modified by Prince, who initially struggled to see the point of the story and became interested only when he started to see Sweeney's story as a metaphor for the dehumanizing effect of the class system and the industrial revolution on the human soul.[37] Prince's concept of the show had an enormous impact on its development, with the physical design and score evolving simultaneously. Sondheim later stated that "I wanted it to be done as a small piece because I wanted to just scare people, but Hal Prince…who is very much influenced by Meyerhold and Piscator, said, 'I know what you want, and you'll lose some of the scariness but I'll give it a large, epic feeling. Perhaps that will serve the piece in a different way.' I thought 'It can always be done small, but things can't always be done big, so let's try it.'"[38] Prince's interest in sociopolitical themes resulted in a production in which the characters' story was played out in a small area dwarfed by an enormous industrial set created from parts of old foundries in Rhode Island. He explained later that "by placing the action in its late nineteenth-century context we could say that from the day the Industrial Revolution entered our lives, the conveyor belt pulled us further and further from harmony, from humanity, from nature."[39] As Sondheim has pointed out, Prince's approach had repercussions not just for the original staging but for the libretto and score of the piece itself: "It could be a show about doors and walls and stuffy Victorian furniture. Hal turned it into something much more abstract, which affected how I thought about the songs."[40]

More than any other Prince–Sondheim show, *Sweeney Todd* is a glorious mixture of cultural sources and typifies their unique talent for simultaneously entertaining and unsettling the audience. The score draws, among other things, on the *Dies Irae* (the Catholic Mass for the dead) and on the suspense-inducing music of acclaimed film composer Bernard Herrmann: "It's an open secret that the music for *Sweeney* is in homage to Herrmann's language…I didn't consciously copy him but it was [Herrmann's score for the 1945 film] *Hangover Square* that started that kind of thought process going in my head."[41] Sondheim has rejected labeling the show an opera, arguing that "when it's done in an opera house it's an operetta, a black operetta. Opera is about showing off the human voice, but *Sweeney* is about telling a story and telling it as swiftly as possible."[42] However, the show clearly draws on operatic traditions in its use of musical leitmotifs and underscoring (80 percent of the piece is scored) and, as music scholar Stephen Banfield has highlighted, *Sweeney Todd* also exhibits a highly sophisticated and subtle use of musical dramaturgy for a Broadway musical.[43] The musical numbers vary greatly in style from pastiche music hall ("A Little Priest," "By the Sea") to operatic ("Epiphany") and contemporary musical theater songs ("Johanna," "Pretty Women"). Thematically and structurally, *Sweeney Todd* combines the Broadway musical's ability to seduce and emotionally manipulate the audience with a more Brecht- and Piscator-inspired focus on social injustice and the corruption of the ruling classes, which begins with the open-ing number, in which the chorus exhorts the audience to "Attend the tale of Sweeney Todd" and warns: "Swing your razor wide, Sweeney! / Hold it to the skies! / Freely flows the blood of those / Who moralize!"[44] The thing that binds all this together is the combi-nation of human tragedy and dark humour—a tone epitomized by "A Little Priest," the startlingly funny music-hall ditty about cannibalism.

Interestingly, the least successful Prince–Sondheim show was also the least themat-ically and theatrically ambitious. *Merrily We Roll Along* is the story of three aspiring young artists whose youthful optimism and friendship is derailed by (respectively) unrequited love, the corrupting influence of commercial success, and professional resentment. The twist is that the story is told backward, starting with the successful but jaded middle-aged Franklin Sheppard giving a speech at his old high school and mov-ing backward toward the bright-eyed young teenagers full of ambition and hopes. This structure helps to give the show a more adult and exploratory feel, starting in middle age and looking back to discover how the characters got there. The idea of middle-aged, middle-class people confronting their thwarted dreams and regrets about the road not taken—and the ensuing reflections on the relationship between material success and happiness—had been previously explored in *Follies*, and there are clear parallels between the characters of Franklin Sheppard in *Merrily* and Ben Stone in *Follies*, but *Merrily* lacked the weight, wider relevance, and the thematic complexity that had bal-anced out the more disturbing aspects of the earlier show.

Despite the structural conceit and a widely admired score, audiences and critics failed to warm to *Merrily* and it closed after only sixteen performances. Prince's later discus-sion of his process is a telling reminder of the limitations that come with creating a show for the Broadway marketplace:

> I called my office staff together and said "Look, it's a Broadway show, you know what the price of tickets is." God knows it's less than now. "But I'll tell you what I would do if I had the guts," I said. "I would have no scenery. I would have racks of clothes and these kids would come in like little kids, and they would pretend to be their parents as they see them. And let's see what happens. So we're talking no production costs, some lights, some kids; put on the story." And everyone looked at me in the office and said, "If that's what you think it should be, do it." And guess
> what? I lacked the courage.[45]

It is perhaps ironic that a show which, among other things, dealt with the corrupting influence of commerce in art should itself fall victim to the populist demands of com-mercial theater.

Although the show has enjoyed some modest success in subsequent productions in the United States and Britain, both Prince and Sondheim have referred to this as a low point in their careers. While the show's structural and thematic flaws are widely acknowledged, the severity of the critical response would suggest that there was an ele-ment of critical backlash against the partnership that had repeatedly challenged the tra-ditional definitions of the Broadway musical for over a decade. The Broadway system of public previews also worked against them. During the prolonged preview period, the show underwent dramatic changes on a daily basis in response to the preview audiences and the creators' own creative ideas. Meanwhile, negative word of mouth began to spread within the Broadway community, and by the (delayed) opening night it seems unlikely that the critics were entering the theater with completely open minds. Clive Barnes, one of the few critics who reviewed the show positively, felt moved to address this directly in his *New York Post* review:

> [T]he word of mouth on the latest Stephen Sondheim musical, *Merrily We Roll Along*, was so bad that all the words seemed dirty and the mouth was twisted in a permanent sneer. Unquestionably the show was beset by trouble, but in my opinion it has equally unquestionably triumphed—at least it should as long as people distinguish between what they are actually seeing on stage and what they heard about the show during previews.[46]

What is indisputable is that the sheer savagery of the critical response to *Merrily*, and the heavily curtailed run, had a devastating effect on both Sondheim and Prince and effectively ended their partnership.[47]

THE PRINCE–SONDHEIM LEGACY

The originality, cultural breadth, and thematic ambition of the Prince–Sondheim musicals might help to explain the appeal of their shows beyond their original place of origin—not least in Britain, where audiences have come to regard Sondheim's work with a sense of ownership usually reserved for native playwrights. While the Prince–Sondheim shows are indisputably American in both theme and style, there is also something very British in the underlying tone of uncertainty and ambivalence about the world and in the exploration of serious issues through the characters' bittersweet and often self-deprecating wit and humor. The combination of demanding subject matter and flamboyant theatrical style is also a good fit with a heritage that incorporates the open acting style of Shakespearean theater, a love of sophisticated language and wordplay, and a tradition of epic social dramas from Shakespeare to Joan Littlewood, David Hare, and Caryl Churchill. Tellingly, the now popular tradition of Sondheim revues started with the British *Side by Side by Sondheim*, whose understated staging—four actors on stools and a grand piano—highlighted the intrinsic dramatic strength of the songs. This is not to say that the relationship of British critics and audiences has always been one of unadulterated praise. In particular, the West End premiere of *Sweeney Todd* met with a mixed critical reception and demonstrated the limits of cultural tolerance. While Michael Billington named it "one of two (the other being *My Fair Lady*) durable works of popular musical theater written in my lifetime"[48] and Sheridan Morley hailed it as "the most exciting and innovative attempt to drag the stage musical into the second half of the twentieth century since *West Side Story*,"[49] some London critics seemed unable to get beyond the original story and format. These included Milton Shulman, who opined that "the theme is as thin as a penny whistle and to burden it with arias, declamatory recitatives and quartets is to give a 'penny dreadful' unseemly pretentions,"[50] and James Fenton, who dismissed it as a "dishonest" reworking of a Victorian melodrama in which the psychology was "a sham" and the lyrics "bogus and painfully contrived."[51] These damning reviews were possibly not unrelated to the fact that this was a British story that had been turned into a Broadway musical and then transported back to London—an act of cultural chutzpah that would be reversed in the 1990s when *Miss Saigon*, a musical about America's painful failure in the Vietnam War, transferred from the West End to Broadway and stimulated similar patriotic outrage among many critics.

Unlike many more initially successful musicals, the Prince–Sondheim collaborations have enjoyed a rich and varied life beyond their original productions, inspiring interesting and sometimes radical reinterpretations. This might to some extent be due to the fact that subsequent directors have the advantage of learning from the revelations of the shows' strengths and pitfalls in their original productions. In addition, there is no question that general shifts in cultural perception, ongoing experimentation with the musical theater form, and a growing appreciation of the Sondheim canon have made today's audiences much more receptive to the ambiguous and unsettling worlds of the Prince–Sondheim musical dramas. The more simplistic, optimistic viewpoint of American musical comedies like *Guys and Dolls*, *The Pajama Game*, and *On the Town* continue to be enjoyed for their craft and as joyous escapism, but the Prince–Sondheim shows speak to us as timely and thought-provoking musical dramas. Far from feeling dated, many of the preoccupations and themes of these shows (the complexities and ambiguities of adult relationships, the effects and repercussions of colonialism, the impact of social injustice on the individual) have become only more pertinent with time. Even *Company*, absolutely a product of its time and very geographically specific, has retained its relevance several decades later. As Banfield points out, "if its attitudes and modes of discourse capture a moment in time, it is a moment that has perpetuated itself to the present day, at least as a cultural topic. Yuppies are already in full flight in *Company*, in all but name... Its postmodernist ways are the ways of Stoppard, Neil Simon, and Woody Allen, of Habitat and Gucci, even, to a degree, of Ayckbourn."[52] Certainly Sam Mendes's 1995 studio production of *Company* at the Donmar Warehouse highlighted the enduring relevance of this musical about thirty-something urbanites negotiating the minefield of adult relationships in a fast-moving consumer culture. And this was only one of many revelatory, high-profile productions of Prince–Sondheim musicals envisioned by directors from nonmusical theater backgrounds who were attracted by the social and psychological complexities of the shows' themes and characters. *Sweeney Todd* has been variously reconfigured as Declan Donnellan's intense studio production at the National Theatre in London; as John Doyle's distinctive 2004 Watermill production featuring actor-musicians, which was restaged on Broadway in 2005; and as Tim Burton's macabre 2007 film version. In addition, both *Sweeney Todd* and *A Little Night Music* have become favorites at leading opera houses such as the Royal Opera House, Covent Garden, and New York City Opera, where they have fostered a crossover between the opera and musical theater communities both onstage and in the auditorium. There have even been attempts to rework the shows themselves, such as the London production of *Follies* (produced by Cameron Macintosh), which gave the show a more upbeat ending and included several new songs supplied by Sondheim. James Lapine's substantial reworking of *Merrily We Roll Along* for his 1985 production at La Jolla Playhouse resulted in a revised version that has formed the basis of most subsequent productions. Among other things, this version repositions "Our Time" as the finale, thus shifting the emphasis from the specific, largely self-inflicted problems of the central character toward the show's more universal exploration of the fragility of friendship and youthful dreams in the face of society's stress on material wealth and the external hallmarks of success.[53]

One striking example of the shows' continuing relevance is *Pacific Overtures*. The original production, while adopting the Japanese viewing position and drawing on Japanese cultural traditions in its music, lyrics, and staging, was very much a Broadway musical intended for American audiences. This caused some critics to question the authenticity, such as Walter Kerr's assessment in the *New York Times*:

> The occasion is essentially dull and immobile because we are never properly placed in it, drawn neither East nor West, given no specific emotional or cultural bearings. The evening is a Japanese artifact with a stamp on the back of it that says, "Made in America." ... [I]t does raise a basic question for us, if not for the Japanese. Why tell their story their way, when they'd do it better?[54]

In 2000, Japanese director Amon Miyamoto's production at the New National Theatre in Tokyo was in many ways a response to critics like Kerr (Figure 6.2). Produced, staged,

FIGURE **6.2.** A scene from Miyamoto's production of *Pacific Overtures* (2004).

and performed by Japanese theater artists in Japanese and drawing on the sparse and highly stylized performance traditions of Noh theater, this production resolved many of the initial issues around authenticity and highlighted the relevance and profundity of the musical's themes. In a 2005 interview, Miyamoto noted that "After the economic bubble burst in the '90s Japanese people began to ask, 'What is our identity?' I thought it was an extremely good time to stage this work. Although *Pacific Overtures* was originally written for American audiences, I wanted to get the message across to Japanese audiences that it was time for us to take a fresh look at where this nation was headed."[55]

In 2002, the show was performed in Japanese at New York's Avery Fisher Concert Hall and at the Kennedy Center in Washington, DC, in the immediate aftermath of the 9/11 attacks and the invasion of Afghanistan. It was subsequently reworked as an English-language Broadway production, opening in December 2004 during the Iraq War. If anything, *Pacific Overtures*—originally performed against the backdrop of the Vietnam War—was even more pertinent to audiences at the start of the twenty-first century, with its probing questions around the issues of national identity, cultural politics, and the use and abuse of power. With images of the World Trade towers and the Afghanistan bombings fresh in our minds, it was at once theatrically thrilling and intellectually sobering to sit as an audience member in the Avery Fisher Hall and watch the arrival of the European trade negotiators depicted as an intimidating procession of grotesque, masked giants through the auditorium. As Ben Brantley commented in the *New York Times*,

> [I]n exchanging the usual fairy-book delicacy for a style both more robust and austere (more Noh than Kabuki), Mr. Miyamoto's version seemed to clarify rather than distort the intentions of the show's original creators. And at a feverishly patriotic moment in American history, Mr. Miyamoto provided a sobering outsider's perspective on Western imperialism. He made his point with some jaw-dropping coups de thé âtres, including an immense American flag that unfurled as a claustrophia-inducing canopy and a gigantic, gruesomely masked Commodore Perry, who stalked up a 60-foot ramp as the ultimate invading barbarian.[56]

Tellingly, while the new production differed technically from the original staging, Miyamoto's stated aims are a faithful echo of the Prince–Sondheim approach to theater:

> I want to put forth a powerful message that's totally different from Broadway's upbeat and glitzy norm. It's not my goal to direct mere entertainment or big hits. I want to provoke an audience to think about the future of humanity... I want people to look at themselves objectively, without getting caught up in the events of our times. It's not a question of who's bad and who's right in the flow of events. The story depicts a world of gray zones, and that's what I like so much about it.[57]

What is clear is that this revelatory production was made possible by the structure, tone and the specific yet more universally applicable themes of the show itself, as Miyamoto himself points out:

> The interesting thing about the songs in *Pacific Overtures* is that although they are written against the backdrop of Japan-U.S. relations 150 years ago, they always come

through with a fresh message relevant to the times…Some people interpreted it as depicting the emotions of the U.S. as invader and as victim of attack. Others in the audience felt that it reflected the entire world situation. They said they felt empathy for humanity struggling to cope with a rapid succession of events in a swiftly changing environment. As it crossed the Pacific Ocean in both directions, this musical has come to carry a truly international, even universal, message.[58]

The great irony of Prince and Sondheim's achievement is that while their work served as an inspiration and springboard to the next generation of musical theater practitioners, the cumulative effect of cultural, social, and economic changes to the theatrical landscape has been that it is impossible for their successors to undertake comparable work on a similar scale. Broadway, the creative incubator of both plays and musicals from the early 1900s until the 1970s, has increasingly become a receiving house for transfers from Off-Broadway, American nonprofit theaters and London's West End. While some musicals do open directly on Broadway, they tend to be feel-good, crowd-pleasing musicals, revivals of popular classics or so-called jukebox musicals based on well-known songs. It seem highly unlikely that we will return to the kind of economic and cultural conditions that would enable a new Prince–Sondheim partnership to survive on Broadway. Today's innovative musical theater writers, directors, and producers look not to Broadway but to the nonprofit theaters for a creative home; as composer-lyricist Adam Guettel (*Floyd Collins, Myths and Hymns, The Light in the Piazza*) points out, "writers like me are going to the regionals and finding some measure of autonomy and decent money. A show has to have a distinctive nature and that can be nurtured more safely out of town."[59] But while the nonprofit theaters may offer greater creative freedom, they impose restrictions in terms of scale and resources and many of the most exciting new musicals are being performed in smaller theaters, on more modest budgets and without the kind of national or international recognition that helped to make the Broadway musical an American cultural ambassador. As Prince has noted, his generation of producers, directors, and writers had the possibility of plying their craft on Broadway from the start of their careers, and even though the first attempt was often unsuccessful,

> we all went back to the same arena, the most difficult arena, the Broadway theater, and did our second show. In almost every instance the second show worked—not in my case, but in theirs. There's a lot to be said for the trappings that professional productions give you: the best scenery if your taste is good, the best designers, the most talented performers, and a large audience. One of the things that is inhibiting the musical form is that wonderfully talented people are forced to work in hundred-seat theatres. That will work for certain material, but I wouldn't want to see *Phantom of the Opera* in a workshop.[60]

Broadway producer and dramaturg Jack Viertel points out that despite the increased dialogue between nonprofit theaters and commercial producers through transfers and enhancement deals,

> the hurdle that's never been overcome is the physical one. You can't do in any resident theatre what you can do at the highest level on Broadway in terms of scenery, costumes, scenic transitions and special effects…So the shows that have been

developed in resident theatres by and large have been physically modest because, having conceived them for a theatre that has limitations, it's not worth reconceiving them for Broadway—you simply dress them up a little bit more.[61]

In this sense, the Prince–Sondheim shows are both an ending and a beginning. With a few exceptions, they represent the end of the era in which serious, complex, and intellectually demanding new musicals could be produced and premiered on Broadway. But their work has also helped to redefine the possibilities of musical theater as a powerful vehicle for exploring complex ideas while simultaneously providing an expertly crafted, entertaining and moving theatrical experience. By drawing on a wide range of different musical and theatrical traditions and challenging themselves and their audiences, Prince and Sondheim have created a body of work that is both a unique milestone in the evolution of musical theater and an ongoing source of discovery, debate, and inspiration for musical theater audiences, practitioners, and scholars.

NOTES

1. Martyn Sutton, "How to Write a Musical without Big Numbers," *Sunday Times*, July 6, 1980.
2. Fosse was also credited as a co-librettist on *Chicago*.
3. Brendan Gill interview with Harold Prince and Stephen Sondheim, Theatre on Film and Tape Archive, New York Public Library, 2 June 1975.
4. Gill, interview with Prince and Sondheim.
5. Foster Hirsch, *Harold Prince and the American Musical Theatre* (Cambridge, UK, and New York: Cambridge University Press, 1989); Carol Ilson, *Harold Prince: A Director's Journey* (New York: Limelight, 2000); Craig Zadan, *Sondheim & Co.* (London: Macmillan, 1987).
6. William Goldman, *The Season* (New York: Limelight, 1969), 285–98.
7. Jackson R. Bryer and Richard A. Davison, *The Art of the American Musical: Conversations with the Creators* (New Brunswick, NJ, and London: Rutgers University Press, 2005), 180.
8. Hal Prince, *Contradictions: Notes on Twenty-six Years in the Theatre* (New York: Dodd, Mead, 1974), 34.
9. Edwin Wilson, interview with Harold Prince. Theatre on Film and Tape Archive, New York Public Library, June 22, 1989.
10. Ilson, *Harold Prince*, 160–61.
11. Ibid., 163
12. Ibid., 229.
13. Zadan, *Sondheim & Co.*, 233.
14. Sondheim and Wheeler, *Sweeney Todd: The Demon Barber of Fleet Street* (London: Nick Hern Books, 1991) 1–2.
15. Zadan, *Sondheim & Co.*, 185.
16. Bryer and Davison, *American Musical*, 169.
17. Prince, *Contradictions*, 32.
18. Harold Prince quoted in Ronald Rand, "Interview with the artists: Harold Prince," *The Soul of the American Actor*, Vol 4, no. 2, 8.
19. Wilson interview with Hal Prince.
20. Stephen Sondheim quoted in "Side by Side by Side," *American Theatre* 19, no. 6 (2002), 68.

21. Raymond Knapp, *The American Musical and the Formation of National Identity* (Princeton: Princeton University Press, 2005).

22. John Bush Jones, *Our Musicals, Ourselves: A Social History of the American Musical Theater* (Waltham, MA: Brandeis University Press, 2003).

23. Prince, *Contradictions*, 23.

24. It should perhaps be noted that European operetta was not a new source of inspiration to American composers: *The Merry Widow* was an enormously successful import as were Gilbert and Sullivan—giving rise to American operettas such as *Rose Marie* (1924) with music by Rudolf Friml and Herbert Stothart and book and lyrics by Otto Harbach and Oscar Hammerstein II and *The Desert Song* (1926) with music by Sigmund Romberg and book and lyrics by Oscar Hammerstein II. However, the innovation in "Night Music" was to use the forms and conventions of the operetta in conjunction with the traditions of the American musical to create a formally experimental work rather than simply a pastiche.

25. Miranda Lundskaer-Nielsen, *Directors and the New Musical Drama: British and American Musical Theatre in the 1980s and 90s* (New York: Palgrave Macmillan, 2008), 26–8.

26. Martin Gottfried first used the term in his review of Harold Prince's production of *Zorba* (1968) by Kander and Ebb.

27. Stephen Banfield, *Sondheim's Broadway Musicals* (Ann Arbor: University of Michigan Press, 1993), 147.

28. Prince, *Contradictions*, 128

29. Ibid., 73–4.

30. For further discussion of the sources for *Company*, see Lundskaer-Nielsen, *Directors*, 33–5.

31. Ilson, *Harold Prince*, 178–81.

32. Zadan, *Sondheim & Co.*, 182.

33. Ilson, *Harold Prince*, 227.

34. Bruce A. McConachie, "The 'Oriental' Musicals of Rodgers and Hammerstein and the U.S. War in Southeast Asia," *Theatre Journal* 46, no. 3 (1994), 385–98.

35. Bryer and Davison, *American Musical*, 199.

36. Ibid.

37. Hirsch, *Harold Prince*, 120.

38. Meryle Secrest, *Stephen Sondheim: A Life* (New York: Alfred A. Knopf, 1998), 296.

39. Hirsch, *Harold Prince*, 120.

40. Mel Gussow, "*Sweeney Todd*: A Little Nightmare Music," *New York Times*, February 1, 1979.

41. Secrest, *Sondheim*, 295.

42. Bryer and Davison. *American Musical*, 202.

43. Banfield, *Sondheim's Broadway Musicals*, 281–310.

44. Sondheim, 379–380.

45. Secrest, *Sondheim*, 317.

46. Clive Barnes, "Rolling Along Quite Nicely, Thank You," *New York Post*, November 17, 1981.

47. Prince and Sondheim reunited briefly in 2003 when Prince was brought in to direct the first full production of *Bounce* by Sondheim and John Weidman, which had previously been workshopped with director Sam Mendes under its original title of *Wise Guys*. However, this was not a Prince–Sondheim collaboration in the same sense as their earlier works as Prince joined the team late in the development process.

48. Michael Billington, "A Cut above the Rest," *The Guardian*, July 3, 1980.

49. Sheridan Morley, "On His Todd," *Punch*, July 9, 1980.

50. Milton Shulman, "Barbarous!" *Evening Standard* [London], July 3, 1980.

51. James Fenton, "The Barbarous Crimes of Sondheim and Prince," *Sunday Times*, July 6, 1980.

52. Banfield, *Sondheim's Broadway Musicals*, 162.

53. For detailed discussion of the revisions, see S. F. Stoddart, "Visions and Re-visions: The Postmodern Challenge of Merrily We Roll Along" in *Reading Stephen Sondheim: A Collection of Critical Essays*, ed. Sandor Goodhart, 187–98 (New York: Garland, 2000).

54. Walter Kerr, "Pacific Overtures is Neither East nor West," *New York Times*, January 18, 1976.

55. "Visionary Director Amon Miyamoto Turns Broadway on its Ear," *Kateigaho*, winter 2005. http://archive.is/0zxka.

56. Ben Brantley, "Repatriating the Japanese Sondheim," *New York Times*, December 3, 2004.

57. "Visionary Director Amon Miyamoto."

58. Ibid.

59. Lundskaer-Nielsen, *Directors*, 158.

60. Bryer and Davison, *American Musical*, 174.

61. Lundskaer-Nielsen, *Directors*, 203.

CHAPTER 7

"GROWING PAINS": REVISING
MERRILY WE ROLL ALONG

ANDREW BUCHMAN

THE saga of the musical *Merrily We Roll Along* falls into three periods: how the work took shape up to the first performances in 1981; the Broadway flop, and how the creators tried to remedy it over the next four years via major revisions; then the series of fine tunings—at least up to 2002—that have combined to make *Merrily* more successful as a stage show. The revisions of *Merrily* could fill a book (or another play). The recent 2012 London revival (the most critically successful production to date) could begin yet another chapter, on revivals of revivals, based as it was on a 1993 production, restocked with a talented, well-matched cast, including an exceptionally likeable protagonist, and with many fine directorial details added (Figure 7.1). The second part of this discussion will turn from literal growing pains to musical depictions of them—considerations of the music and lyrics in *Merrily* that have been retained largely unchanged, especially in the uniquely autobiographical number "Opening Doors." After examining some music closely, this chapter will in conclusion consider further aspects of autobiography and aesthetics.

The study of *Merrily We Roll Along* is significantly hindered by the absence of readily available sources.[1] The libretto is the only one of Sondheim's Broadway shows that has never been published and no complete video version is generally available despite the beautifully staged and lensed Kennedy Center revival in 2002 and the recent London production, which was presented in a fine video version in selected movie theatres internationally in 2013.[2] The revised show's book and music are available via rental, and continue to receive thoughtful productions, such as a student workshop at Yale in 2007 and professional productions at the Watermill Theatre in Newbury, two hours' drive west of London, under John Doyle's direction (2008) and in the aforementioned production by Maria Friedman, which opened at the Menier Chocolate Factory before transferring to the West End in 2013. Rumor has it that the show has even been staged with its scenes in chronological order,[3] a notion perhaps inspired by Sondheim, who once said "if the

FIGURE 7.1 Mark Umbers, Damian Humbley, and Jenna Russell as Frank, Charley, and Mary in *Merrily We Roll Along*, Menier Chocolate Factory, London (2012).

score is listened to in reverse order—although it wasn't written that way—it develops traditionally." [4]

Merrily began as an experiment with the conventions of the genre by "modernism's chief exponent[s] in the musical," [5] Sondheim and producer and director Harold Prince, who brought in George Furth as librettist. Budgeted at $1.5 million and in need of an audience as a result of disastrous word-of-mouth during six weeks of previews, "the show underwent the most radical revision of any Sondheim-Prince show, in fact, one of the most radical revisions any [Broadway] show has undergone." [6] The creative trio had set ambitious and contradictory goals for themselves. Write a musical about writing musicals. Tell the story backwards. Cast the show with unknown young talent and produce it (after costly missteps) with minimal sets and costumes. Make the main character an antihero, difficult to like. Finally, fill this experiment with great old-fashioned show tunes, and turn a profit with it on Broadway.

When you listen to the score as an album, it's a hit. But it wasn't. The songs "soar and linger and hurt." [7] As with so many musicals that flop, the book has generally been held responsible for the failure of *Merrily*. But Furth's "arch, brittle quips" (in the style of its source, the Kaufman and Hart play from 1934) constitute a perfectly good framework for the songs. [8] *Merrily*'s intrinsic problem remains the structural imperative of going backwards. [9] We meet the principal characters in middle age, self-absorbed and unattractive. We only come to like them later, in the second act when they are young and full of pep, ending up (so to speak) twenty-five years earlier as a bunch of enchanted dreamers on a rooftop, gazing toward the stars. Instead of establishing our sympathy before manipulating it, Furth had to alienate us, then progressively engage our sympathy—an almost impossible dramaturgical task within a commercial genre like the musical. Mainstream audiences are said to have trouble with principal characters in musicals who sell out or are otherwise unsavory.[10] Sondheim observed, "A lot of people found the central character [Frank] unlikable. The idea is, of course, that he is unlikable, but you get to like him better as the evening goes on."[11]

The narrative structure of *Merrily* is not linear: it's a discourse, episodic and additive. Like *Company*, Sondheim's other collaboration with Furth, the book is made up of "loosely connected scenes."[12] Grim scenes of spoiled middle age give way in the second act to nostalgic scenes of bright youth. But any sequence of scenes featuring the same characters has a cumulative impact—we come to know them. In this sense, *Merrily* tells the stories of three artists, close friends who help one another make the big time. Furth's book utilizes the structure of its Kaufman and Hart source play, with its series of nine flashback scenes, each ending with a climactic onstage moment. Time runs forward within each scene, but each scene is set further back in time than the previous one.

After the Broadway fiasco—sixteen performances in the autumn of 1981—Prince moved on, "ashamed."[13] But Furth and Sondheim doggedly returned to the work, after Sondheim finished *Sunday in the Park with George* in 1984. By 1985 they had revised the opening and ending, reinstated plot points from the original play and musical materials cut from the first run, and added a new song ("Growing Up").[14] By 1992, they had built up the roles of Frank and his second wife, Gussie, conflating two scenes in the first act and revising the act 2 opening and, with Jonathan Tunick, adjusted orchestrations and arrangements between 1994 and 2002.

In a 1995 interview, Sondheim assessed the 1994 version, emphasizing his collaborations with Furth, with James Lapine, Prince's successor as director, and with a succession of good producing organizations:

> *Merrily* has gone through four revisions over a period of thirteen years. The first and major revision was when Jim Lapine directed it at the La Jolla Playhouse in 1985, and that's when the show took its major turn. It was really terrific, and to this day James regrets not having brought it to New York. George and I tinkered with it further and improved it in Seattle [1988], and then we took it a couple of steps backwards in Washington [1990], and then I had a structural idea to combine two scenes into one and it worked ["Growing Up" parts 1 and 2, in act 1]. We did that version in Leicester, England a year and a half ago and it was swell. The production was wonderful and the English cast was just great. The people at the York Theater have done my shows enthusiastically and well and they'd been pushing me to let them do *Merrily* for years, and I said not until George and I are pleased with what we've done. And when we got through in Leicester, we were pleased with it, so that's why they're doing it now. And I think it's really good.[15]

Originally the musical ended with a high school graduation set in 1955, echoing the 1934 play, which concludes with the young valedictorian Frank rousing his college classmates in 1916 as war raged in Europe by quoting Polonius in Shakespeare's *Hamlet*: "This above all: to thine own self be true, / And it must follow, as the night the day, / Thou canst not then be false to any man" (act 1, scene 3). Future popular playwright Richard Niles (who in Furth's book becomes Franklin Shepard, a popular composer), wishes his class-mates each "a great friendship," like his own with painter Jonathan Crale (who becomes the playwright, librettist, and lyricist Charley Kringas in the musical), and urges them to "value ideals above all else." A minor character in the play is expanded into a triangular "best pal" in the musical—Mary, a novelist. The final setting for the play is a Gothic cha-pel, flooded with sunlight filtered through a stained glass window. The musical ended in 1981 as it began, with the cast arrayed on a bare wagon of bleachers.

Having finished singing "Our Time," a lovely Bernsteinesque anthem sung on a roof-top by the three friends who are joined by the chorus on adjacent rooftops, the cast hast-ily redonned the black high school graduation robes they wore at the outset and stood "as in the opening [scene]," as the older Frank, joined by a "YOUNGER FRANK," recited the lines from *Hamlet*. A few weeks into the run, the actors had traded their black gowns for glowing saffron orange ones, as all the sets and costumes were replaced before open-ing night.[16] The younger Frank then conducted the student body in two verses of the graduation hymn "[Behold] the Hills of Tomorrow."[17] The 1982 libretto concludes, "The younger Frank exchanges smiles with Charley, then with his older self, as the curtain falls slowly."[18] This *Follies*-like symbolic wedding of selves was intended somehow to resolve Frank's decisive break with the ideals of his younger self. It was probably not fully satisfying to an audience already struggling with the modernist challenge of Furth's deliberately disconnected, puzzle-like sequence of scenes. An audience familiar with more conventionally plotted fare, such as the taut melodrama of Sondheim's preceding show, *Sweeney Todd*, may well have found that the nonlinear narrative required them to connect too many dots. By the press night, it also didn't make much sense that older Frank would have any kind expressions to share with his younger self, because the open-ing had been changed, as we'll see. The audience probably felt that older Frank was a thoroughly unpleasant fellow.

Furth, Sondheim, and Prince created an analogous opening scene that is not in the 1934 play—a graduation at the same school set in 1980, with Franklin Shepard of the class of 1955, now famous, invited back as guest speaker. In an early draft of the open-ing scene, with pages dated variously between January 10 and July 14, 1981, Frank is still sweeter than he is foul, someone who indeed might smile fondly at his younger self. Older Frank reverently recalls his high school music teacher, who told him "*everyone* is an artist... [but] it's not enough for someone to paint... or play... or write his master-piece. All of that will come, will just fall into place... (echo)... *if you make your life your masterpiece.*" The echo was presumably added electronically by Sondheim's first credited sound designer, Jack Mann.[19] The chorus then interjects some of the music about tend-ing dreams and traveling along metaphorical roads, bumpy or smooth, that is still in the show, although recast as a choral prologue, like that of *A Little Night Music*. Frank continues with his speech: "[T]hat old man, my music teacher... (*he laughs*) who was probably exactly my age today... was the one person I wanted to *be* like..." At this point a soloist, then a quartet, then an octet, sing more of the opening music. Frank continues his speech, explaining his divergent path since high school, sanctimoniously but reasonably modestly:

> When I began composing, my plan was to repay the world for bumping into that great man and some day just stop and go back and teach what that great man taught me. But along the way I also bumped into success and fame. I suddenly found myself in music publishing and then the recording business and ultimately producing films. . . . But I like to think in going into business that I opened up the way for many people to make *their* lives *their* masterpiece.[20]

The sweet prerehearsal Frank was jettisoned before the show opened, along with spoken dialogue from another group of characters who are getting ready to go to a party. A more cynical Frank is his replacement. Frank's speech has become a call to be "practical" and "compromise."[21] He starts out with a slightly sarcastic tribute to the class of 1980—"Are these kids *swell?*"[22] On at least one occasion, the Broadway audience wasn't sure how to respond to this line, although a few brave souls got into the spirit of the moment and cheered as they would have been expected to at a genuine graduation.[23] Prince reflected ruefully on this and similar moments later, observing, "when an audience gets confused, it gets hostile."[24]

Frank takes a prepared speech out of an inside pocket and begins grimly lecturing the "young innocents" about "a few realities," like "not necessarily doing the best," just "the best you can." A young graduate disagrees quietly, "No, it's doing the best." This speaker is "YOUNGER FRANK." A sonic dialogue develops between the old, boring Frank—speaking or sometimes only miming speech silently, a perfect quasicinematic simulation of what most audience members at a boring speech actually perceive—and a vibrant, lively chorus of young people who gradually unfreeze from their orderly graduation tableau, tear off their robes, and start dancing as well as singing. However, their everyday clothes reveal another irony. These idealistic young people are evidently all headed for lives not as successful dreamers, but as underlings to OLDER FRANK. Their "sweatshirts" (in the script, which became T-shirts in the actual production) read variously: "HIS . . . ATTORNEY / SECRETARY / PUBLISHER / MASSEUR / MANAGER / DEALER / BUTLER / BODYGUARD / MAID / YESMAN / DECORATOR / PRESS AGENT / ASSISTANT / PROTEGE / HOUSEBOY / BARTENDER / ANALYST / PHOTOGRAPHER / BACKER." They join actors who previously have revealed their T-shirts, bearing the legends "FRANKLIN SHEPARD," "EX-MRS. SHEPARD" (Gussie, Frank's second wife), "EX-EX MRS. SHEPARD" (Beth, Frank's first wife), and "NEXT MRS. SHEPARD" (Meg, Frank's new rising star, as we learn in the next scene).[25] Although not specified in this script, presumably two additional T-shirts read something like "BEST FRIEND" (Charley Kringas) and "BEST PAL" (Mary).

These labels confuse matters at the outset, contradicting the lyrics and action. How can Frank's future "hangers-on" be so full of dreams and roads to try? How could all three of his future wives have been high school seniors along with him? Why does our main character start out as such an unthinking boor, so lacking in the requisite social grace of an invited speaker expected to invoke idealistic dreams and future pathways appropriate to graduations that the students themselves are forced to express these traditional platitudes? To confuse matters further, in early previews it was hard to tell the difference between old and young Frank. The 1981 production was performed by an extraordinarily young cast ranging in age from sixteen (Harold Prince's daughter Daisy was fifteen when she auditioned) to Jim Walton, twenty-six, who eventually replaced the original Franklin Shepard, James Weissenbach, a former intern in Prince's office[26] (Figure 7.2). Before opening night, an older actor, Geoffrey Horne, was finally cast as old Frank to make this point clearer.[27] Early attempts to delineate age via hairpieces—twelve, just for Charley—were jettisoned late in rehearsals in favor of much simpler sets and costumes. The onstage swimming pool—actually a pit filled with paper—also disappeared.[28]

In both versions, the original opening made a visually striking beginning, as a frozen graduation scene comes to life. But it was roundly criticized. It may have simply been too ambitious, particularly the multileveled first version. On the one hand, the kinder, gentler Frank of the first version undermined the—still rather diffuse—retrogressive tracking of Frank's career, during which he is exposed as someone his younger self would not understand. But from another point of view the original Frank is more engaging, and might somehow have engaged the audience's interest more than the cynical Frank. Again, *Merrily*'s "backwards" book challenges conventional genre expectations. Frank sold out, abandoned his youthful dreams and his potential greatness, and stopped composing: knowing all this at the outset of the show can be painful and sad.

Many of the 1985 revisions to Furth's book borrow further elements from the Kaufman and Hart play. For example, after a choral prologue consisting of the revised

FIGURE 7.2 Jim Walton as Frank (center, in black trousers) in a scene from *Merrily We Roll Along* (1981).

remains of the high school scene, the second scene of the 1981 show—a party—became the first scene, as it is in the play. The elimination of Frank from this first scene and the removal of the closing graduation scene probably constituted the most crucial revision of *Merrily*. But postponing Frank's introduction didn't resolve the larger challenge of the show for a mainstream Broadway audience, baffled by reverse chronology, characters without depth, and a lack of action. ("Depth" and "action" imply backstory and motivations supplied via dialogue, and the suspenseful narrative strategies typical of Hollywood and Broadway musicals.) While the further borrowings from Kaufman and Hart, particularly the building up of the character of Gussie (actress Althea Royce in the play) and the restoration of a moment of Oedipal violence (a blinding), were widely perceived as improvements to the revised version of the musical's book in 1985. They also make it more conventional, melodramatic, and less jarringly modern.

Some critics have suggested that the first scene was removed from later versions of *Merrily*. For example, Frank Rich in a 1990 review of the revised version labeled the opening as new material, saying: "The original production's confusing framing device, a high-school graduation, has been dropped (though a new and counterproductive prologue has been added)."[29] That's not accurate. Only Frank and the original high school *setting* were removed from the first scene. The music of the new prologue is just as it was in the "cut" graduation scene: complex interplay between solos and chorus, free counterpoint in the chorus climaxing in a bluesy soprano section descant, and the whole punctuated with brass fanfares and Latin rhythms.[30]

The effect is certainly completely different. Instead of the *tableau vivant* (anticipating *Sunday*'s re-creations of Seurat's paintings) of a rite of passage—a high school graduation with a boring guest speaker—we have a timeless Greek-style chorus setting the scene by stating the evening's theme repeatedly: how people and cultures change with age, often giving up their dreams on the road from then to now. ("How does it happen?"[31]) The effect of the revised opening is much closer to that of the choral opening of *A Little Night Music*—an invocation to the audience. However, as Stephen Banfield reluctantly observed, the many choral interludes in *Merrily* get "rather tiresome."[32] Although carried along by the music, the opening remains dramaturgically problematic. The show remains as a whole something less than the sum of its many magnificent parts.

The original opening and ending of *Merrily*, despite extensive revisions in rehearsals, failed to click with audiences or critics. Furth called the 1985 revision the "grown-up" version of *Merrily*, probably referring to the older cast, and the revised opening and ending became the hallmarks of *Merrily*'s coming-of-age as a stageable show.[33] The 1984 piano–vocal score lists nine numbers in the first act and eighteen in the second, reflecting the complexity of the original stage version, astutely streamlined for the original cast recording. Ten songs out of the fourteen numbers recorded on that 1981 album, some of them actually whole scenes, remain largely unchanged from 1981 to today: "Like It Was," "Old Friends," "Franklin Shepard, Inc.," "Not a Day Goes By," and "Now You Know" in the first act; "It's a Hit!," "Good Thing Going," "Bobby and Jackie and Jack," "Opening Doors," and "Our Time" in the second. These set pieces constitute the glories of *Merrily*, the reasons, perhaps, for its enduring appeal. The other musical materials in the show, including the new song "Growing Up" (and the never-restored but published song "Honey," originally part of the second act wedding scene) do not have the same impact as this stable of thoroughbreds. The new opening, a party, was revised heavily in 1985, as were other parts of the first act within which these songs are set. Only the set piece "Franklin Shepard, Inc." is intact as a number; the other four songs in act 1 have been substantially recontextualized and rearranged in ways analogous to—but less drastic than—the revised choral opening. Many shows have second-act problems. In *Merrily*, like the story itself, it's just the reverse.[34] The reworked opening of act 2 features Gussie in yet another brief show within a show—this time a turn as a glamorous chanteuse.[35] Otherwise, the second act is trimmed but largely unchanged from 1981.

"Opening Doors" stands out in several ways. It's arguably the most ingenious of several depictions of shows within this show about show business. The episode wasn't in the source play, and it is avowedly autobiographical. The process of creation depicted is similar to Sondheim's actual working methods. It is also about artistic idealism, and being called a Stravinsky unable to write a hummable melody. Does it perhaps express the anxiety of Richard Rodgers's influence—he who *could* produce hummable tunes like "Some Enchanted Evening"?[36] Many works of fiction attempt to portray creativity as moments of inspiration. Sondheim sticks to portraying the perspiration.

Compared to a through-composed (or sung-through) score, *Merrily*'s score, like its book, is inherently episodic because it is all made of tunes. This is why, Sondheim has said, it was so hard to write. The tunefulness of the score undercuts the perception of motivic relationships. It is easy to perceive *Merrily*'s modular blocks, not as motivic interconnections, but as emblems of the composer Frank's lack of creativity. This is why Swayne's appellation for "one-tune" Frank seems so apt. For example, when Frank suggests, "[we'll write a re]view of our own" in "Opening Doors," he uses the next few notes of the first phrase of "Who Wants to Live in New York?" which becomes the first phrase of "Good Thing Going." "Opening Doors," in a single continuous musical scene without spoken dialogue, incorporates a variety of materials, yet derives stylistically from the generic Broadway showtune, a little miracle we can begin to dissect by charting its structure (Table 7.1)

The scene includes several kinds of "working" music and two discrete songs, "Opening Doors," and "Who Wants to Live in New York?" Charley first "plays" a typewriter solo; then he performs a duet with Mary, complete with carriage-return bell rings, multiple rolls of the platen (the rubber roller), and even a series of "x's" to cross out a bad line, performed as a determined series of straight eighth notes.[37] While Charley and Mary rhythmically write, Frank plays a series of slightly different versions of a bit of melody, a germ of an idea, a motive or motif. It is the start of "Good Thing Going," which we've heard in a previous scene—the fictional hit song from Frank's first hit show with lyrics by his friend Charley. *We* know this, but the conceit of the show is that since time moves backwards, this younger Frank doesn't know it yet. In fact, he's still struggling, quite audibly, to find it. After deciding on the bit of melody, he struggles with how to harmonize it, whistling and humming it over various chords (Banfield counts thirty-three different harmonizations of Frank's motif[38]). Suddenly—implied jump cut

Table 7.1 Listening chart for "Opening Doors," with sectional analysis

time*	Section	narrative description
0:01	A	Charley makes rhythmical manual typewriter sounds, later joined by Mary
0:03		Frank begins melodic variations on his motif (no harmonies yet)
0:20	B	Frank collapses on the keys, then asks Charley "How's it going?" over a vamp and orchestral echoes of Frank's motif
0:24	C	Phone rings, Charley answers ("Chinese Laundry")—it's Mary
0:31		Muted trumpet stabs underline Frank's question to Mary, "What about the book?"
0:36	A²	Frank hangs up and he and Charley go back to work: more motivic variations and typewriter percussion
1:00	D	Charley, Frank, and Mary complete each other's phrases as they recount small accomplishments, punctuated by pizzicato strings and a repeated piccolo falling minor second (scale degrees 4 and 3)
1:13	E	All sing in unison, "We're opening doors..." (A section, made up of one-bar-long "modules": abac abb'd)
1:29	E²	Tuba obbligato (playing A section, accompanied by brass riffs, doubled by trumpet on second half)
1:42	A³	Frank and Charley go back to work; Frank whistles his riff, accompanying it with chords for the first time; the stage is "alive with activity"; accompanying riffs in orchestra continue into...
1:49	D²	Charley, Frank, and Mary complete each other's phrases as they recount small accomplishments, punctuated by pizzicato strings and a repeated clarinet note
1:57		Direct modulation up minor third, from G to B♭
2:04	E³	All sing "We're opening doors..." with prominent tuba bass line, ending in a choral harmony
2:20	A⁴	Direct modulation back to G. Back to work, with a new syncopated treble riff accompaniment played on synthesizer
2:25		Frank sings his motif out loud for the first time, using vocables
2:35	B²	Modulation, prepared via a brief chromatic passage (mm. 86–7), up to A♭
		"How's it coming?" Frank almost yells to Charley. Mary calls. Charley finishes a draft of lyrics for Frank's song.
		Ritardando
2:55	A⁵	Charley begins to sing Frank's first draft of the song based on his motif, "Who Wants to Live in New York?" with riff-based accompaniment on piano from Frank, featuring a falling minor second (scale degrees 5 and ♯4), for Joe Josephson, a potential producer; twice through A section (sixteen bars)
3:16	F	Joe unconsciously provides a nice "middle eight," or B section, then repeats the A section twice, then repeats the new B section all the while commenting on the song (see Banfield, *Sondheim's Broadway Musicals*, 333–4)
3:57		Charley desperately begins the song again, "overselling" *à la* Al Jolson

(Continued)

Table 7.1 (Continued)

time*	Section	narrative description
4:04	G	Joe interrupts again, providing a "refrain," or contrasting C section and repeating closing gesture that he repeats as he exits, then hums an off-key rendition of "Some Enchanted Evening" as an example of the kind of melody he prefers, accompanied by a mournful oscillating minor second on muted trombone (scale degrees 3 and ♭3)
4:29		Grand pause
4:30	D^3	Wind stab; then the three friends trade bits of bad news, punctuated by a soft rasp
4:49	E^4	Trio sings a soft, detached version of the tune, to the words "They're slamming their doors"
5:04	A^6	Frank suggests "a review of our own," singing the "Good Thing Going" motif
5:26	A^7	Frantic auditions, using "Who Wants to Live in New York?" for a female lead (Mary won't perform except at dinner). Direct modulation to F. First girl, "shrill and off-pitch."
5:37	A^8	Beth auditions; Frank calls for two direct modulations "up a step," to G, then A, and she follows the accompanist easily
5:49	G^2	Beth introduces herself, in the new higher key of A, using Joe's "middle eight" tune
5:57	D^4	Quartet trade updates frantically, to a repeated high xylophone note, as they prepare the review of Frank's songs, finally all speaking at once and segueing to…
6:10	E^5	"We're opening doors, singing 'here we are!'…" accompanimental riff changes to a less syncopated march rhythm
6:28		Another direct modulation up a step, to B: "We're banging on doors…," ending: "We haven't got time!"
6:49		End

*Timings and orchestration descriptions refer to 1981 recording.

through time—the music is finished, and Charley must struggle to set words to the new tune, with the deadline of a scheduled audition approaching. The result is the up-tempo number "Who Wants to Live in New York?" affectionately parodying not only the typical "I love it / I hate it" song but also some of the many anthems in celebration of New York City.

Both songs begin with the same motif, a horncall, a leap upwards of a perfect fourth (like "Taps"). The second song interwoven in this scene, "Opening Doors," also begins with this leap, followed by yet another leap of a fourth (separated by a major second): "o-pen-ing doors." These expertly redeployed motifs serve temporally compressed stage action (Mandelbaum states that the number covers two years in the lives of the characters, which is plausible).[39] Each reprise of a tune is punctuated by another work session, moving the action along in a kind of rondo form. Banfield singles out the taste-less Joe Josephson's tasty contrasting melodic materials—which Beth borrows—for praise, in part because they simultaneously serve plot and aspects of show song form (B section and closing vamp, labeled F and G on the listening chart, which Banfield calls "middle eight" and " 'refrain' ending"). In the middle of F, Josephson sings the A section of Frank's melody while complaining that it isn't memorable—a musico-verbal pun.[40] What Josephson wants is Rodgers's tune—"Some Enchanted Evening" to be precise— even though he can't sing that either. Interestingly, "Opening Doors" was finished well before much of the rest of the show, possibly by early November of 1980.[41] The only difference between this version and the one usually performed nowadays is the substitution in 1981of straightforward repetitions of the original first verse of "Who Wants to Live in New York?" during the audition for Frank and Charley's Off-Broadway revue.

To sum up, "Opening Doors" is intriguing on several fronts: motivic density, temporal compression, creative yet historically informed approach to its topic, craft, stylistic nuance. It embodies "Sondheim-ness." Textually, it is perhaps the most striking of a number of self-referential, postmodern shows-within-the-show, along with the offstage hit *Musical Husbands*, represented metonymically by "Good Thing Going" —itself featured in a backer's audition, another kind of show-within-the-show—and "It's a Hit." The trio's debut cabaret show, depicted in the number "Bobby and Jackie and Jack," gets titled *Frankly Frank* by Mary in the course of "Opening Doors." Gussie's Las Vegas-ized reprise of "Good Thing Going" in the new beginning to the second act is a fantasy show-within-a-show, of the kind typified by "Rose's Turn" in *Gypsy*.

"Opening Doors" is original as well as being autobiographical for Sondheim. There is nothing like it in Kaufman and Hart's play. In a nice touch of staging, Beth's instant rapport with the three established friends is signaled in the 1981 production by her being clad in carpenter's pants dyed saffron orange that visually connected her to the high school graduation robes of the opening scene, and to the urban artist's garb of choice in the late 1950s or early1960s (the scene's date is 1959). Augmenting some underwhelming marching dance steps in early previews, the stage's turntable added kinetic energy to the final chorus in the scene in later performances, revolving the players along with an upright piano. Future productions would introduce analogous minor revisions that continued to alter *Merrily*, beyond the major revisions accomplished in the 1985 revival.[42]

The 2002 revival at the Sondheim Celebration Festival at the Kennedy Center in Washington, DC, employed a talented cast of players, bringing strong musical and dramatic skills and yet more insights to the piece, directed this time by Christopher Ashley, and opening memorably with the chorus lounging on, then pushing around, and even playing four gleaming black concert grand pianos. This production starred Michael Hayden (as Frank), Raùl Esparza (Charley), Miriam Shor (Mary), Emily Skinner (Gussie), and Adam Heller (Joe).[43] Although the production was amplified, the dynamics are not compressed as in so many amplified shows. Some musical passages are soft, some are loud, and this makes a great deal of difference. It is, of course, sad to have to make this obvious point—but subtly gradated dynamics are truly a distinguishing characteristic of the 2002 production.

By this time orchestrator Jonathan Tunick had added many felicities to the arrangements, which Rich had described accurately in 1981 as "brassy." Tunick increased the musical role of the piano—augmented initially in 1994 and further in 2002—which is also "played" onstage several times during the show, echoing the many diegetic musical moments in the 1934 play. The former tuba solo in the overture, given to the piano by 1994, is adorned by 2002 with repeated allegro piano triplets reminiscent of Antoine Dominique ("Fats") Domino or Tommy Thompson, for another nice touch of 1950s popular music style, and the many passages of diegetic piano music are enriched throughout with thoughtful interpretive choices such as phrasing, articulation, and dynamics within phrases. The original 1981 tuba, while distinctive, was not perhaps as felicitous a choice as the horn in the opening scene of Sondheim's next show, *Sunday in the Park with George*, and was actually passed over to a trombone on both the 1981 and 1992 cast recordings.[44]

At some date, Tunick also reshaped the overtures to the first and second acts and the bows music, repeating materials more for emphasis, creating a musical da capo frame for the show, analogous in a way to the original formal intent of the long-gone twin graduation scenes. In 1981, *Merrily* ended with a beautiful Stravinskyesque vamp (under dialogue) repeated an unimaginative seventeen or so times in a row in the cut 1950s high school graduation scene.[45] "Our Time" is really a better musical ending. But to be fair, Rich's judgment of the second-act book in 1981, despite its marvelous musical settings, still stands: "all anticlimactic plot exposition." The best David Richards could say of the second act's book after seeing the 1994 New York revival was "moving in a deeply melancholy way." Ironically, as in most operas, the nonoperatic music of *Merrily* packs the expressive punch.

Sondheim discussed the relationship of *Merrily* to his own early career in an interview in 1997:

> *Merrily* was the hardest score I ever had to write, and it was partly because I was trying to recapture what I was like when I was twenty-five without making a comment on it. It's about two young songwriters, and I wanted to convey what they would have written back in the late fifties, early sixties, without making it a take-off or a parody. *And* they're supposed to be talented. Writing it was like pushing a pea up a hill with your nose. What I like about it is it sounds effortless to me now—it just sounds like a nice score—and I know what went into it. . . . To write a thirty-two-bar song that has freshness and style to it and tells the story is hard.[46]

Elsewhere, however, he was more explicit about the autobiographical aspects of *Merrily*. Mark Horowitz asked him in 1997, "So in 'Opening Doors,' . . . when you have the character of the composer trying out the thirty-two different harmonizations of his theme, is that really how you approach it?" Sondheim responded, "You got it. That's what I do. That's my big autobiographical number; everything in that number is me. . . . [Jerome] Kern was not the only one to do this."[47] As Cronin points out, Sondheim's own biography is much more Charley Kringas, the loyal, principled playwright and lyricist of *Merrily* the musical, than Franklin Shepard the fickle friend and tunesmith turned movie producer and "Opening Doors," may be an inspired amalgamation of bits of himself and young friends like Burt Shevelove and Harold Prince from the early 1950s. Sondheim has stated that each character in *Company*, not *Merrily*, had a specific real-life inspiration, but he did so while discrediting autobiographical readings of his works, crediting Furth for creating the characters in *Company*, and highlighting the collaborative nature of musicals.[48] Elsewhere, Sondheim responded unambiguously to over-literal biographical readings by asserting (as paraphrased by Gottfried) that "although his work, like all art, draws on personal experience, it is never literally about himself—with a single exception... 'Opening Doors.' "[49]

Merrily marked the end for a time of Sondheim's collaborations with Harold Prince that ran back to *West Side Story*, but unlike the fictional Frank and Charley, it was not the end of their real-life friendship.[50] The two reunited in 2003 to create *Bounce*—one version of another much-revised work in Sondheim's oeuvre. *Merrily* is potentially Sondheim and Prince's most concept-driven, narratively disjointed stage piece. Many critics have noted that rather than youth, the central theme of *Merrily* is friendship. Without an engrossing central character, the present version of *Merrily* plays as a fine ensemble show.

In another interview, Sondheim grouped *Merrily* the 2003 revision of *Wise Guys* titled *Bounce*, and indirectly addressed its episodic structure:

> The harmonic language [of *Bounce*] is, again, a kind of very tonal language with moderately simple key relationships that I was writing in the late fifties (not on Broadway) and when I was writing things like *Forum*, which is early '60s—what I was recapturing when I did *Merrily We Roll Along*. It's that kind of a score—it's a *Merrily We Roll Along* kind of score. I wanted it to be crisp and bright and simple and direct, with primary colors, because we first started to write the show in a rather cartoony style, a Hope-Crosby kind of musical like the "road pictures." Swiftness is a major element— not that all songs are fast, but all the songs make their point and get off. At least that's the intention. There are very few extended pieces in it.[51]

Those who prefer well-made, coherent narratives may indeed find *Merrily*, like *Bounce*, "a rather cartoony" kind of road show (to cite *Bounce*'s later title), despite its deeply felt themes and, as revised, more conventional narrative. As Sondheim implies here, it is not appropriate to criticize *Merrily*'s book because it is episodic or simple. It was quite deliberately intended as a departure from the epic nineteenth-century worlds evoked by its immediate predecessors, *Pacific Overtures* and *Sweeney Todd*, and perhaps a return to the focus on the present and the topic (coming of age) of *Company*, Furth and Sondheim's first show together in 1970. Although by comparison, *Merrily* was judged a failure, it was bold. Banfield ends his chapter on *Merrily* with some notes Sondheim wrote to himself when working on the show, describing them as nothing less than a brief "to reconstruct the romantic popular song." They also outline an aesthetic for this show that is deliberately not brainy and unironic—two adjectives usually considered inseparable from considerations of Sondheim's work, but anticipating something of the more open expressions of sentiment and humanistic philosophy in *Sunday, Into the Woods*, and *Passion*, for example: "Simple, energetic, sassy, non-intellectual—if anything exaggerate these."[52] Sondheim's personal aims weren't realized, as the whole narrative structure of *Merrily* is designed to create dramatic irony. The music and lyrics are nevertheless conceived to appear as brassy and direct as a traditional Broadway musical comedy even if the stories told are ones of personal and artistic tragedy, and we know how they end from the outset.

This determinedly new venture for its creators developed tentatively, opened disastrously, and has for thirty years been repeatedly revised, revived, and reappraised. The most recently revised version has made *Merrily* more stageable, but what makes it distinctive continues to be what it has always been: a great score and lyrics.

NOTES

1. The easiest way to hear parts of the show is to sample the tantalizing tidbits aficionados post online, including fragments videoed from the balcony of the original production, school, and regional productions, and tracks from the three audio recordings of productions released to date, from 1981 (Broadway), 1992 (Haymarket Theater, Leicester, then London, released 1994, expanded and rereleased 1997), and 1994 (York Theater, Off-Broadway). The producer of the 1981 cast recording claimed, "We spared no expense to prove that no matter what the show was like, it was a fabulous recording," Craig Zadan, *Sondheim & Co.*, 2nd updated ed. (New York: Harper and Row, 1994), 282. It is—but all three are worth hearing. The vocal score, published in 1984, is out of print. Eight selected songs were published in 1981 in piano–vocal arrangements. Good sources for scholars do however exist in New York City. A low-fidelity but fairly complete amateur video of the original 1981 production has been donated to the New York Public Library at Lincoln Center, which also houses archival videos of the 1994 Off-Broadway revival and the major 2002 revival in Washington, DC, where *Merrily* ran in a festival context along with *Sweeney Todd, Sunday in the Park with George, Company, A Little Night Music*, and *Passion*. Jason Alexander— later famous for appearing in *Seinfeld*—who created the role of producer Joe ("I'll let you know when Stravinsky has a hit") Josephson, in the original production later donated his manuscript score, incomplete but with unique prerehearsal materials (some dated 1980 or early 1981) to the Lincoln Center library. Fortunately, the library also houses a copy (dated 1982) of the original script, complete with line scores of all the musical numbers of the type a chorus member would use.
2. This production was filmed for the Library of Congress but never released commercially. *Merrily We Roll Along*. Videorecording of Sondheim Celebration Production at Kennedy Center, Washington, DC, Performing Arts Research Collections, New York Public Library. Gift of the Washington Area Performing Arts Video Archive.
3. The rumor has been circulated on *Wikipedia*.
4. Zadan, *Sondheim & Co.*, 271.
5. Stephen Banfield, *Sondheim's Broadway Musicals* (Ann Arbor: University of Michigan Press, 1993), 322
6. Ken Mandelbaum, "How Did You Get to Be Here, Mr. Sondheim? *Merrily We Roll Along* to Washington, D.C.: Analysis and Review," *Theatre Week*, March 29, 1990, 17.
7. Frank Rich, "Stage: A New Sondheim, 'Merrily We Roll Along,'" *New York Times*, November 17, 1981.

8. Ken Mandelbaum, *Not since "Carrie": Forty Years of Broadway Musical Flops* (New York: St Martin's, 1991), 134.

9. Zadan, *Sondheim & Co.*, 285

10. This is said to be the case in musicals, but not straight plays or operas—see the discussions of *Sunset Boulevard* and *Carousel* in Geoffrey Block, *Enchanted Evenings: The Broadway Musical from "Show Boat" to Sondheim and Lloyd Webber*, 2nd ed. (New York: Oxford University Press, 2009). Brooks Atkinson, in reference to *Pal Joey,* claimed that it was impossible to "draw sweet water from a foul well"; see Geoffrey Block, *Richard Rodgers* (New York: Oxford University Press, 2003), 68–70.

11. Zadan, *Sondheim & Co.*, 282

12. Bruce Weber, "George Furth, an Actor and Playwright, Dies at 75," *New York Times*, August 11, 2008.

13. Martin Gottfried, *Sondheim* (New York: Harry N. Abrams, 1993), 153.

14. "That Frank," sometimes described as a new song, is a reworking of part of "The Blob."

15. Stephen Sondheim, "Sondheim on *Passion* and Writing for the Musical Theater," *Dramatists Guild Quarterly 31*, no. 3 (autumn 1995), 13.

16. A photo of the black robes in the opening can be seen in Gottfried, *Sondheim*, 151; the saffron robes can be seen in the videorecording of a performance of *Merrily We Roll Along* at the Alvin Theatre, New York, in the Performing Arts Research Collections, Theatre on Film and Tape Archive, New York Public Library, Sondheim 1981a. (Note: misdated 1982 in online catalogue as of January 2010.)

17. Ibid. The B section included in *Merrily We Roll Along*, vocal score selections (New York: Revelation/Rilting, 1981), was apparently cut before opening night.

18. Stephen Sondheim, *Merrily We Roll Along*, libretto and line scores (photocopy, 1982). (Note: misdated 1981–2 in NYPL online catalogue as of January 2010.) Stage directions include T-shirt slogan changes for principal characters. Performing Arts Research Collections, New York Public Library. Call number: JPF 98-1.

19. Zadan, *Sondheim & Co.*, 405

20. Stephen Sondheim et al., *Merrily We Roll Along*, vocal score selections (copyist's manuscript: diazo copy, 1981–2). 185 leaves of music in thirteen folios. (Note: some folios are undated, contrary to otherwise accurate detailed information in online catalogue as of January 2010.) Performing Arts Research Collections, New York Public Library. Gift of Jason Alexander. Call number: JPB 01-3.

21. Sondheim 1981a; Sondheim 1981c; Stephen Sondheim, *Merrily We Roll Along*. Sound recording, original cast. CD, RCA, 1986; Sondheim1982; Stephen Sondheim, *Merrily We Roll Along* (vocal score) (New York: Revelation/Rilting, 1984).

22. Sondheim, 1981c, track 2, 1:28

23. Sondheim, 1981a.

24. Zadan, *Sondheim & Co.*, 281.

25. Sondheim, 1982.

26. Secrest, *Sondheim & Co.*, 311–12.

27. Mandelbaum, *Not since "Carrie"*, 132.

28. Zadan, *Sondheim & Co.*, 274; Mandelbaum, "How Did You Get to Be Here," 17–18; Mandelbaum, *Not Since "Carrie"*, 132–3.

29. *New York Times*, February 27, 1990.

30. Compare the second tracks on the sound recordings, Sondheim 1981c, and Sondheim, *Merrily We Roll Along.* Sound recording, York Theatre Company cast. CD (Varèse Sarabande, 1994b).

31. Sondheim, 1981c.

32. Ibid., 318

33. For a detailed discussion and interpretation of the revised book focused on the reworked relationship between Frank and his best friend Charley, see S. F. Stoddart, "Visions and Re-visions: The Postmodern Challenge of *Merrily We Roll Along,*" in *Reading Stephen Sondheim: A Collection of Critical Essays*, ed. Sandor Goodhart, 187–198 (New York: Garland, 2000).

34. Mandelbaum, *Not since "Carrie,"* 132

35. Stephen Sondheim, *Merrily We Roll Along.* Videorecording of Sondheim Celebration Production, summer performance at Kennedy Center, Washington, DC. Performing Arts Research Collections, New York Public Library. Gift of the Washington Area Performing Arts Video Archive, 2002.

36. See Block, *Enchanted Evenings.*

37. Sondheim 1980–81; Sondheim 1984, 199.

38. Banfield, *Sondheim's Broadway Musicals*, 312.

39. Mandelbaum, *Not since "Carrie"*, 134.

40. Banfield, *Sondheim's Broadway Musicals*, 333–4.

41. Sondheim 1980–81

42. These changes are discussed thoughtfully and in considerable detail in Mandelbaum, *Not since "Carrie"*; Banfield, *Sondheim's Broadway Musicals*; and Stoddart, "Visions and Re-visions."

43. Hayden was also known for his portrayals of *Carousel's* antihero Billy Bigelow. See Ben Brantley, "Critic's Notebook: Emotions beneath the Sondheim Chill," *New York Times,* August 8, 2002.

44. See Block, *Enchanted Evenings*, 367, for a discussion of the motivic significance of the horn-call in *Sunday.*

45. Sondheim, 1981a. The vamp is artfully reinterpreted as eleven slowing, fading iterations on 1981c; see also Sondheim,1984, 241

46. Mark Eden Horowitz, *Sondheim on Music: Minor Details and Major Decisions* (Lanham, MD, and Oxford: Scarecrow, 2003), 20.

47. Horowitz, *Sondheim on Music*, 42.

48. Sam Mendes, interview with Sondheim about *Company* (BBC, n.d.). http://www.youtube.com/watch?v=rjO3gXig07E; accessed November 18, 2013.

49. Gottfried, *Sondheim*, 151.

50. Ibid., 153.

51. Mark Eden Horowitz, "Sondheim: 'This is the Show We Meant,'" *Sondheim Review* 10, no. 3 (winter 2004). http://sondheimreview.com/v10n3.htm.

52. Banfield, *Sondheim's Broadway Musicals*, 340

CHAPTER 8

"GIVE US MORE TO SEE": THE VISUAL WORLD OF STEPHEN SONDHEIM'S MUSICALS

BUD COLEMAN

IN *Sunday in the Park with George*, George Seurat's mistress Dot urges the painter to keep "Moving On,"

> Anything you do,
> Let it come from you.
> Then it will be new.
> Give us more to see...[1]

While ardent fans of musicals by Stephen Sondheim understandably find themselves awed again and again by his brilliantly erudite lyrics and his breathtaking music, few come away from a production extolling what the show looked like, perhaps assuming that any praise devoted to the visual elements would somehow diminish Sondheim's contributions as lyricist and composer. But to neglect the *mise en scène* of any Sondheim musical (at least in its original incarnation) is to deny the significant planning and thought that Sondheim devotes to the visual-kinetic realization of his work. In close collaboration with his directors, choreographers, and designers, Sondheim helped to revolutionize not only what the late twentieth-century musical sounded like, but also how it looked.

The eight Broadway musicals that came to be through the partnership of Harold Prince and Stephen Sondheim (and their collaborators), from *West Side Story* to *Merrily We Roll Along* (1981), mark the first phase of Sondheim's career. The second phase began with James Lapine's *Sunday in the Park with George* (1984). It is worth remembering that when *West Side Story* opened in 1957, while it was innovative in form and content, it was only a modest box office success (732 performances); audiences flocked to the more conventional sights and sounds of *The Music Man* and *My Fair Lady*. *West Side Story* not only broadened the scope of the musical to include tragedy, it revolutionized how set changes could contribute to the pacing of the show and it transformed the role of dance as a medium for storytelling. Critic Water Terry noted that Jerome Robbins "has restated for our times the necessity of action for drama and the power of dance as the fullest manifestation of action in drama."[2] As Sondheim was to learn, Robbins was not only interested in how dance could support character development and the show's narrative, he wanted to make sure every element of the production contributed to the dramatic action (Figure 8.1).

> During rehearsals of Tony's solo "Maria," Robbins asked Sondheim, "*What is he doing?*" Sondheim replied, "Well, he sings 'Maria, Maria. I've just met a girl named Maria, and suddenly that name will never be the same to me.'"
> Robbins persisted, "And then what happens?"
> "Then he sings…"
> "You mean," Robbins asked incredulously, "he just stands looking at the audience?"
> "Well, yes."
> "*You* stage it" Robbins said disgustedly.[3]

In the integrated book musical, Robbins was determined that everything about the production would be united in telling the story and revealing character—"*What is he doing?*" This adaptation of Shakespeare's *Romeo and Juliet* was not the place for reflective art songs, it was a musical that insisted on action. Sondheim became convinced that,

FIGURE **8.1** Debbie Allen as Anita in the 1980 revival of *West Side Story.*

Every second should carry you forward in some way. Well, it's up to the songwriter to think those things up before you put the show in the director's lap. If you don't, you get clumsy staging or static songs and you end up throwing lots of things out on the road because they don't work.[4]

For Walter Terry, this goal had been reached: "The great wonder of *West Side Story* is that realistic action flows into dancing and out of it again without hitch or break, just as speech swells or snarls its way into poetry and song."[5] Sondheim was influenced not only by what Robbins expected from the lyrics and libretto, but also from the scenic elements as well.

The visual world that Oliver Smith created for *West Side Story* was essentially abstract; for example, in the rumble scene, Smith created a forced perspective[6] environment to invoke the brutality of Hell's Kitchen. Various scenic elements in *West Side Story* were realistically rendered, but most of the scenes were made up of fragments of a neighborhood: fences, rooftops on crumbling tenements, torn posters, and sections of highway. While the bedroom, drugstore, and fire escapes were three-dimensional, most of the scenery was painted drops so as to leave a maximum area of the stage floor open for dance. Having collaborated with Robbins on six Broadway musicals and at Ballet Theatre, Smith was well aware of Robbins's sense of movement, so for *West Side Story* he created a set whose movements were part of the choreography of the musical. When Tony and Maria danced the dream ballet in "Somewhere," they were confined and hemmed in by moving set pieces and drops which flew in and out. Working in tandem with lighting designer Jean Rosenthal, the creative team paced the show so that one scene dissolved cinematically into the next. As Tony sang the last bars of "Maria" in a spotlight at the gym, the scene shift was already in motion, so that the next scene could take place immediately on the street without a pause. As William Green observed in *The American Theatre*, the integrated book musical had reached its zenith with *West Side Story*: a "total integration of book, lyrics, music, ballet, and set and costume design. None of these items can be divorced from the others."[7]

Although nominated for six Tonys, only scene designer Oliver Smith and Robbins (as choreographer) took home awards for *West Side Story*. While Robbins was often a disagreeable collaborator, he and Sondheim worked closely together to devise the "mash-up" medley of "Rose's Turn," comprising all the songs that were connected to Rose. According to Sondheim:

> Difficult as he [Robbins] was to work with—and he could be really mean and [an] awful man—I would work with him anytime. It's just...it is worth it. The end product is worth it. He does get, not only the best out of you,...some of his invention rubs off on you. You get more inventive when you work with Jerry Robbins.[8]

As with *West Side Story, Gypsy*'s design team was a stellar group of Broadway's best. Set and lighting designer Jo Mielziner came to the project with three Tonys and five Donaldson Awards, providing the production a dizzying number of locations, ending with a bare stage for "Rose's Turn." Footlights had long disappeared from Broadway theaters, but Mielziner brought them back to give the vaudeville and burlesque sequences

FIGURE **8.2** Chita Rivera as Anita in the "Dance at the Gym," *West Side Story* (1957).

a surreal look. Costume designer Raoul Pène du Bois also embraced the idea of "unreal brilliance" for the show-within-a-show scenes,[9] contrasting them with the somber earth tones of the characters' everyday clothing. The curious coats that would appear on Rose and her two daughters were a running sight-gag; they had been created using hotel blankets from a previous scene.

Uncharacteristically for a Robbins show, there is comparatively little dance in *Gypsy*. Having seen early drafts of Laurents's libretto, Robbins thought the musical would be a virtual history of vaudeville as it morphed into burlesque, so was shocked to read the rehearsal draft and realize that this musical fable was an intimate look into the lives of three people: Rose, Louise, and Herbie. After the cutting of much the planned choreography and the a radical editing of the libretto, the end result was not only a personal triumph for Ethel Merman, the team had redefined what the musical biography could be, and in the process they created a classic American musical.

From one vantage point, the original production of *A Funny Thing Happened on the Way to the Forum* looks lean: one set (unheard of in the world of elaborate musicals), only sixteen actors, and no singing or dancing chorus. The principal characters did not have numerous costume changes, and Jean Rosenthal's lighting design was mainly a full stage wash. John Chapman (*Daily News*) felt that Tony Walton's set and costume designs "seem sure enough B.C. Roman,"[10] and Howard Taubman (*New York Times*) noted that while Walton did not get to design much scenery, "he has had his little joke with the odd assortment of leotards, tunics, togas, gowns and wreaths that pass for Roman duds."[11]

Although Sondheim wanted Robbins to direct and choreograph *Forum*, he turned down the project, so producer Prince secured the services of veteran director George Abbott and choreographer Jack Cole. During his long and illustrious career, Cole had created an original style, a fusion of jazz, modern dance, ethnic, and ballet—known as the "Cole Style" —which had been seen in such stage hits as *Kismet, Jamaica*, and *Man of La Mancha*, and in films like *Gentlemen Prefer Blondes, There's No Business Like Show Business*, and *Some Like It Hot*. When *Forum* was in trouble out of town, Abbott agreed to invite Robbins to take a look at the show. Robbins choreographed a new opening number, and was given permission to "doctor" *Forum*'s other musical numbers. Sondheim remembered that Cole "was a great genius" but one who "had a serious problem in finishing things.... So there were numbers that were dazzling numbers that would just stop. And the audience was completely baffled how come there was no big finish."[12] But Robbins did his magic, and at long last, although he was only thirty-two years old, Sondheim had his own show—and a hit—on Broadway.

After working with Laurents on two previous musicals, Sondheim was not surprised that the libretto for *Anyone Can Whistle* called for an extensive dance segment in act 3. Unlike most musicals, where a dance arranger adapts melodies from the score to fit existing choreography, Sondheim composed original dance music, to which Herbert Ross choreographed. Laurents added some rhythmic dialogue to "The Cookie Chase," turning the number into a "unique sung-danced-dramatized sequence"[13] full of "inventive whirlwind waltzes."[14] Howard Taubman of the *New York Times* was especially impressed with the sequence where a ballerina waltzed up the proscenium arch, assisted by three male dancers. "The Cookie Chase" is the only lengthy instrumental composition that Sondheim has written for the theater.

Like Jerome Robbins, Ross was a classically trained dancer who had choreographed both concert dance and for Broadway musicals, and who was also a performer and director. Sondheim biographer Meryle Secrest calls Ross's contribution to *Whistle* "brilliant,"[15] and Taubman thought *Whistle*'s dancing to be the "cream" of the production, yet noting that "Not even a remarkable dancing ensemble, which executes Herbert Ross's amusing and dazzling patterns, can right the balance of a concept weighed down by its own crudity."[16]

In addition to raising the funds for a production, the lead producer has an enormous impact in that he hires members of the creative team. Harold Prince had already worked with set designer Boris Aronson on *Fiddler on the Roof, Cabaret*, and *Zorba*, but Aronson still seemed like an unlikely candidate to design a concept musical set in contemporary New York City. Hiring Michael Bennett as chorographer of *Company* also seemed a gamble as his previous Broadway work had received mixed notices (negative: *Promises, Promises*; positive: *Coco*). Nevertheless, joined by D. D. Ryan (costume design) and Robert Ornbo (lighting design), this team would create the show that producer and director Prince claimed "changed people's definition of musicals."[17]

The two-level urban "jungle gym for actors," which Aronson designed for *Company*, was greatly informed by the Russian Constructivist style which he studied during his early training. The space contained several compartments made of plastic and chrome, which looked either like apartments or glass cages. The levels were connected by two elevators; with sliding panels, a revolving door, and flying props inspired by the paintings of Francis Bacon, *Company* was meant to evoke the alienation of "contemporary New Yorkers who are at once trapped and exposed in their glass enclosures."[18] A minimal amount of furniture was brought onto each scene, as place was often defined by projections: 600 slides on twenty-eight carousel projectors.[19] The entire basic unit set was positioned on an angle, an asymmetry that created visually dynamic rhythms in the design. As the actors moved up and down and around all the hard angles of the set, Aronson hoped it would evoke a mechanized New York where walking on the sidewalk is a contact sport and crossing the street a high-stakes game of dodge-the-cab—not an easy effect to achieve with a musical which only had fourteen performers.

Bennett was thrilled to find that "the *Company* set had levels, elevators, and still a playing space to dance in. I could move one dancer—Donna McKechnie, the only dancer in the show—all over the set. Because the set and the winches all ran on angles, I had a staging concept for the show—the choreography was all on angles, too."[20] Based on his experience with *West Side Story*, Sondheim had acquired the habit of precisely timing everything that would happen while the character was singing.

> The director is free to change it or not but he has the blueprint. He never has to turn to me and ask, "What am I going to do here?" I always give him more than enough.... If you want the character to cross from here to there, or he has to pick up a coffee cup and drink it or whatever it is, I time those things here in my studio. Then I say,
>
> "Okay now, during these beats or in between, he empties his coffee cup." The director may say, "I don't want a coffee cup in this number" and that's all right. But that's the idea and almost no other composers do this. When I first worked with Michael Bennett and I did the opening number for *Company* he couldn't believe it.... He'd always had to invent out of nowhere....I staged the entire number in my head around the elevator. I asked Boris how long it would take the elevator to get from the top to the bottom so that I knew I could get the people off the stairs and onto the stage level and that's what that climax is about.[21]

The team of Sondheim, Prince, Bennett, and Aronson moved directly from *Company* to *Follies*, joined by Florence Klotz (costumes) and Tharon Musser (lighting). For *Follies*, Aronson created three primary acting areas, three steeply raked platforms on the Winter Garden stage. Upstage and hanging from batons was a jumble of demolition scaffolding, rubble, and faded drops. This world of decay was completely obliterated by the design for the last thirty minutes of the production; the "Loveland" sequence is a flashback to the glory of the 1920s and 1930s revue. In contrast to the jarring asymmetry of the rest of the set design, Aronson's visual world for "Loveland" was symmetrical, containing a riot of old-fashioned color and sparkle, and pointedly two-dimensional. Prince and Aronson wanted the nostalgia for the romanticized 1930s revue to be perceived as "dead weight—the psychological burden of the past that the characters must escape."[22] When the "Loveland" sequence was over, the stage returned to the decrepit Weismann Theatre, but now the back wall of the theater had been demolished, revealing a New York street glistening in the bright sunlight. Aronson's goal was that "When all is broken down again and we see the daylight, it must be like a breath of fresh air!"[23]

To complement this large, moveable set with many possible configurations, costume designer Florence Klotz designed 140 elaborate costumes for *Follies*. The complexity of presenting two radically different worlds (the past and present) demanded almost more of lighting designer Tharon Musser than the technology of the day was able to deliver. With *A Chorus Line* (1975), she was able to use the newly invented memory lightboard, whereas *Follies* (1971) had to make do with manually executed light cues. Similarly, the scale of many of Klotz's revue costumes created a particular challenge for the actors making their entrances and exits through narrow doorways. The Marie Antoinette costumes featured in the "Loveland" sequence were so large (six feet wide) they had to be flown off-stage in the wings as it was impossible to store them elsewhere in the theater.[24] The production was designed to go from scenes in the present day (color) to the past (black and white) in seconds. In some scenes, characters from the past would watch a scene set in the present, providing a commentary on the contemporary action. These theatrical simultaneity moments were in contrast to movie-like close-ups of a character isolated onstage. Realized in Aronson's elaborate stage settings, *Follies* paved the way for the megamusicals of the "British invasion": *Evita, Cats, Les Miserables, The Phantom of the Opera*, et al.

The *Follies* creative team was inspired by the famous *Life* magazine photograph of a valiant Gloria Swanson standing in the rubble of the partially demolished Roxy Theater (1960) (see Chapter 24, Figure 24.1), and an image of a backstage scene in Fellini's *Juliet of the Spirits* (1965) which contains a black staircase framed by two enormous statues of Greek goddesses.[25] The later inspired Bennett to create the showgirl ghosts who appeared ominously in the production's opening number. Representing the theater's bygone era of glamorous revues—but like the show's poster of a showgirl's face with a crack running through it—*Follies* "ghosts" were not seen through the lens of rose-colored nostalgia, but rather the harsh light of a carbon-arc spotlight. In keeping with the fragmentation that occurs with memory, Aronson chose elements that were leftovers and remnants because memory is never complete. "The audience helps all evening in re-creating the past, because we only suggest it," he explained. "I took full advantage of this duality, this juxtaposition, to try to create an image of a monumental theatre of bygone days."[26]

Perhaps no musical number better synthesized this thrilling and nightmarish collision of the past and present than "Who's that Woman?" (aka "The Mirror Song") where seven former chorus girls recall a dance turn and not only try to remember the steps but also question who they are. As the retired, old chorus "girls" began their number on the downstage platform, Bennett had their younger alter egos appear on Aronson's upstage platform with their backs to the retired performers, dancing the way the women want to remember their youthful selves.

> The Memories upstage move in mirror image to the "chorus girls" down front. The tempo and excitement rise, the steps and turns grow harder, faster. Then the explosion comes as past and present mingle: the Memories join the "chorus girls" downstage…the two tunes mesh and all the girls sing out and dance at once.[27]

"It is a tumultuous, terrifying, unforgettable number," declared Coby Kummer in *Atlantic*. Sondheim considers Michael Bennett's staging of the song to be "maybe the most brilliant musical number in terms of the staging I have ever seen in the theatre."[28] Kummer agreed, stating that Bennett's choreography "surpassed his work on *A Chorus Line*, the musical he created four years later. Although *A Chorus Line* is thought to be his masterpiece, his work in *Follies* was wedded to ideas that had shading and ambivalence, Sondheim's favorite emotions, rather than the straightforward, heart-on-leotard emotions of *A Chorus Line*."[29]

Adapted from Ingmar Bergman's *Smiles of a Summer Night* (1956), Hugh Wheeler's libretto for *A Little Night Music* is about a weekend of emotional and sexual roulette played out in turn-of-the-century Sweden. *Night Music*'s designers were faced with realizing a weekend in the country with twenty-eight changes in location. Prince and Aronson solved the challenge with staging the musical so that all the scenes, even the interior ones, would take place surrounded by birch trees. Painted on silk, the "trees" were then attached to several twenty-four-foot-tall screens made of a new plastic, Lexan. The screens moved to create entrance and exit positions, as well as to mask, and then reveal, set changes. As Sondheim had not written the act 1 finale before he saw Aronson's set, he was able to tailor the construction of the song to the possibilities of the set. "I'd call Hal," Sondheim recalled, "and ask if I could get a character from here to there with a screen move—and he'd say yes or no, or that he'd need more time for a move. The movement of the screens was what allowed me to feel the sense of flow from place to place."[30]

Douglas Watt (*Daily News*) celebrated the fact that "director Harold Prince and choreographer Patricia Birch have given the movement sweep and flourish"[31] thus reinforcing the motion of Aronson's tree panels. On the other hand, Martin Gottfried (*Women's Wear Daily*) complained that *Night Music*'s, "Movement and musical staging is minimal. The songs are sung with barely a gesture, in fact some are performed sitting and one is actually done with a man in bed, his eyes closed. Despite a credit for choreography (Patricia Birch) there is virtually no dancing, which is not only unusual for a musical...but is positively amazing for a show whose music is all in waltz-time, perhaps the dancingest time in music."[32] *Night Music* was not only a critical success—the *New York Times* crowed, "Great God! An adult musical!" —it was also a commercial success (running for 601 performances, investors received a 125 percent return).

For the fourth Sondheim production Prince was to direct on Broadway, they looked East for inspiration. Focusing on Commodore Matthew Perry's mission to persuade the Japanese to open Japan to trade with the West in 1853, the libretto by John Weidman and Hugh Wheeler for *Pacific Overtures* was not a documentary, rather it sought to unpack "the conflict between an ancient, traditional society and a foreign, mechanized, modern approach to life."[33] In what was to be his final design for Broadway, Boris Aronson gave the production "a Japanese garden as imagined through Western eyes."[34] At times a low border was used to frame the proscenium in the Winter Garden Theater so as to approximate the horizontal look of a Kabuki stage. Other times in the production an enormous, stylized "curtain" of kimonos filled the full height of the stage space. This curtain had the ability to change shapes so that it could appear as a solid surface and then open up to reveal the individual silhouettes of the colorful kimonos. Also following the architecture of a Kabuki theater, Aronson constructed a runway (*hanamichi*) from stage right to the back of the auditorium for entrances and exits through the house. Unfortunately, due to budget cuts, several elements of Aronson's original design were never realized. An origami treaty house was supposed to grow, unfold out of the floor, and then disappear as the Japanese wanted no visible memory of this meeting to be extant. Ultimately, the treaty house was suggested by three portable screens, and the finale ("Next") had to make do with using the backs of existing set pieces. Yet, despite all the cuts and corresponding adjustments to Aronson's designs, *Pacific Overtures* "received the greatest acclaim of his career."[35] While some thought Florence Klotz's costumes and Tharon Musser's lighting revealed the work of inspired professionals at the peak of their creative powers, the collage of Broadway (Western) and Kabuki (Eastern) aesthetics ultimately confused many critics and audience members. Edwin Wilson of the *Wall Street Journal* queried, "Are we seeing a Japanese work through Mr. Prince's eyes, or are we seeing an American musical through the eyes of his imaginary Japanese counterpart?"[36] Stephen Holden (*New York Times*) felt that the elaborate, original production overwhelmed the show's "reflective delicacy" with "spectacle and bombast."[37] On the other hand, Martin Gottfried (*New York Post*) was very impressed with what he saw: "a Broadway musical in the Kabuki style to an end that is definitely American—musical—theatre. Although the show's externals are Japanese, its structure and staging are American and so although it is exotic it is not alien."[38]

For *Pacific Overtures*, producer and director Prince not only hired Broadway veteran choreographer Patricia Birch, he also engaged a Kabuki consultant to work with the all-male Japanese cast. No doubt many western audience members were unsure how to evaluate a Kabuki aesthetic—Douglas Watt (*Daily News*) could say only, "Patricia Birch devised the dance interludes." Nevertheless, the closing number, when the Asian performers appeared in Western dress and executed traditional Broadway choreography, was striking, providing the musical with a jarring juxtaposition of East and West.

Drawn to stage settings that were grand and imposing, when *Sweeney Todd, The Demon Barber of Fleet Street* was booked into the biggest theater in New York at the time, the Uris (now the Gershwin), Prince asked set designer Eugene Lee to create a setting that would dominate the cavernous auditorium. Even though Sondheim had conceived of *Sweeney* as a chamber musical, Prince explained, "I know what you want, Steve. You want antimacassars and curtains parting. What I'll give you is an epic style. You'll lose on the scary part but you'll gain the size."[39] To contextualize this nineteenth-century melodrama, Prince not only wanted a factory on stage (to symbolize the Industrial Revolution), he wanted a *real* factory on stage. (Lee found one in Rhode Island that he moved into the Uris Theatre, removing its proscenium arch to make the imported factory parts seem even larger.) The monumentality of the Lee set for the Broadway premiere of *Sweeney Todd* aggressively announced itself; a catwalk bridge and enormous traveling girder delivered Todd's new barber chair, but mainly was there to create atmosphere. When asked why he wanted a factory setting for the story, Prince replied, "They make Sweeney Todds."[40] By using the framework of the Industrial Revolution and the socioeconomic inequalities it created, Prince hoped to give the production a social commentary so that it was more than the story of revenge. Like most of Sondheim's musicals that Prince directed, there was very little dance in the original staging of *Sweeney Todd*, save for a nightmarish flashback of the masked ball when Judge Turpin seduced Lucy Barker. Choreographer Larry Fuller's main contributions were limited to using the ensemble to creating whirling street crowds as the large scenic unit center stage (Todd's barbershop upstairs; Mrs. Lovett's pie shop and the basement on the lower level) turned.

Sondheim would have to wait until 1989 to see a production of *Sweeney Todd* that was closer in scale to his original concept of the show, one with just some "fog and a few street lamps." In 1979, he went along with Prince's grand concept since he had come to trust Prince's vision; "[Prince] has a sense of a whole evening, a sense of an arc, a sense of design, of what an evening of the theater is about." And Sondheim correctly reasoned, "Someday it could be done small…why not try it large? Hal is the one I want to do it so let's see how it works this way."[41] Director Susan H. Schulman first staged *Sweeney Todd* in 1989 in the Off-Broadway venue the York Theatre Company; subsequently this production (with fourteen actors) moved to Circle in the Square. The 1993 staging by Declan Donnellan at the Royal National Theatre, London, won Sondheim's praise for its chamber approach. And then British director John Doyle reduced the scale even further for his 2004 revival which featured only ten performers (who also performed the score, since this version did not have a separate orchestra). On the other hand, audiences also had the option to see versions of *Sweeney Todd* that retained its original grandeur. Prince, using Lee's Broadway design, staged *Sweeney* for the Houston Grand Opera in 1984, and then with a simplified (although still large) Lee setting which has been in the repertoire of New York City Opera since 1984.

Kaufman and Hart's *Merrily We Roll Along* ran only 155 performances when it opened in New York in 1934, but Prince nevertheless suggested musicalizing it as a way of returning to *Follies'* themes of "failed hopes and blasted expectations."[42] George Furth's libretto follows the conceit of the Kaufman and Hart play—that of telling the story in reverse. Even though Prince believed that *Merrily We Roll Along* should have been done without any scenery at all, like *Our Town*, "I didn't have the guts—I didn't think you could charge Broadway prices for a show without scenery."[43] To highlight the energy and vigor of his youthful cast, Prince uncharacteristically allowed more dance in *Merrily* than was present in the rest of his Sondheim musicals. Nevertheless, in his scathing review, Frank Rich (*New York Times*) dismissed Fuller's choreography as "uninspired to the extent that it exists at all."[44] Fuller's "Old Friends" was a spirited romp and "Bobby and Jackie and Jack" included some Irish step-dancing, but when done by a cast who were between fifteen and twenty-five years of age, many in the audience could see *Merrily*'s choreographer only as another liability. Nevertheless, Robert Simonson and Kenneth Jones, reviewing a reunion concert staged in 2002, found Fuller's original choreography to be "sprightly and charming." After devastatingly poor reviews, the original production ground to a halt after sixteen performances. Looking back, Prince was still baffled. "[T]he score is beautiful. *We* let *him* down. I never knew how to direct it, because I work so much from 'What is it going to look like?' That becomes the motor of the show. I could never figure it out."[45] Although they remained friends, Sondheim and Prince would not work together for the next twenty-two years, until the 2003 Chicago production of *Bounce*.

When producer Lewis Allen suggested a meeting with playwright and director James Lapine in June 1982, Sondheim enthusiastically agreed. Having been impressed with Lapine's *Twelve Dreams* the year before at the New York Shakespeare Festival, Sondheim was especially struck by his visual approach to writing and directing. Twenty years Sondheim's junior, Lapine had been a photographer and had taught graphic design before he migrated into playwriting and directing. While Prince was unique in that he was a brilliant auteur who was also a producer, in collaborating with James Lapine, Sondheim was in a way returning to his early professional experience with Robbins on *West Side Story* and *Gypsy*. As choreographer, Robbins was the author of the movement text of these two musicals, not "just" the shows' director. As the author of *Sunday in the Park with George*'s libretto, Lapine was the author of one of the texts of the musical as well as the production's director.

Since Sondheim had started his career at the top, on Broadway with *West Side Story* and *Gypsy*, he had no experience with the Off-Off-Broadway, Off-Broadway, and regional theater world. Working with Lapine on *Sunday*, Sondheim did not want to preview the production in New York as *Merrily* had done, so agreed to a three-week run of workshop performances at Playwrights Horizon, an Off-Broadway group which Lapine had worked with before. Just as Richard Rodgers's music changed when Oscar Hammerstein replaced Larry Hart as his lyricist, Sondheim knew that his compositions were transformed by the poetry of Lapine's writing. Inspired by George Seurat's theories of painting, Sondheim sought to create a musical landscape which constructed music the way pointillists use paint. Frank Rich (*New York Times*) wrote, "*Sunday* is itself a modernist creation, perhaps the first truly modernist work of musical theater that Broadway has produced. Instead of mimicking reality through a conventional, naturalistic story, the authors of *Sunday* deploy music and language in nonlinear patterns."[46]

Tony Straiges's set design took its cue from the first words in the libretto, "White. A blank page or canvas. The challenge: bring order to the whole." With only George at his easel on a white environment, set pieces gradually move into the space until the stage becomes a three-dimensional replica of Seurat's famous painting. Indeed, the first act not only recreates *A Sunday Afternoon on the Island of La Grande Jatte*, it also creates tableaux of three other Seurat paintings. Most of Ann Hould-Ward's costumes in act 1 were painted in a pointillist style so that they could play their part in re-creating the four paintings. The show's choreography (musical staging by Christopher Gattelli) was pretty much limited to Dot kicking up her heels in a very brief fantasy of going to the Folies Bergère with George in "Color and Light."

Act 2 takes place one hundred years later and we meet George, a kinetic sculptor, who might be the great-grandson of the famous Impressionist painter. After the brilliance of "Putting it Together" —an extended musical number which magnificently partners satiric dialogue and lyrics, music, and inventive staging (the numerous pop-ups of George give all the cocktail party guests "personal" time with the artist)—the actual appearance of George's Chromolume #7 was an anticlimax in the 1984 production. What made act 1 and "Putting It Together" dramatically powerful was that people brought the stage to life. Straiges's chromolume, on the other hand, was an inert object center stage which pathetically flashed with a couple of dozen colored lights, looking for all the world like a large-scale model of a cheap, disco-party light fixture from the 1970s. The dialogue tells us that this performance by Chromolume #7 stopped due to the electrical power going out at the museum, however most theatergoers assumed that it died of its own accord due to a lack of imagination. Nevertheless, the rest of Straiges's designs for *Sunday* were lauded by his peers, earning him three prestigious Best Scenic Design awards (Tony, Drama Desk, Outer Critics Circle). Far more successful in making a dramatically effective Chromolume #7 was the one created by set designer David Farley and projectionist Timothy Bird for the 2005 London revival, where they removed the machine itself from the stage, so that the audience only sees the light (colors and patterns) it creates. The *Washington Post* applauded this production's "astonishing computer-generated images,"[47] as this revival utilized technology that did not exist when the show opened on Broadway in 1984.

The Lapine–Sondheim collaborative relationship continued in 1985 with two projects: a new musical and Lapine's direction of a revised version of *Merrily We Roll Along* for the La Jolla Playhouse. Gone were the sweatshirts with characters' names on them, a high school gym set, and the youthful cast. Sondheim called the 1985 score to *Merrily* "definitive."[48] *Merrily* returned to New York in 1994 for a successful run at the York Theatre, this time directed by Susan H. Schulman. In this production, choreographer Michael Lichtefeld proved once again that the right choreographer can integrate dance effectively into a Sondheim musical if it is done with intelligence and creativity. The *New York Times* applauded his "witty parody of Bob Fosse's socket-wrenching brand of dancin'"[49] and *The Hartford Courant* applauded his ability to "define the times as they slip backward" through dance.[50]

There was almost no dance in the 1987 original Broadway *Into the Woods*, save for the vaguely folk-dance-like round at the end of act 1, but as *Playbill* notes, the show's original choreography was more accurately labeled "musical staging." Two seduction duets (Wolf and Little Red; Prince Charming and the Baker's Wife) were subtle and effective, and Straiges's *passarelle* and moving sidewalk downstage meant that most of the show's movement patterns involved walking, as indeed the entire conceit is "Into the woods / Then out of the woods / And home before dark." *Into the Woods* is one of the few musicals Sondheim wrote for characters to literally stand and sing to the audience. While Cinderella and Little Red Riding Hood's act 1 solos are physically static, the two Princes in "Agony" and its act 2 reprise are doing something—each one is trying to top his brother in a classic example of one-upmanship. It seems surprising, given the relative absence of dance in *Into the Woods* that the production was given the modern dance luminary Lar Lubovitch[51] as its choreographer. For his Broadway debut with *Woods*, Lubovitch received a Tony nomination for Best Choreography, but this had more to do with a dearth of musicals featuring dance that year (*The Phantom of the Opera*, *Sarafina*, *Chess*, and *Romance, Romance*) than groundbreaking or stunning choreography.

While Tony Straiges's *Into the Woods* set stayed the same as it had been in act 1—a series of moving panel "trees," the moving sidewalk downstage, a platform moved by winches— Richard Nelson's lighting was much darker and ominous as characters were forced to flee their homes and delve deeper into the woods in act 2. Similarly, Ann Hould-Ward had designed a dirty and distressed version of the characters' act 1 costumes so that the picture-perfect world of fairy tales was replaced by ones much more realistic and gritty.

Arguably, *Assassins* would never have come to be if it had not been for the safe space provided by Playwrights Horizons. With a book by John Weidman and directed by Jerry Zaks, *Assassins* started in the 139-seat main theater at Playwrights Horizons in 1991. On its tiny twenty-five-foot stage, there was not much in the way of scenery or choreography, so director Jerry Zaks put the emphasis on character. While the overall tone of the reviews from New York critics were lukewarm to savage, the London critics embraced *Assassins* as an insightful assessment of a nation obsessed with easy access to firearms. A twelve-week run of the show by the Donmar Warehouse in 1992 was SRO. Set designer Anthony Ward took an environmental approach and turned the entire theater into a fairground, where each of the eight assassins had their own shooting booth. *Assassins* would not appear on Broadway until 2004, produced by Roundabout Theatre and directed by Joe Mantello, with musical staging by Jonathan Butterell. This production's only real dance choreography occurred when Charles Guiteau (James Garfield's murderer) did a cakewalk up and down the steps of the gallows he dies on.

Passion reunited Sondheim not only with Lapine, but also orchestrator Jonathan Tunick, conductor Paul Gemignani, and lighting designer Beverly Emmons. While no choreographer (or "musical staging") credit was listed in the program of this intermission-less musical, Lapine's associate director was Jane Comfort. Just as he had done with *Into the Woods*, Lapine engaged a luminary from the modern dance world to assist him with musical staging. While *Passion* contains even less "pure" dance than *Woods*, Comfort (like Lubovitch) was there to assist Lapine with stage pictures and to coach the actors on body language.

Like *Sunday* and *Woods*, the visual world of *Passion* is flat, with Adrianne Lobel's scenery parallel to the proscenium arch. As William A. Henry III noted in his review for *Time* magazine, "*Passion* is ably staged but so austere that it provides little visual pleasure."[52] Other critics (like John Simon, *New York Magazine*) found that Lobel's scenery, while minimalist, deftly moved the show from bedroom to exteriors to drab military rooms, evoking "the world of such Italian modernists as Ardengo Soffici and Carlo Carra."[53] Simon found Emmons's lighting "suitably romantic; Jane Greenwood's costumes for the women, paragons of tasteful opulence,"[54] with Clara's costume providing the only vibrant color in the production. John Lahr (*New Yorker*) found strength in Lapine's "strong, if sedate, stage pictures" but felt that the grandness in Lobel's "design trivializes rather than enhances the play's statement."[55]

The 2003 staging of *Bounce* at Chicago's Goodman Theatre brought back together Sondheim, Weidman, and Prince, who had not collaborated since *Pacific Overtures* in 1976. Like most Sondheim musicals post-*Follies*, there was not much dance in *Bounce*. Critic Jonathan Arabanel wrote that,

> Choreographer Michael Arnold has few opportunities to shine; most of the 19 cast members are not dancers and there are no big production numbers, though "The

Best Thing That Ever Happened to Me" in act 1 and "Boca Raton" in act 2 approach that status and are devoured hungrily by the audience.[56]

For over fifty years, Stephen Sondheim has been changing not only what the American musical sounded like, but also what subject matter it explored, and ultimately, what it looked like. He also influenced the pacing of the Broadway musical. According to Frank Rich and Lisa Aronson, with *West Side Story* and *Gypsy*, "Robbins and his collaborators had begun a radical transformation in the style of the Broadway musical. The Robbins shows still had conventional musical plots, but they also had serious themes that coexisted with the various love stories of their librettos. The staging techniques, meanwhile, became more and more cinematic. Robbins musicals didn't necessarily have more dancing, but, increasingly, they were choreographed to achieve a seamless flow in which scenes, dances, and songs were inextricably interwoven."[57] Robbins could not have realized this innovation without the contributions of Bernstein, Styne, and Sondheim.

While still a teenager, Sondheim was a production assistant on *Allegro* (1947) and was thus able to observe the process of Agnes de Mille—one of the first choreographers to direct a Broadway musical—staging Rodgers and Hammerstein's third production. No doubt this experience, coupled with working with Robbins easily convinced young Sondheim of the powerful narrative potential of brilliant choreography. But after *A Funny Thing Happened on the Way to the Forum* (1962)—with the exception of *Anyone Can Whistle* (Herbert Ross, choreographer) and *Follies* (Michael Bennett, choreographer)—Sondheim would never again create a large dance show.

If the Golden Age of the director–choreographer stretches from *West Side Story* (1957) to *Jerome Robbins' Broadway* (which closed in 1990) and *The Will Rogers Follies* (1991), we see that Sondheim's work was not appealing to Gower Champion, Bob Fosse, Tommy Tune, or Michael Bennett (after *Follies*, 1971), as these auteurs were more interested in properties which either originated with their idea, or those that could be altered to contain a lot of dance. The second wave of the director–choreographer as star could be said to start in 2000 with Susan Stroman's revival of *The Music Man;* other second wave director–choreographers like Twyla Tharp, Kathleen Marshall, Graciela Daniele, Rob Marshall, and Jerry Mitchell have been exploring not only the use of dance in the traditional book musical, but also creating a new musical form, the dansical (*Movin' Out, Contact*, etc.).[58] It is worth noting Sondheim did not work with any of the director–choreographers who came after Jerome Robbins.

Another reason why Sondheim employed less and less dance in his later musicals has to do with his progression as a composer and Harold Prince's evolution as a director. As Sondheim told biographer Mark Eden Horowitz, "I think the older you get, the fussier you get about 'less is more.' I think that's why so many classical composers end up writing string quartets. It's called: I don't need the oboes and I don't need the trumpets; let's just do the music. Let's do a piece and limit the colors to black, white, and blue—no reds and no greens and no oranges.... What's necessary?"[59] Increasingly for Sondheim and Prince, dance did not seem to be necessary as they visualized how the musical would tell its story.

This move towards simplicity is mirrored in the set designs of Broadway productions of Sondheim musicals over the years. Despite the scale of megamusicals like *Les Misérables, The Phantom of the Opera,* and *Wicked,* some have remarked that no one today has the budget to stage something like the premiere of *Follies* in 1971. While the settings for Sondheim's musicals have been shrinking over the years due to reduced budgets, they also became simpler as he challenges himself and his collaborators, "What's necessary?" The visual world also changed with Sondheim's directors: Prince was drawn to the asymmetry and angles in the set designs of Boris Aronson and the large-scale works of Eugene Lee, while Lapine preferred the more symmetrical and flat work of Tony Straiges and Adrienne Lobel.

Like Shakespeare, although armed with music as well as poetry, a Sondheim musical is so aurally rich, so that while each can (and has) been framed by stunning and evocative *mise-en-scène,* it is not essential to the storytelling or emotional engagement of the musical. When Dot challenges George to "Give us more to see...," she not only means in a literal sense (new paintings and new ways of seeing), but also begs for more images for her mind's eye, for ways of making sense of life. Fosca continues this line of thinking:

> I read to live. In other people's lives.
> I read about the joys, the world
> Dispenses to the fortunate,
> And listen for the echoes.
> I read to live,
> To get away from life![60]

Clearly lyrics like this do not lend themselves to helicopter landings or precision kick lines. For Sondheim's fans around the world, his soundscapes make us feel like Little Red Riding Hood,

> And I know things now,
> Many valuable things,
> That I hadn't known before.[61]

In typical Sondheim fashion, Little Red realizes that knowledge itself does not necessarily bring power, insight, or happiness: "Isn't it nice to know a lot! / ...and a little bit not..."[62]

Whether a Sondheim musical is staged with all the scenery and costumes and lighting and choreography that money can buy, or is presented in a nontraditional theater space by actors wearing their own clothing, Sondheim reminds us that there is no right or wrong approach to his work: "A blank page or canvas. His favorite. So many possibilities."[63]

Notes

1. James Lapine and Stephen Sondheim, *Sunday in the Park with George* (London: Nick Hern, 1990), 107.

2. Walter Terry, *I Was There: Selected Dance Reviews and Articles, 1936–1976* (New York: Audience Arts, 1978), 326.

3. Original emphasis; Keith Garebian, *The Making of "West Side Story"* (Oakville, ON: Mosaic, 1998), 121.

4. Meryle Secrest, *Stephen Sondheim: A Life* (New York: Alfred A. Knopf, 1998), 123.

5. Terry, *I Was There*, 327.

6. Forced perspective refers to the optical illusion that makes objects appear larger than they really are by manipulating the point of view of the observer.

7. Tom Mikotowicz, *Oliver Smith: A Bio-bibliography* (Westport, CT: Greenwood, 1993), 64.

8. Amanda Vail, *Jerome Robbins: Something to Dance About*. Produced by Judy Kinberg for Thirteen/WNET's "American Masters." DVD (Kultur, 2009 [130 minutes]).

9. Keith Garebian, *The Making of "Gypsy"* (Toronto, ON: ECW Press, 1994), 93.

10. John Chapman, "*Funny Thing* Happens in Rome but not in Today's Funny Rome" (review of *Forum*), *Daily News*, May 9, 1962.

11. Howard Taubman, review of *A Funny Thing Happened on the Way to the Forum*, *New York Times*, May 9, 1962.

12. Martin Gottfried, *Sondheim* (New York: Harry N. Abrams, 1993), 62.

13. Gottfried, *Sondheim*, 73.

14. Taubman, *New York Times*, May 9, 1962.

15. Secrest suggests that Ross's choreography inadvertently led to the show appearing to be cursed. Ross asked dancer Tucker Smith to move downstage during a dance in the second act. Temporarily blinded by the stage lights, Smith fell into the orchestra pit during a performance. Smith was not seriously injured, but the string player he fell on had a stroke and eventually died. Shortly thereafter, the actor playing the role of Comptroller Schub (Henry Lascoe) suffered a heart attack and passed away. Alas, these deaths were the tip of the iceberg of bad news for the production.

16. Taubman, *New York Times*, May 9, 1962.

17. Barbara Isenberg, "In Sondheim's Company," *Los Angeles Times*, April 18, 2010.

18. Frank Rich, with Lisa Aronson, *The Theatre Art of Boris Aronson* (New York: Alfred A. Knopf, 1987), 221.

19. Ibid., 228.

20. Ibid., 230.

21. Secrest, *Sondheim*, 195.

22. Rich and Aronson, *Boris Aronson*, 23.

23. Ibid., 237.

24. Ibid., 243.

25. Rich and Aronson, *Boris Aronson*, 232.

26. Ibid., 234.

27. Gottfried, *Sondheim*, 95.

28. Ibid., 95.

29. Corby Kummer, "Their Show of Shows: Backstage with a Troubled, Now Legendary Sondheim Musical," *Atlantic*, November 1, 2003. http://www.theatlantic.com/doc/200311/kummer.

30. Rich and Aronson, *Boris Aronson*, 260.

31. Douglas Watt. "'A Little Night Music': Operetta that's Exquisite but Fragile," *Daily News*, February 26, 1973.

32. Martin Gottfried, review of *A Little Night Music*, in *Women's Wear Daily*, February 26, 1973, 349.

33. Rich and Aronson, *Boris Aronson*, 264.

34. Secrest, *Sondheim*, 280.

35. Rich and Aronson, *Boris Aronson*, 280.

36. Secrest, *Sondheim*, 282.

37. Ibid., 282.

38. Martin Gottfried, "'Overtures' —A Remarkable Work of Theatre Art," *New York Post*, January 12, 1976.

39. Gottfried, *Sondheim*, 123, 125.

40. Ibid., 127.

41. Ibid., 125.

42. Secrest, *Sondheim*, 309.

43. Gottfried, *Sondheim*, 146.

44. Frank Rich, "A New Sondheim: 'Merrily We Roll Along,'" *New York Times*, November 17, 1981.

45. Secrest, *Sondheim*, 317; original emphasis.

46. Rich and Aronson, *Boris Aronson*, 53.

47. Peter Marks, "A Grand 'Sunday in the Park,'" *Washington Post*, February 22, 2008. www.washingtonpost.com/wp-dyn/content/article/2008/02/21/AR2008022102840.html.

48. S. F. Stoddart. "Visions and Re-visions: The Postmodern Challenge of *Merrily We Roll Along*," in *Reading Stephen Sondheim: A Collection of Critical Essays*, ed. Sandor Goodhart, 187–98 (New York: Garland, 2000), 187. Sondheim's statement was made two years before further revisions were undertaken for a 2002 revival of *Merrily*.

49. David Richards, "A Sondheim Musical Keeps Evolving," *New York Times*, June 10, 1994. http://www.nytimes.com/1994/06/10/theater/review-theater-a-sondheim-musical-ke eps-evolving.html?pagewanted=all&src=pm.

50. Malcolm Johnson, "Streamlined 'Merrily' Rolls Better," (review of *Merrily We Roll Along* at the Theater at Saint Peter's Church), *The Courant* [Hartford, CT], June 19, 1994. http://articles.courant.com/1994-06-19/entertainment/9406160058_ 1_ franklin-shepard-sondheim-wendall-k-harrington/3.

51. Lubovitch established his own company in 1968, but his work has also been performed by Alvin Ailey American Dance Theatre, American Ballet Theatre, New York City Ballet, Paris Opera Ballet, Royal Danish Ballet, Stuttgart Ballet, and Mikhail Baryshnikov's White Oak Dance Project.

52. William A. Henry III, "Miserably Ever After" (review of *Passion*), *Time*, May 23, 1994.

53. John Simon, review of *Passion, New York Magazine*, May 23, 1994.

54. John Lahr, "Love in Gloom" (review of *Passion*), *New Yorker*, May 23, 1994.

55. Lahr, "Love in Gloom."

56. Jonathan Abarbanel, "Bounce" (review of *Bounce* at the Goodman Theatre, Chicago), *TheatreMania*, July 2, 2003. http://www.theatermania.com/content/news.cfm?int_news_id=3693.

57. Rich and Aronson, *Boris Aronson*, 187

58. The dansical is a work where the emphasis is on dance; often there is no dialogue or sung lyrics, and in many cases the work does not feature original music: *Dancin'* (Bob Fosse,

1978), *Big Deal* (Fosse, 1986), *Dangerous Games* (Graciela Daniele, 1989), *Chronicle of a Death Foretold* (Daniele, 1995), *Contact* (Susan Stroman, 2000), *Movin' Out* (Twyla Tharp, 2003), *Come Fly Away* (Tharp, 2010).

59. Mark Eden Horowitz, *Sondheim on Music: Minor Details and Major Decisions* (Lanham, MD, and Oxford: Scarecrow, 2003), 43.

60. James Lapine and Stephen Sondheim, *Passion* (New York: Theatre Communications Group, 1994), 22.

61. James Lapine and Stephen Sondheim, *Into the Woods* (New York: Theatre Communications Group, 1987), 35.

62. Ibid., 36.

63. Lapine and Sondheim, *Sunday in the Park with George*, 174.

CHAPTER 9

··

ORCHESTRATORS IN THEIR OWN WORDS: THE SOUND OF SONDHEIM IN THE TWENTY-FIRST CENTURY

··

NATHAN R. MATTHEWS

THERE are various widely available conceptions of the art and craft of orchestration.[1] Sid Ramin, an orchestrator for *A Funny Thing Happened on the Way to the Forum*, *West Side Story*, and *Gypsy,* worked out the instrumentation, the menu of what musical instruments would end up in the shows' orchestras, with the shows' composers. Then, he would get to the business of what he calls "orchestration: who's going to play what." Ramin says that by contrast the art of arranging is "added embellishment."[2] In contrast, Paul Gemignani has said that the orchestrator's is "as much a creative job as the composer's... The same thought process, the same agonizing, the same artistic decisions made by an actor have to be made by the orchestrator.... Orchestration is the warmth in a love scene, the electricity in the kiss, the thing that makes you start to tear up. And it has to come from the gut."[3] Michael Starobin has described orchestration in this way:

> You're like a running back and the composer's the quarterback and he's handing you the ball and saying, "There's the hole: go run." And you basically go run. Along the way something may come up that you have to go a different method than he pointed you at, but the basic is, you're moving the ball further down the field for *him* as if you were him. And so that's sort of what you're doing. I just need to understand what his theatrical choices were.[4]

Starobin and Jonathan Tunick, who were the original orchestrators for most Sondheim shows and who provided them with some of the best orchestrations ever written for Broadway, have both spoken of their early work as musicians who orchestrate, and their understanding of the need for a solid music education. Tunick reminisces: "when we were kids, we got together and played chamber music...[which] invited in sophistication...[we] played Beethoven quartets with any four instruments we had handy.... We didn't just hack through, [but] I wouldn't have wanted Beethoven to hear it." He mused that perhaps people said, "Gee, isn't it nice these kids are playing and aspiring to bigger and better things."[5]

Starobin also makes references to classical music in his comments on orchestration style, and his training is obvious in his work. He has said, "there's nothing to teach you about orchestration like really doing it. There is *no* manual on theater orchestration...and so the best book on it right now is on-the-job training."[6] Starobin considers college as a proper training ground for becoming a theater musician. As a freshman in college he began to do what eventually became his career. While he says "there was a bit of fudging and pushing things around," in order to do shows with whoever he had available to play, he cautions against lessening the opportunities that college offers by "synthesizing with orchestral libraries":

> If it just becomes about doing..."synthestration," as someone once called it, it is not theatrical. It's not live. What's so wonderful about orchestration for the theater is that you're doing [it with] live players contributing to a live piece of *theater*—a live *performance*.[7]

Starobin cautions against sequencing saying that it is,

> giving up the chance to reconceive it for your particular production at your school and your particular players that you have who can do things. It's such a great opportunity, I hate passing it up...I mean the reason I am in the business I'm in is I love responding musically to a theatrical situation. You know, that I have this number that's being sung, and in my head I imagine the whole play that's going on even though it's just being staged, and I respond musically to it. And that's sort of the joy of doing it and there's no reason that it can't be done on an amateur level. Will it be done as well as I'm doing it? I hope not, but somebody will and there's my future competition—as it should be...When you get to New York you're competing with so many people to just do the smallest job, and when you're in college...[y]ou can be the big fish in that pond and be doing all this great work that teaches you so much.[8]

While Sondheim has close relationships with his orchestrators, he has never been involved "in terms of specific instruments."[9] Sondheim studied composition with Milton Babbitt, who told Sondheim that he hears orchestrally: "And what he meant by that is I hear lines. I hear the interplay of horizontal lines as opposed to just vertical chordal structures, which is what most Broadway composers hear."[10] Sondheim's scores are therefore completely composed, the notes are all his, unlike those of many Broadway composers. He says that he goes "over the score carefully with the orchestrator to show what I mean by individual contrapuntal lines and where, if I have five voices that become four, where I think the fifth voice is combined with one of the other voices to make the four, etc."[11] After the orchestrator has come to rehearsals and after he has played the orchestrator the score on the piano and discussed it, Sondheim says that he reviews

> the music of that number bar by bar with the orchestrator for his questions, his suggestions, or anything I feel should be in the orchestration that might not be apparent in the piano copy...[What the orchestrator] does is take a general description from me because I don't really know enough to say this should be oboes, this should be

a clarinet. And with an orchestrator with the kind of sensitivity that Jonathan and Michael Starobin have, they translate that into their own terms, into the specifics of the orchestration.[12]

An example of this occurred during the course of the orchestration process for *A Little Night Music*, when Jonathan Tunick asked Sondheim what kind of sound he wanted, and Sondheim said, "It's like perfume coming out of the orchestra pit…is what I want." Tunick then said, "Oh, you mean strings."[13]

Jonathan Tunick has defined orchestration poetically as "lighting for the ears."[14] He has said that he attempts to "find an orchestral language for each show."[15] He says that when it comes to Sondheim, he "does it for you" and reconfirms that Sondheim has composed every note of his music. Tunick's process begins when he receives a copy of a song. He watches the number in rehearsal, taking perfunctory notes on the combinations of instruments that he thinks might be good for the number. Before actually scoring, Tunick works out a well-developed sketch of the piece. Then, he lays out the number on staff paper. First, he goes for critical points like endings and rhythm tracks. Later, he fills in the middle. Sometimes the introduction is the last thing he writes. Part of Tunick's aim is to create orchestrations that serve to guide the singer through the song and through the show. He has said that he admires Puccini's orchestrations and how Puccini doubles or semi-doubles melodies in a lower octave in order to darken thin voices and vice versa. Beyond that he sees orchestration as providing subtext and color to a piece. That is part of why Tunick works away from the piano and works on paper and not at a computer keyboard—because he finds that if he does work at the piano, his work falls into the piano idiom and that it places a wall between him and the music.[16]

Starobin, like Tunick, attempts to get away from the piano, both during his work process and within the orchestrations he writes. There seems to be an inherent problem in reducing an orchestra, particularly an orchestra for a Sondheim show, when it comes to dealing with the piano or keyboard. While a Sondheim score has all of the notes composed and ready to orchestrate, Starobin nevertheless points out,

> the problem that's endemic to orchestrating Sondheim in general—and this isn't a problem just for him—but he's an extremely pianistic composer. … There are a number of them…and it's not just that they're writing at the piano and on the piano: they write very pianistic figures. And those don't always translate well to instruments. Particularly around the time of *Into the Woods* he was doing a lot of added notes in his chords. You know, a major chord always had the fourth just thrown in…a lot of color notes, and you know, when you have limited forces you can't do all of those notes unless you leave some of it on the piano. You would need a symphonic orchestra to get all those rubs orchestrally. And I know both myself and Jonathan have had to deal in the score with how to get the rubs without enough instruments, and a lot of it is about leaving it on the piano. On the other hand the big challenge…is that if the piano's playing all the time, it sounds like a rehearsal, and the piano ceases to be an orchestral color and becomes just this ongoing palette that's already there. And for me a big challenge with small orchestras is leaving the piano every time I can—going away from it…it may only be for…sixteen bars—but when I do come back, it's a

color, it's an orchestral choice, not an orchestral substitute that's omnipresent and therefore sort of disappears without any color meaning.[17]

The early twenty-first century has witnessed a wealth of Broadway revivals of Sondheim's musicals. Concurrently, economic strictures imposed by Broadway producers, who are allocating less and less money and pit space to orchestras, are changing not only how new works sound; they are changing the sounds of well-known Broadway shows, as they are revived with smaller orchestras. This period is also seeing a growing interest from theater audiences, popular journalists, as well as from academic researchers and writers in the rich traditions and history of Broadway orchestras and orchestrators, stimulating a debate over the shrinking orchestra. While this is bemoaned by all except the producers—the renowned orchestrator Elliot Lawrence, for instance, has said that he is "very hurt" when he hears Sondheim played by five players[18]—it is possible to exploit the situation as an opportunity to discover new insights into how one might do the Sondheim shows well with less.

Professional and amateur theater companies and educational institutions, groups that historically have not been able to field a full Broadway pit orchestra, have gained new resources in the work of orchestrators such as Tony Award winner Sarah Travis, who orchestrated the acclaimed John Doyle actor–musician production of *Sweeney Todd*; and Drama Desk Award winner Jason Carr, whose work has been heard in the revivals of *Sunday in the Park with George* and *A Little Night Music*. Even Michael Starobin, who orchestrated the first productions of *Sunday in the Park with George* and *Assassins*, has, with the production of *Sondheim on Sondheim*, rescored many of the songs from the Sondheim canon for eight players.

Sondheim himself has sanctioned the adaptation of the original orchestrations[19] by those who love and respect his shows and have only small theaters or inadequate funds for the full orchestras:

> My only advice for people who do not have the ability to hire an orchestra would be either to just use a piano accompaniment or any group of musicians that they can get together on their own. Or there are also reduced orchestrations that are available through Music Theatre International, which is the licensor of most of my shows.... But you know if those orchestras still are too big, the reduced ones, then I think the only thing to say [is] that the people who are putting on the show have to make their own music.... As far as changing the orchestrations goes, obviously if they have to they have to. But if they don't have to, I would advise not doing so.[20]

In addressing this problem, Michael Starobin advised:

> You should be getting permission to do the piece, but if you don't have the instruments, and [you] get the books and want to rewrite it, there's no orchestration police. No one comes around and says, "You didn't use..." if you don't have strings because you are in a high school or you're in a small college that doesn't have a music department that wants to participate, but you have a student who's a really good musician, you orchestrate. We do it.... It's what they're making us do for Broadway. I mean I'm about to do ... *Sondheim on Sondheim* ... I'm doing it for only eight pieces, which is,

you know, way too small. But that's what they can afford.... You know for three quarters of this I'll be taking Jonathan [Tunick]'s beautiful orchestrations, and I'm not going to reduce them; I'm just going to rethink the number for eight because [to] reduce it to eight and try and sound like, you know, that big *Follies* orchestra is foolish. I'm going to try and do something new with it. And that's what I think people should do if they're doing it. They should *not* take samplers and just sample it all in. That's foolish, and it's not *theatrical*.[21]

Whether it is an original production or a revival, the orchestrator's role is that of an aural designer, a person who makes major choices concerning how the audience hears the story. Jason Carr wisely advises that the sound world needs to chime with the design—all elements must work together. In other words the orchestrator must be sure that he or she is doing the same show as their collaborators. Carr believes that in determining a show's instrumentation a good orchestrator will look at the *whole* score and not fixate on a couple of moments.[22] Starobin says that orchestrating Sondheim's music is "simple" because he has already responded so completely to the play in musical terms that much of what he does for the play is planned out, obviating the need for the orchestrator to do the work of making the piece theatrically relevant.

It's sort of like, here's the song, you know, and go...do your thing. I do remember asking him as I was starting work on *Sunday*, I said, "Talk to me," I asked him to talk to me about the opening number, 'cause here was this arty show, you know, *very serious*, so involved in what it was trying to say. And I said, "Tell me about this opening number. It feels like from a different show, like it's musical comedy." He said the opening numbers say: "Yes, you are going to see art and serious matters, but you are allowed to laugh, kick back, and take it in."...That may be more what I'm discussing with him—what his intentions are with something. He doesn't discuss instruments. No one's involved in my day-to-day work, ever....In *Sunday* there's two spots where at the end of a song he has "ba-ba-ba-ba-ba" [*MS sings the signature Sunday horn call*], and he wrote "horn or trumpet." That's it. That's the only spots where he said he wanted something. And he doesn't do that for me or Jonathan. And as you can see from his support of the John Doyle productions, he's open to new interpretations, musically, of his work. Which to bring this all back to your main subject is: if you're being creative and supporting the play and the characters, go do something different. Go do *Sweeney Todd* with string quartet, piano, clarinet, and horn. I mean, I think that would be a great—sort of like a Brahms piano quintet.[23]

For an orchestrator, "doing all this great work," as Starobin put it above, begins with the production budget. While Broadway producer Harold Prince says that he has "little or no role in setting the instrumentation of a score" and states that "I work with composers who are genuine musicians, and respect them mightily. I cannot recall an occasion when I interfered in that department"[24], Jason Carr is correct in saying, "The producer tells you what the budget is, for starters—if they can only afford three musicians, then that's the gig, take it or leave it. Of course, there might be room to bargain for more."[25] Sondheim confers with a "production team" regarding a show's budget only when he attempts to convince producers to budget for the number of instruments that the orchestrator finds to be "ideal or optimal." Although he finds it "much harder do than it was when [he] was in [his] early twenties and there were orchestras of twenty-five, twenty-eight, and thirty people. We had twenty-eight people in the *Follies* orchestra originally. Nowadays *no* new show has over twenty instrumentalists."[26]

Likewise, the Watermill, the theater where Sarah Travis worked with John Doyle on developing their production of *Sweeney Todd*, holds an audience of only two hundred, and Travis says that therefore the budgets are "tiny."

> I'm handed that *fait accompli* before I even start. So, whatever choices you make, you have to do something radical and you have to reduce.... You have to reinvent to do it, to make the production work.... In a way it's quite good 'cause you're forced into a corner to create something different.[27]

Jason Carr echoes this sentiment: "there's a discipline involved in working with limited resources that can be an exciting challenge—you certainly have to make sure everyone has a meaningful part—*counterpoint*!!! [*sic*]."[28] Carr explains how he arrives at his decisions for an orchestration:

> The [theater] building tells you what scale you should be working on—no point putting a deafening brass section in a studio space and then expecting it to sit well under lightly miked actors. Working with the director and design team is, as I've said, crucial—you have to all be working on the *same show*, which sounds like a truism, but it's too easy to pull in different directions and then the trouble starts.[29]

Carr had originally reduced the orchestration of *Sunday in the Park with George* for the 180-seat Menier Chocolate Factory in London, though the production eventually transferred to Studio 54 in New York City.

Although Starobin agrees with Carr's view of the need for orchestrations to be adapted to suit the size of a venue, he has nevertheless commented:

> Jason Carr's *Sunday*...that small five-piece would work great for me in a little Off-Broadway 150[-seat] house....It makes sense for that....[Since] the original *Sunday* orchestration is eleven and they had done *Assassins* [in the same theater, Studio 54] with thirteen...they certainly could fit the eleven within the two boxes on either side....So, there was no reason not to...bring in the original eleven since what he did was a very good and intelligent reduction basically of what I had done. So...that felt really small for that space."[30]

In speaking with Starobin I pointed out that when I attended the Doyle production of *Sweeney Todd* on Broadway, I fell into it as a live theatrical event. While I found the production to be successful in live performance, I prefer listening to the original recording partially because the piano is almost continuous in the revival recording, and I feel like I am listening to a rehearsal. Starobin agreed that "those things don't come off well at all on recording," and went on to say,

> [I] was enthralled with it [the Doyle *Sweeney Todd*] because playing instruments became a dramatic action that meant so much to what the piece was. You know that when Michael Cerveris picks up a guitar to sing, it just turns Sweeney into a different

kind of much more contemporary angry character seeing him hunched over a guitar. It was a great look that said a lot of things.[31]

My conversation with Sarah Travis provided a "snapshot" of the work involved in orchestrating a specific revival of a Sondheim show and revealed the way this orchestrator has reimagined the aural language of *Sweeney Todd*. Travis collaborated with the director John Doyle more intimately and regularly than the standard orchestrator. Typically, the orchestrator retreats into the studio to work. Travis participated in the discovery of this new version of the show beginning with auditions and continuing throughout day-to-day rehearsals. In discussing her work on *Sweeney Todd*, Travis reconfirmed her peers' statements that Sondheim fully composes his scores. Instead of working from the full score, she chose to work from the show's piano–vocal score because she felt that the piano–vocal reductions are so full that she could get everything from them, because "every note has been carefully chosen, and there's nothing there that shouldn't be there."[32] She felt bound to honor the composition but free to be "adventurous" with the texture of the sounds she would create. Travis said that the only sections she "really fiddled" with were the parlor songs and the wigmaker sequence, in which she said that she changed quite a lot of the passages. She knew that she wanted "some sort of string section, however primitive, and some sort of woodwinds, and a couple of brass, and a little bit of percussion—and the keyboard led."[33]

Travis's process of orchestrating an actor-musician show is notably different from that of conventional orchestration. Doyle's and Travis's casting process at the Watermill necessarily included each potential actor's ability to play a musical instrument. She goes into auditions with an orchestration "wish list," the actor-musicians who walk through the audition door inspire her, and she tailors her orchestrations to those who eventually make up the production's cast. Travis's "real work" comes when she is in the rehearsal room with the actor-musicians. Doyle, Travis, and Fraser (who ran the Watermill) found what Travis called "an interesting way forward" in casting the characters of Anthony and Johanna with actors who were both cellists (strings). They discovered their brass player when they found a Mrs. Lovett who played trumpet, an instrument Travis referred to as "bawdy." When the production transferred to Broadway, Patti LuPone, the New York Mrs. Lovett, played a tuba (brass), which Travis said had "that same sort of slightly bawdy, sort of dirty sound… it just seemed cheeky and big and a brash statement that seemed to work."[34] That Pirelli was a woman in the Doyle production grew out of an actress playing the accordion at her audition. The idea of using the instrument and the woman as Pirelli appealed to them in the moment. Despite there being no accordion in the original orchestration of *Sweeney Todd*, Travis found the choice to be perfect for their version of the show. She said that she "immediately found it a bit eerie; and you know you could write long floating lines. It hangs over what you've got and yet it seems to mold it together."[35]

Travis revealed that when the production transferred and Stephen Sondheim became involved, she chose to redo and "refine" her orchestrations in those rehearsals. She added that Sondheim was very accepting of what they were trying to do and made no changes to her orchestrations. She said that Sondheim helped with some dramatic choices and "insisted quite rightly"[36] that some material that they had cut went back into the show. Also, John Doyle wanted to take the button off the end of "God that's Good" because he wanted to do away with having applause as much as he could, and Sondheim helped them connect it with the next section. The experience led her to laud Sondheim as "a very unselfish man, willing to let his work go through different processes."[37] After talking at length with Travis, I believe Sondheim's openness allowed her to become braver as the process continued. Still, her ultimate aim was to represent the piece well,

> to always keep the piece intact and to respect what the composer has written and to honor what's there. But...you also have to tailor it to your needs and the director's needs and your version of the piece....It's just a sort of constant negotiation....You just have to go with your instincts and hope you're doing a good job and hope that if the composer comes to see it, he's going to be happy and interested in what you've done. Ours wasn't necessarily right or wrong; it was just a different way of looking at the piece.[38]

Travis reconfirmed what others have said about Stephen Sondheim and his compositional style as well as the effect orchestration within the context of the performance venue has on the audience's theatrical experience. Before doing *Sweeney Todd* with Doyle, she had seen the show at the Royal Opera House in London with a cast of sixty people and a full orchestra, an experience that she found to be powerful and said, "It's a testament to a strong piece that it can take lots of different interpretations. But each interpretation honors the piece as theirs."[39]

The Doyle–Travis process resulted in an orchestration for *Sweeney Todd* that supported the story and the actor-singers in their production, which may be why it also resulted in Tony Awards for both of them. Their version did not attempt to get around the piano issue. Instead it went through it, and made the piano what Carr calls the "key *continuo* sound."[40] Centering on what Sondheim himself has said and all of his orchestrators confirm, that he provides a completely composed piano copy, Travis provided an orchestration that included Sondheim's notes in ways that worked dramatically and created a visceral theatrical experience when I saw it at the Eugene O'Neill Theatre in New York. I had seen the original production of *Sweeney Todd* and have since been musical director of a two-piano version of the score in a 150-seat theater. Still, I literally leapt from my seat in the back row of the theater in reaction to this version's musical and dramatic action. As I believe it does in the Doyle–Travis cast recording, I felt the "piano problem" presented itself when I saw this production at the Princess of Wales Theatre in Toronto. Seating nearly twice as many people as the O'Neill, the Toronto playhouse altered the audience's experience and confirmed my belief that successful orchestration is tied to a work's specific production, which must be sensitive to the physical dimensions of its venue.

One of the major ways that Doyle stoked the engine of his version of *Sweeney Todd* was his incorporation of the playing of musical instruments into the physical life of each character and thereby into the story. Just as Sondheim had challenged musical theater conventions from the time he wrote the lyrics for *West Side Story*, so are directors like John Doyle and Trevor Nunn breaking the rules anew.[41] As the theatrical landscape is reimagined and the stories are told again, Harold Prince, the original director of most of these shows, has taken the lead once more in saying, "I suppose there is no sanctity about original orchestration. . . . I personally am in the drama business, and storytelling is foremost in my mind—clarity and the motor energy of a production."[42]

According to Paul Gemignani, Sondheim remains "very generous with his own work" and believes that "[h]ad that been Jule Styne or Richard Rodgers, the response would have been: 'Excuse me, this score was originally orchestrated for twenty people. Get them in here, or the show's not happening.' "[43] Stephen Sondheim has himself supported the idea of the "chamber approach" to his works by saying that "you get to concentrate on the piece of work rather than on the production."[44] It is through these artists' experimental productions that we are given new ways of seeing and hearing the original work. In the later part of his career, Stephen Sondheim continues to "give us more to see" by embracing the changes in theatrical economics and consequently those of his shows' orchestrations. He mentors and supports the reimagining of his works, thereby giving orchestrators and other theater artists the pleasant opportunity to learn and examine his works within their own resources and to "make their own music."[45]

Appendix

At Michael Starobin's suggestion, I decided to poll various well-known orchestrators to give artistic suggestions for reduced orchestrations of some Sondheim shows. In order to make the list manageable I limited it to *Company, A Little Night Music, Sweeney Todd,* and *Sunday in the Park with George*.[46]

Orchestrator	orchestrated for	Company	A Little Night	Sweeney Todd	Sunday in the Park
Michael Starobin	5 instruments	2 synths, guitar, bass, drums	piano, woodwind doubler, horn, violin, cello	piano, woodwind doubler, horn, violin, cello	piano, synthesizer, horn, 2 woodwind doublers
	8 instruments	2 synths, guitar, bass, drums, trumpet, 2 woodwind doublers	piano, woodwind doubler, horn, violin, violin, viola, cello, bass	piano, woodwind doubler, horn, violin, violin, viola, cello, bass	piano, synthesizer, horn, 2 woodwind doublers, violin, viola, cello
	Comments	"These instrumentations are suggested for *rearranging* the score into more contemporary pop feels (which is probably not something that would meet with the composer's approval). The opening number might have a techno feel to it. "Sorry-Grateful" might have a gentle Latin feel to it. Moving the piano-based grooves onto guitar would be a key to much of this working. This is all probably a bad idea—but that is the dilemma of shows written within the pop sound of the moment—they don't necessarily translate well as the years go by."	"I chose the same instrumentation for *Night Music* and *Sweeney*."	"I would look to bring out classical chamber textures, as in a Brahms piano quintet or horn trio. In the eight-piece, I would have enough strings to get away from the piano for a bit."	"As in the original, I would use the left hand of the synthesizer for bass. The five-piece I'm suggesting would lose some warmth without strings. But I would also look to moving a lot more of the keyboard parts onto the synth than was possible in the early 1980s: quirky keyboard textures that would avoid pop textures, and instead reflect Seurat's refraction of colors."

Larry Blank[47]	5 instruments	keyboard, guitar, bass, drum, sax/woodwind doubler	keyboard, woodwind, harp, cello, bass	keyboard, woodwind playing several instruments, horn, percussion, bass	2 keyboards, horn, woodwind, percussion
	8 instruments	keyboard, guitar, bass, drum, sax/woodwind doubler, trumpet, trombone	keyboard, woodwind, harp, violin, viola, cello, bass	keyboard, woodwind playing several instruments, woodwind II, a brass instrument, horn, percussion, cello, bass	2 keyboards, horn, woodwind, percussion, harp, violin, cello
	Comments	"Company is an eclectic sounding show of the 70s.... While I think guitar can usually be excluded, I would make an exception because of the period sound of Company."	"[I included bass] because some kind of pulse is vital and it's just not sufficient with either the harp or keyboard."	"Sweeney Todd is the difficult one because of all the textures. Regarding the five-piece instrumentation: I think the string sound would be unnecessary with that grouping."	"I would use Michael's original orchestration and just cut something. I think the nature of the show requires keyboard sounds for the 'pointillism' [effect]."
Sarah Travis	5 instruments			Keyboard, woodwind, clarinet/sax, violin, cello, bass	
	8 instruments			Keyboard, clarinet, trumpet, percussion, violin, cello, bass, and either another woodwind, viola, or cello	
	Comments				

(Continued)

(*Continued*)

Orchestrator	orchestrated for	Company	A Little Night	Sweeney Todd	Sunday in the Park
Jason Carr[48]	5 instruments				piano, keyboard, woodwind on flute/clarinet/bass clarinet/alto saxophone, violin, cello
	8 instruments		keyboard, woodwind, bassoon, harp, violin, viola, cello, bass [Broadway revival orchestration]		
	Comments				"In trying to make *Sunday* work for five players, I realized that, despite a couple of iconic moments (including the big tune right at the top), a French horn would not easily blend in such a small ensemble (and such a small, live acoustic space as the Menier Chocolate Factory)—and once I got my head round that moment sounding different (an alto sax, with its Paris conservatoire associations), the line–up fell in to place."

NOTES

1. The author and editor wish to thank Dr. Olaf Jubin for his assistance in preparing this chapter.
2. Jonathan Tunick, Sid Ramin, Elliott Lawrence, and Larry Blank. "The Sound of Broadway Music: Broadway Orchestration, Panel I: Broadway Orchestration." New York Public Library for the Performing Arts, New York. October 19, 2009. Public address.
3. Susan Elliott, "Off the Stage, What's Behind the Music," *New York Times*, August 17, 2008.
4. Michael Starobin, telephone interview with the author, September 29, 2009; email correspondence, October 19, 2009.
5. JonathanTunick, telephone interview with the author, December 16, 2009.
6. Starobin, telephone interview, email correspondence.
7. Ibid.
8. Ibid.
9. Stephen Sondheim, audiotape interview with the author, November 2009.
10. Ibid.
11. Ibid.
12. Ibid.
13. Ibid.
14. Tunick, telephone interview.
15. Ibid.
16. Tunick, Ramin, Lawrence, and Blank, "The Sound of Broadway Music."
17. Starobin, telephone interview, email correspondence.
18. Tunick, Ramin, Lawrence, and Blank, "The Sound of Broadway Music."
19. Jonathan Tunick advises that one needs to get the licensing company of the shows to provide a correct orchestration list because many of the published orchestration lists for the Sondheim musicals are incorrect.
20. Sondheim, audiotape interview.
21. Starobin, telephone interview, email correspondence.
22. Jason Carr, email interview with the author, October 26, 2009.
23. Starobin, telephone interview, email correspondence.
24. Harold Prince, email interview with the author, September 28, 2009.
25. Carr, email interview.
26. Sondheim, audiotape interview.
27. SarahTravis, telephone interview with the author, September 27, 2009.
28. Carr, email interview.
29. Ibid.
30. Starobin telephone interview, email correspondence.
31. Ibid.
32. Sarah Travis, telephone interview.
33. Ibid.
34. Ibid.
35. Ibid.
36. Ibid.
37. Ibid.
38. Ibid.
39. Ibid.

40. Carr, email interview.
41. Patrick Healy, "Sondheim Makes His Entrance again, Intimately," *New York Times*, January 4, 2010.
42. Prince, email interview.
43. Elliot, "Off the Stage."
44. Healy, "Sondheim Makes His Entrance again."
45. Sondheim, audiotape interview.
46. I am very grateful to Sarah Travis, Larry Blank, and Michael Starobin for contributing the suggestions and comments that comprise this appendix.
47. While Larry Blank has not done Sondheim shows on Broadway, he was nominated for a Tony Award for his orchestrations for *Irving Berlin's White Christmas* and for a Drama Desk Award for his orchestrations for *The Drowsy Chaperone*.
48. The instrumentations for Jason Carr's orchestrations cited here are listed at http://www.ibdb.com/person.php?id=72181.

CHAPTER 10

"NOTHING MORE THAN JUST A GAME": THE AMERICAN DREAM GOES BUST IN *ROAD SHOW*

GARRETT EISLER

STEPHEN Sondheim's first new musical of the twenty-first century is based on one of his oldest ideas. As early as 1952 the budding composer-lyricist became fixated on the real-life misadventures of Addison and Wilson Mizner—a pair of brothers from a bygone era whose only legacy seemed to be their colossal failures. The older Addison (born 1872) made some impact in the 1920s as an architect to the Florida elite; Wilson (born 1876) was at times a playwright, boxing promoter, restaurateur, and criminal. Despite their differences, their fates have been inexorably linked ever since their deaths in 1933 (within weeks of each other, no less), and they have fascinated chroniclers of their time—like Pulitzer Prize-winning journalist Alva Johnston, whose serialized profiles of the brothers for the *New Yorker* magazine and subsequent book (*The Legendary Mizners*, published 1953) were devoured by the young Sondheim. The show that would be *Road Show* might well have been the first Sondheim musical, had Broadway producer David Merrick not already optioned the Johnston book himself for a never-completed project for Irving Berlin and S. N. Behrman. "I gloomed heavily," Sondheim later recalled of his response to this news, "and went on to other things never forgetting my original crush."[1]

What allure did the relatively unremarkable Mizners hold for all these master storytellers? Both brothers were well-liked raconteurs in their day; Addison wrote colorful memoirs of his travels and Wilson was, as one of Sondheim's lyrics puts it, "Always ready with a quip or a quote."[2] But more importantly, they left behind an irresistible case study in both the potency and the pitfalls of the American Dream. Their respective rollercoaster rides through the United States of the early twentieth century mirrored the ups and downs of the burgeoning nation itself. In their contrasts—Addison the respectable artist, Wilson the scandalous huckster—they also illustrate contrasting archetypes of American success; or, as Sondheim has written, they "represent two divergent aspects of American energy; the builder and the squanderer, the visionary and the promoter, the conformist and the maverick, the idealistic planner and the restless cynic, the one who uses things and the one who uses them up."[3]

The musical Sondheim and librettist John Weidman finally wrote about the Mizners underwent many changes over a nearly ten-year period; songs and characters were continually added and jettisoned, along with new titles and new directors for the project. But the most significant changes were less plot-related than tonal; the key question facing the authors turned out to be one of the most basic in the history of drama: comedy or tragedy? While Sondheim's Mizners were initially conceived of as a vaudeville team or classic comedic "odd couple" (with the Bob Hope–Bing Crosby "Road" movies serving as a model), by 2008 the musical—try as it might—could not escape the cynicism and sadness inherent in their story.

PRODUCTION HISTORY

According to Sondheim's own published account, he began working on the project in earnest soon after the opening of *Passion* in 1994, when he returned to his forty-year-old notes on the subject and finally approached a librettist, Weidman, about writing the book. Sondheim and Weidman had already worked together on two other iconoclastic American history musicals, *Pacific Overtures* and *Assassins*. (As Associated Press critic Michael Kuchwara wrote, "*Road Show* impressively completes the trilogy" which together "provide a sterling look at what has shaped the way America is today."[4]) This resumed collaboration marked a significant return for Sondheim to quintessentially American subject matter. After the Italian romance of *Passion*, the French impressionism of *Sunday in the Park with George*, the Victorian penny dreadful of *Sweeney Todd*, and even the ancient Greek comedy of *The Frogs* (which he revisited in 2004), the Mizners' story brought him back to similar geographic, thematic, and/or historical territory as *Assassins, Follies*, and *Merrily We Roll Along*—all of which, incidentally, were initially reckoned ambitious box office failures.

The show had its first unveiling in 1999 under the title *Wise Guys* in the form of a highly exclusive, yet highly publicized "workshop" that was closed to critics. Hosted by the normally experimental Off-Broadway New York Theater Workshop, the three-week preview (part open rehearsal, part backers' audition) boasted big Broadway names despite its seemingly modest setting.[5] Leading the cast were Sondheim stalwarts Victor Garber as the seductive pleasure-seeker Wilson and Nathan Lane as the more sensitive and cautious Addison; to direct, the authors tapped Sam Mendes—at that time a relatively new name to Broadway, but who had just scored two successive hits with his *Cabaret* revival and David Hare's play *The Blue Room* (starring Nicole Kidman) and whose first film, *American Beauty*, had just opened to career-boosting acclaim. Mendes first caught Sondheim's attention at the Donmar Warehouse in London, where he had staged hit revivals of *Company* and *Assassins* that pleased the composer.

But rather than a polished pre-Broadway tryout, the *Wise Guys* workshop ended up being hampered by the need for constant revisions, as well as having minimal production resources and little rehearsal time. (According to Michael Riedel's reporting in the *New York Post* at the time, "For nearly half its run at the New York Theater Workshop, only the first act of *Wise Guys* was performed as Sondheim and Weidman furiously reworked the second."[6]) In the face of cool industry reception, plans for an April 2000 Broadway opening were called off.

Undeterred, Sondheim and Weidman continued revising, but now with the help of a new director, Harold Prince. Although Sondheim and Prince hadn't worked together since *Merrily We Rolled Along* two decades earlier, their relationship dated all the way back to *West Side Story*, and their string of collaborations in the 1970s (*Company, Follies, Pacific Overtures*, and *Sweeney Todd*) was instrumental in forging both men's stellar reputations. The renewal of this legendary partnership sparked new excitement around the show and led to a fully staged premiere at Chicago's Goodman Theatre (one of the nation's leading nonprofit venues) in the summer of 2003 (Figure 10.1).

Renamed *Bounce*, the new version very much reflected Prince's desire to inject the material with more humor, romance, and showmanship. A female love interest was added ("Where are the girls?" was Prince's quoted response to the workshop),[7] designer Eugene Lee was engaged to provide elaborate sets, and—as indicated by the new title and eponymous opening number—vaudevillian levity was highlighted. But Chicago reviews were tepid; New York critics were held at bay until the production traveled to the Kennedy Center in Washington, DC, that autumn, but response there was only

FIGURE 10.1 Howard McGillin (left) as Addison Mizner and Michele Pawk (left, rear) as Nellie in *Bounce*, Goodman Theater, Chicago (2003).

marginally more favorable. The all-important *New York Times* review by Ben Brantley offered this commonly shared judgment:

> [*Bounce*] never seems to leave its starting point. The map lies tantalizingly before you, its routes and destinations marked in bright colors. But it remains a wistful diagram, rarely closer to three dimensions than the outsize, hand-tinted tourist postcards that frame the set. It's like a travel agent's pitch for a wondrous vacation.[8]

Hopes for a Broadway opening were yet again deferred and, in some quarters, written off entirely.[9]

With relentless adaptability though, Sondheim and Weidman shifted gears yet again and eventually entrusted the project to a third director, John Doyle. Doyle burst suddenly upon the New York scene in the fall of 2005 with the Broadway transfer from London of his minimalist ensemble staging of *Sweeney Todd*; and, the following year, he mounted a similar production of *Company*. In Doyle, Sondheim found, in many respects, an anti-Harold Prince: spare staging instead of expansive, "organic" rehearsal process instead of top-down vision, and London fringe-style "rough theater" instead of consummate Broadway slickness. If *Bounce* had shown the Mizners' story was too small to support Prince's razzle-dazzle, a turn inward towards Doyle's more intimate *mise-en-scène* seemed the answer to the musical's woes. And just as crucially in an age of drastically increased austerity in the American theater, a Doyle staging promised to be a less expensive—and therefore more producible—solution, as well.

Rather than wait for Broadway producers to come calling, Sondheim and Weidman also decided to keep the show in the nonprofit realm and turned to the New York's Public Theatre. (Since New York Theatre Workshop, the Goodman Theatre, and the Kennedy Center are all nonprofit institutions, the project had always lived in the nonprofit world.) The Public—virtually the nucleus of downtown Off-Broadway, with a long history of innovative musicals from *Hair* to *Chorus Line* to *Passing Strange*—hosted an exploratory reading in January 2006,[10] which led, after yet more delays, to an announcement two years later of the project's long-awaited official New York premiere in a new production of a new script with an entirely new cast under Doyle's direction.[11]

The change from the big, Broadway-bound *Bounce* to the lighter, more portable *Road Show* involved more than a change in names and budgets. (The name changed when the old title-song "Bounce" became one of the casualties of the move.) While Prince's version was a self-referential showbiz romp, Doyle's would turn out to be a more melancholy dissection of American archetypes—with perspective, perhaps, only a non-American could supply. And while many were shocked that another new Stephen Sondheim musical would not be opening on Broadway, *Road Show* actually marked a continuing interest of the composer in the form of the "chamber musical," returning him to an environment similar to the small Off-Broadway Playwrights Horizons nonprofit theater, where he had premiered *Sunday in the Park with George* in 1984 and *Assassins* in 1991—two works, incidentally, whose respective treatments of lonely artistic obsession and self-destructive capitalist democracy can be seen in retrospect to have significantly prefigured *Road Show*.

At an intermission-less 100 minutes (as opposed to the two-act, well over two-hour *Bounce*) and with just seventeen numbers (to *Bounce*'s twenty-one) *Road Show* ended up in a form Sondheim probably couldn't have written back at its inception in 1952: an antiromantic one-act chamber musical with an unhappy ending. While not through-composed, the compression and cutting of large amounts of book meant Sondheim's score would do more work than usual in dramatizing the story from beginning to end. A song-by-song analysis of the piece, therefore, reveals much about both its narrative and thematic impulses.

FROM WASTE TO WASTE: *ROAD SHOW* SONG BY SONG

The fundamental change that took place in Sondheim and Weidman's vision between *Bounce* and *Road Show* is evident in the evolution of the opening number. In both versions, the play begins in a nondescript purgatory, where the brothers meet up after their deaths. In the earlier song, "Bounce," a jaunty vamp and foxtrot pace accompany their reflections, celebrating resilience and indifference to setbacks.

> ADDISON:
> You hit a few bumps,
> You make a few gaffes
> You learn how to bounce.
> WILSON:
> You take a few lumps,
> You have a few laughs,
> And all the while you bounce.[12]

By *Road Show*, Sondheim does not let them bounce back so easily. The exact same tune (and vamp) now provides a more ironic counterweight to a harsh indictment of the brothers' lives, sung not by themselves, but by the ensemble—a Greek chorus of past Mizner victims casting posthumous judgment on their lives. The contented shrug of "Bounce" has become the more dismissive "Waste."

> A MAN: Think that he's dead?
> ANOTHER MAN: Has been for years.
> A WOMAN: God, what a waste.
> A MAN: Genius, they said.
> A WOMAN: Opened frontiers.
> ANOTHER WOMAN: Really, such a waste.[13]

These sarcastic opening comments soon lead to more full-throated indictments, a series of cacophonous overlapping testimonies from individual chorus members (each beginning, "Remember me I'm the one that you..."), detailing offenses great and small perpetuated upon them by one of the Mizners. This litany is broken off abrasively by the young man we will later meet as Addison's male lover, Hollis, who silences the crowd with the cutting line: "Remember me, I'm the one that you fucked."[14] In what is probably

Sondheim's most profanity-laden score, this lyric and others puncture at every turn—as he has so often done before—the traditional Broadway musical's idealized romanticism. This line in particular also introduces in a deliberately shocking way Sondheim's first depiction of a same-sex relationship in one of his plays.

The opening afterlife scene serves as prologue and framing device for a narrative that now begins in flashback. Doyle's production may have lacked the star wattage of a Lane or Garber, but his casting of two younger actors as Wilson and Addison (Michael Cerveris and Paul Gemignani, respectively) had the advantage of making the early scenes of their beginnings more dramatically credible. It also highlighted the characters' childlike qualities, especially in their relationships with their parents. The inciting incident for the Mizners' adventures is a song they hear at their father's knee; after attempting a somewhat comic version of this scene in *Bounce* (with the song "Opportunity"), in *Road Show* Sondheim returned to the more solemn ballad he wrote for *Wise Guys*, "It's in Your Hands Now." According to Sean Patrick Flahaven, the melody is borrowed from a number discarded from *Assassins*, "Flag Song"[15]—and indeed the music's stately progressions and open tones recall familiar anthems from patriotic lore and even musical theater, such as Rodgers and Hammerstein's "You'll Never Walk Alone" from *Carousel*.

While delivered in earnest by Papa Mizner, the sentiments of the lyric signal a pathetic fallacy that will both inspire the brothers and lead them astray. Set in the 1890s the scene is situated dramatically to launch not only the brothers but the nation itself upon what Henry Luce would later hubristically dub "The American Century." Papa's generation of true pioneers now makes way for a new wave of men who will attempt to profit from those earlier achievements without putting in the hard labor.

> PAPA:
> There's a road straight ahead,
> There's a century beginning.
> There's a land of opportunity and more.
> It's in your hands now.

Sondheim counters the lyrics' optimism with many oblique references to capitalism's pitfalls and contradictions. He alludes to Herbert Hoover's careless laissez-faire when Papa tells the boys to "never paus[e] in your quest / for something better just around the corner," and also talks of Americans' obsession with reinventing themselves in terms that ominously anticipate his sons' personal fates: "Keep your eyes on what's afar, / Not on what we are, / But what we can become!" The American Dream is invoked as "dreams to be fed," not an idealistic goal but a voracious appetite, and, at the coda, Papa's exhortation musically mimics the brothers' own obsessions with perpetual forward motion, as the pitch and volume steadily rise:

> As the road extends,
> It gets rough as it ascends,
> And it often bends,
> But it never, ever ends.

No wonder he collapses and literally expires at the end of the number—giving the lie to his promise of everlasting good fortune.

The ultimate cloud hanging over "It's in Your Hands Now," of course, is the audience's memory of the song immediately preceding it. As Papa says in his lead-in, "It was my generation's task to make of [the] New World a nation. Now, with the dawning of a new century, your work begins. The work of determining what type of nation we shall be." The stakes could not be higher as he charges Addison and Willy with this mission; and yet we already know they will only make a "waste" of it.

The Mizners' quest for material wealth begins in Alaska, with the Klondike Gold Rush of the 1890s. *Gold* was yet another title considered for the musical itself (in the revision period after *Wise Guys* and before *Bounce*), and the powerful resonance of the word survives in the song "Gold!" which—with its exaggerated syncopations recalling Copland's *Rodeo*—whisks the brothers away from California at the beckoning of a chorus of prospectors. Indeed, the use of song to convey leaps in narrative time became an essential feature in *Road Show*, in order to compress the much longer book of *Bounce*. In "Gold" the ensemble joins in, with manic Sondheimian rhyming and repetition:

> The century's beginning,
> Gold will make it tick!
> Dig in any mountain, pan in any crick.
> All you need's a bucket and a shovel and a pick
> And with a little bit of luck it
> Means you get rich quick!
> Get rich quick! Get rich quick![16]

Addison, ever the more sensitive and cautious of the pair, is at first reluctant, but the incessant musical pressure ultimately persuades him.

Arriving in the Yukon, the two Californians are at first unprepared for the bracing weather and even harsher open-season capitalism of what is still a Wild West territory.

In the song "Brotherly Love" the two share a sleeping bag on a freezing Alaskan night. Wilson squirms at first but warms up as Addison recalls fond childhood memories of his brother taking care of him as a sickly child and sneaking him off to see fireworks; "You always looked out for me, no matter what," Addie sings in a fond falsetto. Although in real life Addison was the older brother, in *Road Show* Wilson is consistently implied to be dominant partner of the two. By establishing Addison's deep-seated adoration of Wilson, the song sets up the stakes for Wilson's ultimate betrayal and sabotaging of his brother's trust, the emotional climax and endpoint of the narrative.

"Brotherly Love" also marks a significant departure from *Bounce* in foregrounding the brothers' own relationship as the primary "love story" of the show. Added by Sondheim during previews (it was the one entirely new song in *Road Show* that did not appear in any previous version[17]), it effectively substituted for one of *Bounce*'s seduction songs, "What's Your Rush," sung in that version by Wilson and his romantic interest, Nellie. Since the dearth of tangible affection between Addison and Wilson may have contributed to early criticisms of *Wise Guys* and *Bounce* (which lacked such a moment),

FIGURE **10.2** Michael Jibson and David Bedella as Addison and Wilson Mizner in *Road Show*, London (2010).

dramatizing their deep emotional bond early in the play was crucial, since they spend so much of the story apart and at odds. (Figure 10.2)

The irreconcilable difference between the brothers' psychological make-ups first becomes evident when, after they strike gold, Wilson immediately bets their claim in a card game. His guilt-free celebration of his recklessness is expressed in a sublime musical summation of the capitalist ethic, "The Game."

> The whole thing's nothing more than just a game.
> And, Addie, what I'm good at is the game.
> They said, "Come on in, sucker!"
> Now they're sorry that I came.
> I tell you, kid, there's nothing like the game.

Sondheim's music here (and actor Michael Cerveris's delivery as recorded on the cast album) is utterly serene, befitting the gambler's narcotic "high." The mark of a true addicted gambler is not the love of money—it's the rush of the risk. Wilson's greatest pride is as a "player" of the game, not necessarily a victor. ("It's more than just the winning," he sings, "it's the game.") Capitalism—for which poker provides a handy stage metaphor—depends upon the constant willingness of players to pour money into the system, in only the *hopes* of a return. "The Game," a recurring leitmotif for Wilson throughout the score no matter how bad things get, reveals him as a definitive American businessman in spirit, even if he will remain a largely unsuccessful one in practice.

Wilson is unsuccessful in musically reassuring Addison, who promptly takes his share of the winnings and splits from his brother for what will be the first of many times to set out and make his own fortune. An extended musical set piece, "Addison's Trip," charts his journey of self-discovery, again encompassing a long duration of time through the use of comically compressed stage conventions. Taking the character through an eight-minute travelogue across many continents, the song is the clearest trace in *Road Show* of the Hope–Crosby films from which Sondheim and Weidman originally drew inspiration.

Perhaps that broadly comic influence from another time explains the cartoonish shorthand depictions in the song of Hawaiian, Indian, Chinese, and Latin American cultures. But the stereotype-risking tone also reflects Addison's point of view as a Teddy Roosevelt–era economic imperialist, albeit a pathologically unlucky one. In Hawaii he buys a share in a pineapple plantation that soon goes up in flames; in Bombay, his warehouse of "precious gems" is totaled in a cyclone; in Hong Kong his fireworks factory, unsurprisingly, explodes; and in Guatemala he is ousted from ownership of a coffee plantation by a populist uprising. In real life, Addison Mizner's trips to these places were spread out over many years, but the minidrama "Addison's Trip" skillfully creates an accumulation of misfortunes that leads to the protagonist's realization that he is not a born capitalist like his brother but, rather, an artist.

Even his chosen medium of architecture, however, derives from the epic spending sprees of his travels. Greeted at every stop by locals hawking "souvenirs," he brings home more knick- knacks and *tchotchkes* than he knows what to do with:

> What I need to have is space
> That holds crucifixes,
> A Bombay chest,
> A temple bell
> And a condor's nest
> And commodes and mirrors and all the rest—

A breakthrough comes when he finally beholds all the pieces of other cultures he has consumed and realizes their potential for interior decorating:

> Build a marble niche for the Ming tureen
> And a mezzanine for the lacquered screen,
> And an archway here and a skylight there
> Until everything has a place somewhere—
> I'll build a goddamned house![18]

With its steady *crescendo* and *accelerando*, this exciting climax to "Addison's Trip" once again musicalizes a mania for materialism, as does so much of the *Road Show* score. It also pleases the ear as a "list song" in the Cole Porter tradition—dazzling the listener with surprising rhymes that connect unlikely pairings. Sondheim deploys that classic songwriter's device here to enter the mindset of the privileged international "collector." Addison Mizner's eclectic cross-cultural borrowing informed his unique—some would say kitschy—"Mediterranean Revival" brand of architecture, characterized by jarring blends of disparate styles and periods. In the later song, "You," Sondheim has him describe one house as "a hacienda, a happy fusion / Of Indonesian and Andalusian—/

I see gingerbread, / I see Chinese red / And a huge Victorian potting shed." Again the constantly surprising "list" lyrics inevitably subsume and level all the cultural differences under that always marketable commercial label: *exotic*. "There's a whole new way America should look," he says in a line from Weidman's dialogue, summing up the nation's paradoxical quest for its own identity via the appropriation of others.

As Addison settles into an artist's life in Greenwich Village, Wilson comes pleading for help, having lost his Alaska fortune. He soon rebounds by wooing a rich New York widow who funds his next endeavors as a showman-at-large. And so ensues another narrative-synthesizing musical set piece, "That Was a Year," which parallels "Addison's Trip" as a travelogue, but instead of going around the world, this song's hero just descends deeper into Broadway debauchery.

The structure of "That Was a Year" resembles classic narrative songs of scoundrels' exploits (like Kurt Weill and Ira Gershwin's "Saga of Jennie" from *Lady in the Dark*) as each verse recounts a different highlight from the hero's unabashedly sinful life. Here, four of Wilson's seduced and abandoned business partners (all loosely based on real people) come forward: a boxer he managed goes to waste after too much partying with his boss; a Broadway playwright who collaborated with him is left stranded with an unfinished script that flops; the jockey of his thoroughbred goes to jail when he fixes the race; and even Wilson's wife, Myra Yerkes, discovers she was nothing more than a business partner to him all along, singing, "Perfect in looks, / Perfect at sex, / Not so god-damn perfect at forging my checks."[19]

The rhyming of "sex" and "checks" sums up the nature of the marriage, prompting Myra to leave him after just one year. But for his other victims, what they suffered with Wilson was worth it because "oh, what a year" it was. And as a counterweight to all the tales of chicanery, we get literally a chorus line of showgirls (as if out of one of Wilson's plays) singing his praises:

> Everybody wants
> Broadway Willie Mizner!
> Knocks 'em silly,
> Lowlifes and Duponts,
> Cops and debutantes...
> Night club fillies,
> Writers, racketeers,
> Everybody cheers
> Good Time Willie Mizner![20]

This fantasy of high and low, where Wilson is loved by simply "everybody," might be the tipoff that the number is in fact all in his head—an impression inescapable to Sondheim fans who recognize in the chorus girls' ending repetitions of "Broadway Willie, Broadway Willie..." echoes of the delirious coda to "Who's that Woman?" from *Follies* ("Mirror, mirror...").[21]

In *Bounce* the character of Wilson's wife, Nellie (who briefly takes on the name of Yerkes, Wilson's wife in real life), was much more prominent, so her removal from *Road Show* left Mama Mizner as the most prominent female character in the otherwise male-centered world of the play. Still, Mama's stage time altered throughout the three versions of the show, and in *Road Show* is the most reduced. (In *Bounce* she was played by former MGM star Jane Powell and at the 2006 Public Theatre reading by Bernadette Peters.) Her one remaining solo number, "Isn't He Something," is hardly a mother's song. One in a long line of Sondheim's dysfunctional, self-destructive love songs, it essentially expresses the contradictory love we can have for those who are bad to us. In a more conventionally romantic situation, the song might contrast two lovers, one boringly faithful, one a more exciting scoundrel. Here the competing lovers are Mama's two sons: the stable and dutiful Addison versus the prodigal and unreliable Wilson. Appropriately she addresses the song to Addison, who is there supporting her, even while clearly expressing a preference for Wilson, who is not.

> Some men are tender souls
> With worthy goals
> They keep fulfilling.
> Some men ignore the rules,
> Are rogues and fools,
> And thrilling.

As with Wilson's willing victims from "That Was a Year," Sondheim grasps the psychology of abusive or exploitative love—which extends, by implication, to America's celebration of hoodlums and conmen, as well. As Mama says, it's all about the vicarious pleasure we want to experience but can't: "I've had the time of my life, / Living through him."[22]

Just as "It's in Your Hands Now" was for Papa, this turns out to be Mama's death song. In *Bounce*, this same scene—in which Wilson returns once again, but too late to see his mother alive—marks the end of act 1 and the intermission point. But in the whirlwind pacing of *Road Show* there is little time for mourning and, just as the gold prospector steps on Papa's final words, now a Florida real estate agent bursts onstage with a reprise of "Gold!" now called "Land Boom!" hailing the new frontier in schemes:

> All you need is capital,
> A little does the trick.
> Beg or steal or borrow,
> It'll double by tomorrow.
> Only get your ass to Florida
> And get rich quick!

Hopping the next train down south, Addison has a fortuitous meeting with Hollis, young scion of a metals magnate. Hollis is about to awaken Addison's seemingly dormant sexuality, but he will also effectively become his patron. The song that introduces him, "Talent," is a classic case of Sondheimian irony, since it's actually about how Hollis's *lack* of talent ("Just enough talent to know / That I hadn't the talent") makes him want to consume art (and artists) instead of create.

Hollis sees himself as not just any patron, but Louis XIV, and his artists as his riches. (He sings of a "Versailles by the Florida sea"[23]). The song's title might as well refer to what Hollywood today commodifies as simply "the talent."

The subject of patronage in the artistic marketplace—and its connections to eros—is as prominent a theme in *Road Show* as it was for Sondheim in *Sunday in the Park with George*. The parallel between the two shows is most evident in the music accompanying Addison's unveiling of his houses—a shimmering arpeggiated chord just like the one that opens the song "Sunday" that reveals Seurat's painting of *La Grande Jatte*. The song in which this happens, "You," is a love song between both Hollis and Addison and between Addison and his new clients, simultaneously. In the midst of wowing and wooing the Florida nouveau riche (to whom Hollis has introduced him) with his personalized designs for their mansions, the two men sing to each other over the crowd: "You, where have you been all my life?" But by song's end, the exact same words are directed at Addison by the Floridians, overlapping in ecstatic multivoiced harmony.

The Addison–Hollis relationship is deepened further by a second love song, "The Best Thing that Ever Has Happened," a song originally intended for Wilson and Nellie in *Bounce*. But the removal of Nellie once again casts more focus on the same-sex (and male-centered) romance in the story by transferring the song with particulars altered but essentially unchanged. The song recalls the beloved Rodgers and Hammerstein "antilove songs" (like Billy and Julie's conditional declarations of "If I Loved You" in *Carousel*), as is evident in the comic hedging each partner engages in while trying to express pure emotion:

> ADDISON:
> You are the best thing that ever has happened to me,
> You are.
> *(Hollis waves him away, blushing)*
> Okay then,
> One of the best things that's happened to me,
> You are.

And then:

> HOLLIS:
> You might just be the best thing that has happened to me.
> So far.
> Of course not much ever really has happened to me,
> So far.[24]

In *Bounce*, we get a much more undercutting and vulgar variation, to the same tune:

> WILSON:
> You're still the best thing that ever has happened to me.
> NELLIE:
> Bullshit.
> WILSON:
> Okay, the best thing that could ever happen to me.
> NELLIE:
> Bullshit.[25]

Either way the song reminds us how preoccupied the Sondheim canon is with the ambivalence of love (like *Company*'s "Sorry-Grateful" and *Follies*' "Losing My Mind"). And Sondheim's invocation of the Rodgers and Hammerstein model in reference to Addison and Hollis makes the song in its *Road Show* incarnation particularly subversive by bringing a gay relationship into the fold of the "Golden Age" musical theater tradition.

The song would be charmingly coy, were the relationship not in fact doomed to fail. In pursuing his wildest artistic dreams in his designs for the then-new resort city of Boca Raton, Addison ends up losing his reputation, his brother, and his lover. Wilson, destitute yet again after his divorce and Broadway failures, shows up at Addison's and Hollis's Palm Springs doorstep with nowhere else to turn. But working his old magic (through a reprise of "The Game") he goads Addison, with Hollis's help, into making Boca Raton his greatest legacy (the song "Addison's City"). While Addison dives into the art, Wilson takes over the marketing to bring the necessary buyers down to Florida to occupy these houses. Like all advertising, Wilson needs to create a demand that isn't necessarily there.

In a show of several extended set pieces "Boca Raton" shows Sondheim and Weidman's collaborative powers at their best, as song and speech comingle to tell the story of the venture's rise and fall in a compressed five minutes of stage time. While Addison and Hollis gradually realize the deal is going bust, Wilson (high on "whiskey and cocaine," it is remarked) and a team of yet more chorus girls take to the airwaves to sell Utopia. "It's time to wake up to tomorrow," he exhorts the nation, "Time to wake up to opportunity! . . . Now comes the most magnificent piece of real estate to hit the market since the Good Lord foreclosed on the Garden of Eden."[26] Almost mocking the language of Papa Mizner's generation, the chorus promises glory to listeners but simply for buying property, not for hard toil: "Come and see / The new frontier! / Come and be / A pioneer!" And they are not above appealing to Americans' sense of competitive acquisition when Sondheim cunningly rhymes cries of "You'll love it" with "You'll covet."[27]

At the center of all the frenzied action, Wilson's increasingly megalomaniacal narration overwhelms the proceedings—just as, in the grand scheme of things, he is eclipsing and undermining Addison's plans. John Doyle's staging held back nothing in dramatizing the dark side of the pitch, placing Michael Cerveris at a 1930s standing "ring" microphone, lighting him from below, and supplying audio cues of applause and cheering crowds. The evocation of fascist rallies—as well as Cerveris's recent association with the role of Sweeney Todd—drew a clear line between *Road Show* and other more genial musical depictions of con artists, like *The Producers*' Max Bialystok or *The Music Man*'s Harold Hill. In this nightmare version of Boca Raton, we're not in River City anymore.

Cerveris's almost self-hypnotizing delivery of Wilson's "hard sell" became especially eerie at the rousing yet ominous-sounding conclusion, where (over a darker arrangement of the music for Papa's anthem "It's in Your Hands Now") he reveals more about his own tragically insatiable appetite for "the game" than anything to help sell real estate.

> What is life? I say it is a journey. A road down which we travel, ever seeking, never satisfied. . . . Onward we go, restlessly reinventing ourselves. Searching for something that already lies before us. For in America, the journey *is* the destination! Or it has

been, until now. Until tonight. Because the road which I have just described to you
will take us someplace so spectacular that finally we can cease our searching, stop our
wandering and be content. Where does it lead? To journey's end. Behold my friends,
Boca Raton![28]

"Journey's end," unfortunately is where the Mizners soon end up. Hollis exposes the
fraud and overselling behind the campaign and will have nothing left to do with either
brother. Addison then launches into a quarrel with the one lover he has left, Wilson.
The combined numbers "Get Out" and "Go" dramatize their final reckoning with each
other. "I thought we could go from scheme to dream," Addison confesses (although the
rhyme suggests the two are not so different), then demands his brother finally leave him
alone: "You owe me a life, / A life of my own."[29] Wilson's response, drowning out Addison's
protests, is at once touching and devastating, contented and fatalistic. Mock-triumphant
music bolsters his plea—part pep-talk, part prophecy—as he wears his brother down:

> WILSON:
> And this isn't the end of the trip.
> No, it's just the reverse.
> Face it, Brother, we're joined at the hip.
> And that is our curse.
> ....
> Though I'm not worth a lot,
> I'm what you've got,
> Which you'll never outgrow.
> We were stuck from "hello,"
> It was bound to explode.
> Don't you see we're the same,
> That whatever the game,
> This was always our road?

Addison finally relents, but his response signals (once again) the ambivalence of abusive
love and dangerously codependent relationships:

> All right, yes!
> I love you, I always have loved you!
> Does that make us even?
> Does that make you happy?
> And I want you to go.
> (Beat)
> And, no,
> I don't want you to go...[30]

In the end they must stay together since no one else will have them. And as much as
Addison wants "his own life," the whole play itself stands as a reminder that Wilson is
right: the two brothers' names will be forever inseparable.

This scene seamlessly segues back to the opening purgatory setting, bringing us full
circle now that we have seen how the brothers came to such a "waste." Even the ghost of
Papa briefly surfaces to pronounce final sentence: "I expected you'd make history, boys.

Instead, you made a mess."[31] When "Bounce" was reprised at the end of *Bounce*, it projected a defiant whimsy; now, as the same jaunty vamp plays, the brothers' own rendition of the song about their "Waste" leaves us on a less certain note.

> WILSON:
> Why should we dwell
> On the past?
> Looking ahead—
> Addison:
> Willie, we're dead.[32]

One could say Wilson still seems stuck in the "Bounce" version; he never got the rewrites. And while the script's final moment (where the brothers have a vision of yet another "road") remains unchanged, the preceding context now highlights Wilson's obliviousness, albeit with a wink:

> WILSON: Addie, look at it! You know what that is? It's the road to opportunity!
> ADDISON: It's the road to eternity.
> WILSON: The greatest opportunity of all. Sooner or later we're bound to get it right.
>   (*Blackout.*)[33]

It wouldn't be the first time Wilson tried to put a price on heaven.

CONCLUSION

With no further intentions to revise, Sondheim and Weidman seem to have settled on *Road Show* as the final form the piece will take. The 2004 cast recording of *Bounce* will always be available as a partial record of its past life. But with the 2008 Public Theatre opening (and 2009 recording), *Road Show* does indeed appear to be the end of the road for the composer's long-gestating Mizner project, and, no doubt, he prefers future audiences to focus on the final product, not its difficult production history.

But opening when it did at the Public on October 28, 2008, the show may have fortuitously found its moment. In the midst of a Wall Street collapse—mostly triggered by inflated housing values and shell-game salesmanship—and a vicious presidential campaign debating the nation's economic future, the Mizners' story could not have been more relevant. To the traders of stock "derivatives" and sellers of "subprime" mortgages, the whole thing really *was* nothing more than just a game. Against such a backdrop of capitalism run amok, the Mizners' epic cross-country adventure from Alaska to Florida could not help but recall the same landscape (and even same time frame) of an earlier musical dissection of American business: Brecht and Weill's *Mahagonny*. While Sondheim has often disavowed any influence from the Brecht–Weill canon, it might have at least been on the mind of director John Doyle, who had staged *Mahagonny* for the Los Angeles Opera and PBS television the year before.

Road Show's lasting value, though, will probably be in the emotional impact it delivers—far more than previous versions of the show and more than many previous works of this notoriously "all head, no heart" dramatist (as he mocked himself in *Sunday in the Park*). The changing titles of the show's three versions actually offer a clue as to why the final one is the most moving. *Wise Guys*—presumably the closest to Sondheim's initial impulse—took its inspiration from the storied chutzpah and amusing idiosyncracies of its two lead characters. *Bounce* captured a mood, an optimistic and carefree "can-do" attitude; but as Ben Brantley wrote, the result was "a quaint distance from its subjects, as if viewing them through a stereopticon."[34] But the phrase *Road Show* itself already conjures up so much more. For a country that has always prided itself on its road stories (from Lewis and Clark to Twain to Kerouac), American folklore rarely acknowledges the price paid for the constant itinerancy of both body and soul. As Doyle's own scenic design of "an eclectic pyramid of trunks, old furniture, and packing crates"[35] immediately signified in performance, the Mizners' story is ultimately one of detritus, of "waste," and of everything we associate with being "on the road": short-term highs and one-night stands; perpetual loneliness, homelessness, and impermanence; always travelling, never arriving. In a word, limbo.

In his "Boca Raton" broadcast, Wilson at one point compares Addison's luxurious properties to "the Emerald City of the legendary Oz himself."[36] But by invoking that other classic (yellow-brick) road story, he willfully ignores the irony that there is no "Oz" —just a "man behind the curtain." Dorothy at least finally realizes "there's no place like home," but the Mizners instead seem destined to fulfill that other road-related prophecy of Thomas Wolfe: "You can't go home again."

Road Show the musical, at least, did finally find its home and "arrive." And it stands as a testament to a similarly great writer's continuing excursion through the ways and paths of the American psyche.

NOTES

1. Stephen Sondheim, "A Musical Isn't Built in a Day, but This Took 47 Years," *New York Times*, September 12, 1999.
2. Stephen Sondheim and John Weidman, *Road Show* (New York: Theatre Communications Group, 2009), 49. Wilson Mizner's most famous quote is still perennial: "Be nice to the people you meet on the way up, because they're the same people you're going to meet on the way down."
3. Sondheim, "A Musical Isn't Built in a Day."
4. Michael Kuchwara, "Two Brothers Forever Seek Success in 'Road Show,' " *Associated Press*, November 19, 2008.
5. The New York Theatre Workshop presentation in fact reflected a hybrid of nonprofit and commercial interests; Washington's Kennedy Center for the Performing Arts (which commissioned the piece in the first place) was listed as a coproducer, as was maverick theatrical and independent cinema mogul Scott Rudin. Rudin and Sondheim subsequently engaged in a lawsuit when the musical went forward with production (as *Bounce*), sidestepping

Rudin's original exclusive option. The two parties settled out of court by the time *Bounce* opened in Chicago in 2003.

6. Michael Riedel, "'Wise Guys' is Going Bust," *New York Post*, November 26, 1999.

7. Bruce Weber, "Adding a Sexy Spring to Levitate 'Bounce,'" *New York Times*, July 30, 2003.

8. Ben Brantley, "Sondheim Guides Two Brothers on a Tour of Life," *New York Times*, November 1, 2003.

9. *Bounce*'s Broadway chances were not helped by the absence of stars of the caliber of Lane and Garber. Prince cast two lesser-known but veteran actors, Richard Kind and Howard McGillin, as Addison and Wilson, respectively.

10. Michael Riedel, "Bernadette's Bounce Back," *New York Post*, January 18, 2006.

11. Doyle's role in the *Road Show* revision apparently went far beyond staging. In his acceptance speech for the 2009 Obie award for the show's score, Sondheim thanked both Doyle and Public Theatre Artistic Director Oskar Eustis for their contributions as "dramaturgs," suggesting that they were instrumental in the condensing and restructuring of the script. The published *Road Show* text is notably dedicated to both men.

12. Liner notes, *Bounce: Original Cast Recording*, CD (Nonesuch, 2004).

13. Sondheim and Weidman, *Road Show*, 9–10.

14. Ibid., 13.

15. Liner notes, *Road Show*, CD (Nonesuch, 2009).

16. Sondheim and Weidman, *Road Show*, 23–4.

17. Liner notes, *Road Show*, CD.

18. Sondheim and Weidman, *Road Show*, 41–2.

19. Ibid., 50.

20. Ibid., 48–9.

21. It is worth noting that this is one number in *Road Show* that underwent significant expansion; its analog in *Bounce*, "I Love This Town," runs a minute and a half shorter on CD (3:57 as opposed to 5:31) and is missing the jockey story entirely.

22. Sondheim and Weidman, *Road Show*, 52–3.

23. Ibid., 59.

24. Ibid., 71–2.

25. Liner notes, *Bounce*, CD.

26. Sondheim and Weidman, *Road Show*, 83–4.

27. Ibid., 85.

28. Ibid., 91.

29. Ibid., 94.

30. Ibid., 94–6.

31. Ibid., 98.

32. Ibid., 98–9.

33. Ibid., 99.

34. Brantley, "Sondheim Guides Two Brothers."

35. Sondheim and Weidman, *Road Show*, 9.

36. Ibid., 86.

PART III

SONDHEIM IN PERFORMANCE

"IT TAKES TWO": THE DOUBLING OF ACTORS AND ROLES IN *SUNDAY IN THE PARK WITH GEORGE*

OLAF JUBIN

THE aim of Stephen Sondheim and James Lapine in writing the musical *Sunday in the Park with George* was to create a musical on a theme and its variations.[1] In order to examine the role art and the artist play in society and how this role has changed over the course of 100 years Sondheim and Lapine divide their story into two acts that take place in different centuries (in 1884 and 1984, respectively) and feature two sets of seemingly different characters. Nonetheless, the audience is expected to draw certain parallels between the action before and after the interval. This is made clear first and foremost by having at the center of both acts an artist who is named George.[2]

Act 2 represents variations on ideas introduced in the first part of the show, with Sondheim and Lapine using thematic motifs to knit the two halves of the show into a coherent whole. The repetition of bits of dialogue and certain lyrical and musical motifs provides many parallels between the two acts. In addition to this, some characters in the second half mirror characters in the first half: both acts feature colleagues of the artist, a love interest, his closest family member, and critics. As with most musicals, the second half is much shorter than the first, and that means that there is considerably less time to supply each of the new characters with enough individual detail to give the audience a clear impression of who they are.[3] Therefore it is not surprising that many people had a problem caring about the characters in act 2, who were criticized as being less interesting than those in act 1. This is probably the main reason why, ever since the earliest incarnations of *Sunday in the Park with George*, there have been many proposals to scrap the second act altogether.[4]

So one might conclude it was either brave or foolish of the authors to start the second act with new protagonists whom the audience doesn't know and are required to become acquainted with. On closer inspection, though, it becomes evident that these are not wholly *new* characters, but versions of the characters in act 2. Aside from characters that serve the same function in both parts of the show, each of the actors in act 1 morphs into another character in act 2. Early on in the development of *Sunday*, Sondheim and Lapine experimented with casting the same actors in different parts in each act. In the

FIGURE **11.1** Mandy Patinkin as George the Painter, with the cast in act 1 of *Sunday in the Park with George* (1984).

FIGURE **11.2** Mandy Patinkin in "Putting It Together" in act 2 of *Sunday in the Park with George* (1984).

workshop production at Playwright's Horizon that preceded the Broadway version in July 1983 they had already used the same six actors in both acts: the actors playing George, Dot, Mrs./Nurse, Franz, Mr., and someone called Bette all also played characters in the second half of the show.[5]

No doubt one of the reasons for this doubling was financial. But a detailed reading of the musical reveals that parallels in casting are not just "practical and *to a certain extent* [my emphasis] conceptual" as Stephen Banfield put it.[6] I would argue that Sondheim and Lapine found a way of turning an economic necessity into an artistic means of expression that actually enhances the spectator's understanding of the characters and underlines what the authors have to say about the artist and his or her place in a society that admires creativity while at the same time being suspicious of it.

Most people would agree that the characters in the second half of the show are not as vividly drawn as the Parisians who stroll through "La Grand Jatte" (Figure 11.1)[7] In this respect the double casting is very helpful, because the audience (whether conscious of doing so or not) is likely to carry over associations and traits from characters in the first act and ascribe them to those characters played by the same actors in the second half of

Table 11.1 The same actor in different parts

No	Actor/Actress	Act 1 (1884)	Act 2 (1984)	Trait(s) in common
1	Mandy Patinkin	George, *painter*	George, *multimedia artist*	creative, socially aloof
2	Bernadette Peters	Dot, *mistress*	Marie, *grandmother*	serve as inspiration for the artist
3	Barbara Bryne	Old lady, *mother*	Blair Daniels, *art critic*	make demands on the artist
4	Charles Kimbrough	Jules, *painter*	Bob Greenberg, *head of museum*	interested in art without having real talent
5	Dana Ivey	Yvonne, *wife*	Naomi Eisen, *composer*	Collaborator
6	Brent Spiner	Franz, *servant*	Dennis, *technical assistant*	harbor false ideas about the artist's life
7	Nancy Opel	Frieda, *cook*	Betty, *artist*	defend the artist
8	William Parry	Boatsman	Charles Redmond, *curator*	offer a unambiguous perspective
9	Cris Groenendahl	Louis, *baker*	Billy Webster, *boyfriend*	ignorant about art
10	Robert Westenberg	Napoleon, *soldier*	Alex, *artist*	are prepared to attack and conquer
11	Kurt Knudson	Mr.	Lee Randolph, *public relations*	spread the news
12	Judith Moore	Mrs./Nurse	Harriet Pawling, *board member*	interested in sponsoring
13	Melanie Vaughn	Celeste 1, *shopgirl*	Waitress	hired help
14	Mary D'Arcy	Celeste 2, *shopgirl*	Elaine, *ex-wife*	hanger-on

the show. This strategy of cross-reference does not merely add depth to the minor characters in act 2. Because it also works retrospectively, the double casting in addition sheds new light on some of the characters in act 1, thereby completing the picture Sondheim and Lapine draw of certain types in the art world and the function they have for the artist.[8]

If one compares the characters each actor plays in both parts of the show and compares those roles that are similar in outline, it becomes clear that most of the roles in act 2 either present another facet of the parallel character in the first act or demonstrate another side of the function these characters serve in the overall scheme of the show—all in order to accentuate those respects in which the art world has changed or remained the same in the century between 1884 and 1984. Thus the whole musical represents several series of variations on a theme.

The Same Actor in Different Parts

Let us first consider what can be inferred from comparing the two roles played by the same actor. The following table schematizes the doubling of actors (Table 11.1).

1. George I and George II

In both acts the artist represents creativity—creativity in full bloom in 1884 and creativity more and more undermined by self-doubt in 1984. The two Georges want what all artists crave for: to make something startling and original that might surprise themselves as much as the rest of the (art) world. Both figures use the identical phrase when talking about their artistic goal. The painter George I says: "I am trying to get through to something new."[9] Later, "sculptor-inventor" George II sings (in "Move On"): "I want to know how to get through, / Through to something new, / Something of my own—" (106) but apart from this common aim there are several noteworthy aspects in which George II deviates from his forebear.

In both acts the artist utters the phrase "Connect, George" as a reminder to himself (59; 101), and the different meanings of that phrase in act 1 and act 2 highlight the major difference between George I and George II. George I has hardly any social contact at all, which is how he wants it to be. He seems awkward with the other Parisians who stroll through the park and quite often is considered to be either rude or arrogant, which, in turn, may be one of the reasons why he prefers to be alone. Not given to compromises either in his work or in his personal relationships (he flatly tells his mistress "I cannot be what you want" [53]), George I comes across as self-contained. Dot puts it like this: "You are complete, George" (53). Up to a certain point that's true: he can still go on as a painter without Dot or any of his other acquaintances. So when it becomes clear that even Dot cannot be what George I needs her to be, he lets her go without putting up much of a fight. Knowing that he, too, can never be what she wants him to be (he simply "cannot give [her] words," [53]), George I accepts Dot's decision to leave. But his longing to "con-nect" with other people remains, showing the astute awareness that in the end he *has* to find ways of opening up to friends, lovers, and his family, because even George I cannot live completely cut off from the rest of the world: like every human being he needs love, understanding, and reassurance.

George II's urge to "connect" on the other hand refers to the "family tree," meaning the artistic tradition that he too is part of. Artistically speaking every artist must know where she or he comes from, because this is a prerequisite if she or he doesn't want to repeat her- or himself or others. First she or he needs to understand what the artists that came before have done and how they have expressed their ideas and feelings and then she or he has to decide for her- or himself which of these artistic modes and means of expression to develop and which to cast aside in order to explore something new. So George II has to reconnect with the artistic tradition, to find a way of experiencing it as inspiring instead of restrictive. Only then will he be able to go on.

In that respect the focus has shifted in act 2, which shows the artist at a crossroads in his career, trying to navigate his way to a new beginning. What hasn't changed is that George II feels as insecure working the room and connecting with other people as his great-grandfather did a century earlier. The reception at the museum makes this abun-dantly clear: Always looking for "the perfect excuse...to leave early" (98), George II would rather go home.

But in contrast to the painter in 1884, the sculptor-inventor in 1984 cannot avoid socializing if he wants to continue being an artist, because it would jeopardize his work if he is not able to "network." In more ways than one, nowadays "[k]eeping at a distance doesn't pay" (89). Social contact in the twentieth century has become the starting point to secure funding for creative work and is therefore an economic necessity. So George II has chiefly one aim to accomplish at the reception: "Putting in a personal appearance, / Gathering supporters and adherents..." (94).

2. Dot and Marie

The characters played by Bernadette Peters signify the artist's inspiration, first (act 1) through Dot's sensuality and in act 2 through the sense of (family) history that Dot's daughter conveys: it is Marie who urges George II to find a connection to the "family tree" and then gives him the little red book that will make such a connection possible. Marie's insistence on referring back to the artistic tradition represents the first step in the process that finally enables George II to go ahead and start something new. In addi-tion both characters have aspirations to do something outside the norm. Dot entertains (and finally rejects) the idea of becoming a "Follies girl" (18) and Marie explains to the visitors of the museum that she once was a "Floradora" girl (76).

Moreover, both women have problems with concentration, Dot because she has not yet mastered the technique of being a model and Marie because of her age. So when we first see them the two digress from the task at hand: to stand still in the first half of the show and to introduce the chromolume in the second part. There also is a connection between Dot's reproach to George I "I am something you can use" (52) and George II's way of incorporating his own grandmother into the presentation of his newest piece of work. In a way the artist is "using" Marie for his own means. Mother and daughter both think that George is too much preoccupied with his art. This leads Dot to storm out angrily when George I doesn't make good on his promise to take her to the "Follies." Marie too expresses her regret that for George II, there only is "Work. Work. Work" (86).

Marie ("I don't understand what it was…" [98]) and Dot would be hard pressed to explain what real art is. The latter's idea of an immortal creation—"Something nice with swans" (7)—is rather commonplace if not downright bourgeois. But both intuitively sense that George has extraordinary talent and is up to something amazing, with Dot confirming that George is "good" (7) and Marie proudly announcing, "Mama, he makes things—/ Mama, they're good" (98). What they also have in common is a sense of family. The knowledge that she is going to have a baby finally gives Dot "[a] mission to see" (54). Marie for her part lectures Blair, Harriet, and Billy: "Family. You know, it is all you really have" (86), adding "there are only two worthwhile things to leave behind when you depart this world: children and art" (97). It is obvious that it was Marie's mother Dot, who instilled that idea of what is important in her daughter, because when Dot goes to America her concern is to take two things with her: her baby and the painting in which she is powdering herself—children and art.

3. The Old Lady and Blair

The two matrons played by Barbara Bryne both make demands on the artist. George I's mother presses him to "[q]uick, draw it all" (56) before it fades and thus is lost forever. In other words the old lady wants George I to bear witness. Art critic Blair Daniels urges George II to get over his fascination with chromolumes which to her have become a dead end. She challenges him to develop something new and more substantial. Both women are anxious that "George" may have lost his way, one (the old lady: "I worry about you" [58]) because of the instability in his personal life and the other because he isn't fulfilling the promise that his earlier work held. So Blair criticizes George II because: "I think you are capable of far more" (93). The two characters both complain about a lack of warmth in George's behavior and in his work: whereas his mother in Act 1 informs the audience that, for her, artists are "unfeeling" (26), Blair congratulates George II on his idea of incorporating his grandmother in the presentation of his latest piece of work as it "added a certain humanity to the proceedings" (92).

George I's mother says: "I do not like what I see today…" (27). That line could be uttered by Blair as well who seems to be very critical of today's artists and their accomplishments. The old lady is upset about the "lack of discipline" (27) in the younger generations and chides them for not going "in the right direction at all" (27). This sentiment is mirrored in Blair's short summary of what is wrong with the latest installment in George II's ongoing series of sculptures: "We've been there before, you know" (93). Nevertheless, they also both have great trust in his talent, the old lady knowing that her son will render her world "beautiful" (56) in his paintings, and Blair reminding George II, "I have touted your work from the beginning" (93). Of the old lady, it is said that "[s]he's everywhere" (3), a feeling that many artists must have about the critics that pester them with their comments and often unwanted opinions. George I's mother's comment, "George was always off and running, and I was never able to keep up with him" (74), could also serve to illuminate the relationship between George II and Blair. The same thing might be said about the gap between artists and those who review their work: the history of the arts is full of critics who were unable to see how far certain artists were ahead of their time. When it comes to discovering and praising the kind of work that is really innovative, reviewers can seldom keep pace with art.[10]

Both women are single: George I's mother is a widow and, judging from her abrupt departure following Marie's question, "Are you married, Miss Daniels?" (97), Blair has obviously never had a husband.

4. Jules and Bob

Bob Greenberg, the head of the museum, where George II presents his newest creation, admits that when it comes to art and the direction it takes, "[n]o one can be an oracle" (83). Certainly Jules, Bob's counterpart in the first act, cannot see into the future. Although he is a painter himself, Jules never really understands what George I is up to. In spite of having encouraged him "since they were in school" (49), he does not recognize George I's uniqueness. In addition, both Jules and Bob remark on the speed with which trends in the art world come and go ("Jules: These things get hung—/ . . . / And then they're gone." [12]; "Bob: . . . something new pops up every day" [81]). As Jules is not based on a real artist such as Seurat he comes across as someone who is interested in art, but does not possess the special something that would make him and his work immortal. (Even though George I is of the opinion that "Jules is a fine painter" [14], the audience never gets a chance to judge for itself.) That is why Jules's greatest asset seems to be not his questionable talent but his ability to get paintings into an exhibition. It is therefore fitting that the character played by Charles Kimbrough after the interval is the head of a museum, a man who can help other artists without being one himself and whose aim it is "to form collections" (88). Bob's real status is probably summed up best in his remark, "Ladies and gentlemen, dinner is served" (96); over the course of history Jules, the minor artist, has been reduced to the role of a domestic.

Insisting that the artist must keep company and maintain social contacts, Jules advices George I: "Your life needs spice, George. Go to some parties. That's where you'll meet prospective buyers" (36). This is exactly what George II is doing in the second half of the musical, presumably following Bob's advice. It is also very apt that Jules should say to George, "I have touted your work in the past and now you are embarrassing me!" (50), because it is Bob, giving George II the opportunity to display his talent, who has to save the situation after the blackout during the presentation of Chromolume #7 by appearing before the audience and diverting it while the artist and his assistant sort out their technical problems.

5. Yvonne and Naomi

The two characters played by Dana Ivey, Yvonne and Naomi, have in common their dependence on other people's opinion. Yvonne is hurt by the fact that Dot doesn't like her and formulates her impressions of George I's work with great care so that her husband won't take offence. It's obvious that Jules agrees with her observations about George I's accomplishments only as long as they coincide with his own. The number "No Life" is staged in such a way that it gives the impression of the art pupil Yvonne trying to please her art master with the appropriateness of her remarks. Jules seems to examine her, at one point even consenting to something she has said with a rather patronizing "Good" (12). Naomi, the composer, seems to have no opinion of her own. She agrees with whatever the person she's talking to says, veering between "Well, yes" and "Well, no" (82). In addition, the composer's complaint that in artistic collaboration it is "all compromises" (83) could be taken for a description of Yvonne's marriage, which does not seem a happy one. She spends her life with an artist, although, as she admits, "Talk of painting bores me" (48). Lack of interest in one's partner's profession surely is a poor basis for any sort of relationship. The marriage seems to work mainly because Yvonne makes compromises, giving in to her husband's urges and wishes.

6. Franz and Dennis

Brent Spiner played two highly strung characters, the servant Franz (act 1) and George II's technical assistant Dennis (act 2). Each of these hired helps is told to "relax"—by Frieda and George II, respectively (36; 90)—and both suffer from delusions about an artist's life. Franz believes that to create a painting is a pleasurable pastime for lazy people: "I should have been an artist. I was never intended to work" (35). In a way it seems that Lapine and Sondheim cure Franz of his false notions in the second act. Dennis obviously quit his job at NASA because he labored under the false impression that creating art would be less stressful and competitive. He started working for George II, only to realize that the pressure in the art world is not only much higher than he anticipated but is in fact even higher than in a governmental or high-tech work environment (9). In the end, each character stops being a hired help: Dennis quits and Franz gets fired.

7. Frieda and Betty

In turn, both Frieda and Betty defend the artist from what they feel is undeserved criticism. The German cook corrects her husband who thinks that painters are lazy by stating, "Artists work, Franz. I believe they work very hard" (35). Betty on the other hand is very angry with fellow artist Alex for sharply criticizing George II and retaliates by declaring that he is "talking crap" (82). Frieda's view of art and the artist is somewhat unusual for the characters in the first act. In that respect she represents the opposite of Jules. Jules should know better, but "can only see [George] as everyone else does" (51). Therefore he is reduced in the second half from being an artist himself to being "merely" the head of a museum, whereas Frieda becomes creative in her own right. Another explanation for why Frieda is promoted to the status of an artist (Betty) is that she—like Yvonne who "rather fancied George" (74) and later on becomes the composer, Naomi— is attracted to the painter ("George had beautiful eyes" [73]). It is the case that Sondheim and Lapine have rewarded those characters in the first act that feel attracted to George by making them creative in the second act, although this may not have been a conscious decision. They do, however, deliberately "punish" those that are too critical (Jules and the old lady) by turning them into figures on the periphery of the creative process.

8. The Boatman and Charles

The roles played by William Parry offer the audience a sense of perspective. As Stephen Banfield has pointed out, the one-eyed boatman in act 1 praises his own unambiguous viewpoint[11] whereas (to him) George is saddled with seeing things in three dimensions, with all the problems that this may bring: "One eye, no illusion—/ That you get with two" (38).

Charles Redmond, curator of the County Museum of Texas, gives us a clue how George II's work is perceived in the art world. The comments of his friends, colleagues, and critics are less trustworthy, as they all seem likely to judge George II subjectively. As the only one who is knowledgeable about art and still praises the artist's work (Charles deems it "just tremendous" [87]), without knowing George II personally, Charles's opinion is that of an outsider and therefore especially valuable. The boatman and the curator also both appear to have achieved what George I and II are striving for: by being even more rude to his fellow beings than the painter, the boatman safeguards his privacy ("No one comes near" [23]), and the curator has no problem at all with networking, because he is clearly more outgoing in nature than George II. Finally, the boatman complains about the arrogance of certain painters ("Condescending artists" [25]), something the curator must also have encountered in his work.

9. Louis and Billy

In both parts of the show the characters portrayed by Chris Groenendaal are rather simple men who get brought to the artist by the woman they love. Neither Louis the baker, whose "thoughts are not hard to follow" (39), nor Billy Webster ("I can't say that *I* understand" [80]), could be categorized as intellectuals. The only other information the audience receives concerning Louis is that he is "lovable" (39), loves Dot very much, and is good in bed. (Dot tries to make George jealous by hinting at Louis' hands-on sexual approach: "he kneads me / I mean, like dough" [39]). If one assumes that Billy, Harriet's boyfriend, possesses the same qualities, it would explain why she hooked up with him.

10. The Soldier and Alex

The soldier whose name, as he later confesses to the two shopgirls, is Napoleon, returns in the second part of the show as Alex the artist, who in his own estimation may be too radical to be successful ("My stuff is a little too inaccessible" [91]). Both characters mix socially "[t]rying to make connections" (88). Napoleon, on the lookout for food and female companionship, clearly introduces himself and his fellow soldier to the two Celestes in order to seduce them. With this plan of attack he behaves like a true soldier, prepared to go into battle and conquer. This is exactly what Alex does: he attacks George II in order to force the artist into submission by having him admit that his chromolumes are merely "pleasant" and too unthreatening to be true art. Moreover when the soldier says to his deaf-mute friend that, "We may get a meal and we might get more" (44), the remark also indicates what motivated Alex in choosing to attend the presentation of George II's newest creation in spite of Alex's distaste for his colleague's work. The dinner reception after the presentation not only offers food but also the chance to get one of the all-important commissions.

11. Mr. and Lee

Both Mr. and Lee Randolph, who is in charge of public relations for the museum, like to seize opportunities. Disappointed with Paris which "looks nothing" like the paintings (40), Mr. turns his trip to Europe into a success by exporting the one thing the French can do better than the Americans—pastries. In that respect he is as much "spreading the news" as is Lee, who values the dinner reception at the museum because it offers "a lot of opportunity for some nice press" (89). So the character played by Kurt Knudson is simply transformed from promoting pastries to promoting art, thereby indicating that in the twentieth century art has become just one more product in a line of commodities.

12. Mrs. and Harriet

Lack of understanding characterizes both Mrs. and Harriet Pawling. Mrs. has no command of the French language and doesn't know what to make of French culture. Harriet may be a board member, but she does not really know what to make of George II's "Sunday: Island of Light" ("I mean, I don't understand completely" [80]). In addition to this, she also has to ask Marie what exactly "that square form" (96) in the painting signifies and greets George II with the not very intelligent remark: "This is the third piece of yours I've seen. They are getting so large" (84). Nonetheless, the two wealthy ladies are willing to shell out money to sponsor what they think are worthwhile causes—the sea voyage of a baker and his family in act 1, so that America will get a chance to taste Louis' culinary inventions, and new art projects in act 2, so that America will get a taste of the newest development in the arts.

13. Celeste 1 and Waitress

The shopgirl Celeste 1 returns in act 2 as another hired help, a waitress. For the latter, it would seem natural to have the same feelings about her job as Celeste 1 gives vent to in act 1: "Do you like your work? I hate mine" (60).

14. Celeste 2 and Elaine

Just as Celeste 2 seems to be a hanger-on to the more forthright Celeste 1, the character Mary D'Arcy plays in the second half of the show (Elaine) seems to be a hanger-on to her ex-husband George II. Elaine's character is very difficult to grasp as she isn't on stage for long and doesn't say very much when she is. As the audience only gets informed by Marie that "these children have remained close" (85), we can only guess what went wrong with their marriage. One possibility is that Elaine and George II simply experienced a variation of the problems that finally lead to the separation of George I and Dot. Another imaginable scenario is hinted at in the following exchange between the two shopgirls. Celeste 1: "They say that George has another woman." Celeste 2: "I'm not surprised" (24).

Table 11.2 Parallel roles in act 1 and act 2

No	Role	Act 1 (1884)	Act 2 (1984)
1	artist	George, *painter*	George, *sculptor-inventor*
2	love interest	Dot, *mistress*	Elaine, *ex-wife*
3	family member	Old lady, *mother*	Marie, *grandmother*
4	colleagues	Jules, *painter*	Betty and Alex, *artists*
5	Caretaker	Nurse	Elaine, *ex-wife*
6	Critic	Jules, *painter*, and Yvonne, *wife*	Blair Daniels, *art critic*
7	the significant other	Yvonne, *wife*	Billy Webster, *boyfriend*

Parallel Roles in Act 1 and Act 2

A completely different set of parallels and meanings is revealed when one compares those roles in *Sunday in the Park with George* that are similar in both acts (Table 11.2). Here, not every role in the first act has its equivalent in the second half of the show.

1. The Painter and the Sculptor-inventor

Although the two Georges have a lot in common when it comes to their understanding of art and its functions, their working conditions are completely different. The environment in which George II works is much more complicated and in many ways more hostile to the creative mind than the Parisian society of the 1880s. George I (alias Seurat) experiments with the approximation of natural light by means of a special painting technique. The painter's artificial light has its counterpart in the use of laser beams for the sculpture in act 2. This is the closest connection between the painting "A Sunday afternoon" and the chromolume "Sunday: Isle of Light," as art has become three-dimensional: The flat canvas has turned into a sculpture that sends laser beams in all directions. Moreover, art today is often a mixture of several art forms that were once displayed separately. As the stage directions describe it, the chromolume is "a coordinated performance of music, text, film projections and light emissions" (75). But this new rather complicated approach to being creative has the disadvantage that the meaning of art is no longer self-evident. Like most modern art it needs to be—to paraphrase George I—taken apart and put back together again (51). To help the audience in the museum (and the Broadway audience) George II gives a short presentation before activating his latest invention.

The dominance of positivist science in the nineteenth century resulted in an absolute separation between the sphere of science, which established the facts of the material world, and the realm of the art, which expressed the visions of the imagination. This is why George I's paintings at first meet with derision and misunderstanding. Even Jules, a fellow artist, insists, "You're a painter, not a scientist" (50). In 1984 no one either takes offence or is irritated when George II proclaims: "I think of myself as an inventor as well as a sculptor" (84). In the 1980s it has become customary, virtually the norm, for artists to use any available device in order to execute their vision. In the 1980s we inhabit a world where everything has become faster: it takes two years to paint *La Grande Jatte* (76), whereas the chromolumes can be finished in only one (86).

Although George I, too, has "image problems" (his infamous visit to the zoo has most of the characters in act 1 gossiping), nowadays the way in which the artist is perceived by others—especially by the people who give out commissions or fund the arts—is much more important. George II knows about the necessity of "[b]uilding up the image" (89). Sometimes the personality or the image of the artist can become more important than his work. Image and agenda, artist and artistic creation can become so entwined that even the artist can get confused. George II at first informs us networking is necessary "[s]o that you can go on exhibit-," only to correct himself: "[s]o that your *work* can go on exhibition." (92)

There is also a difference in the artist's perception of himself. Missing from act 2 are the abundant allusions of the first half of the show (especially in "Finishing the Hat"), that represent the painter as god-like creator. George I proclaims: "I revise the world" (56), because like an all-powerful being he arranges what he sees into something that "is beautiful" (55). Later it is said of the painter that the other visitors to the park "hated him because they knew he would always be around" (74)—like God. The understanding of the artist as a person who can create whole new worlds has long been supplanted by a less romantic idea or ideal.

Today artists seem to be less sure of themselves and their power to invent a universe of their own, and are more given to introspection and doubt. That is because the artist is in a position of greater dependency: he is dependent on other people's contributions (in the form of money, creative input, or technical assistance). This perhaps is the major difference between George I and his great-grandson: the latter is dependent on collaborators. George II needs a technician for his chromolume to work at all and he has hired a composer to heighten the impact of his creation.[12] George I on the other hand isn't really dependent on others to be creative. Although he uses Dot for sketching, for example to study the light and to try out certain poses for the characters in his painting, it becomes obvious later on that he can work without models as he has drawn most of the other people in the park without them noticing it and without their permission (28).

But if one is forced either to collaborate with other artists or to work for conglomerates, foundations, or other corporate sponsors, obligated to "put the names of [your] contributors" on your creations (86), it quickly shatters any delusions of grandeur. That the artist's position in modern society can be a demeaning one is illustrated by the simple fact that today when there's "no electricity," there sometimes is "no art" (78).The attitude of the artist towards his peers changes as well. In 1884 George I rebuffs Jules with: "I do not paint for your approval" (37). But in 1984, George II admits that it "means a lot" (91) to him when fellow artist Betty confirms: "I like the new machine, George" (91). The reason for this new attitude simply may be that George II cannot say "I am what I do" with the same conviction as his great-grandfather (53). George I when talking to his painting as if it were another person—a companion in his rebellion against the whole (art) world—underlines: "But we will not let anyone deter us, will we?" (51).

Such a position is more difficult to maintain a hundred years later. It never becomes quite clear what George I actually lives on (it seems likely that his mother supports him), but colors and a canvas are cheap when compared to lasers and state-of-the-art computers. This is why George II can work only when he gets a commission. Therefore, in the time-honored way of (American) politics, what he does at the reception is fundraising. This is why he needs "a little dab of politician" (88). What hasn't changed is the attention the artist pays to "every little detail" (86) and the overall construction of the whole: "Putting it together—/ That's what counts" (87). And as every work of art is an offer to communicate, an invitation to start a discussion, no creative work ever was produced merely for the benefit of the artist. George I admits: "I want it to be seen" (50). This is the one point where he seems to be truly vulnerable. That still holds true for George II who in the second act sings: "If no one gets to see it, / It's as good as dead" (86).

2. and 3. The Mistress and the Ex-wife; The Mother and the Grandmother

The personal relationships of the artist are depicted through the way George I and II behave towards their "love interests" and their one remaining family member. In both cases the ties grow more distanced in one respect while becoming closer in another, reminding us that although relationships may in the abstract seem less intimate they can actually be warmer and full of understanding. Dot, the mistress, turns into Elaine, the ex-wife, as if to cut short any discussion about whether George and Dot, the artist and the woman in his life, would have been happier together if he simply had asked her to be his wife. Sondheim and Lapine make it clear that marriage alone is no guarantee of a successful relationship. But even though George II and Elaine are no longer a couple, they "have remained close" (85). In act 1, the physical attraction between George and Dot not only inspires the artist, but also makes their affair combustible and volatile. With sexual desire and jealousy no longer leading to aggressive (and creative) outbursts, the relationship between the partners calms down, and George II and Elaine can become friends. But obviously the artist will never get the "woman that [he] wanted" (45) because either she will not put up with the fact that his art always comes first (as in act 1, maybe even in act 2, as we don't know what led to the divorce) or because her empathy for the artist is limited. Elaine cannot for instance really understand the self-doubts of George II that have already started to set in during the reception, insisting: "You're the toast of the party. You should feel wonderful" (98). Moreover, both of the young women urge George to seek out social contact and enjoy a little diversion: Dot wants him to take her to the "Follies," and Elaine persuades George to stay at the party, even though he'd rather be at home or—which is more likely—at his studio.

The mother turns into a grandmother which means there literally is a "generation gap" between the artist and his closest relative in the twentieth century. Nevertheless, the bond between George II and Marie is much closer than the one between George I and the old lady. In 1884 the latter seems to be embarrassed that she has a painter for a son. When he reminds her of who he is she answers only with "Shh," described by the stage directions "as if it is to be a secret"(15). In contrast to this behavior, Marie in 1984 tells everyone who will listen to her how proud she is of her creative grandson. Both George II's great-great-grandmother as well as his grandmother at one point do not recognize George. In the first act the line "It's George, mother" (15) always gets a laugh, and in the second act Marie admits, "I thought you were your father for a moment" (99). They both also adore the artist for being able to render the world as it is. That is why the old lady demands of George I, "Quick, draw it all!" (56), and Marie gushes to George II,

"Isn't it lovely how artists can capture us?" (100). Furthermore, both women think that George and his work are not emotional enough. The old lady chides her son for being "unfeeling" (26) and Marie, too, gently presses George II to show "a little more feeling" (100) in his sculptures.

4. Jules and Betty/Alex

In the first act the audience meets only one of George I's colleagues, Jules. In the second act the number of "other visual artists" has doubled to include Alex and Betty. This not only indicates that more people are trying to make their living by being creative nowadays, but also that it is no longer considered unusual for women to do so. (Naomi, the composer, could serve as another example.) But now as then the art world is a competitive place, where painters are struggling to get their new work into exhibitions (act 1) or compete with one another for attention and commissions (act 2)—"fighting for prizes," as Betty puts it (83). That leads to professional envy (Jules and Alex are accused of being jealous of George by Dot and Betty respectively [49, 95][13]). The put-downs of artists critical of one another's work haven't changed much. There is not much difference between Jules' snide remark that George I's paintings show "no presence. / No passion. / No life." (11) and Alex's view that George II's chromolumes can be faulted for having "[n]o nuance, no resonance, no relevance" (95). Dot accuses Jules and his wife of "spying" on George, and it is possible that Betty and Alex are doing just the same when visiting the presentation in act 2, even though at least one of them (Betty) is deeply sympathetic and offers generous praise for the chromolume.

But what is different in 1984 is the part that artists play in acquainting the public with new talents. In 1884 it is through the recommendation of Jules, a fellow painter, that George I might have his *Sunday Afternoon on the Island of La Grande Jatte* presented in an exhibition. A hundred years later a whole array of curators, board members, heads of museums, and art critics has the power to decide which artist to feature or nurture next. In that respect the artistic community is no longer self-contained and artists are no longer judged merely by their peers.

5. The Nurse and Elaine

George's desire for privacy will not allow him to accept help from other people. The nurse informs us at the beginning of act 2 that she "offered to take care for him, but he would let no one near" (74). It is not far-fetched to assume that this remark would also make sense when uttered by Elaine. But more important for our judgment of the artist is that he never takes care of his ailing family members himself, probably because he doesn't want to be distracted from his work. George I has engaged a nurse for his mother, and it seems fine with George II to leave his grandmother mostly in the care of his ex-wife. This behavior also goes to show that in the 1980s nursing is still commonly considered a woman's job (and George II himself shares the prejudice).

6. Jules/Yvonne and Blair

In the 1880s paintings are mostly criticized by other artists and their relatives, but a century later art criticism has become a fully-fledged profession. The negative comments by Jules and his wife about George I's *Une Baignades Asnières* mostly seem to be the result of differing concepts of art (Dot also suspects it to be a sign of jealousy). So the opinions of the couple come across as merely expressions of taste and therefore as subjective. With Blair Daniels it is different. She is prepared and knowledgeable: "I've read all there is to read about this work" (97).[14] But instead of just putting George down, as Jules and Yvonne do, Blair encourages George II to try something different: "there are new discoveries to be made, George" (93). But every artist is wary of critics, and therefore George II at first contradicts Blair's views on his work with "I disagree" (93). He decides only later that Blair may have a point and turns down the commission from the "County Museum of Texas."

So all in all the portrait of the critic and the uses she or he may have for the artist could be considered to be balanced: Sondheim and Lapine are not simply taking cheap shots at reviewers in general. Nevertheless in this respect it is important to take note of the fact that even though the critic's advice may be enough to start George II thinking he may be going in the wrong direction, it is only after his technical assistant and close friend, Dennis, points out to him that Chromolume #7 is just more of the same ("I've helped you build the last five, and now I want to do something different" [102]), that George II's crisis of self-doubt reaches its climax as expressed in the song "Lesson #8." In the end, the critics' reaction to an artist's work certainly can be helpful, but may not be sufficient. It needs friends to help the artist see the errors of her or his ways. Obviously it takes someone trustworthy to finally convince the artist that she or he has painted her- or himself into a corner, and the critic is not necessarily that person.

7. Yvonne and Billy

Yvonne and Billy are dragged along by their respective partners to artists and exhibitions even though in Yvonne's case they don't really care about art ("Talk of painting bores me" [48]) or, like Billy, they can't really figure out what it is all about ("I can't say that I understand" [80]). But it is interesting to note that there is a change of gender: in the twentieth century it is also possible for men to be the "significant other."

Conclusion: The Art World Now and Then

In the first act only two people (George and Jules) make a living out of art. Two more (Dot and the Old Lady) are interested in it purely for personal reasons, Dot because she wants to gain immortality and the Old Lady because she needs someone to preserve her favorite views of Paris for her. Most of the others, like the two Celestes and Franz, are curious about the artist, but finally are more concerned about their own hopes and wishes. In 1884, many of them spend their leisure time in pursuit of romance or sex (Jules, Frieda, Franz, the nurse, the shopgirls, and the soldiers come to mind). A hundred years later all of ten people including artists (George, Betty, and Alex) and composers (Naomi), curators (Charles), heads of museums (Bob), board members (Harriet), art critics (Blair), public-relations experts (Lee), and even technicians (Dennis) dabble in the arts or at least on the fringes of the art scene, and each and every one of them has his or her own agenda (Figure 11.2).

The preoccupations of the characters have changed. Even in their spare time (most exhibition openings take place in the evening after the day's work is done) people in the twentieth century use social gatherings mostly as an excuse for making business transactions: art is something to negotiate after careful networking. Schemes for romantic involvements give way to economic schemes. The artists try to get sponsors or commissions, because as George II reminds himself and us, "Machines don't grow on trees, George" (84), whereas the curators, heads of museums, and board members are on the look-out for the next artistic sensation that can bring prestige and paying customers to their institutions. Several occupations that were performed by the artistic community itself, such as criticizing the artist or promoting him, have turned into professions (the art critic, the head of museum, the curator, the board member, the public-relations expert). Art has become an industry. Now the art scene offers job opportunities to many people and only a minority of those (four out of ten) actually are artists and thus could really be called creative; the others simply feed off the artists. Because of that, the artistic scene is a much more crowded arena than it was a century ago. But for the artists it is still a world full of envy and rivalry, even though most of them realize that up to a certain point they must either work together to create anything at all or at the very least fight for the same goals (arts subsidy for instance), as artists are an endangered species in a society that operates on strict capitalistic principles: "Advancing art is easy—/ . . . / Financing it is not" (86). The whole situation is neatly summed up in "So you should support the competition / Try to set aside your own ambition / Even while you jockey for position—" (91).

Striking the right balance between asserting oneself and fighting side by side with one's fellow artists is something that every creative person must achieve—one detail more in the eternal struggle of "putting it together."

NOTES

1. See Craig Zadan, *Sondheim & Co.* (New York: Harper & Row, 1989), 296.
2. To differentiate the two, the painter of act 1, inspired by Georges Seurat, will be called George I, while his great-grandson, the "sculptor-inventor" of act 2, will be called George II.
3. At first the creators had a completely different approach to those characters featured prominently in the painting that is at the center of the first act of *Sunday, A Sunday Afternoon on the Island of La Grande Jatte.* James Lapine is quoted as saying: "The original idea was for all the secondary characters to have songs. What we discovered in the workshop was that people weren't interested in them" (Zadan, *Sondheim & Co.*, 303). Therefore, the focus of the show shifted back to George and Dot.
4. See Zadan, *Sondheim & Co.*, 307.
5. Without having seen the production at Playwrights Horizon or having access to the authors' notes, one can only speculate whether Bette who in act 2 turned into Betty the artist, later in the history of the show developed into Frieda, the cook. This is very likely though, as both roles were played—as were Frieda/Betty on Broadway—by Nancy Opel.
6. Stephen Banfield, *Sondheim's Broadway Musicals* (Ann Arbor: University of Michigan Press, 1993), 365.
7. Analyzing the second half of *Sunday in the Park with George*, Banfield for instance states that "[a]ll that the shorter Act 2 lacks is the series of miniature studies for the minor characters." (Banfield, *Sondheim's Broadway Musicals*, 367)
8. It could be argued that most of the later productions of *Sunday in the Park* (like the London and German productions) did not adhere to the casting scheme as proffered by the Broadway version, and that therefore the following reading of the play is based on the specifics of a single (or singular) production. But casting always depends on the abilities of the respective ensemble and at least for the original production Lapine and Sondheim knew the cast members well enough and early enough—many of them had already taken part in the workshop production of *Sunday*—to tailor the parts to the specific talents each of them could bring to the show. The previews that preceded the Broadway opening on May 2, 1984, then gave the authors several weeks to fine-tune the combination of actor and role.
9. Stephen Sondheim and James Lapine, *Sunday in the Park with George* (London: Nick Hern, 1990), 50. Copyright © 1990 by Nick Hern Books, London. Used by permission. All further page references to the published libretto will be given within the text.
10. Case in point: most of the reviews for *Sunday in the Park with George* and the Tony Award Committee, which opted for the mildly risqué but essentially dated *La Cage aux Folles* as "Best Musical of the Year."
11. See Banfield, *Sondheim's Broadway Musicals*, 369.
12. That there is a close connection between painting and composing is established in act 1, when George I describes his painting technique as "fixed laws for color, like music," thus preparing us for the combination of sculpture and music in act 2.
13. Jules may also resent George for having such a "pretty" (Jules' word) mistress (36) while he himself is saddled with a shrill, middle-aged, rather unattractive wife and a brat of a child.
14. On the other hand this remark may also indicate that her understanding of art consists mainly of book knowledge.

CHAPTER 12

....

"SOMETHING JUST BROKE": *ASSASSINS* AFTER THE IRAQ WAR—A PRODUCTION AND ITS RECEPTION

....

JOANNE GORDON

To what extent is every artistic act political? Growing up in the repressive atmosphere of the rigid apartheid system in South Africa, the answer seemed self-evident. Even though my taste tended toward the lush melodic world of Rodgers and Hammerstein rather than the seething anger of agitprop, I knew that everything we did in the theater could be a protest against the immorality that permeated our lives. I remember vividly the huge public furor when Inia Te Wiata, the Maori bass, led the chorus of black singers in *Showboat* on the hallowed stage of the exclusively white Civic Theatre. The issue, as I recall, centered on bathrooms. At the theater everything was segregated. The actors' bathrooms were designated for the use of whites only and the powers that be did not know what to do with the cast of black singers. Things became progressively more absurd when, in response to his huge success and popularity, Te Wiata was invited back to the Civic to play the lead in *Most Happy Fella*. He was declared an "honorary white" so he could kiss Olive King, the bubbly white ingénue, without breaking the law, and we assumed he was entitled to use the bathroom in the star's dressing room. Olive King's daughter was a schoolmate of mine and I vividly recall the guilty thrill of seeing someone we knew publically flaunt the rigid repression of the Nationalist government.

This surreptitious rebellion continued when as a young woman I directed *South Pacific*. I was working at an exclusive Jewish day school and I was aware that the song "You've Got to Be Taught" had been cut both from the film and the professional theatrical production in South Africa. Including the song was a tiny act of insurrection, but it empowered my students and me. This act was given deeper significance when, after working through all kinds of bureaucratic red tape, and of course promising to utilize separate bathrooms, I gained government permission to invite a group of students from the Indian High School to see our play. As my beautiful young blond Jewish Lieutenant

Cable began to sing, "You've got to be taught to be afraid," the entire audience began to weep. It is a memory I cherish.

What has all this to do with Stephen Sondheim? In the past when I have written about Sondheim's work I have endeavored to be as dispassionate and objective as possible. I saw my task to be that of the analyst, disentangling the complexities, highlighting the intricacies, and sharing my understanding of the theatrical impact of words and music. I assiduously avoided speculation about the artist himself, and other than conveying my obvious enthusiasm for the work, I attempted to remove myself entirely from the text. In discussing the California Repertory Company's production of *Assassins* at the Long Beach Armory, objectivity is impossible. My political conscience and perspective are intrinsic. From a deeply personal place I hope to reveal the broader political resonances of *Assassins* and the impact that the production had on both cast and audience.

The initial decision to stage *Assassins* as Cal Rep's inaugural production at the Armory was an obviously political one. I had grown up profoundly suspicious of and antagonistic to anyone in uniform. As a typical child of the sixties, the armed forces and the police represented a despised repressive authoritarianism. This sense of fear and loathing was exacerbated within the South African context of apartheid. Young and dutifully idealistic, I marched in protest against the daily horrors of the Nationalist regime. With my fellow undergraduates I stood on Jan Smuts Avenue outside the University of Witwatersrand, waving my placard, and laughing at the passing motorists' frustrated attempts to pelt us with eggs. As inequities escalated and freedoms were curtailed our disgust with those who enforced the immoral system grew. Many of my friends and the male members of my family chose to flee South Africa rather than agree to compulsory military service. With the vivid images of Sharpeville, Steve Biko's battered corpse, and the Soweto riots indelibly etched in my mind, my suspicion of anyone in uniform became deeply engrained. It was a prejudice I carried with me as decades later I acquired permission for Cal Rep to perform in the home of the California National Guard.

Our journey to the Armory had been circuitous. The Cal Rep Company had spent the previous ten years in a charming small theater in downtown Long Beach. Then, in late 2006, two weeks prior to the opening of a show, we were forced to vacate as a result of seismic concerns—the joys of living in Southern California. We were homeless, and as artistic director of the company I became progressively more despondent as the months passed. Finally, it was one of my alums who came to our rescue. She is a colonel in the National Guard and with her assistance we were invited to set up shop in a vacant drill hall in the Long Beach Armory. It was less than ideal and I had many reservations and misgivings. The space was large and the acoustics horrible. In addition, I retained my profound suspicion of anyone in uniform.

The relationship began tentatively—with a cricket bat. I had never seen this particular symbol of British imperialism in California before. Swinging in a leisurely pendulum from a pair of strong hands, it evoked images of elegant English gentlemen in immaculate white, crouching behind the wickets. The crack of the ball against the bat conjured up scenes from my own youth—of over-eager pink-cheeked schoolboys emulating their heroes in seemingly endless innings—in the insular world of apartheid. But this bat was held by a young member of the 640th Aviation Support Battalion of the National Guard. He had been given it as a gift by his translator when he served in Afghanistan. The bat suddenly seemed to me the perfect metaphor for the crazy quilt of our contemporary globalized experience. Isolation is impossible—our world has contracted and in a very real sense we are all intimately connected. This fusion of people and cultures gradually compelled me to abandon my preconceived prejudices against people in the military. As we began rehearsing at the Armory, I found myself sharing a space with a generous, hospitable, dedicated, and—I had to acknowledge—idealistic group of people. It was both an enlightening and humbling experience.

The National Guard opened their home and their hearts to welcome our rag-tag band. Our sojourn at the Armory created some interesting challenges and some evocative juxtapositions. Mingling with men and women in uniform opened my eyes. Knowing that anyone of them could be shipped off to the war zone personalized my politics and prevented any slick or easy moralizing. As I thought about our responsibility as artists and citizens facing the daily barrage of news from the front, I realized that I dared not offer any trite platitudes about the artist's noble calling and civic duty. I could not pretend to have any answers. The servicemen and women were living the dangers that we could only simulate and imply in our art. Without any obvious pontificating, I was intent that our first theater piece would gain resonance from its context. *Assassins* proved to be an ideal choice. The musical dramatizes the terrifying fault line that cuts through the American psyche using the sound and language of the American musical. It reveals our society's horrific fascination with guns and the power and impotence of violence in a uniquely American way. Yet, at its core it retains an innocence and idealism that consistently, night after night, brought tears to the eyes of both actors and audience. This fusion of naïveté and chauvinism is inherent in the form and expectation of the musical and Sondheim capitalizes on this implicit duality throughout *Assassins*. Both in musical form and lyric Sondheim evokes a cavalcade of American history in music and word choice. From the somber resonances of "Hail to the Chief," through the jaunty Sousa-like marches, to the sentimental chords of the Carpenters—Sondheim brilliantly recreates periods and attitudes that are thematically united in their distinctly American connotations. He writes of two hundred years of bloodshed and pride and pain; of ideals realized and dreams lost. The musical evokes the past but more significantly cautions about the future.

It is this link between past and future that resonated deeply throughout our production. *Assassins* was first produced during the dark days of the first Bush presidency and in the midst of the bellicose chauvinism of Operation Desert Storm. We went into production during the waning days of Bush the younger and the horrors of the Iraq war filled our television screens. Barack Obama's bid for the presidency was in full swing. I have been teaching at American universities for almost thirty years. During most of this time I have been appalled by the political apathy of my students. I teach at a state school. The majority of my students comes from blue-collar families and appear to be totally politically disaffected. They do not vote; they do not care. They are passionate about their work in the theater—but do not seek or require any kind of political resonance in their art. With Obama's candidacy all this changed. Suddenly here was a young charismatic leader with whom they could identify—and perhaps more significantly in terms of *Assassins*—for whom they were dreadfully afraid and protective. The tragic flaw at the center of the play was suddenly terrifyingly apposite.

Controversy started early in the production process. The designer, Danila Korogodsky, who had been born, educated, and reached artistic maturity during the height of Soviet power in Leningrad, Russia, and I were two passionate voluble Jews. Our production manager was a smart, efficient young female Republican from the Midwest. During our initial design meetings she sat in barely repressed disgust as these two "foreigners" appeared to denigrate her country. We did not want the piece to reflect only our outrage at the current administration or any simplistic didactic message. Danila and I focused on the fascination with guns and violence, murder and the death penalty, and the connection between power and impotence that lie at the heart of the play. Danila had been unaware of the notorious film clip in which Edison boasts of the safety of his electric current by electrocuting an elephant. We watched it, appalled yet transfixed. It seemed to reflect the circus sideshow horror echoed in the style and musical language of *Assassins*. Our discussion ranged from capital punishment, to assassination, to guns, to fairground freak shows, to genetic proclivity to violence. The result was an extraordinary scenic design in which these ideas were fused. Danila created a wild steel sixteen-foot high merry-go-round of death. At its center was an oversized electric chair which served as a nucleus around which this vast

FIGURE **12.1** Craig Fleming as Charles Guiteau in Joanne Gordon's production of *Assassins* (2006).

atomic structure spun. It was poetic, fanciful, and totally appropriate. I had marvelous fun directing on it and the actors shared many moments of abject terror and riotous delight. Our production manager was inflamed. She wrote a long missive of censure condemning us as virulent foreign agents who were mocking and condemning her beloved country. Within weeks she had packed her bags, tendered her resignation and returned to the Midwest. She had missed the point completely. But, our controversial artistic journey had begun.

From the eerie chords of the opening we strove to fuse the two primary themes of the play—perverse patriotism and violence: idealism and impotence. Like the undead, the characters slowly emerged from the gloom to explore the huge steel structure that dominated the stage. (Figure 12.1) The idea of ghosts haunting our history is echoed throughout the piece, culminating in the revivification of all the assassins in the final scene in the Texas book depository. Our ghosts were present from the start—connected yet essentially alone as they climbed slowly up to their seats on the atomic merry-go-round of death. Above, and insular, the actor playing Lee Harvey Oswald sat caressing his rifle. From the start his presence is noted and emphasized. He was never part of the ensemble and this feeling of isolation while intrinsic to the effect of the play proved difficult for the actor to maintain. He felt disconnected and rejected and I encouraged this separation. Oswald embodies both the pinnacle and nadir of the destructive force that permeates US history. His act will provide the climax for the play and the focus for our cathartic feelings of terror and pity. His isolation from the band of assassins was deliberate and effective.

The actor playing Oswald, Scott Fielding, had spent many years studying and teaching in Europe and was a disciple and master teacher of the Michael Chekhov technique. Initially he was very resistant to my approach. He found the notion of being simultaneously present and not present, interacting with a world that he was both part of and separate from, at odds with his notions of actor integrity and character truth. In contrast with Jerry Zaks's original production, in which Oswald made his appearance only very late in the piece, I saw Oswald as a central force from the beginning. He was on stage throughout the play, a lurking malevolent presence absorbing and reflecting the history of violence as it occurs. He is observed by the contemporary audience, but acknowledged by the other assassins only in the penultimate scene of the play. The actor's deliberate exclusion from the group felt to him like rejection and fed his anxiety. This tension reflected the psychological truth of Oswald's character and assisted in the creation of the complex loner. Ultimately the actor embraced the isolation, utilizing Stanislavsky's notion of public solitude and divided consciousness.[1] He realized that he was not acting alone, but was constantly interconnecting with the events on stage and the audience. He could not alter history, but had to absorb it. He was carrying the responsibility for all Americans to understand the source and accept culpability for the assassinations, for the destruction of the dream. It was this sense of guilt and responsibility in the actor and audience that I sought to evoke.

Booth on the other hand exuded the certainty of the fanatic. He was smooth, charismatic, and sanctimonious in his rectitude. His belief in his own ideals is so unflinching that any act is justified. Jeff Paul, an actor I had directed many times over the years, who had played roles as diverse as Henry in *The Lion in Winter*, Salieri in *Amadeus*, and recently the egocentric corrupt father in *Festen*, possessed precisely the kind of demonic charm the character required. His influence was palpable and comprehensible as he inspired and shaped the course of history. The dangers of fanatical belief were self evident; there was no need to belabor the threat or emphasize the contemporary parallels and dangers.

On a very simplistic and superficial level, *Assassins* educated my predominantly young multi-ethnic student audience about pivotal events and attitudes in US history. In an entertaining and accessible way they learned of the exploits of this band of losers. Without effort they experienced the success and failure of the various assassins. By combining characters that were familiar, Booth and Oswald, with the most esoteric of the murderous bunch, like Zangara, Czolgosz, or Byck (an audience favorite), Sondheim and Weidman enlivened the civics lesson. Historical accuracy and verisimilitude are eschewed as the characters encounter each other in an ahistorical limbo. The hilarious scenes between Squeaky Fromme and Sara Jane Moore invite caricature—but when the real Squeaky appealed for clemency our students knew who she was. Moreover, the actress playing Sara, Debbie McLeod, who has had a distinguished musical theater career, found again and again that the songs would not permit her to choose simple caricature or a one-dimensional style. Sara is funny because she is real and authentic in her crazy excesses. The play is anchored by the two most famous central assassins, but *Assassins* revivifies the other bizarre misfits and saves them from the ignominy of being mere historical footnotes.

But the lessons learned were far more profound than a mere accumulation of esoteric historical facts. The broad appeal and relevance of the piece were initially emphasized by my choice of actor to play all the presidents. Dom Magwili is a mature, very politically active, Philipino artist. We spent hours discussing the marginalization of the Asian American actor and his belief that white is still the "default face" of America. Undoubtedly discrimination and stereotyping still exist in the contemporary American theater and society and by choosing to cast the figurehead of power in a nontraditional manner, Dom felt we were compelling the audience to react to their unquestioned assumptions about race and governance. He was delighted with this prospect and utilized the role as the focus of his MFA thesis. However, the interesting fact that emerged was that all that the audience observed was an actor portraying the symbol of authority. No one commented or even appeared to notice that a nonwhite actor was playing the US presidents. The audience brought in its expectations of the truth and made meaning. We had hoped that Dom's presence in the piece would serve as a "visual counternarrative" and evoke the history of racism in the United States. This did not prove to be the case. However, for Dom, discovering that his race truly was irrelevant was illuminating, and enabled him as an actor of color to accept that there is a place for him in the national imagination to dream his American dream.

What was perhaps even more interesting was the impact on and response of our young audiences to the thematic structure. It was chillingly evident that the vast majority of our students came into the theater sharing the cynicism of the assassins themselves. They had given up on the promises of America and readily identified with the bleak contemptuous tone of "Everybody's Got the Right." They shared the sentiments and pessimism of "Another National Anthem." They were the "ones who could not get into the ballpark." Many of them had grown up in neighborhoods scarred by urban violence and neglect. They were angry, disenfranchised and too often distressingly apathetic. I have dedicated my life to empowering these young people through theater. In South Africa I had seen at first hand the ability of the theater artist to change the world—both through the global impact of Athol Fugard and in the vibrant street performances that refused to be suppressed in the shanties and beer halls of Soweto. I am determined to infuse that same commitment into my laid-back Southern California kids. I need them to believe they can change the world.

But as our knowledge of the world expands so it seems our awareness contracts. The attention span of the millennial generation is so attenuated that all political argument or philosophic insight has to be reduced to the easily digested sound bite. As a society we tend to avoid the complex and convoluted. We want all content to be fast, fun, and facile. We have become so addicted to our virtual reality that real life has become incidental. Our ability to experience truth and art and reality has been reduced to the crude interconnections of social networking on the web: Facebook and YouTube, blogging, instant messaging, smartphone addiction, and the gratification and control of a DVR-dominated culture. But theater as a form does not readily relinquish its heft. It is, of necessity, a communal experience that demands of its audience time and commitment. If successful, the theater engages and provokes. It compels us to explore our connections and untangle all the implied ramifications of the theme and plot of a piece. It emphasizes the commonality of experience and the universality of human response. It is alive and real and immediate and dangerous. If effective, it demands that we pay attention to the here and now. "Attention must be paid!" Booth quotes Willy Loman to convince Oswald—but this could be Sondheim's and Weidman's rallying cry. Without didacticism or an overt political agenda *Assassins* compels its audiences to experience the issues and take a stand.

It was the political dimension of *Assassins* that compelled me to direct the piece as our inaugural show at the Armory and it was the political resonance that validated the choice. Without any overt didacticism or preaching, both actors and audience took a journey from cynicism to passionate concern as they experienced the production. The combination of the environment: its ancient cannons outside the doors, the monster Hummers parked in the rear, the slew of young people in uniform, and the knowledge that a huge cache of weapons lay in the basement below our stage, combined with the dawning of a new hope and political awareness inspired by Obama's candidacy, created a febrile atmosphere of tension and expectation. Our audiences were ripe for a cautionary tale and I observed with delight as they plunged willingly and passionately into the world of Sondheim and Weidman. They laughed at the ridiculous antics of so many of the bizarre characters but, as the play moved inexorably towards its tragic climax the dread was palpable. Oswald's presence on stage had been the unavoidable reminder of the inevitable climactic event. The issues Sondheim and Weidman chose to drama-tize are difficult, and they offer no easy solutions. They shy away from trite platitudes and dare us to look into our own heart of darkness—challenge our certitudes—and stir the frightening stew of our complacency. But, for me the poignancy was even more personal.

Something miraculous occurred at each performance. With "Something Just Broke" the reality of loss flooded into the theater. We were performing in a military installation. There were always men and women in uniform in the audience and in the halls of the Armory. These young people were getting ready to be deployed in Iraq. The reality of their service and sacrifice was inescapable as they faced horrors we could only pretend to understand in our theater. The conjoining of their world and ours revealed both the infinite range of theatrical truth and its limitations. We create art in order to shed light on the intractable problems of our contemporary life—they live a life we only imagine. This was coupled with the new incarnation of idealism embodied in Obama. The for-merly cynical young audience had a new leader—one they believed in and one who was so patently vulnerable to the horrors of violence that they had just seen on stage. They wanted to believe in the hope he represented and were dreadfully afraid of the history lesson they had just been taught. Our production was staged almost two years prior to the disgusting spectacle of gun-toting fanatics at the "right wing Tea Party assemblies". Yet, night after night tentative hope collided subconsciously with racist fear as my young ensemble sang "Fix it up fast, please," with tears pouring down their cheeks. They knew what could happen—they knew what was at stake—and they were very frightened.

Our work at Cal Rep is focused on student power and activism and we struggle to nurture aspiring young artists and challenge audiences by developing relevant and thought-provoking work. Over the years as artistic director of the company I have remained intent on proving that as makers of theater, teachers of theater, and students of theater we are profoundly privileged; that in dedicating our lives to the creation of art we must possess the unwavering passion of the fanatic. Despite our location in the center of the Hollywood dream machine we should not solely be driven by the desire for fame and fortune—but rather should develop an unflinching fervor. I have attempted to prove that if theater is merely an intellectual exercise; a casual entertainment; or a self-serving ego trip, it is empty. I want my students to believe that great theater can induce a visceral, vital, life-altering epiphany, that it can change the way we see the world and each other. We are a society in crisis. America is at war. Our environment is threatened and social problems are proliferating. We have to act in the theater and in our community

I have always accepted that it is the theater's responsibility to provoke; that good art is iconoclastic, contentious, and disturbing. Yet, in the past couple of years these assump-tions seem to be in question. A tsunami of censorship has battered artistic institutions in the United States. From the early banning of Mapplethorpe's photography, through the furor over Serrano's provocative work, to the reversal of grants by the NEA and the riots in Denmark in response to the cartoons of the prophet Muhammad, art is under attack. Perhaps the most pernicious form of censorship is self-censorship. It is here that the danger is most imminent. Not only commercial producers are cowardly. Within the rarified cocoon of the nonprofit world, theater companies are afraid to offend. Even in companies as brave and independent as the New York Theatre Workshop, plays have been withdrawn; seasons have been changed in response to a vaguely disguised fear and threat. In backing away from the provocative, these companies are violating the most sacred principles of art. One has only to trace the tangled production history of *Assassins* to understand the tenuous control the artist has over their work and the powerful force of capitalism that controls the marketplace of commercial theater. The first Gulf War caused critics and audiences alike to distort the intention of the musical and undermine its impact. The tragedy of September 11 further highlighted the delicate symbiosis of theater and society. Both these events prevented or delayed a commercial Broadway production of the piece. Yet, Sondheim's musical has prevailed and in many ways has been invigorated by its troubled production history. Certainly I experienced a visceral energy and political awareness stirring in my youthful student audience during every performance of *Assassins* in the Armory. It renewed my passion, both for the genius of Sondheim and for the regenerative and provocative power of art.

The conclusion of this very personal excursion is a rather sad. With the collapse of apartheid and Mandela's ascendancy to power my annual visits to South Africa were filled with naïve optimism. To return to the place where my ruminations began—the bathroom—it was in this most private public place that the miracle of the relatively peaceful transfer of power really hit me. I was standing in line at the Market Theatre— home of much of the brave protest theater during the seventies and eighties—and there we were—black women and white women politely holding the door to the stall for each other. No fuss—no drama—just simple civility. Again my tears flowed. It seemed the long nightmare was over. But, I had not properly learned *Assassins'* brutal lesson.

A couple of months after the production closed I returned to Johannesburg for my annual pilgrimage to visit my aging parents. It had been fifteen years since Mandela's emotional walk to freedom and the realities of poverty, lack of opportunity, and education were evident everywhere. The brutality and hopelessness of people who felt betrayed was evident on every street corner. "Where's my prize—I want my fucking prize" was the new anthem. The AIDS rate was soaring, unemployment was well over 50 percent and Johannesburg had become the murder capital of the world. My parents are in their eighties and like many well-meaning white liberals of their generation have retreated behind looming walls and alarm systems. The Johannesburg of my youth has been transformed. I walked around the neighborhood where I had grown up. As children we rode our bikes, played on sidewalks, young mothers with strollers jostled by toddlers cruised the streets in this quiet suburb—it was all white "Leave it to Beaver" territory. The only nonwhite faces belonged to the nannies and gardeners who maintained the manicured perfection. But now the streets were empty. I was often the only person strolling down desolate lanes shrouded by huge purple blooming jacaranda trees. Where once each house was open and inviting, now only the paranoia of terror was evident in the high walls, electrified fences, alarm systems, and warnings of rapid armed response and ubiquitous barbed wire. I resolutely ignored all these signs of fear and each day set off on my lonely pilgrimage visiting my old haunts and walking around the isolated paths of Emmarentia Dam, determined to ignore the dire warnings of the violence that filled the headlines each day. My visit that year proved to be a difficult one. My mother was clearly not well and after much vigorous persuasion I got her to the cardiologist and within days she was undergoing major heart surgery. But her spirit was indomitable and I was finally able to return to Los Angeles confident she was well on the way to recovery. A mere five days after I returned home the dreaded call came. My parents' home had been ransacked. For two terrifying hours in the middle of the night, they had been held hostage while two men methodically desecrated their home of forty years. Closets were emptied—and with their possessions strewn and trampled all over the floor, their faith destroyed forever. My parent's dream of a postapartheid utopia lay in shambles, lost in the jumble of crumpled clothes in the wreckage of their home.

The harsh reality of shattered illusions was not confined to my personal experiences in South Africa. The election of America's first black president had not resulted in the Mandela-like euphoria I had expected. Rather than signifying the end of racism and the dawn of a post-racial United States, Obama's election resulted in an explosion of fear, insecurity, and bitterness. I now lived in an America in which television images depicted a never-ending flood of hate-filled faces spewing forth vile racist rhetoric at US town-hall meetings. The sight of crazy gun-toting fanatics preening at the rallies where President Obama was scheduled to speak brought the horrifying truth of *Assassins* brutally alive. The threat of the lone assassin taking the law into his own hands is terrifyingly alive and present in the blood-soaked images on the T-shirts worn by so many fundamentalists as they hoist their misspelt placards adorned with brutish slogans and obscene caricatures of their president sporting a Hitlerian moustache. With Kennedy's assassination, something pure and good "broke." The idealism of my generation was tested and the subsequent history of the baby boomers has done little to "fix it up fast please." We wanted to believe that goodness could triumph—that our idealism would flourish. But it is the thumping martial chords of the dispossessed and disengaged who have prevailed. "Everybody's got the right" is the prophetic anthem as the angry, the ignorant, the bigoted, the dispossessed and the violent crowds gather. *Assassins* has proved to be horribly insightful as those of us who cherish the symbolism and hope manifest in the election of the first African American President of the United States now live in terror of the violence that threatens his every move.

In the early days of Sondheim scholarship and criticism, it was the composer and lyricist's supposed cynicism and nihilism that was emphasized. I will never forget the virulent attack that John Lahr[2] launched against *Company* almost forty years ago. Where Lahr saw only harsh chords and sophisticated brittleness, I experienced from the start the soaring, aching melodies and idealistic longing of each new score. My response to Sondheim's work has not really changed. While it would be easy to see only a dark pessimism in *Assassins*, I believe the ultimate message that my student cast and audience retained was the pure idealism of the dream inherent in the glorious melody and heartbreak of "Something Just Broke." The musical both fans the flames of hope and faith in a better America and lays bare the dark currents of violence.

We are all inevitably the products of our environment. The political, aesthetic, and moral forces that shape our individual responses may seem invisible and innocuous—but in seeking to delineate our artistic standards we are inevitably forced to confront and articulate our defining values. As an artistic director, a teacher, and a manager this obligation has become increasingly urgent. My inherent guilt growing up as a very privileged white South African has always been at the forefront of my consciousness. I have glibly defended the art I respected in terms of my response to its political and moral dictates. While consciously avoiding didacticism—I sought to direct plays that espoused the purest of ideals and satirized the greed, racism, and cruelty of my world. But in our increasingly complex world, moral imperatives have become less clear. Certainty is far more difficult to achieve. Fanaticism and idealism are so easily conflated. Ironically, it is in Sondheim's melodies that I have been able to find the balance between the soaring longing of the ideal and the cynical brutality of reality. Music can inspire without being dogmatic. It has been many years since any foolish critic has dismissed the extraordinary melodic range of Sondheim's work. No one questions the ineffable beauty of the scores. But this recognition was a long time in coming. For decades Sondheim's work has enabled me to retain and give voice to my idealism. My professional life has been steeped in the study of his work—and it is with a deep and abiding gratitude that I recognize that even in the darkest hours—his words and music are a beacon; that the political exploration I undertook in directing *Assassins* served as a culmination of my personal journey from passionate political protest to a quiet celebration of the healing power of his art.

NOTES

1. The notion of *public solitude* is the sense the actor has of being alone while surrounded both by other actors on stage, and more importantly fed by the tangible energy of an audience. Stanislavsky describes it: "[T]he feeling of solitude in public which we do not know in ordinary life…is a marvelous sensation. A theater full of people is a splendid sounding board for us. For every moment of real feeling on the stage there is a response, thousands of invisible currents of sympathy and interest streaming back to us. A crowd of spectators oppresses and terrifies an actor, but it also arouses his truly creative energy. In conveying great emotional warmth it gives him faith in himself and his art" (Constantin Stanislavski [sic], *An Actor Prepares* [New York: Routledge, 1989], 282–3). Public solitude is a psychological state that is invisible to the spectator but demands complete concentration from the actor. Despite all the emphasis that American theorists placed on truth in acting in their evolution of Stanislavsky's method, Stanislavsky himself was profoundly influenced by Diderot's "actor's paradox." In his work he makes clear that the actor needs to embrace the *divided consciousness* by being both aware of himself as the actor and as the character.
2. John Lahr, "Sondheim's Little Deaths," *Harper's*, April 1979, 71–8.

CHAPTER 13

SONDHEIM ON THE LONDON STAGE

MATT WOLF

It's not often that the Royal Albert Hall gives over an evening of its annual summertime Proms to a composer drawn from the world of Broadway, but Stephen Sondheim's eightieth birthday was never going to be a commonplace milestone, especially in a capital that takes both its music and its theater as seriously as does London. And so it was on July 31, 2010, that a capacity crowd of some 6000 or so packed out the hall as the likes of Simon Russell Beale, Julian Ovenden, Bryn Terfel, Judi Dench, and many more cantered through the Sondheim canon with affection, enthusiasm, and inordinate skill.

Come the finale, the man himself took to the stage to roars of approval that are doubtless ringing in his ears still, Sondheim's confession that he cries easily borne out by an adoring public that was with him every step of the emotional way. All this enthusiasm for a visiting American and in this most British of settings too? (It simply doesn't get more English than the Last Night of the Proms.) Yes, and why not? The fact is, Sondheim may indeed be a Broadway baby—as the title of one of the most beloved of specialty numbers from *Follies* puts it—but he's always held unique pride of place in Britain, a country he has long adored and that has reciprocated his affection many times over.

As an expatriate American myself, albeit one who has lived in the United Kingdom far longer now than I ever lived in the United States, I have felt privileged to savor Sondheim's output on both sides of the Atlantic over the years, one of my first exposures to his work being the Broadway première of *Side by Side by Sondheim*, a musical revue that was in fact (and perhaps against the odds) spawned in Britain, from which the show, and its quartet of performers, travelled westward to great acclaim. And once I moved to London late in 1983, I hadn't been in my newfound home long before it became clear that Sondheim has pretty well been adopted as an honorary Brit, and not just because he happens to share a birthday with, of all people, Andrew Lloyd Webber: same date (March 22), different year.

Why the admiration abroad? His love of language offers one obvious reason, not to mention an appreciation of wit and irony that allies him more closely to the British theatrical community than to some of his American compatriots. But there's a more practical explanation, as well. The British system of theatrical subsidy allows Sondheim to be done time and again in London freed from the commercial pressures that inevitably bedevil Broadway, where even the most celebrated of Sondheim shows have often lost money, *Follies* being a famous example (indeed, in both its first New York production and the superlative 2011 Bernadette Peters–led revival). I'm not sure that Sondheim's shows do that much better commercially in London than they do in New York—the original West End *Into the Woods*, directed by Richard Jones and starring Julia McKenzie as the Witch and Imelda Staunton in an Olivier Award–winning turn as the Baker's Wife (Figure 13.1), did a fast fade at the Phoenix Theatre in 1991, a victim (or so it was claimed at the time) of dwindling theatrical attendance caused by the first Gulf War. But such is the theatrical ecosystem in London that virtually all Sondheim's shows can find some sort of home that allows them to play to a dedicated audience liberated from the commercial dictates that rule on Broadway—the very same imperatives for which Sondheim professed great affection when he told an audience during an Oxford University Q & A that he was pleased and delighted to be (and have been) a product of Broadway, this despite the interlocutor's having remarked how fervently he wished Sondheim were English so that Britain could lay exclusive claim to him.[1]

As it happens, Sondheim initially came to London in 1952, then age twenty-two, and was first represented on a British stage with the West End premiere in 1958 of *West Side Story*, on which, of course, he worked only as lyricist, not as composer. But in his capacity as a practitioner of both, Sondheim points to the London reviews of *A Funny Thing Happened on the Way to the Forum* as better and more encouraging than he had previously received for the same show on Broadway: the beginning of a mutually enthusiastic love affair that has scarcely let up, even if the occasional individual production (the West End bow of *Sweeney Todd*, for instance) underperformed at the box office or with the critics.

In some respects, it doesn't matter hugely that the first London *Sweeney*, with Sheila Hancock and Denis Quilley as Mrs. Lovett and the vengeful barber, respectively didn't take the town the way Hal Prince's staging had previously done on Broadway. London also allows for frequent go-rounds of the same show on a more regular basis than happens in New York, where audiences are tougher on repeat visits of titles they regard as familiar; the result, in the case of *Sweeney*, possibly more than any other Sondheim piece, is that I have seen some seven or eight different London takes on that surprisingly flexible show, two of which fell within the confines of the opera repertoire. London has recently witnessed the transfer to the Adelphi Theatre for a commercial run of a 2011 Chichester Festival Theatre *Sweeney* from the director Jonathan Kent, which starred a recessive, introspective Michael Ball in the title role and Imelda Staunton as a notably impish Mrs. Lovett. In the West End the production gained huge critical acclaim. Among the *Sweeney*s come and gone, the first of the opera reckonings of the musical to come my way was David McVicar's version for Opera North in 2002, with Steven Page an ashen-faced, outstandingly sung Sweeney, Page positing the title character in the tradition of outsized outcasts that includes Wozzeck and Peter Grimes, to cite just two figures from the repertoire who are also granted the titles of their respective works; the other, late in 2003, was drearily proffered by the Royal Opera House, with Thomas Allen too benign a Sweeney and Felicity Palmer the only Mrs. Lovett in my experience not to garner a single laugh. (Well, leaving aside Helena Bonham Carter in the Tim Burton film, a venture whose provenance itself speaks to the British hold over material that is, of course, the one Sondheim musical actually set in London.) A further two London *Sweeney*s were concert performances, one of which, at the Royal Festival Hall in February 2000, invaluably returned Len Cariou to the eponymous assignment that he had originated in New York in 1979, this Sweeney's chilling thirst for justice, not to mention the nakedness of his fury, as remarkable as ever, even if the voice was somewhat frayed.

Like many a Sondheim show, *Sweeney* has shown that it can be adjusted in virtually any direction: enlarged or made more intimate, as required.[2] So it wasn't altogether a surprise when the Anglo-Irish director Declan Donnellan mounted his own *Sweeney* for London's National Theatre in 1993, deliberately opting not to open the show at the largest of the National's three auditoriums—the Olivier—but going instead for the black-box Cottesloe and for an ensemble feel that extended even to the bows: on press night, I recall to this day Julia McKenzie and Alun Armstrong being denied solo bows in favor of a company ethos that saw the entire cast taking a collective call. The thinking was of a piece with the National Theatre practice of billing everyone in alphabetical order, though it seemed slightly cruel to the two leads not to be given at least a fleeting moment of glory (Figure 13.2).

Armstrong reportedly found the title role difficult to sustain, though he brought a craggy and altogether thrilling intensity to the part that gave rise to perhaps the least showbizzy Sweeney I have come across in any context (he, McKenzie, and Donnellan all won 1994 Olivier Awards for their contributions). But when the same staging moved to the mid-sized Lyttelton auditorium to capitalize on its success, Armstrong had been replaced by Denis Quilley, London's first Sweeney back in the hot seat, having in Donnellan's version first taken the role of the self-flagellating Judge Turpin—which meant that Quilley had spent some months watching Armstrong reinterpret the very role which he had originated and to which he would later return. The abiding glory of the piece remained McKenzie, who discovered in the comic/pathetic Mrs. Lovett a battered grace that remains forever etched on my mind, the actress appearing in the opening number abjectly blank-eyed, as if to portend the psychic depletion that would accompany Mrs. Lovett's grievous fate. A superlative singer (and not just of Sondheim), McKenzie also made room for vocal embellishments that even the sublime Angela Lansbury on Broadway never managed, while Imelda Staunton, in turn, may be among the strongest vocalists to have ever essayed this role.

Another tiny *Sweeney*—this one so small that it dispensed with an orchestra, turning its superlative ensemble into so many actor-musicians—hit London in 2004, courtesy of the veteran English director John Doyle, who in effect asked each company member to become his or her own instrumentalist. (When the production later transferred in triumph to Broadway, gaining Patti LuPone as its Tony-nominated star and winning Doyle his own Tony Award in 2006, one found it hard to think of Mrs. Lovett not toting around her own personal tuba.) Doyle brought this same approach, one arrived

FIGURE **13.1** Imelda Staunton as the Baker's Wife in Richard Jones's production of *Into the Woods* London (1990).

FIGURE **13.2** Alun Armstrong, Julia McKenzie and cast in *Sweeney Todd*, London (1994).

at out of financial necessity but fine-tuned into an aesthetic trademark, to several other Sondheim musicals on both sides of the Atlantic, among them a Tony-winning *Company* in 2007 on Broadway, starring Raul Esparza, and, back in England, a not terribly impressive *Merrily We Roll Along* at the Watermill Theatre, in Newbury, Berkshire, early in 2008. That particular go-round was notable mainly for the presence as Franklin of Sam Kenyon, the same actor who had made a tremulously impassioned Tobias in the earlier Doyle *Sweeney*.

Sweeney for all its British incarnations remains one of the few Sondheim shows not (so far, anyway) to have graced any of the Donmar, Menier Chocolate Factory, and Bridewell spaces, to name the three Off–West End venues that have turned to Sondheim with greatest frequency. The Donmar, under its former artistic director Sam Mendes, in fact launched both his regime and an entirely refurbished, rebuilt playhouse with the European premiere in 1992 of *Assassins* (Figure 13.3), reclaiming in the process an Off-Broadway curiosity that at the time hadn't yet come into focus in Sondheim's home country, though it would do in time—largely thanks to the director Joe Mantello's belated Broadway premiere of the same piece in 2004. (Indeed, so provocative was *Assassins* during that first London sighting that there were reports of visiting Americans

FIGURE **13.3** The world premiere of *Assassins* in London, directed by Sam Mendes (1992).

threatening to bomb the Donmar, so enraged were they by Sondheim's galvanizing musical pastiche of America at its most murderous.) Eager not just to replicate what had been done in New York but to revisit the material anew, Mendes prompted from his composer a new song—an 11 o'clock number called "Something Just Broke"—that brought into bold relief the grief coursing through an interval-free account of the various assassins who had beset the American presidency over the years: the song was given to the so-called "bystanders," observers to the sorrowful theme of a show that sounded bigger in London than it had Off-Broadway, a function of the musical trio heard in New York giving way to an eight-person London band.

Sondheim's willingness to be led into uncharted territory by a keen director has been an ongoing constant of London productions of his work—both the Sean Mathias and Trevor Nunn stagings of *A Little Night Music* incorporated songs, albeit different ones in each instance, that had been discarded along the way: "My Husband the Pig" as sung with acidic brilliance by Patricia Hodge, in crackerjack form as the hapless Charlotte at the National in 1995, and "Silly People," a number for the servants that amounted mostly to further lengthening an already long evening when Nunn mounted *Night Music* at the Menier in 2008.[3]

But *Assassins* showed the composer not just allowing extant material to be inserted anew but to compose afresh in keeping with a particular director's wishes, as Sondheim had previously done when the 1987 West End production of *Follies* opened at the Shaftesbury Theatre with a host of new songs. Among them were a tricky, musically jagged duet, "Country House," for that musical's unhappily married sophisticates, Ben and Phyllis, as well as entirely new numbers ("Ah, but Underneath" and "Make the Most of Your Music") for two of the four climactic solos of the "Loveland" sequence of *Follies*, even if it's fair to say that in both instances, their better-known predecessors ("The Story of Lucy and Jessie" and "Live, Laugh, Love") have tended to prevail in subsequent revivals of the same show.[4] Richard Jones's biting, often gleefully vicious West End *Into the Woods* introduced a duet between the Witch and Rapunzel, "Our Little World," that sits seamlessly in that show and some years later transferred well to the al fresco environs of the Open Air Theatre, Regent's Park, where the director Timothy Sheader directed at once the most slippery and muddiest *Into the Woods* in my experience in the summer of 2010, a staging that went on to win an Olivier Award for Best Revival of a Musical (and was re-staged for the Delacorte Theatre in New York's Central Park in 2012). An austerely wigged Hannah Waddingham was the Witch in Regent's Park in a complete about-face from the same performer's beautifully melancholic, unusually comely Desirée Armfeldt in the Nunn *Night Music*, a staging that moved from the Menier across the Thames to the Garrick Theatre for a limited run.

Assassins won the 1993 Critics' Circle Award for Best Musical—an encomium one would have thought unimaginable on the basis solely of reaction to it Off-Broadway—and an Olivier (the actor's first of two) for Henry Goodman as the chillingly jaunty Charles Guiteau, and got Mendes's Donmar off to an adventurous start, signaling an interest not just in Sondheim but in the American repertoire that would guide the same director through to winning an Oscar for his first-ever film, the tellingly titled

American Beauty. The same 250-seat Covent Garden venue has since mounted five further Sondheim shows to varying degrees of acclaim: John Crowley's 1998 revival of *Into the Woods* was notable for bringing the same piece back quickly after its premature West End demise (and for pairing the then-fledgling—or relatively so—Irish director with his elder brother Bob, the awards-laden designer), but the show was arguably both overdesigned and undersung, one notable exception being Sophie Thompson, who won her own Olivier for playing the Baker's Wife—the role from this show that tends to attract the trophies.[5] The production also introduced, as Red Riding Hood, a pert, gleaming-eyed teenage talent from the north of England by the name of Sheridan Smith. This was well before her ascendancy in the worlds of both TV and the West End and such shows as *Legally Blonde* and *Flare Path*.

Far better was Mendes's own *Company* at the Donmar late in 1995, a landmark staging not least in casting a black performer, the sensational Adrian Lester (Anthony in the National's *Sweeney Todd*), in the defining role of Bobby, the eternal (or is he?) bachelor whose friends fete him on his thirty-fifth birthday only to leave him alone on stage, tussling with the very notion of "Being Alive"—the musical's tumultuous finale. The show transferred to the West End's Albery Theatre (now the Noël Coward) to indifferent box office but continued acclaim and was not only captured on disc but also broadcast by BBC television; in autumn, 2010, it was offered up as the second of a pair of Donmar Sondheims that got revisited for two gala concert performances each at the Queen's Theatre, Shaftesbury Avenue. Almost fifteen years on, Lester cut a bulkier, even more emotionally bruising figure who as before placed Bobby at the very core of a musical from which its central character can seem strangely absent. The event was further lifted by the added presence as the cynical Joanne (a song forever associated with Elaine Stritch) of a fiery Haydn Gwynne, who stepped in triumph into a part that had been played during the 1990s by Sheila Gish, who during the intervening years had sadly died of cancer. Gwynne made an entirely worthy inheritor, both vocally and affectively, and the *Billy Elliot* alumna announced herself as a smashing Phyllis-in-waiting as and when *Follies* next comes around.[6]

But it was the first of the two Sondheim-themed Donmar gala concerts (seen the Sunday before *Company*) that really set the pulse racing: *Merrily We Roll Along*, the famously short-lived Broadway flop from 1981, seemed entirely reborn under Michael Grandage's compassionate yet incisive eye when premiered at the Donmar late in 2000. Its director, interestingly, had seen the very first London performance of the piece presented by drama students at the Guildhall in 1983, at the same time that he was studying to be an actor. A subsequent, if little-known, *Merrily* involved the quartet of young lovers from the 1987 West End *Follies*, who found time during the eighteen-month run of that show to do their own late-night *Merrily* concert, directed by Julia Mackenzie. The Grandage *Merrily*—that director's first musical—saw off competition from some notable big guns, including Andrew Lloyd Webber's *The Beautiful Game* and the Cameron Mackintosh production of *The Witches of Eastwick*, to win 2001 Olivier Awards for Best Musical as well as for two of its three leads (Daniel Evans and Samantha Spiro), a happy outcome that had seemed unthinkable from a musical that on Broadway brought to an end the long run of acclaimed collaborations between Sondheim and the director Hal Prince. In part, it was clear that a better London design and smaller auditorium shone a more focused spotlight on a mournful but often witty and funny tale told in reverse of the splintering relationship of three friends whose ideals and dreams exist to be eroded and deferred. At the Donmar, there was some initial panic when leading lady Spiro lost her voice during previews, though she recovered in time to give a near-definitive performance as the lovesick Mary, while the object of her (romantically unreciprocated) affections—the composer Franklin Shepard—was played by a then-unknown twenty-four-year-old, a former cathedral chorister called Julian Ovenden whose soaring tenor was later pressed into service at that 2010 Sondheim Prom, resulting in an exultant but also angry "Being Alive." It was no bad thing, either, that Ovenden was himself a piano-player, a skill of invaluable use both to the musical as a whole and very specifically to his part. (Daniel Evans, by the way, got his own chance at "Being Alive" in an eccentric if affecting Crucible Theatre, Sheffield, revival of *Company* late in 2011, a staging so belligerently set in the era in which the piece was written that the verisimilitude was almost too much—enough psychedelia already!)

So there were Spiro, Ovenden, and Evans on October 31, 2010, back together for afternoon and evening concerts, joined as they had been the first *Merrily* go-round by Anna Francolini in a revelatory supporting turn as Gussie, Franklin's predatory, tart-tongued wife who, in turn, shows up her husband as being not so much bad as weak: an important distinction, not least in light of Sondheim's lyric in *Into the Woods* to the effect that "nice is different than good." A show very much about the effects of the passage of time, beginning in 1980 and ending with the launch of Sputnik in 1957, *Merrily* in concert seemed to be commenting on itself in reverse, which is to say that even as George Furth's book insists on the gathering sourness of the creative types at its center, the cast of the concert performance looked even more robust and capable (talk about being alive!) than they had ten years earlier. Ovenden at that point was headed Off-Broadway to star in a Maury Yeston musical, *Death Takes a Holiday*, from which he then had to withdraw for vocal reasons, while Evans in the intervening decade had stormed both the West End and Broadway in *Sunday in the Park with George*, playing the title character of Georges Seurat. Those runs, in turn, had immeasurably strengthened a voice that was firmer and more robust in every way from the appealingly frazzled Charley Kringas, the frenetic lyricist whom Evans had played the first time round and returned to as if meeting the sort of "old friend" celebrated in one of the many knockout numbers in *Merrily*'s score, each encounter with this show adding to my feeling that it may be Sondheim's most defiantly and thrillingly "Broadway" show, even if the irony is that it did so poorly on Broadway.[7]

Merrily remained a Sondheim–Donmar bellwether, notwithstanding the American director Gary Griffin's summer 2003 revival of *Pacific Overtures*, which went on to win its own Olivier Award for Best Musical Production (as the category was then called) for a staging spawned at the Chicago Shakespeare Theatre and, in London, utilizing ten performers and four musicians. More exciting, in my view, and cast with an acumen that completely rethought the work at hand was the director Jamie Lloyd's 2010 revival of Sondheim and Lapine's *Passion*, a show seen previously in the West End, with Maria Friedman and Michael Ball, and at the Bridewell, with Clare Burt. A piece often as difficult to like as its creepily tenacious heroine, the sickly Fosca, *Passion* at the Donmar gave the diminutive Elena Roger a chance to revisit the auditorium where the Argentinian dynamo had performed her scorching Edith Piaf.[8]

But the abidingly transformative aspect of this *Passion* lay in the prominence it gave to the central male character of Giorgio, the army officer who falls under the devouring eye of the ailing Fosca and is himself transformed by a love that borders on the obsessional.[9] Arguably the story primarily of Giorgio, *Passion* benefited in director Lloyd's scalpel-sharp take from the musical theater performance of that or any season by comparative newcomer David Thaxton (Figure 13.4), a *Les Misérables* alumnus (who isn't?) who played the Italian army officer as someone both bowled over and hollowed out by the force field of feeling communicated by Roger's tiny if towering Fosca. It's always been said that where London productions of Sondheim have gained the upper hand over those elsewhere has been in the ability of British performers to treat the works as acting opportunities—plays with music attached, not just a collection of songs—which is why Judi Dench's aching, shimmering National Theatre Desirée reigned, and remains, supreme. That's why Lloyd's *Passion* proved itself the finest interpretation I have yet encountered of this eternally knotted show—and also why such follies as the dreadful 2002 Raymond Gubbay and Royal Festival Hall summer revival of *Follies* let the

FIGURE **13.4** David Thaxton as Giorgio in *Passion*, Donmar Theatre revival, London (2010).

side down. Sure, Henry Goodman, Louise Gold, Kathryn Evans, and David Durham could sing that demanding *Follies* score perfectly well, but there wasn't a trace of the nerve-rattling connection to the material that coursed all the way through the Donmar *Passion.*

Follies, as it happens, gave London one of those landmark Sondheim performances in its 1987 West End premiere at the Shaftesbury Theatre, a mix of Anglo-American talent in which Julia McKenzie yet again asserted her affinity for Sondheim as an unusually rending Sally, the abject one-time chorus girl-turned-housewife who returns to New York in a wildly self-deluded attempt to sort out a love affair that exists mostly in the mind she is clearly losing (as her second-act torch song so memorably tells us). McKenzie, her American accent as pitch-perfect as her musical phrasing, was sublime in a role in which she was replaced by Jill Martin, only for Martin to cede the last few performances of the production in turn to McKenzie: an act of noblesse oblige that, in context, made perfect sense. The remainder of the company of the late Mike Ockrent's revival—designed by another talent who died before time, namely Maria Bjornson, here fresh off *The Phantom of the Opera*—folded several Americans into the mix, all of them excellent. David Healy brought a battered avuncularity to the near-desperate high jinks of Buddy, the man Sally married, if not necessarily the one she actually loved, while first Dolores Gray and then Eartha Kitt, legends both, blasted Carlotta's death-defying "I'm Still Here" halfway to New York. Amongst the Brits, Diana Rigg was a coolly leggy Phyllis, the theatrical Dame dipping a toe into the musical repertoire that she had dabbled with in America during the ill-fated pre-Broadway tryout of a (non-Sondheim) show called *Colette.*

Follies itself continued to be done in unlikely venues around the capital, from a Walthamstow pub theater production to one at Clapham's Landor that I loved. That last, most unexpected of ventures found a cast of twenty-two performing to an audience at capacity of little more than twice that number. How did it work? Very well, actually, though purists would have disdained the use of a lone piano in place of the orchestral heft from which the lushly eclectic score of *Follies* especially benefits. But there was something about seeing and hearing up close the pain that pulsates through Sondheim and Goldman's 1971 ground-breaker. You wouldn't want to see every *Follies* done this way of course but as an alternative take on a show that can against the odds take it, Robert McWhir's hyperintimate staging in 2006 reconsidered *Follies* as John Doyle had done *Sweeney Todd*: two musicals deemed to be inextricably wedded to a certain size revealing a malleability no one could have guessed.

And so it has gone with more or less every Sondheim show in London, whether *Sweeney* was being seen in a studio theater or at Covent Garden, or *Pacific Overtures* was first playing the capacious London Coliseum in Keith Warner's English National Opera outing or the Donmar seventeen years on. (I may be alone in having preferred Warner's production.) *A Funny Thing Happened on the Way to the Forum* survived the indifferent voice of star Roy Hudd to charm audiences outdoors in Ian Talbot's 1999 Regent's Park revival of Sondheim's 1962 Burt Shevelove and Larry Gelbart knockabout romp, whereas the same show indoors five years later at the National Theatre allowed leading man Desmond Barrit to casually bring down the house, remarking po-faced during the first act: "Silence, I am about to say the sooth." (What else would you expect a soothsayer to, well, say?) That second production, directed in the Olivier auditorium by Edward Hall, got both physical and aural mileage out of the oversized lung power of costar Philip Quast, playing a feather-festooned Miles Gloriosus in a performance that—to a degree custom-made for so flesh-happy a show—seemed to be about the Australian performer's thighs.

In taking on *Forum*, Quast was returning to the address where the notable Javert in *Les Misérables* had first distinguished himself in Sondheim, winning a 1991 Olivier Award as Britain's first Seurat in the National Theatre premiere of *Sunday in the Park with George*, opposite Maria Friedman's Dot/Marie. Friedman, for her part, became an ongoing Sondheim interpreter and was a lovely Mary when Paul Kerryson directed *Merrily* at the Leicester Haymarket. I doubt many performers could rival the vocal ease and finesse of that role's originator, Mandy Patinkin; however Quast did aurally in a star turn that on occasion seemed explicitly to evoke Patinkin, even if the late Steven Pimlott's Lyttelton staging was in the end fussier and less moving than James Lapine's 1984 New York incarnation of the same, ever-daunting, always wondrous show.

The same piece returned as if remade in November 2005, to south London's comparatively pocket-sized Menier, the very venue that would further its affinities for Sondheim via the Nunn *Night Music* and, in July 2011, a so-so UK première of *Road Show*, John Doyle's version of Sondheim and John Weidman's long-aborning piece about the real-life Mizner brothers, Wilson and Addison, here seen as dual embodiments of dueling American energies. (Some central miscasting—no way did leading men David Bedella and Michael Jibson seem like they were from the same planet, much less brothers—and an overeagerness of tone didn't help this English account of a problematic show that resonated more fully in its Off-Broadway version, also directed by Doyle, several years before.)

No such cavils attended the Menier *Sunday*, which was directed by a young unknown, Sam Buntrock, whose résumé to that point had included a feisty 1997 fringe production of *Assassins* at Hampstead's New End Theatre, a venture produced by a then nineteen-year-old called David Babani, the Bristol University undergraduate who in the intervening years had relocated south of the river to run the Menier (and feature fairly regularly at the Tonys on the occasion of his venue's various Broadway transfers, of which *Sunday in the Park* was the first). Buntrock's coup on both sides of the Atlantic was to utilize projections to knit together the potentially disparate halves of a wounding and beautiful show that some have—wrongly, in my view—argued doesn't need a second act. Once Seurat's signature canvas, *A Sunday Afternoon on the Island of La Grande Jatte*, is painstakingly recreated at the tumultuous close of the first half, bring down the curtain, or so the assertion goes. But no: as reimagined by Buntrock, with the crucial assistance of Timothy Bird's computer animation and David Farley's sets, the show's separate acts were knit into an indissoluble whole whereby projections gave literally animated force to the pointillist landscape of French Impressionist Georges Seurat while tilting toward the mixed-media innovations of the artist's American grandson, George, who takes center stage in the second act as a deviser of what are known as chromolumes.

Daniel Evans offered an elfin, gimlet-eyed Seurat entirely different in affect from the emotionally omnivorous Patinkin, an approach to the part that in fact suited the fastidiousness of the pioneering painter whom Evans was playing.[10] And following his Donmar success as Charley Kringas, the *Sunday* revival confirmed Evans as a dedicated Sondheimian who joined Maria Friedman in a summer 2007 anthology of Sondheim's work called *Good Thing Going*—the title lifted self-evidently from one of the songs from *Merrily*. Evans also figured invaluably as part of that 2010 Prom, where he scampered about with Terfel, Ovenden, and Russell Beale on "Everybody Ought to Have a Maid" from *Forum*: sheer bliss.

His leading lady in *Sunday* changed as the production moved on, Anna-Jane Casey departing the show at the end of the Menier engagement to be replaced by Jenna Russell, both wonderful performers who lent a genuine sweetness and wit to the roles first of Seurat's inspiration and muse and, after the interval, of the avant-garde George's nonagenarian grandmother who represents a connection to the past that we've seen unfold before us in act 1. Russell was amongst the haul of 2007 Olivier Awards (five in all) accomplished by a production that was later picked up by Broadway's Roundabout Theatre Company, just as the Doyle *Sweeney* and Nunn *Night Music* were also snapped up for New York consumption on the basis of earlier kudos in London.

Indeed, that's the abiding irony—and a pleasurable one it is, too—about the proliferation of Sondheim in London, a capital that views the composer and lyricist simply as part of the canon whose work is worth perpetual examination, in much the same way that one returns regularly to Stoppard, Chekhov, and, of course, Shakespeare. His songs—playlets in themselves—are well suited to a culture that has then been able to reevaluate the work and ship it back to its source, as has been happening to varying degrees ever since *Side by Side by Sondheim*, a revue that was itself followed by numerous British-conceived variations—*Putting It Together* and *Moving On*, among them.[11]

It's worth noting that London doesn't shy away from lesser-known Sondheim shows: *Saturday Night* got an airing at the Bridewell Theatre in 1998 some forty-five years after it was first commissioned and well before it was then staged Off-Broadway in a separate version (and was revived, additionally, in London). Even such Sondheim esoterica as *The Frogs* got done in the summer of 1990 at a west London baths in a blink-and-you-missed-it engagement that whetted the appetite for the far fuller Lincoln Center version of the same piece in New York in 2004. There have been good, and quite a few great, Sondheim productions in London, and a whole slew of era-defining performances among which McKenzie's Sally and Mrs. Lovett, Ovenden's Franklin, Thaxton's Giorgio, Dench's Desirée, and Lester's Bobby are just a few seared on the memory for all time. And when the productions have offered bum times as opposed to good? So what: the fact remains, Stephen Sondheim's extraordinary output is still here.

NOTES

1. This was all during the composer's 1990 residency at St Catherine's College, Oxford, where he inaugurated an annual professorship in contemporary theater that was timed to coincide with rehearsals for the National Theatre premiere that same season of *Sunday in the Park with George*.

2. Broadway relabeled the show *Teeny Todd* when the director Susan H. Schulman reconceived the piece in 1989 in a staging first seen at the tiny Church of the Heavenly Rest on Manhattan's Upper East Side that then found its way to one of the smallest Broadway houses, the Circle in the Square.

3. That production, recast in all but the leading male role, later transferred successfully to New York, winning Catherine Zeta-Jones a 2010 Tony Award in her Broadway debut.

4. Sondheim will no longer license the 1987 London version of *Follies* for performance.

5. Joanna Gleason got a Tony for the same part in 1988.

6. Trevor Nunn has long spoken of wanting to do it – at one point while he was running the National in a regime rife with classic Broadway titles – but that has yet to materialise, the director in 2011 instead mounting a separate James Goldman work, *The Lion in Winter*.

7. A 1996 play coauthored by Sondheim and George Furth, *Getting Away with Murder*, did marginally better, running for seventeen performances—one more than the original Broadway *Merrily*.

8. Roger won an Olivier for Pam Gems's musical play *Piaf* and was nominated two years later for *Passion*. In 2012, she made her Broadway debut playing the title role in Michael Grandage's revival of *Evita*.

9. Many commentators have in fact argued that this 1994 Broadway musical should in fact be titled *Obsession*, not *Passion*.

10. Friedman has long been inextricably linked to Sondheim, appearing additionally in 1996 as the first London Fosca, for which she won an Olivier, and in 2007 concert stagings of both *Follies* and *Sweeney Todd*. She was an invaluable part of the birthday Prom and has given Sondheim pride of place in numerous one-woman shows. In November 2012 she directed *Merrily* for the Menier Chocolate Factory.

11. *Side By Side*, incidentally, often gets revived in London, where the role of the narrator fell in a 1997 go-round to the comedienne Dawn French, who was the best thing about the director Matthew Francis's otherwise inadequate run-through of what can devolve into a series of poorly thought-out party pieces.

CHAPTER 14

....

"AND ONE FOR MAHLER": AN OPERA DIRECTOR'S REFLECTIONS ON SONDHEIM IN THE SUBSIDIZED THEATER

....

KEITH WARNER

HAVING taken time to welcome the musical into their elysian fold, subsidized theaters have more recently focused a large amount of attention upon the work of one man, Stephen Sondheim. In recent years he has become firmly established as a unique cross-over act: from commercial to state-funded theaters. This is as surprising as it is wholly deserved, but there are dangers inherent in this bipartisanship. Not artistic dangers either; despite early murmurings, there is no dumbing down or "slumming it" involved in placing his works alongside Pinter and Stoppard or Britten and Henze. Quite the reverse, the real questions arising here actually lie buried deep within our theatrical life and times rather than in Sondheim's elevation. This association, in the current climate, may in fact do more harm to his works themselves and particular harm to their performance history, due to the way they are often treated and viewed within the "public sector" theaters. Rather than explore his ceaseless innovation and pay attention to his larger reforming quest, there is a tendency now to view Sondheim as a brilliant boulevardier, a lucky charm for cash-strapped times. Sondheim has often quipped that his pieces are musicals when performed on Broadway or in the West End and operas when done in opera houses. He is of course right, but there is a lot more riding on this business of cultural differentiation than that.

One can argue, as he himself has, certain of his pieces are right for opera houses and other roomy palaces of culture, and some are not. I would suggest that this business of "appropriateness" is now more a question of architecture rather than cultural classification. Nowadays surely there's no need to feel artistically disorientated attending any of his works, even those that are more like chamber pieces, undertaken by an opera company, if they have theaters appropriate to the scale of each individual piece and production.

The performing artists within opera certainly can be extraordinarily versatile; it could even be argued that many opera singers today have a far wider range of acting styles and spectrum of vocal delivery than some "straight" actors who remain cemented into a naturalistic tradition and lack any true musical training. It is a given that nobody can easily imagine seeing *Assassins* or *Passion* performed on the main stage of the Royal Opera House, but probably you would not want to see them at Drury Lane either. On the other hand, *Follies* is not so readily conceivable in a small studio (although some have had fun trying), because there is something about the piece that needs a larger dimension. You almost need to see and feel the time theme central to the show physically realized, as the "then" enshrined in the show's brilliant musical parodies vies with the "now" of the central characters' problems. This needs to be writ large in the audience's imagination. Surely the needs of each individual show are no longer a question of the cultural status of the producing house, high or low, mainstream or fringe, but can be judged only by the appropriateness of each experience, physically and aesthetically.

When the Royal Opera House produced *Into the Woods* in the Linbury Studio (2007, directed by the Royal Ballet choreographer Will Tuckett), the black box auditorium seating a few hundred or so seemed right enough and nobody questioned it being a project promoted by the Royal Opera, nor scrupulously examined who in the cast was an actor, who a dancer or who an opera singer. On the other hand, in the case of *Into the Woods*, the piece did not seem dwarfed by having the entire Regent's Park as its set and theater (2010, director Timothy Sheader) even in a day-lit matinee. The pieces simply need to be conceived to fit the circumstances—and, with Sondheim's output, one must never be resistant to the occasional wholly unexpected reversal. They were nearly all designed to surprise and to be presented audaciously. Indeed, this is one of the most important aspects that any new production should try to capture—their sheer theatrical originality. His earlier creations, those made in collaboration with Harold Prince, were all based on what they both called "secret metaphors"—theatrical concepts or ideas that encapsulate the idea of the piece, and then in some subtle way take a central role in the dramaturgy of each show. During Sondheim and Prince's genre-changing collaboration these metaphors were writ large within the physical life of the production, visually and hermeneutically.

In recent years we have become more used to studio representations of Sondheim's shows, be they at the Donmar Warehouse, the Cottesloe, Playwrights Horizon, any number of Off-Broadway houses, Edinburgh Fringe venues, or American regional companies, but sometimes there can be another kind of liberation for these pieces by returning them to their conceptual origins as large-scale entertainments, and by utilizing a full panoply of theatrical devices, impossible in studio productions.

Sondheim's shows are all wonderful vehicles for actor–singers and as such one needs to read facial details and comprehend the filigree craft of the lyrics at close hand, yet they are also pieces that treat ideas and issues, politics and passions, lives and times, so in order to be true to such a scope of drama, it is also crucial to give them a larger context, in order that the sheer size of Sondheim's ambitions for the genre are not compromised. This is why the home for them in the future might well prove to be with the subsidized sector companies, which are still—just about—the only places where it is possible to play and see such expansively "theatrical" work, although the chance for risk and innovation here too is fast disappearing as a consequence of the financial situation.

So the alternative in the last decade has been regularly to reduce Sondheim's works to studio pieces. There is much to be gained by this process. Sondheim the lyricist, the dramatic miniaturist, is often served well by small-scale productions, but I am not so sure about Sondheim the theatrical innovator or the composer. The gain in focus, in intimacy, can also become an avoidance of the "bigger picture." These productions are often as much the outcome of current financial constraints as they are of artistic choice. And it has to be admitted that they have also kept us constantly and often brilliantly in contact with the works.

Here I must declare some personal professional interest. In September 1987, I was fortunate enough to direct the London premiere of *Pacific Overtures* for the English National Opera (ENO) at the Coliseum. This was the culmination of a two-year process that had started with workshops for opera singers, mostly members of the resident company, to find ways to perform Sondheim without the vocal production sounding over-emphatic, classically produced, and plummy, and—beyond this—how to deliver text in songs as a trained opera singer. This transformed itself into a workshop or rehearsed reading of *Pacific Overtures* which, adhering to the traditions of Japanese theater, has an all-male cast.[1] At some point in the summer of 1986 Stephen Sondheim himself got involved and I think none of us will forget the marvelous sessions we had with him coaching, guiding, training and encouraging us. By the end of this process it was pretty obvious to all involved that we wanted to perform this piece in a full-scale production, and following a private presentation within the company of the whole show in workshop form, the combination of public subsidy and the enlightened artistic leadership of David Pountney and Mark Elder allowed us to carry on and to schedule a full production for autumn of the following year. By then many within the company believed passionately in this piece (Figure 14.1).

FIGURE **14.1** Keith Warner's production of *Pacific Overtures* for English National Opera (1984).

What strikes home now is this: we could at that point have chosen any of his shows, but in those heady, generously Arts Council–funded days, it seemed right and fitting that a subsidized company should be looking at the least commercial and, at that time anyway, the most esoteric and controversial of his output. The fact that it had closed on Broadway and had received mixed reviews and a slightly quizzical public response was exactly the reason why we *should* have taken it on. It is an enormously interesting, worthwhile, but challenging piece of theater with an astonishingly original score. That was reason enough, allied with the belief that a public could be wooed towards it, however strange the piece may seem. As within my lifetime with Pinter, Beckett, Benjamin Britten, or Hans Werner Henze, any difficulty in dealing with the different or unfamiliar was unimportant in contrast to the artistic gains of making these works familiar. When did we in the arts give up on difficulty?

I also believed then and still believe now that publicly funded companies such as ENO should be standard bearers for such a unique figure as Stephen Sondheim, just as others were advocates for, say, Harrison Birtwistle or John Adams. In the United Kingdom, although some great Sondheim performances were emerging from regional companies like the Forum Theatre, Wythenshawe, none of the major subsidized companies had at that time gone anywhere near his works, which seemed to me an outrage that had to be corrected. (You could afford wild disdain about decisions within the subsidized sector in those days!)

When *Pacific Overtures* opened at the Coliseum in 1987 (although it can be no part of mine here to evaluate the production), I readily admit that the Coliseum was simply too large for the longer dialogue sections. I must also add that if you believe a representation of Japanese traditional theater is an important factor of this show's "metaphor" as it transforms itself from a kabuki-styled performance into a vulgar American musical by the finale, then it is also true to say that this style is far removed from the subtle chamber atmosphere of a studio production. However what we did have at ENO were many weeks of workshops even prior to the show's final rehearsal period. We tried hard to engage and experiment with kabuki style; we could do this only because of the ensemble existing within the company, supported by government money. Kabuki actors, instructors for onagatas (kabuki female impersonators), a bunraku puppet master, Japanese martial arts experts, all of these were lavished upon us as we tried to do the piece justice. It still seems to me that this is exactly why subsidized theater exists: to take on the great challenges that certain visions present; to allow us all, performers and audiences alike, to explore in a body of work like Sondheim's their multifaceted greatness and their openness, not necessarily to do them better—no one can guarantee that—but to do them other. In other words, not merely to ape the criteria of commercial productions, but to explore, to reach further. There's no Noh business in showbusiness.

It is interesting to note how far Britain has traveled down the monetarist trail in the arts since then, for now no ensemble theater companies, like the old ENO, exist in the United Kingdom—not one, in opera or in theater. This type of work is lost and a whole system of beliefs has been lost with it. Nowadays, all theater is to a greater or lesser degree commercial; its principles of financial success and failure resulting in a conservative aversion to risk and experiment—and the same criteria in production are shared more or less by all state-subsidized pleasure domes.

At ENO we all found from working closely with Sondheim the composer that the notes, exactly as written, matter—at least at the first level of preparation. This is simply because Sondheim's scores emerge from a considered compositional technique, the rhythms, the markings, the exact pitch of notes, contribute to the meaning, and prepare the expressivity. They should be adhered to, as they should in Janáček or Wagner. Precisely because Sondheim is a very good composer indeed, he writes accurately for the voice and what he notates gives you a key to the expression. He sets words with the skill of a Schubert or Benjamin Britten. And from the lyricist we learned that the words are in many ways the primary source, that for the performer in the moment of the action the lyrics are a means of getting the meaning across, but that this in no way conflicts with the composer's demands. From the show's creator we learn that meaning, not style, is all; that the way you sing, the contribution you as a performer make is about interpretation, not vocalization. This is why an expressive voice, a technique that can adapt itself freely and unselfconsciously toward character, emotional truth, and clarity, is worth more in the Sondheim world than a highly trained "instrument." From the man of theater I discovered how everything must be considered, balanced, and made clear. A show is an accumulation of a million choices and details but these are made correctly only if each contributes to the overall power of the theatrical moment and hence bit by bit, ounce by ounce, to the show—and to the clarity of its meaning.

Within the opera house the size and quality of the orchestra also play an important part. Orchestration alters a piece radically—for after all, as with opera, the sound world is what finally marks it out as a musical not a play. Sondheim himself admitted in a radio interview for the American Theatre Wing, Downstage Center, broadcast on January 3, 2010, and widely available on the Internet and as a podcast, that, "In small revivals, I miss the full-sized orchestra." We have readily come to accept even in the major revivals of his works that a small instrumental combo, artfully rescored, is giving us a full experience of the score. In fact, we have almost forgotten what that full sound experience was like. When buying a ticket for a studio-type production an audience understands that a small band rather than a full orchestra is a part of the deal; but when we attend one of our large national companies, do we not deserve a little bit more? You certainly would normally get this in an opera-house version and this is not a feature to be easily undervalued. So too with the musical preparation, both vocal and instrumental; these things take time to absorb and expertise to deliver and the tight rehearsal schedules of a commercial production does not always allow for such careful, painstaking artistic work. Sondheim's songs and ensembles really repay detailed coaching in all areas. In production terms a show in a subsidized house should surely attempt to explore more, to delve deeper, to follow paths that a commercial producer would not be comfortable with, which also means that you probably need to rehearse for longer and have a design budget and technical time on stage that allows a production team to spread its wings. Any chance to risk more and therefore to conceive, design, and direct the works as they were first conceptualized is almost certainly the first victim of budgetary hard times. It is important to note here that a "conceptual" production does not imply a large-scale scenic show: it might, but then again it might involve ten white chairs in a black space. "Conceptual" merely indicates the thematic organization of ideas behind the production.

If subsidized companies are to do these pieces—and they certainly must—should they not be attempting to do them differently from their commercial rivals? The luxury of subsidy should demand more than money: quality and innovation should be the two requirements for a public grant. So often, subsidized institutions, great and small, put on musicals as a way of filling the theater and generating huge popular success rather than to explore the art form. Aren't these institutions just the places, the only places, to pick up the gauntlet Sondheim himself threw down in creating his startling musical visions, and then ride like hell with it?

To understand this at one remove: if Rodgers and Hammerstein are to be done by these institutions, should it not be *Allegro*, that team's fascinating early commercial failure, that they tackle not *Carousel* or *South Pacific*? *Allegro* possibly inhibited the extent to which Rodgers and Hammerstein would ever really experiment in the future—and yet it opened up a pathway for Sondheim. He has admitted:

> Right away I accepted the idea of telling stories in space, of skipping time and using gimmicks like the Greek Chorus. All the stuff that's in *Allegro*, of playing with the idea of theatre, Pirandello-ish almost.... That's why I am drawn to experiment.... I realize that I am trying to recreate *Allegro* all the time.

So is it not with *Anyone Can Whistle, Pacific Overtures, Assassins, Merrily We Roll Along*, and *Passion* that subsidized theater should be concerning itself? Even perhaps *Follies* these days—based on the argument that it may well be too expensive ever to mount commercially again. But if so, let's have a *Follies* showcased in a visual world that allows it to be more than a mere string of camp, nostalgic numbers in a production that isn't scared of the darkness of the original vision. Many of the shows in the Sondheim canon may now fall outside the range of the commercial sector because of finances, and that's why state theaters must pick them up and nurture them. Moreover, shouldn't our companies provide the workshops and conditions to mount *Road Show*, or better yet, to help the young blast survivors of Sondheim develop the art form—John LaChiusa, Ricky Ian Gordon, Stephen Flaherty, and Adam Guettel (to name just a few)? This is really the challenge that Sondheim has set up for the future of musical theater.

The status of Stephen Sondheim in our culture seems thoroughly intertwined with the question of whether we want a serious theater and a serious music-theater or just mindless entertainment? British Arts Council funding was born with that overused motto, "the right to fail," hung above its cradle. Nobody has failed again and failed better than Sondheim and as is the way of all great artists he has transformed our very perceptions of "failure," redefining it and in time proving that he was usually right all along. With hindsight, a different interpretation offers itself. Critics failed. Productions failed. We failed. The shows really didn't. They refuse to disappear because their force of innovation keeps them fresh in every revival. That's another justification for an unfettered subsidized sector: first impressions can be dangerously wrong. Masterpieces need to be viewed from many different angles and over time.

The subsidized sector should prove Sondheim's truest ally in helping us all escape from the hall of mirrors that reflects success and failure on the basis of commercial considerations. In some ways the New National Theatre in Tokyo shamed everyone when they presented *Pacific Overtures* (2000, director Amon Miyamoto). On paper this must have seemed a somewhat obscure repertory choice: a postmodern Japanese take on Sondheim's American take on a kabuki take on nineteenth-century American expansionism—the biggest take of all. And it was a great show. Now that's what a subsidized theater is for.

In the United States the trend for "art houses" to champion Sondheim's pieces started quite early on, and it was opera companies that led the way. *Sweeney Todd* finally convinced the culture barons in charge of these fiefdoms, which are still run on the nineteenth-century German model, based on the tastes and education of one or two men (and, very rarely, women) at the top. What was crucial to this work being accepted into the opera canon was, in the opera house at least, the sheer quality of its musical invention coupled with the best libretto written for any "opera" since Hoffmanstahl. Sondheim pays tribute to his period of study with Milton Babbitt, a guru of American modernism, as a key influence on his compositions:

> It stood me in very good stead for shows I've written which have extended developments in them because I am pretty good (not quite as good as I'd like, but pretty good) at writing what Lenny [Bernstein] would call scenas, something that goes on for twelve and fourteen minutes that's more than a song.

It is the sense of development, musical allied with dramatic, that perhaps marks out *Sweeney Todd* as an important composition as well as a great show. To some extent all of Sondheim's works share this sense of architecture over long spans, evenings, and it is this that attracted serious musical attention as much as the polished brilliance of individual songs. All of a sudden opera houses had a composer and a work that they could feel at home with to sit alongside *West Side Story* and *Porgy and Bess*, neither of which, because of their ethnic subject matter and cast requirements, have been easily assimilated. Following its Broadway premiere in March 1979, while giving a wide berth to its original run and national tour, Houston Grand Opera presented *Sweeney Todd* as part of its opera season in June 1984. This company was under the mercurial leadership of David Gockley and Music Director John De Main, both of whom have an almost unrivaled track record in commissioning and presenting world premiere pieces. Interestingly, they chose also to present it in a slightly revamped production of the Harold Prince original.

New York City Opera was to follow suit in doing *Sweeney Todd* later in the same year, and both companies used a version of the original production, in itself a seminal masterpiece, and although it might have been exciting to view a different interpretation of the piece, the casting of opera singers in both venues did make it different. In later years, Opera North (1998, director David McVicar) in a superbly dark but intimate production and Chicago Lyric Opera (2002, director Harold Prince) followed the trend. A hugely important moment in the show's history occurred when it was taken into the rep of the Royal Opera, Covent Garden (2003, director Neil Armfeld), one of the world's most prestigious opera houses. It was more significant perhaps because the music director of the house, Antonio Pappano, one of the leading classical conductors of our times, having played the piano for the New York City Opera production early in his career, scheduled the performances and affirmed it as a modern masterpiece. Nobody, in this generation at least, need ever argue its case again. There was a hugely significant première when the demon barber set up shop in Unter den Linden in Berlin at the Kommische Oper (2004, director Christopher Bond) which turned into a sadly missed opportunity. The production was originally to be directed by a real iconoclast of Deutches Regietheater (director's theater), Dietrich Hilsdorf, who in the end withdrew on health grounds, and Christopher Bond, the writer of the pastiche melodrama that had originally attracted Sondheim's interest in the subject, was co-opted at the last moment. The Germans, pursuing the path of Lessing and Goethe, still expect their theater to concentrate on ideas rather than entertainment and the right production, embracing their conceptual tradition of theater (and not aping a commercial musical), might attach Sondheim firmly back to one of his historical roots: the American musical as a descendant of nineteenth- and twentieth-century German music-theater traditions. *Sweeney* set in an abattoir, anyone? Actually this is not so far from Harold Prince's original vision.

When finally the National Theatre in London got around to bringing Sondheim into their fold they made the exciting choice of *Sunday in the Park with George* (1990, director Stephen Pimlott). The show had not yet been seen in Britain. Pimlott's production was daring and found very different solutions to the necessarily demanding visual challenges of the subject. Like it or loathe it, this was a cool, deconstructionist view of the piece and exactly the kind of enterprise that a national theater should be sponsoring—a first-class choice and a provocative production that would never have happened in the commercial world.

The reception of Sondheim's work provides one key to understand the vagaries of our uncertain theatrical times. When we performed *Pacific Overtures* at ENO, attitudes were changing. The 1980s saw the beginning of a major cultural shift that has and will continue to shape the arts. Money mattered, and money above all else. The ethos of the subsidized arts was gradually forced to change with the times too; from the end of the 1980s there would be no show in town that wasn't concerned above all with box office success. If you quietly whittle down the amount of subsidy by freezing the grant or by increasing it below the rate of inflation it soon means that the people running these companies have to pay much more attention to box office receipts and to "success," whether natural or manufactured (which is what the producers of West End shows became virtually Mephistophelean at doing during the decade). In the case of our *Pacific Overtures*, the marketing and sales department at ENO suddenly sighted a yellow brick road towards a potential financial Oz, and scheduled twenty-seven performances.

A "musical" could only mean money. It didn't matter that no opera at the Coliseum, the home of ENO, even a new *Carmen* or other popular opera titles, ever did more than a dozen or so performances in its initial run, nor that the ENO lacked the advertising expertise to fill the Coliseum (over 2000 seats a night) for almost a month of performances, or that it was necessary to find a different audience for a different product. The marketing gurus forgot that the very reason that some artists had chosen to do this particular piece was that it was our duty to do difficult, not popular, masterpieces. You could not assuage this new appetite for commercial success. So rather than undertake a safe eight performances, sell them out, and build a taste for it then revive the show two seasons later, reason was thrown to the great wind of imagined box office receipts. I must add that, unlike with a West End producer, there was never any pressure to make the show more commercial, only better, richer, but it was clear that the temptation to view not the challenging side of Sondheim, but the commercial possibility was, is, and always will be hard to resist for companies looking for cash cows. So the distinction began to blur between opera houses and a commercial theater becoming less amenable to the visions of Sondheim and big spenders like his early directorial collaborator, Harold Prince. Not surprisingly the subsidized sector would then prove to be a little too interested in anything perceived to have "popular" appeal. The heads of the big subsidized companies were suddenly desperate to secure their survival so no one was to blame except perhaps governments; no longer believing that the arts, just as much as health and education, are socially cohesive and educational, especially when they ask the more challenging questions, they turned back the clock on proper subsidy for the arts.

It is poignant to observe how many of Sondheim's shows have a sense of this economic realpolitik at their very heart. In their leisured introspection, the cocktail-set characters of *Company* sing of their frustrations and emptiness almost by reason of their financial security. They endure idle lives while watching at a distance as "another hundred people" come out of the ground. *Pacific Overtures* is a virtual treatise on the ugliness of global capitalism. By *Sweeney Todd* everything is economic, and Sweeney himself even analyzes this as he clearly becomes the king of savage cuts: "The history of the world, my sweet—.../—Is who gets eaten, and who gets to eat!"[2] The cast of *Assassins* are sleepwalkers, financial misfits stumbling away from the American dream of plenty into deep darkness. And financial success is the motoric force behind the brothers' journeys in *Road Show*, which, even when found, proves hollow and ephemeral. Sondheim knows and writes his times like no one else in this genre, deeply questioning all our values. This is also why he sooner or later needs to be performed by any company, high or low, that considers itself a serious theater.

The original Germanic music-theater tradition that Sondheim springs from has suffered badly from these new financial constraints. Wagner's ideal of *Gesamtkunstwerk* (total work of art) glows distantly somewhere over Sondheim's shoulder and is most evident in the degree of seriousness that he has imagined and then drafted within the frame of the musical genre. What a musical might be has been changed radically by him in work after work. But has his revolution now got anywhere to call home? These negative financial effects do not impede his actual writing, of course, which has continued remarkably unaffected, but they have not only reduced the possibilities for presentation but affected his legacy to young writers, inspired by this revolution—a matter he cares about far more passionately than his own personal reputation. It feels as if there is little chance for any genuine development in this field at present, at least in the English-speaking theater.

The final irony of this situation is that the subsidized theater now tends to absorb his pieces as guaranteed box office—core rep that is presented with little of his sense of experimental vision. In Britain we can certainly recognize Stephen Sondheim as part of the zeitgeist, the bold innovator finally tamed as the perfect artist for monetarist times, the creator of the sophisticated musical that has been made to serve two masters, art and money. But he is also a last remaining symbol, to a few of us, of a paradise lost; an ever-imaginative, innovative, popular modern music-theater developed through the subsidized sector that would change the future of the musical. To imagine that the tendency towards increased commercialization can now be reversed within the United Kingdom, that we can somehow return to Sondheim and his successors the chance to try out some challenging new ideas—to put the barbed wire back in the soufflé, or in general, to return to the halcyon days of proper levels of funding-is as unlikely as winning the prizes in "Another National Anthem."

Following their bravely curated Seurat exhibition, the National Theatre tackled *Sweeney Todd* (1993, director Declan Donnellan), *A Little Night Music* (1995, director Sean Matthias), and *A Funny Thing Happened on the Way to the Forum* (2004, director Edward Hall). None of these productions were anything other than commercial, and in accordance with the changing times they became increasingly so. Even though these were all very well executed shows and did much for Sondheim's serious reputation, none of them justified revival as a new interpretation produced as a special event by one of Britain's two major theater companies.

A Little Night Music has proved to be the second most popular of Sondheim's works to be championed by opera companies. It is perhaps the most perfectly formed operetta ever written. No wonder New York City Opera jumped in early with a production (1990, director Scott Ellis) and Houston Grand Opera once again kept the faith (1999, director Michael Leeds), this time with major opera stars in the lead roles: Frederica von Stade, Evelyn Lear, Sheri Greenawald, and Sir Thomas Allen. But again, even more so in the American context of almost entirely unsubsidized companies, they were lacking in new directorial concepts—watered down, nonconceptualized attempts to render Broadway in an unfamiliar setting, as Broadway itself became ever more estranged from Sondheim's continuing output. Australian Opera in Sydney, which had also performed *Sweeney Todd* in 2000, added *A Little Night Music* to its repertory (2009, director Stewart Maunder). So it is now true to say that Sondheim's cultural adoption is a worldwide phenomenon. One further somewhat unexpected development has been that the Théâtre du Châtelet, Paris (2010, director Lee Blakeley), presented *A Little Night Music* very successfully for a notoriously *sang-froid* Parisian audience, and as a result produced a new *Sweeney Todd* with the same director in spring 2011. This conquest can only end with *A Little Night Music* in Salzburg or *Sweeney Todd* in Bayreuth.

In 2002, I was asked to lead a workshop program funded by the Belgian-based Centre International de Formation en Arts du Spectacle (CIFAS), an organization funded by European Union and local Belgian government subsidy. I invited a dozen teams of young directors and designers, chosen by competition, to work on any show by Sondheim in Brussels. This two-week event took place at the opera house, Le Théâtre de la Monnaie, which also participated in hosting the event. The aim was to find a fresh and individual approach to presenting these works in mainland Europe, and the results were spectacular; the productions devised, scenic models built, scenes rehearsed with local professional actors and opera singers in English, the quality of the fresh cultural views on these pieces, were eye-opening. It suggested to me that the discovery of the broad possibilities of Sondheim's music-theater has scarcely begun for us, and that it might be in some of the great European companies—all subsidized to the hilt—that this would happen. It has. While in the English-speaking world we are stagnating with old hand-me-down styles of presentation of musicals, a new chapter in Sondheim's performance history will begin elsewhere. The borders are open: the possibilities boundless. One example: a new production of *Sweeney Todd*, sung in English, took place in the Lithuanian National Opera in Vilnius (2009, director Dalia Ibelhaubtaite).

One other strong, alternative line has emerged out of the innovative stagings of John Doyle; for although these have all the trappings of a studio production, they seek to rethink the ambitious ideas behind the original shows in each case. He has shown us that studio productions can also be highly sophisticated conceptually, starting with his *Sweeney Todd*, which originated in Newbury (2004) before transferring to London's West End and Broadway, and going on through his brilliant *Company* (Cincinatti Playhouse in the Park, in March 2006, followed by its Broadway transfer six months later), before culminating in both the New York and London premieres of *Road Show* at the Public Theatre (2008) and the Menier Chocolate Factory (2011). Starting in small, state-subsidized or sponsorship-funded companies, he has found a way to reinvent these shows. The use of singers who also play the musical instruments to become their own band is only one level of originality in these productions, but the sheer innovation of the reimagined performance style of the dialogue in *Company*, for example, and the bold stylization of *Road Show* have shown that in spite of constant pressures to downsize there are ways of being true to the vision of Sondheim, by moving away from the usual compact naturalism of almost all other previous studio realizations. By being audacious and imaginative, by reconnecting with the bold theatricality within each show he has somehow been truer to the spirit of these pieces—a startling glimpse of one way forward.

But still, something else lingers: have any subsequent productions of *A Little Night Music* had anything like the scope of the Harold Prince original, which delivered so much more than a naturalistic weekend in the country? Visually, at least, it found a way, with its waltzing trees and faded grandeur, in its elastic interplay of inside-outside locations, human nature versus animal nature, to recapture a sense of its source, the film *Smiles of a Summer Night*, by Ingmar Bergman, one of the world's greatest conceptual directors. Harold Prince and his Broadway designer Tony Walton visualized it beautifully. We may have had better acted, wittier, more grotesque productions of *Sweeney Todd* than the Prince original, but have any of these productions ever delivered the sheer vision of a society rotten to its core, or analyzed the way it functioned, as the Prince original did in those humanly diminishing Eugene Lee sets? The incredible thing is that that these were productions mounted on Broadway and in the West End in the 1970s that would nowadays seem too ambitious even for the subsidized sector. I am not hankering for reproductions of the original versions here, just seeking to encounter once again the brave vision they represent, not just of the pieces themselves, but of the power of music theater at its bold best.

The initial impact of Sondheim's pieces was as much to do with their audacious spirit as their brilliant writing. The early Harold Prince productions were all theatrically innovative, and no matter which book-writer collaborates with Sondheim, be it Wheeler, Furth, Weidman, or Lapine, they create together an idea, a concept, as much as incidents and characters. Surely this is *his* current running through the electric wire that connects all the pieces—the courage to explore; the quest to change the status quo of a brain-dead, heart-stopped Broadway; the challenge art offers to business; and the search in all of this for a new audience. Isn't that why Sondheim's work will increasingly need to find a future in the subsidized sector? His work will survive if that sector survives; for if this sector ceases to fund productions that explore, and becomes instead a kind of extravagant commercial showplace, it is too easy for its enemies to claim that it needs no financial help whatsoever.

Sondheim once said wistfully, "You know, I had the idealistic notion, when I was twenty that I was going into the theater. I wasn't; I was going into show business, and I was a fool to think otherwise." Perhaps implied in each of his works is a plea that in every new encounter with it, either as audience or as practitioners, we revive his initial idealistic enchantment in theater as an art—if not for him, at least for ourselves: "Look I made a hat.../ Where there never was a hat!"[3]

NOTES

1. At the time, the male members of the ENO company were more often available.
2. Stephen Sondheim and Hugh Wheeler, *Sweeney Todd: The Demon Barber of Fleet Street* (New York: Dodd, Mead, 1979), 105.
3. James Lapine and Stephen Sondheim, *Sunday in the Park with George* (London: Nick Hern, 1990), 45

PART IV

SONDHEIM ACROSS THE MEDIA

CHAPTER 15

··

EVENING PRIMROSE: SONDHEIM AND GOLDMAN'S TELEVISION MUSICAL

··

ROBYNN J. STILWELL

Charles, what is sadder than a waltz?

Mrs. Monday

"EVENING Primrose,"[1] John Collier's dark little short story about people living in a Manhattan department store, may seem a curious choice on which to base a musical. In retrospect, however, its appeal to Stephen Sondheim in the mid-1960s is not so surprising. Elements of the macabre fairy tale, the outcast hero (even if a near-parody of one), a compressed or repressed social sphere, and claustrophobic spaces emphasizing psychological states permeate the story, as does rhythmic and alliterative language, mimicking the voice of the narrator, a young poet, "Charles."

Evening Primrose came in a transitional time for Sondheim. He had made the move from lyricist to songwriter–composer in *A Funny Thing Happened on the Way to the Forum* (1962), but wouldn't have another Broadway success until *Company* (1970), placing *Evening Primrose* directly in the middle, relatively close on the heels of the notorious flop *Anyone Can Whistle* (1964). At the time, Sondheim was collaborating with James Goldman on what would become *Follies*; Goldman's wife was pregnant and the family needed a new apartment, which meant that Goldman needed more money. He proposed that he and Sondheim collaborate on a project for *ABC Stage 67*, an adaptation of John Collier's short story "Evening Primrose,"[2] and the resulting musical aired on November 19, 1966, in a production by John Houseman, starring Anthony Perkins, Charmian Carr, and Dorothy Stickney, directed by Paul Bogart.

The production is an intriguing snapshot that captures a number of intersecting impulses: Sondheim's own predilection toward mystery, fantasy, and the macabre; the shifting ground of mid-century popular culture, both in style and medium; and a yearning for the urban pastoral, an escape from the urbanization, mechanization, and alienation of the modern condition, particularly in New York City. Although perhaps a little odd, even in the output of the man who wrote *Sweeney Todd* and *Assassins, Evening Primrose* is a work in which one can find Sondheim's distinct voice in tune with a cultural moment that is just about to pass.

GENRE IN FLUX

The 1960s were a period of contraction and reorientation for the musical in all its guises. In part because of the shift in commercially popular musical styles—a generational shift in which the Tin Pan Alley style kept most of its audience, but the newer rock and rhythm and blues styles were capturing the younger listeners—the massive interpenetration of Hollywood, Broadway, the recording and sheet music industries, and early television started to recede, almost like islands emerging as an ocean retreats. The Broadway musical was moving from its central position in the popular music field toward a more elite theater-going experience, even as smaller, more experimental musicals like *The Fantasticks* and later rock musicals like *Hair, Godspell*, and *Jesus Christ Superstar* were transforming the expectations of the stage musical.

As an hour-long television musical, *Evening Primrose* is an anomalous example of even such a manifold genre. Most discussion of musicals focuses on either the theater or the film as a medium, for very good reasons, including sheer numbers, influence, and cultural dominance; even the academic disciplines involved differ: film musicals are usually the province of film studies, theatrical musicals of performance studies, with musicology either lagging behind or running between the two. The television musical is an orphan, a manifestation of the genre that never really got a chance to develop fully but had potential to become something distinct. The medium of television arose in the 1950s, at a time when the film and the theatrical musicals were at a peak of their classic production; but by the end of the decade, they were beginning to lose their cultural centrality. (Television has frequently been accused of being the *reason* for this loss, though that is almost certainly an exaggeration, as many forces were at play in that change). The television musical never really established itself as an independent genre; on the other hand, television itself was finding its way as a medium, in part through mimicry of genres from other media, like the sitcom and soap opera from radio or the musical from theater and film.

Television musicals tended to range from one to two hours in length, though yielding running time to commercials, and to fall into two major groups: adaptations of theatrical musicals, like *Annie Get Your Gun, Kiss Me Kate*, and *Anything Goes*; and fairytale musicals aimed at the family, like *The Pied Piper of Hamelin, Pinocchio*, and *Hansel and Gretel*. There is overlap, of course: the Broadway version of *Peter Pan* starring Mary Martin was staged three times for television, in 1955, 1956, and 1960. And perhaps the most famous of all television musicals, *Cinderella* (originally 1957, refilmed in 1964 and 1997) was written by Richard Rodgers and Oscar Hammerstein II. The original television musical was more prevalent in the 1950s and began to fade in the 1960s, mirroring the cinematic and, to some extent, theatrical realms.

The aesthetic frame of the television musical is primarily theatrical, in large part because of the limitations of technology and budget. In the era of live television, the liveness of theater was an obvious parallel, and film—so reliant on realistic sets and continuity editing—was not a practical model. The television camera could, however, allow a more flexible, multifronted set than a theater and close-ups that counteract the technological alienation of the black-and-white image, creating a language that was a hybrid of the cinematic and the theatrical. Each time the Mary Martin *Peter Pan* was televised, for instance, the staging was essentially the same, but changes of camera angle significantly affect the clarity and mood of some scenes: the scene in which Wendy stitches Peter's shadow to his feet is shot from opposite sides in 1955 and 1956, privileging Wendy's actions and reactions in one and Peter's in the other; perhaps more subtly, in a scene in which the camera lurks behind Tiger Lily and her tribe in the jungle to watch Hook and his crew cavort in a clearing, the camera is closer and the scene darker in the 1955 version. In this version, the audience seems to be "one of" Tiger Lily's band, but in the 1956 version, we are far enough away to be watching them. The 1956 version looks technically superior, but the 1955 version seems to have more intimacy and visceral impact.[3]

Like most television musicals until the 1990s, *Evening Primrose* was shot on videotape,[4] though it is somewhat more "cinematic" than most. The exteriors and some of the interiors of the department store were shot on location, and director Paul Bogart created a number of shots, particularly in the store, that give it a scope and some suggestively expressionistic moments often lacking in the predominantly brightly lit, cheerily artificial fairytale musical.[5]

STORY

Evening Primrose is an odd, dark little tale, but also very much a part of mid-century American popular culture in at least three overlapping ways: as a television musical, as a modern take on a fairy tale, and as an urban pastoral, a product of increased urbanization, isolation, and alienation. A young man named Charles takes up residence in a department store, renouncing the distractions and limitations of the bourgeois world to dedicate himself to poetry—or rather, to living his life as a poet, which is a significant distinction.

The musical opens with external shots of Stern Brothers Department Store, a nervous Charles (Anthony Perkins) checking his watch and running his hand through his hair before entering, and the closing of the loading dock doors. We then move inside, see the security guard locking the door and turning off the lights, and Charles hide in a display. The first musical number is his "If You Can Find Me, I'm Here," a song which foreshadows not only "I'm Still Here" from *Follies*, but "Being Alive" from *Company*.

As Charles hides from the night watchman, he discovers that he is not the only permanent resident of the store, most of them now elderly children of wealthy parents who
had taken refuge there during successive economic crises, the last group having arrived
in the Crash of 1929. The doyenne of the denizens, the elegant and imperious Mrs.
Monday, has taken as her maid a young woman named Ella (surely an intentional reference to Cinderella, another fairytale maiden treated poorly). Unlike the older residents,
Ella is not there as the result of an active escape; she was lost in the store at the age of six.
Her song, "I Remember," strongly references nature, even if that of "ponds and zoos"
within an urban landscape. Charles, of course, falls in love with Ella, and abortively pens
awful poetry ("Ella, gay as a tarantella") to a tune that will eventually become their duet,
"When?" Although not a song, or even a duet, that can really stand on its own outside
the context of the musical, it is one of the most striking televisual musical numbers of
the era, dependent on camera and prerecorded vocals for its effect.

Mrs. Monday and the others would not approve of their relationship, and Ella, who
dwells in the basement among the seconds and damaged goods, is particularly aware of
this. Anyone who endangers the clandestine world of the store, whether an intruder like
a security guard, a burglar, or a transgressing member of the community, is threatened
by the "Dark Men." Ella informs Charles that the Dark Men come from the "Journey's
End" Mortuary, and, in the morning, there are new mannequins.

Charles and Ella create a sanctuary for themselves in the sporting goods department,
where he can teach her to read and tell her about the world beyond ("Take Me to the
World"). Unfortunately, in his zeal to provide nature sounds for their mock campsite,
Charles turns on every sound-producing device he has gathered around them. This
accidentally includes the PA system, alerting Mrs. Monday and the Dark Men. A chase
ensues, and Charles and Ella hide among the boxes in a truck, figuring to escape in the
morning when they leave. (Reprise of "Take Me to the World.")

At the end, with exterior shots of Stern Brothers bracketing the musical, the security
guard turns on lights, the loading dock doors open and trucks emerge, and we see a
young couple looking at a bridal display in the window. From behind, they look like
Charles and Ella, but as the camera moves closer, we see that Charles and Ella are the
bride and groom mannequins in the window.

The adaptation makes some significant changes from John Collier's short story,
which is in the form of journal "found in a pad of Highlife Bond, bought by Miss Sadie
Brodribb at Bracey's for 25 cents" (16). Some of the changes reflect a shift toward realism: "Bracey's Giant Emporium" is a more fanciful name than the real "Stern Brothers."
Similarly, Collier's Charles makes himself a nest behind a towering pile of carpets, lined
with "eiderdowns, angora vestments, and the Cleopatraean tops in pillows" (16), while
Goldman and Sondheim's Charles is assigned a display furnished like a study, with a
desk and sofa. That their Mrs. Monday keeps her room unusually cold is a small touch
that recalls refrigeration, a sense of keeping old or stale things fresh, and is even a
reminder of the Dark Men's connection with a mortuary.

Other changes isolate the denizens of the department store and to some extent generalize or universalize the location. The short story evokes a sense of an alternate society,

an element lost in the transformation from page to screen. In the story, the society of Bracey's not only mount their own theatricals and soirées, but sneak out at night to attend those at Macy's, Gimbel's, and Bloomingdales, and there are asides about a disgraced colony at a five-and-dime and a lonely outcast who lives a "beachcomber existence" at a delicatessen. There's even the suggestion of cannibalism at "Journey's End" ("But what can they live upon, Ella, in a funeral home? / "Don't ask me! Dead people are sent there, to be embalmed. Oh, they are terrible creatures!"; 22), which is made more subtle—and funny—in the musical, when Charles responds to her mention of "Journey's End," his voice dropping in horror, "What do they live on?" The specificity of New York also resides in the original name of the grand dame: in the story, her name is "Mrs. Vanderpant," a Dutch name redolent of old New York society; in the musical, the more Anglicized "Monday" heightens a sense of time passed—her name may be the first day of the week, but she is in the "Saturday" of her life. Ella's name, of course, recalls Cinderella, but her last name, Harkins, not only carries a Dickensian quality but also the double meaning of listening. Ella has no real voice of her own in the store's society, but she does listen, a seemingly passive activity that can be turned to her advantage.

The most significant difference between the short story and the musical is the relationship between Charles, Ella, and the night watchman. In the musical, the relationship between the poet-prince and the young "Cinderella" is the fairytale (however dark) love story we expect in a musical, with the night watchman as the threat lurking in the forest. The short story, however, thwarts these conventions: Charles finds Ella entrancing and declares himself in love with her, but she is in love with the night watchman; so Charles becomes their enabler, their matchmaker. Their escape at the end is much more ambiguous, though Charles recognizes the possibility that the Dark Men will catch them, that one might "Look for three new figures: two men, one rather sensitive-looking, and a girl. She has blue eyes like periwinkle flowers, and her upper lip is lifted a little." The story ends with a melodramatic exhortation: "Smoke them out! Obliterate them! Avenge us!" (27).

We may laugh at the Charles in the short story, with his melodramatic prose and self-indulgent actions, but we have to feel more connection with Charles in the musical. He is made into a more sympathetic young man; the casting of Anthony Perkins undoubtedly helps, as sensitive, vulnerable young men were his stock in trade, from *Friendly Persuasion* to *Green Mansions*; and even Norman Bates is a victim turned victimizer. We see Charles struggle with his poetry, finding awkward rhymes for Ella (tarantella, umbrella, larks singing a capella). He recites a fragment of a poem to Mrs. Monday:

> Crack, crack, ConEdison, and crush the streets
> As cruel Vanessa does my heart
> She shatters me, and yet my heart still beats.
> Oh, happy pavement to be torn apart.

Her response, "Yes, yes, that's really terrible—the boy's a poet," is both cruel and affirmative of his calling. When, later, Mrs. Monday refuses to let him go, even if he promises not to tell, her assertion that she cannot because "It's too good a story not to tell," reaffirms his status. We can laugh at the juxtaposition of dismissal and praise in one utterance, but she reaffirms Charles's poethood. Similarly, the Ella in the musical is fleshed out, made more human, by her desire for contact with the natural world, and the human world within it (and by Charmian Carr's charming performance). In the story, those traces are certainly there, but by building entire scenes around Charles teaching her to read and giving her not one, but two, songs about the world outside ("I Remember," looking back, and "Take Me to the World," looking forward), the musical gives her significantly more dramatic weight. She is not just a function of Charles's adventure, as in the story, or a love interest, as one might expect, but a person the equal of our leading man.

Evening Primrose makes "Evening Primrose" into a musical—a dual-focus narrative, to recall Rick Altman's analytical frame,[6] making our leading characters sympathetic and equal and in love with each other. In this traditional musical structure, Stephen Sondheim's distinctive voice becomes fully recognizable. The four songs emerge smoothly from the dramatic texture and not only convey the inner state of the characters but also elucidate aspects of their story that reflect larger societal concerns. The staging ranges from simple and spare set pieces to spectacles that challenge the boundaries of the small screen.

"If You Can Find Me, I'm Here"

The music sneaks into *Evening Primrose*. The opening shots of the exterior of Stern Brothers are accompanied only by street noise, but as we follow Charles inside, a slightly dampened hand drum begins a two-note rhythm with just enough lift on the second note to make it clearly sound like a heartbeat. Charles finds a hiding place in a covered bed that even in the black and white video evokes the opulence of an Orientalist fantasy (resonating with the "Cleopatræan tops"). The connection of the "heartbeat" with Charles is strengthened when it drops out as the closing bells ring and the scene cuts away to the loading dock doors closing. The "heartbeat" then returns to follow the night watchman locking up and turning off the lights, as if Charles is watching. He peeks out from behind the curtain (an eerie intertextual reference that may seem creepier than intended, merely through the familiarity of Anthony Perkins's peeping in *Psycho*), and the reverberation increases on the last few beats before an ad break.[7] The heartbeat returns after the break, but now clearly more musicalized, orchestrated. Charles emerges from the pavilion and begins to speak in rhythm across the heartbeat.

Charles's first utterance in the short story is the source of "If You Can Find Me, I'm Here." The first paragraph of the journal is Charles's decision to turn his back on the "bourgeois world that hates a poet," corresponding to the shots of Charles hiding in the store. The second paragraph, expressing his exuberance at finding sanctuary in the store, is the closest approach of the lyrics to the source text. Sondheim has testified that Ella's song, "I Remember" is the closest he's ever come to writing directly from a source text, in this case Goldman's book rather than Collier's story,[8] but that connection seems primarily thematic: the changing of "I remember snow," for instance, to "I remember sky" so that Sondheim can achieve the ultimate rhyme with "die"; and still, the images of snow "soft as feathers, sharp as thumbtacks" are some of the most striking among the lyrics.

These kinds of similarities are also found between the short story and the lyrics, although the lyrics find a sharper distinction between Charles's poetical ways and his surroundings. "The bourgeois world that hates a poet" offers a weak, self-indulgent conflict; in the lyrics, by contrast, Charles bids farewell to "bloodsucking landlords, pouring their threats in my ear" and "Neanderthal neighbors, swilling their pretzels and beer," suggesting a more working-class environment. The bourgeois world may hate a poet, but a working-class one might have no sense of what that *is*.[9] The Charles in the musical may be self-indulgent and emotionally adolescent, but his sense of alienation is clearer and more concrete, which can generate a stronger connection with an audience than the melodramatic, polysyllabic narrator in the short story.

The spoken transition into the main body of "I'm Here" is one of the most distinctively "Sondheimian" moments of the score, and yet also a moment that seems to arise from Collier's writing. The second paragraph starts with a short, emphatic, "And I have done it." The declaration of action is sharp, clear, assertive, its dynamism increased by the anacrusis of "And." It creates a meaningful tension that connects it back to the desire to break away, while increasing the potential energy to land on the verb, the point of action. The "it" is less important metrically, but encompasses all that has come before, the turning away, the rejection, the leaving, negative actions that are themselves negated, rejected, or activated by Charles's action.

This second paragraph expands in celebration of Charles's freedom:

> I am free! Free as the mote that dances in the sunbeam! Free as a house-fly crossing first-class in the largest of luxury liners! Free as my verse! Free as the food I shall eat, the paper I write upon, the lambswool-lined softly slithering slippers I shall wear. (16)

The emphasis on the declaration "I am free!" is obviously taken up by Sondheim's lyrics, but the rhythm of the phrasing is striking. A short, assertive phrase is developed by a longer phrase, and then by one that is longer still, stretching the bounds of both metaphor and breathing; then the entire process is repeated, the third phrase both amplified and cramped by the assonance of first a liquid "l" and then a sibilant "s," creating an internal resistance to the forward flow if one imagines, or attempts, oral realization. The implications, rhythmic and semantic, of Collier's prosody are realized in Sondheim's setting (see Table 15.1).

Across the heartbeat rhythm, Charles begins to speak softly, in short, urgent phrases. "*Is it done? Are they gone?*" The two-eighth-note anacrusis falls to the verb on the downbeat, and the staccato of the second beat in the bass and drum pattern (the "dub" of the lub-dub heartbeat), finishes the arc described by the phrase, as if a ball were bouncing on the downbeat. This rhythm is intensified in the next phrase with the addition of a third eighth-note to the anacrusis: "*Am I alone?*" The two-bar iteration pattern established

Table 15.1 The rhythm scheme of the spoken transition into "If You Can Find Me, I'm Here"

			Is it	
done?	Are they	gone?	Am I a-	
lone?			I am a-	
lone. It's	done. They're	gone. I am a	ge-nius.	
Charles, you are an	un-a-dul- ter- at-ed	ge- nius, you are an	in- dis- put- ab-ly,	
			ex-	
traordinary…What	that?			Not a
was				
thing.	You're a	fool.	You are a-	
lone.			And it be-	
gins.				
Careful.	Careful.	Mustn't get excited,	mustn't over do it.	
Softly.	Tip-toe.	You'll get used to	no time.	
		it in		
Look at it.	Beautiful.	What a place to	live! What a place to	
write! I shall be in-	spired. I shall turn	elegies and sonnets,	Verses by the ton. At	
	out			
last I have a home.	nobody will know,	No one in the world,	Nobody will know	
And			I'm	
here!	(sung) *I am*	*here!*		

in the first two phrases is both maintained and disrupted by the silent third and fourth bars, an implied beat of "listening" that is confirmed with the consequent phrase, "I *am* alone," which suddenly shifts the emphasis from the downbeat to beat three and the confirmation of his state of being: he *is* alone.

The metric tension is further intensified by his immediate "It's done, they're gone" on the next two bars, landing firmly on the downbeat and then completing the mirror structure of the phrase by repeating the rhythm of the first bar and adding another weak beat on the end ("I am a genius."). This symmetry conceptually closes off the phrase, but the weak ending and the semantic content pull forward into the next phrase, as Charles excitedly congratulates himself.

The addition of his own name creates the first isolated downbeat of the phrase, and the extension into full measures composed almost entirely of eighth notes intensifies the rhythmic drive until the phrase overflows its four-bar pattern and is interrupted by the displaced next phrase. The stream of eighth notes completes the process of filling in the bar, but introduces an internal tension as the first syllable of "extraordinary" starts on the sixth eighth note of the fourth bar of the phrase, placing the diphthong "traor" on the downbeat of the fifth bar, and the interruption "What was that?" comes on beat three, leading to the downbeat on "that?" While natural diction, this also creates an effect rather like an elastic band being stretched, creating both increased length and tension as the phrase is extended but the internal rhythm shortens. An arrival that *feels* like it should be on the fifth or ninth bar happens on the sixth. But then the rests, as he "listens," push the eight-bar pattern to nine before the reiteration of the first, tentative rhythmic phrases as he calms himself. At the larger scale, this phrase's repetition creates another arch, once again closing rhythmically but with an expectant "And it begins," leading forward.

The next section creates a new set of rhythmic expectations, sharply accentuating the downbeat without the cushion of the anacrusis and amplifying the heartbeat rhythm: "Careful. Careful. Mustn't get excited, mustn't overdo it. / Softly. Tiptoe. You'll get used to it in no time." Here, instead of being stretched, the last phrase is compressed, losing a full bar of eighth notes and placing the two quarter notes ("no time") in a weak position on the downbeat of the fourth bar, rather than the expected downbeat of the next four-bar phrase.

The metric quality shifts once again in the thirteen-bar build-up to singing. The rhythm "Look at it! / Beautiful!" is the same two-eighth-note–quarter-note rhythm that was prevalent at the beginning ("Is it done?"), but now across beats two and three, rather than three and one, giving it a breathless, rushed quality that races into "What a place to live! What a place to write!" This places the verbs at the downbeat again, but now extends the anacrusis to four eighth-notes, building momentum. Streams of eighth notes ensue as Charles lists his aspirations, and the rhythm hits two emphatic, repeated measures that shift the four-eighth-note–quarter-note patterns from 2–3–1 to 1–2–3 (the only combination not yet used) "[and] Nobody will know, / No one in the world," with the third iteration extended to the downbeat "Nobody will know I'm here!" on the downbeat of the thirteenth bar. In bar 14, two quarter notes pick up the declarative arpeggio on the first sung phrase, "I am free!" landing firmly on the first beat with the all-important "free!" From this point, the metric structure of the sung part settles down into steady four-bar phrases, with occasional two-bar vamps for spacing.

The song proper is a brisk waltz in one, with circulating melodic phrases that outline the chord changes but build to the heraldic leaps upward on "I'm Here" that arrive strongly on the downbeat of the measure. The resemblance to "I'm Still Here" from *Follies* is undeniable in the similarity of the lyrics and the upward leap on the salient word "here" —a statement not just of location but of a state of being in both songs. But while "I'm Still Here" is a celebration of survival, "If You Can Find Me, I'm Here" is a declaration of self, of identity, though one that also needs a second term to the equation. The song subtly foreshadows Ella, another incomplete personality who needs someone to see her, to recognize her humanity, and Charles needs someone to find him, perhaps even to look for him, that alienation of the individual among the masses, bordering on anomie, that is not only a common condition of mid-twentieth-century urban life, but a recurring state in Sondheim's characters. The circular phrasing with a driving asymmetrical rhythm highlights similarities to another Sondheim standard of the era, "Being Alive," from *Company* (1970). The fast waltz in "I'm Here" has the same forward impetus as the suggestion of a rhumba in "Being Alive," and the lyrics in both often focus on that which confines the singer (whether bloodsucking landlords and Neanderthal neighbors, or someone who loves them too much, holds them too close). And both songs build to an assertive declaration of selfhood at the high peak of a melody on the downbeat.

The song is staged rather like a Gene Kelly street dance among the aisles of the department store, often shot from slightly above, showing the depth of field and the vastness of the store. The Kellyesque street dance often uses the familiar frame of the street for spectacularized movement, with the everyday nature of the background "magicked" by the dance. In this number, Perkins is not really dancing, merely moving rhythmically along the aisles, occasionally interacting with the items in the store, placing him *in* the store the same way that Kelly might hang on a lamppost or stomp in a puddle. Notably, Charles puts on house slippers that illustrate not only Sondheim's "forty pianos and ten thousand shoes" but recall Collier's "lambswool-lined softly slithering slippers."

The slightly elevated camera angle, although conditioned by the space in the location,[10] also suggests the surveillance already implied in the opening by the shots of the night watchman, which will intensify throughout the musical with the eerie references to the Dark Men. The sense of "overlooking" is amplified by Perkins's eyeline, which approximates direct address to the camera, but is slightly too high and to the right of the camera; Perkins has said that this eyeline was Sondheim's suggestion[11] and acknowledged its awkwardness. However, the "off" eyeline heightens the sense of unease, perhaps unconsciously, because it is neither direct address nor directed outward in a more natural performance style. The oblique look seems to recognize the camera, but avoids making eye contact; more appropriately to the context, it may suggest Charles feels safe with the camera but is looking outward for threat in the shadows.

Charles eventually wends his way up the stopped escalator at the top of the frame, and his last declaration "I am—" is interrupted prophetically by the steps of the nightwatchman, and he jumps over the side. This escalator is where the final chase ends, and the spot from where he jumps is the place where Charles and Ella are captured by the night watchman and the Dark Men.

"WHEN"

While "I'm Free" is a cinematic moment, in its staging and its smooth elision between speaking and singing, "When" is arguably the most televisual. It is certainly dependent upon the apparatus of a camera for its multiple camera angles and quick edits from one character to another, and for its heavy reliance on nondiegetic sound. The singing is in voiceover, as if imagined by each character: Charles begins by urging Ella to look at him and concentrate, suggesting that they are making telepathic contact. Occasional interjections are made diegetically by the card players, but the bulk of the number is a duet in semirecitative form, shot mostly around a bridge table, as Charles and Ella exchange longing glances.

The melody is composed only of a couple of arpeggiated melodic phrases, sung first over held chords, then a simple, upbeat chordal pattern. The primary melody is the one to which we have heard Charles attempting his awful poetry ("Ella, gay as a tarantella," "Let my poem be your umbrella," lines which recur in the duet), and as such, it comes conditioned with a kind of awkward *naïveté*, bolstered by the downward tonic arpeggio, followed by an upward arpeggio on the minor supertonic, or one full step higher. As their romantic intensity and/or curiosity about the other increases, the meter changes from 4/4 to 3/4 and the melody curls around a few notes at the bottom of the range, creating a sense of urgency and breathlessness that heightens the sense of natural conversation, or even a sense of speaking under one's breath.

While the music itself is effective, the staging and editing are what make it distinctly televisual. The camera has to contend with a card party around a round table—always a difficult shooting arrangement, as shooting has to be "covered" from all angles, meaning a great deal of redundancy in filming—plus additional characters, watching around the table. Tight close-ups and comparatively quick editing on angles higher or lower than the normal eyeline are striking and to some extent draw attention to the "cinematic" aspects of the camera, but in doing so, reflect the nature of television, its history, and interaction with film.

On first viewing of this scene, I was strongly reminded of the famous garden club and brainwashing scene of *The Manchurian Candidate* (1962), which was directed by John Frankenheimer. The scenes are similar in their circular composition: the *Manchurian Candidate* is less so in real physical space: the brainwashing chamber is circular, but the garden party set alternates between an audience and a semicircular setup on a stage, making both spaces much more expansive than the bridge game set-up in *Evening Primrose*. The distinctive 360° camera pan, though, reinforces the sense of enclosed circularity. The relatively swift cutting rhythm between speakers and reaction shots, the low and high camera angles and unusually close close-ups may well reflect a common televisual language, albeit one with a cinematic accent. Frankenheimer had honed his craft directing live drama for television, particularly for *Playhouse 90* and *Climax!* The striking visual style of his production of *The Days of Wine and Roses* (1958), for instance, with its sharp angles and unusual perspectivizing shots recall 1920s and 1930s expressionism, but conditioned by the limitations of a television camera. In *The Manchurian Candidate*, Frankenheimer's wide screen often is composed of a close-up at one side of the frame with other characters ranged in mid and deep focus across the width, expanding the language of his television productions (Figure 15.1).

In "When," the alternating shots on each character as they think or sing a line is composed in shot–reverse-shot fashion, a conventional technique from cinema, but the close-ups are more close up than most cinematic versions, and especially with their yearning expressions, the scene looks distinctly like a soap opera interchange. The legibility of faces on the relatively small, indistinct television screens of the 1950s, and even the dominance of the voice and utterance in genres such as soap opera or news broadcasts—both of which were early transfers from radio to the newer medium of television—led to heavy reliance on close-ups.

This is not meant to be disparaging at all—the more one is aware of the difficulties of shooting such a scene, the more one can admire the relative ease with which it presents the song, and while the resemblance to *The Manchurian Candidate* can be seen as an appeal to art,[12] the similarity to soap opera can underline the romantic element even as it

FIGURE 15.1 Anthony Perkins as Charles Snell, Dorothy Stickney as Mrs. Monday, and Charmian Carr as Ella Harkins in *Evening Primrose* (1966).

recaptures a little of Collier's sense of parody, more obvious in the overheated language of his first-person narrator.

"I Remember"/"Take Me to the World" and the Urban Pastoral

Ella's two ballads from the song score, particularly "I Remember," have had the most life outside the bounds of the musical, having been performed and recorded more often than the others.[13] Musically and lyrically, they are less tightly bound into the texture of the drama than "If You Can Find Me, I'm Here" or especially "When." Both are relatively simple, rhythmically, melodically, and harmonically, though "I Remember" also has a couple of short phrases that mimic a waltz topic ("soft as feathers / sharp as thumbtacks" is arpeggiated across beats 2–4 in two successive measures, with the rest on the downbeat hinting at an elongated breath and the implied downbeat on beat 2 creating a slight metric tension).

The way that Ella's two songs are staged and shot—much more simply than either "If You Can Find Me, I'm Here" or "When" —concentrates on Ella's personhood and her relationship with Charles. Both of them are markedly static (and, in that stillness, theatrical, since it would be impractical to move much while singing the expansive tunes); both show Ella's face in close-up, unedited, for long stretches, using the back of Charles's head and shoulder to frame and support her. These close-ups, not unlike those in "When," give us entry into Ella's thoughts, though this time we also can see the physical effort of singing as well as the flickers of emotion across her eyes and mouth and the slight shifts of her head position as she looks up to the imagined sky, or casts her eyes down in shyness. In "I Remember," she is seated on the bottom steps of the basement stairs, with Charles crouching below her, looking up at her. This adoration could be romantic, or could be admiring deference to the imagery she evokes. In "Take Me to the World," we see them as a couple, lying in a hammock in tennis gear, or at a (fake) campfire. The majority of the song frames them in an embrace in front of the tent, with the camera looking over Charles's shoulder, down on Ella. The angle seems unusually severe, but was the product of the difference in height between Perkins and Carr; this strengthens the echo, however, in the reprise, as we see them crouching in embrace among the boxes in the back of a truck, awaiting escape. The high angle, again, was largely practical but evokes surveillance—and, in fact, when Charles accidentally turns on the PA system, that surveillance is realized, although through aural rather than visual means.

In addition to their more recognizably "song-like" aspects and more conventional functions in the narrative of the musical, these two songs also tap into more universal tropes of longing. In particular, they are part of a strong subtext of the urban pastoral that permeates *Evening Primrose*.

Collier's story (perhaps consciously) is an urban pastoral of a sort not uncommon in mid-twentieth-century American popular culture. A person who may be a poet, like Collier's Charles Snell, or even a precocious child like E. L. Konigsburg's Claudia in *From the Mixed-up Files of Mrs. Basil E. Frankweiler* (1967), finds some place of escape within the city, a city which is almost always New York City, even if unnamed. (One could imagine it being Chicago, but population and architectural density, particularly skyscrapers, seem to be a prerequisite.) Both are escaping a bourgeois existence: Charles explicitly renounces "the bourgeois world that hates a poet," while Claudia is running away from a suburban home in which she feels unappreciated, but the motivation seems to be the same—Charles is simply "poet" enough to hyperbolize.

The pastoral elements of "Evening Primrose" start in the title itself, evocative of nature, fragility, and a liminal time in the circadian cycle. It is the descent into darkness, the last glimmers of light. The Dark Men are a shadowy (literally) evocation of the coming of night. The pastoral is, for all its simplicity, the eye of a storm, light holding the darkness at bay. It is a space created by the centripetal force of distinctions between urban and rural, cultivated and wild, work and leisure. The pastoral is a kind of familiar exotic, a seductive other. The pastoral is always conditioned by the urban; the periods in which the pastoral flourished most prominently in Western culture—the Hellenic, the Renaissance,[14] and the Industrial Revolution—are periods of increased urbanization. The "peace" of the rural existence is available only in contrast to the "noise" of the city, and the work of the shepherd is idleness only to the person whose livelihood is not dependent upon animal husbandry. The pastoral landscape is also a tamed landscape; it is the "civilized" rural, implicitly surrounded by the wild forest that harbors a threat like the wolf—a real threat, a fairytale threat, and a gothic fantasy (the werewolf) such as that of the Dark Men.

This escape from the urban features in the postwar suburban boom, captured in frenetic irony by Eric Hodgins's *Mr. Blandings Builds his Dream House* (1946) and Betty McDonald's *The Egg and I* (1945) and the films thereof; even the Ricardos made their escape from their Manhattan apartment to a "farm" in Connecticut in the last season of *I Love Lucy*. In the early 1960s, popular Brill Building songs, such as "Up on the Roof" and "Under the Boardwalk," not only depict places of peace and possible romance or sex within the cityscape, but in their prepositional form, emphasize removal, distance, the act of moving away from the city. The later 1960s pushed the borders of escape further in the hippie commune movement, but also brought the pastoral into the cities with "flower power."

The sense of a unique, personal identity under threat in a modern urban existence is a theme of many stories, movies, and television shows at mid-century, and the link with corporate culture is often pivotal; marketing and advertising, public relations, and insurance feature heavily, as they are both modern fields and ones in which labor is indirect and parasitic on the creativity and/or production of others. In both *The Apartment* and the film version of *Days of Wine and Roses*, Jack Lemmon's characters (an insurance statistician and public relations agent, respectively—men who are busy, but not productive in an older sense) find a conflict between integrity and success; *The Man in the Gray Flannel Suit* has to choose between the demands of family in the suburbs and a successful career as a PR man for a television network in Manhattan.

The story that most often arises in comparison with *Evening Primrose* is the *Twilight Zone* episode "The After Hours" (no. 134, June 10, 1960), in which a confused young woman in a deserted department store at night discovers that she is, in fact, a mannequin whose chance to roam the city as a Pinocchio-like "real girl" has come to an end. The resemblance may be stronger than mere thematic similarity: in his introduction to the 2003 edition of *Fancies and Goodnights*, the 1951 collection of Collier short stories that first included "Evening Primrose," Ray Bradbury relates that he met *Twilight Zone* creator Rod Serling at a dinner soon after the commissioning of the series, and Serling was uncertain about the genre; Bradbury took him to his basement to load him up with books by Richard Matheson, Charles Beaumont (both of whom would write for *The Twilight Zone*), and Roald Dahl. "On top of the stack," reports Bradbury, he placed John Collier and told Serling, "There's your *Twilight Zone*" (x).

Though both question the reality of individual identity, the two stories form conceptual bookends. In "The After Hours," Marsha is aware that her identity is unsteady, marginal, but doesn't know why; it makes sense in the end that she is, in fact, a mannequin, but her feelings of isolation and lack of recognition in modern urban life circa 1960 were hardly particular to briefly animated mannequins. Ella and Charles *become* mannequins, but is it worse for them to have lost their personhood, compared to Marsha, who never had one? In fact, one can even question the distinct personhood of Charles, who so strongly fancies himself a poet that he has very little personality other than that constructed around that stereotype, and Ella, who has had no independent life since the age of six. They are certainly immature, and even incomplete personalities, each cut off from a sense of belonging: Charles rejects the bourgeoisie he perceives as hating him, and Ella, as an abandoned child growing up as a servant, is the only involuntary resident of the department store.

This sense of isolation from society is even more intense in the musical than in the short story. Though an understandable casualty of the transformation from page to screen, the short story's evocation of a covert, nocturnal, alternate society in New York's commercial establishments is narrowed down to an isolated colony in a single store. The isolation and separation are emphasized by the composition of that society, those who were attempting to escape economic disenfranchisement—not poor people, or even rich people who lost their wealth, but the children of the wealthy who did not know how to survive without money and so escaped into a mercantile fantasy of plenitude. Wealth and youth are similarly placed as "lost," when Collier describes "elderly ingénues," or a distracted Mrs. Billby loses her way to the (outmoded) parasol department in the musical; when confronted by the nightwatchman, she evokes another kind of "lost," when she quotes *Peter Pan*, "The clerk said first left and straight on 'til morning, but that can't be right." The eternal childhood of Peter and his lost boys "can't be right" for a colony of lost children who are growing old without growing up.

CONCLUSION

In both its literary and telemusical versions, *Evening Primrose* reflects many of Sondheim's ongoing concerns. The dangers of conformity were a major cultural theme during his formative creative years, but like his near-contemporary Pete Townshend, he was also critical of excessive romanticizing of the outsider at a time when the counter-cultural revolution was gathering steam and breaking out in full force. While realistic, this acknowledgement of the tension between "fitting in" and "standing out" is bleak. Understanding Sweeney Todd's victimization doesn't excuse his indiscriminate murder, any more than understanding Lee Harvey Oswald's, Squeaky Fromme's, or John Hinckley's need to be "seen" excuses theirs. The political act of assassination is only a mask that dramatizes much smaller, more human ends. These later examples are magnifications—perhaps similar masks—of the conflicts of Bobby, who wants but doesn't want connection, or Charles, who escapes society, only to be trapped in one even more claustrophobic.

Much more remains to be said about *Evening Primrose*, as a television musical, as a manifestation of cultural anxieties of the mid-twentieth century, and as an early utterance of Sondheim's mature voice. The underscore deserves more attention than I have been able to give it here, two sequences in particular. The chase sequence composed by a young David Shire is intriguing not only as an early chance to hear his work but in its striking modernist language that at one point strongly recalls Igor Stravinsky's *Agon*—a work that was only nine years old at the time and would have been familiar if not to a television audience, then to an audience who also attended the New York City Ballet with some regularity. Also resonating with the Franco-Russian line of American art-music heritage are the short waltzes that the "elderly ingénues" play at Mrs. Monday's dance. Although the two ladies mime playing recorders onscreen, we hear two clarinets. Stephen Banfield says that they sound as if they were written by a student of Nadia Boulanger[15] and emphasizes the work's "neoclassical containment."[16]

This last phrase strikes me as particularly pertinent. "Neoclassical" is an indirect historical evocation of the pastoral of the Industrial Revolution, and "containment" is a form of "isolation." So many of Sondheim's mature works are, musically as well as thematically, about the tension between isolation and connection, between grand emotional musical expression and a "civilized" restraint. In this respect, *Evening Primrose* is a clear sign of things to come.

NOTES

1. Page ref?
2. "Evening Primrose" indicates the short story, *Evening Primrose* indicates the television musical.
3. I have written elsewhere about the three television productions of the Rodgers and Hammerstein *Cinderella* and how the differences reflect stages of aesthetic development of television, corresponding roughly to theatrical (1957), televisual (1964), and cinematic (1997). Robynn J. Stilwell, "The Television Musical: Rodgers & Hammerstein's *Cinderella*," in *The Oxford Handbook of the American Musical*, ed. Raymond Knapp, Mitchell Morris, and Stacy Wolf (New York: Oxford University Press, 2011)
4. Only a black-and-white videotape of the original color version survives (as far as we know); a commercial DVD was released in October 2010.
5. Bogart himself was disappointed in his ability to create the sense of threat and darkness that he envisioned, particularly surrounding the Dark Men. This was a function of technological limitation (microphone technology, lighting, videotape) and a lack of money and time (personal communication, July 16, 2010)
6. See Rick Altman, *The American Film Musical* (Bloomington: Indiana University Press, 1987). Although the *Evening Primrose* musical is not a film musical, it shares similar narrative strategies and, as mentioned above, has more cinematic aspects than most television musicals of the era.
7. The videotape studied excludes the commercials, but the blackout and the distinct shift of orchestration upon return are characteristic, and Paul Bogart confirmed that this was, indeed, a break (personal communication, July 16, 2010).
8. Stephen Citron, *Sondheim and Lloyd-Webber: The New Musical* (New York: Oxford University Press, 2001), 142.
9. This is not at all to say that the working class does not produce artists, and might not even revere the talent of artists, but that practicalities may make such pursuits more difficult and separated from everyday lived experience.
10. Paul Bogart, personal communication, July 16, 2010.

11. Video of roundtable on *Evening Primrose*; Museum of Broadcasting 6th Annual Television Festival, Los Angeles, March 2, 1989 (viewed at the Paley Center for Media, New York City). Bogart acknowledges that because he dislikes direct address in television, he was uncertain which way to go with the moment, and left the decision to Sondheim (Paul Bogart, personal communication, July 16, 2010).

12. In an interview, Paul Bogart chuckled at the comparison to *The Manchurian Candidate*, but as we talked about it, we agreed that it was likely that Frankenheimer's work in television had influenced his cinematic style. The soap opera comparison, Bogart said, was necessitated by the "internal" singing and the need to connect their faces and reactions with their voices (Bogart, personal communication, July 16, 2010). Robert Allen's work on soap operas accentuated the importance of *telling* (an utterance eliciting a response, verbal or nonverbal); see Allen, "Reader-oriented Criticism and Television," in *Channels of Discourse: Television and Contemporary Criticism*, ed. Robert C. Allen, 74–112 (Chapel Hill: University of North Carolina Press, 1987). It makes sense that action and reaction would best be conveyed by a familiar televisual strategy.

13. Drawn from compiling searches on Amazon.com, allmusic.com, and iTunes.

14. When Claudia escapes the suburbs in *Mixed-Up Files*, she runs to the Metropolitan Museum of Art, where she becomes embroiled in a mystery about Renaissance art, a statue of a cherub that might be by Michelangelo.

15. My initial reaction was not dissimilar, musicologically, although as a former clarinetist, my first thought was that the waltzes would provide a nice addition to the sparse repertoire for two clarinets in a conservatory setting.

16. Stephen Banfield, *Sondheim's Broadway Musicals* (Ann Arbor: University of Michigan Press, 1993), 45.

CHAPTER 16

FROM SCREEN TO STAGE: *A LITTLE NIGHT MUSIC* AND *PASSION*

GEOFFREY BLOCK

OVER the past few decades, movies, usually Hollywood movies, have gradually replaced plays, novels, and short stories as primary sources for Broadway musicals. Movies great and small, from classics like Joseph L. Mankiewicz's *All About Eve* and Federico Fellini's *8½* (adapted, respectively, into *Applause* and *Nine*), and Billy Wilder's *Sunset Boulevard* to film diversions such as *Urban Cowboy* to *Legally Blonde* have joined juke box retrospectives as the most usual suspects for a new musical. Prior to 1960 such adaptations were rare. In fact, perhaps alone among the generation of Broadway composers active from the 1920s through the 1950s, and not until his final show, did a major composer, Cole Porter, adapt a film into a musical, the modest hit *Silk Stockings* (1955) based on *Ninotchka* (1939). Dozens of film adaptations would follow, increasing exponentially over the next four decades. Among the best known are *She Loves Me* (adapted from *The Shop around the Corner*) and *Promises, Promises* (*The Apartment*) in the 1960s, *Applause, A Little Night Music, The Wiz*, and *On the Twentieth Century* in the 1970s, *Woman of the Year, Little Shop of Horrors, Nine, La Cage aux Folles, The Phantom of the Opera*, and *City of Angels*, in the 1980s, *Sunset Boulevard, Beauty and the Beast, Passion, Victor Victoria, Big, The Lion King, Footloose*, and *The Full Monty* in the 1990s, and in the past decade, *The Producers, Sweet Smell of Success, Thoroughly Modern Millie, Hairspray, Spamalot, Billy Elliot, 39 Steps*, and *Shrek*, among others.

Significantly, in contrast to earlier generations, nearly all of the major figures who arrived on Broadway after 1960 have adapted one or more Hollywood or European films for the musical stage.[1] This chapter will explore how Stephen Sondheim, in collaboration with director Hal Prince and librettist Hugh Wheeler and later director-librettist James Lapine, adapted two films to the musical stage: *A Little Night Music* in 1973 and *Passion* in 1994. *Night Music*, which opened on February 25, 1973, was based on Swedish director Ingmar Bergman's comic masterpiece *Smiles of a Summer Night* (1955). Two decades later *Passion* arrived (on May 9, 1994), an adaptation of a less well-known film by the Italian director Ettore Scola, *Passione d'Amore* (1981), a film based on the novel

Fosca, which its Italian author Iginio Ugo Tarchetti almost completed in serial form the year he died (at almost exactly the same age as its central character).[2] Bergman, one of the most internationally acclaimed film directors of his generation, was known primarily for such brilliant, psychologically rich, if somewhat gloomy, films as *The Seventh Seal* (1956) and *Persona* (1967). In the larger context of his film career, *Summer Night* must be considered unrepresentative.[3] Scola, along with Michelangelo Antonioni, Federico Fellini, Bernardo Bertolucci, Pier Paolo Pasolini, and Francesco Rosi followed in the wake of the post-Second World War neorealists, Vittorio De Sica, Roberto Rosselini, and Luchino Visconti. Although film historian Ephraim Katz assessed Scola as "one of the most highly regarded figures in European cinema today," perhaps the only Scola film widely shown in the United States (and even recognized with an Oscar nomination in the foreign film category), was *Una giornata particolare*, released as *A Special Day* (1977), starring the leading Italian romantic film partnership of their day, Sophia Loren and Marcello Mastroianni.[4]

Prince and Sondheim, a devoted cineaste since his teenage years, turned to *Smiles of Summer Night* after failing twice in their efforts to secure the rights to Jean Anouilh's play *Ring Round the Moon* (1948).[5] On viewing *Passione d'Amore* in 1983 in a movie theater across Broadway from Lincoln Center, Sondheim was moved to tears by the frightfully ugly central character Fosca and her effect on the handsome soldier Giorgio, remembering the film more than a decade later, and managing to persuade a reluctant Lapine to adapt it into a musical.[6] Along with *Sweeney Todd*, which was greatly influenced by if not directly based on a film, *Hangover Square* (1945), with its score by Bernard Herrmann, *Passion* is the only show that Sondheim initiated himself (Prince or other collaborators initiated all the others).[7]

When Bergman was interviewed by reporter Marie Nyröd on Svensk Television in summer 2003, he freely acknowledged *Smiles of a Summer Night* as the "turning point" in his career. The unexpected success of *Smiles* at Cannes (where it was entered without Bergman's knowledge) gave the struggling director the financial and artistic freedom he craved: "Since the success of a *Summer Night*, I've never had anybody interfering in my business. I've always done whatever I wanted."[8] After the "cheerful and carefree" *Smiles* "with its slightly serious tone," Bergman was able to turn to the more somber *The Seventh Seal* (1957).[9]

Night Music occupies an analogous place in the work of Sondheim. After the huge financial losses incurred with *Follies*, *Night Music* was the hit Sondheim and Prince needed in order to continue writing and producing the shows they wished to. Although they began with the idea of creating an "elaborate, quite experimental memory piece" (an idea that was eventually incorporated to some extent in Wheeler's screenplay for the 1978 film, also directed by Prince), in the end they decided to write a more conventional and traditional show.[10] Earlier in the process Sondheim had a different take on the show's tone, but concluded at the second reading of the play that some of his songs "were so dark—because I was really writing to Ingmar Bergman rather than to Hugh Wheeler—that we could see it going right off the track," and "threw out practically all the songs."[11] Somewhat surprisingly, although Prince influenced Sondheim in moving the adaptation in a more traditional direction, his later somewhat cynical assessment exhibited less joy, both in the process and in the result:

> I didn't enjoy doing *A Little Night Music*. I suffered no sleepless nights. I wasn't digging deep into myself. Of course, there are things I learned: the dinner-table scene, of which I'm very proud, and the final scene, on the lawn, are extensions of techniques begun with *Cabaret* and better realized with the birthday parties in *Company*. But mostly *Night Music* was about having a hit.[12]

Night Music was the third of the Prince–Sondheim collaborations that began with the path-breaking *Company* in 1970 and ended with the financial and critical failure of *Merrily We Roll Along* in 1981 (the others are *Follies* in 1971, *Pacific Overtures* in 1976, and *Sweeney Todd* in 1979). Although at 601 performances it fell far short of the nearly 2000 performances enjoyed by *Pippin*, *Night Music* followed *Company* as Sondheim's second show to win the coveted Tony Award for Best Musical, besting *Pippin*. In welcome contrast to *Follies*, *Night Music* also managed to pay back its entire investment within six months, long before it closed on August 3, 1974.[13] In short, *Night Music*, a show "about having a hit," *was* a hit.

On one level the subject of both the *Smiles* film and its musical adaptation is the circuitous process of discovering the right partner. More ambitiously, both versions are also investigations of the meaning of love itself. The summary below identifies the four pairs of lovers—and two nonlovers—in their *Night Music* personae (with parenthetical jottings concerning their counterparts in *Smiles*):

Anne and Henrik

- *Anne* (eighteen; sixteen in *Smiles*), the virginal bride of the prosperous middle-aged lawyer Fredrik for the past eleven months (two years in *Smiles*), does not realize she loves Fredrik's nineteen-year-old son Henrik.
- *Henrik*, a repressed theology student, suppresses his love for Anne and instead tries, unsuccessfully, to make love to Petra, the Egerman's sensual young maid, before discovering and professing his love for his stepmother. In the end, Anne and Henrik elope in full view of and without opposition from the sadder but wiser Fredrik.

Fredrik and Desirée

- The prosperous middle-aged lawyer *Fredrik*, who is suffering an unconsummated marriage to Anne, does not realize he loves the actress Desirée Armfeldt, with whom he had an affair fourteen years earlier (five years in *Smiles*).

- *Desirée*, Fredrik's former mistress, tiring of the "glamorous life" of an aging, end-lessly touring actress, is having a dalliance with the married Count Malcolm but wants to marry Fredrik, the love of her life and the father (unbeknownst to him until act 2) of their thirteen-year-old daughter, Fredrika (in *Smiles* they had a son, Fredrik, now four, of whose existence Fredrik senior learns much earlier in the story). By the end of act 2, Fredrik not only accepts the marriage of his son and his own virginal wife, he comes to realize his "want and/or love" for Desirée.

COUNT CARL-MAGNUS AND CHARLOTTE

- The self-absorbed dragoon *Count Carl-Magnus* is having an affair with Desirée and takes his wife Charlotte for granted.
- His long-suffering wife, *Charlotte*, both loves and hates her husband the Count in equal measure and tries, successfully, to make him jealous. Among the many plot machinations of act 2, Carl-Magnus loses a bet that his wife could not seduce Fredrik in fifteen minutes and promises to be faithful in his fashion.

PETRA AND FRID

- Fredrik's sensual young maid *Petra* is initially attracted to Henrik but meets her match in Madame Armfeldt's footman and butler Frid, a less ethereal man of her own station.
- *Frid* is also attracted to Petra but prefers sex to marriage. Despite his inherent reluctance to settle down, Petra seizes the moment after their carefree lovemaking and Frid agrees to wed.

Two other important characters do not find love. For one, Madame Armfeldt, love comes too late, and for the other, Fredrika, it is too early:

- Desirée's mother *Madame Armfeldt*, formerly a courtesan, laments that modern liaisons lack the class they possessed when she was young. In the Prologue of *Night Music* Madame Armfeldt explains to Fredrika that the summer night smiles "at the follies of human beings."[14] The first smile is "at the young, who know noth-ing" (Fredrika, and Anne and Henrik); the second smile is directed "at the fools who know too little, like Desirée." (Figure 16.1). At the end of the play Madame Armfeldt dies peacefully after the third smile of the summer night smiles on her, an exemplar of "the old who know too much."[15]
- Desirée's daughter in *Night Music*, *Fredrika* (thirteen), plays a part in the match-making of Anne and Henrik and in the end gets her parents back.

FIGURE **16.1** Nima Wiefstrand as Madame Armfeldt and Eva Dahlbeck as Desirée in Inmar Bergman's *Smiles of a Summer Night* (1955).

At the close of the curtain everyone, with the exception of Madame Armfeldt and Fredrika, has found their appropriate partner. As a young woman, the former courtesan thoughtlessly cast aside a lover who offered what she mistakenly thought was a worthless wooden ring. Only much later in life did she learn that the sentiment behind the gift of the ring, a family heirloom for many centuries, was priceless.

In transferring Bergman's film into a work for the musical stage, Sondheim and Prince successfully took advantage of the film's inherent theatrical and musical qualities[16] and potential for a rich musical adaptation. In one important change, the creative team of *Night Music* altered the character, identity, and dramatic function of Desirée's four-year-old son, Fredrik. In *Smiles*, little Fredrik is discovered in Desirée's room during her meeting with the lawyer, and despite her denials, even audiences unfamiliar with the story might suspect that their liaison had produced a son. The metamorphosis from Fredrik to Fredrika adds a third female link to the generational chain of Madame Armfeldt and Desirée and her greater age now brings her to the verge of womanhood (Figure 16.2). Her relative maturity also gives Fredrika the opportunity to have meaningful conversations with her grandmother, Anne, and Henrik, and to sing knowingly about her mother in "A Glamorous Life." Unlike the mute Fredrik, Fredrika consequently plays an important role in the musical play.

On the other hand, by making Fredrika thirteen, the abandoned love affair between Fredrik and Desirée seems more distant and arguably less convincing. In the film, much

FIGURE **16.2** Glynis Johns and Hermione Gingold as Desirée Armfeldt and Madame Armfeldt in *A Little Night Music* (1973).

has happened in a comparatively shorter time frame. The breakup, initiated by Desirée, occurred only five years earlier and the platonic marriage with Anne has lasted for the last two of these years. Consequently, it is more plausible in the film that Fredrik still dreams of his sexual encounters with his former mistress. In the musical, the affair with Desirée had ended fourteen years earlier, and the marriage has been unconsummated for a marginally more bearable eleven months.

One of the central tasks of *Night Music* was to make Bergman's play sing. A major step in this direction was to give all the major characters an opportunity, not only to sing but to sing in a musical style appropriate to their character. In the case of act 1, the transition from screen to stage was a relatively painless one. By the time the show went into rehearsal in December 1972, much, but by no means all, of what we know now as act 1 had been written, or at least planned. Not all of these act 1 songs contained lyrics (for example "Later" and "Liaisons" did not), and other songs would eventually be renamed ("Reminiscences" became "Remember") or given shorter titles ("We're Off for a Weekend in the Country" shortened to "A Weekend in the Country"). Nevertheless, with the exception of "In Praise of Women," which is anticipated first by "Bang" and then by "My Husband the Pig," all the songs from act 1 are more or less in their rightful positions ("Later" and "Soon," however, would trade places), and no song we now know from the show failed to make some form of an appearance in the December 10th script (see Wheeler [17] for more information on this and earlier drafts).

By contrast, according to the libretto draft of December 10, the shorter second act lacked four of the five songs that would eventually be seen and heard on opening night: "It Would Have Been Wonderful," "Perpetual Anticipation," "Send in the Clowns," and "The Miller's Son."[18] Anne and Henrik's "Two Fairy Tales" and "Silly People," with its acerbic class commentary by Frid the country servant, would soon disappear, and a song called "Tonight in Your Room," first sung by Fredrik and Desirée and then by Carl-Magnus and Desirée, would evolve into "Send in the Clowns" (first sung by Desirée to Fredrik and later as a duet). Although the December 10th script indicates a reprise of "Tonight in Your Room" and a reprise of "A Weekend in the Country," now designated "We're Going to the Country," there are no tangible signs of Prince's innovative idea to conclude the show with the series of reprises we know today.

The departures of "Two Fairy Tales" and "Silly People" are significant. Without the former, Henrik and Anne lose the opportunity to express their passion in song. While the removal of this particular talky and somewhat impersonal musical exchange may not be lamentable, audiences are now unable to hear these lovebirds sing to one another. The removal of Frid's angry outburst against his masters in song, "Silly People" completed the downward trajectory of Frid's character as a dramatic presence from film to the theater and the complementary elevation of Madame Armfeldt. In *Smiles* it is Frid, the servant, not Madame Armfeldt, who emerges as the poet who explains the meaning of the three smiles and it is the earthy nonromantic liaison between Frid and Petra that dominates the last few scenes of the film. Further reducing Frid's role in *Night Music*, it is Fredrik and Desirée, not Petra and Frid, who get the last musical word in their reprise of "Send in the Clowns."

After Fredrik and Carl-Magnus survive Russian roulette, Charlotte points out to her husband she has won the dinner bet that she could seduce Fredrik in fifteen minutes (it took only eight minutes but she chose not to reap the spoils of victory). Charlotte then asks her husband to swear fidelity, and Carl-Magnus responds as follows: "I'll be faithful to you until the last gasp separates us. In short, I'll be faithful to you in my way."[19] One wonders whether Bergman (or his translator) was familiar with Lois Lane's pledge of fidelity to Bill Calhoun in *Kiss Me, Kate*: "I'll always be true to you darling, in my fashion / I'll always be true to you darling in my way."

One of the most surprising aspects of the transformation from film to stage is that relatively few of the songs that ended up in *Night Music* are direct outgrowths of the *Smiles* plot, and all of these are found in act 1:

- "Now," "Later," and "Soon." This consecutive trio of songs early in the show are sung respectively by Fredrik, Henrik, and Anne before Sondheim cleverly and unexpectedly combined portions of each into a trio.
- "You Must Meet My Wife." Fredrik sings his thoughts about his young wife with Desirée in her room after her play.

- "In Praise of Women." Carl-Magnus sings his thoughts to himself when Fredrik leaves to put on one of the dragoon's nightshirts, and continues the song to his long-suffering wife, Charlotte, when recapping the events of the previous evening over breakfast.
- "Every Day a Little Death." Charlotte's visit with Anne (to report the liaison between Fredrik and Desirée) creates a natural opportunity for a duet.
- "A Weekend in the Country." The expectations, preparations, and eventual arrival at the country estate of Madame Armfeldt lead to the elaborate act 1 finale that Sondheim delayed composing until Prince had plotted and blocked the number after rehearsals had begun.[20]

The newly imagined songs include all of the Liebeslieder songs ("Night Waltz" and "Remember" in act 1; "The Sun Won't Set" and "Perpetual Anticipation" in act 2); "The Glamorous Life" for Fredrika, Desirée, Malla (her servant), Madame Armfeldt, and the Liebeslieders; and Madame Armfeldt's "Liaisons" in act 1; and in act 2, "It Would Have Been Wonderful" (for Fredrik and Carl-Magnus); Desirée's "Send in the Clowns"; and Petra's "The Miller's Son."[21]

Another difference between *Smiles* and *Night Music* concerns the contrasting treatments of Fredrik and Desirée's reunion (as noted earlier, five years later in the film vs. fourteen years in the musical). In Bergman, the separation had ended badly and not enough time had passed to alleviate the painful memories. In *Night Music* rancor has been transformed into wistfulness and healing and Fredrik has suffered Anne's virginity for only eleven months compared to the insufferable two-year agony in the film. In the musical we learn of a thirteen-year-old daughter, now under the tutelage of Madame Armfeldt, but we won't learn her tell-tale name Fredrika until act 2. Bergman's four-year-old Fredrik, whom we meet in Desirée's dressing room, neither sings nor plays the piano, nor does he play cards or converse about life, love, and the meaning of the smiles of the summer night with his grandmother. Also in the film, neither Fredrik nor Desirée are able to withhold their bitterness. After Fredrik asserts that his former lover is "not fit to have a child," he receives a "lightning-like slap that sends his nightcap down over his ears."[22] Although their reunion is marked by hard feelings and acrimony, the intensity of their feelings and honest conversation makes it clear they still love each other.

Nevertheless, a happy end remains in doubt in the film, and until its final minutes, Fredrik and Desirée do not meet again privately to sort things out. Only the morning after Fredrik has been compelled by Carl-Magnus to play roulette and, covered with the soot propelled from the blank bullet in Carl-Magnus's gun, do Fredrik and Desirée finally get a chance to speak. They do not say much. Instead, Bergman allows actions to speak louder than words. After cleaning up the worst of the soot with a sponge, and asking him whether it still hurts, Desirée covers Fredrik with a blanket, pockets the artistic photographs of Anne that we have seen Fredrik admire earlier in the film (photos Broadway audiences could not and do not see), lights a cigar in quiet triumph, and takes out a script. When her servant Malla arrives and inquires whether she is studying her new role, the actress replies "Yes, you might say that" and "the old woman grins insinuatingly."[23]

In contrast, the reunion of Fredrik and Desirée in the musical reveals an easy camaraderie that leads to a casual sexual reunion. "What are old friends for? Wait till you see the bedroom!" says Desirée.[24] Although in *Night Music* Fredrik claims in speech and song to be in love with Anne, neither Desirée nor the film viewers are fooled. With the possible exception of Fredrik, who is not even initially persuaded by "Send in the Clowns," everyone else knows that these foolish former lovers will be reunited in the end. In contrast to a film, the musical stage cannot easily rely on minute facial expressions or silent pocketing of photographs, but why should it want to when it has a chance to sing about it? In any event, "Clowns," which originally was going to be sung by Fredrik to Desirée after a long speech, has no direct counterpart in the film.

This central act (2 conversation between Fredrik and Desirée) underwent extensive revision from the four drafts created between March and August 1972, the October draft, and the December 10th rehearsal draft.[25] In the four early drafts, the scene includes far more dialogue. Fredrik wants Desirée to like his child bride and wants Desirée to persuade his Anne to give up her virginity. Desirée refuses to play this role and instead lays her cards on the table and explains why she invited Fredrik for a weekend in the country. She was convinced she could use her charm and beauty and that Fredrik would be overwhelmed by her "well-worn allurements and rush to the Divorce Court and the Marriage Bureau in that order."[26] Fredrik knows Anne doesn't love him, in truth he knows she finds him physically repulsive. He also knows that Desirée can offer "everything that any man of sense would long for." Nevertheless, during the weeks of rehearsal he remains obsessed with Anne, apologizes to Desirée, and leaves without a song.

A month into rehearsals Sondheim and Prince realized that Desirée needed to respond to Fredrik's words in a song of her own and that Glynis Johns, who was cast for her acting, not her singing, could, if given the right song, succeed in carrying it off. Two days before the run-through on January 14, Johns sang "Send in the Clowns," a song expressly designed for her. In his examination of the history and compositional genesis of this song, Mark Horowitz discusses its dramatic purpose:

> In singing the song, Desirée is making a serious attempt to make it clear to Fredrik that she finally believes they belong together and regrets that it appears not to be. For once she is being as honest and straightforward as she knows how to be, but at the same time she knows that even honesty and laying oneself bare has a certain manipulative quality to it—that it is a technique. That very self-awareness adds to the layers and the bittersweet quality of the song; ultimately, it's one of the reasons she realizes that the *clowns* are here.[27]

After Desirée finishes a chorus of "Clowns," Fredrik asks her to forgive him, leaves, and the actress privately reprises the final A section of the song with new lyrics. The scene then shifts to Henrik's failed suicide, Anne's rescue, and their declaration of love.

The scene shifts again and Petra sings the last new song in the show, "The Miller's Son," to her sleeping lover and future husband, Frid. After that, following the director's suggestion, Prince and Sondheim tie up all the loose ends interspersed by no less than six reprises in the final scene (scene 8):[28]

1. Charlotte explains to Fredrik that her motive for seducing him was to make her husband jealous. Henrik and Anne elope (Reprise No. 1, "Soon").
2. Fredrik and Charlotte observe the elopement of Henrik and Anne (Reprise No. 2, "You Must Meet My Wife").
3. Desirée ends her dalliance with Carl-Magnus. Carl-Magnus sees Fredrik with his wife and leaves hastily to fetch his dueling pistols. Madame Armeldt tells Fredrika about the man who might have been the love of her life, the man she discarded because he gave her an apparently worthless wooden ring (Reprise No. 3, "Liaisons").
4. Carl-Magnus challenges Fredrik to a game of Russian roulette (Reprise No. 4, "A Weekend in the Country").
5. Fredrik and Carl-Magnus survive the duel and Charlotte and Carl-Magnus kiss and make up (Reprise No. 5, "Every Day a Little Death").
6. Desirée and Fredrik reconcile (Reprise No. 6, "Send in the Clowns," sung as a duet). Madame Armfeldt dies as the summer night smiles for the third time.

In his critical exploration of *Smiles of a Summer Night* John Simon remarks on the breadth of Bergman's accomplishment:

> In a relatively short compass and with a very modest cast of characters, Bergman here explores virtually the entire range of human love, from youthful adoration to avuncularly sentimental benevolence; from neurotic, vengeful passion to easeful indulgence of the appetites; from foot-stamping, infantile capriciousness to wistful, autumnal resignation.[29]

Sondheim captures a comparable diversity within what at first seem like the narrow framework of the waltz, the emblematic signifier of love in fin-de-siècle Viennese operetta (transported to fin-de-siècle Sweden). As Steven Swayne and others have long realized, the waltz itself plays a relatively small role in *Night Music*, although everyone recognizes that the music emphasizes groups of three.

In an introduction to *Night Music* written in 1990, the show's orchestrator Jonathan Tunick points out the compound duple meter organization in "Send in the Clowns," the twelve measures of duple meter near the end of the middle section of "The Glamorous Life," three six-measure duple passages between the opening slow triple melody (3/4 time) and the contrasting fast triple section in "The Miller's Son," and a section of underscoring in duple meter in no. 22 of the vocal score (eleven measures).[30] He also notes that "the remainder of the score consists exclusively of various permutations of triple time, utilizing for the main part eighteenth- and nineteenth-century generic forms."[31] Tunick offers five such genres and lists one or two songs that fit each:

WALTZ: "Soon," "You Must Meet My Wife" [to which can be added "Night Waltz,"
    "The Sun Won't Set," and the main section of "The Miller's Son"]
MAZURKA: "Remember," "The Glamorous Life"
SARABANDE: "Later," "Liaisons"
POLONAISE: "In Praise of Women"
ETUDE: "Now," "Every Day a Little Death"
GIGUE: "A Weekend in the Country"[32]

Concerning Tunick's last-named genre, it should be said that the metrical organization of the gigue, indeed all music in 6/8 in a moderate tempo or faster, is actually compound duple (i.e., *two* groups of three) and invariably conducted in two rather than three. On the other hand, the underlying groups of three in "Send in the Clowns" (plus the occasional but conspicuous employment of 9/8 meter, 3 + 3 + 3) highlight the triple metrical dimension of this song. Perhaps even more significantly, the apparent rhythmic allusions to Johann Strauss's "Blue Danube Waltz" on the opening phrases of the song starting with "Isn't it rich?" and the *luftpause* reminiscent of "The Emperor's Waltz" on "You in midair" and "One who can't move" add to the unmistakable waltz feel.[33] The parallels in rhythm on certain key phrases and the basic accompaniment figure in the famous melody of Rachmaninoff's *Rhapsody on a Theme of Paganini* Variation 18, with its clear triple meter, also contribute to the waltz character of "Clowns."

Like *Night Music*, *Passion* is about the nature and power of love. But the love depicted in *Passion* is a markedly different kind of love: love as a disease. Poets from Petrarch to Lorenz Hart have made a similar connection, for example in the latter's "It's Got to Be Love" (since it "couldn't be tonsillitis" although "it feels like neuritis") in *On Your Toes* and its sequel in *The Boys from Syracuse*, "This Can't Be Love" ("because I feel so well"). In *Passion*, an obsessive love based on pity and capable of overcoming physical attraction contrasts with the confused but amiable lovers in *Smiles* and *Night Music*, working their way to their rightful and attractive (if not equally young) partners. Also in marked contrast to the stylistic musical diversity of *Night Music*, Fosca's obsessed and diseased love in *Passion* finds its musical counterpart in Sondheim's choice to obsessively confine musical ideas to a bare minimum and to repeat them—obsessively.

Compared with the many details in plot and changes in tone that occurred in the process of adapting Bergman, *Passione d'Amore* and *Passion* are remarkably similar in most respects. Most significantly, the film and the musical share the same basic structure, a structure largely based on letter exchanges, an idea in turn based on Tarchetti's original epistolary novel. In one notable difference, *Passion*'s Giorgio is allowed to finish the letter Fosca (Italian for "dark") started to dictate to him in *Passione d'Amore*. In another departure, Colonel Ricci tells Giorgio in the film the story of Fosca's past while the two soldiers are on horseback, and the story is told without visual flashbacks, whereas on stage, Lapine and Sondheim use this as another opportunity to stage and sing a somewhat different and more dramatic back story.[34] Lapine and Sondheim also take advantage of the many letter readings to bring Clara (Italian for "light") physically and musically on stage, although she is more imagined than real.

Despite the strong similarities between *Passion* and its film source, however, some of the ideas that are clear in the film (and novel) are lost in the translation to the stage. If it were not for Sondheim's interviews with Mark Horowitz published in *Sondheim on Music* or the composer's audio commentary on the *Passion* DVD, it might be difficult to perceive that the opening dissonant chords heard at the outset of the show were meant to capture Clara's orgasm, moments before the curtain opens on their lovemaking. Similarly, if it were not for various interviews and commentaries with and by Sondheim, the meaning of Giorgio's scream at the conclusion of his duel with Colonel Ricci might also be unclear, even if audiences notice a common denominator between Giorgio's scream and Fosca's frightening offstage screams which announce her character aurally before we meet her in person. In the novel especially, but also in the film, readers and viewers learn that Giorgio's scream and subsequent illness were transmitted directly through Fosca's illness.

In his Dramatists Guild interview of 1995, Sondheim states that "this story is about how Giorgio gets infected by love."[35] Broadway audiences who are moved by Giorgio's willingness to abandon the celestial beauty of Clara and declare his unequivocal love for the fiendishly ugly Fosca might still not realize that the love that infects him now has ravished his body with a disease far more intense than tonsillitis, from which he may not recover. Sondheim tried to convey this infection in his songs, but concedes that "it's hard to tell an audience about being infected by a disease."[36] Sondheim correctly observes that although the transmission of illness is made verbally explicit only once in the movie by Doctor Tambourri, the combination of dialogue and a close-up combine to convey this idea. This idea too might go undetected in the stage musical, although we will observe how Sondheim manages to take advantage of music's ability to convey the infection of Fosca's obsessive love.

Additionally, in the film the physical presence of the character playing Fosca (the actress Valeria D'Obici) is skeletal and her facial features, aided by evocative lighting and distorted camera angles, are truly frightful (Figure 16.3), especially, perhaps ironically, at the moment of her vocal orgasm with Giorgio late in the story. In fact, the intensity of this climactic moment and its visual and aural manifestation makes it believable that she would die from a combination of ecstasy and exhaustion only days later. Donna Murphy, the actress who introduced the role of Fosca on the stage was fleshier and her physiognomy more sinister than frighteningly ugly (Figure 16.4). With a less severe hairstyle and the removal of a mole, the addition of some makeup and a smile, the stage Fosca could have been physically alluring, and might even start to resemble Murphy, who is beautiful offstage and in other dramatic roles.

Just as the stage version and the silent film of *The Phantom of the Opera* (1925) contrasted with the physically hideous silent screen image of Lon Chaney by presenting a character who, while less conventionally handsome than his rival Raoul, could definitely serve as a romantic alternative for the heroine, Fosca's ugliness is by no means the central obstacle to a love match. The reason *Phantom*'s Christine Daaé eventually abandons the Phantom is not because his face is ugly but because of his murderous, vindictive, and ugly soul. Similarly, the stage Fosca is repellent primarily because she is obsessive, humorless (for the most part), jealous, obnoxious, vindictive, self-absorbed, and manipulative in her love for Giorgio. Fosca is not, however, cruel (although she

FIGURE **16.3** Bernard Giraudeau as Giorgio and Valeria d'Obici as Fosca in Ettore Scola's *Passione d'Amore* (1981).

FIGURE **16.4** Jere Shea and Donna Murphy as Giorgio and Fosca in *Passion* (1994).

does at one point threaten to blackmail Giorgio). She also possesses positive qualities that partially offset her neurotic disposition, including intelligence, a love of books, and a sensitivity to people, art, beauty, and ruins. In all these areas she is a perfect match for Giorgio.

In both the film and on stage, the turning point in the love story occurs as a result of Fosca's unexpected appearance on the train, moments before it is about to take Giorgio back to Clara in Milan. While sitting in the train depot waiting for a return train to the barracks, the Fosca in *Passione d'Amore* expresses her total devotion to Giorgio, predicts that he will be compelled to love her after she dies for him, and begs him to kill her without further delay. A few days later (about three minutes later in the film), Giorgio, who has by now decided to return permanently to his outpost in order to be near Fosca, visits the sensitive Clara, who understands viscerally that, despite his disclaimers, her physical beauty is no match against Giorgio's pity and Fosca's neediness:

GIORGIO: For that poor wretch I only feel pity.
CLARA: That can be stronger than love.
GIORGIO: She's a monster.
CLARA: Maybe it's a nobler love. She needs you.
GIORGIO: Don't you need me?
CLARA: I need you to be happy. She, to survive.[37]

A few minutes later in the film, Giorgio explains further to the Doctor how pity has turned to love:

"That woman" risked humiliation for me, and ridicule. She endured my rejection, my anger. She surrendered her pride, her self-respect. For me. It's easy to love when one is loved. But she, though spurned, loved me more than anyone. I love her too! Go ahead and be surprised. I love Fosca.[38]

When Giorgio goes to Fosca that night he tells her he loves her more than he loved Clara. Moments later the unlikely lovers consummate a reciprocal love.

If Fosca in *Passione d'Amore* plays on pity, *Passion*'s more manipulative Fosca plays on altruism. In the final words of her short but powerful song on the train, "Loving You," she says, "I would die for you," and answers Giorgio's skepticism by offering a pure and selfless love, a love she argues is purer than what Clara can offer:

GIORGIO: Die for me? What kind of love is that?
FOSCA: The truest love. Would Clara give her life for yours! Would she, Giorgio?
(*A beat; he doesn't answer, realizing the truth of his situation*)
I would. Happily. In the end, you'll finally see what is beautiful about me.[39]

Although love's pity is an implicit causal factor in Giorgio's transformed feelings for Scola's Fosca, in Lapine and Sondheim's *Passion* pity ultimately takes a back seat to the more unstoppable force of Fosca's unreasonable love. Clara may have given Giorgio her heart, but she is unable to recklessly abandon her obligations to her son (until a more reasonable time in the future when he would be away at school). This reasonable—one might say, adult—approach to an adulterous love affair, is devalued by Giorgio as less meaningful than Fosca's unreasonable love. Stacking the deck in her own favor, Fosca neglects to point out that she was already on the verge of death and without any comparable personal obligations. Consequently, she convinces Giorgio that hers is the greater love. As Giorgio tells Fosca, "Love within reason—that isn't love. And I've learned that from you…"

In an allusion to Tarchetti's novel, in which we learn that it was Clara's pity for the disease-ravaged Giorgio that initially led her to love him, the words of the opening love duet in *Passion*, "Happiness," refer to the sadness in Giorgio's eyes at their glance in the park that allowed the illicit love affair to begin:

GIORGIO: We were both unhappy.
CLARA: Unhappiness can be seductive.
GIORGIO: You pitied me…
BOTH: How quickly pity leads to love.[40]

Sondheim makes Fosca's musical presence felt in two prominent ways. First, her six-note "obsession" motive, which she introduces three times in succession starting on the words "I do not read to think"—"Fosca's Entrance (Part I)"—within a surprisingly short time infects Clara and Giorgio, for example when Clara sings the words "To feel a woman's touch" from Giorgio's letter (scene 3).[41] The motive is so ubiquitous that, as Swayne demonstrates, its absence becomes more significant than its presence.[42] In fact, I cannot think of another work for the musical stage, opera or musical, in which a single motive pervades all the central characters so thoroughly and relentlessly as it does in *Passion*. As the *coup de grâce* in Fosca's final letter, the last words sung, "Your love will live in me" (Finale), repeats as a musical phrase no fewer than *eleven* times.[43]

A second important motive, the "happiness" motive which pervades the opening love duet between Giorgio and Clara, appropriately called "Happiness," is eventually usurped by Fosca. Before that happens we hear Clara sing the motive one more time in her farewell duet with Giorgio. Here Clara returns to the "happiness" motive ("All that happiness we had then"), but underneath her musical line Giorgio tellingly sings Fosca's obsession motive, a motive which belongs now to him as well ("Is this what you call love?").[44] Just as Giorgio and before long Clara sing Fosca's obsession, Fosca, fittingly, sings the "happiness" motive shortly before Giorgio tells Fosca he loves her. In her weakened condition she is able to sing only a few phrases, but this is more than enough to get the point across.

The musical contains one other ubiquitous idea. Its material consists of one of the simplest ideas in music, the outline of an ascending major triad (for example C–E–G). As Sondheim notes in the *Passion* interview of 1995, these triads appear most frequently as accompaniment figures:

The accompaniments are often based on bugle calls, though more hidden. The bugle only plays three notes, and I decided to use them as the basic figuration for all the Giorgio/Clara stuff, though with a dissonant underpinning to make them restless as well as less blatant.[45]

The triadic accompaniment appears most insistently throughout the opening "Happiness" duet between Giorgio and Clara. In a more active form it permeates the accompaniments of the First and Second Letters and the melody of Clara and Giorgio punctuated by choral soldier interjections in the Third Letter. Just as Fosca usurps the "happiness" motive shortly before her sexual liaison with Giorgio, Fosca takes the rising accompanying triad as the starting point for the main melodic material of "Loving You," her quietly impassioned love song at the train station.[46] This is the music in which Fosca gives voice to her explanation that loving Giorgio is not a choice. It is who she is, what she lives for, and she will gladly die for Giorgio. Strikingly, but perhaps not surprisingly, the "obsession" motive itself occurs only twice in "Loving You," successively on the words "That is why I love" and "You are why I live."

One more important but less frequently employed musical connection should be mentioned. This is the opening phrase of Fosca's piano music, which first underscores the dialogue between the First and Second Letters. The stage direction informs us that "we hear elegant Chopinesque piano music from upstairs as Clara exits."[47] It isn't quite the "love at first sound" that occurs when Ravenal hears Magnolia's piano theme in *Show Boat*, but the idea of an aural awareness preceding the visual is the same in both shows and fits especially well with what Giorgio will soon be facing. In the film we see Fosca from the back playing her own version of Chopinesque music. Once viewers have seen Fosca's face, the soundtrack, composed by the award-winning Italian Armando Trovajoli, will continue to display numerous manifestations of pseudo-Chopin throughout the film (music not quite up to the master, but appealing and stylistically appropriate). In *Passion*, audiences will hear Fosca's piano theme far less often, but many songs later it is this theme that will provide the starting point for Giorgio's pivotal song, "No one has ever loved me as deeply as you."[48]

Both *Night Music* and *Passion* respond imaginatively to the demands of their respective sources. In the former, Sondheim offers a musical counterpart to the diversity of love explored in *Smiles of a Summer Night*, while in the latter he captures the obsessive love of Fosca and demonstrates that obsessive and altruistic love can triumph over a more conventional romantic love based on sexual attraction. The score of *Passion* is beautiful and powerful in its own right and Sondheim manages to create musical diversity within its purposefully constrained musical range. Furthermore, in contrast to other totally integrated musicals of its era in which characters indiscriminately sing virtually anyone and everyone else's motives, it makes sense in *Passion* that Giorgio sings Fosca's piano music, that Giorgio and Clara eventually acquire Fosca's obsession and that Fosca transforms the bugle call into song and in the end acquires Giorgio and Clara's happiness motive, or at least the first part of it.[49]

The concentrated musical ideas of *Passion* match the intensity of its one-act drama (albeit an act nearly two hours in length), a show deliberately without applause, in Sondheim's description, "one long song."[50] In contrast to perhaps all other Sondheim shows, including or perhaps especially *Night Music, Passion* also eschews two Sondheim trademarks, irony and humor (although the soldiers do provide some relief, if not always genuinely comic relief, from the musically incestuous love triangle).

This is the first show I've written that has no irony in it at all. Irony is the greatest shield against that kind of audience reaction.[51] There is nothing wry in *Passion*; everybody is earnest. The three principals have no humor—well, Fosca does have some—but when people say *Passion* breaks new ground, I say yes, it's the world's first humorless musical."[52]

Passion bears the dubious distinction as the musical with the shortest run of any Best Musical Tony Award recipient (280 performances). Although Sondheim's last award-winning show contains probably more dialogue than *Sweeney Todd*, enough to disqualify *Passion* as an opera, Sondheim has pointed out that "Fosca is an opera-sized character in a musical" and that *Passion* "is an opera in its attitude towards people."[53] In their own way and in their own time *Night Music* and *Passion* adapt their worthy foreign film sources with great skill and inspiring finesse. In the process Sondheim and his collaborators have successfully demonstrated that even when love is blind, theatrical and musical imagination can be far-sighted.

NOTES

1. What follows is a partial list of musicals by major composers and their lyricists since 1960 adapted wholly or in part from films: Jerry Bock and Sheldon Harnick (*She Loves Me*), Cy Coleman (*Sweet Charity, City of Angels*), John Kander and Fred Ebb (*Woman of the Year*), Charles Strouse (*Applause, Nick and Nora*), Jerry Herman (*La Cage aux Folles*), Maury Yeston (*Nine, Grand Hotel*), Alan Menken (*Little Shop of Horrors, Beauty and the Beast*), Andrew Lloyd Webber (*The Phantom of the Opera, Sunset Boulevard, Whistle Down the Wind*), Lynn Ahrens and Stephen Flaherty (*My Favorite Year*), and Sondheim (*A Little Night Music, Passion*).

2. Tarchetti's novel was translated into English by Lawrence Venuti the year of *Passion*'s debut and was renamed to match the musical rather than the film: Iginio Ugo Tarchetti, *Passion* [original title *Fosca*], trans. Lawrence Venuti (San Francisco: Mercury House, 1994).

3. Bergman is the subject of numerous critical and biographical studies. For an insightful and detailed examination of *Smiles of a Summer Night* that devotes special emphasis to its theatricality, dance-like qualities, and inherent musicality, see John Simon, *Ingmar Bergman Directs* (New York: Harcourt Brace Jovanovich, 1972), 106–39.

4. Ephraim Katz, *The Film Encyclopedia*, 2nd ed. (New York: Harper Collins, 1994), 1217. In Manuela Gieri's chapter-length survey of Scola, neither *Una giornata particolare* nor *Passione d'Amore* receives more than cursory mention; see Manuela Gieri, *Contemporary Italian Filmmaking: Strategies of Subversion* (Toronto: University of Toronto Press, 1995). In the other half-dozen books on Italian cinema published in English since 1980, Scola himself is treated as a minor figure and receives scant critical attention.

5. Sondheim: "I don't think we have gotten further than two or three talks on any aborted project. Usually, by the time we are in the fifth talk we can see it's a year hence and it happens. We wanted to do Anouilh's *Ring Round the Moon* in 1959. He wouldn't give us the rights. We asked again in 1972, and he still wouldn't give us the rights. But by that time we were committed, so we found another kind of weekend to write about, *A Little Night Music*. The day the show opened in Boston there was a wire saying, 'O.K., you can have the rights to *Ring Round the Moon*.' We sent back a note saying, 'Too bad.' It was his agent we were

trying to deal with, of course, not Mr. Anouilh." Sondheim, "On Collaboration between Authors and Directors," *Dramatists Guild Quarterly* 16, no. 2 (1979), 30.

6. See the commentary on the DVD, *Passion* (Image Entertainment, 2003 [115 minutes]). Featuring audio commentary with Stephen Sondheim, James Lapine, Donna Murphy, Jere Shea, Marin Mazzie, and Ira Weitzman. Sondheim offers a helpful survey of how *Passion* took shape as a show in "Sondheim on *Passion*," *Dramatists Guild Quarterly* 31, no. 3 (autumn 1995), 3–4.

7. Geoffrey Block, *Enchanted Evenings: The Broadway Musical from "Show Boat" to Sondheim and Lloyd Webber*, 2nd ed. (New York: Oxford University Press, 2009), 353.

8. Interview with Bergman by reporter Marie Nyröd for SVT Svensk Television, *Smiles of a Summer Night*, DVD (Criterion Collection 237, 2004 [108 minutes]).

9. Despite its acknowledgment as a turning point, however, Bergman barely mentions the film in his autobiography, *The Magic Lantern*, beyond a hurtful review, the fact that Desirée Armfeldt, among other women, was modeled on his wife, Gun Hagberg, and the psychosomatic health problems he experienced after its filming. See Bergman, *The Magic Lantern: An Autobiography* (New York: Viking, 1988).

10. Sondheim, "Author and Director: Musicals," 367. Although Sondheim found "nothing experimental with the form" of *Night Music,* he did believe he had achieved "something experimental with the texture of the piece" ("Musical Theater," 229).

11. Sondheim, "Author and Director: Musicals," 360.

12. Hal Prince, *Contradictions: Notes on Twenty-six Years in the Theatre* (New York: Dodd, Mead, 1974), 183.

13. Craig Zadan, *Sondheim & Co.*, 2nd rev. ed. (New York: Harper and Row, 1986), 192 and 194.

14. Hugh Wheeler, James Lapine, Burt Shevelove, and Larry Gelbart, *Four by Sondheim: A Little Night Music, Sweeney Todd, Sunday in the Park with George, A Funny Thing Happened on the Way to the Forum* (New York: Applause, 2000), 180.

15. Wheeler et al., *Four by Sondheim*, 180.

16. See Simon, *Ingmar Bergman Directs*, 106–39.

17. Wheeler, libretto drafts for *A Little Night Music*, New York Library for the Performing Arts at Lincoln Center, Billy Rose Theatre Division.

18. In the libretto drafts of August and October 1972 (New York Public Library librettos #4124 and #2588), a song called "The Miller's Song" is indicated for Petra to sing with a guitar. By the December 10 libretto, the song had disappeared, and "The Miller's Son" was not added until much later in the rehearsal process.

19. Ingmar Bergman, *Four Screenplays of Ingmar Bergman: Smiles of a Summer Night, The Seventh Seal, Wild Strawberries, The Magician*, translated from the Swedish by Lars Malmstrom and David Kushner (New York: Simon and Schuster, 1969), 120.

20. Prince, *Contradictions*, 179.

21. Madame Armfeldt's "Liaisons," which in *Night Music* appears as commentary that links mother and daughter during Desirée's friendly sexual reunion, is dimly based on a conversation between Desirée and her mother at the latter's estate, in which the former courtesan explains that she earned her lavish mansion by agreeing not to write her memoirs. The contents of these memoirs are captured in the lyrics of "Liaisons."

22. Bergman, *Four Screenplays*, 65–6.

23. Ibid., 123.

24. Wheeler, *Four by Sondheim*, 220.

25. Wheeler, *Four by Sondheim*.

26. The quotations in this paragraph can be found in the March–August 1972 typescripts (New York Public Library at Lincoln Center, #4124). See Wheeler, "Libretto Drafts for *A Little Night Music*," New York Library for the Performing Arts at Lincoln Center, Billy Rose Theatre Division: Typescripts, 1st–4th drafts, March–August, 1972 (#4124 A–D); typescript, "October, 1972" (#2588); this version contains no lyrics and a few song cuts [Harold Prince Collection]; typescript, "December 10, 1972" (#2606) [Harold Prince Collection]; typescript, screenplay by Hugh Wheeler, "First half of first draft" "March 4, 1976" (#1744); typescript with corrections, additions, and notes from Wheeler, Revision, May 26, 1972, 2–26.

27. Mark Eden Horowitz, "Send in the Clowns," *Sondheim Review* 11, no. 3 (spring 2005), 16.

28. Sondheim credits Prince with this idea: "Hal has always been very fond of a technique that I think works very well. We discussed it last summer in Majorca when I went there to work with him and Hugh. It actually started in *Night Music*. Hal wanted to have in *Night Music* a series of reprises of all the songs at the end. We didn't get in more than five songs, but it was very effective." "On Collaboration between Authors and Directors," 27.

29. Simon, *Ingmar Bergman Directs*, 139.

30. Jonathan Tunick, "Introduction," *A Little Night Music*, in Wheeler et al., *Four by Sondheim*, 163.

31. Tunick, "Introduction."

32. While agreeing with most of these assignations, Swayne, who offers a detailed examination of genre in *Night Music*, argues that "Liaisons" shares more common properties with the Bolero. Of the songs left out, he suggests that "It Would Have Been Wonderful," despite its 9/8 meter, shares much with the Minuet, and while he doesn't entirely dismiss those who identify Waltz elements in "Send in the Clowns," finds more in common with the Barcarolle.

33. In his interview with Sondheim about *Passion*, Horowitz mentions that the sketches of the "Flashback Sequence" contain a quote from the opening of "Emperor Waltz," *Sondheim on Music: Minor Details and Major Decisions* (Lanham, MD, and Oxford: Scarecrow, 2003), 51.

34. Sondheim spoke of the flashback as the major departure from the film and a cause of major indecision, especially since when Louis Malle and John Guare came to see the workshop and were asked whether they should retain it, the former emphatically replied "Absolutely!" and the latter with equal conviction said "Take it out!," "Sondheim on *Passion*," 5.

35. "Sondheim on *Passion*," 9.

36. Ibid.

37. *Passion of Love* (1982), directed by Ettore Scola. VHS (New York: Kino on Video, 1994). Italian with English subtitles.

38. *Passion of Love*.

39. Stephen Sondheim and James Lapine, *Passion* (New York: Theatre Communications Group, 1994), 101.

40. Stephen Sondheim and James Lapine, *Passion* (vocal score) (New York: Rilting, 1994, 1996), 3–4.

41. Sondheim and Lapine, *Passion* (vocal score), 36, 55.

42. Steven Robert Swayne, "Hearing Sondheim's Voices," PhD diss., University of California, Berkeley, 1999, 230.

43. Ibid., 196–7.

44. Sondheim and Lapine, *Passion* (vocal score) (scene 13), 171.

45. "Sondheim on *Passion*," 6.

46. It also serves as an accompanimental figure to her piano playing (known as an Alberti bass).

47. Sondheim and Lapine, *Passion* (vocal score), 13.

48. In the vocal score, Fosca's piano theme is first heard on page 22; "No one has ever loved me as deeply as you" begins on page 178.

49. For a critique of the dramatic limitations in what I have called the "totally integrated" musical see Block, *Enchanted Evenings*, 394–5, and Joseph P. Swain, *The Broadway Musical: A Critical and Musical Survey* (New York: Oxford University Press, 1990; 2nd ed., Lanham, MD: Scarecrow, 2002), 403–8.

50. "Sondheim on *Passion*," 8.

51. Sondheim is referring to the unwanted laughter that broke the mood in a number of places during rehearsal before he and Lapine figured out ways to circumvent these intrusions.

52. "Sondheim on *Passion*," 8. In the commentary to the DVD Sondheim notes another unique feature of *Passion*: "It's the world's only epistolary musical—everybody reads letters all evening long and then the curtain falls." *Passion* also made history as the first mainstream musical to begin with a musical orgasm (which some, including me, managed to miss) and significant female nudity. The orgasm remained but the nudity was greatly curtailed.

53. "Sondheim on *Passion*," 8.

CHAPTER 17

MORE SONDHEIM: ORIGINAL MUSIC FOR MOVIES

ROGER HICKMAN

STEPHEN Sondheim is generally recognized as the leading figure of contemporary American musical theater, and this *Handbook* naturally focuses on his music and lyrics for musicals and revues. But, borrowing a title from a song, there is more. Sondheim has frequently referred to his passion for film and readily admits to growing up watching movies. Steve Swayne has provided an insightful analysis of cinematic influences on Sondheim's musicals.[1] In addition to maintaining a general interest and adapting film-making techniques, Sondheim has also composed original music for five films: *Stavisky* (1974), *The Seven-Per-Cent Solution* (1976), *Reds* (1981), *Dick Tracy* (1990), and *The Birdcage* (1996).[2] Sondheim's contributions to these films range from a single song to an entire score. In this survey, we will begin with the songs and then turn to the larger compositional endeavors.

THE SEVEN-PER-CENT SOLUTION

It is hard to imagine a topic that would excite a cinéaste more than a film about Sherlock Holmes. *The Seven-Per-Cent Solution* is loosely based on Nicholas Meyer's 1974 novel about Sir Arthur Conan Doyle's legendary fictional detective. Meyer combines two intriguing aspects of Sherlock Holmes's career. The first is his drug addiction. According to the faithful chronicler Dr. Watson, Holmes was a habitual user of cocaine, which was legal in England at the time. Concerned that the drug would have a harmful effect on Holmes's mental health, Watson claimed to have helped cure him of the habit at an unspecified date. The second is Holmes's mysterious disappearance. In 1891, Doyle wrote what he thought would be the last adventure of Sherlock Holmes, and he had the hero fall to his death off a cliff with his arch nemesis Moriarty. Three years later, Doyle, bowing to public pressure, resurrected the detective, leaving fans to speculate as to what happened during the "Great Hiatus." From these elements, Meyer fabricated a fanciful fiction in which Holmes descends into cocaine-induced madness, is taken to Vienna by Watson to seek treatment from Dr. Sigmund Freud, and is cured while engaged in a new adventure. Holmes then takes a well-needed vacation with a female companion.

Meyer adapted his novel for the film directed by Herbert Ross. An excellent cast was assembled that included the London stage veteran Nicol Williamson (Sherlock Holmes), Robert Duvall (Watson), Alan Arkin (Freud), Laurence Olivier (Moriarty), Vanessa Redgrave (Lola), and Joel Grey (Lowenstein). Popular reception was mixed, undoubtedly due to its shocking nature for devoted Sherlock Holmes fans and its odd mixture of moods that range from the realism of drug withdrawal to slapstick comedy. Indeed, the film can be seen as a parody of itself (and of the Holmes tradition), an approach that is found in Hollywood classics such as *The Bride of Frankenstein* (1935) or *Kill Bill* (2003 and 2004).

John Addison, who received an Oscar for *Tom Jones* (1963) and a BAFTA award for *A Bridge Too Far* (1977), supplied a supportive musical score that captures the necessary range of moods to suggest an altered state, action, and humor. Particularly notable is his mimicking of traditional Viennese styles to reflect the central location of the story. The music for the opening credits shifts from the style of Brahms to that of Mahler, two composers associated with Vienna. A later reference to Brahms's Hungarian Dance No. 5 is humorous, since the climactic train ride will take us from Austria to Hungary.

The film calls upon a rich tradition of clichés from the canon of Sherlock Holmes films and other mystery stories based in the late nineteenth century. One stock scene is a bawdy pub with a singer. In this case, Ross recreated a Viennese brothel, and Régine, the celebrated French singer and nightclub entrepreneur, played the role of the madam. Referred to in the film as "Madame's Song," Sondheim composed "I Never Do Anything Twice" for Régine's performance (1:16:15). In its full version heard in *Side by Side by Sondheim*, the song contains three verse–chorus alternations and a coda, a common form for nineteenth-century parlor songs. Sondheim's lyrics, as described by Swayne, are "deliciously scandalous."[3] Each verse tells of the sexual idiosyncrasies of three former lovers—a captain of the guard, a baron, and an abbot—and the choruses sparkle with the consistent rejection of repetition in sexual encounters. Unfortunately for those who appreciate a good song, the film's adaptation involves cutting over half of the original. Sherlock enters the parlor just as Régine is singing the second chorus (she substitutes "vice" from the third chorus for the word "price"). Following the third verse, the song jumps to the coda, which is a variation of the chorus sung a half step higher. In the film, the concluding repetition that humorously contradicts the title is omitted.

In addition to choosing a standard parlor structure, Sondheim provides the song with the simplicity and squareness of popular music of the time. Melodic phrases move in four-measure units, and the range falls largely within a single octave. It is the type of song that amateurs could have sung while accompanying themselves at the piano. The artistry of the song can be seen on several levels. In keeping with Addison's score, the chorus is a waltz, at once a mimicking the popular song type of the era and serving as another reference to Vienna, the home of the waltz. But the song also reflects a

Hungarian quality. Like the popular "gypsy" melodies of the region, it alternates a slow, rhythmically free parlando section in minor with a bright, strong-pulsed passage in major. Both sections are unified with a general descending motion, and Sondheim links the two sections together aurally by having the repeated descent of C to C♭ of the verse echoed in the third measure of the chorus with a C to B♮ motive.

THE BIRDCAGE

Sondheim composed "Little Dream" for Mike Nichols's *The Birdcage* from 1996. This movie is one of several adaptations of Jean Poiret's 1973 farce *La Cage aux Folles*; earlier versions include a 1978 French film (with two sequels) and a 1983 Broadway production with music and lyrics by Jerry Herman. With *The Birdcage*, Sondheim is associated once again with a strong cast, headed by Robin Williams (Armand), Gene Hackman (Senator Kevin Keeley), and Nathan Lane (Albert), who would win a Tony Award in this same year for his performance in *A Funny Thing Happened on the Way to the Forum*. The Screen Actors Guild awarded this ensemble the "Outstanding Performance by a Cast" for 1996. The plot centers on the desires of a young couple to get married, which properly involves having their parents meet. Her father is a Republican Senator, the leader of the "Coalition for Moral Order," and is desperately trying to avoid any scent of a personal scandal. The young man's parents are a gay couple; his dad is the owner of a South Beach drag club, and his "mom" is the club's star drag queen.

"Little Dream" functions quite differently in this film than "I Never Do Anything Twice." While the latter is largely used for ambience, "Little Dream" is more intimately involved with the plot, since the singer is a main character in the story—Albert. We hear a nearly complete version of the A–B–A′ song during a rehearsal (0:30:30). Interruptions for comic dialogue occur at the end of B and just prior to the completion of the song. This is a love ballad, and Albert is singing under Armand's watchful eyes. The lyrics, while primarily dealing with the dream-like state of love, contain a suggestion of Albert's insecurities in his relationship with Armand, which is critical to the plot. Note that the second interruption follows the questioning of his lover: "Are you a dreamer, too? And of who?" The association of this song with Albert and his insecurities is later reinforced when the A portion of the tune is heard as diegetic bar-room piano music (0:41:20), just as Armand is trying to decide what to do with Albert during the Senator's visit.

In the song, Sondheim creates a dreamy atmosphere with a tinge of uncertainty through chromaticism, dissonance, and tonal ambiguity. The piano prelude consists of light flourishes and concludes with four bars of chromatically descending parallel chords. The "fluffiness" of these gestures is reflected in Albert's clothes (high heels, tights, scarf wrapped as a skirt, and pink accessories) and his ballerina-like hand movements. The descending chords, which also appear in the accompaniment during the A sections, contain a first-inversion triad in the right hand and a nonchordal pitch set a major seventh below the root of the triad in the left. The chromatic descent and the mild dissonances continue after the voice enters. The lingering chromatic descents in measures eight and twelve of the vocal melody gain harmonic significance, which adds to the overall sense of ambiguity. Although E♭ is the implied central pitch, a convincing E♭ cadence is constantly averted. The A section does come to a melodic close on E♭, but Sondheim harmonizes this moment with C-minor harmony. The B section, which melodically centers on D♭, E♭, and D♮, also avoids cadential resolution. The only clear arrival on the tonic is at the final cadence, a moment that is excluded from the performance in the film. For Albert, life is a dream, and his love is insecure and seemingly unresolved.

"Little Dream" is the only music Sondheim wrote specifically for the film[4] but two other previously composed songs are quoted. Both are known from *Side by Side*, and both were originally written and rejected from earlier musicals: "Can that Boy Foxtrot" was dropped from *Follies*, and "Love is in the Air" from *A Funny Thing Happened on the Way to the Forum*. The first of these appears briefly just as Albert begins his portion of the show (0:12:15). The provocative meaning of the lyrics takes a humorous twist in the context of a drag show. "Love is in the Air" is sung unaccompanied when Armand and his former wife (the boy's actual mother) recall their earlier stage appearances, recreate some of their dance steps, and rekindle some of their sexual energy (0:59:40). Implied in the choice of this song is that the two met in a production of *Side by Side by Sondheim*, and there is humor in the lyrics, as Armand salaciously emphasizes the words "act queerly."

DICK TRACY

Sondheim's music is integrated into the plot of *Dick Tracy* (1990) more thoroughly than in any of the movies in this survey other than *Stavisky*. The film, Warren Beatty's third as director and his second collaboration with Sondheim, brings the classic comic strip detective and his odd assortment of arch villains to life with the colors of the Sunday funnies. For this endeavor, Beatty assembled an all-star cast, which includes himself in the title role and Al Pacino as Big Boy Caprice. The latter is a caricature of Pacino's role in the *Godfather* trilogy. Beatty must have enjoyed this comic disfiguration of Pacino, since the role of Michael in *The Godfather* was originally offered to him, and he turned it down. Other prominent figures include Madonna (Breathless Mahoney), the popular Sondheim interpreter Mandy Patinkin (88 Keys), Dustin Hoffman (Mumbles), Dick Van Dyke (DA Fletcher), and another former *Godfather* figure James Caan (Spaldoni). Danny Elfman composed the score, and he replicated several of the qualities heard in *Batman* released one year earlier (1989). The march-like theme representing Dick Tracy is not as captivating as Batman's theme, but the love theme is much more effective.

Dick Tracy is a playful mixture of film genres and draws freely upon their diverse conventions. This pastiche of movie clichés includes characteristics of two genres popular in Hollywood's Golden Age, film noir and the musical. The noir qualities are a natural outgrowth of the comic strip. Created by Chester Gould in 1931, *Dick Tracy* reflected the era's concern with crime and fascination with hard-boiled detective stories, such as those written by Dashiell Hammett. In essence, Dick Tracy is a comic-noir detective. Beatty's film incorporates a number of stock scenes (city views at night with wet streets) and situations found in film noir, foremost of which is Tracy's choice between two women, the faithful redeemer Tess Trueheart and the seductive femme fatale Breathless.

A fan of film noir, Sondheim composed five songs for the film (Table 17.1). Moving beyond mere ambience or momentary illuminations of a plot, these songs are often central to the drama due to their prominence, length, and reprises. Most involve a montage or crosscutting that forwards the drama. As is standard for musicals of the 1930s and 40s, one of the principal characters in the drama is a performer. Reflecting its noir conception, the performance venue is a nightclub, where much of the story unfolds, and the singer is the femme fatale Breathless, a true siren luring men to destruction.

The two songs not performed by Breathless in the film, "Live Alone and Like It" and "Back in Business," function in a similar fashion; both reflect song and lyric traditions of Tin Pan Alley, both have an ambiguous diegetic quality, and both accompany a montage, one showing Tracy's love interest, and the other showing Tracy losing ground to the crime syndicate. "Live Alone and Like It" is a standard rag song, complete with drums, a Dixie-styled clarinet accompaniment, and lyrics containing metaphors to nature. The snappy delivery by Mel Tormé suggests the character of a gimmick song, a trademark of the music publishing industry at the time. The one verse melody assumes a standard A–A–B–A′ –Coda structure. The A portions contain three four-measure phrases, all of which center on the pitches of an E♭ major triad, with some lingering on C. In the first two phrases, the melodic content of the first measure returns playfully in the fourth, where the lyrics make a side comment on the verse. The eight-measure B phrase

Table 17.1 Songs in *Dick Tracy*

Song	Plot	Performer	Timing
"Sooner or Later"	Nightclub entertainment	Breathless	0:04:55
"More"	Nightclub rehearsal; crosscuts of interrogation	Breathless and dancers	0:15:40
"Live Alone and Like It"	Montage with Tracy, Tess, and Kid	Offscreen voice	0:25:15
"Sooner or Later," reprise	Nightclub entertainment; crosscuts of imminent raid	Breathless and dancers	0:50:20
"What Can You Lose"	Private performance; crosscuts of Tracy and Tess	88 Keys and Breathless	1:01:15
"Back in Business"	Montage of gang activity	Chorus	1:12:40
"More," reprise	Nightclub entertainment; crosscuts of saving Tess	Breathless and dancers	1:21:10
"More," reprise	Closing credits	Breathless and dancers	1:40:22

predominantly remains in the upper register of the octave range, and the coda, with its emphasis on the lower register, provides melodic balance.

In the film, "Live Alone and Like It" is first heard with a radio-like tone quality that suggests source music. The excerpt begins with A′ but quickly skips to the coda. Notably, Elfman adds dissonant scoring beneath the song at this point to foreshadow the shooting that will occur near the end of this scene. The song begins again, now heard more distinctly—less like source music—and almost in its entirety during a montage showing the bonding of Tracy, Tess, and the Kid, with the rondo-like punctuation of Kid's question, "When are we going to eat?" Once again the A′ portion cuts to the coda, but the end of the song is never heard. Sondheim's lyrics make a direct reference to the dialogue, in which Tess declares that she "likes living alone," and Tracy says that they share this in common. The irony is that, during the song, Tracy is working up courage to propose marriage, and Tess is obviously more than anxious to change her tune. But just as he explains that he really may not like living alone, the shooting begins. At the close of the scene, Tess says that she understands Tracy's life, but contradicts the title of the song by saying, "Just don't ask me to like it." With a brief song, montage, and some action, one of the critical threads of the story is humorously and somewhat poignantly furthered.

In Tracy's professional life, the tables are turned against him after he has been framed for murder. "Back in Business" also takes its lead from the dialogue, as it immediately follows Caprice's declaration, "Boys, we're back in business!" The song also hearkens to the 1930s with its ragtime character, showgirl chorus presentation, and dance band accompaniment. The music could be interpreted as diegetic, since dancing showgirls are one of the components of the montage, which also includes scenes of rampaging crime, Tracy in jail, and money rolling in. The montage is synchronized well with the song, creating numerous humorous links to the lyrics, such as Tracy's spinning image to "let the good times roll," a head conk with the word "bang," and the contradiction of seeing the depressed police chief as the song refers to "no more gloom and doom."

The lively tune has a verse-chorus structure, with the verse in C minor and the A–B–A chorus in C major. Each segment, as befitting a dance tune, is sixteen measures in length. The montage is nearly two minutes in length, but this still necessitates some cutting— the second verse, the second half of the initial A of the reprise, and the coda are omitted. A more exuberant tune than "Live Alone and Like It," "Back in Business" is less stable harmonically and playfully flirts with harmonic ambiguities.

"What Can You Lose?" is a love song in a more contemporary musical style. The melody centers on four-note motives that initially encompass the ranges of a minor or major third (Example 17.1). As the melody ascends, the interval expands to a fourth and fifth. The song is performed in its entirety; 88 Keys renders the first portion (1:01:15), and he is then joined by Breathless. The lyrics apply to three relationships, Tracy and Tess, 88 Keys

EXAMPLE **17.1**

and Breathless, and Breathless and Tracy. Tess has left Tracy, and the couple's separation is the primary focus of the montage; the sentiments that urge, "Say it to her, what can you lose?" are easily tied to Tracy's difficulty in declaring his love. With cuts showing 88 Keys staring longingly at Breathless, the montage also suggests his devotion and love for the femme fatale. Since 88 Keys is the primary singer, the words imply rather directly his inability to be anything other than a devoted friend to Breathless, a state that does not change in the film. Less explicit, but more fundamental to the plot, is Breathless's desire for Tracy. Since the song is sandwiched by two failed attempts on her part to seduce the stoic detective, one can easily read that her thoughts are of Tracy as she joins in the song. Furthering this connection, 88 Keys, acting for Breathless's alter ego No Face, propositions Big Boy with the ultimate argument, "what can you lose?" just prior to the song.

Sondheim received his only Academy nomination and won the Best Song Oscar for "Sooner or Later (I Always Get My Man)." In its complete version, the song has an A–B–A' form. The initial A section has an expanded antecedent–consequent phrase structure that suggests a blues with its tempo, low register, text repetition, sustained cadential pitches, and flattened notes. The principal motive is a rising triplet figure, a traditional figure for a seductress. In the antecedent phrase, the triplet motive occurs in the first and third measures. The fifth measure also contains triplets, but without the rising motion, as Sondheim prepares the listener for the imminent cadence. The consequent phrase is extended by a four-measure insertion that begins with the cadential triplets and moves to the melody's emotional climax. The B section has two distinct sections delineated by two other motivic ideas, one in E♭ minor and the other in E♭ major. The first is a syncopated rhythmic gesture that lies with the interval of a third, and the second (starting after "It's a question of when") is a more disjunct figure, generally lying with the range of a minor sixth (or augmented fifth).

Breathless performs "Sooner or Later" twice in the film, and each scene connects the meaning of the text with her desire for Tracy. The first takes place during the drama's exposition. The piano introduction begins as we observe Tracy and Tess walking away from reporters. Just after Tracy states, "there is about as much chance of me getting behind a desk as of me getting a new girlfriend," the voice of Breathless enters to take up that challenge; we initially hear the consequent phrase; "sooner or later you're gonna decide," alluding to the temptation that Tracy will soon face. While she continues singing, the film provides us with an overview of the city (a standard noir vision), an establishing shot of the Club Ritz, and then the Breathless performance accompanied by 88 Keys in front of her current boss, Lips Manlis.

The reprise of the song (0:50:20) allows the performance, through crosscutting (Table 17.2), to encompass an entire scene that extends more than five minutes. The diegetic nature of the performance is maintained, as music is not heard during the moments when the eavesdropping bug is being planted in a distant room, and the dynamics are diminished for scenes outside the club. When the song bleeds into the outside action, it is always linked with images of Tracy.

This second performance of "Sooner or Later" shows Breathless with her new boss, a scene that parallels its first performance. A small instrumental combo has been added,

Table 17.2 "Sooner or Later," reprise

Song section	Plot	Timing
A and first half of B	Crosscutting between performance and raid preparations	0:50:20
No music other than a brief fragment	Drilling hole for the bug	0:51:55
B from beginning	Tracy enters club in the raid	0:52:05
No music	Planting the bug	0:52:28
B from where it stopped	Return to club; no evidence found; Tracy leaves	0:52:35
No music	Tracy in car with Pat	0:53:05
A beginning at m. 3; musical cadence from consequent phrase	Club	0:53:20
B (skips closing measures); A′	Montage of Tracy closing down Big Boy's activities	0:53:42

reflecting Big Boy's interest in show business. The frequent visions of Tracy in action accompanied by the voice of Breathless tie the lyrics to her infatuation. Two moments are particularly striking. The first is just after Tracy enters the club during the raid. He momentarily stares at Breathless, she looks directly back at him, and the lyrics reach the most seductive moment: "and no one I've kissed, babe, ever fights me again" (she has kissed Tracy in an earlier scene). The second is at the conclusion of the scene. A brief double exposure shows Tracy walking towards us with his Tommy gun (a not too subtle erotic image) and Breathless, who sings, "my man." Throughout the film, Tracy never gives any overt indication that he would consider a relationship with Breathless. But visions such as these coupled with his inability to express emotions to any woman, suggest that he is not impervious to her obvious charms.

"More" is the longest song in *Dick Tracy*. Sondheim gives it a verse–chorus structure, but with some innovative twists (Table 17.3). The opening verse provides an additional link to the time period by quoting lyrics and some of the melodic motives of "I Got Plenty of Nothing" (1935) and "I Got Rhythm" (1930) by George Gershwin, and "The Best Things in Life Are Free" by Lew Brown, Buddy DeSylva, and Ray Henderson (1927). The chorus continues with other references to Gershwin. The opening phrase, which is later heard with the text "I got rhythm, music too," has the same rhythm as the chorus of Gershwin's "I got rhythm." The A phrase appears to follow the same structure as Gershwin's song with the repeat of the opening phrase and then a contrast. But the expected return of the opening material is abandoned, and the melody greedily and prematurely leaps to a cadential "more" on a D♭. In the repetition of this material, that moment is extended with the word "more" symbolically rising higher to a D♮ and then an E♭. The lyric B phrase is extended by a bit of patter and then the first choral entrance with the word "More!"

Table 17.3 "More," structure

Song structure	Opening words
Verse 1	Once upon a time
Chorus: A	Got my diamonds
Chorus: A'	Count your blessings
Chorus: B	I'm no mathematician / More
Chorus: A"	I got rhythm
Verse 2	One is fun
Chorus: B	Or does that sound too greedy
Chorus: A"	Each possession
Coda	Except all

Sondheim introduces a second verse, but with new musical material. The basic motive recalls Gershwin's "Fascinatin' Rhythm," a song that is played by the stage band just prior to the actual performance of this number at the Club Ritz. While maintaining the patter quality characteristic of a verse, the choir enters with the word "more" on sustained pitches that again ascend C–D♭ –D♮, which allows Madonna to provide the climactic E♭. This is another reference to "I've Got Rhythm," in which Ethel Merman repeatedly belts out "More" during the instrumental break in the musical *Girl Crazy*. As is often the case in Tin Pan Alley songs, the reprise of the chorus is abbreviated and begins with the B phrase. The choir returns in the coda, once again emphasizing "More" in successively quicker statements.

The two principal songs performed by Breathless represent her emotional split. "Sooner or Later" is linked with her attraction for Tracy, and "More" is an expression of her desire for wealth and power, which she pursues under the guise of No Face. "More" is heard three times during the film. It is first heard during a scene that crosscuts between Tracy interrogating Mumbles and a rehearsal at the Club Ritz accompanied by 88 Keys on the piano. Tracy is convinced that Big Boy has murdered Lips Manlis, the owner of the Club Ritz. His questioning over the whereabouts of Lips occurs just as Big Boy, having murdered Lips and taken over as the new owner of the club, is actively directing Breathless and dancers with grand visions of going into show biz. Because of the numerous interruptions, the song is heard at various moments; the opening verse is omitted, the second verse and the return of the Chorus are heard after a brief break, and the scene essentially ends with the coda. At this point, the song and its lyrics would be interpreted merely as a typical 1930s entertainment number reflecting the spirit of the popular gold digger movies of the era.

The second appearance of "More" is a performance with a dance band. Once again, crosscutting extends the song so that it encompasses an entire scene in which Tracy is closing in on Big Boy. The performance includes passages that were heard in the rehearsal, and all of the excerpts occur within the proper order of the song. Once again the crosscutting is not without humor. As Tracy is calculating how to get out of a locked room, Breathless sings the portion highlighting the word "mathematician."

Once Tracy asks Pat for his weight and Pat's response reluctantly moves through several increasing numbers, the cut returns us to Breathless singing, "I find counting a bore." A couple of other crosscuts foreshadow the surprising twist that Breathless is No Face. As she observes Big Boy running through the club with Tess as a prisoner, she sings, "Now, however, I own the view," and when Tracy and the police are eliminating the gang, Breathless and the dancers reach their most exuberant moment. Breathless's unfolding plan is approaching her desired goal.

Still, the full meaning of the song remains ambiguous. Audiences could interpret her need for "more" as another statement for her desire for Tracy and perhaps for a "good" life. Her apparent sadness in the moments following the performance, especially as she sees Tracy's anxiety over the wellbeing of Tess, adds to this impression. It is the presentation of the song during the closing credits (after the revelation that Breathless is the mastermind No Face) that the true implications of the lyrics are made clear. For the first time, we hear the opening thirty-two-measure verse. The texts of all three of the quoted songs suggest that money is not essential to happiness, but Sondheim takes the twist from Gershwin's line, "who could ask for anything more?" This leads directly into the chorus that demands "more." The casting could not have been better, as Madonna's best-known song at this point was "Material Girl" (1985). Madonna's video includes a reference to "Diamonds Are a Girl's Best Friend," which may account for Sondheim's opening words of the chorus, "Got my diamonds."

REDS

Sondheim and Warren Beatty collaborated for the first time with *Reds* (1981), an epic film about the life of the American communist Jack Reed and his love affair with writer Louise Bryant. This movie received twelve Academy Award nominations, putting it into lofty territory.[5] Beatty won the Best Director Award, and Oscars were also earned for Cinematography and Supporting Actress (Maureen Stapleton). It lost out on the Best Picture Award to *Chariots of Fire*, a bit of a surprise. Warren Beatty, Diane Keaton, and Jack Nicholson (as Eugene O'Neill) were also nominated for acting awards. Gene Hackman, a two-time Best Actor winner, also has a minor role.

Music was not one of the nominated categories, which may be attributable to a number of trends. When we think of typical Hollywood epics, films like *Gone with the Wind* and *Ben-Hur* come to mind with their monumental symphonic scores. But a new style of epics had been created, largely through the work of English director David Lean. Beginning with *The Bridge on the River Kwai* (1957), stories set in twentieth-century history began to dominate the genre, and the new sparse scores tended to feature a single melody with popular appeal. Such formulas can be found in *Exodus* (1960), *Lawrence of Arabia* (1962), and *Doctor Zhivago* (1965), all of which won Oscars for Best Score.

Two films appeared in 1977 that would have a dramatic impact on Hollywood music—*Star Wars* ushered in the return of the full symphonic score, and *Saturday*

FIGURE 17.1 Diane Keaton and Warren Beatty in *Reds* (1981).

Night Fever showed the potent market for popular music soundtracks. These films also mark the beginning of an enormous gulf between box-office hits and critically acclaimed films. Both the symphonic scores of John Williams and popular music scores were relegated to the former. Hence, the quality epics of the early 1980s that are based on twentieth-century historical plots, including *Reds, Gandhi* (1982), *Passage to India* (1984), *Out of Africa* (1985), and *The Last Emperor* (1987), avoided either approach and sought a musical style in which simplicity was essential.

Beatty used music sparingly. He relied upon either source music or a recurring piano tune that serves as the love theme for Jack and Louise. Sondheim published this melody with words under the title "Goodbye for Now," but it is never sung in the film. The cueing of the tune is quite simple. All seven appearances (Table 17.4) are in F major, and many end abruptly with no sense of closure. Most are set for the piano with the occasional addition of strings. Because of a thin tone quality, several of the cues suggest an unseen diegetic source—someone playing on an upright rather than a grand piano. The two cues in Russia (not related directly to the romance) employ a balalaika with string harmonies underneath.

The melody primarily moves in eight-measure phrases; the overall shape can be described as A–B–C–A′ –codetta. The unifying element is the opening three-note motive, which is repeated a fourth lower in measures 3 and 4 (marked with brackets in Example 17.2). This idea is treated sequentially at the beginning of the B phrase, and it appears twice in succession at the beginning of C. Although A′ clearly refers back to the first phrase in its pitch center and content, this phrase also contains elements of B and C,

Table 17.4 Appearances of the Love Theme in *Reds*

Scene	Melodic material	Instrumentation	Timing*
Provincetown montage; romantic	Expanded intro; A' material cuts to codetta	Piano	0:39:25
Marriage proposal	No intro; 14 measures	Piano, strings	0:56:20
Marriage; Christmas	No intro; ends just after the beginning of A'	Piano, strings	1:02:20
Montage of letters from Louis	New intro; 12–13 measures	Piano	1:16:40
Jack flees Russia	No intro; A B codetta	Balalaika, strings	0:41:10
Jack flees train	No intro; 10 measures	Balalaika, strings	1:16:10
Closing credits	No intro; full tune with repeat	Piano, strings, flute	1:28:00

*Timings are from the CD. For ease of locating the cues, the timings after the intermission reflect those of the second CD in the set.

EXAMPLE 17.2

EXAMPLE 17.3

nicely rounding off the tune. The melody in the codetta closes on the third scale degree of the tonic chord, creating an inconclusive sound, much like the love affair itself.

The most important source music of the film is the singing of the Socialist anthem "Internationale." Sondheim links these two melodies together. The principal motive of the love theme is taken from the first measure of the anthem (marked with brackets in Example 17.3). Moreover, the first seven pitches of Sondheim's theme correspond to those of Internationale without the pickup and with the substitution of a B♮ for an A. In addition, Sondheim also adopts the descending motion in the third measure of the Socialist anthem to his melody, which is most notable in the A phrase. The close relationship of the love theme to the anthem is reinforced in the film just prior to the intermission. The Russians break into a choral rendition (1:39:30) and the ensuing montage includes several views of Jack and Louise making love.

STAVISKY

For his first venture into film music, Sondheim worked with one of the most prestigious directors of the era, Alain Resnais. Associated with the French New Wave, Resnais created two of the most provocative films of the era, *Hiroshima Mon Amour* (1959) and *Last Year at Marienbad* (1961). *Stavisky* (1974) would be Resnais's sixth feature film and the first to enjoy popular success. Although receiving mixed reviews, the film balances broad appeal with intellectual complexities, which leads biographer James Monaco to suggest that this is arguably Resnais's greatest artistic achievement.[6] One reason for the acclaim garnered by the film is the strong acting of Jean-Paul Belmondo, who had become a major screen star in France following his role in Godard's *Breathless* (1960), and of Charles Boyer, who received the Best Actor award at the Cannes Film Festival for his portrayal of the Baron Jean Raoul. *Stavisky* received a nomination for the Golden Palm at this festival as well.

Looking beyond the superficial differences between Resnais and Sondheim, the pairing of these two figures is a natural. Resnais describes several of his films as stemming from a musical conception, and Sondheim's cinematic approach to musical theater has been previously noted. Both sought to balance popular accessibility with intellectual content and form, both manipulated the time continuum, and both had great respect for each other. Resnais freely talked about inspiration derived from Sondheim's musicals. According to Jore Semprún,[7] the screenwriter for *Stavisky*, Resnais was not particular about what subject they chose for his next film, but simply wanted to make a movie staring Belmondo and Boyer with music by Sondheim.[8]

Resnais's wish was fulfilled, and his dream team produced a drama based on the life of the embezzler Alexandre Stavisky, the central figure in a scandal simply known as the Stavisky Affair. The revelations of fraud involving Stavisky and a number of prominent officials sparked a riot and toppled the French government in 1934. The film focuses on the events from July 1933 to Stavisky's suicide or murder in 1934.[9] A number of flashbacks relate earlier incidents in his life, and flashforwards show his funeral and the postmortem parliamentary enquiry. Intermixed with the various components of the Stavisky story are scenes involving Trotsky, who was granted asylum in France in 1933 and was asked to leave in the wake of the Stavisky Affair. Underlying the plot are the volatile political events that would soon lead to war and to the Vichy régime, including the prevailing anti-Semitism in Germany, Russia, and France. Both Stavisky and Trotsky were Russian Jews.[10]

While Resnais illuminates details of the affair and various moments of Stavisky's life, he bathes the story in a haze of nostalgia. "Resnais makes a film that is of its decade and yet also, in its colors, its textures, its grand sensuality, of another decade imagined and artificially reconstructed."[11] Music plays a significant role in this effort, as Sondheim captures the vibrant musical character of France in the early 1930s. Many of the cues incorporate the styles of contemporary dances. The title theme is a slow foxtrot, the

FIGURE 17.2 Jean-Paul Belmondo (center) in Alain Resnais's *Stavisky* (1974).

most popular dance of the time, and waltzes are heard frequently, especially in scenes suggesting elegance. As such, these dance segments suggest the smoothness and superficiality of Stavisky as well as the decadence of the era.

During the 1920s and 30s, concert composers active in France assimilated the rhythms and gestures of popular dances, including ragtime. Igor Stravinsky was an active force in Paris, and the most prominent French composers were the Eric Satie-inspired "Les Six," headed by Milhaud, Poulenc, and Honegger; Honegger wrote several outstanding film scores, including those for Gance's silent film epic *Napoléon* (1927) and for *Les Misérables* (1934). Sondheim's orchestration, with its emphasis on woodwinds and economy (lacking the full orchestral string sound of Hollywood films), the angular and often syncopated melodies, and neotonal harmonies,[12] reflect the Parisian style of Stravinsky and Les Six. Notably, the woodwind introduction to the title theme includes a number of quartal chords (Example 17.4),[13] a standard harmonic practice of French concert music in the early 1930s.

Sondheim composed a relatively lengthy orchestral score. Each cue creates a specific mood for a given scene, generally with few contrasts. Some are cut off abruptly without the dovetailing that is prevalent in Hollywood scoring. There is a significant amount of recurring thematic material, but none of the associations are consistent enough to be considered as leitmotifs in the Hollywood sense. Sondheim did not write any songs for the film, which makes this his longest foray into the realm of strictly instrumental music. His score reveals an excellent understanding of orchestration, both for the popular and

EXAMPLE 17.4

EXAMPLE 17.5

neoclassical styles, a full grasp of contemporary harmony, and a lyric conception of melody. Many of the themes are song-like, as they are in instrumental works of great song composers such as Schubert and Gershwin. The most beautiful of his themes is a rising melody associated with Erna (first heard at 0:32:00 and expanded shortly thereafter). In spite of the variety of the melodic materials, the score is remarkably unified.

The title theme not only establishes the mood of the film, but also provides much of the thematic material for the remainder of the score. The sinuous saxophone melody (Example 17.5) moves mostly by step and incorporates a number of chromatic shifts. The overall effect recalls Chopin's Prelude No. 4 in E minor, written for Parisian salons in the 1830s. The melodic repetition of long and short durations is common to both compositions, although the *Stavisky* theme generally includes syncopation. Each melody initially centers on the pitches B–C–B and A–B–A, and the Sondheim tune and key signature imply E minor as a tonal center. The accompaniment for both is a repetitive pulse, but while the Chopin accompaniment shares in the chromatic shifting, the Sondheim accompaniment maintains an ostinato alternation of E and B. One additional parallel is the overall form. Both are simply a melodic statement and a varied repetition.

During the narrative, the title theme is generally associated with Stavisky in relation to his beautiful wife Arlette. Its initial appearance is when Stavisky places a necklace on the sleeping Arlette (0:47:20). Other variations of the theme occur when, at a cemetery, he recalls his father's suicide and ends up in Arlette's arms (0:54:40), when he is anxiously burning his files before looking at Arlette's picture (1:30:25), during his funeral procession led by Arlette (1:35:05), and when flowers are sent to Arlette in prison (1:49:00). The cue for the funeral procession is particularly effective, as it grows dynamically in a fashion similar to the music of Honegger, and then transforms into a carnival-like waltz when a cut shows Stavisky's files in the hands of the authorities.

The title music presents three other important musical ideas: the introduction (Example 17.4), a countermelody played with harmonics and glissandos heard in the second half of the theme (Example 17.6), and an active motive heard during the brief interlude (Example 17.7). The latter features a repeated pattern of three notes in duple

EXAMPLE 17.6

EXAMPLE 17.7

meter over the first phrase of the principal theme (Example 17.5). These three thematic ideas recur throughout the film, either independently or in various combinations.

The introduction idea, which begins with a melodic descent of a major sixth, is heard in several transformations; notable developments occur during a flashback to Stavisky's youth (0:23:30) and in the scene at the cemetery (0:54:50). The thematic material of Examples 17.6 and 17.7 are frequently combined in scenes involving Arlette and cars. In these appearances, the active motive is played quickly as an accompaniment, and the countermelody becomes the principal theme, which will be referred to as the "Arlette theme." The Arlette theme is first heard when Stavisky and the Baron are walking to their car and talking about Arlette (see the discussion below and Table 17.5). The same material returns when Stavisky and the Baron are driving to see Arlette (0:44:05). This cue incorporates the plush string sound heard during the opening credits and turns into a waltz when they approach the hotel where Arlette is sleeping. Further variations of the Arlette theme occur in the cue underscoring Stavisky's visit to his father's house, while the Baron, Arlette, and Montalvo wait in the car (1:11:40).

Dances are important throughout the score. One recurring theme is a light dance tune with two pick-ups. First heard in a flashback to a meeting of the Baron and Arlette (see Table 17.5 below), it seems to accompany moments of infatuation (rather than serious or passionate love). The waltz, though, is the most prevalent of the dance types. Three of the thematic ideas from the titles music are presented at least once with a waltz character (Examples 17.4–17.6). Several motives from this melody recur and mix with other material.

The two most prominent waltzes in the score are associated with the elegant life at the Claridge Hotel. Both share the same introductory material. The first of these simulates a diegetic presentation with its setting for piano, violin, and cello, a common ensemble in fine European hotels (0:05:20). The A–B–A form of the theme strongly resembles a waltz–trio–waltz. The other waltz presents a lazy chromatic melodic descent and suggests the sensual and extravagant side of Stavisky's high life. Near the end of the film, the waltz cadence that generally coincides with images of the Claridge façade closes the narrative with a touch of bitter irony, as we now observe the façade of a prison, Arlette's new residence.

Table 17.5 Recollections of Arlette

Plot	Music
Stavisky and Baron leave hotel; begin to discuss Arlette's triumph of the previous day	Arlette theme
Flashback: Baron comes to meet Arlette	Dance theme; touch of title theme at end
Backseat of car: discussion of Arlette continues	Arlette theme
Flashback: Baron and Arlette meet Montalvo	Dance theme; more elegant in strings
Flashback: car show	Popular tune heard in previous flashback to show
Car arrives at the theater	Music stops

The variety of these musical ideas helps to delineate the threads of the story. No music is heard during segments devoted to Trotsky or during flashforwards to the testimonies. For flashbacks in the lives of Stavisky or Arlette, music generally reinforces the jumps in time. The scene in which the Baron recalls the events of the previous day involving Arlette (0:11:50), for example, involves several flashbacks (Table 17.5). The overall musical shape is A–B–A–B′ –C, which corresponds to the five segments of the scene. The A portions in the present time are accompanied by the Arlette theme. The B portions are flashbacks to the previous day when the Baron met with Arlette. Both are accompanied by the light dance tune described above; the first is a lively version and the second is more elegant. The final segment is a cut to the car show, and the popular music from an earlier flashback to this scene returns. In this manner, Sondheim crafts a remarkably unified score that both contributes to the nostalgic atmosphere of the film and illuminates the interweaving segments of the drama.

* * * * * *

Sondheim's music for *Stavisky* is his most ambitious cinematic collaboration and is especially notable for its absorption of the styles of both popular dance and the composers of Les Six. His other music for film is written for voice and piano or, in *Reds*, just piano. All five movies are critically acclaimed productions with strong directing and acting, and Sondheim enhanced each with his melodic gifts, ability to generate appropriate moods, and sense of dramatic placement. Although small in number, these contributions are strong in quality. They leave those of us who study film music simply wishing that there were more.

Notes

1. Steve Swayne, *How Sondheim Found his Sound*. (Ann Arbor: University of Michigan Press, 2005).
2. Omitted from this survey are the song "Water under the Bridge" composed for the film *Singing out Loud*, which was never produced, and the clever mystery *The Last of Sheila* (1973), which Sondheim co-wrote with Anthony Perkins.

3. Swayne, *How Sondheim Found*, 194.
4. "It Takes All Kinds" was also written for the film but not used; it was later recorded for *Sondheim at the Movies*, CD (Varése Sarabande: VSD-5895).
5. The fourteen nominations for *Titanic* and *All about Eve* remain the all-time record.
6. James Monaco, *Alain Resnais* (New York: Oxford University Press, 1979), 168–9.
7. Semprún has enjoyed a colorful career that includes work as a politician and an organizer for the Communist party in Spain. Among his screen credits is the Greek political thriller *Z* (1969), for which he received an Oscar.
8. For additional details on the relationship between Sondheim and Resnais, see Swayne, *How Sondheim Found*, 181–91.
9. Officially, Stavisky committed suicide, but there was speculation that the police shot him.
10. For a study of the political implications of the film, see Naomi Greene, *The National Past in Postwar French Cinema* (Princeton: Princeton University Press, 1999).
11. Emma Wilson expands upon the nostalgia of *Stavisky* in *Alain Resnais* (Manchester: Manchester University Press, 2006), 123.
12. Neotonality maintains tonal centers but rejects the use of functional tonality, in which a key is established by the progression of a dominant-seventh chord to tonic.
13. Quartal chords are based on the intervals of a fourth, as opposed to triads, which are based on thirds. The first chord of Ex. 17.4 includes three pitches related by fourths (C♯, F♯, and B), and the second chord has four pitches (F♯, B, E, and A).

CHAPTER 18

··

ATTENDING THE TALE OF *SWEENEY TODD*: THE STAGE MUSICAL AND TIM BURTON'S FILM VERSION

··

DAVID THOMSON

AT what time of year should DreamWorks open a movie like *Sweeney Todd*? Well, no, it's hardly a reliable family outing, and while it does offer a great deal of red in its otherwise gunmetal imagery, it doesn't really feel like Christmas entertainment. Beneath the credits we see a snake of blood like grease in the cogs of the city's machinery. We have been warned. The blood will come in a flood. But December is the month that draws movie producers nowadays, because if you can squeeze your picture in before the close of the year you qualify for the Academy Awards. Better still, if you open in early December and build at the box office then your chance at an Oscar is improved. So they opened Tim Burton's *Sweeney Todd* on December 21, 2007. I daresay they thought it was a prestige package, meant for Sondheim fans and anyone who didn't mind an astringent touch-up on the Christmas spirit. I say Tim Burton's *Sweeney Todd*, because it is that, and because for a while now film criticism has been duty-bound to regard movies as the work of their directors. But as a marketable commodity, everyone knew this was in the Sondheim field, which is to say the work of a pronounced and famous theatrical talent, with a fervent and loyal following, but never quite the unquestioning sentimental attachment that has been given to Andrew Lloyd Webber, or Rodgers and Hammerstein.

One reason why so few Sondheim musicals have been filmed is that the tone of his work doesn't always like or trust people and their feelings. A musical is bound to be expensive and the system has never been sure that Stephen Sondheim is comfortable enough for the large crowd. The film fared reasonably well. It is supposed to have cost $50 million. It grossed $52 million in its first American run, and it has grossed $152 million worldwide. Those numbers seem adequate, but gross revenue is a long way from net (the money returned to the producers) and I doubt anyone is close to profit yet on *Sweeney Todd* the movie. Christmas wasn't fooled. This is a very grisly picture and Todd isn't simply a wicked man. He's a delicate and tricky dramatic project.

So, although Stephen Sondheim himself has made charitable comments on the picture, and seems to have been content, we don't have to follow suit.[1] Sondheim has lamented that he can't see himself as a dramatist, or a writer of plays.[2] It's not that the music in *Sweeney Todd* is less than extraordinary. Still, this is a play and that's one reason why the film is so disappointing. The great difficulty in doing *Sweeney Todd* is to accept its story as a plot that can be followed without drastic shifts in mood or tone. So is this really the story of Benjamin Barker, falsely convicted and transported to Australia after which his wife was seduced and killed, his daughter kidnapped, in his absence? Does he return, at last, with vengeance in his heart? Can he destroy the Judge Turpin who has done him such damage? Or is there another purpose, far more malign, to becoming a demon ready to murder anyone who sits in his barber's chair? Will he keep our allegiance in that relentless progress? Must he finally die in the bloodlust of vengeance, or can he be redeemed?

And how does that foul pie shop fit in? Or to put it another way, is there a world where we can believe in his daughter Johanna and her boy, Anthony, existing together "in love," where he sings her name forever, or is there truly a hole in the world that is bound to grow and consume the entirety of this dark and convincingly wretched London? Johanna is a strange heroine: her lovely yet shrill song about birds can't compete with the earthiness of Mrs. Lovett. She and Anthony may end up singing together in a cage.

A warning sign about the film's compromised intentions comes very early. Instead of keeping the arresting stage opening—"Attend the Tale of Sweeney Todd" (1),[3] as delivered by various citizens but culminating in the first, exultant appearance of Todd himself—the movie suggests it is going to tell us a regular story. The gap left can be put very simply: on stage, we are meeting Sweeney immediately, not just as the demon barber of Fleet Street, but almost an epic, legendary figure, an eternal demon, as fearsome and emphatic as Mr. Punch. Whereas in the movie the story begins with the ship coming through the fog into London—beneath a Tower Bridge that was not in fact opened for another forty years. The first voice we hear, to the hopeful strains of "No Place like London," is Anthony's. When we find the two men on deck, it is plainly Barker talking to Anthony, albeit a Barker who is using the alias of Todd. This Barker is chill yet on terms with the young man. He owes him his life. The movie wants us to like him—and, of course, it has cast Johnny Depp in the part (Figure 18.1).

Depp must have been responsible for a fair portion of the film's gross, and no one wants to berate him. He may be the decisive element that let the picture go ahead. He is a handsome charmer, droll enough to make fun of himself, a naturally relaxed and slightly hidden or recessive actor. He sang in a rock band once, and he sings passably well—which is a little like saying Sweeney makes a fair job of cutting a throat. But Sweeney needs to roar, and to possess immense power and strength. Call it fury, call it vengeance or the demonic—it can hardly be introspective or recessive. When he hits the word "Attend," there can be no arguing or half-heartedness. On stage, that song and his appearance put him in charge. He may be a victim in life, but he has surpassed victimhood at the outset. Yet Depp often sings in a kind of interior monologue, where the

FIGURE **18.1** Johnny Depp as Sweeney Todd in the film by Tim Burton (2007).

classic Sweeneys of Len Cariou and George Hearn are blasts that fill the hall, and even the hole Todd recognizes in the world:

> There's a hole in the world that's a great black pit
> And the vermin of the world inhabit it
> And its morals aren't worth what a pig would spit
> And it goes by the name of London. (9)

This is already a reworking and sinister acceleration of the far more idealistic "London" song begun by Anthony. But the "pit" rhyme in Sweeney's lyrics swiftly takes the turn the ear is waiting for: "There's a hole in the world like a great black pit / And it's filled with people who are filled with shit"(11). That lyric is very telling: the first line is misanthropic, but poetic; it could be the cry of a pessimist who knows he's fighting to preserve hope or sanity against great odds. But the second line is lost, plunged in despair, and as dementedly insistent as the repetition of "filled." I don't think that's saying too much of a writer who takes lyrics and their craft so seriously. So the couplet embodies Sondheim's essential notion of Sweeney: a lost soul at the brink of authentic madness, a depressive whose only relief is the hideous glee of slaughter and Mrs. Lovett's cannibalistic transaction.

It's not that the couplet needs to be sung in different voices or even with altered dramatic stress. So the requirement on acting and voice is not very demanding. It's like the
suddenness with which Anthony Perkins' Norman Bates goes from amiability to mania
in *Psycho*. I say that not just because there's a bond between *Psycho* and *Sweeney Todd*
(to be explored), but because Perkins was a close friend of Sondheim. They collaborated
on the screenplay of the movie *The Last of Sheila*, which opened in 1973, just six years
before the debut of *Sweeney Todd*. In addition, Sondheim has mentioned the influence
of Bernard Herrmann, who composed the music for *Psycho* and many other great films,
so it's hardly possible to make Sweeney inward, reflective, or wistful, but these are Depp's
preferred areas of expression. It's more dangerous to have a Mrs. Lovett with whom this
quiet barber might fall in love. Helena Bonham Carter is a natural beauty, only forty
when the film opened and hardly less ravishing than she had been in her melancholy
masterpiece *The Wings of the Dove*, made for Iain Softley, where her guilt is expressed
in silent nakedness. Her Mrs. Lovett is untidy, sluttish, and entirely lowlife, but her dark
eyes are emphasized by make-up, her dress is cut low, and the white of her skin is not just
attractive but has a hint of some spiritual feeling beneath her bruising. She photographs
like a fallen beauty, not a cheery witch (Figure 18.2).

Of course, she is also partner to Tim Burton, the mother of two children with him,
and a light-voiced, intimate singer. So, one can hardly blame the director for loving his
actress. Bonham Carter has the humor Mrs. Lovett needs and she can deliver the nasty
edge. But if Sweeney is Punch she is a long way from Judy. A romantic possibility has
been introduced in this casting, and we need to remember that her great predecessors
in the role were Angela Lansbury, who was fifty-four when she created the part on stage,
and Patti LuPone, who has occasionally played it since then.

FIGURE **18.2** Helena Bonham Carter as Mrs. Lovett (2007).

You can see LuPone (with George Hearn) in the DVD of the concert performance given in San Francisco in 2001. It is not just that LuPone is sexy, lewd, and funnier than Bonham Carter. Once more, it is a matter of her ferocious, devouring energy—she eats people long before she gets the idea of priest or poet pies. Nor is it enough to say that in a movie, as close as a camera can come, her role needs to be played more softly or with more restraint. The great trouble with movie and the close scrutiny of an inner life is that it easily falls into the self-love in most actors, that willingness to look good for the camera and to be available for our fantasies. Patti LuPone's Mrs. Lovett is external, aggressive, pathologically confident, but Bonham Carter shows us the wounded soul that was there once and might be rescued. Once you start to turn Sweeney or Mrs. Lovett into needy people, the puppet-like grotesquerie of their interaction dwindles. When that happens Sweeney is at risk of becoming an unpleasant trickster, instead of an operatic madman.

The performance history of *Sweeney Todd* suggests the rewards in simplifying and stripping away "atmosphere." The original 1979 production already seemed nervous of recreating the logistics of a barber shop upstairs and a pie kitchen below, not just for the expense of it, but because the more real that factory became the queasier the audience might feel. It's worth adding that *Sweeney Todd* ran for only a modest 526 performances (*Evita*, which also opened in 1979, ran for 1,567). Further, when the show went on the road, it met with less success, as if to suggest that provincial audiences found the mixture of the exalted music and the barbaric action harder to digest.[4]

Although the Broadway premiere was a *success d'estime*, the show "still only repaid 59 percent of its investment" while the London production "opened [in June 1980] to very mixed reviews and closed four months later."[5] But the show has grown in reputation, as if its daring and its fraught use of disaster and dream found our shaky hearts in an age that acted both those things out wherever we cared to look. There is something prescient in the show, as there was in Hitchcock's *Psycho*—a feeling that death is a modern rapture. There have been revivals, of course, and in that series the most impressive have been the "in concert" performances, with cursory gestures toward scenery or props, and the version conceived and directed by John Doyle, which is a deliberate minimalization of the work, where the orchestra gives way to just a few instruments played by members of the cast. Having seen both those productions (the "in concert" in San Francisco), I believe the show benefits from simplification and a reluctance to attempt an 1849 London where Todd might have existed, to say nothing of the mechanics of Mrs. Lovett's establishment (so much larger inside in the film than the exterior view can sustain).

By contrast, the movie believes we won't be satisfied without the authenticity of the London of the time. Of course, it's not the real London, or even extensive studio sets (though it was shot in England, at Pinewood). It's a clever balance of set-building and computer generated imagery, all done in the hues of winter, smoke-darkened stone and the lack-luster metallic tones of unpolished razors. This look (photographed by Darius Wolski) is sophisticated and impressive, and there are sudden swooping camera movements that draw us down streets and alleys that are giddily persuasive. There is a sense of the London of Mayhew or Dickens, and you feel it's a directorial attempt to get at the "black hole" theme. Still, it's painfully factual, or realistic, and a diversion from the very theatrical game of the show. Dante Ferretti was responsible for the production design, and he won the only Oscar given to the film for a tour de force that steadily depletes the spirit of the stage musical. Ferretti is remarkable for creating worlds, or turning existing places into movie worlds: thus, he previously did *Casino, Cold Mountain*, and *Gangs of New York*. The last is especially relevant in that it is approximately the same period as *Sweeney Todd* for a film in which director Martin Scorsese was eager to recreate the nineteenth-century look of New York City. This design scheme is supported by the brilliant and precise work on costumes by Colleen Attwood, which did not win an Oscar (it was nominated) but did secure several other awards.

So the film has set out to win over the eye—what else can films do, even if that risks some loss of sense? It is anxious to have us feel we are in a real place (albeit with the dark gloss of computerization, a thing that young audiences today hardly seem to detect or dispute). And that atmosphere is intended to assist the psychological realism of this outline: poor Sweeney, so put upon, meets Mrs. Lovett, who might have been "right" for him—but no, it's too late. Whereas I think the only way to play their meeting is more along these lines: here's Sweeney, nearly crazed, but here comes Mrs. Lovett—she'll tip him over. The paraphernalia of London in the 1840s has nothing to do with that savage thrust. And the expensive fuss devoted to appearance and the visual only exposes embarrassment—that Depp and Bonham Carter, modishly delectable perhaps, do not sing well enough and never reach the natural habitat of monsters who despise rescue.

The movie does have other assets: Sacha Baron Cohen is surprisingly effective as Pirelli, the fraudulent barber who knows Barker when he sees him again; Timothy Spall is unctuous and hateful as the Beadle Bamford; and then there is Alan Rickman as Judge Turpin. It's unlucky for Depp that he should find himself alongside one of the best actors anywhere, and it's not too hard for the viewer—angling for a better deal—to wonder if Rickman might have made a fearsome Sweeney. Not just because the part requires an actor raised in theater's stronger voice, but because Rickman does feel like someone who might have served twenty years in a penal colony, and suffered the emotional damage in Barker's life. Rickman has the age, the heft, and the battered, world-weary gravitas that was there in George Hearn's performance. Perhaps he can't sing well enough—that may be deduced from his singing in the movie—and that would be reason enough to kill the idea. But Rickman's Turpin has a level of pained experience that Depp does not match.

So the movie falls short in many ways, and it's hardly an excuse to say, well, didn't a motion picture bring Sondheim and the power of this great work to a new audience? Any individual saved is to be appreciated. But there are other versions of *Sweeney Todd* that would be so much more useful and they are available on DVD. Sooner or later, anyone caught by the show's turmoil of lyricism and horror knows they must see it on stage. Perhaps certain kinds of death need to be done "live" —in blatant masquerade—for them to be shocking (as opposed to repulsive). Remember, you can't cut real throats on stage; you have to do something more interesting. The safe distance of the screen and the impersonation of reality only turn us into helpless voyeurs. So, the greatest error in the movie—for me—is the decision to pretend to have a river of blood. We get the sight and sound of a razor severing a throat, the spurt and gurgle of blood. There is a whole sequence where Todd's face is wreathed in splashed blood—it looks like war-paint. But this mask detracts from the drama of vengeance gone mad; it leads us into the dead-end of being armchair connoisseurs of slaughter.

I daresay Burton and the powers behind the film decided that was what a young audience would expect. The stylization of red ribbon and light, the piercing scream from the stage production, those things would be regarded as old-hat, tame, and evasive. So *Sweeney Todd* drifts towards being a horror film, whereas its horror is so much more effective if left to the imagination. Because the core of the drama has to be in Sweeney's head, I mentioned *Psycho* earlier as a point of comparison, and this is the moment to return to it. *Psycho* was a landmark in art or entertainment in that Alfred Hitchcock managed to make horror or slaughter into popular entertainment. Yes, there had been horror films before. But it was the genre of Bela Lugosi and Boris Karloff, or Peter Cushing and Christopher Lee. It derived from familiar material, folklore or popular literature. It had set conventions trusted by the audience, and they included make-up blood and the artificial brutalization of bodies always kept within bounds by the censorship codes that guarded us from mayhem at the movies.

There had been murder stories, too, since the beginnings of cinema, but the murders were seldom graphic. In *Laura* (1944), a young woman has been shot in the face so there's no face left, but we never have to see the act or the result. No modern director would be so lenient. *Psycho* broke down these barriers. It is a murder story, and it was horrific: the shower scene remains a landmark in film experience, even in black and white—with the appropriate amount of red blood I don't think *Psycho* could have emerged victorious from its tricky struggle with the censor of the time. But *Psycho*'s murder is a montage of action and reaction in which—as the director boasted—a blade never pierces skin. Just try convincing an audience they didn't see that.

Psycho was a departure in so many other ways: in offering us an appealing character, Marion Crane (Janet Leigh), who would then be ripped out of life, leaving us no one else to identify with but this shy, slightly awkward fellow, Norman, who proves the most dangerous person around. Norman is mad, or movie mad, yet he has extended lucid moments and a capacity for insight. His line about us all being in our traps is a gentler version of Todd's vision of the black hole. The most provocative thing in *Psycho* is the question: is Norman himself, and what is that self? The same question hangs over the drama of *Sweeney Todd*.

I said "movie mad," and that is important. For *Psycho* treads on dangerous ground in introducing a psychotic and then turning him into an entertainment game. In other words, Norman slips in and out of the boyish charm of Anthony Perkins as the hectic plot requires. If you think about it, we only ever see Norman as normal—the engaging and sympathetic fellow from the touching supper scene, the warmest company Marion finds in the film. When he goes abnormal, we don't actually see him—because Hitchcock wants to keep his plot device secret and because the part is close to unplayable at those demented heights. The closest we come to abnormal Norman is the last scene, where he is confined, talking to himself and to so many watching eyes. It is a cunning get-out, but it doesn't obscure Hitchcock's lack of interest in the psychosis he has pioneered. He used it for a roller-coaster engine.

These thoughts are relevant to the dramatic problems in *Sweeney Todd* that exist in the stage musical as much as in the film. Is this a flagrant blood-and-horror show, a lurid murder story, or a portrait of a depressive and vengeful mania? Is Sondheim out to put on a Broadway musical or is he interested in murder—for its own sake, as it were? The question is the more intriguing if you recall that in 1990 Sondheim introduced *Assassins*, a fairground panorama of American attempts at presidential assassination, a work so dark and controversial it has never had a long run.

Vengeance is a legitimate and frequent dramatic urge: Hamlet ponders the matter, but in the end he is helplessly caught up in avenging his father. Sweeney has been wronged sufficiently for us to believe in his just cause, and Turpin is so hateful we could relish his demise. It may be necessary or prudent for a comfortable or box office play to have Sweeney dead, too, at last, as some quasi-judicial rebuke to his violence. That sort of contract with the audience still operates in movie making. But the arc is clear and viable. Sweeney is not like that, however, and in the end there is a risk that the killing of Turpin gets lost in the run of killings—including that of the Beadle; the wife from the past, who was not dead after all, but who had become a beggar-whore; of Mrs. Lovett (a frightening moment in the film where we see the aghast rag-doll of Helena Bonham Carter on fire); and then the execution of Sweeney himself, by the boy Toby. And it is worth pointing out here that Sweeney never has a scene with his Johanna, not so much as a moment of discovery or reunion. There is a brief meeting, but he thinks she is a boy and is ready to shave her and kill her before distraction intervenes. Is this really what we would call a family man? Does he feel any ties—except the one with his razor, and the stunning "I am complete" line as he holds the blade aloft? Remember that he fails to recognize both wife and daughter. It always feels as if his own saga of ruined family is a pretext for his impacted homicidal energy.

This Sweeney Todd has acquired a hatred of the world, and it is a matter of unease in many productions as to how he slips over from being a justified vengeance-seeker to a serial killer. But how does either of these men take the business of the pies seriously? Of course, the corpses-into-pies trick is many people's favorite moment in the show and it is as accomplished and macabre a scene as the shower killing in *Psycho*. It changes the game and the tone in a very violent way. For, all of a sudden, amid the manic death-knell songs Sweeney sings, Mrs. Lovett has made him laugh with what is one of Sondheim's merriest lyrics:

MRS. LOVETT: It's priest.
Have a little priest.
TODD: Is it really good?
MRS. LOVETT: Sir, it's too good, at least.
Then again, they don't commit sins of the flesh.
So it's pretty fresh. (99–100)

There is a key moment in the sprightly, ghastly song, with Sweeney's "Ah," and Mrs. Lovett's "You've got it," which is impossible to play as less than fun and togetherness. He calls her "my love." They dance to the lurching waltz of the song. She will even hope they might one day be together "By the Sea." In the film this breaks into a picnic under a fine tree and then a seaside interlude. It is fantasy, of course, and shot with mockery, but still it is a scene where sunlight, the spreading tree, blue sky, and clouds have ousted persistent dark. But where does that world exist?

The pie song is their closest moment of affection, and it is in what one might call "delicious bad taste." Audiences relish it, and hardly notice what is happening or where it will lead. The madness in Sweeney and in Mrs. Lovett (for it is her bright idea) has suddenly been tamed or house-trained—we are into black comedy, before we can even smell the pies, let alone taste them. It is a superb theatrical set piece, but it cuts across the dramatic logic of what we are asked to attend to. It is the gimmick that the press might seize on in the scandal, rather than take up the greater challenge of how it is a man decides to murder everyone.

In *Psycho*, the plot begins to veer into excess and the film loses the tight control of its first hour; in *Sweeney Todd*, the second act spills over with ideas that are not completely organized or fulfilled. Hitchcock knew he had a problem with the ending of *Psycho*, a problem founded in his lack of real interest in madness, which was how to explain Norman. When he shot the psychiatrist's explanation scene (a rather stilted, talky interlude to most critics), Hitch embraced the actor, Simon Oakland, and told him he had saved the picture. That hadn't happened, and I don't think *Sweeney Todd* is complete either. The conclusion of the stage musical brings Todd's ghost back to tell us how anyone can be carried away by vengeance (this coda is absent in the movie). But the musical has been swept up by so many wilder forces. The film includes the stage production's freeing of Johanna from Fogg's Asylum, and Burton takes a few moments to make that asylum terrifying. But the film does not bother with the headlong escape of the inmates or the riveting "City on Fire" number which is the proper pay-off to the black hole song.

> "City on fire!
> Rats in the grass
> And the lunatics yelling in the streets!
> It's the end of the world! Yes!
> City on fire!" (167)

That implies a complete abandonment of order in this London and the onset of violence and madness. Is it worthwhile surviving? One can see why John Logan's film script foregoes this daunting perspective, for it is too much to expect of an audience who may still be wondering how they were led to entertain romantic hopes for Todd and Mrs. Lovett. And it could unsettle an audience hoping to get out of the theatre alive, and asking itself what's for Christmas dinner.

In fact, the movie turns to Mrs. Lovett more and more in its last half hour. As Sweeney is slashing anyone he can think of, she has her seaside dream (and it is hers—he is present, but only as a sleepwalker) and a well-developed scene with Toby in which a prospect of motherhood sinks in on her. By now, more prosperous from the pies, Mrs. Lovett is better dressed and more artfully groomed. So Helena Bonham Carter becomes more beautiful, as well as more thoughtful. Our distress at the whole enterprise—our nausea even (there is a close-up of a fingertip Toby finds in his pie!)—begins to find solace in her distress and in a few poignant close-ups where Bonham Carter the actress is on display, and in scenes where she has very little to sing.

Her murder—waltzed into her own oven—is the cruelest in the film. You can see all the reasons why Burton might give Mrs. Lovett this pathos and make her the ultimate victim, and this helps offset the sunken stupor of Todd—his depression appears to be taking him over. I said earlier that the core of the drama needed to be in his head, but he becomes catatonic in the movie. Just as his triumphant voice is omitted from the start of the film, he is silent at the end. The opera has been abandoned.

So the film is misguided, and often unpleasant in ways that might confirm the worst fears of Sondheim's critics. We can say with reason that it was a commercial compromise, though it is unduly naive to marvel at compromise in a project costing $50 million. More interesting, perhaps, the stage original has its own conflicts, or confusion, over what to make of Sweeney. No doubt, in the full musical onslaught, with restraint in the staging, and with a Todd and Mrs. Lovett who grasp Grand Guignol, the musical is an enormous and consuming experience. Its best songs are always studies in the subversion of fondness or attachment. They are, at an underground level, a way of questioning the nature or rights of the Broadway musical, a challenge that consumes Sondheim and breathes air on the flame of his endless struggle between romanticism and despair. The thought that remains from the movie is how the ponderous and highly skilled effort of enlargement and reality has killed off this fierce game. That may be the worst murder.

NOTES

1. At a press conference in Los Angeles, Sondheim opined, "I found the film stunning and was quite surprised at how stunned I was even though I knew what was gonna be done," in Brian Gallagher, "Stephen Sondheim Dishes on *Sweeney Todd*," December 18, 2007; http://www. movieweb.com/news/stephen-sondheim-dishes-on-sweeney-todd. At a press conference in London, he claimed "This is the first musical that has ever transferred successfully to the screen." Quoted in Norman Lebrecht, "When a Movie Outshines the Outstanding Original," February 12, 2008; http://www.scena.org/lsm/sm13-5/sm13_5_sweeneytodd_en.html.

2. Although Sondheim cowrote the screenplay for *The Last of Sheila* (1973) with Anthony Perkins and was coauthor with George Furth on *Getting Away with Murder*, he has opined that he cannot write books for musicals without a collaborator. See his comments in Meryle Secrest, *Stephen Sondheim: A Life* (New York: Alfred A. Knopf, 1998), 236–7.

3. All citations from lyrics and libretto refer to Stephen Sondheim and Hugh Wheeler, *Sweeney Todd: The Demon Barber of Fleet Street* (New York: Dodd, Mead, 1979).

4. See Craig Zadan, *Sondheim and Co.*, 2nd updated ed. (New York: Harper and Row, 1989), 260.

5. Zadan, *Sondheim & Co.*, 260–61.

PART V

SONDHEIM ACROSS GENRES

CHAPTER 19

··

A LITTLE NIGHT MUSIC:
THE CYNICAL OPERETTA

··

JOSEPH SWAIN

THE trio begins with tearful farewells. The husband, off for a short stay in the local prison for a petty crime, hears his beloved wife sing "So muß allein ich bleiben" (So I must remain alone) to a minor-mode melody made of a rising sequence. The strings sob on offbeats in the background; her language is histrionic. Barely able to speak, he replies "O je, wie rührt mich dies" (Oh yes, how this moves me). But his lingering half cadence resolves unexpectedly into the major mode and the loving couple, now joined by their housemaid, reiterate that last line *accelerando* until the trio turns into a wild and joyful Czech dance number.

The audience needs no explanation of this apparent musical malapropism. They know what the three characters do not, that the prisoner-to-be has been suborned by his good friend to report late to his cell and instead spend the evening frolicking with pretty girls at a costume party, that the maid sees his departure as the way out of her household duties so that she may attend the same ball, that the mournful wife has been visited by a secret admirer whom she desires to know a little better while her man is in jail. Playing on the ambiguity of the German verb *rühren*, the composer Johann Strauss creates a triple irony in the explicit contrast of musical affect. The audience of *Die Fledermaus* is delighted.

What is the source of the smiles, the comedy of the moment? The obvious answer is true: seeing respectable and proper members of posh society trying to get away with amorous infidelities, seeing human foolishness played out in the mutual deceptions of a supposedly loving couple. But for this comedy to work, that is, to be actually funny, it must presume something deeper: that fidelity in love is possible, real, and an absolute good. Without this foundation the humor has nothing to stand on, nothing to measure its irony against. If fidelity is merely a social option, something to be taken or left at will, so what if Eisenstein and Roselinde have a little fling? The choice is no more comic than having a whisky or not. It is only when the whisky is forbidden can such a choice offer the possibility of comedy.

At first acquaintance, Stephen Sondheim and Hugh Wheeler's *A Little Night Music* appears to takes its place in the proud tradition of operetta. Indeed, the idea for the piece is one of the few in all his musicals originated by Sondheim himself, and the operetta tradition seems to have been his explicit intention.[1] Here are the high society, the vaguely exotic, foreign locale, the opulent settings, the fantasy world of graceful speech, and larger-than-life characters. Certain musical effects even recall *Die Fledermaus* in particular: the maid Adele's vocalization in her opening aria parallels the first things heard in *A Little Night Music*; both feature big parties full of dissimulation, and both have contrapuntal combinations of previously isolated melodies. And of course there are the romantic intrigues. But in the end, *A Little Night Music* is far from the typical operetta; one might even call it an anti-operetta. For it lacks that essential presumption of the value of romantic fidelity; and its romantic intrigues have an entirely different significance. *A Little Night Music* is not merely farcical. It is cynical.

"Cynicism is a matter of the individual's relationship to society at large. From its earliest appearance in Athens in the fifth century BC, cynicism has signified a spirit of antagonism towards cultural values."[2] In contrast to farce or satire, cynicism does not ridicule the behavior of society's members in the face of social norms, or attempt to draw moral lessons from such behavior. Rather, it undermines the norms themselves and claims that they are fictitious, harmful, or simply irrelevant to good living. *A Little Night Music* does not merely mock high society's behavior with respect to its professed proprieties about romantic and sexual norms. It claims that any such norms are quite silly and have no bearing on romantic relationships. How does it make such a claim?

HUGH WHEELER'S BOOK

The source for the plot of *A Little Night Music* is Ingmar Bergman's 1956 film *Smiles of a Summer Night*, a romantic farce. The essential cast of intertwined romantic couples remains the same: Frederik, the middle-aged well-to-do lawyer and his virgin child bride, Anne; the ridiculously overdrawn dragoon Carl-Magnus and his embittered wife, Charlotte; the sensuous maid Petra and Frid the butler; and the two wild cards, Frederik's son Henrik, who eventually replaces his father as Anne's husband, and the "one and only" Desirée, Carl-Magnus's current flame, who returns to her real desire, Frederik, to bring the entire ensemble into socially respectable harmony, having begun, in the manner of all classical comedies, with a situation quite out of tune. But the show's book writer Hugh Wheeler, with admirable skill, introduces a number of subtle plot changes and one crucial new element into the staging that grounds the cynical thrust, transforming *A Little Night Music* into a new kind of operetta.

In both versions a key scene is the reunion of Frederik and Desirée early on after he sees her act in a French farce on stage. In Wheeler's book, what drives Frederik to sneak out of his own house to find her is naked desire. In his chat with Desirée he is forced at last to admit this only after he has admitted that his young wife has never permitted the consummation of their marriage. In the song "You Must Meet My Wife," Desirée takes this peculiarity to be the height of cruelty on Anne's part, and it leads Frederik and Desirée directly to the bedroom. In *Smiles of a Summer Night* there is little of this libidinous atmosphere. She asks directly:

> DESIRÉE: Have you got a pain in the old pump, or the heart as most people call it?
> FREDERIK: That isn't why I came. (55)[3]

And later he explains why he did come:

> FREDERIK: You must help me, Desirée. You must help me for the sake of an old friendship.... You are my only friend in the world. The only human being to whom I've dared show myself in all my terrible nakedness. (58)

Furthermore, when she learns the truth about the child bride, far from calling it a callous sin, Desirée thinks it quite funny and attributes the cause to Frederik, not Anne:

> FREDERIK: ...in short, she is still untouched.
> DESIRÉE: Now the world is really going awry when the wolf turns into a tender shepherd. (56)

In the film, Frederik actually falls into a large puddle which requires him to don Carl-Magnus's robe, fortunately hanging nearby. When the officer unexpectedly appears, the farcical scene is complete, but Frederik need invent no patently ridiculous lie about tripping into a hip-bath as he must in the musical. Finally, lest there remain any doubt, Desirée tells her mother in a frank interview that Carl-Magnus threatened her with bodily harm as punishment for infidelity, "For once, I was really innocent" (74).

Despite all allusions to feelings of the past, in Bergman no trust is violated. The humor is utterly traditional: a haphazard circumstance that is awkward precisely because of the presumption of the value of fidelity in love. In Wheeler, the worth of any such fidelity is quickly made counterfeit. After the disclosure of Frederik's long abstinence, Desirée acquiesces readily but can summon nothing more momentous to consecrate the occasion than an old cliché, "What are old friends for?" and then mock the Virgin Mary. Any presumed symbolism, any sanctity, any lasting importance of the sexual union is destroyed.

The other key scene is the entire second act, the "weekend in the country" that unites all the principal players in a farcical set piece. In *Smiles of a Summer Night*, Desirée engages her rival Charlotte in a simple plan: Charlotte will a make play for Frederik, thus arousing the tiger Carl-Magnus to a fit of jealousy, detaching him from Desirée and allowing Desirée to recover the man she really wants, Frederik. The plan in the musical is not Desirée's at all, but Charlotte's. In the act 1 finale, "A Weekend in the Country," Charlotte suggests to Anne that a direct confrontation with the aging Desirée can only show off her innocence to advantage. Anne seizes upon the idea. In act 2, Charlotte offers to expedite matters by romancing Frederik. Anne is too stupid or naïve to see that making Carl-Magnus return to Charlotte can only make her own situation precarious, but the important thing in the plot alteration is that Anne loses her innocence by her involvement in the scheme,[4] and then casts aside any loyalty that remains by running off with Henrik at his first protestation of love.

But the real transformation in Wheeler and Sondheim's adaptation of the Bergman story is an entirely new operatic element, the Liebeslieder singers, a quintet of three women and two men who are given Swedish surnames in the list of dramatis personae but are dramatically anonymous, a kind of Greek chorus that creates an essential semantic context for scenes that precede and succeed their unpredictable appearances. The Liebeslieders open the musical and are present at the final curtain. They interpret every important scene and dominate the underlying dramatic action.

And what do they have to say about it? In the opening scene they allude unmistakably to an illicit affair: "The proprietress's grin…" (20).[5] The "Remember" theme is resumed, in much the same words, just when Frederik and Desirée see each other at the play. They sing again, with bawdier lyrics, directly preceding their reunion backstage. This is their last appearance in the first act, and by this point their meaning is all too clear. They personify infidelity as the norm, as a worthy thing—their surnames are all different and include three "Mrs." —and so act as the prime source of cynicism for this cynical operetta. Everything in their movement and appearance is anonymous and abstract, but "the Liebeslieders, for all their abstraction and surrealism…, only sing music and lyrics that complement, extend, and share the material of the central characters rather than oppose it."[6] At the same time they mock any hint of longer-term faithfulness: "I'm *sure* it was you." Their cynical attack upon the very possibility of fidelity in love is built into their ensemble. As they sing their reminiscences of various assignations, they pair off severally, recombining as the musical progresses, but no permanently satisfactory coupling is ever possible. After all, they are a quintet.

Sondheim's Lyrics

The significance of "Remember" of course depends heavily upon Sondheim's witty and allusive lyrics. The lyrics of other songs, and the careful placement of those songs within the musical, are also important cynical elements. "Liaisons" captures the peculiar brand of comedy that characterizes the whole show: it is very funny in many particulars, but the whole effect is not humorous at all, but rather depressing. "Liaisons" is sung by the grand dame of the operetta, Desirée's mother. Madame Armfeldt, and at a choice moment, when Frederik and Desirée move offstage to the bedroom in act 1. This context provides the cynicism. The song becomes an ironic commentary on Desirée's behavior, in the classic manner of an elder sage admonishing the youth, "When *I* was young…" (Figure 19.1) Sondheim's delicious humor arises from the unabashedly pragmatic Madame's reminiscences, not of her many men, but of what material profits she extracted from each, all cued by a single line in the Bergman film "Dear daughter, I got this mansion from

FIGURE **19.1** Angela Lansbury as Madame Armfeldt and Catherine Zeta-Jones as Desirée in Trevor Nunn's revival of *A Little Night Music*, Broadway, New York (2010).

promising *not* to write my memoirs" (75). But elder sages promote conservative values that they believe the new generation is about to forsake. In a situation where an audience would expect someone like that to preach fidelity, the criticism is not of liaisons instead of faithful relationships, but of liaisons that are profitless rather than profitable. By this point, fidelity in love is so far gone over the moral horizon that it is not even entertained.

The one possibly ingénue romance of the operetta is undermined by the appearance of Petra, the maid, singing "The Miller's Son." We have just witnessed Henrik's profession of love to Anne, her epiphany, and her ardent response. What is next? Wedding bells in the distance? Dreamy lyricism from the strings? Rather, it is Petra's cynical ballad about her future as a lower-class domestic. But the point is not social criticism; that is merely the vehicle. In every verse Petra envisions her eventual marriage as the onset of decrepitude, a crashing bore at best, while the real living is to be had in the momentary embraces of one man after another. Marriage is set to a mournful, slow tune in aeolian mode, the embraces to a spirited dance, the only duple-meter passage in the entire score. Poor Anne and Henrik, how completely naïve they are![7]

The other direct perspective on what married life is like is "Every Day a Little Death." The dramatic context here is the corruption of innocence, the first task of the cynic. Charlotte has been sent by Carl-Magnus to inform Anne about her husband's nocturnal visit to Desirée. The two married women are former acquaintances through Charlotte's younger sister Marta. The tone is set a moment before the song begins, when Anne politely asks about her. Charlotte reports that she is "Ecstatic. Dear Marta has renounced men and is teaching gymnastics in a school for retarded girls in Bettleheim"

(81). Again, funny only until brutal significance sinks in. The song's lyrics and title speak for themselves. Charlotte delivers a schizophrenic portrait of the married state that more or less equates the commitments of fidelity with being trapped. The music is composed in Sondheim's mature idiom of weak harmonic functions and tonal ambiguity, giving Charlotte's assessment the cool detachment of truth undisturbed by passion. The mild melodic climax sets "I think love's a dirty business," at which point Anne suddenly makes the piece a duet with "So do I!" In fact, this moment is the most significant one of the song for the dramatic action, since it signifies the beginning of the loss of innocence, the cynicization if you will, of the one innocent character of the show.

Sondheim's Music

The composer of this cynical operetta attempts a feat of musical drama even more complicated than that of the routine musical play, which is quite complicated enough. Two kinds of music are required. For those songs such as "Every Day a Little Death" and "Liaisons" where the cynicism is explicit, Sondheim's music merely has to be sincere, an amplifier and, as in Anne's entrance in the former song, a clarifier of the semantic content of the lyrics and mover of the dramatic action. This is the usual task of the musical dramatist of whatever genre.

What about those songs where the lyrics, on the surface, say one thing while their significance must be entirely opposite? The satirical, the sarcastic, and the cynical expressions in music would seem to contradict the nature of the union of words and music that has obtained in the Western tradition since the sixteenth century. In this tradition the composer seeks to match the meaning of the text he sets with a musical creation whose semantic range can accommodate that meaning, so that both text and music are amplified and clarified in a feedback perceptual relationship. As in spoken language, the context at all levels makes the meaning of any utterance precise while at the same time that meaning advances the context, and in music drama all the relevant contexts—textual, dramatic, musical—illuminate one another to move the action forward.[8] These perceptual habits are so strong that in those unusual cases where there is a mismatch of what the character's text says and the music by which he says it, we always believe in the sincerity of the music, not the words. When, in Monteverdi's *L'Incoronazione di Poppea*, Ottone protests to Drusilla that he really has forgotten Poppea and loves only her, his short boilerplate affirmations, entirely without the chromatic and lyrical expressions once bestowed on Poppea, tell the audience that he lies. *A Little Night Music* must accomplish similar things, not occasionally but frequently. In fact much of the score is infected with cynicism. One Sondheim critic points out that the very triple-meter fabric that is perhaps this musical's most famous compositional feature undermines the value of fidelity "by rescandalizing a previously scandalous dance through making it the sign of decoupling instead of coupling."[9] But what is the

technical grounding of such a feat? How does a composer create music that undermines its own semantic range—that communicates a connotation and at the same time
tells us not to believe it?[10]

A key instance of Sondheim's cynical expressions is the music that begins the play
after the vocal medley "Overture," the "Night Music" (no. 2). Its *Tempo di valse* begins
with an utterly stereotypical waltz vamp, the bass sounding degrees 1 and 5 on strong
beats while the strings with an offbeat gesture that stresses the third beat of every metric group. The waltz, and all the connotations that come with it, is unmistakable. When
the woodwinds enter in the fifth bar (measure 63 in the published score) however,
strange things happen to the harmonies implied by the waltz pattern. The fifths are
augmented (A♮ over the bass D♭), and the seventh flatted. The curtain rises on a slow
tune in the high register, waltz-like in rhythm over the 1–5 bass but highly chromati-
cized. The result? In a very short time Sondheim has brought to mind the connotations
of the waltz that he needs for this show and then undermined them with pitches that
fit metrically but not tonally. The perceptions and musical cognitions of the listeners,
naturally unwilling to let go of a known conventional meaning of long association,[11]
contemplate this musical contradiction *without giving up the waltz frame of reference*.
The sentimental waltz connotations are perceived and yet not believed. That Sondheim
may have heard such sounds or similar ones in his long acquaintance with Maurice
Ravel's *Valses nobles et sentimentales* matters no more to this dynamic than the fact that
"intercourse" was once regularly uttered in polite conversation matters to its current
delicacy. The meaning of a musical utterance depends upon the current musical community that hears it interacting dynamically with the context of its immediate use.[12]
At this point early in the musical, "Night Waltz" cannot yet mean something as precise
as "decoupling" but it is quite arguable that very soon it will. Sondheim has created a
cynical waltz.

An example of the contradiction of text and music such as that in *Poppea* occurs
in the most consistent leitmotif for the irrelevance of fidelity, "Remember," which is
always sung by those most responsible for articulating the themes of the musical, the
Liebeslieder singers. Now Sondheim can profit from his personal definition of the cynical waltz, which can begin to acquire the associations necessary to come to mean "decoupling." Once again the *tempo di valse*, once again the downbeat waltz bass frames the
utterance. The music and the Liebeslieder ensemble dominate the quick scene changes
that set up the rendezvous of Frederik and Desirée with connotations of increasing erot-
icism. The title "Remember" is a cue for the many little insignificant details that lovers remember about a romantic encounter, particularly a secretive one, and Sondheim
makes a virtue of the waltz melody being sung chiefly on the weak beats, playing off
the strong-beat bass. The melodic fragments sung by the five anonymous characters
fly in bewildering succession like so many non sequiturs, ending on strong beats only
occasionally to articulate high-level structure. Curious pitches of the manner already
described give the piece its cynical air throughout, but the most explicit cynical expression comes when the audience will best remember it, at the end. In the first rendition,

after Frederik and Desirée make eye contact for the first time, the song ends with "I think you were there," a less than subtle jab at the worth of fidelity in love. It is harmonized with a tonic triad plus an added minor sixth degree, a harmonic compromise that could agree with the hesitation of the last thought. In the reprise, sung as Frederik makes his way across town back to the theater to meet Desirée, the line is strengthened to "I'm sure it was…you," but the same augmented harmony, combined with a delay of "you" until the weak half of the third beat, reveals its falsehood as surely as the barebones melody revealed Ottone's.

These several strategies of musical cynicism combine in Carl-Magnus's reflection on the encounter with Desirée and Frederik in her boudoir, the delightful "In Praise of Women." Given Sondheim's determination to compose *A Little Night Music* entirely in triple meter, the choice of the *tempo di polonaise* is obviously appropriate for the insufferable military buffoon of the operetta, but the adoption of such a familiar *topos* also gives the composer a semantic basis for cynical music. As with "Night Waltz," Sondheim begins with a bare accompaniment so stereotypical that its cultural associations spring to mind immediately: a long tonic pitch deep in the bass on the down beat, followed by a mid-range dotted figure leading to a subdivided second beat and finishing the bar with the long third beat on dominant harmony. Jonathan Tunick's military orchestration helps out a great deal here too: timpani and trumpets join the romantic strings and winds for the first time. Then the subversion begins: added chromatics that twist the dominant harmonies on every third beat, and a most unromantic modulation scheme.

Sondheim's pattern of keys leads with ruthless logic to one of the most distilled cynical moments of the musical. Carl-Magnus sings his first phrase in F major, accompanied to the highly colored tonic and dominant alterations characteristic of Sondheim's *tempo di polonaise*. The second phrase is a near melodic match to the first, beginning with a fanfare-like descent through the tonic triad, except that the tonic pitch F is raised to F♯. This small detail completely changes the tenor of Carl-Magnus's half-agonized, half-supercilious musings by substituting a diminished triad for the stable major. At the same time Sondheim justifies the F♯ harmonically by setting the reformed melody in D major, a minor third down from the home key of F. Now the pattern is set. The release of the tune—"Fidelity is more than mere display…" —moves down another minor third to B major. But the composer's consistency has placed Carl-Magnus's pompous pontification about the nature of fidelity in the key a tritone away from the overall tonality of the song. Need one say more? But that is not the last cynical gesture, nor the most brilliant. The next key in the algorithm should be A♭. But as Carl-Magnus climbs to a melodic climax with "Fidelity like mine to Desirée," Sondheim wrenches the tonality prematurely yet directly back to F major, with "And Charlotte, my devoted wife." With the skill of coordination that must be second nature to one who composes his own lyrics, the composer sets the name "Charlotte" to the high F, the melodic climax which shocks and satisfies us with the tonal return and at the same time gives the lie to any concept of "fidelity" by subverting the logic of the modulation pattern so pointedly established.

THE CYNICAL OPERETTA

A Little Night Music would appear to end as does *Smiles of a Summer Night* and, for that matter, *Die Fledermaus* or any of the classic romantic operettas.[13] All the romantic mismatches are rematched so that everyone conforms at last to what society expects of them. Carl-Magnus, having seen the attraction of his wife through the eyes of another, returns to her, unbowed perhaps, but returns nonetheless. Petra abandons any fleeting predilection she might have shown earlier for Henrik and instead makes the happy peasant couple with Frid, her social equal. Henrik, for his part, can hardly believe that he has won the object of his long-smoldering and barely repressed obsession, his father's child bride. And Frederik, having lost her, gains someone far better for him, his one true friend.

And they lived happily ever after? Sondheim, who in 1970 wanted a cynical song called "Happily Ever After" to express Robert's disillusion with all things matrimonial at the end of *Company*, by 1973 has the confidence to let sing his perspectives on such matters in *A Little Night Music*.[14] "I feel *any* relationship with one person is increasingly difficult these days [1976], as the world shrinks and we are pushed and pushed by time."[15] In Bergman, there is no reason to believe that the four couples do not live happily ever after in their fantasy world. In *A Little Night Music*, the music and lyrics have taught us time and again that what we see at the end is not at all likely to last for long. *Die Fledermaus* and *Smiles of a Summer Night* show to great humorous effect how weak human beings are in the face of the responsibilities demanded by faithful love, but never for a moment do they question its absolute value. *A Little Night Music* goes far beyond questioning it: the cynical operetta shows fidelity in love to be untrustworthy, inconvenient, boring, slavish, ridiculous, and ultimately irrelevant. "At the very least, cynics foresee a future in which individuals have little chance of fixing their problems or improving their conditions in life or at work."[16] There is no reason to believe that Frederik and Desirée, Carl-Magnus and Charlotte, Petra and Frid, and even the delirious Anne and Henrik will stay together for long, not even in their fantasy world. And why should they? What would be the point?

And that is why we don't laugh at a performance of *A Little Night Music* in the way we laugh at *Die Fledermaus*. To be sure, we do laugh; Sondheim's lyrics alone provide more than enough witticisms for the evening's entertainment, to say nothing of the antics of an imaginative staging. But not in the same way, for lyrics and staging are not the principal sources of comedy in a traditional operetta. Rather, it is the contrast of ideal social norms and real human behavior. Because *A Little Night Music* dismisses fidelity altogether, failure to live up to it as the essential dramatic action of the piece cannot be funny. Indeed, this cynical operetta can be a rather bitter, even dangerous, pill to swallow. Happily for listeners, it comes with a sugar coating to say the least: the musical coherence, intrinsic dramatic interest, and brilliant lyricism that obtain throughout have long been lauded by Sondheim critics. It is certainly a most ingenious transformation of the venerable genre of operetta: a sheer delight to experience, most sobering upon reflection.[17]

NOTES

1. "For many years Sondheim and Prince wanted to do an unabashedly romantic musical. As early as 1957, they attempted to acquire the rights to Jean Anouilh's *Ring around the Moon*. When in 1971 their request was turned down a second time, Sondheim suggested adapting Ingmar Bergman's 1956 film *Smiles of a Summer Night*, a film containing precisely the elements of intricate romance, of 'love and foolishness,' for which they had been looking." Joanne Gordon, *Art Isn't Easy: The Achievement of Stephen Sondheim* (Carbondale: Southern Illinois University Press, 1990), 123.

2. Timothy Bewes, *Cynicism and Postmodernity* (London: Verso, 1997), 1.

3. All film citations are taken from *Four Screenplays of Ingmar Bergman*, trans. Lars Malmstrom and David Kushner (New York: Simon and Schuster, 1960).

4. A loss of innocence is the explanation for the bawdy double entendres that Anne sings in "A Weekend in the Country," which otherwise seem out of character.

5. All citations are taken from the published libretto of *A Little Night Music*, music and lyrics by Stephen Sondheim, book by Hugh Wheeler (New York: Applause, 1991).

6. Stephen Banfield, *Sondheim's Broadway Musicals* (Ann Arbor: University of Michigan Press, 1993), 214.

7. Again, Petra's worldview here contrasts starkly with that of the Petra in the film. "As foil for the turn of the century formalities and posturing of their employers, the maid and coachman react to one another instinctually and simply; they meet, flirt, rendezvous outdoors away from the artificiality of the house, make love, talk and finally resolve to marry. The relationship is natural and uncomplicated." Richard A. Blake, SJ, "Sexual Themes in the Films of Ingmar Bergman," in *Ingmar Bergman: Essays in Criticism*, ed. Stuart M. Kaminsky (New York: Oxford University Press, 1975), 34.

8. For a detailed exposition of this semantic theory, see Joseph P. Swain, *Musical Languages* (New York: Norton, 1997), chap. 3.

9. Stephen Swayne, *How Sondheim Found his Sound* (Ann Arbor: University of Michigan Press, 2005), 15–16.

10. A more detailed discussion of this general problem of music drama may be found in Joseph P. Swain, "Musical Disguises in Mozart's Late Comedies," *Opera Quarterly* 13, no. 4 (summer 1997), 47–58.

11. The claim here is an application of a basic principle of music perception, indeed of all Gestaltist formal perception, often called the Law of Good Continuation, which is that the perceiver does not easily abandon a pattern once established until the perceptual data make it necessary.

12. This claim is part of the semantic theory referenced in note 8.

13. The most glaring exception would be George Bizet's *Carmen*.

14. See the discussion in Banfield, *Sondheim's Broadway Musicals*, 169.

15. Swayne, *How Sondheim Found*, 146–7.

16. David Mazella, *The Making of Modern Cynicism* (Charlottesville and London: University of Virginia Press, 2007), 4.

17. I would like to thank Robert Gordon for suggesting that I consider *A Little Night Music* as a kind of operetta for this essay.

CHAPTER 20

CROAKS INTO SONG: SONDHEIM TACKLES GREEK *FROGS*

MARIANNE MCDONALD

THE transformation of a classical play into a Broadway-style musical can result in the production of a disfigured monument from the past or the creation of a new work of art that has validity in itself and may very well become a future monument. Operas based on classical myths and plays have had both outcomes.[1] Aristophanes seems to be a safe candidate for revival; Sondheim also has his masterpieces.

Sondheim has many talents: he is as verbally gifted as he is musically. Sondheim loves crossword puzzles, games like charades, and scavenger hunts, and dotes on mysteries, the more macabre the better. He also creates them. His plots often feature dysfunctional parents, particularly women who are domineering, manipulative, and cruel, as he used to describe his own mother.[2]

Based on his reading and his attraction to wordplay, *The Frogs* (1974) takes its place with other reworked classics; even those based on films could be called classics. For instance, Ingmar Bergman's *Smiles of a Summer Night* (1955) led to *A Little Night Music* (1973), whose title recalls another classic, *Eine Kleine Nachtmusik* (1787) by Mozart. Sondheim was literate, but also eclectic in his range of references, both in his writing and his compositions: his selections ranged from Roman and Greek literature through Shakespeare, to modern plays, films, and musicals, and through composers like Mozart, Ravel, and Stravinsky, to jazz and popular music. Sondheim studied both Latin and Greek, which not only helped him solve puzzles, but also helped him enormously in his selection of words for his rhymes.

In a way, Sondheim's penchant for puzzles attracted him to classics, and how he could transform them. He studied them when he was at Williams College in Massachusetts, and played a member of the chorus in Sophocles' *Antigone* and Tiresias in his *Oedipus Tyrannus*.[3] Instead of tragedy, he inclined toward comedy, which perhaps satisfied his satirical bent. The first ancient classic for which Sondheim wrote the music became his first Broadway musical as both composer and lyricist: *A Funny Thing Happened on the Way to the Forum* (1962). This was a composite derived from Greek New Comedy,

Menander, and from Latin, Plautus (a combo of *Miles Gloriosus, Pseudolus, Menaechmi, Mostellaria*, and *Casina*), with a script by Burt Shevelove and Larry Gelbart.[4]

Frogs was initially adapted by Shevelove as a graduate student at Yale in 1941 and performed in a campus swimming pool. Some thirty years later, Robert Brustein, director of Yale Repertory Theatre asked Shevelove for a revival, with lyrics and music by Sondheim, for another performance in a swimming pool (1974). They had collaborated before: Shevelove had directed a musical tribute to Sondheim in 1973, and the next year directed Sondheim in a production of George S. Kauffman and Ring Lardner's *June Moon*. The cast of this 1974 *Frogs* included Sigourney Weaver, Meryl Streep, and Christopher Durang, all products of Yale Repertory Theatre. Wendy Wasserstein, in her second year of studying to be a playwright, was an usher at the performances.

This performance used over a hundred people: many in the cast, an orchestra of twelve, thirty-five backstage, a singing and dancing chorus, plus a chorus of swimming frogs. It had too brief a rehearsal period, and ran for only a week. Durang said, "members of the chorus sat at the side of the Yale swimming pool, a cast of undergraduate swimmers played the frogs in green mesh jock straps, and the star, the late Larry Blyden, was in a rowboat, surrounded by frogs as he was about to make his descent into Hades."[5] Many words would be swallowed by the large hall; the chorus were supposed to dance, but weren't professional, and they kept slipping as they emerged soaking from the pool.

The opening was black tie and it received a standing ovation; the following week's run was sold out every night. Brustein complained that the cast and resources grew way past what had been originally suggested, but welcomed the acclaim. He thanked everyone but the orchestra, which annoyed Sondheim no end, spurring him to say, "I know you don't like my work, but the least you could do. . . ."[6] Sondheim, if nothing else, was passionate in his opinions, likes and dislikes, besides his music. In July 1990, *Frogs* was performed in London, again in a swimming pool.[7] This version featured an introductory piece and choral work by Sondheim. *Frogs* was again adapted for New York in 2004 (Vivian Beaumont Theatre at Lincoln Center) by Nathan Lane, who relied on the version by Shevelove, who had died in 1982. Sondheim was persuaded to add more songs to this version. Lane also added a lot of political commentary (anti-Bush, though Bush is never named, and antiwar). He also dumbed it down a bit with his stand-up jokes (he is a professional comedian, and starred in this production as Dionysus). This version was directed by and included choreography by Susan Stroman. Sondheim had worked with Lane for a concert at the Library of Congress in honor of his seventieth birthday (2000), in which songs from the 1974 production that Jonathan Tunick newly orchestrated for the occasion were included.[8] Lane sang several as Dionysus. Tunick's earlier orchestration suggested the classical in reducing the instruments to woodwinds, harp, and percussion, possibly to reflect the lyre, flute, and percussion featured in Greek drama. For the Broadway version, strings were added and Sondheim wrote seven more songs. He also added the love interest requisite in traditional Broadway productions (Ariadne, for Dionysus). Shevelove, who wrote plays and librettos, and directed, was more literate than Lane, and stayed closer to the Aristophanic original.

Note that when Sondheim turned to the classics he chose ancient comedy rather than tragedy. Nevertheless he could never escape his own pessimistic commentary or interpretation. In a certain sense, he is the most modern of the present-day composers writing musicals in that he reflects not only the blackness of the times, but doubts about the future. One might say that, of the three major ancient Greek tragedians whose work has survived, Sondheim is closest to Euripides, Dionysus's own favorite when he first goes down to Hades to bring back a tragedian.[9] Aristophanes' biting edge was a good choice after New Comedy and the Romans, though the latter seemed to lend themselves to the type of musical that was popular on Broadway, if the success of *A Funny Thing Happened on the Way to the Forum* is any criterion.

Aristophanes' *Frogs* was performed the year before the Peloponnesian War between Athens and Sparta ended (404 BC), with the latter defeating the former.[10] The war had begun in 431 BC. Athens, the birthplace of Greek drama, was war-weary, and its plays reflected that weariness. Euripides in 415 BC had written a scathing antiwar play and, during the intervening years Athens had suffered through a mixture of victories and defeats, with the war party consistently playing more to wishful thinking than commonsense and convincing the populace to continue a war that was draining all their resources (sound familiar?). The war had begun over resentment of the Athenian empire and the coercive influence that it exercised. It called itself a democracy, and was in fact the first the world had known, but that did not prevent it from creating what amounted to an empire.[11]

The basis of Athenian democracy was free speech, and there was no place it was exercised more freely than in the theater. Tragedy lets audiences face their worst fears, but also allows them to heal through the vicarious feelings they experience. Tears help wash away their sorrow. Comedy, on the other hand, lets them at laugh at those fears and all they can't control, such as gods, fate, death, and those in authority, particularly those who abuse it. Old comedy, of which Aristophanes was the foremost proponent, had biting satire of politicians, the gods, and every human flaw imaginable. No subject was off limits, and sexual jokes abounded. At times Aristophanes, and it seemed Euripides, was fined (the equivalent of being sued for slander), but that did not prevent them from continuing. It was only the defeat of Athens that gagged Aristophanes' biting political satire and led to a new type of domestic comedy in the hands of Menander.

The first half of Aristophanes' *Frogs* makes fun of Dionysus, the god of theater and wine, son of Zeus and Semele. Heracles the great Greek hero is also shown to be a buffoon, and he dresses the effeminate Dionysus for his trip to Hades in a lion skin. Dionysus then proceeds to Hades dressed as Heracles, after dismissing various forms of suicide suggested by Heracles. He prefers the long way that Heracles took. There were various reputed entrances to Hades in Greece, and one was at Eleusis just outside Athens, where initiates were taught what to do when they arrived. Demeter, the earth goddess, mother of Persephone, who married Hades the king of the underworld, was the patron of these rites and this location. Hymns to Iacchus (another name for Dionysus) were sung there, and the singers greet Dionysus when he arrives. Later in the play, this chorus sings the *parabasis*, the section that allows the playwright to step out of his usual role and speak directly to the audience, giving them advice, besides criticizing his rivals in the theater and politicians.

Dionysus's slave, Xanthias, is braver than his master as they confront monsters in Hades. People alternately welcome "Heracles" or revile him for what he did on his last visit to Hades. For the latter reason, Dionysus wants Xanthias to be disguised as "Heracles". At one point there is a contest to prove who is the slave and who is the god, and Aeakos is the judge. This leads to both being whipped, but the outcome is as indecisive as the later contest between the two playwrights. It just leads to a lot of sadistically oriented jokes meant to titillate the audience. Many of the earlier jokes were scatological, directed against politicians, homosexuality, and other sexual proclivities. Most of the political jokes are lost on a modern audience.

The god and slave arrive at Pluto's palace to witness a competition for the chair of tragedy. Sophocles does not claim it (he's said to be too obliging), and that is probably because he had just recently died, so Aristophanes had little to say about him. The contest is between Aeschylus and Euripides. They compete on prologues and lyrics, and then they weigh verses. The final contest is for Dionysus to decide who can give the best advice to the city, not just simply to bring the best tragedian back, so the rules seem to have changed as the play has progressed.

Euripides speaks ambiguously but basically tells Athens to change its leaders, whereas Aeschylus advocates trusting in the fleet, and describes what was once the winning tactic during the Persian Wars. Dionysus doesn't make an intellectual choice, but says that he inclines now toward Aeschylus, although Euripides had been his choice at first. The entire contest showed that Aeschylus was patriotic and urged all to be the same. He also appeared to be the representative of conventional morality and the old values, in contrast to the iconoclastic and, according to Aeschylus himself in this play, the immoral Euripides. Dionysus, that supposedly learned god of theater, never says this, but shows that his choice is rather whimsical, since he gives no reason for it. He is somewhat like the viewer in a painting gallery who says, "I know nothing about art, but I know what I like." This is Aristophanes' final joke about audience preferences and the inevitable voting for prizes that followed ancient Athenian dramatic performances. It is also the way Sondheim and his librettists make fun of critics for their arbitrariness and personal bias.

The adaptation of a classical text, myth, play, or story to opera or musical involves many approaches. First of all, the text has to be made more concise and passages adapted for song. This may lead to a loss in meaning. Sometimes one needs simply to relay the gist of the original to understand the scene or business that follows. Obviously, one tries for both meaning and the brevity necessary to compensate for the added length of the music. The ancient text also used meters that had their own rhythms, but opera varied the rhythms throughout the ages, and often used rhyme in its verses. Many if not most Broadway musicals rely on rhyme. Sondheim doesn't stop there, but uses inner rhymes, and many of the same verbal devices that ancient Greek poetry did.

Sondheim, like Aeschylus and Aristophanes, enjoys coining words. Translation itself presents problems, and different languages pose different ones. Different times set new puzzles. The intention is to engage the audience, and the ancient writer knew his audience, but the present translator or composer has to make some sort of bridge that still allows the audience to appreciate the original work. Aristophanes—and comedy in general—poses particular problems because his jokes were often topical. Tragedy deals more in universal themes that easily cross time. Whether Cleocritus was given wings that made him look like Cinesias (*Frogs* 1437) doesn't make us laugh, or even elicit a giggle. Many jokes per se are also dated, and they should be brought up to date. There are just so many jokes about farts that can still get people laughing.

Both of Sondheim's versions (1974 and 2004) begin with a fanfare and an invocation, followed by instructions to the audience. In the Broadway version there is an explosion, and when the smoke clears Dionysus appears. Shevelove had a challenge. He took some of the jokes that could be in the category of universal slapstick, but he cleaned them up. For instance, the Aristophanic sequence of scatological jokes about releasing various contents of the body, from vomit to weightier matters, is excised; instead we have Xanthias threatening to say something "dirty" or "run around bare-ass."[12]

So also, instead of Aristophanic scatological references, we have a song by Sondheim about travelling ('Travelling Music,') in which Xanthias initially shows a "slave" mentality by not wanting to travel, while in the extended version of the song written for Broadway ('I Love to Travel') he is finally coerced into agreeing that he loves to travel. He anachronistically mentions visiting Paris, and that he'd like to have "a Ménage à trois (French pastry, right?)." So also instead of Dionysus wetting himself out of fear, he steps in something that he wipes off the sole of his sandal, which, as in the original, gets Xanthias to note that this is not very becoming for a god.

They reach Heracles's door, and Heracles reacts when he sees Dionysus dressed in a lion skin. In the original he said: "Sorry. It's no good. I can't help laughing. A lion skin over that yellow dress. What's it all for? High heels and a club! Where in the world are you going dressed like that!" He points out the absurdity of the imitation.[13]

Heracles goes on to tell Dionysus the vine leaves have to go, and replaces them with the lion's head. He also tries to teach the effeminate Dionysus how to swagger and at least make a stab at masculinity, though they both admit their proclivity for boys. Heracles fails in his lessons, and Dionysus minces out. In Shevelove's *Frogs*, it is Heracles who tells Dionysus that he should wear his lion skin, and he takes it off, showing himself nude underneath. This explains the advice to the audience at the beginning:

> Do not intrude, please,
> When someone's nude, please...
> Let's not be too strait-laced—
> The author's reputation isn't based
> On taste.
> So, please, don't fart—
> There's very little air and this is art. (289)

Dionysus tells Heracles he wants to bring back George Bernard Shaw. It's amazing that Heracles hardly reacts, but the dramatic device here is that any name can be mentioned and accepted without explanation, since there is no way that Heracles could recognize a modern playwright. Some reaction like "Who's Shaw?" might be in order. That is used as a joke on Xanthias, who, as a slave, lacked education and would hardly have any way of knowing who Shaw is, even if he were his contemporary. Heracles in the original suggests bringing back Sophocles instead of Euripides, so obviously he isn't simply the strongman of myth.

There are no jokes in this version about committing suicide in various ways as there are in the original, but Shevelove's Heracles directly points out the way to the river Styx and to Charon. Charon refuses passage to Xanthias, claiming he's not first-class material. The anachronisms abound. In the second version by Lane, Xanthias is allowed to take a seat in the boat. This allows him to hear Dionysus's song about Ariadne. The frogs also sing, and this puts both Charon and Xanthias to sleep in the Lane version. In the earlier pool version, Dionysus wakes Charon to say they've reached the other side, but in the later one Dionysus is dragged into the River Styx. In the earlier version, the frogs are not as intrusive or threatening as they are in the later version, but they are hopelessly conservative in their advice in both versions (see below). In Aristophanes' original, the frogs say that they once sang in honor of Dionysus when revelers from feast days came through. They also boast that the muses love them. These frogs are also a bit irritating in that they do not stop singing when Dionysus wants them to stop, and they claim they have won the contest of shouting him down. (Figure 20.1)

Xanthias threatens to go back home, so Dionysus starts inventing monsters, first the Thanaglebe: "if its droppings fall on you, you fertilize to death," then the Hippodrool, with "the head of an eagle, the body of a rhinoceros, and the insatiability of a rabbit"

FIGURE 20.1 Nathan Lane as Dionysus with the chorus in *The Frogs*, Vivian Beaumont Theater, Lincoln Center, New York (2004).

(47–8). These inventions are a tribute to Shevelove's virtuosity with words, which perhaps owed something to Sondheim. Xanthias decides to stay. In the original, the monster was the Empusa, whose antics Xanthias describes in detail to Dionysus, relishing the fright it puts him into: Dionysus is a dedicated coward.

They meet a chorus praising Dionysus: in the original they are a chorus of initiates, but in the musical versions, the Dionysians. They give political advice in the original, and sing praises to Demeter and Dionysus. They also give instructions to the two about where to go next. The Dionysians simply praise Dionysus and the blessings of wine. This certainly is another simplification, but Sondheim's music saves the day once again.

They encounter various pretty women, whom Dionysus asks if they had seen Shaw—Irish with a red beard. It seems everyone in Hades knows everyone else. They tell him about him having dinner this night with Pluto. These characters also know each other's schedules. Aeakos here is the doorkeeper for Pluto. When they knock on the door, he opens it and threatens Heracles (Dionysus). Heracles switches the lion skin with Xanthias. Just then, a beautiful maiden (named Charisma in the 2004 version), invites Heracles to have a lovely bath in hippopotamus milk. They switch roles again. But then the queen of the Amazons, Virilla, threatens Heracles (these names could come from the house of prostitution in *A Funny Thing Happened on the Way to the Forum*). Xanthias, however, is attracted by her, and at the end opts to stay in Hades with Virilla.

They switch costumes again, after Charisma returns with the feast invitation but Aeakos enters with guards. Dionysus disguised as Xanthias and Xanthias disguised as Heracles accuse each other of being the other. They are each whipped to try to identify the god. The slave is sure he will win, since he's so accustomed to beatings, but the result is interrupted by the arrival of Pluto, who sees through their disguises. The section itself is reduced and the jokes are also changed and brought up to date for Shevelove's version. When he is lashed, for instance, Dionysus quotes Shakespeare with a cute anachronism, "What a rogue and peasant slave am I" (*Hamlet*, act 2, scene 2). In this soliloquy Hamlet curses himself for not having the courage that an actor has as he enacts his "dream of passion." Dionysus shows the same cowardice. These allusions are fun for the literate, but Nathan Lane was not as sympathetic to them. In fact, in the Broadway version this whipping scene is eliminated.

In Shevelove's version, Pluto appears and puts an end to the whipping, and immediately sees that Dionysus is no Heracles. Dionysus identifies himself as a relative. This is expanded from the original. Pluto is shown as affable, and hell as a great place to be. The songs that Sondheim later added for Broadway celebrate Hades, or as Pluto says:

> Everybody dumps on Hades—
> People yelling, "Go to Hell!"
> Well,
> Let me tell you, life in Hades
> Is just swell.
> (*Some semi-nude six-foot-ten chorus girls, called Flame Girls, begin their dance*)…
> Where whatever you regret
> You just forget

Or better yet,
Forgive.
Where you're not afraid to die,
And when you're not afraid to die,
Then you're not afraid to live.
And you're living here in Hades—
And I mean you're living well. . . .
In the grand scheme of things, life is a test really.
A little pop quiz. Nothing more. Some pass, some fail.
But it's ultimately meaningless. Just something to
Amuse the gods. This is where reality begins.
Here no one has a need any more
To commit a murder, wage a war.
Who're you going to murder, and what for?
They're all like dead.
All
Deceased.
Kaput, defunct, released. . . .[14](297)

This chorus shows another aspect of Sondheim's musicals, repetition. He loves the word-play in choosing amusing synonyms.

"Evoe for the Dead," also shows Hell as the place to be if you want a party, "They do an awful lot of dancing, the dead." Still they point out that it can get boring: "It's very comforting, and yet you can put up with just so much."[15] Sondheim deconstructs myths, as he does so well in *Into the Woods*, where he takes conventional stories and shows they can turn out the opposite of "happily every after." Pluto delivers this philosophical *parabasis*, which in its own way taps into the spate of plays and movies on the theme of the afterlife, from Rodgers and Hammerstein's *Carousel* (1945) to *Defending Your Life* (1991) with Meryl Streep. However, Sondheim rarely delivers the "feel-good" endings that Rodgers and Hammerstein and other "golden age" musicals did.

This is another changed theme from the original, in which Aristophanes' Dionysus just wants a good poet, but ends up wanting the one who would be best for Athens at this time, and who would give the best advice. Here Shakespeare's winning song "Fear no More" is exactly on the theme earlier voiced by Pluto in the song about getting over the fear of death, so that one can live. This also brings the musical into the realm of later Sondheim works that explore what constitutes a life of quality: he never can confine himself to being simply entertaining.

After Pluto's defense of Hades the chorus delivers a *parabasis* that includes more advice:

(*SOLO VOICES, SINGING*)
It really doesn't matter.
Don't worry, relax.
What can one person do?
After all, you're only human.
And it's all been said before.

> And you've got enough to think about...
> Things fix themselves.
> Don't worry, relax.
> ALL
> It's only a play...
> The world's still afloat
> So it's hardly a note
> For today. (298)

This is comparable to the philosophy of the frogs, namely complacency, and is meant to indict the audience. It is opposite to the approach of Aristophanes, whose chorus gives direct rather than ironic advice.

The substitution of Shaw (1856–1950) and Shakespeare (1564–1616) for Euripides and Aeschylus works up to a point. They are not in the same time zone, Shakespeare being Elizabethan and Shaw relatively modern, besides one being English, and the other Irish. Shakespeare quotes the St. Crispin's Day speech by Henry V at Agincourt to show his patriotism. Shaw being Irish, instead mocks patriotism, particularly patriotism to England ("Patriotism is the conviction that this country is superior to all other countries because you were born in it").[16] Other playwrights could have been chosen; several are mentioned but dismissed with one-liners. On the whole though, the more traditional Shakespeare versus the iconoclastic Shaw does provide a contrast that very roughly parallels Aeschylus and Euripides. The format of prologues, lyric verses, and the ultimate weighing contest is rejected in favor of bringing out the volumes—one large one for Shakespeare, and about forty for Shaw. Shaw if nothing else is wordy.

Shaw simply criticizes Shakespeare as he criticizes society, but Shakespeare says he writes about the many splendors of life. Shakespeare chooses his "seven ages of man" speech, and the *Henry V* speech mentioned above. Shaw quotes the critics who prefer his work, the likes of Kenneth Tynan. Shakespeare asks who he is, and Shaw responds, "The creator of *Oh! Calcutta!*" (98), an allusion that in a few years will fall as flat on an audience's ears as the allusion to Cleocritus and Cinesias quoted above. The muses are invoked before the contest begins, and they are all listed with one-liners saying what they do, for instance Urania: "Searcher of the Starry Night" (99–101). Their euphony is marked by the chords that Sondheim gives each, and a type of *recitative*. The Dionysians ask for inspiration. Shaw shows himself to be arrogant and also secular, by claiming that they should invoke him instead of vice versa. Shakespeare shows himself to be more respectful.

Shevelove cannot resist the occasional dig at critics: Dionysus has the aside, that he wishes he were infallible, "like an old scholar, or a young critic" (102). Critics suffer whenever they are mentioned, and scholars also bear the brunt of the Sondheim and Shevelove rapier. In the *parabasis*, advice is sarcastically given to the audience to let the critics, along with the politicians, make your decisions for you. This *parabasis* is the opposite of Aristophanes', in which he was seriously advising the citizens.

A woman crosses Dionysus's path and the topic chosen is women. Shakespeare quotes from his Sonnet 130, "My mistress' eyes are nothing like the sun," which concludes,

"And yet by heaven I think my love as rare / As any she belied with false compare." Shaw tackles the subject as usual from the social point of view: "Women have to unlearn the false good manners of their slavery before they can acquire the genuine good manners of their freedom"…and ends with a joke: "The fickleness of the women I love is only equaled by the infernal constancy of the women who love me." Shakespeare adds something complimentary, showing respect for women. He quotes, "From women's eyes this doctrine I derive," claiming that he can learn all there is to know from women's eyes, which in the original was "from whence doth spring the true Promethean Fire" (*Love's Labour's Lost*, act 4, scene 3), but in our *Frogs* is altered to "that show, contain and nourish all the world" (105).

The next subject is man, and Shakespeare quotes his "What a piece of work is man, how noble in reason…" (*Hamlet*, act 2, scene 2). Shaw begins with criticism, saying essentially that man is a blunderer. Shakespeare contributes; Shaw subtracts. The next subject is the life force, and Shaw is finally creative, praising the human brain with lines from *Don Juan in Hell*, originally a long scene in act 3 of *Man and Superman* (1902–3): "Whatever man wishes to do, he will finally discover a means of doing." Shakespeare quotes from *Macbeth* (act 5, scene 5): "life's but a walking shadow…" Shaw completes his lines for him.

What we don't have in Aristophanes' surviving work is the music; nevertheless much additional commentary on the text can come from the music. Sondheim was certainly not confined to writing dramatic music that simply illustrated the text; he would stimulate new thoughts and new reactions in the audience, sometimes by the lack of resolution in chords, which expressed his own doubt to the audience about what had just been sung. His music can work against the text, or express the doubts of the singer, or make the singer's meaning absolutely clear.

Then love is the subject, and, Shakespeare quotes again from his sonnets, this time the "Marriage of True Minds" (Sonnet 116). Shaw once again jokes where Shakespeare praises, completing his entire sonnet. They go on and Shakespeare quotes "How this spring of love resembleth the uncertain glory of an April day" (*Two Gentlemen of Verona*, act 1, scene 3). Shaw dismisses it saying it's all style, no content. Even Dionysus notes the difference: "Bernard, no offense meant, but must you be so…brutal?" (299) In Aristophanes, this accusation about empty style is leveled at both Aeschylus, who is accused by Euripides of redundancy, and Euripides, accused by Aeschylus of padding his rhyme, in order to add the same line in various places without altering the metrics. Obviously the particulars differ, but not the accusation.

The final contest is appropriately about death, and Shaw quotes a beautiful passage from *St. Joan* (1923) showing that she would prefer death to a life that deprived her of her freedom and the beauties of the world, concluding "But without these things I cannot live, and by your taking them from me…I know that your counsel is of the devil and that mine is of God" (scene 6)[17]. After some quotations by Shakespeare, beginning with Duke Vincentio: "Be absolute for Death, either Death or Life / Shall thereby be the sweeter" (*Measure for Measure*, act 3, scene 1), the glorious words from *Cymbeline* that Sondheim sets to achingly lyrical notes win Shakespeare his return to earth. Shakespeare has song, but Shaw only words, and this message seems to be that the world needs song once again, some poetry and music to celebrate life. Aristophanes on the other hand, pits Euripides against Aeschylus for their advice to the city. Aeschylus seemed to be the more traditional, whereas Euripides spoke obscurely and critically in a way that was a bit reminiscent of Shaw in the modern version.

By the time of the Lane revisions for the 2004 production, 9/11 had occurred, and the play clearly implies that the misguided Bush policies brought Americans to a situation resembling that of fifth-century Athens and were continuing to undermine any possibility of achieving a peaceful resolution of the West's conflict with radical Islamists. So both Aristophanes' play and Sondheim and Lane's version were investigating how to find peace with honor. This is shown particularly in the threat the frogs pose by too much complacency, a theme that was also introduced in the Shevelove version.

The frogs are anticreativity and against freethinking in general. They speak rather like the Republican Fred Cady, who, in Sondheim's *All that Glitters* (1948), dissuades his daughter's potential fiancé from writing "art music" and urges him to write more popular music, but most of all, to join his firm and make a proper living. Wendy Wasserstein compared the swim team of frogs with their synchronized swimming to "all the clean-cut, mechanized President's men."[18] The frogs say:

> We're the frogs ...
> Not your hoity-toity intellectuals,
> Not your hippy-dippy homosexuals
> Just your easy-going simple ...
> Frogs ...
> Whaddaya care the world's a wreck?
> Leave 'em alone, send 'em a check,
> Sit in the sun and what-the-heck,
> Whaddaya wanna break your neck for? ...
> And who in the world are you saving the world for?
> For the frogs! ...
> Not for fancy-pants humanitarians,
> Not for chatty platitudinarians ...(293)

It seems they are anti-Dionysus, but are particular voluble for being anti words. They want to prevent him from changing the status quo and letting the "Athenians" think for themselves. These lyrics sounds rather like an attack on McCarthyism and the trials that condemned people for their freethinking politics: being branded a "communist" became a criminal accusation.

Lane's additions make it much more explicit and the later version has Dionysus saying:

> The frogs are everywhere. At first glance, they seem harmless enough, but in the blink of an eye they've got their tongues wrapped around you and they've pulled you into their sick sedentary little universe. They hate change. They hate new ideas. They just like what's good for them. And they'd like everyone to think the way they do. They'd like to turn us all into frogs.[19]

By the end of the revised version, when Shakespeare is returning, and planning a new play, Dionysus comments on the frogs' silence and advises:

> But citizens of Athens
> If you're smart,
> Don't sit around while Athens
> Falls apart [...]
> And now—
> (*Quietly speaking*)
> ALL
> We start.[20] (300)

Although he is always original, Sondheim is eclectic in his use of musical and literary allusions. Sondheim's greatest musical debt is to classical composers, and these were the only works he said he would take along with him, besides his own, if he were ever confined to a desert island.[21] Many of these influences come out in *The Frogs*. For instance, in his "Hymnos" in the 1974 *Frogs*, there is a debt to the chordal sequence that occurs at the beginning of the third movement of Stravinsky's *Symphony of Psalms*. The invocation "Alalalalalalalai" is even verbally reminiscent of the "Alleluia" that Sondheim particularly admires in that passage. Besides obeisance to that master, this "Alleluia" quote in "Hymnos" gave it a type of classical solemnity with a hint of modernism, so that it didn't stand out totally from the rest of the piece. He also adopted the ionic meter, of two shorts followed by two longs, for Dionysus's invocation, "DIO-NY-SUS," which is in fact the meter of the lyric invocation in Aristophanes' original.

Sondheim even quotes from himself, as he did in his "Invocation and Instructions to the Audience," which he had originally intended to use to introduce *Forum*. This whole section is as metatheatrical as the *parabasis* in the original play, since the actors address the audience directly. Some remarks were especially appropriate for *The Frogs*' setting in the Yale swimming pool, and the last lines didn't survive the 2004 move to Broadway:

> And when you disapprove, don't clear your throats
> Or throw your crumpled programs, coins and coats,
> Or tell your neighbor scintillating anecdotes,
> And please—no grass,
> This is a classic, not a class. (288)

On Broadway this was altered to schtick on cellphones. There was also advice at one point not to strip even though it is hot, advice that directly applied to the pool setting of the original at Yale. The *parodos* at the end used quarter-tones and semitonal progressions and harmonies, and along with the "Hymnos" led to "an achievement without which the still greater idiomatic adventure of *Pacific Overtures*, written the following year, would probably not have been possible."[22]

The Frog Chorus is a type of barcarolle, reminiscent of songs by Venetian gondoliers (see also Chopin's *Barcarolle*, or the beginning of Offenbach's *The Tales of Hoffmann*). It has a lulling rhythm (often 6/8 time), reminding one of waves gently rocking the boat. This is well suited to the "status quo" philosophy the frogs sing about. Gradually, with the repetitions, this music begins to spin out of control, and suggests danger, somewhat like Ravel's *La Valse*, which begins benignly, but soon becomes unsettling. Dionysus feels under attack by the frogs, and Sondheim's music corroborates this. The revised version also features a quotation from the theme song of *Into the Woods* that suggests people take the wrong path by overexertion:

> Forget your
> Troubles,
> Wallow with us,
> Squat and take
> A mud bath!
> What's it get 'em,
> Making a fuss?
> Just another blood bath. (293)

The song "Into the Woods," and the play itself suggested an escape into a world where supernatural creatures could appear, and the mythical added a new perspective on what one thought was familiar. The talking frogs are naturals for this. There is also the threat of danger, or the eternal escape becoming permanent, as Dionysus is first dragged down a hole, but emerges to be swallowed by a giant frog at the end of the Broadway production.

Sondheim has the frogs sing "Row, Row, Row your boat," which is maddeningly repeated. This characterizes the frogs themselves, who advocate the status quo, adapting to what is, not thinking too much about anything, but lulling oneself into an unthinking life, the opposite of what Sondheim himself has lived. He is eclectic if nothing else, setting musical puzzles to titillate those with broad musical education.

The Frogs also features choruses, typical of Greek tragedy, and contrapuntal effects, another allusion to older classical music. These latter owe as much to Hindemith as Bach. Sondheim investigates contrapuntal devices and interesting unexpected harmonies. His particular addition was to mix the various voices in an unpredictable way. He likes the vamp approach (in popular music, a theme that is repeated or varied until the soloist is ready to begin), mingling the voices behind them as if they were going one way, and then surprising the listener by going another.[23] This becomes a trademark of his work; he is never content to be predictable or boring. These choruses also lead to Sondheim's use of choruses in ways that differ from conventional musicals, not simply to underline the solo action, but to advance both the plot and commentary, sometimes reaching surprising conclusions.[24]

Tunick helped with advice when Sondheim was despairing about his choruses in *The Frogs*: "I wrote this elaborate chorus for *The Frogs,* and it sounded squeaky and thin, and yet there were like twenty-five voices…and Tunick said: 'No. First of all the key was a little too high, and you're doing it in the swimming pool at Yale, and the reverberation's muddied all the harmony.'…I should have known: if you're writing for a chorus in a swimming pool, you've got to thin out the harmonies."[25] The later musical director, Paul Gemignani, applied first aid by simplification and lowering of the voices.[26] In the song about Ariadne, Sondheim uses his favorite chord, the suspended dominant, but he does not resolve it into the tonic. This creates a lack of resolution, obvious in the parallel with Dionysus losing his beloved Ariadne to death, and his love remaining unfulfilled. This contrasts with the Aristophanic original that had sex, and sexual jokes, not love.

Sondheim's music characterizes the subjects. The song the chorus sing describing Dionysus wanders over keys, suggesting his ambiguous nature (and perhaps the nature of theater itself).[27] The final tour de force in Sondheim's *Frogs* is his setting of the Shakespeare lines from *Cymbeline,* "Fear No More the Heat o' the Sun." It relies on many fourths and fifths in its progressions and resolutions, just as the rest of *The Frogs* does. Its sheer beauty in praise of death which comes to all is also a tribute to the underworld that Dionysus has just visited. He has a song in which Pluto praises the merits of the underworld and what fun the people have (rather different from the Aristophanic Hades, in which criminals were punished), so the entire musical tends to argue that man must fear death no longer. This choice provides an appropriate Sondheim ending, bittersweet.

Many will debate which of these two versions, 1974 or 2004, is closer to the original and how well they succeed in equaling or surpassing the original. However, given the success of all three, isn't this debate irrelevant? Aristophanes wrote at a time when Athens was fighting for its life and for civilization as he knew it. Isn't much of the world doing the same thing now? The political decisions of these last years have involved us in wars that are not only draining our economy, but cannot be won. Economic greed has bankrupted what was left. Aristophanes and the two modern versions tackle these problems in their own way.

Shevelove's earlier version was closer to Aristophanes' play in its literary-critical debate, and also other sections that paralleled the original. Lane's additions bring the work closer to Aristophanes in the politics of a war that was exhausting the country's patience, but the ideology is totally different. The additional songs "I Love to Travel," "Dress Big," "On the River Styx," "Hades," "It's Only a Play," and "Ariadne" contain the Broadway requisites of a certain "feel-good" quality and love interest that Aristophanes avoided in his bitter stinging zingers. However, there are some negatives: that love interest is only a memory, and there are negative insights into what is happening on earth that contrast with the peace of the dead. That peace can be a relief, but for eternity, as the chorus points out, it can get boring.

Dionysus has his own *anagnorisis* when he sees that the world needs Shakespeare's broad humanity, which is getting lost, rather than Shaw's unrelenting criticism. The music has given us some great songs, and the final "Fear no More" is a masterpiece, a true and skillful marriage of two minds. What Sondheim, Shevelove, and Lane have done is make Aristophanes topical and accessible to a modern audience. Whereas professional classicists may complain that the literary-critical information about Aeschylus and Euripides is sadly missing, and also, if truth be told, if they miss some of the scatological explicitness, nevertheless what is gained is a new work that entrances audiences to this day, as evidenced by different new recordings of the works, and reactions to each revival. This is a play/musical that, given the foibles of humanity, will always be topical.

We can truly say that Sondheim has fulfilled the wishes expressed in the final chorus of the *Frogs*:

> Dionysus,
> Bring a sense of purpose,
> Bring the taste of words,
> Bring the sound of wit,
> Bring the feel of passion,
> Bring the glow of thought
> To the darkening earth.
> Evoe.
> Alalalalalalalai. [28](300)

Sondheim brought it, and continues to deliver.

NOTES

1. See Marianne McDonald, *Sing Sorrow: Classics, History, and Heroines in Opera* (Westport, CT, and London: Greenwood, 2001), *passim*.
2. See "An Institutionalized Child," in Meryle Secrest, *Stephen Sondheim: A Life* (New York: Alfred A. Knopf, 1998), 3–22.
3. According to Meryle Secrest, Sondheim claimed playing this role embarrassed him, and he only did it as a favor to Shevelove (Secrest, *Sondheim*, 233).
4. Larry Gelbart started the series *M*A*S*H* for television and wrote close to 100 episodes. He also adapted Ben Jonson's *Volpone* for Broadway as *Sly Fox*, starring George C. Scott. See also Lois Kivesto, "Comedy Tonight! *A Funny Thing Happened on the Way to the Forum*," in *Stephen Sondheim: A Casebook*, ed. Joanne Gordon, 35–45 (New York: Garland, 1997).
5. Secrest, *Sondheim*, 234
6. Secrest, *Sondheim*, 235
7. Shevelove moved to London in the sixties, collaborating again with Gelbart, but was born and educated in America. Philip M. Parker, ed., *Stephen Sondheim: Webster's Timeline History, 1913–2007* (San Diego: Icon, 2009), 7.
8. There is a recording of this by Nonesuch Records (2000).
9. See J. Michael Walton discussing Sondheim's relation to classics in *Euripides Our Contemporary* (London: Methuen, 2009), 207–9.
10. Marianne McDonald and J. Michael Walton translated and wrote an introduction for Aristophanes' *The Frogs* in 2006, with performances at The Theatre, Inc., in San Diego, 2007. For a good edition with extensive footnotes see Alan H. Sommerstein, *Frogs*, in *The Comedies of Aristophanes*, vol. 9 (Warminster, UK: Aris and Phillips, 1996). See also Mary-Kay Gamel, "Sondheim Floats Frogs," in *Aristophanes in Performance: 421 BC–AD 2007*, ed. Edith Hall and Amanda Wrigley (London: Legenda, 2007), 209–30.
11. It called itself a democracy, but in fifth-century Athens at the beginning of the Peloponnesian war the population was roughly 30,000, of whom 10,000 were male citizens, the rest being women, children, and slaves, all with limited rights. One might argue that pre–Civil War America was not much different.
12. Quotations from the lyrics are taken from Stephen Sondheim, *Finishing the Hat* (New York, Virgin, 2010); quotations from the dialogue of the 1974 version from *Aristophanes, The*

Frogs, freely adapted by Burt Shevelove, with music and lyrics by Stephen Sondheim, the words of William Shakespeare and Bernard Shaw, selected by Jo Durden-Smith, and then later in revisions by Michael Feingold (Woodstock, IL: Dramatic Publishing, 1976).

13. McDonald and Walton translation, see note 10.
14. No. 12. "Hades," in Stephen Sondheim, *Finishing the Hat.*
15. See S. F. Stoddart, "'Happily...Ever...NEVER': The Antithetical Romance of *Into the Woods*," in *Reading Stephen Sondheim: A Collection of Critical Essays*, ed. Sandor Goodhart, 209–220 (New York: Garland, 2000).
16. No. 14. "Shaw," in Stephen Sondheim, *Finishing the Hat.*
17. Bernard Shaw, *St Joan* (Harmondsworth: Penguin, 1983), 138
18. Libretto accompanying Stephen Sondheim and Nathan Lane, PS Classics, PS 525, Image Entertainment 2005, *The Frogs*, CD produced by Tommie Krasker.
19. Libretto, *The Frogs*, 2005.
20. No. 19. "Final Instructions to the Audience," Stephen Sondheim, *Finishing the Hat.*(300)
21. Steve Swayne, *How Sondheim Found his Sound* (Ann Arbor: University of Michigan Press, 2005), 39
22. Stephen Banfield, *Sondheim's Broadway Musicals* (Ann Arbor: University of Michigan Press, 1993), 33.
23. In a Q and A session with Stephen Sondheim: Part I with Frank Rich for *Dramatists Guild Quarterly* 28, no. 1 (1991), 8–15.
24. See Barbara Means Fraser, "Revisiting Greece: The Sondheim Chorus," *Stephen Sondheim: A Casebook*, 223–49.
25. Sondheim, in Mark Eden Horowitz, *Sondheim on Music: Minor Details and Major Decisions* (Lanham, MD, and Oxford: Scarecrow, 2003), 109.
26. I remember a comparable experience with Monteverdi's *Orfeo*, which was played in a cathedral in Salzburg, and the reverberations created a whole new piece, losing some of the original brilliant clarity. *Orfeo* also began as *The Frogs* did with a fanfare, and just as Ariadne's crown was placed in the heavens, likewise Orfeo and Euridice, after their deaths, took their place in the firmament.
27. *Sweeney Todd* well illustrates this with the song of the innocent boy Tobias telling Mrs. Lovett he will protect her, all simply written in major keys with predictable transitions ("Not While I'm Around"). This contrasts with the relentlessly dark and unpredictable music that surrounds Sweeney.
28. "Hymn to Dionysus," in (295)

CHAPTER 21

SWEENEY TODD: FROM MELODRAMA TO MUSICAL TRAGEDY

MILLIE TAYLOR

IT is debatable, though possible according to Peter Haining, that the story of *Sweeney Todd* is based on a true story that became an urban myth. Haining suggests that the story derives from the *Newgate Calendar* of 1802, which records that a Sweeney Todd was executed in 1785.[1] On the other hand, Joseph Marchesani states categorically that "Todd remains, of course, a literary creation."[2] Dick Collins claims to have deduced the most likely source when he suggests that it derives from "a short piece in *The Tell Tale* for 1825 entitled 'A Terrific Story of the Rue-de-la-Harpe, Paris.' "[3]

Whether based on truth or not, there appear to have been a number of tales in Britain and France about a murderous barber whose victims were cooked and sold in pies that arose in nineteenth-century popular fiction. Helen Smith suggests antecedents for the story including *The Tell-Tale* (1824), *The Murderous Barber* (1825), and *Joddrel, the Barber* (1844).[4] The serialization of *The String of Pearls* appeared in 1846, written by Thomas Peckett Prest, in which the fictional character of Sweeney Todd first appeared.[5] Michael Kilgarriff records that the play is "taken from the much admired Tale of that name (founded on fact) in *Lloyd's People's Periodical*." However, Kilgarriff was not able to discover this "mysterious publication."[6] Dick Collins has now proposed evidence to suggest that it was *The People's Periodical*, published by Edward Lloyd, and that the serialization was predominantly written by James Malcolm Rymer.[7]

Whoever the author of the serialization was, in 1847,[8] George Dibdin Pitt dramatized the story, even before the serialization had reached its end, a play which seems to be variously called *The String of Pearls, or, The Barber Fiend of Fleet Street* or *Sweeney Todd, The Barber of Fleet Street*.[9] This was followed by a number of appearances of the story and the character both in this version and others, including a film version in 1936, directed by George King and starring Todd Slaughter, and a play by Christopher Bond in 1970, on which Sondheim and Wheeler based their 1979 musical. All this suggests at least a measure of continuity between the nineteenth-century melodramatic story and Sondheim and Wheeler's musical version of the work, and a host of potential influences on the musical.

However, in the Dibdin Pitt version of the story there are just four scenes. Todd is an outright villain whose reasons for killing are not justified, and right from the start he kills his victims solely for their wealth. His first victim in the play is Mark Ingestrie, a young sailor who has returned from India with a string of pearls to claim his bride, Johanna. Todd is discovered by his apprentice, Tobias Ragg, and Mrs. Lovett's assistant, Jarvis Williams. Tobias is taken by Todd to Mr. Fogg's asylum, from which he escapes with Jarvis's help. Meanwhile Colonel Jeffery, who had sailed with Mark Ingestrie, offers to help Johanna find her lover. Todd tries to frame the colonel for the theft of the pearls and the murder of the sailor, but the sailor has survived and appears in the courtroom to resolve the situation, "preserved from death by a miracle, [he] returns to confound the guilty and protect the innocent."[10]

In this melodramatic version of the play there is a clear demarcation of good and evil; the lovers are clearly good, fine, and innocent, while Todd is entirely evil. Colonel Jeffery is not so clearly polarized; he offers to help Johanna, perhaps for good reasons, but almost immediately decides that in the absence of her lover he wants her for himself. Perhaps this character is the precursor of Judge Turpin. Clearly Tobias and Jarvis are combined in the contemporary Tobias, and Mrs. Lovett remains the pie maker who is complicit in Todd's crimes. The characters do not change or develop as a result of events in the course of the play. Todd begins evil and remains so until the end; the lovers are barely more than outlines but are entirely innocent, loyal, and true. The story is told through action and has a kinetic structure that can proceed of its own momentum because, as in farce, all of the characters "have one thing they want."[11] This leads to a feature of melodramatic characters; that they are "essentially 'whole,'" as opposed to tragic man, who "is essentially 'divided.'"[12]

The other important feature is the morality of the play in which the evil Todd is captured and punished for his crimes by a community of people, including the victims of his crimes, other just people, and the institutions of society—the justice system. This conforms to Charles Nodier's description, noted in 1841, that in the early French form of the genre an important feature was its moral function, "its emphasis on justice and humanity, its stimulation of virtue, its arousal of tender and generous sympathy," and its demonstration that, "even here below, virtue is always rewarded and crime is never without punishment."[13] Alongside this, François Ponsard concluded in 1852 that any play "which seeks only to astonish and move the spectator by a rapid succession of adventures and unexpected turns would be a melodrama."[14] This corresponds to James Smith's description of melodrama as "a dramatic piece characterized by sensational incident and violent appeals to the emotions"[15]. These appear to be the most important features of nineteenth-century melodrama: the thrill of sex and violence, an overarching morality, and a story told through action by characters who don't change.

Sondheim and Wheeler's version of the story was developed directly from Christopher Bond's play *Sweeney Todd, the Demon Barber of Fleet Street* (1970), which is credited on the title page. The main events of the plot are that Todd has escaped from a ship transporting him to Australia, where he was sent on a trumped-up charge by Judge Turpin, and has returned to London with Anthony Hope, a sailor who "saved his life."[16] The first scene (after the prologue) is their arrival in London, with Todd vowing vengeance on those who had wronged him. Todd sets up his old barber's shop above Mrs. Lovett's meat pie shop in Fleet Street, while Anthony, wandering the streets of London, sees and immediately falls in love with Judge Turpin's ward (and Sweeney's daughter), Johanna. Todd's first victim is Pirelli, a rival barber who recognizes and tries to blackmail Todd. The Judge then arrives at Todd's shop, but before he is dispatched Anthony enters singing of his love for Johanna. The Judge vows to incarcerate her where she can't be found and never to come to Todd's parlor again. In a rage at being denied vengeance, Todd sings "Epiphany" and changes his mode of behavior. Henceforth, all men are the subjects of his vengeance. Mrs. Lovett intervenes, calms him, and suggests that a perfect use for the bodies is to cook them in her meat pies.

In the second act the barber shop and pie shop are successful. Anthony searches for Johanna and finally discovers her in Mr. Fogg's asylum. Todd teaches him how to pass himself off as a wigmaker to rescue her, while secretly he writes to Judge Turpin tempting him back to the parlor with the news that Johanna will be brought there. But in the chaos that ensues, with the asylum residents and the Old Beggar-Woman running round the streets, the rescue of Johanna by Anthony, and her disguise as a sailor, Todd ends up killing the Beadle, the Old Beggar-Woman (who he finally realizes was his wife), the Judge, and Mrs. Lovett (as well as almost killing his daughter). Finally Mrs. Lovett's shop boy, Tobias, who has gone mad, kills Todd as he bends crying over his wife's corpse in the silence of what is effectively Todd's second moment of epiphany or revelation.

On the cover of the vocal score, Sondheim and Wheeler's work is designated "A musical thriller." This is in some ways a vague term but a thriller implies a suspenseful narrative style in which sex and violence may play a part.[17] Stephen Banfield also discusses the term "thriller," concluding that it requires not only an intellectually satisfying plot but that it relies on atmosphere and suspense, which are created by setting and music.[18] Cuddon identifies the derivation of the thriller from the nineteenth-century melodrama tradition,[19] and indeed, Sondheim himself implicitly refers to the work as melodrama when he is arguing that *Sweeney Todd* is not Grand Guignol: Sondheim saw what he referred to as three extremely bloody and boring plays and remarked that, in contrast, "Melodrama, for me, has to be a great deal purer than that, and it has to be at least as interesting as other drama."[20] So clearly a thriller derived from melodrama.

But there are other influences. Banfield and Swayne both identify the importance of film thrillers, or film noir, especially *Hangover Square* on Sondheim's score and the plot for *Sweeney Todd*.[21] The influences of film noir include "a partial flashback; assumed identity; a powerful and corrupt womanizer; six deaths (including the male and female leads); the ingénue couple brought together at the end; and the presence of the childlike innocent."[22] Other features of noir are that a single character propels the drama, and that the character struggles against an inexorable fate searching for a solution to an insoluble problem.[23] In this final respect, noir perhaps combines melodrama and trag-edy. The partial flashback at the masked ball and the numerous murders are claimed by Thomas P. Adler as features of Elizabethan revenge plays,[24] and Swayne also cites the device of narration, a feature sometimes adopted by the *nouvelle vague*, where it was used to introduce criticism, and the use of montage to pit the past against the present, as evidence of the influence of noir.[25] Given that most of these are devices developed from either melodrama or revenge tragedy, it is apparent that noir's derivation from these forms confuses any attempt at genre categorization. However, there are other features of melodrama; the use of love triangles, urban settings, and—derived from film melo-drama—family groupings.

The first love triangle is in the narrated past and concerns Todd, his wife, Lucy, and the Judge, who lusts after her and maneuvers Todd out of the way before raping her. The next obvious triangle is Anthony and Johanna, again with the Judge as the third party holding them apart, making Anthony and Johanna a reflection of the naïve and foolish Todd and Lucy. Todd and Mrs. Lovett's partnership is conducted under the watchful eyes of the Beggar-Woman, later revealed as Todd's wife Lucy, forming another triangle. The same triangular patterning is apparent in the family relationships, where in the past Todd, Lucy, and Johanna had formed a family group that was broken up, and for the whole of the first act that history and memory drive Todd. In the second act Todd forms a new family group with Mrs. Lovett and Tobias that leads to the downfall of them all. As for urban settings, the story is set in Victorian London, and potentially the critique of society it offers reflects contemporary urban life.

According to Adler, Sondheim uses the form of Grand Guignol in *Sweeney Todd* to present a darker, subversive critique of socioeconomic culture. He makes the case that there is a binary patterning in the work's images and motifs, such as "victim/victimizer, vengeance/forgiveness, lust/love, caged/free, sanity/lunacy, angel/devil, high/low,"[26] but that the boundaries between the opposites bleed into each other, producing ethical ambiguity and thence critique. This, he argues, is best seen in the treatment of Johanna, who kills Mr. Fogg the asylum keeper, to protect herself and her rescuer Anthony, but is also present in the various imprisonments to which she is subject.[27]

Raymond Knapp discusses the work as a blend of melodrama and farce with a pat-tern of "first scaring the hell out of its audience and then rescuing the situation through humor, each time by introducing Mrs Lovett into a situation saturated with Sweeney Todd's wrenching angst."[28] For J. L. Styan, writing in 1962, in order to suit a modern con-sciousness drama needs to swing between the extremes of tragedy and farce in order to rouse spectators to the highest degree and to encompass the greatest range of human experience.[29] Such a blend of comedy and tragedy results in irony, and according to Eric Bentley, comedy is not present to lighten tragedy but to render it deeper, and simultane-ously to imply a kind of transcendence in the triumph over chaos and hopelessness[30]. So the binary juxtaposition of dramatic and comic scenes might allow audiences to per-ceive the tragic implications of the work, while the complexity of the characterization of Todd himself, wavering between tragic victim and melodramatic villain, allows audi-ences to understand the depth of the tragedy.

CHARACTERS

There are substantial differences between the nineteenth-century melodrama and the twentieth-century musical theater version, but the most important is that Todd is changed by the events that befall him. In the first scene Todd describes himself as having been "naïve" and "foolish" in his early years before transportation, but the actions of the Judge in framing and transporting him have caused bitterness, such that he wants to avenge these crimes. At this point his actions seem justified, as he was the victim of a crime against him by an officer of the justice system, which also implies the corruption of that institution. The audience then learns about what befell his wife and child as a result of his absence, and his vengefulness appears to be, if not appropriate, then at least understandable.

Throughout the first act Todd's actions are designed to achieve vengeance on the perpetrator of the crime, and Todd has music and lyrics that allow the audience to understand his mental state. He is introduced in the first scene with the angry "There's a hole in the world like a great black pit . . . ," concluding that "the cruelty of men is as wondrous as Peru, / But there's no place like London!" However, he then begins to tell his story ("There was a barber and his wife") with the repeated reference to her beauty and his love for her. The accompaniment that Banfield describes as the "Ballad" accompaniment motivically links with the prologue, relates to the Dies Irae theme and, as it comes to rest, prefigures the motif of Anthony and Johanna.[31] More important than the motivic complexities for this argument, though, is that the song is *mezzo piano*, lyrical, not very dissonant, and *rubato*. It gives Todd the opportunity to draw the audience to him, explain his motives, and to connect with his voice, his loving emotion, his righteous indignation, and the beautiful melody.

Audiences subvocalize in response to musical gestures or vocal melodies, so that some parts of an audience's brains are activated almost as though they were singing themselves. This triggers similar emotional states in the audience to those of the performer and emotional contagion within the audience through mirroring.[32] In fact Istvan Molnar-Szakacs and Kate Overy have argued that "Music has a unique ability to trigger memories, awaken emotions and to intensify our social experiences."[33] Though all these stimuli can be resisted, it has also been shown that audiovisual stimuli engender a greater degree of "entrainment" or similarity of response than other stimuli, and that responding as a community of watcher/listeners stimulates the reward areas of the brain.[34] This means that Todd's music is likely to stimulate similar emotions in the audience in response to the emotion in the vocal and musical gestures, and that the beauty of the music and the emotion of his singing will lead the audience to empathize with his plight more fully than had he simply spoken of it.

In the next scene Mrs. Lovett, having recognized him, gives Todd his razors, which she has kept hidden. Taking them he sings, again softly and sweetly, crooning a lullaby to them; "These are my Friends." The beautiful melody, poetic lyric, calm and gentle sentiment, and slow waltz time are at odds with the intention revealed in the final lines: "you shall drip precious rubies." In the accompaniment there is some dissonance, and the key is often ambiguous as it vascillates between A♭ and A major, but the song is built in an arch shape, beginning quietly under speech and drifting quietly away again at the end, before the *crescendo poco a poco* in the coda. Thus the song appears to be a moment of soliloquy out of time, with Todd remaining apart from Mrs. Lovett's interruptions. After Todd has finished singing, the music continues building to a climax as Todd raises the razor into a spotlight for the sudden interruption of silence and the spoken line, "My right arm is complete again!" The combination of beautiful music, slow, lyrical singing, and the understanding generated through the lyrics gives audiences the opportunity to empathize with Todd and so the complexity of his character begins to be revealed (Figure 21.1).

Even after he has killed Pirelli and the Judge is in the chair, the duet Todd and the Judge sing, "Pretty Women," is again in waltz time, lyrical, poetic and beautiful, in stark contrast to Todd's murderous intent. These moments could be read as moments of binary opposition where the most beautiful and consonant music occurs as a prelude to murder, but simultaneously the music continues the audience's attachment to Todd even as he prepares to carry out his vengeance. In "Pretty Women" it also offers a hiatus, a delay to increase suspense before the fulfilment of Todd's ambition and the audience's release from tension.

However, the killing of Pirelli for attempted blackmail begins Todd's downward spiral, and after his failed attempt to kill the Judge, Todd is transformed, a transformation that

FIGURE **21.1** Imelda Staunton as Mrs. Lovett and Michael Ball as Todd in *Sweeney Todd*, London (2012).

is revealed in the song "Epiphany,-" to which I will return. In the second act Todd more closely resembles the evil character of the Victorian melodrama, and the action flows kinetically as events become unstoppable, albeit that even now audiences might feel a sense of sympathy with his plight because of the empathy that was established in the first act. Although he has little solo vocal material in act 2, Todd's music remains lyrical in the Johanna act 2 sequence and again in the reprise of "My Friends" after his vengeance is completed. It is only when he is confronted with the fact that he has killed his wife—now an old, half-mad beggar-woman—that his downfall is complete and he realizes what his lust for revenge has wrought.

This is the moment of tragedy, as Richard B. Sewall, writing in 1954, describes it: tragedy exposes the paradoxical nature of man and the universe. Tragic suffering and insight come when the hero confronts the ambiguities within and without. "The confrontation, suffering, and insight make up the 'tragic form.' "[35] On the other hand, the tragic hero, according to Karl Jaspers, is the exceptional man who, by calling into question the established political, social, moral or religious order, exposes both its limitations and his own, revealing not triumph but the whole situation.[36] So there is a tragic moment of revelation for the character, and tragedy is revealed through his suffering for audiences as a result of the humanity of the character who through his actions and those of others around him exposes the corruption of society. The effects of this are magnified by the attachment of audiences to Todd and his plight produced by the character and quality of his music. In this sense, tragedy is at work in *Sweeney Todd*.

Joseph Marchesani equates three stages of Todd's transformations with Lacan's three registers, the Imaginary, the Symbolic, and the Real. The first point of transformation between these registers that Marchesani notes is when Todd is transformed into a criminal by the court's conviction, removing his naïve identity. The second point occurs when Todd fails to kill the Judge, so that "the wronged barber metamorphoses into the world's avenger."[37] This is when, according to Marchesani, Todd is transformed into a psychotic murderer and his Symbolic register is subsumed by his Imaginary one.[38] And this is when Todd sings "Epiphany."

The other characters are perhaps more melodramatic as they appear to be less changed by the events, though all are combinations of good and bad characteristics rather than stereotypes. Mrs. Lovett, though a comic character, is always villainous; it is revealed that not only did she do nothing to help Lucy, but she encouraged her to take poison. Later, she tricks Tobias into the bakehouse, worried that Tobias's attempts to protect her from Todd will reveal her own complicity. The complexity here is in the audience's feelings toward her, since she draws goodwill through comedy and music, and appears to have maternal feelings for Tobias (especially in "Nothing's Gonna Harm You"), even as she manipulates and tricks her way to what she wants. Even the Judge, who might be considered the most clearly or stereotypically evil, has the opportunity in his "Johanna" (Mea Culpa) to reveal his self-loathing and his catholic guilt alongside his overwhelming sexual drives, and thus also becomes more complex.

Johanna is perhaps always slightly crazed since at the start she already sings of the madness wrought by "sitting in cages." In the first version of "Kiss Me" she chatters incessantly first about the Judge's return and then telling of her fear that she won't see Anthony again, even though she does not yet know his name, while in the second part she sings of herself as a "silly little ninnynoodle" and a fool. In the second act she kills Fogg before chattering incessantly as she and Anthony escape, singing, "Will we be married on Sunday? That's what you promised," before recollecting, "That was last August" and still insisting, "Kiss Me" as Anthony drags her off.[39] The tone and pitch of her singing, especially in the "Kiss Me" sections, characterize her both as heroine in a nineteenth-century operetta tradition (always a soprano), and as altered, nervous, frantic, or mad. Certainly Judith Schlesinger argues that "[e]veryone on Fleet Street is warped in one way or another."[40] And it is true that even among the lesser characters Pirelli is a liar and a cheat, and the Beadle kills Johanna's bird and holds Lucy for the Judge to rape.

However, Tobias, who might be argued to be Todd's nemesis, also changes from the lively young sales assistant apprenticed to Pirelli to the insane and unknowing killer of Sweeney Todd. Lucy has changed before the musical begins from the beautiful, faithful wife and mother to the crazed hag who haunts the streets. But nothing in the world is changed and the institution of the law is not overthrown; only its representatives, Judge Turpin and the Beadle, are murdered. So it might be possible to argue that while the majority of characters are warped and odd, they are not really changed by the events of the story. Only Todd and Tobias are further changed during its course. Perhaps first his victimhood, then his change of strategy after Epiphany, and finally his realization of his crimes all render Todd a tragic figure. And perhaps the audience comes to some realizations about society and its institutions, justice, and vengeance, thus rendering the work tragic or at least tragicomic.

STRUCTURE

Todd's moment of transformation occurs as a result of not killing the Judge and is evident in his singing of "Epiphany," and so this moment becomes the focus from which the plot plays out. It also provides a pivot for a binary pattern in which the two acts reflect each other, not as a palindrome, but as direct repetition of the structure, location, and character of each scene, as can be seen in Table 21.1.

The prologue, its narrative reprises, and the epilogue are removed for this comparison, but beyond that there is a remarkable degree of comparability. One of the least obvious parallels is the opening scene of revelation, "There's no place like London," with "Epiphany." The first scene introduces Todd, Anthony, and the Beggar-Woman, and provides part of the back story and therefore the motivation for Todd that is to be played out subsequently, and the history of his first transformation. Its parallel scene is "Epiphany," followed by the black comedy of "A Little Priest," in which Todd, with Mrs. Lovett, reassesses his position and, I would argue, transforms from tragic victim to melodramatic villain. It also instigates the action that is to follow.

Table 21.1 Parallels emerge in a structural analysis of acts 1 and 2

Act 1: Place: song	Principal character (others in both acts)	Mood	Act 2: Place: song
London Docks	Todd (with Anthony, Beggar-Woman and Mrs. Lovett)	history, anger, comedy	Epiphany (transformation)"A Little Priest"(Interval)
Pie Shop: "Worst Pies"	Mrs. Lovett (with Todd and others)	comedy	Pie shop and barber shop: "God, that's Good"
Fleet Street: Johanna and Anthony	Johanna and Anthony (with Judge, Beadle, Todd)	romance and lust	Streets: Searching for Johanna
St Dunstan's market place: Pirelli shaving contest	Todd	comedy / suspense	"Mrs. Lovett's parlor: 'By the Sea', 'The Wigmaker Sequence', and 'The Letter'"
Mrs. Lovett's parlor: "Wait"	Mrs. Lovett (with Todd, Tobias, Beadle)	lust, filial love	Mrs. Lovett's parlor and bakehouse: "Not While I'm Around" and "Parlor Songs"
Barber shop: "Pirelli's Death"	Todd (and victims)	murder	Barber shop: Beadle's Death
Judge's house and street: "Kiss Me," etc.	Johanna and Anthony, Judge and Beadle (and others)	love, lust	Streets of London: "Fogg's Asylum," the rescue, "City on Fire"
Barber shop: "Pretty Women" (Judge in chair, Anthony interrupts)	Todd and Judge	vengeance	Barber shop: Johanna hiding, Judge in chair, Judge's death
Barber shop: "Epiphany" (transformation)	Todd (Mrs. Lovett and Tobias)	tragedy	Bakehouse in the cellar: Todd's transformation and death

In each sequence these scenes of plot exposure are followed by comic pie-shop scenes featuring Mrs. Lovett, first with "The Worst Pies in London" (followed by "Poor Thing" and "My Friends") and in the second act with "God, that's Good." The meeting of Johanna and Anthony in act 1 on Fleet Street is paralleled by the search for Johanna through the streets of London in act 2. This is followed by two quite different scenes. In act 1 the comedy scene of the shaving competition with Pirelli is replaced in the second act by "The Letter," in which Todd betrays Anthony and potentially puts Johanna in danger. Both of these scenes are opportunities for Todd to manipulate events so that the Judge will come to his tonsorial parlor, though they are different in character.

Parlor scenes focusing on Mrs. Lovett follow. In act 1 this is Mrs Lovett's exhortation to Todd to "Wait" for the opportunity to arise, and in the second act there is the calm beauty of Tobias and Mrs. Lovett's "Not While I'm Around," that leads Mrs. Lovett to the conclusion that Tobias has guessed the secret and must be disposed of. Both demonstrate Mrs. Lovett's manipulation and treachery. In act 2 this scene also contains the comedy and suspense of the Beadle sitting in the parlor singing while Mrs. Lovett sits anxiously by and Tobias sings along in the bakehouse.

In each act this is followed by a scene in the barber shop in which first Pirelli and later the Beadle are despatched. These are the tense and suspenseful scenes followed by more street scenes in which, in act 1 Anthony and Johanna are together at her home as the Judge and Beadle walk home and are about to discover them, before deciding to go to Todd's tonsorial parlor. In act 2 the scene again centers on Johanna, who is rescued by Anthony as the asylum inmates run around the streets, and Mrs. Lovett and Todd search for Tobias in the sewers below. A final scene in the barber shop follows, as in act 1 Todd attempts to kill the Judge and in act 2 accomplishes it, before the two epiphanic scenes conclude each sequence. In the first, Todd vows vengeance on the "whole human race," and in the second realizes he has killed his wife, Lucy—"what have I done?"—before pushing Mrs. Lovett into the oven and after the music ends, being killed himself.

These scenes represent a parallel structure between the acts, in which scene type, location, and to some extent characters are reflected. But the internal construction of the scenes varies. In act 1 there are fewer montage scenes, fewer occasions when suspense is created by parallel stories being played out simultaneously. In fact this occurs in act 1 primarily in "Kiss Me (Part II)," in which Anthony and Johanna are together, and the Beadle, having walked almost to the Judge's house with Turpin, persuades the Judge to go for a shave. The suspense occurs outside the songs, though, as "Kiss Me (Part I)" is sung, followed by "Ladies in their Sensitivities," and only after the decision is made to go to the barber does the montage of scenes and the musical quartet of "Kiss Me (Part II)" take place. So in act 1, scene follows scene, building to a climax in what might be considered a nineteenth-century or melodramatic theatrical style.

In act 2 the scenes contain more internal complexity and montages of divergent events, although they can be separated into a parallel structure, as seen above. This is apparent right from the start of the act as "God, that's Good!" takes place in the pie shop *and* the barber shop above. The act 2 Johanna sequence takes place on the street but overlays Anthony searching for Johanna, Todd singing and slashing throats, the Beggar-Woman trying to draw attention to her suspicions, and Johanna singing from the asylum. The parlor scene was mentioned above, and then the "Searching" sections continue this sequence of montages in which locations transform so that the pace increases and moments of action are juxtaposed to create intensity and suspense. It is only after the Judge is dead and Todd is in the bakehouse that the pace falters to allow the moment of revelation. This second act appears much more filmic in the fluidity of movement between places, characters, and situations, but also melodramatic as the kinetic process becomes unstoppable. The use of montage throughout this act allows juxtapositions that contribute to the tension and intensity of the work. Possibly, this use of montage creates the tragedy that is revealed in the swings between comedy and dramatic violence, between times, places, and actions, and between involvement and critical reflection.

This act, then, is constructed in a way that is perhaps more modern, drawing on filmic influences and contemporary dramatic practices. So despite the parallel construction of the two acts, there is a marked contrast in the style of their construction that may to some extent account for some of the difficulties of genre delineation noted above. It is interesting that Todd has become the vengeful and evil melodramatic villain in this second act that is constructed in a more fluid or filmic way, whereas in the first act, constructed in a format comparable with a nineteenth-century melodramatic aesthetic, he is perceived to be more sympathetic. In this sense at least, he is always out of step with his context, a fact that contributes to the perception of his tragedy.

Music and Melodrama

Some of the functions that have been identified in relation to the music of nineteenth-century melodrama are to point character, underline mood, and heighten tension,[41] for entrances and exits, for mechanical necessities such as scene changes, to enhance spectacle, and as motifs.[42] For David Mayer, one of the features is that memorable themes for characters and incidents are repeated for sentiment, subliminal association, or deliberate irony or mockery.[43] Some more concrete functions are furnished by Thomas Elsaesser, who suggests that music, with other devices, serves "to dramatise a given narrative, is subjective, programmatic. But because it is also a form of punctuation...it is both functional (that is, of structural significance) and thematic (that is, belonging to the expressive content) because used to formulate certain moods—sorrow, violence, dread, suspense, happiness"[44] Caryl Flinn suggests that melodrama music "picks up where something else leaves off, veering in the direction of what might appear to be pure surfeit or excess"[45]

Stephen Banfield has identified many of these features in *Sweeney Todd* in his seminal study *Sondheim's Broadway Musicals*. He provides a chart of the use of musical motifs and their recurrence in the work (288–9); makes reference to the range of musical styles included in the score, "ballads, burlesques, marches, waltzes, patter songs, and so forth" (291); examines the use of diegetic song and atmospheric evocation of London (293); and discusses the use of the Dies Irae symbol of doom in what he describes as the "Lucy" motif (297–300), and the use of "motivic repetition, transformation, combination, and reprise" as the structural processes of the score (300–305). In *The American Musical and the Performance of Personal Identity*, Raymond Knapp also discusses the use of recurring motives and their transformations, especially the Dies Irae that provides the basis of "The Ballad of Sweeney Todd," and identifies the pervasiveness of the music as underscore and song throughout about 80 percent of the work (333). These features, which have parallels in the descriptions of melodrama music above, need not be rehearsed here.

"Epiphany" begins with the "Nemesis motif." It occurs as Todd is horror-struck at what has happened and says, "I had him... and then," and sings, "I had him! His throat was bare beneath my hand..." This motif has already appeared as Todd sang "No Place Like London" and "There's a hole in the world like a great black pit." It occurs again, transformed in the accompaniment to "My Friends," and clearly in the underscore and accompaniment to represent the tension that Mrs. Lovett dispels in "Wait." After "Epiphany" it recurs in "God, that's Good!" when Todd confronts the Beggar-Woman in "Searching (Part II)," again in 'The Judge's Return," and when he almost kills Johanna. It is a clearly audible motif that, with its sharp, fast, dissonant, attacking sound, represents the violent pain and anger in Todd.

Todd and Mrs. Lovett reprise a few short phrases of "Wait" as Todd blames her for telling him to wait, with a harshly dissonant stabbing accompaniment. This is followed by a section of "There's a hole in the world" before the main march theme, developed from "There's a hole in the world," begins, "They all deserve to die." This is loud, raucous, and angry, and is now Todd's anthem. It is followed by a sudden transition to a memory of his wife and daughter that is accompanied by the Beggar-Woman's motif. Suddenly the whole framework of the work alters as Todd addresses the audience directly "All right, you, sir, How about a shave?" This switch is a sudden reminder of the distancing and narrative of the prologue, but is simultaneously more immediate and threatening, as Todd interrupts his keening, aching, longing for his wife and daughter with these moments of violent, sardonic passion directed at the audience. The Beggar-Woman's motif is extended to conclude the song with a loud, dissonant, and maddened phrase from Todd, "I'm alive at last, And I'm full of Joy!" which has a similarity to his sentiment in the final line of "My Friends": "At last my right arm is complete again!" In both cases he expresses joy at having the tools that, in his hands, become the instruments of vengeance.

In "Epiphany" there are juxtapositions of many different motifs accompanied by dissonant music, sudden switches between styles, between narrative "realism" and direct address, and between angry attack and keening loss. And if that were not enough, the excessive heightened emotion is immediately undercut by the black comedy of "A Little Priest." Not only is "Epiphany" the most motivically and melodically diverse in the score, it is also extremely dissonant, emotionally excessive and timbrally harsh, enhancing the expression of Todd's violence and anger, and giving full orchestral vent to his passion and suffering. Knapp describes it as cascading chaotically from blind rage to foreboding, to resolution, before Todd wails at the realization that he will never see his wife and daughter, interrupted only by the manic and maniacally improbable recollection of a classic music-hall routine ("Who, sir? You, sir?")."[46]

"Epiphany" is the turning point for Todd from tragic victim to melodramatic villain, it disrupts linear narrative through direct address, it disrupts melodic line by rapid juxtaposition, and it is accompanied by raucous and dissonant harmonies. The story changes at this moment, Todd's character is fatally transformed, and the binary structure of the whole work hinges on this transformation.

Conclusion

In the first act Todd could be viewed as a tragic victim, and in the second act, after the transformation of "Epiphany" and until the second epiphany when he realizes what he has done, he could be viewed as melodramatic villain. But this is confused by the empathy that has been generated for him in the first act, by the beautiful music he has sung and by the attachment and understanding that music has created in the audience. Moreover, in act 2, the pace and the juxtapositions of scenes demonstrate that everything is out of control. Todd's melodramatic striving for vengeance has set a tragic process in motion that becomes unstoppable. This is both melodrama and tragedy, and the highpoint of this tragedy is Todd's realization of his crimes in the final scene, the return of the music "There was a barber and his wife," that brings the story full circle, and the silence that precedes his death at Tobias's hand. The music is melodramatic in its excess and in its use as underscore, to create atmosphere, and to create a motivic web that tells the story through its repetitions and transformations. Comedy is used to undermine excessive emotions and angst, and to contrast with tension or danger, making the contrast greater and the critique darker and deeper. But principally Todd is presented as an antihero, whose empathetic music renders him an everyman, the dominant consciousness who allows us to see the world in a new and tragic light.

Notes

1. Haining, Peter. *The Mystery and Horrible Murders of Sweeney Todd, the Demon Barber of Fleet Street*. London: Frederick Muller, 1979. Referred to in Knapp, Raymond. *The American Musical and the Performance of Personal Identity* (Princeton: Princeton University Press, 2006), 426, n. 30.

2. Joseph Marchesani, "Arresting Development: Law, Love, and the Name-of-the-Father in *Sweeney Todd*," in *Reading Stephen Sondheim*, ed. Sandor Goodhart (New York: Garland, 2000), 171.

3. James Malcolm Rymer, *Sweeney Todd and The String of Pearls* (London: Wordsworth, 2010), xix.

4. Knapp, *American Musical*, 426.

5. Helen R. Smith, *New Light on Sweeney Todd, Thomas Peckett Prest, James Malcolm Rymer and Elizabeth Caroline Grey* (London: Jarndyce, 2002), 21–8.

6. Michael Kilgarriff, *The Golden Age of Melodrama: Twelve 19th Century Melodramas* (London: Wolfe, 1974), 244.

7. Rymer, *Sweeney Todd*.

8. Stephen Banfield records the date of Dibdin Pitt's play as 1842, which further confuses the derivation in *Sondheim's Broadway Musicals* (Ann Arbor: University of Michigan Press, 1993), 283; but Dick Collins accounts for this in his introduction to the 2010 version of the serialization of *Sweeney Todd and The String of Pearls* by suggesting that Dibdin Pitt's play-text was published as a Standard Play by John Dicks in the 1880s, in which its original date was wrongly stated as 1842 (xxiv).

9. The play text contained in Kigarriff, *Golden Age*, 242–72 lists a cast for *The String of Pearls* from a playbill for the first performance at the Britannia Theatre, Hoxton, London, on March 1, 1847. A second, and markedly different, list of dramatis personae is then listed, also for the Britannia Theatre in 1847, before the play text entitled *Sweeney Todd, The Barber of Fleet Street*. There is an editorial note that the second cast list is that given in the published edition of 1883. Kilgarriff remarks that "[t]he play was probably altered in subsequent performances, and it is doubtless the improved version which was eventually published," Kilgarriff, *Golden Age*, 245.

10. Dibdin Pitt, in Kilgarriff, *Golden Age*, 262.

11. Stephen Sondheim, "Larger than Life: Reflections on Melodrama and *Sweeney Todd*," in *Melodrama*, vol. 7, ed. Daniel Gerould (New York: New York Literary Forum, 1980), 14.

12. Banfield, *Sondheim's Broadway Musicals*, 291, quoting Smith, 7, who is paraphrasing Bechtold.

13. Marvin Carlson, *Theories of the Theatre*, expanded ed. (Ithaca and London: Cornell University, Press, 1993), 214.

14. Carlson, *Theories of the Theatre*, 214.

15. Smith, *New Light*, 5, quoted in Banfield, *Sondheim's Broadway Musicals*, 291.

16. Sondheim, "Larger than Life," 21.

17. J. A. Cuddon, ed., *The Penguin Dictionary of Literary Terms and Literary Theory* (London: Penguin, 1992), 915.

18. Banfield, *Sondheim's Broadway Musicals*, 281.

19. Cuddon, *Dictionary of Literary Terms*, 919.

20. Sondheim, quoted in Steve Swayne, *How Sondheim Found his Sound* (Ann Arbor: University of Michigan Press, 2005), 280.

21. For Banfield, see this volume, Chapter 1.

22. Swayne, *How Sondheim Found*, 167.

23. Ibid., 168.

24. Thomas P. Adler, "The Sung and the Said: Literary Value in the Musical Dramas of Stephen Sondheim," in *Reading Stephen Sondheim*, ed. *Reading Stephen Sondheim*, ed. Sandor Goodhart (New York: Garland, 2000), 41.

25. Swayne, *How Sondheim Found*, 177.

26. Adler, "The Sung and the Said," 42.

27. Ibid.

28. Knapp, *American Musical*, 333

29. Carlson, *Theories of the Theatre*, 451

30. Ibid., 453

31. Banfield, *Sondheim's Broadway Musicals*, 298–9.

32. J. D. Smith, D. Reisberg, and M. Wilson, "Subvocalisation and Auditory Imagery: Interactions between the Inner Ear and Inner Voice," in *Auditory Imagery*, ed. Daniel Reisberg, 95–119 (Hillsdale: Psychology Press, 1992); J.D. Smith, M. Wilson, M. and D. Reisberg, "The Role of Subvocalisation in Auditory Imagery," *Neuropsychologia* 33 (1995), 1433–54.

33. Istvan Molnar-Szakacs, and Kate Overy, "Music and Mirror Neurons: From Motion to 'E'motion" *Social Cognitive and Affective Neuroscience* 1, no. 3 (2006): 235–241.

34. Christian Keysers, "From Mirror Neurons to Kinaesthetic Empathy," keynote presentation at *Kinaesthetic Empathy*, Manchester University, April 22–23, 2010.

35. Carlson, *Theories of the Theatre*, 449.

36. Karl Jaspers, *Tragedy Is Not Enough*, trans. H. A. T. Reiche et al. (London, 1952), 31, 52 [*Von der Wahrheit* (1947)]. Referred to and quoted in Marvin Carlson, *Theories of the Theatre*, 446.

37. Marchesani, "Arresting Development," 173

38. Marchesani also makes the case that each register is also articulated Todd's interactions with a pair of characters: Anthony and Johanna inhabit the Imaginary, The Judge and Mrs. Lovett articulate the Symbolic, and the Beggar-Woman and Tobias articulate the Real (Marchesani, "Arresting Development,"174).

39. Stephen Sondheim and Hugh Wheeler, *Sweeney Todd: The Demon Barber of Fleet Street*, based on a version of *Sweeney Todd* by Christopher Bond (New York: Revelation/Rilting, 1981), 325.

40. Judith Schlesinger, "Psychology, Evil, and *Sweeney Todd* or, 'Don't I Know You, Mister?'" in *Stephen Sondheim: A Casebook*, ed. Joanne Gordon (New York: Garland, 1997), 130.

41. James L. Smith, *Melodrama* (London: Methuen, 1973), 50.

42. Anne Dhu Shapiro, "Action Music in American Pantomime and Melodrama, 1730-1913" *American Music* 2, no. 4 (1984): 49–72.

43. David Mayer, "The Music of Melodrama," in *Performance and Politics in Popular Drama*, ed. David Bradby, Louis James, and Bernard Sharratt, 49–64 (Cambridge, UK: Cambridge University Press, 1980).

44. Thomas Elsaesser, "Tales of Sound and Fury." in *Home is Where the Heart Is: Studies in Melodrama and the Woman's Film*, ed. Christine Gledhill, 43–69 (London: British Film Institute).

45. Caryl Flinn, "Music and the Melodramatic Past of New German Cinema," in *Melodrama: Stage, Picture, Screen*, ed. Jacky Bratton, Jim Cook, and Christine Gledhill (London: British Film Institute), 108.

46. Knapp, *American Musical*, 339.

CHAPTER 22

"CAREFUL THE SPELL YOU CAST": *INTO THE WOODS* AND THE USES OF DISENCHANTMENT

BEN FRANCIS

> If we hope to live not just from moment to moment, but in true conscious-
> ness of our existence, then our greatest need and most difficult achieve-
> ment is to find meaning in our lives.[1]

THE opening line of Bettelheim's work on fairy tales accurately sums up the main theme
of *Into the Woods*. It was Bettelheim's book that first inspired James Lapine to write a
show that would take a darker view of fairy tales. The title itself indicates one of the
main themes of the show. When so many musicals aim simply to enchant their audiences, *Into the Woods* asks a deeper question: what use is enchantment? Enchantment
and disenchantment are themes running all the way through Sondheim's work. The
songs "Take Me to the World" from *Evening Primrose* and "Our Time" from *Merrily We
Roll Along* are about young people trembling with excitement as they are on the verge
of discovering the world and its infinite possibilities. As the disenchanted characters in
Follies put it, youth was a time when "everything was possible and nothing made sense."[2]
But Ella Harkins, who sings "Take Me to the World," is destined to become a shop window's dummy (a fate reminiscent of a fairytale character turning to stone), and of the
three young people who sing "Our Time," one becomes an alcoholic and one becomes a
Hollywood producer (in Sondheim's eyes an even worse fate). If the world is enchanting,
it is also dangerous.

   Into the Woods was Sondheim's second show with James Lapine, and develops one
of the major themes of *Sunday in the Park with George*: the relationships between parents and children. In *Sunday* it is mostly the parents who sing, but in *Into the Woods*
we also hear the children's point of view as they begin to journey away from home. The

woods themselves are a kind of Forest of Arden: an enchanted space where roles are reversed and magical transformations are possible. They are also, of course, as they are in the original fairy stories, a metaphor for the uncertainties of life, especially when one is growing up.[3] And much of the show takes place in an enchanted twilight; at the beginning the characters are seemingly confident, but easily frightened:

ALL:
No need to be afraid there –
BAKER, CINDERELLA (*Apprehensive*):
There's something in the glade there ... (20–21)[4]

At the end of the show the light is the same but the characters have changed:

BAKER, JACK, CINDERELLA, LITTLE RED RIDINGHOOD (*Softly*):
The light is getting dimmer...
BAKER:
I think I see a glimmer— (137)

The characters are all more aware of how fragile the light is, but instead of being afraid, they make the best of it.[5]

The show's first words, after the traditional "Once upon a time" spoken by the Narrator, are Cinderella's "I wish." The characters are defined mostly by their wishes: Cinderella wishes to go to the ball, Jack and his mother wish not to be so poor, Little Red Ridinghood wants lots of pies and cakes from the Baker, and the Baker and his Wife wish for a child. The Baker and his Wife are then visited by the Witch who lives next door. She reveals to them that she had stolen the Baker's sister Rapunzel when a baby, and also that she has cursed the Baker with childlessness. She committed both these crimes in revenge for the Baker's father having once stolen vegetables from her garden: a neat conflation of the story of the Garden of Eden with Greek myths that saw children such as Electra cursed by the impiety of their parents. The Witch demands that the Baker gives her four items before she will let him have a child. She needs these items to undo the curse of ugliness that her own mother had put on her.

Like Prospero she uses magic on a disparate number of people for revenge; but unlike the magician of *The Tempest* she grants no forgiveness (when the Witch later finds that she can't cast a spell over Rapunzel any more she breaks her magic staff out of petulance, not renunciation). The Witch has kept Rapunzel locked in a tower for fourteen years and, when later Rapunzel angrily confronts her, the Witch's response is "I was just trying to be a good mother" (95). This line usually gets a laugh of recognition. But the world is a dangerous place, and the Witch was right to be afraid.

In this show, as in many of the stories, wishes can rebound on the people who make them. When Cinderella visits her mother's grave she says "I wish," only for her mother's ghost to interrupt:

CINDERELLA'S MOTHER:
Do you know what you wish?
Are you certain what you wish
Is what you want? (22)

The last words of the show are Cinderella saying, once again: "I wish." Few musicals would admit the uncomfortable truth that wishing is a perennial human state, that somebody has only to have their wish granted for them to want something else.

But the main characters have all learned to be more careful of what they wish for. All gradually realize the need to grow. As Little Red Ridinghood sings after being rescued from the belly of the Wolf: "Isn't it nice to know a lot! /. .. and a little bit not ..." (36).

She recognizes that an increase in knowledge also means lost innocence. The Wolf persuades Little Red Ridinghood to try different paths in the woods, bringing in a recurring Sondheim motif of a path or road equaling a choice in life ("The Road You Didn't Take" from *Follies* is a key example). But the path the Wolf is ultimately thinking of is his gut: a "dark slimy path," the opposite of the new world that Jack later finds in the sky. This part of the story is echoed in the scene in act 2 where the Prince (who is usually played by the same actor as the Wolf) seduces the Baker's Wife, underlining the fact that the Wolf's eating people is a metaphor for sex. Not that Little Red Ridinghood *is* sexually abused when she is eaten by the Wolf, but it is the way that a child might displace their sexual anxieties in their dreams.

Jack's personality also begins to develop: when we first see him his principal attachment is to his cow. He is so simple that he thinks the cow is male. When he has to sell it to the Baker and his Wife he sings a goodbye that is both poignant and funny. Hopelessly naive though he is, his feelings are real. But later, after he has returned from the beanstalk, he sings "Giants in the Sky," where he explains that, in the Giant's kingdom, he has felt things that he never felt before. This is partly to do with dawning sexual awareness: "And she gives you food / And she gives you rest / And she draws you close to her giant breast, / And you know things now that you never knew before" (43), but it is more than that. He is another of Sondheim's characters who express the thrill of discovering a whole new world that shimmers with possibilities. Like Red Ridinghood, he is "excited and scared" (35).

Into the Woods adopts the bipartite structure of *Sunday in the Park with George*, in that the first act seems to bring the story to a close. But unlike *Sunday*, in which the unresolved tensions of act 1 are brought to a harmonious resolution in act 2, the second act of *Woods* disrupts the seemingly happy ending of the first act. The concept of a happy ending implies stasis. Act 2 shows that this is impossible. The perfect marriage of Cinderella has become a bore and the Prince is following a new impossible love. Sondheim explained that Lapine was "skeptical about the possibility of 'happily ever after' in real life and wary of the danger that fairy tales may give children false expectations."[6] Children aren't in danger of believing that stories about dragons or witches are literally true; they know that they are made up. What is dangerous is that they might believe the underlying pattern; the implicit promise that everything will always turn out all right—that at the hour of darkest need somebody will come and help them.

The Narrator doubles as the Mysterious Man who turns out to be the Baker's long-lost father. He emerges at the end of act 1 and helps the Witch perform the magic spell that restores her beauty. In other words, he doesn't just tell the story, he breaks into it to ensure all is resolved happily. The fact that he is suddenly revealed as the Baker's father—enabling the Witch to end her curse on the Baker—and then seemingly dies, all within a few minutes, is a satirical comment on the kind of story that sacrifices credibility to bring in a *deus ex machina* to ensure a neat happy ending.

Into the Woods, on the other hand, guides the audience through the process of facing disillusionment and then finding that life is still worth living. It does this partially by bringing back the violence of the original stories. For instance Lapine restores the fact that one of Cinderella's Ugly Sisters cuts off her toes, and the other cuts off her heels, in order to fit into the gold slipper offered by the Prince. The show acknowledges the violence that is often in children, and that they love to read about in stories as it acts out their frustrations. And the casual callousness of childhood is caught well in Red Ridinghood's line about her grandmother: "For all that I know / She's already dead" (10), which she sings while being more interested in how much she can eat.

The show then, like *Follies*, is a reexamination of a particular genre. *Follies* took musical comedy apart and reassembled it again, and *Into the Woods* does the same for the fairy tale, and for the same reason: both genres can build unrealistic expectations of trouble-free lives. Neither *Follies* nor *Into the Woods* is simply a piece of literary criticism, but rather an attempt to reclaim a genre and put it to real use.

Near the start of act 2 a Giant's foot comes through the sky and brings death to the enchanted forest—perhaps provoked by the hubris of the characters who declare that they have never been so happy. The foot belongs to the widow of the giant whom Jack had killed in act 1. The second act dramatizes the beginning of maturity for the characters as they start to realize that actions have consequences, and by the end of the act there are no parents left to guide Jack or Little Red Ridinghood, but instead there is a community.

The first onstage casualty of the vengeful Giant is the Narrator. Just as the characters are arguing about what they should do about the Giant they notice the Narrator for the first time.[7] They fight over whether they should pretend he's Jack and offer him to the Giant, and just as they seem to agree to let him go the Witch grabs him and pushes him towards the Giant who picks him up and drops him. The killing of the Narrator is symbolic of the moment when the growing child begins to realize that the stories are not always to be trusted. The Narrator could be seen as a representative of the kind of official morality that says justice is always done and that nobody need worry about anything. His is the voice of the parent or the political propagandist, and in both cases their ultimate aim is to stifle any form of dissent.

If Sondheim's shows don't have conventional happy endings, it is not because he doesn't believe in happiness, but because he doesn't believe in endings. His message is that only those who can adapt to a changing world can survive; to be in a happy ending is to be trapped in a fantasy, and that is death. For instance, at the end of act 1 Cinderella marries one of the Princes. (The fact that there are two princes, just as there are two ugly sisters, makes them more comical; instead of being unique figures, they are shown to be cut to a pattern.) But the Prince is a fantasy figure who is himself trapped in fantasy. Both he and the other Prince dream only of what they cannot have. The song "Agony" wittily shows this, as the Princes admit to being:

> BOTH:
> Always in thrall most
> To anything almost,
> Or something asleep. (97)

They are in love with the unattainable; the very fact that Rapunzel is trapped in a tower or Sleeping Beauty is held in an unbreakable glass coffin is what attracts them. It is not difficult to see why this is so: if someone is unattainable then you never have to face the disappointment of turning your dreams to prosaic reality. This is why the Princes get a laugh with the exchange:

> CINDERELLA'S PRINCE:
> Did you learn her name?
> RAPUNZEL'S PRINCE:
> No,
> There's a dwarf standing guard. (97)

It is so clearly an excuse for Rapunzel's Prince not to get what he wants.

"I was raised to be charming, not sincere" (127), says Cinderella's Prince in a rare moment of honesty. And once he has finished charming somebody he can only move on and charm someone else. He is the kind of man who doesn't realize that the first enchantment of love never stays, and is always looking to recapture that thrill: a wraith in pursuit of a chimera.

But he is not the only one who lies. As Sondheim wrote: "What interested James was the little dishonesties that enabled the characters to reach their happy endings."[8] The Baker's Wife lies and cheats to get the things they need to have a child, and in the song "Maybe They're Magic" she proves adept at self-justification. She argues that it was all right to trick Jack out of his cow by pretending she was giving him magic beans in return: "If the end is right, / It justifies / The beans!" (31). In the second act, however, she has a momentary fling with Cinderella's Prince. He pretends that her decision will have no consequences: "Best to take the moment present / As a present for the moment" (109).

As far as the Prince is concerned, the woods are Las Vegas. She justifies herself more ingeniously.

> WIFE:
> Just remembering you've had an "and,"
> When you're back to "or,"
> Makes the "or" mean more
> Than it did before. (113)

In other words she tells herself that by betraying her husband she appreciates him better.

But after her fling, the Baker's Wife falls victim to the Giant and dies. This part of the story has sometimes been criticized as an overly severe punishment of her infidelity; but there is no hint that, even though she has betrayed the Baker, she *deserves* to die. In traditional fairy tales death is a punishment for the wicked, but in this story the deaths are arbitrary—people die because they happen to be standing in the wrong place. As she says earlier:

> WIFE:
> This is ridiculous,
> What am I doing here?
> I'm in the wrong story. (109)

However, the Narrator, who kept everyone to their appointed story, is now dead and anything can happen. It might be that the Baker's Wife dies because she lives in a fantasy; she had dreamed of Prince Charming even more than Cinderella did. In act 1 she eagerly asks Cinderella: "Is he sensitive, / Clever, / Well-mannered, / Considerate, / Passionate, / Charming, / As kind as he's handsome, / As wise as he's rich / Is he everything you've ever wanted?"[9] This is almost word for word Cinderella's Prince's description of himself in "Agony."

Fairy tales have always had morals but this show calls them into question: in the First Midnight sequence the characters take it in turns to sing a number of different morals; then they start to drown each other out and soon all is confusion. It becomes a veritable thicket of conclusions, which in turn casts doubt on the idea of drawing conclusions at all. But in the show's finale they sing different morals that show a deeper knowledge; for instance in the First Midnight sequence Jack's Mother sings: "Slotted spoons don't hold much soup" (40), meaning that Jack isn't very bright. At the end she sings, "The slotted spoon *can* catch the potato ..." (133). This doesn't contradict the first statement but shows a more profound and generous knowledge: she now realizes that there are qualities in Jack that she hadn't appreciated. The audience is being led to understand that reliance on pat little maxims is not enough. As the Baker puts it in "It Takes Two":

> BAKER:
> It takes care,
> It takes patience and fear and despair
> To change.
> Though you swear
> To change,
> Who can tell if you do?
> It takes two. (54)

In order for wishes to come true they have to be acted on, which means making choices and, as the Narrator reminds us, "these were not people familiar with making choices" (101). The characters often try to duck their responsibilities; as Jack puts it in "Giants in the Sky," "you wish that you could live in between" (44). This is true for Cinderella, who like Petra in *A Little Night Music*, dreams of marrying a prince. In "On the Steps of the Palace" she explains that the Prince has tried to trap her by spreading pitch on the stairs. "It's your first big decision" she sings, but she backs away from the responsibility.

> CINDERELLA:
> Then from out of the blue,
> And without any guide,
> You know what your decision is,
> Which is not to decide. (64)

She leaves her shoe behind to see if the Prince will find her, thus putting the onus on him. And when she is married to him she tries to be what he wants, showing that she hasn't yet outgrown the slave mentality that was imposed on her by her Stepmother and Ugly Sisters.

In act 2 the characters start to realize just how ambiguous and complex the world is (Figure 22.1). They are not aware of having strayed from the path through the woods but they find that, as the Baker puts it to Little Red Ridinghood, "The path has strayed from you" (99). Understanding does not come easily and they argue, which leads to the comic recrimination number, "Your Fault," as the characters start to blame each other for the Giant's rampage. But they won't surrender Jack to the Giant when the Witch suggests it. So the Witch rejects them.

> WITCH:
> You're so nice.
> You're not good,
> You're not bad,
> You're just nice. (121)

FIGURE **22.1** The Ensemble in *Into the Woods*, Regent's Park Open Air Theatre, London (2011).

So many plays and films are predicated on their characters being nice all the time and never doing anything that might threaten their popularity with the audience. But, as the Witch sees, niceness isn't enough. Niceness is only possible in a world where all difficult moral choices have been ironed out, as they are in badly written stories.

We have already seen the perils of niceness; when we first see Cinderella with the Ugly Sisters she tries to tolerate their bullying by telling herself:

> CINDERELLA:
> Never mind, Cinderella,
> Kind Cinderella—
>
> ...
> Nice good nice kind good nice— (11)

Cinderella feels the pressure felt especially by girls—boys are allowed to misbehave more—of society's demand that they be unfailingly nice, even when they are not treated well. Nice is simply pretending nothing is wrong. As Red Ridinghood sings after her encounter with the Wolf, "Nice is different than good" (35). In her song "Last Midnight" the Witch adopts the role of truth-teller.

> WITCH:
> I'm the hitch,
> I'm what no-one believes,
> I'm the witch. (121)

In this lyric Sondheim recognizes that it is the villain who often states uncomfortable truths that the heroes are all too nice to mention. It is the Witch who, in her earlier song "Lament" faces the uncomfortable fact that "Children can only grow / From something you love / To something you lose" (106).

The Baker is similarly disgusted and runs off into the woods. He has reached a point of total disillusionment as he sings "No More," a song in which the character tries to opt out of responsibility: "No more questions. / Please" (123). As the Baker wanders in the woods, his father reappears. He is not dead after all, but instead has come to help him. But rather than helping his son out of his difficulties by giving him props, this time he gives advice. He suggests that the Baker should run away with him. But the Baker's father is not seriously suggesting this; instead he is making the Baker understand that he is abandoning his baby son, just as he himself was abandoned as a baby. This scene echoes the scene in *Carousel*, where Billy, who has committed suicide, sees from the afterlife his daughter growing up without a father. "Something like what happened to you, when you was a kid, ain't it?" says the Starkeeper. It is also reminiscent of the song "Come Home" in *Allegro*, where the ghost of the hero's mother returns in act 2 to call her son back to where he can practice his true vocation of medicine. *Into the Woods* is perhaps Sondheim's most Rodgers and Hammerstein-like show, the only one that offers explicit morals, and the only one where the community's final celebration of together-ness is not undercut by irony, as it most definitely is in Sondheim's next show, *Assassins*. Even the togetherness expressed in the finale of *A Funny Thing Happened on the Way to the Forum* is that of a theatrical troupe reminding you that there are no morals, you have simply been watching a comedy.

The Baker realizes that his father is right, so he goes back to rejoin the group and begins to look after his son. The survivors finally learn to work together and kill the Giant although this in itself is morally ambiguous. Little Red Ridinghood says that the Giant's widow is a person and they should learn to show forgiveness. And the Giant's widow does have some justification for what she is doing: her husband was killed by Jack. But Jack is not really a murderer, just a simpleton who blundered into an adventure (and the male Giant had been planning to eat Jack for lunch). The group must choose: either Jack or the Giant's widow dies. No literary *deus ex machina* will rescue them now. In this the show resembles *The Wizard of Oz*, where Dorothy and her companions realize that the Wizard is a fake whose only gift is to enable them to believe in themselves. Dorothy and her friends are the ones who work together to defeat the Witch, although the film shows Dorothy killing the Witch by accident, so the heroine is free of any blood guilt. *Into the Woods*, on the other hand, doesn't give the characters any easy way out. They must make a moral choice and live with the consequences.

After the Giant's widow is killed, Cinderella's Prince arrives and Cinderella tells him she is leaving him: "My father's house was a nightmare. Your house was a dream. Now I want something in-between" (128). This time her desire to live "in between" isn't an avoidance of making decisions; it is the opposite. Now Cinderella wants to live somewhere away from the slavery of her past or the fantasy of the Prince's palace—to live somewhere where she will live her own life. Cinderella then shows her compassion to Little Red Ridinghood by singing "No-one Is Alone" (another echo of *Carousel* and its anthem "You'll Never Walk Alone") after Little Red Ridinghood discovers that her grandmother is dead. This could be seen as wishful thinking; many people are alone, but the song is really saying that no one *need* be alone.

> BAKER, CINDERELLA:
> People make mistakes,
> Holding to their own,
> Thinking they're alone. (131)

How much the characters have learned can be shown when we compare their intentions at the beginning with their intentions at the end. At the end of the first scene they sing:

> ALL:
> To see—
> To sell—
> To get—
> To bring—
> To make—
> To lift—
> To go to the Festival—! (21)

In the final song they sing:

ALL:
To mind,
To heed,
To find,
To think,
To teach,
To join,
To go to the Festival! (138)

They are no longer just out for what they can get.

The show's final number is "Children Will Listen." Previously the Witch had sung that children won't listen as a bitter lament for Rapunzel, who had disobeyed her, and been crushed by the Giant. Now she sings that they will listen; not necessarily when you tell them what to do, but they will listen when you tell them stories. They may also listen when you don't want them to: they will listen to how you act, and how you are. As the Witch adds, "Careful the tale you tell. / *That* is the spell" (136). In this show, the morals are mostly for the parents.

Family is a central theme in Sondheim's work, albeit the families in his shows are usually provisional. With the Jets in *West Side Story* ("You got brothers around, / You're a family man"[10]), Rose's theatrical troupe in *Gypsy*, Erronius's cry of "I get a family"[11] at the end of *A Funny Thing Happened on the Way to the Forum*, the less-than-cosy domesticity of Sweeney Todd with Mrs. Lovett and Toby, Dot's assertion that the two things that matter most are "Children and Art." Even in the assassins' encouragement of Lee Harvey Oswald to kill Kennedy, as "We're your family…,"[12] we can see how family has always been a major concept in Sondheim's work. Although many of these families are sick or warped, Sondheim never attacks the underlying idea of family; rather he acknowledges the need for family relationships as so fundamental that people may be drawn into a bad family rather than do without one altogether. He has written, "To be part of a collaboration is to be part of a family, and…every new show provides me with one. It may be a temporary family, but it always gives me a solid sense of belonging to something outside of myself."[13]

Both the Witch and Jack's Mother are single parents and, by the end of the show, Jack's Mother and Red Ridinghood's Granny are dead, the Witch has lost Rapunzel, and the Baker has become a father but has lost his Wife. Yet in the finale the dead characters reappear and the Baker's Wife sings, "No-one leaves for good" (135). Again, this echoes *Carousel* and the Heavenly Friend's remark to Billy that, "As long as there is one person who remembers you, it isn't over." *Into the Woods* doesn't make any guesses one way or another about an afterlife, but does assert, along with *Carousel*, that even though people die, we remember them and they still help us live.

We see the Baker trying to calm his son by telling him the story of what has happened: "Once upon a time…in a far-off kingdom…lived a young maiden…" (136).

Like the Narrator, he is both storyteller and father, but he doesn't pretend, as the Narrator did, to be outside the story while simultaneously entering it in disguise. Instead he starts to tell the tale hesitantly, feeling unsure of himself. But it is by telling stories that man preserves his creativity and the truth as he sees it.

Just what happens if we tell the wrong stories is dealt with in Sondheim's next show. *Assassins* is full of people who believed that something good was going to happen to them, and who cannot get over the fact that they are being ignored. Sam Byck's embittered refrain: "Yeah, it's never gonna happen, / Is it?"[14] reminds us of the irresponsible foolishness of pretending to children that they will have everything they wish for. The Balladeer in *Assassins* represents the voice of official morality, just as the Narrator does in *Into the Woods*; in *Assassins*, as in *Into the Woods*, the characters rebel and force him off stage.

But *Into the Woods* reminds us that even if there is constant disillusion you need not lose your nerve. If many shows enchant you without ever bringing you back to reality, Sondheim and Lapine do the opposite, showing their characters learning to tell stories in order to cope with disenchantment. In doing this they show the audience how to do the same: how to choose the spell they cast.

NOTES

1. Bruno Bettelheim, *The Uses of Enchantment* (London: Thames and Hudson, 1976; reprinted Harmondsworth: Penguin, 1991), 3. Page references are to the Penguin edition.
2. "Waiting for the Girls Upstairs," collected in Stephen Sondheim, *Finishing the Hat: Collected Lyrics (1954–1981) with Attendant Comments, Principles, Heresies, Grudges, Whines, and Anecdotes* (New York: Virgin), 207.
3. Bruno Bettelheim put forward a similar idea in *The Uses of Enchantment*, a book that is often supposed to have inspired Sondheim and Lapine, though in fact both men were hostile to Bettelheim's strictly Freudian readings of the stories; see Stephen Sondheim, *Look, I Made A Hat: Collected Lyrics (1981–2011) with Attendant Comments, Amplifications, Dogmas, Harangues, Digressions, Anecdotes and Miscellany* (New York: Virgin, 2011), 58. Lapine in particular is more drawn to a Jungian view of fairy tales as expressions of a collective unconscious. See Lapine's play *Twelve Dreams* (New York: Nelson Doubleday,1982.)
4. Stephen Sondheim and James Lapine, *Into the Woods* (New York: Theatre Communications Group, 1989). Unless otherwise stated all quotations from the text are taken from this edition.
5. Thematically this show is closest to *A Little Night Music*: both take place in enchanted landscapes full of shimmering light and menacing shadows where, "Perpetual sunset / Is rather an unset- / Tling thing." (*A Little Night Music* collected in *Finishing the Hat*, 272) Both shows deal with morally ambiguous enchanters (Mme. Armfeldt, the Witch) and both contain a duet where two vain, preening men have a verbal duel ("It Would Have Been Wonderful," "Agony").
6. Sondheim, *Look, I Made a Hat*, 58.
7. They notice the Narrator just after he has said to the audience: "It is interesting to examine the moral issue at question here. The finality of stories such as these dictates—" (102) In other words, The Narrator is killed when he stops being a storyteller and starts to be a critic.
8. Sondheim, *Look, I Made a Hat*, 58.
9. This line does not appear in the libretto, but does appear in Sondheim, *Look, I Made a Hat*, 70.
10. *West Side Story*, collected in Sondheim, *Finishing the Hat*, 31.

11. Collected in Sondheim, *Finishing the Hat*, 108.
12. Collected in Sondheim, *Look, I Made a Hat*, 138.
13. Sondheim, *Finishing the Hat*, 30.
14. Sondheim, *Look, I Made a Hat*, 135.

PART VI

SONDHEIM, IDENTITY, AND SOCIETY

CHAPTER 23

KEEPING COMPANY WITH
SONDHEIM'S WOMEN

STACY ELLEN WOLF

THERE's much company to be found among the women in *Company*.[1] Sondheim's female characters, in this groundbreaking 1970 ensemble musical about a bachelor's encounters with five married couples and three girlfriends, occupy a striking range of types within one show.[2] From the bitter, acerbic, thrice-married Joanne to the reluctant bride-to-be Amy, and from the self-described "dumb" "stewardess" April to the intense, free-spirited Marta, *Company*'s eight women are distillations of femininity, intensely sketched in the short, singular scenes in which they appear.[3] This chapter examines the eight women in *Company*, what they do in the musical and how they function in the show's dramaturgy. I argue that Sondheim's women in this musical elicit the quintessential challenge of analyzing musical theater from a feminist perspective, because the characters tend to be stereotypically, even misogynistically, portrayed but the actor has tremendous performance opportunities in portraying complicated psychologies through rich music and engaging lyrics.[4]

Critical conversations about *Company* have coalesced around a series of extraordinarily interesting if predictable topics: the groundbreaking status of this fragmented, nonlinear, non-character-driven, thematically oriented musical; the four differently inflected final songs that were attempted at points in the production process and the decision to use "Being Alive," which lent the show a more optimistic conclusion than Sondheim desired; the question of Bobby's sexuality, which a later version of the script attempted to clarify by installing a scene in which he admits to having had sex with a man, states for the record that he is not gay, and deflects Peter's pass at him; the complementary theme of dehumanization in the urban landscape, which makes human connections and the possibility of a successful marriage all the more difficult; the question of the musical's "reality" —that is, whether the characters are real or in Bobby's head; and the ever-present question of the musical's revivability, the dilemma that all productions need to tackle, given the 1970s specificity of its setting and its rock-oriented musical style.[5]

Company's emotional and sociological "argument" about marriage has also settled into an interpretation that accepts a position of ambivalence.[6] As Sondheim said early on, the husbands' number, "Sorry-Grateful," sums up *Company*'s message about marriage: it's difficult, complicated, and necessary. The artistic team wanted the audience to laugh their heads off for two hours and then not be able to sleep. No doubt most continue to find the musical's withering portrait of marriage upsetting, but *Company* reinforces the importance of marriage even as it criticizes it. Not only is Robert not gay, but he can't remain happily single. The palpable, perhaps pathetic desire of the three single women to marry underlines this polemic. The decisive ending that situates Robert as having grown and matured merely caps off an evening that never offers an alternative way of being. In this way, however radical *Company* may have seemed (or still seems) to mainstream audiences because it articulates a critique of marriage, the musical hardly supports an innovative model of social affairs.

Whatever the ideological project of *Company*, it remains a musical; that is, an intensely collaborative performance form that communicates meaning and feeling through song and dance, speech and bodies on stage. *Company* is at once a historical artifact of 1970 and a performance text that shifts with each remounting. Every discussion of this (or any) musical relies on "texts" that the author temporarily and strategically renders stable for the purpose of being able to say something. These texts or archival materials include (but are not limited to) published script and libretto, score, cast album, taped versions, reviews that describe the show, interviews and other commentary in the popular press, scholarly analyses across the disciplines of theater studies, musicology, literary studies, and cultural history, plus extensive primary materials (what we typically consider "archives") and, of course, one's experience seeing or working on the musical. Any one of these texts or a combination would facilitate a different interpretation of the musical. So even as I want to analyze and offer a reading of *Company*'s women, I simultaneously want to attend to the musical's various texts and foreground the inherent instability of musical theater's objects. In other words, it's not merely the passage of time that makes it impossible to declare *Company* "revivable" or not, but that the multiple texts that comprise "*Company*" suggest different, varied, and potentially contradictory routes to interpretation. Moreover, these texts are constantly being remade by artists who (re)produce and (re)perform the show, by critics who comment on it, and by scholars who analyze it. The "women" of *Company* never stand still.[7]

Company's women, like those in many of Sondheim's musicals, defy many stereotypes of female characters in musical theater, in part because they are quirky, often unlikable characters, in part because Sondheim's music is more aurally challenging than that of Rodgers, Loewe, or Loesser and so defies clear characterization, and in part because these musicals eschew "Golden Age" structural conventions that delimit what women can do. Women in traditional musicals fall into two basic types: feisty women who fall for their men and troubled women who fall for their men.[8] Because the plots of most mid- to late twentieth-century musicals are built around the formation of a heterosexual couple, many female characters—Laurey and Ado Annie in *Oklahoma!* (1943), Marion in *The Music Man* (1957), Charity in *Sweet Charity* (1966), Audrey in *Little Shop of Horrors*

(1982)—are primarily concerned with getting and keeping a man, even though their first step is typically avoidance.[9] Sondheim's musicals, in contrast, invariably include heterosexual couples in the cast of characters, but eschew romantic simplicity and matrimonial happiness. As Laura Hanson argues, his female characters express "doubts and ambivalences" as they try to "sort out, through song, their conflicting feelings towards love, marriage, men, their own self-images, and the pursuit of their dreams."[10]

The women of *Company* established "grown up" expectations for Sondheim's oeuvre, emerging in 1970, when "'women's lib' was on everyone's lips."[11] In the first few months of the year, notes historian Sara Evans, "substantial stories on the women's liberation movement appeared in virtually every major journal and broadcast network."[12] Just around when *Company* opened, what became major classic feminist works were published, including Shulamith Firestone's *Dialectics of Sex*, Kate Millett's *Sexual Politics*, and Robin Morgan's *Sisterhood is Powerful*.[13] As Evans explains, "The power of the women's movement lay in its capacity to stimulate such deep rethinking, to pose, as a problem, concepts such as femininity and motherhood, relationships previously taken for granted. Most Americans, both male and female . . . were not converted. They were angry, defensive, confused, but they were thinking about gender nonetheless."[14] Although neither Sondheim nor his collaborators (nor the characters in the musical) were radical feminists, the issues were in the air.

Like much of mainstream America in 1970, *Company* equivocates, at once valorizing women and demeaning them. First, the very project of *Company*—scrutiny of marriage and the conclusion that it's both terrible and necessary—emerges from a masculine perspective, which is especially interesting since Furth originally conceived of a series of seven (nonmusical) scenes about marriage, starring Kim Stanley.[15] However Bobby's friends comment on, critique, and fret about extended bachelorhood, he's still attractive and desirable, and suffers nothing like the still-present spinster image that haunts unmarried women. The story puts the women in the position of being judged: the single women as potential wives and the married women as unattainable fantasies. The narrative itself, then, objectifies women. On the other hand, *Company* figures the women more vibrantly than the men, with the differences among them more sharply defined. The women sing more songs and more memorable ones; audiences especially remember Marta, Amy, and Joanne.

Critics' responses to *Company* reveal an anxiety about women's visibility and vitality in the show. In his review in the *New York Times*, for example, Walter Kerr clearly identifies with husband Harry, describing Sarah as "looking like one of those marshmallow chickens you find in Easter basket . . . Miss [Barbara] Barrie has a magnificent [karate] chop, and is otherwise admirable, if a good girl to stay away from."[16] He calls the single women "wenches of no particular character," although it's impossible to confuse the clearly contrasting threesome, and sums up Amy and Paul's conflict by trivializing her contribution versus his: they "cannot get along because he is too loving while she burns the toast."[17] Clive Barnes, in his *Times* review, criticized the characters' simultaneous recognizability and unlikeability, writing that "these people are just the kind of people you expend hours each day trying to escape from. They are, virtually without exception—perhaps the airline stewardess wasn't too bad—trivial, shallow, worthless, and horrid."[18] If he tolerates April, whose name he fails to mention, Barnes admits of the actors, "I liked the whole cast, the men perhaps more than the women."[19] Kerr agrees that "they're not a bunch you'd care to save, or even spend a weekend with," but the examples of characters he names whom he doesn't like ("On the whole I had difficulty in—what do you call it?—empathizing") are all women.[20]

In addition, each couple's scene, except for the penultimate one with Joanne, Harry, and Robert in a bar, takes place in the couple's home, and usually the living room, even as the design avoids excessive detailed "living room" set pieces. The domestic setting resonates in several ways. First, it links *Company* to the long history of modern "drawing room dramas" beginning with Ibsen's *A Doll's House* (1879) and Chekhov's *Three Sisters* (1901), where intimate emotional scenarios are played out in private domestic spaces. Unlike Ibsen's plays, though, which offer detailed psychologizing, explanatory family histories, and a late point of attack in the plot, *Company*'s brief, unconnected scenes begin in the middle of the action, even in the middle of a conversation. *Company* is interested in characters in snapshots, and Mark Eden Horowitz, who supports the oft-cited reading of the musical as entirely in Bobby's head, argues that every song comprises snippets of conversations that he remembers. Every scene, every song, Horowitz observes, seems to answer a question that the audience hasn't heard Bobby ask.[21] Furth's dialogue provides neither backstory nor an overall conflict with rising action, but like the modern masters, Furth uses everyday conversation to convey middle-class conflict in a culture in crisis. Setting the scenes at home also crystallizes struggles over the meaning of home and domesticity around 1970, when women's liberation was becoming part of mainstream society: do the women have jobs outside the home? Do the men see the home as their castle? *Company* doesn't answer.

The innovative structure of the musical—a series of vignettes, woven together by Robert's often quiet or passive presence—at once enhances and challenges women's presence in *Company*, since the audience's knowledge of and relationship with each woman is extremely limited.[22] With the exception of Joanne, who leads "The Little Things You Do Together" near the beginning and sings "Ladies Who Lunch" near the end—songs that articulate key ideas and emotions—each woman in *Company* appears in only one solo or book scene, plus one of two female group numbers: the wives' quintet, "Poor Baby," or "You Could Drive a Person Crazy," the single women's trio. The women also participate in the ensemble numbers that thread through the musical, although the stage directions imply that the actors come out of role to play members of the "company." As in any musical, a character with a solo number has the better chance to imprint herself on the audience's memory; when she sings alone, she gathers focus and presents her perspective. The musical's vignette structure upends the traditional book musical's convention of psychological change, so a woman's one solo—her first and last—combines the standard "I want" song with every other emotional expression.

While *Company*'s fragmented structure has rightly garnered it the label of "revue" from both scholars and Sondheim himself, and while the musical indeed lacks a linear story, such a designation fails to account for the time-bound experience of spectatorship, wherein the sense of time passing allows spectators to compose (or impose) narratives onto events that follow one another.[23] Spectators make links between and among scenes, constructing characters' development as we see them in different scenes or songs over the course of the show. Interestingly, Sondheim himself perceived the songs in performance order when he composed the score in that order (except for "You Could Drive a Person Crazy"). Even if the scenes are disconnected and no character development is portrayed, the audience has a journey, if a short one, with each character, who becomes crystallized, singular, and unique, if a type. In what follows, I discuss the songs and scenes in order here to evoke how the audience engages with the show, takes in information, and is moved emotionally over time.

Company opens with the sound of recorded messages left on Robert's answering machine, at once announcing the musical's contemporary setting and allowing each character's message to leave an impression of her relationship with Robert. Marta's, for example, "Yo, Bob...Long time no hear. Well, the doctor said false alarm, I'm not pregnant. So, hey, you can feel free to return my calls again, huh?" (4).[24] In one short line, the audience learns that they may have had unprotected sex, which would have had dramatic implications in 1970—three years before Roe v. Wade legalized abortion—and that he's been avoiding her.

The first couple's book scene (act 1, scene 2) finds Sarah and Harry both trying to break addictions: he claims that he's stopped drinking, and she is on a diet. They chat, with Sarah and Harry contradicting each other's every word, and they ply Robert with the tastes they desire—bourbon and brownies—which they also sneak when he's not looking. The scene signals how Robert is the object of displacement and projection for the married folks.[25] Robert demurs sweetly, and the already-combative conversation moves to the karate lessons that Sarah as been taking, and Harry scoffs, "All those fat broads in her gym learning karate. What wouldn't you give to see that"? (25), and she replies, "Strangely enough, darling, I'm terribly good at it" (25). He insists on giving it a go, and Sarah repels two of his three attacks, throwing him to the floor, and once he manages to pin her, to cry "uncle, my ass!" The karate "dance" takes the form of a back-and-forth argument. In the final moment of the scene, after Robert exits, each again succumbs to the preoccupying temptation of the scene: Harry helps himself to a drink and Sarah eats a brownie. Their disciplined behavior in front of Robert was pure performance.

Sarah and Harry's battle is punctuated by Joanne's first number when she enters the stage, typically on a level above the action, and she observes them fighting. "The Little Things You Do Together" introduces the musical's convention of commentary songs, of nonrealist staging, and of a musical number broken up with verses interspersed with book scene. A perky, ironic summary of marriage, the number sets up early *Company*'s bitingly humorous tone and unromantic perspective. As Sarah and Harry almost kill each other, Joanne outlines the "little things" that "make perfect relationships" in lines that rhyme internally and end with "together" over and over in an obviously sarcastic mantra. The first line tends to be something positive that couples "do together": "The little ways you try together," but the next line is a bit troubling: "Neighbors you annoy together," and then the lyrics take a turn: "Children you destroy together, / That keep marriage intact" (28). Each verse shifts from a positive pronouncement to something terrible: "Becoming a cliché together, / Growing old and gray together, / Withering away together" (29). All of the couples participate in the song and comment on the violence they witness. Because the lyrics are all about the plural second-person "you," it doesn't distinguish between men and women, and underlines the couple as the social, relational unit in the musical's theatrical world. In addition, the unison bridge of "I do and you don't and nobody said that" tracks the dissolution of a marriage from the wedding ("I do") to accusation ("you don't") to denial ("nobody said that").[26] Joanne's solo lines and her lower-pitched voice reveal more about her edgy sarcastic character than the others': she sings "withering," "getting a divorce together," and "I've done it three or four times." The song, then, functions both to comment on Sarah and Harry's marriage, to generalize about all of the marriages' repressed rage and difficult power struggles, and to express Joanne's cynicism. This first solo is important, as Sondheim said, "Generally, if you want things heard by an audience, it has to be solo or tutti—all together."[27]

The scene's choreography of physical attacks and defenses is at once a hilarious counterpoint to Joanne's commentary and a ridiculously obvious symbolic representation of their marriage's gendered power dynamics. The physicality in this early scene, not evident elsewhere in the musical, implants a violent, if humorous memory for the audience through which to consider the subtext of each couple's interaction through the course of the musical. Harry presumably could overtake Sarah, but he fails, repeatedly. Is she that powerful? Independent? Skilled? The movement suggests she is, and yet, at the song's end, when the characters move back into the scene, Sarah is stereotypically self-deprecating about her looks, and she exits their scene by telling Harry that she loves him, her mouth full of brownie. He doesn't reply, and the scene ends with a sense of her vulnerability and his ultimate power in the relationship. Their game was just a game, but the audience's visual memory of her throwing him to the ground lingers on.[28]

In the next book scene with a nonsolo singing woman (act 1, scene 4), Jenny also caps it off by expressing her love for David as she exits, with this relationship even more unnervingly unbalanced. The scene is divided into two parts by the single women's "You Can Drive a Person Crazy," whose effect spills over to the second part of the scene. Robert witnesses David speak for Jenny, demean her, and misunderstand her, as the three smoke pot and get high, and all the while David claims that Jenny doesn't like it and is a "square." As David barks at her to feed them in their post-high hunger, Jenny (admittedly stoned) cheerfully complies, representing a woman who accepts and normalizes the power differential. There are, of course, other women in Sondheim's musicals who exhibit masochistic tendencies, such as Sally in *Follies*, Charlotte in *A Little Night Music*, and Dot in *Sunday in the Park with George*, but these women are aware of the abuse or neglect. More importantly, each sings—"Losing My Mind," "Every Day a Little Death," and "We Do Not Belong Together," respectively—three of the most beautiful, wrenching, and memorable in Sondheim's repertoire.[29] Although the female character weakly suffers in unrequited or unbalanced love for her man, the actor playing any of these women has the chance to occupy center stage and to garner sympathy for the character and admiration for the performer. Jenny, in contrast, is stranded in *Company*, verbally abused by her husband, oblivious, and without a song to sing her perspective.

The appearance of Marta, April, and Kathy, Bobby's three girlfriends, interrupts the pot-smoking scene. *Company* presents three contrasting types of single women, who, like the married women, reveal different levels of dependence and autonomy through their scenes and songs.[30] If the married women form a triangular relationship with their husbands and Bobby, then the single women do the same with Bobby and New York City, a force to navigate more powerful than a person. Gerald Mast labels them "three sexual flings—a sensualist, a stewardess, and a kook," which says more about his masculinist perspective, even in 1987, than it offers insight into the characters.[31]

Before becoming acquainted with any of the three individually, the audience meets the girlfriends as a unit in "You Can Drive a Person Crazy," an Andrews sisters–style number with close harmonies, a series of doo-doo-doo-doos, solid four-lined verses in rhyming couplets, and structured and repeated verses.[32] Mark Eden Horowitz observes in the "jaunty and playful" tune "aspects that suggest a piece from the 1920s or 30s, particularly in the rhythms," including "the opening *Doo-doo doo-doo*s, with their syncopated downbeat on an eighth note followed by the quarter note on the offbeat."[33] The boppy, light, musical comedy feeling contradicts the venom underneath, as the women try to fathom why Bobby loses interest. The word "person," repeated in almost every line (not unlike the repetition of "together" in "The Little Things You Do Together"), takes on multiple meanings, as the women refer to themselves, to him, and to the commonsense human behavior that seems to elude him. The B section opens with a hilarious condensation, "When a person's personality is personable, / He shouldn't oughta sit like a lump" (42), as they outline his sadistic behavior: "But turning off a person is the act of a man / Who likes to pull the hooks out of fish" (42). They call him "troubled," "a zombie," and "deeply maladjusted, / Never to be trusted" (44), and the song's quick wit turns on the fact that he makes them crazy and that he himself is crazy. The girlish melody opposes the women's well-observed sharpness, their cynical humor, and their barely concealed rage.[34] Vulnerable in their relationships with Robert, whom they all seem to want in spite of his coldness, since he is attractive, good in bed, and evidently neither gay nor dead.

The women are powerful in the funny, angular song. The Andrews sisters' reference supplies another layer of commentary, since the style is a protofeminist throwback while the lyrics are feminist in their forceful critique of Robert's emotional flaws. Finally, the women know they are performing and presenting their perspective to the audience, to whom they bow at the end. They call attention to themselves as actors and make a direct connection with the audience, wink and nod in collusion. The next number (after the scene with Jenny and David ends and the Ensemble repeats a short "Bobby Baby" refrain) is the married men's "Have I Got a Girl for You," where the married men fantasize about wild sexual encounters with girls who are "dumb—and with a weakness for Sazerac slings" (47); with the two different perspectives juxtaposed, the audience might hear the men's version as a corrective to the single women's frustration, or they might judge the men as ill informed about the reality of single women's lives, since the female subjects "speak" before the men objectify them.

The single women's perspectives expand in act 1, scene 5, which features all three of them in scenes with Robert. Marta's solo "Another Hundred People" opens the scene and is interspersed between the spoken dialogue. "Another Hundred People" is the single woman's answer to "Little Things You Do Together"; that is, while "Little Things" encapsulates the essence of marriage in the frankest, scariest way, "Another Hundred People" evokes what it's like to be alone in New York City, with its simultaneous stimulating, exciting intensity and its alienating, lonely anonymity. The lyrics enumerate what one sees when coming up out of the subway, a "city of strangers," "crowded streets and guarded parks," "postered walls with crude remarks" (55). She stages how one tries to make plans, to connect with people: "And they meet at parties through the friends of friends / Who they never know," leave messages, change arrangements. Because the lyrics repeat verbatim several times over the course of the song, the audience can recall the image of the relentless throngs of "another hundred people" who "just got off of the train" who "are looking around," who "are looking at us" (54).

The number's music, like the lyrics, captures the double-edged sense of the city. Energetic and driving in the first section ("Another hundred people..."), but minor and despairing when she sings "city of strangers," and then shifting again to an optimistic sound in "find each other in the crowded streets," the song expresses the sense of needing to harness one's resources over and over, gearing up and reenergizing to face the city's assaults and pleasures. The song provides an accurate commentary on daily life. As Sondheim said, "If I'm not writing a kind of standard thirty-two bar song say, where I want the melodic line to be fairly even and strike the mind as a melodic line—I will use rhythms according to the rhythm in the inflection of the speech...It's to echo the rhythm of how we talk."[35] When Marta speaks in the book scene that follows the song, she expresses a similar intensity of phrasing if a less ambivalent message.

What Clive Barnes described in 1970 as "Sondheim's most perfect and imaginative song,"[36] provides a powerful moment for the performer, and while the lyrics are not explicitly gendered, it locates the single woman singer as a tough New York adventurer. Walter Kerr was impressed but also (again) undone by a woman occupying a strong place on stage. In his review, he said that Pamela Myers, as Marta, "looks like a bullet and sings like a subway rail, but we see her long enough...to be bowled over by the brass-band bravura of her 'Another Hundred People.' "[37]

April is equally memorable in two scenes and a song with Robert that reinforce the stereotype of the "dumb stewardess" but also grant the actor ample stage time. The first girlfriend in the park bench scene who outlines her relationship to New York, April explains to Robert that she grew up in Ohio and wanted to live in Radio City. "I thought it was a wonderful little city near New York. So I came here. I'm very dumb" (51).[38] Each line of April's is ditzier than the next, but the scene ends with a twist: Robert asks April what she and her male roommate will do if one gets married, and without missing a beat, she answers, "Get a bigger place, I guess" (52). Unlike Robert, who is bound by convention, April can imagine a different kind of living arrangement, which anticipates collective households in the future. Perhaps April is not as dumb as she seems.[39]

Kathy's scene in the park with Robert (again, between verses of "Another Hundred People") suggests that part of his lack of a mate might have to do with timing and serendipity. Longtime friends, Kathy and Robert once had crushes on each other but at different times. Kathy meets with Robert to tell him that she's getting married and that she's leaving New York. Decidedly unromantic, Kathy is ready to move onto the next stage of her life. Like most of the women in *Company*, Kathy can be interpreted in two ways. On the one hand, she is the one who got away, who proves that Robert can be rejected as well as reject, and who makes a mature life choice: "I want real things now. A husband, a family. I don't want to keep running around this city like I'm having a life" (54). On the other hand, her decision seems a defeat, a too-conventional choice because she was waiting for Robert to propose marriage. "But, see," she says, "it [New York] and I, we just don't fit. I think there's a time to come to New York and a time to leave, Enjoy your party" (54). The tone of this scene and the audience's perception of Kathy very much depend on the actor's interpretation and performance.[40]

Marta's extended book scene with Bobby follows the song, and she raves about why she loves New York, why she is New York, and explains her philosophy by using her fist to represent Bobby's very tight asshole.[41] As Marta sets out her position, the audience comes to realize that the singer of "Another Hundred People" reveals more ambivalence about New York that the speaking Marta. Two readings surface here. On the one hand, perhaps the form of a musical number allows a general commentary on the single girl's life in the city; just as the song toggles back and forth between effervescence and despair, Marta sings the perspective of all Single Girls, including April, Kathy, and herself. On the other hand, perhaps the mode of music enables the character to access deeper, mixed feelings that she won't share with Robert in unmusicalized speech, despite her assertion of absolute honesty and directness. Either way, the discrepancy between the song and the scene creates a schism or a gap and adds a layer onto the character of Marta, an aspect that neither Bobby nor the audience can completely access, explain, or explain away. The fierce representation of the Single Girl sidesteps complete knowability.

The gender balance shifts with Amy's tour-de-force solo, "Not Getting Married," and the woman steals the scene. The number is the hilarious, frantic expression of a woman with cold feet at the last minute, but with a perfectly reasonable fear of losing her autonomy and individuality and a persuasive, feminist critique of monogamy. She calls a wedding "a prehistoric ritual / Where everybody promises fidelity forever, / Which is maybe the most horrifying word I've ever heard" (59). The lyrics move at breakneck speed and the music revolves in a melodic whirling dervish as Amy spins herself into hysteria.[42] The song reveals that Amy sees a therapist—less discussed in 1970s—and that she's contemplating suicide, as she tells her therapist, "by Monday I'll be floating / In the Hudson with the other garbage" (60). After the song, Robert actually *does* something in this scene: he proposes to Amy, "Marry me! And everybody'll leave us alone!" It clicks, and she responds, "Thank you, Robert...it's just that you have to want to marry *some*body, not just some*body*" (68). Like Joanne's proposition near the end of the musical that pushes Robert to sing "Being Alive," his absurd offer to Amy pushes her down the aisle.

"Not Getting Married" is complicated in *Company*'s performative project. On the one hand, Amy expresses a resistance to marriage more typically associated with men, a pleasant detour from a woman's stereotypical obsession with getting married. On the other hand, the song is so silly that her reluctance is never credible or sincere, and the scene that follows, where she quickly and anxiously exits to look for Paul, undercuts the power of the song's statement. Although the character believes that she is serious, and she chases Paul away when she tells him that she doesn't love "him enough," and even Robert finds her credible, the audience knows that she will return to Paul in due time, even if she hurts his feelings along the way. The song and scene's trajectory undermines the character's strength and suggests that women don't know their own minds, since Paul, as it turns out, was right all along. The musical supports his puppy dog affection more than her uncertainty. For the performer, though, this song is without a doubt a winner, a fantastic opportunity for an actor to spit out words and act up a storm.[43]

The single women reappear in act 2, scene 2, April's sex scene and "Barcelona." Even though Bobby presumably has a lot of sex with a lot of women (and men?), *Company* stages an encounter with the least intelligent among his three girlfriends to ensure that the audience won't confuse fun sex with love or commitment.[44] As April and Robert have sex, the five married women comment with "Poor Baby," a mournful, funny, almost dissonant dirge. The number casts the women as pathetic, catty, and nasty, as they over react to his girlfriends and to his bachelorhood. The wives are deluded, since they have no idea how Robert's life actually works, which the audience sees. He may be lonely but he is hardly "staring at the walls and playing solitaire" (88). The degree to which they exaggerate his solitude points to an undercurrent of their own desires for sexual freedom and unencumbered adventures. The number parallels the married men's "Have I Got a Girl for You," but while the men want to be Robert, the women want to have him. "Poor Baby," in the end, ridicules the married women for their misperceptions and diminishes the audience's empathy for them (Figure 23.1).[45]

"Barcelona," then, is a dark little duet, the closest thing to a love song that *Company* proffers, an enactment of a scene that Bobby no doubt plays out countless times, and among the few noncommentary, nondiegetic songs in the score. Not quite a pastiche, "Barcelona" echoes folk songs of the time, like the Byrds' "Turn, Turn, Turn" (1965), the Mamas and the Papas's "Monday, Monday" (1966). The light Latin feeling, which Sondheim uses frequently in this musical to suggest urban sophistication and sensuality, also evokes where April is going. The words are banal, conversational, and repetitive, and the accompaniment mostly consists of two chords. The song's punch line hinges on Robert's misreading of April. When they finish having sex, he is ready for her to leave and merely feigns interest and affection, assuming she'll simply go to work as planned, but she surprises him by changing her mind.[46]

FIGURE **23.1** Barbara Barrie, Terri Ralston, Merle Louise, Beth Howland, and Elaine Stritch sing "Poor Baby" in *Company* (1970).

APRIL: Oh well, I guess okay.
ROBERT: [spoken] What?
APRIL: I'll stay.
ROBERT: [spoken] But... (*As she snuggles down*) Oh, god. (*Blackout*) (99–100)

He sings, "Oh god" on the same notes as "okay" and "I'll stay." He is stunned and stuck with her: it's not what he planned. The scene and the song announce that Bobby isn't quite as slick as he seems, that even the most practiced bachelor can't control all women, not even the ones who seem to be "dumb." The encounter, though, also makes her the butt of the joke, oblivious to the contract of their liaison.[47]

After this scene, *Company* moves to the second scene with Peter and Susan. She is the third nonsolo-singing woman who presents a completely negative view of marriage, but she too, is disempowered in the book scenes. She and Peter have decided to divorce but not separate and they are both the happier for it. In this late scene, which includes Marta, who is amused by the couple's blissful divorce, Susan and Peter present an agreeable, unified front. "We're so much more married now than when we were married," Peter crows (101). Only when the two women leave for the kitchen does he open the conversation with Robert about gay relationships and not so subtly proposition him.[48] This brief scene works dramaturgically to "prove" Robert's decisive heterosexuality, but Peter's expansive confession—"sometimes you meet somebody and you just love the crap out of them. Y'know?" (102)—and his thrill in imagining gay relationships highlights that Susan can't fulfill his desires, whether they're married, divorced, living together, or not. Indirectly but surely, the scene diminishes her value, first, by secrecy: although they're no longer married, Peter can't tell Susan that he is attracted to men; she must leave the room for him to confess his feelings to Robert. Second, the scene reveals something complex about Peter that *Company* doesn't offer to the woman in kind. Susan, like Sarah and Jenny, is denied both the musical opportunity to sing her feelings and a revelation book scene like her husband's. Although the character says she is happy, the audience knows what she lacks.

The musical moves to the setting of a private club for the penultimate scene with Joanne, who is not only the female center of this musical, but also the "voice" of *Company*, the commentator, the one who knows this society, marriage, and Robert, too. If Bobby is *Company*'s subject and object, then Joanne is its performative speech act, whose saying—"When are we going to make it? . . . I'll take care of you"—becomes a doing: the simultaneous promise and threat that propel Bobby into self-disclosure and the real possibility of change. From the start, Joanne stands out from the other women because she is older, richer, multiply married, and she talks about it. Joanne's two numbers bookend the show and present the first and last word on society, marriage, and gender, and the most honest and most cynical perspective on the life project the musical explores.[49] The scene opens with Robert and Joanne watching Larry dance, as Joanne scowls at her husband, "I only dance when you can touch. I don't think standing around and making an ass out of oneself is a dance. I find it unbelievably humiliating watching my own husband flouncing around the dance floor, jerking and sashaying all over the place like Ann Miller. Take off the red shoes, Larry. Off" (105). Larry, meanwhile, enjoys himself and Robert praises his dancing, but Joanne is drinking and is drunk, "Betty Friedan with a vodka stinger."[50] Critic Walter Kerr finds her "at a table measuring pickups through heart-of-stone eyes."[51] After a waiter delivers yet another round of drinks, "lights fade on the nightclub," and Joanne "raises the glass again and sings to the audience" (106).

Joanne's last number, "The Ladies Who Lunch," takes up the bitter, sharply observant perspective of her earlier number in a stylized extension of her conversation with Robert.[52] Yet this song is not specifically about men or about marriage but enacts the toll wealthy passivity takes on women's psyches. This Joanne is Martha in Albee's *Who's Afraid of Virginia Woolf?* (1962, film 1966), smart and powerless, alcohol unleashing the rage that simmers barely beneath the well-coiffed surface. Like Martha, Joanne sees that men, even lazy, mediocre, and not very smart men, have access to power and influence. Women, though, are doomed to few choices. They can obsess about their bodies, going "off to the gym, / Then to a fitting, / Claiming they're fat"; or accrue cultural and intellectual capital, "rushing to their classes in optical art," taking in "a matinee, a Pinter play"; or play the perfect housewife and mother, "keeping house but clutching a copy of Life," and "meet[ing] themselves at the schools" (106–7). Joanne, no doubt having tried and tired of all of those lives, opts to "just watch," which gives her "another chance to disapprove, /

Another brilliant zinger, / Another reason not to move," as she washes down her frustration in "another vodka stinger" (107).[53] This brutal, half-sung, half-spoken bossa nova enunciates the fury of a rich but impotent woman.

After the song, Joanne propositions Robert, not for marriage, but for an affair. Oddly, this gesture pushes him to assert that he is ready to be committed. She says she will take care of him and he answers ingenuously, "But who will I take care of?" Joanne compels Bobby's instantaneous transformation, and she recognizes and encourages the change. "Did you hear what you just said, kiddo?" she says, "I just heard a door open that's been stuck for a long time" (111). Yet this climactic turn in *Company*, from a feminist perspective, cuts both ways. On the one hand, she compels his self-realization; on the other hand, the self-knowledge comes from his unhesitating, unthinking rejection of her. The moment is a plot device and the older, desexualized woman the necessary pawn to enable the man's emotional growth. She is even pleased with herself: "I just did someone a big favor," she tells Larry (111). The focus of the scene quickly shifts away from her and toward him and his newly articulated readiness for intimacy.[54] She, meanwhile, seems unfazed by his sexual rebuff and quickly moves into Ensemble mode to encourage him in the spoken lines in "Being Alive."

Critics of the 1970 production admired Elaine Stritch's pitch-perfect performance. Walter Kerr, for example, observed that Joanne "stands alone in the group in making no pretty pretenses about the pleasures of matrimony," but "we are still not prepared for what happens to us and what happens to the theater when she reaches a left-field snarl, complete with a snappy, snide foot-tap called 'The Ladies Who Lunch.'" Stritch "spends a good bit of the evening inhaling cigarette smoke; what smoke she exhales during the song I don't know, but it is hers alone and it is scathing. A great number, perfectly done."[55] Male critics could take some comfort not being the target of Joanne's ire, even as they failed to see the feminist future whose need Sondheim and his collaborators somehow articulated.

Joanne's scathing attack on the very women who sat in the audience of *Company* became the musical's iconic moment as much as if not more than the ending. Stritch's characterization thereafter ghosted the role, and every later Joanne was compared to her, even if favorably.[56] For example, David Rooney in *Variety* praised Barbara Walsh, in John Doyle's production, as "bone-dry as brittle, world-weary Joanne. She reveals the emotional hunger beneath the character's hard shell and adds fresh nuances to 'The Ladies Who Lunch,' a song indelibly associated with Elaine Stritch."[57] Wendy Smith compared the two as well: "When Elaine Stritch sang 'The Ladies Who Lunch,' a sneering, self-loathing song was bearable, even thrilling, because her whiskey-drenched, cigarette-stained rendition recalled generations of Broadway divas. Barbara Walsh gave the lyric every syllable of its meaning in a chilling, honorable effort; as Doyle staged it, the audience wasn't even allowed to relieve the agony by clapping at the end."[58]

Walsh can re-embody and re-envoice Joanne, which gets to the heart of performance: each actor makes the role her own. Walsh's body, voice, interpretation, and inflections put a slightly different spin on the character—as do the actors who play Amy, Susan, Sarah, Jenny, Marta, Kathy, and April—situated within a unique production at a certain historical moment. And yet, *Company*'s very premise is a masculinist one, the privilege of a man in 1970 who might yet choose to remain single. That *Company* meant something different in 2006 than it did in 1995 or 1970, and that future productions will take on new meanings is due in no small part to changing gender roles in American society and contemporary women actors' determination to inflect their characters with agency. *Company* will always present such gendered contradictions.

NOTES

1. Thanks to the students in "The Musical Theatre of Stephen Sondheim" seminar in spring 2010 for their remarkable work. Thanks, too, to Marty Elliott for useful conversations about singing Sondheim, to Liz Wollman, who read *Company* material in the context of my book, and to Ray Knapp and Jill Dolan, for their astute comments on an earlier draft of this chapter.

2. Although *Company* includes more female characters than other Sondheim musicals, collections of vibrant women appear in almost every one of his shows, including *Anyone Can Whistle* (with Arthur Laurents), Cora and Fay; the collaborations with Harold Prince: in *Follies*, Sally and Phyllis, both older and young; in *A Little Night Music*, Desirée, Anne, Charlotte, Mme. Armfeldt, and Petra; in *Sweeney Todd*, Mrs. Lovett, Johanna, and the Beggar-Woman; in *Merrily We Roll Along*, Mary and the wives; with James Lapine: in *Into the Woods*, the Baker's Wife, the Witch, Cinderella, Rapunzel, and Little Red Riding Hood; in *Sunday in the Park with George*, Dot and Marie; in *Passion*, Fosca. Fewer women appear in Sondheim's work with John Weidman: *Pacific Overtures* is cast with all men, kabuki-style; the cast of *Assassins* includes two women in its crew of killers, Sarah Jane Moore and Squeaky Fromme, who might be among the least memorable characters in the show; *Road Show* has a Mother, who mostly functions to provide a familial back story for the troubled and interdependent Meisel brothers. I note Sondheim's creative partners over almost forty years because musical theater is deeply collaborative, and the production that emerges is the result of countless decisions made in the daily labor of creating performance. If Sondheim is no more invested in teamwork than other musical theater artists, he admits his love for collaboration more readily and is often quoted as saying that working on a musical makes a family. Ideas for the musicals sprung from his collaborators as much as from Sondheim himself. This chapter, then, approaches *Company* as a "Sondheim" musical but it is equally a Prince or George Furth or Boris Aaronson or Michael Bennett musical, or even an Elaine Stritch musical, a 1970 musical, or a New York musical. The point here is simply that the inquiry's framework determines the perspective on the show. The 1970 Broadway production won six Tony Awards, including Best Music and Lyrics, Book, Scenic Design, Director, and Best Musical. *Company* was Sondheim's first Tony Award. The show also won the New York Drama Critics' Circle Award for Best Musical. The musical's attention-getting first production and its two most significant revivals launched considerable commentary on the show. The collaborating artists for the 1970 production had established and growing reputations as musical theater innovators. As Prince said, "[W]e did *Company*, and we changed people's definitions of musicals. We changed taste and what was acceptable." Barbara Isenberg, "In Sondheim's Company," *Los Angeles Times*, April 18, 2010; http://www.latimes.com/entertainment/news/la-ca-sondheim18-2010apr18,0,1540 924,print.story.

3. This musical invites a parallel essay to explore in detail masculinity in *Company*. The male characters are fascinating. With a focus on female characters, this chapter doesn't consider the men's perception of them. See Paul Puccio, "Waiting for the Girls Upstairs: How Men Imagine Women in Sondheim Shows," *Sondheim Review* 12, no. 4 (summer 2006): 30–32.

4. This dilemma—of the difference between what the character does and what the actor does—isn't unique to Sondheim musicals, of course. In *Cabaret*, for example, the actor who plays Sally Bowles must perform badly to be believable as the character, but the audience is challenged to perceive the difference between the actor and the character. Jill Haworth, who originated the role, was criticized for her poor singing, but director Harold Prince insisted that a weak singing voice was appropriate for a character who worked in a seedy, mediocre cabaret. No doubt Prince's nuanced understanding of the dynamics of performance and his ambition to portray a layered theatrical world contributed to this double quality in Sondheim's collaborations with him, including *Company*. See Stacy Wolf, *Changed for Good: A Feminist History of the Broadway Musical* (New York: Oxford University Press, 2012).

5. Much has been written about *Company* in a range of critical contexts. When it opened, for example, *Company*'s musical numbers, most of which comment on the action from outside of the scene, initially confused and baffled audiences. This extranarrative function was later well used by Sondheim himself in, for example, *Sweeney Todd, Into the Woods*, and *Assassins*, and eventually became a convention of the form in self-reflexive musicals like *Urinetown, Bat Boy*, and *Spamalot*, to name only a few. At the time, most critics admired the show but didn't like it. Forty years after its premiere, musical theater historiography now comfortably locates it as the first "concept musical," even tracing a logical development from director Harold Prince's excursions into theme- or metaphor-dominated musicals in *Fiddler on the Roof* (1964), which he produced and Jerome Robbins directed and choreographed, and *Cabaret* (1966)—both designed by Boris Aronson, who designed the set for *Company*, too. See, for example, Miranda Lundskaer-Nielsen, *Directors and the New Musical Drama: British and American Musical Theatre in the 1980s and 90s* (New York: Palgrave Macmillan, 2008). For an historical contextualization, also see Amy Henderson and Dwight Blocker Bowers, *Red, Hot, and Blue: A Smithsonian Salute to the American Musical* (Washington, DC: Smithsonian Institution, 1996); Eugene K. Bristow and J. Kevin Butler, "*Company*, About Face! The Show that Revolutionized the American Musical," *American Music* 5, no. 3 (1987): 241–54. For critical work on *Company* in the context of Sondheim's life and work, see, for example, Jim Lovensheimer, "Stephen Sondheim and the Musical of the Outsider," in *The Cambridge Companion to the Musical*, ed. William A. Everett and Paul R. Laird, 181–96 (Cambridge, UK: Cambridge University Press, 2002); Meryle Secrest, *Stephen Sondheim: A Life* (New York: Alfred A. Knopf, 1998); Steve Swayne, *How Sondheim Found his Sound* (Ann Arbor: University of Michigan Press, 2005); Stephen Banfield, *Sondheim's Broadway Musicals* (Ann Arbor: University of Michigan Press, 1993), 147–74. Other useful sources are Raymond Knapp, *The American Musical and the Performance of Personal Identity* (Princeton: Princeton University Press, 2006), 293–302; Elizabeth L. Wollman, *Hard Times: The Adult Musical in New York City in the 1970s* (New York: Oxford University Press, 2013); Foster Hirsch, *Harold Prince and the American Musical Theatre* (New York: Applause, 2005), 85–92; Mark Steyn, "The Genius," *Broadway Babies Say Goodnight: Musicals Then and Now* (New York: Routledge, 1999), 138–184; Scott Miller, *From Assassins to West Side Story: The Director's Guide to Musical Theatre* (Portsmouth, NH: Heinemann, 1996). Other sources cited specifically below.

6. For a psychological reading of the play and the theme of ambivalence, see Diana Calderazzo, "Sorry-Grateful," *The Sondheim Review* 15, no. 3 (spring 2009): 14–16. The men's song of the same title encapsulates the musical's perspective most directly, and yet the women offer more varied, complex, and nuanced observations about marriage, relationships, and intimacy.

7. Another challenge to musical theater scholarship is which production to study. All of Sondheim's musicals underwent revisions at various stages and saw important, even radical revivals, and this one did as well. The artistic team of each of *Company*'s most significant revivals to date—director Sam Mendes's 1995 Donmar Warehouse production, which transferred to the Roundabout, and John Doyle's 2006 production, in which the actors also performed as the orchestra—both made changes to the 1970 version of greater or lesser effect. Books with photographs of the first production capture the staging, as well as Aronson's architectural set design, which defined the Manhattan urban setting that was so crucial to the musical's resonance in 1970. In addition to those sources, I rely on the 1996 published script, which is "an amalgamation of the Roundabout and Donmar Warehouse productions"; my memories of the 1995 Roundabout and 2006 John Doyle productions; and three taped performances: 1970 Broadway (housed at the Theatre on Film collection at the New York Public Library), 1995 Donmar, and 2006 Doyle. Thanks to Bryan Vandeventer, for sharing his paper about variations among the different versions.

8. Laurie Winer, "Why Sondheim's Women Are Different," *New York Times*, November 26, 1989, H1+.

9. See Wolf, *Changed for Good.*

10. Laura Hanson, "Broadway Babies: Images of Women in the Musicals of Stephen Sondheim," *Stephen Sondheim, A Casebook*, ed. Joanne Gordon (New York: Garland, 1997), 14.

11. Sara Evans, *Born for Liberty: A History of Women in America* (New York: Free Press, 1989), 287. Indeed, Hanson argues, Sondheim's representation of "increasingly complicated and ambiguous relationships between men and women" is grounded in the musical's historical context (Hanson, "Broadway Babies," 14).

12. Evans, *Born for Liberty*, 87.

13. Ruth Rosen, *The World Split Open: How the Modern Women's Movement Changed America* (New York: Viking, 2000), xxi–xxii.

14. Evans, *Born for Liberty*, 289.

15. Stanley was an Actors' Studio–trained actor who starred in William Inge's *Picnic* (1957) and *Bus Stop* (1959). In some ways, in fact, the men in *Company* are fairly stereotypical: conventional, privileged, self-interested. That the central dilemma of the musical is a man's is consistent with some of Sondheim's musicals—*Sweeney, Sunday, Merrily, Assassins, Road Show*—and not others: *Follies*. In some of the shows, male and female principals both take focus: *A Little Night Music, Into the Woods.*

16. Walter Kerr, "'Company': Original and Uncompromising," *New York Times*, May 3, 1970, 97.

17. Kerr, "Company," 97.

18. Clive Barnes, "Theater: 'Company' Offers a Guide to New York's Marital Jungle," *New York Times*, April 27, 1970, 40.

19. Barnes, "Company," 40.

20. Kerr, "Company," 97.

21. Mark Eden Horowitz, "Biography of a Song: 'You Could Drive a Person Crazy,'" *Sondheim Review* 13, no. 2 (winter 2006): 25–33. Also, see Stephen Kitsakos, "Make Me Aware: An

Expressionistic Production of 'Company,'" *Sondheim Review* 15, no. 4 (summer 2009): 33, which discusses a production at SUNY, New Paltz in 2008, directed by Frank Trezza.

22. In this way, *Company* differs from other Sondheim musicals in which women grow, change, and have realizations about their lives and choices, such as Sally in *Follies*, Mrs. Lovett in *Sweeney Todd*, Dot in *Sunday*, The Baker's Wife and the Witch in *Into the Woods*, and perhaps most movingly, Desirée in *A Little Night Music*.

23. On *Company* as a "revue," see, for example, Stanley Green, *The World of Musical Comedy: The Story of the American Musical Stage as Told through the Careers of Its Foremost Composers and Lyricists*, 4th rev. ed. (Cambridge, MA: Da Capo, 1984), 3–4. Sondheim also notes that Robert does develop as a character, changing and learning from his experiences.

24. George Furth, *Company: A Musical Comedy*, music and lyrics by Stephen Sondheim (New York: Theatre Communications Group, 1996. Lyrics copyright 1971). Page numbers refer to this version of the script.

25. In his article that judges the relevance of *Company* in 1995, John Olson notes that psychological ideas that moved into mainstream culture between 1970 and 1995 render the characters' relationships all the more recognizable and definable for a later audience. How the characters "act out" on Bobby is clear forty years after its premiere. See John Olson, "*Company*—25 Years Later," *Stephen Sondheim, A Casebook*, ed. Joanne Gordon, 47–68 (New York: Garland, 1997).

26. Thanks to Ray Knapp for pointing this out to me.

27. Sondheim said, "Audiences cannot distinguish between two tunes, two melodic lines, or two different lyrics going together—unless they've heard each one before." See Mark Eden Horowitz, *Sondheim on Music: Minor Details and Major Decisions* (Lanham, MD, and Oxford: Scarecrow, 2003), 110.

28. Mrs. Lovett in *Sweeney Todd* exhibits a similar polarity: she is clearly as smart as Sweeney but she wants him too much and he takes her for granted.

29. "Every Day a Little Death" is a duet with Charlotte and Anne. "We Do Not Belong Together" begins in a scene with George and Dot, but she sings the number.

30. On the representation of the Single Girl in 1960s musicals, see Wolf, *Changed for Good*, chap. 2.

31. Gerald Mast, *Can't Help Singin': The American Musical on Stage and Screen* (Woodstock, NY: Overlook, 1987), 326.

32. For an extended reading of this song and an account of its development through Sondheim's sketches and drafts, see Horowitz, "Biography of a Song."

33. Horowitz, "Biography of a Song."

34. "While perhaps not his most distinguished tune, it is and includes some artful turns of phrase," writes Horowitz, "Biography of a Song."

35. Horowitz, *Sondheim on Music*, 121.

36. Barnes, "Company," 40.

37. Kerr, "Company," 97.

38. This monologue may have influenced Val's character in *A Chorus Line*, which Michael Bennett conceived and directed five years after *Company*.

39. Ray Knapp observes that April's performance of dumbness also converses with Goldie Hawn's character on *Laugh-In*, which played from 1968 to 1973, and would have been a clear intertext for *Company*. Personal email September 6, 2010.

40. Donna McKechnie originated the role of Kathy, who also performs the "Tick Tock" dance, which comments on April's and Robert's sex scene and his distracted state of mind. Michael

Bennett choreographed the dance for her, and reviewers agreed that it was an extremely sexy number. "Tick Tock" provides a performance opportunity for a strong dancer, but this requirement in part motivated the production team to cut it from the published version, according to Sondheim. Since most productions cut the dance, Kathy ultimately plays a small role in the show. For an argument for the importance of this scene, see Michael Ellison, "Dancing Intimacy—and Its Loss," *Sondheim Review* 15, no. 1 (fall 2008): 36.

41. Marta also appears in the scene with the newly divorced Susan and Peter, the only scene outside of the ensemble-populated, repeated birthday party in which the marrieds and the single women meet one another. This scene shows that Robert's married friends occasionally meet his girlfriends, but that no one sticks around long enough for them to identify her.

42. In her memoir, *Time Steps*, Donna McKechnie describes an always anxious Beth Howland rehearsing her lyrics during every free minute at rehearsal. McKechnie remembers how committed the entire cast was and how Barbara Barrie and Charles Kimbrough worked on the karate scene until they were black and blue.

43. Amy's type, as characterized in her solo, repeats in Sondheim's other musicals, in which the fast and funny patter song reveals the woman's sharpness: Mrs. Lovett, especially in "A Little Priest," in *Sweeney Todd*; Petra in *A Little Night Music*; Cinderella in *Into the Woods*. All of these women are smart and clever, good with words. Both Petra and Cinderella explore emotional situations of complexity and contradiction.

44. The sex scene is preceded by some discussion: April's long butterfly monologue, which ends with her rescuing from her cat the newly born butterfly, injured but not dead, and Robert's response about losing his way back to a motel, after buying champagne and baby oil, where a women was waiting for him, are both stories of misunderstandings, misdirections, and hurt feelings. April somehow manages to wrest meaning from Bobby's strange tale, and she provides an interpretation that persuasively links their stories, but when he looks up thankfully, any insight that the audience may have credited to April is undercut by his sarcasm. She also compliments his decorating in the apartment, as if she cannot imagine a man who knows how to decorate (another suggestion of his homosexuality).

45. This song complements the "Bobby Baby" sequences that thread through the show, as the women are not together in "reality" but provide a unified perspective. Like the full group ensemble numbers in *Company*, it's presumed that the women don't know each other and aren't friends but just happen to have the same violent feelings about the women in Robert's life.

46. The end of the song follows the same structure as the cap on the parallel monologues, with different consequences for Robert and the same effect for the audience. April surprised him earlier by contriving a linkage between their stories. In the first instance, he looked to God, thankful that she felt satisfied enough by his story to be willing to have sex with him.

47. Clive Barnes observes that April is the only character in the musical with a job; he describes Susan Browning as "the wistfully wistful airline stewardess who is doubtless eternally on her way to barcelona [*sic*]" ("Company," 40).

48. This scene was in the original version, then cut before the 1970 opening, then put back in 1995. On debates about this scene's persuasiveness of Robert's heterosexuality, see for example, Bruce Kirle, *Unfinished Show Business: Broadway Musicals as Works-in-Progress* (Carbondale: Southern Illinois University Press, 2005); Knapp, personal information; Hirsch, *Harold Prince*; Elizabeth Wollman, *Hard Times*.

49. Structurally, Joanne's numbers create a frame within a frame of *Company*: Bobby's journey traces the outermost frame; the "Bobby Baby" ensemble numbers and the repeated birthday scenes form a second frame; Joanne's two songs forms a third frame.

50. Ann Pellegrini, "Closing Ranks, Keeping Company: Marriage Plots and the Will to be Single in *Much Ado about Nothing*," in *Shakesqueer*, ed. Madhavi Menon, 245–53 (Durham, NC: Duke University Press, 2011).

51. Kerr, "Company," 97.

52. My thanks to editor Robert Gordon for pointing out this aspect of the number to me.

53. The song also mentions Pinter, the absurdist playwright who critiqued contemporary family relations with a vengeance. Like Sondheim's, Pinter's women, especially in *The Homecoming*, seem at once powerless and absolutely the ones calling the shots.

54. The ending of *Company* is famously ambiguous, with Sondheim's four-time effort to compose a final number equally famous. Hirsch finds Robert's change of heart unconvincing and improbable, and Prince said that he wanted it to be unclear what would happen to Robert from this point on.

55. Kerr, "Company," 97.

56. See Marvin Carlson, *The Haunted Stage: The Theatre as Memory Machine* (Ann Arbor: University of Michigan Press, 2001).

57. David Rooney, "Review: 'Company,'" *Variety*, November 29, 2006. http://www.variety.com/review/VE1117932218.html?categoryid=33&cs=1.

58. Wendy Smith, "Sondheim 101: Good Thing Going," *Sondheim Review* 15, no. 2 (winter 2008): 14.

CHAPTER 24

FOLLIES: MUSICAL PASTICHE AND CULTURAL ARCHAEOLOGY

ROBERT LAWSON-PEEBLES

FOLLIES begins. A timpani crescendo introduces a slow waltz, with a sad, fragmentary melody played initially on a soprano saxophone.[1] This is not a waltz of Vienna in mid-nineteenth century. It is, rather, of Paris in 1920, recovering from the "Great War," as it was then called, and beginning to absorb the impact of ragtime and jazz. Musicians in Paris such as Ernest Ansermet and Maurice Ravel welcomed the opportunity for renewal offered by the African American music.[2] Some sixty years later, Stephen Sondheim claimed that Ravel had, in turn, been responsible for the harmonic structure of much twentieth-century popular music.[3] The hyperbole is a recent instance of Sondheim's deep and abiding interest in Ravel. As a youngster, Sondheim had begun the education of his mentor Oscar Hammerstein II in "modern" music with the gift of a recording of Ravel's Piano Trio.[4] Ravel's influence is also clear in the "Prologue" to *Follies* (no. 1), with Jonathan Tunick's orchestration emphasizing a relationship with *La Valse*. It is therefore worth examining *La Valse*. It will give an insight into Sondheim's working method, into the structure of *Follies*, and into the theme of nostalgia for the revues from which *Follies* takes its name.

In 1928, Ravel described his composition as "un tournoiement fantastique et fatal" and, certainly, during the course of its dozen minutes, *La Valse* moves from delicate celebration to giddy demolition of the ghost of a Strauss waltz. Ravel chose the term "tournoiement" with care, for it carries the double burden of cause and effect. The English translation is "whirling" and "dizziness," providing an account of the movement of the waltz, and also of its physiological outcome if undertaken without restraint. Ravel insisted that with *La Valse* he was looking back at the Vienna of 1855—the time when the young Johann Strauss was trying to ingratiate himself with the Imperial Court.[5] In a 1922 interview, Ravel said that *La Valse*

> doesn't have anything to do with the present situation in Vienna, and it also doesn't have any symbolic meaning in that regard. In the course of *La Valse*, I did not envision a dance of death or a struggle between life and death.... I changed the original

title "Wien" to *La Valse*, which is more in keeping with the aesthetic nature of the composition. It is a dancing, whirling, almost hallucinatory ecstasy, an increasingly passionate and exhausting whirlwind of dancers, who are overcome and exhilarated by nothing but "the waltz."[6]

In a 1924 interview, Ravel asserted that "*La Valse* is tragic, but in the Greek sense: it is a fatal spinning around, the expression of vertigo and of the voluptuousness of the dance to the point of paroxysm."[7] Aristotelian tragedy arose from *hamartia*, an error of personal judgment—in this case, waltzing too vigorously. In contrast, Roman tragedy, of which the best-known exponent is the stoic philosopher and statesman Seneca, had a more public dimension, involving murder, ghosts, revenge, and widespread carnage. In that 1924 interview, Ravel compared Greek and Roman tragedy in order to distinguish Mozart from Beethoven. "Mozart is perfection: he is Grecian, whereas Beethoven is Roman. The Greek is great, the Roman is colossal. I prefer the great."[8]

Several critics have challenged Ravel's insistence that *La Valse* was inspired by aesthetics and physiology.[9] Ravel had seen "the present situation" of Vienna, wracked by starvation and violence, during a visit in October 1920. An experience four years earlier made an even deeper impact. Ravel was a driver in a French artillery regiment, and on one occasion had to go to the front, in the midst of a German barrage, to pick up an abandoned vehicle:

> I saw a hallucinatory thing: a nightmarish city, horribly deserted and mute.... [I]t's not this formidable and invisible struggle which is anguishing, but rather to feel alone in the center of this city which rests in a sinister sleep.... Undoubtedly, I will see things which will be more frightful and repugnant; I don't believe I will ever experience a more profound and stranger emotion than this sort of mute terror.[10]

There were more frightful and repugnant sights in Vienna, but this hallucination has a potency that cannot be ignored by a musician—for a city that is mute is musically dead.

The orchestral version of *La Valse* was first performed in Paris on December 12, 1920. It takes its place alongside another musical codicil to the First World War, which had received its premiere just eight days earlier. *Die tote Stadt*, by Erich Wolfgang Korngold, the young Viennese composer, was produced simultaneously in Cologne and Hamburg on December 4. Korngold's plot is set in the crumbling city of Bruges, and involves a "Temple of Memories" to a dead wife, a young lookalike dancer, and psychopathic hallucinations.[11] Korngold's opera may have been both too successful and too Senecan for Ravel, prompting him to insist that *La Valse* was simply an Aristotelian exercise. Yet the image of the dead city provides an appropriate binary framework for *La Valse*, in which the gaiety of mid-century Vienna is viewed with the knowledge of the carnage of the First World War and the consequent dissolution of the Austro-Hungarian Empire. *La Valse*, then, may have an agenda that is political as well as aesthetic, apocalyptic as well as simply physiological. As the conductor Manuel Rosenthal (who was both a student and a close friend of Ravel) put it: "*La Valse* has two things in it...a tribute to the genius of Johann Strauss...[and] a kind of anguish, a very dramatic feeling of death."[12]

This discussion of Ravel and *La Valse* may help to illuminate the particular qualities of *Follies* and of Sondheim's working methods. Sondheim's musical has a binary framework that contains a structural irony holding in delicate balance both a tribute to earlier American music theater and a critique of it. The framework has a political, a stylistic, and a personal dimension, each one indebted to Ravel. The politics are those of evolution rather than revolution. Manuel Rosenthal, reminiscing about Ravel, affirmed that he "hated revolution." Rosenthal asked Ravel to describe the difference between evolution and revolution. The composer responded by using the metaphor of the window, saying that it was better to open a window to let in fresh air than to break it.[13] The stylistic dimension is eclectic. Ravel used sources as diverse as Couperin and the Blues. Sondheim's sources may come from a briefer period, but there is no doubting their variety and richness, for they include—as well as Ravel—Rachmaninoff, Prokofiev, Britten, Stravinsky, Copland, Hindemith, and the great tradition of twentieth-century American popular song in which Sondheim is deeply versed.[14] Sondheim's eclecticism is of a specific kind. In a 2003 conversation he remarked, "I write in a lot of styles, because I'm often imitating a milieu."[15] Sondheim often makes use of pastiche, and in this he follows Ravel rather than his early collaborator Leonard Bernstein, whose eclecticism might be said to lack critical distance. The personal dimension is reserved, unobtrusive, oblique. (Obliquity was never one of Bernstein's qualities.) This dimension acts to create a disjunction between feeling and revelation, distilling emotion into artifice. It is here that the gift to Hammerstein of the Ravel Piano Trio is significant. The Trio, particularly its third movement, *passacaille*, is regarded as Ravel at his most emotional, responding to the outbreak of the First World War.[16] Yet the work's emotionality is held in check by Ravel's formal reticence. The gift, had Hammerstein attended to it, might have let some fresh air into his lyric writing, ever wearing its heart on its sleeve. Even this early, Sondheim was using Ravel to distance himself from Hammerstein.[17]

In that 2003 conversation, Sondheim noted that he listened to "authentic Victor Herbert and Jerome Kern" in preparation for writing *Follies*.[18] If this sounds like self-defense, it is because of critical attitudes toward pastiche that can be traced to the privileging of originality over craftsmanship. The division of art from craft has a long history: it begins with Vasari's *Lives of the Artists* (1550, 1568) and is still greatly influential in music criticism, largely through the writing of Theodor Adorno (1903–69). In this view craftsmanship is derivative, a second level of creativity. It is a view that can be sketched quickly by comparing Adorno's approach to Beethoven and Ravel. Adorno believed that Beethoven's artistry was central to the history of music. Ravel's work was merely peripheral. Adorno said of *La Valse* that it "seals the fate of the waltz...to be a revenant [ghost] means that you have first to have died."[19] In contrast, Tin Pan Alley was all too alive. Adorno brought his Marxist sensibilities to bear on popular music, asserting that the mass production of such music created a false consciousness, a "catharsis for the masses...which keeps them all the more firmly in line."[20] Later critics have been similarly scathing about pastiche, regarding it as merely "clever," lacking the critical attack to be found in parody. The pejorative terms used for pastiche range from "forgery" to "blankness" or "blindness," being a complaisant lackey of late capitalism.[21] It is little wonder that, when interviewed by *Time* about the first, 1971, production of *Follies*, Sondheim insisted that "in each of the pastiche songs, there is always something of me added to the imitation of Kern or Arlen or whoever it is. That's something I couldn't avoid—my own comment on the style."[22] In short, Sondheim's approach to earlier American songwriters presents a parallel with Ravel's approach to Johann Strauss. The mask cannot be separated from the man; neither can craftsmanship from originality.

Of course, Sondheim operates within an advanced capitalist arena. But this does not mean blind servitude. In a 1985 interview he said that every show should have "a secret metaphor that nobody knows except the authors."[23] Yet Sondheim had already revealed the secret metaphor of *Follies* in 1974, ascribing it to his collaborator James Goldman, author of the book:

> The reason Jim chose the Follies as a metaphor was that the Follies represented a state of mind in America between the two world wars. Up until 1945, America was the good guy, everything was idealistic and hopeful and America was going to lead the world. Now you see the country is a riot of national guilt, the dream has collapsed, everything has turned to rubble underfoot.[24]

In an interview that same year, Sondheim answered the critics of *Follies* by saying that the show was good because of Goldman's book. The book was essential: it was both "the scheme" and "the style" of the show.[25] Sondheim has in the past been accused of evasiveness, but a more accurate, and certainly kinder, interpretation of these remarks would be that Sondheim is using Ravel's antinomy, playing Greece to Goldman's Rome, deploying Ravel's witty musical language among the rubble. For as the waltz is played a fire-curtain, "caked with dust," is raised to reveal the enormous stage of Broadway's Weismann Theater, where "vast chunks of the proscenium are missing."[26] The dramaturgy thus creates a double meaning, at once an obeisance to and a critique of the past, sharpening the pastiche with an ironic edge, replacing Ravel's Franz Joseph I and the First World War with Richard Nixon and the Vietnam War.

In his 1985 interview Sondheim talked positively of "the abrasion of collaboration" with Harold Prince.[27] For Prince, who produced *Follies*, "rubble" became the governing metaphor for the show's complex handling of time. He had already employed staging techniques used by such experimental directors as Peter Brook in order to move away from naturalism, for instance in the 1966 production of *Cabaret*.[28] Now he drew on Federico Fellini's *8½*, using the space of the stage to transform the intermittent flashbacks of that film into a simultaneous treatment of past and present, represented by the presence, firstly of the "ghosts" of showgirls, and secondly of the younger selves of the characters.[29] Prince's handling of time may also derive from an intellectual environment that includes Einstein's physics, William Faulkner's "metaphysics" of "a closed future" (to use Sartre's words), and a Rodgers and Hart song:

> When you're awake, the things you think
> Come from the dreams you dream....
> Sometimes you think you've lived before
> All that you live today.
> Things that you do come back to you,
> As though they knew the way.

This is from the verse of "Where or When," written for the 1937 Broadway show *Babes in Arms*. The verse was dropped from the 1939 Hollywood version, and is now rarely sung, making the refrain seem even more enigmatic:

> Some things that happen for the first time
> Seem to be happening again . . .

The song is about déjà vu or paramnesia, a condition previously linked with dissociative identity disorder; and today sometimes ascribed to falling in love, and sometimes to exhaustion.[30]

Paramnesia is one of the themes of *Follies*, and so too is the evolution of *Babes in Arms*. The show concerns the attempts by a group of teenagers to arrest the decline of vaudeville by staging their own updated version. The Broadway production contained several of the best songs of Rodgers and Hart, including "I Wish I Were in Love Again," "My Funny Valentine" and "The Lady is a Tramp." These songs, like the verse of "Where or When," were dropped from the 1939 Hollywood version and replaced by others, some (like "I'm Just Wild About Harry") looking back to the beginning of the twentieth century, and one ("Good Morning") much better known in a later Arthur Freed production, *Singin' in the Rain*. The film partnered Mickey Rooney with Judy Garland, fresh from *The Wizard of Oz*—as was Margaret Hamilton, trying to escape her role as a wicked witch. *Babes in Arms* marked a change in the career of Busby Berkeley, from Warner to MGM; a change in the career of Arthur Freed, from lyricist to producer; and the beginning of the collaboration of Judy Garland and Mickey Rooney as hopeful young showbiz innocents. The film also responds to European political events. It was produced between May and July, after the German invasion of Czechoslovakia and the Italian invasion of Albania, and had its premiere in October 1939, one month after the outbreak of the Second World War. *Babes in Arms* had earlier asserted its American credentials in a comic conflict between swing and opera. Just before the dissolve into the final song, the promoter Madox (Henry Hull, with wagging finger and hectoring voice) demands that Rooney become the messiah of the American Dream. *Babes in Arms*, Rooney responds, "is bigger than just a show . . . it's everybody in the country." The final song is "God's Country," by Harold Arlen and E. Y. Harburg, imported from a 1937 antiwar musical, *Hooray for What!* Including quotations from "Yankee Doodle" and "The Stars and Stripes Forever," the song becomes a spectacular exercise in xenophobia, pitting Americanized Hollywood stars against European dictators:

> We've got no Duce, we've got no Fuehrer,
> But we've got Garbo and Norma Shearer.

Perhaps James Goldman had *Babes in Arms* in mind when he chose the metaphor for *Follies*. For Busby Berkeley transformed *Babes in Arms* into an exemplar of the interwar "state of mind" of the United States, with Rooney and Garland as its "idealistic and hopeful" —but innocent—leaders.[31]

One acknowledged inspiration for Harold Prince was a photograph, originally in a 1960 issue of *Life* magazine, of Gloria Swanson in a long black sheath dress and an even

FIGURE **24.1** Gloria Swanson in the ruins of the Roxy Theater, New York.

longer pink feather boa, standing among the ruins of the Roxy Theater (Figure 24.1). The Roxy had opened in 1927 with the premiere of *The Love of Sunya*, a silent film starring and produced by Swanson. The ironic contrast, of a glamorous yet aging star amid the rubble of a vast cinema that she had opened, was compounded by Swanson's recent career. In *Sunset Boulevard* (1950) Swanson plays a passé silent film star, Norma Desmond, who murders her young lover, Joseph Gillis. The corpse of Gillis introduces the flashback that lasts the entire film, revealing "the facts" that precipitate the murder. Those facts are caused by Desmond's failure to cope with the process of aging and the loss of fame, recorded most famously in her riposte: "I am big, it's the pictures that got small." The 1960 photograph could therefore be regarded as Swanson's pyrrhic victory, the desolating triumph of the present over the past.[32]

The Swanson photograph suggested that the stage could be used to treat the simultaneity of past and present ironically. Those ironies are revealed in the counterpoint between the older and younger characters, reminding the audience of the pathogenic inescapability of the present that undermines any celebration of the past. *Follies* thus draws on F. Scott Fitzgerald's 1925 novel *The Great Gatsby*, particularly Gatsby's wish "to recover something, some idea of himself, perhaps, that had gone into loving Daisy … if he could once return to a certain starting place and go over it all slowly, he could find out what that thing was." The wish is fatal, not only for Gatsby but, as Nick points out at the novel's elegiac close, for all those who believe in "the orgastic future that year by year recedes before us."[33] If we heed them too lovingly, the siren songs of America will draw us onto the rocks of the Roxy Theater. Indeed, the deadly trajectory can take us further, from *Follies* to *Assassins*.

The receding past makes its presence felt in the opening speech of Dimitri Weismann. Weismann had staged a variety show here for each year between 1919 and 1941. Since then the theater has suffered a declension: from "ballet, rep, movies, blue movies and now, in a final burst of glory, it's to be a parking lot." So, before the theater is torn down, Weismann holds a reunion. Reunions are vexatious events, best approached with irony, and Weismann is ironical when he says he has created:

> a final chance to glamorize the old days, stumble through a song or two and lie about ourselves a little. I have, as you can see, spared no expense. Still, there's a band, free food and drink, and the inevitable Roscoe, here as always to bring on the Weismann Girls. So take one last look at your girls. They won't be coming down these stairs again. I don't trust any music under thirty. Maestro, if you please![34]

The song that follows is a palsied pastiche of one that, in 1971, was fifty-two years old. "Beautiful Girls" (no. 2) alludes to "A Pretty Girl is Like a Melody," composed by Irving Berlin in 1919 for the *Ziegfeld Follies*. Doris Eaton Travis, a Ziegfeld girl, recalled that Berlin wrote his song to accompany a parade of girls, each suggesting a familiar nineteenth-century melody:

> The curtain parted on an empty, dark stage. As the music started, the spotlight picked up John Steel. . . . John had a beautiful, clear tenor voice, and he sang the verse and a chorus of the Berlin song. Then as each girl appeared—one at a time—the music switched to refrains of well-known classical compositions, such as Mendelssohn's "Song of Spring" and Offenbach's "Barcarolle." With each "haunting refrain," the spotlight picked up a showgirl, dressed to match the mood of the music.

The scene closed with a final chorus of Berlin's song, with the girls surrounding the tenor. "A Pretty Girl is Like a Melody" therefore began its life in homage to European popular classics, and then superseded them by becoming "the quintessential Follies song."[35] As sung by "the inevitable Roscoe," "Beautiful Girls" in turn becomes an ironic comment on Berlin's song. In 1971 Roscoe must have become so inevitable that he would have been in his seventies. The final sustained note of "Beautiful Girls" is an A nearly two octaves above middle C, close to the top of the tenor range and hence a cruel task for an elderly tenor. Indeed, in the 1971 recording Michael Bartlett could reach the note only by shouting.[36]

Although there were a number of annual revues—such as *The Earl Carroll Vanities* and *George White's Scandals*—that could have been models for *Follies*, Sondheim's pastiche and Harold Prince's memoir make it clear that they had Florenz Ziegfeld in mind.[37] Ziegfeld is best remembered for his *Follies*, staged annually between 1907 and 1931. They presented a mixture of variety acts, comedy and satirical sketches, and songs. Fanny Brice (memorialized in *Funny Girl*, the 1964 musical and 1968 film), Bert Williams, Will Rogers, and Eddie Cantor all performed in Ziegfeld's *Follies*. The centrepiece of the *Follies*, however, consisted of the women who paraded in front of lavish and elaborate settings. As its name suggests, the *Follies* assimilated the dancing from the Folies Bergère to New York middle-class tastes. In Paris Josephine Baker danced with or without a girdle of bananas, and nude showgirls were suspended from chandeliers. This latter spectacle is recalled in Howard Hawks's film *Gentlemen Prefer Blondes*, while Marilyn Monroe sings "Diamonds are a Girl's Best Friend." Ziegfeld despised such "orgies of nakedness," and so his girls were dressed exotically if scantily, or distributed motionless amongst the scenery.[38] Hawks dressed his chandelier girls in black bikinis and plastic straps in a suggestion of bondage that represents one of his flirtations with the censors of the Hays Office.[39] Ziegfeld's aim was less lurid. He wished, he said, to "glorify the American girl," and he did so by turning her into an expensive commodity. In 1922, for instance, the Ziegfeld girls paraded in "Laceland" as if they were catwalk models for a bridal trousseau. Outside the theater, the girls were required to behave in a "ladylike" manner, and were paid accordingly. The "Ziegfeld girl" thus became a brand name.[40]

Ziegfeld died in 1932, two years after Sondheim was born, but his style and brand name was disseminated, to the envy of competitors, by a 1934 biography, and in a number of Hollywood movies, including some by his former assistant, Busby Berkeley. The biography was cowritten by the singer and comedian Eddie Cantor, who begins by uniting medieval chivalry and modern technology:

> The beginning of the Twentieth Century developed three great inventions—the telephone, the telegraph and the American Beauty—and Florenz Ziegfeld was the leading exponent of all three. He was the Knight Errant of American Womanhood. The telegram was his sword and the telephone his coat of arms.
>
> To glorify the American girl he went out and gave battle to an army of comedians, costumers, scenic designers, authors, composers, press agents and rival producers. With his telegram pad in one hand and his telephone in the other, he kept the wires sizzling to make the world safe for beauty.[41]

Cantor's depiction of Ziegfeld as American entrepreneur in search of the Grail of Womanhood is reminiscent of *The Great Gatsby*, shorn of its ironic narrative frame and toxic environment. As Linda Mizejewski has shown, the 1936 biographical epic *The Great Ziegfeld* made even clearer, if still unshadowed, reference to *The Great Gatsby*.[42] That obscure object of desire, the green light at the end of Daisy's dock, is replaced in "A Pretty Girl is Like a Melody" by a thirty-two-foot-high revolving wedding cake of a volute, replete with top-hatted men and frill-bedecked girls.[43] Irving Berlin's song is interspersed with dramatized extracts from Dvořák, Puccini, Mendelssohn, Johann Strauss, Verdi, and Gershwin, and sung by Allan Jones, best known in the 1936 *Show Boat*. Jones had a classically trained voice that could easily reach top A, so he sang the song while Dennis Morgan, equally uncredited, wore white tie and tails—and moved his lips. As the volute turns, the camera moves upwards and inwards to focus on the Spirit of the *Follies*, in the form of Virginia Bruce.[44]

This sequence was so extravagant that MGM used it again, to close the 1941 film *Ziegfeld Girl*, with musical numbers directed by Berkeley. An uneasy Judy Garland substituted for Virginia Bruce, and Irving Berlin's anthem was replaced by "You Never Looked so Beautiful before," by Walter Donaldson and Harold Adamson.[45] Five years later the dead impresario was given the ultimate accolade in Vincente Minnelli's *Ziegfeld Follies*. William Powell, who played Ziegfeld in the 1936 film, has now been translated to Heaven. Here he looks back to "the Broadway of 1907 . . . an innocent world believing in a golden future, full of peace and love and beautiful girls." In this world he treats people like animated dolls: "children playing with the dreams of tomorrow, [just as] all men play with the memories of yesterday." Ziegfeld–Powell continues:

> The New York night still burns for me with the names I have branded into the sky. Great shows that were part of the dreams of America. How many millions of people today remember their courtship, their honeymoon, their anniversary, their happiest moments in terms of a Ziegfeld show. The world will never forget the Ziegfeld *Follies*.

These sentences mark an imperial inflation of a brand name (perhaps not unlike some other American brand names), from Broadway, to New York, to America, and finally to the world. Ziegfeld–Powell's pride inflates in unison and so, with a little help from God, he plans a new *Follies*. It occupies the rest of the film.[46]

Sondheim's *Follies* repeats the warnings of *The Great Gatsby*, telling us that if we follow Ziegfeld–Powell's belief and "play with the memories of yesterday," we will begin a dance that will end in collapse. Prince pointed out the irony in the name *Follies*: it means, "in the British sense, foolishness, and in the French, 'folie,' which is madness."[47] The irony is woven into the texture of *Follies*. The musical texture often consists of fragmentary melodies and broken chords, creating an unsettling feeling of incompletion. Similarly, characterization and narrative structure are limited. Sondheim remarked that the characters spoke in phrases rather than complete sentences because they were not fully realized. They were, rather, "essences," reduced to the "most succinct form." *Follies*, said Sondheim, "is a mood piece." That is why he and Goldman took most of the incidents out, denying the audience the satisfaction of narrative and even, in their aim to maintain a mood, insisting that there be no intermission.[48]

To an extent, Goldman and Sondheim revisited the format of the revue. Revues had little or no narrative structure. As Fred Astaire remarks in Minnelli's *Ziegfeld Follies*, a Follies "never had a story—it was itself a story of an era."[49] *Ziegfeld Follies* avoided the narrative drive of the earlier Ziegfeld films, and of Hollywood film in general. In doing so, Minnelli's film returned to the form of musical that preceded the so-called "integrated" musicals of Kern and Hammerstein (*Show Boat*) and Rodgers and Hammerstein (starting with *Oklahoma!*). And so did Sondheim. Drawing further away from Oscar Hammerstein II, Sondheim voiced his objection to the "integrated" narrative form in a group of interviews in the 1980s. "The form that Rodgers and Hammerstein developed tells a story through character and song," he said, "the characters therefore cause the things to happen in the story, and it goes song-scene, song-scene, song-scene, song-scene." Such a process, he thought, was "naïve." This does not mean, however, that Sondheim can be regarded as a postmodernist lyricist and composer, revealing the meaninglessness of life. Rather, Sondheim applies his avowedly experimental methods to that earlier tradition of songwriting, which he calls "the vernacular of the musical theatre," for the purposes of ironic commentary.[50] Two instances may help to explain Sondheim's dislike of the "integrated" format. In Kern and Hammerstein's "Make-Believe" (from *Show Boat*, Broadway 1927, film 1936 and 1951), the lyric suggests that "Our dreams are more romantic / Than the world we see," but the refrain that ends the first and last stanza finds the lovers admitting "Might as well make believe I love you, / For to tell the truth I do." The "dreams" of the song, in short, drive the characters from pretence into truth, with all the unhappy consequences that follow.[51] Rodgers and Hammerstein's "If I Loved You" (from *Carousel*, Broadway 1945, film 1956) operates in a similar way:

> Longin' to tell you but afraid and shy,
> I'd let my golden chances pass me by!
> Soon you'd leave me
> Off you would go in the mist of day,
> Never, never to know
> How I loved you,
> If I loved you.

This moving song draws on Miltonic imagery, and is magnificently sung by Shirley Jones and Gordon McRae in the film. Its final line nevertheless shows the characters hiding their "true" feelings behind the subjunctive afterthought.[52] Once again, as in tragic opera, things inevitably get worse. It could be said that Sondheim's project in *Follies* is to reveal the mendacity and unhappiness created by the integration of song, character and plot. When Dimitri Weismann says he does not "trust any music under thirty," he may partly be speaking for Sondheim.

The major characters in *Follies* therefore cannot be described as protagonists, and the plot is skeletal. Sally and Buddy Plummer, an unhappy middle-class couple, meet Phyllis and Ben Stone, an unhappy upper-class couple, at Weismann's reunion. Ben and Buddy were stage-door Johnnies, paying court to the two Weismann girls. Sally had an affair with Ben before marrying Buddy on the rebound. The four reveal their frustrations and disappointments, and at the end of the reunion they prepare to go home. Sondheim talked of "the Chekhovian quality" of *Follies*, and the mood of nostalgia and passivity is discernible.[53] But not futility. Whereas the sisters Prozorov long to be back in Moscow, the Chekhovian mood of *Follies* is moderated in some of the songs, a reminder of Sondheim's belief in the importance of the songwriting tradition to American cultural history.

Mark Steyn suggested that Heidi Schiller's song, "One More Kiss" (no. 17), presents the essence of *Follies*.[54] It is in fact the only song where an older character and her younger counterpart are in agreement, with the younger singer decorating the melody sung by the older. "Dreams are a sweet mistake / All dreamers must awake....Never look back." It is instead the allusion that provides the irony, for the song is sung in a manner that looks back to old Vienna. Heidi earlier asserts that "Franz Lehar wrote it for me in Vienna." Lehár (1870–1948) would be an appropriate choice, for he celebrated Vienna long after it became cloaked in morbidity; and the Nazis used his music for propaganda purposes. Yet Heidi immediately corrects herself: "Facts never interest me.

What matters is the song." Indeed it does. "One More Kiss" bears a closer resemblance to "Kiss Me Again" from *Mlle. Modiste*, with music by Victor Herbert and lyrics by Henry Blossom, and a lasting triumph for the Viennese-born soprano Fritzi Scheff. However, Scheff played no rich merry widow, but rather Fifi, a poor Parisian milliner. Hiram Bent, a self-made American theater promoter, helps Fifi to become a famous singer, and later to marry a French aristocrat. *Mlle. Modiste* was a success on Broadway in 1905, confirming the belief that even a French girl, granted American glorification, can overcome the rigid European class structure. The name of the theater promoter would nowadays suggest an ironic treatment; but in 1905 he personified the American Dream. Instead, Herbert apparently intended "Kiss Me Again" as a satire on Victorian sentimental ballads, but was confounded by Scheff's success. It took Fanny Brice to realize Herbert's satire, and Sondheim to provide the answer to Blossom's mawkish lyric of "sleepy birds dreaming of love."[55]

The reference to *Mlle. Modiste* is just one strand in an enormous network of parallels and counterpoints, augmenting the musical and contextual allusions that are central to pastiche. The network can be extremely complex and difficult to untangle. Critics are forced into playing guessing games; and sometimes may simply be led down the garden path. Sondheim, who once was a professional puzzle-writer for *New York Magazine*, is known as an enthusiastic, even intrepid games player.[56] The discussion of the songs that follows can be no more than hints that acknowledge Sondheim's superiority as both practitioner and antiquary of music theater. The songs can be organized into two groups: those that pay homage to the old vaudevillians and those sung by the four main characters. The vaudevillians appear in a "Montage" (no. 6) of three nostalgic songs. The first are an old-time duo, Emily and Teddy Whitman, singing "Rain on the Roof." Stephen Banfield suggested an allusion to Irving Berlin's "Isn't This a Lovely Day?" which Fred Astaire sings to Ginger Rogers as they shelter in a gazebo in *Top Hat*.[57] The song could also allude to Sammy Cahn and Jule Styne's "Let It Snow," written during a Hollywood heatwave in 1945 and turned into a pseudo Christmas carol by, among others, Vaughan Monroe, Ella Fitzgerald, Bing Crosby, and Frank Sinatra. (The song has achieved a latter-day fame in *Die Hard 2*.) The phrases "Pit-pitty-pat" and "Plunk-planka-plink" recall the tongue-twisting patter songs of Gilbert and Sullivan, revived for instance in "Mischa, Jascha, Toscha, Sascha" of George and Ira Gershwin (ca. 1921). In "Tchaikovsky (and Other Russians)" in *Lady in the Dark* (Broadway 1941, film 1944), Ira Gershwin, now writing with Kurt Weill, would test the patter song to destruction by requiring the singer to give a *presto* rendering of the names of forty-nine Russian composers and one Yiddish playwright.[58]

Solange La Fitte follows the Whitmans. She sings a hymn to a Paris that, for "ooh-la-la," outdoes all other cities of the civilized world. Solange has in mind the Folies Bergère, and also Maurice Chevalier, less the nostalgic Chevalier of *Gigi* (1958) than the saucy "Apache" of Rodgers and Hart's "That's the Song of Paree," in Rouben Mamoulian's innovative *Love Me Tonight*:

> It has taxi-horns and klaxons,
> To scare the Anglo-Saxons,
> That's the Song of Paree.
> It has men that sell you postcards,
> Much naughtier than most cards,
> That's the Song of Paree....
> You'd sell your wife and daughter,
> For just one Latin Quarter.
> That's the Song of Paree.[59]

A hymn to Broadway concludes this group. Hattie Walker sings "Broadway Baby." Her tired feet have been pounding the street for many years "to be in a show." Sondheim's suggestion of the models for the song confirms that she is not disheartened by her failure. The team of DeSylva, Brown, and Henderson wrote for a number of revues and produced such jaunty feel-good songs as "The Best Things in Life Are Free" (from *Good News*, 1927), and "Button up Your Overcoat" (from *Follow Thru*, 1929). As Joanne Gordon points out, Sondheim's three songs are presented with sympathy as well as irony, showing a respect for the tenacity of the old troupers. This is endorsed in a later song, "I'm Still Here" (no. 14). Sung by Carlotta Campion, this is again a hymn, not to Broadway, but to the survival of the trouper through "good times and bum times," presented by Sondheim as a bravura list of contextual allusions occupying some hundred lines.[60]

The four main characters are treated with much less sympathy. Their songs confirm that they are the fools of the *Follies*. The first, "Don't Look At Me" (no. 4) begun by Sally and then joined by Ben, highlights the conflicting emotions, false bonhomie and game-playing that characterize many reunions. Ben's concluding remark, "what we need is a drink," may well be his last honest emotion. Thereafter, the quartet fail to break out of the illusions about their youth because they surround themselves with lies. The next song, "Waiting for the Girls Upstairs" (no. 5), set in ABA form, contrasts "the remembered joy of being young," with a petty quarrel between their younger counterparts over the after-hours "joint" they will visit. The song then returns to the reminiscences of the older quartet: "Waiting around for the girls upstairs—/ Thank you but never again." Of course they don't mean it. The first and third sections alternate memories, sung in a jaunty tempo, with slower, longing interludes: "Hey, up there! / Way up there!" A wistful and sad five-note phrase, played initially on the oboe, is repeated rather than completed. Their present-day unhappiness has locked all four into a time when the major event for them was to wait.[61]

Both sad and jazzy, "Waiting for the Girls Upstairs" has a predecessor in "Ain't We Got Fun," which first appeared in the revue *Satires of 1920*, and then became a popular recording:

> In the winter, in the summer, don't we have fun,
> Times are bum and getting bummer, still we have fun,
> There's nothing surer,
> The rich get rich, and the poor get—children,
> In the meantime, in between time, ain't we got fun.

The song appears in *The Great Gatsby*. Sung by Ewing Klipspringer, it causes "bewilderment" on Gatsby's face and prompts Nick to reflect on "the colossal vitality of his illusion," which, decked out "with every bright feather that drifted his way," far exceeds the human frailty of Daisy. Nick concludes, "no amount of fire or freshness can challenge what a man can store up in his ghostly heart."[62] Klipspringer's song, then, sums up the complex issues of wealth and desire, illusion and transience that are the essence of *The Great Gatsby*. Fitzgerald's novel is a premature requiem to the Jazz Age. *Follies* performs a similar, now posthumous, function for the whole interwar period.

The "Montage" of three vaudeville songs follows. In the meantime, Sally and Buddy, Phyllis and Ben have been thinking about their present lives. Ben's song, "The Road You Didn't Take" (no. 7), in a whirling 3/4 time, is constructed as a series of questions that undermine Ben's self-confident assertion of success. The song may have three literary sources, indicating Ben's cultural pretensions. The title may refer to Robert Frost's 1916 poem "The Road Not Taken," where the narrator is confronted with a choice and its consequences. A phrase in the song suggests Kierkegaard's *Either/Or* (1843), in which the Danish philosopher contrasts the hedonistic and ethical views of life. The questioning phrases hint at Henry James's frightening ghost story "The Jolly Corner" (1907), where the Europeanized protagonist, Spencer Brydon, enters into a conflict with the mutilated ghost of his alternative self in a large and decaying Manhattan house. The music too reflects Ben's unease, with a muted horn note in F natural creating what Sondheim called "a stabbing dissonance" to the dancing flute accompaniment.[63] A similar melody in slower 3/4 time introduces Sally's song (no. 10), in which she tells of her perfectly "ducky" suburban life and her eternal youth and beauty "In Buddy's Eyes." The uneasy parallel between Ben and Sally's dissimulating songs is separated, first by angry exchanges between Buddy and Phyllis, who are now aware that Sally still loves Ben; and second, by the "Bolero d'Amour" (no. 9). This is a tango, taken at a more urgent tempo than Ravel's *Bolero*, but (fortunately for the dancers) occupying less than a quarter of its time. A vaudeville dance-team, Vincent and Vanessa, dance it with their younger counterparts. They are able to complete this demanding dance because, after the Follies, they say they bought a franchise from the Arthur Murray Dance Studio, and kept in shape. This may be a laudatory reference to Doris Eaton Travis. She danced in the 1920 *Follies*, premiered the song "Singin' in the Rain," became an Arthur Murray instructor, marrying one of her pupils and eventually owning eighteen Arthur Murray studios in Michigan. She began dancing again on Broadway at the age of ninety-four, and died in May 2010 at the age of 106, the last Ziegfeld Girl.[64]

The more common physical consequences of nostalgia are enacted in "Who's That Woman" (no. 12), often known as "The Mirror Song." The music echoes the typical revue production number, as well as Gershwin and Dixieland Jazz. It is sung and danced by a chorus line comprising Phyllis, Sally, and five others, shadowed by their younger selves. They ask the Queen's question from *Snow White*, get an unhappy answer, and as their dancing ends, the younger selves withdraw to leave "seven breathless middle-aged ladies."[65] In a complex trio, Ben sings his love song, "Too Many Mornings" (no. 15), to Young Sally, but it is the present-day Sally who mimics the embrace with Ben, and then sings her response. The sense of loss created by wrong choices is broken by Buddy's song, "The Right Girl" (no. 16), where with crudely thrusting, syncopated interjections, "Yeah," Buddy reveals his affair with Margie and his self-doubts, summed up in his uncertainty about his "home."[66] The bad temper that breaks out in Buddy's song is amplified in Phyllis's "Could I Leave You?" (no. 18). The song presents the clearest reference to the whirling conclusion of Ravel's *La Valse*. Phyllis's question "shall we dance?" therefore has nothing to do with the "urgent solicitude" of the Gershwins' title tune in the Astaire–Rogers movie *Shall We Dance*.[67] It is also as far as possible from the thumping, ungainly waltz in the Rodgers and Hammerstein musical *The King and I*.[68] Instead, "shall we dance?" is merely one of an increasingly passionate list of rhetorical questions, which finally brings the waltz to a shuddering halt with "Guess!"[69]

Buddy and Sally, Phyllis and Ben now turn on each other, and then on their younger selves, in a raucous and demented babble. This is the sign for "Loveland" (no. 19-1) to begin, in what can only be described as a *coup de théâtre*. The backdrops, "all valentines and lace," suddenly descend, and beautiful young dancers appear, "all dressed like Dresden dolls and cavaliers," parading to a slow waltz. It is difficult to come to grips with this sudden change. Sandor Goodhart, in a detailed account of the 1971 production, compares *Follies* with Jerzy Kosinski's novel *The Painted Bird* (1965) to suggest that we are experiencing a break in narrative but not of context.[70] We could also resort to mathematics where, in catastrophe theory, a small change in values causes a sudden, unpredicted shift in behavior of a system. A third way of looking at the change would be in terms of temporal reversal. Instead of comparing the past from the point of view of the present, we are comparing the present from the point of view of the past. Sondheim's "Loveland" therefore projects us back into the exotic "Loveland" sequence from the 1929 film produced by Ziegfeld, *Glorifying the American Girl*.[71] The childish words of the chorus project us even further back, to "Toyland," from the 1903 operetta *Babes in Toyland*, by Victor Herbert and Glen MacDonough: "Toyland! Toyland! / Little girl and boy-land!" The comparison is not flattering to the present, for the closing two lines of "Toyland" —"Once you pass its borders / You can ne'er return again" —contain a warning that is not repeated in "Loveland." Therefore, while "Loveland" silences the octet, it only begins a catharsis that is the opposite of the "happiest moments" suggested in Minnelli's *Ziegfeld Follies* (Figure 24.2).[72]

As Harold Prince put it, Buddy and Sally, Phyllis and Ben are forced to "confront in lavish production numbers the lies that had led them relentlessly to the brink of madness."[73] Young Ben and Phyllis sing "You're Gonna Love Tomorrow" and are joined by Young Buddy and Sally in "Love Will See Us Through" (no. 19-2). Sondheim suggested that the young quartet's song could draw on "Jerome Kern and Burton Lane, with an Ira Gershwin-E. Y. Harburg lyric." This reads like a puzzle-writer's trick, but two songs come to mind: the jaunty "Who," from the Broadway musical *Sunny* (Kern–Harbach–Hammerstein, 1925), and Lane and Harburg's list song "How About You," from the Rooney–Garland sequel, *Babes on Broadway*. Allusion to those songs would support Joanne Gordon's remarks that, "there is a painful irony in the buoyant and carefree assertion of [the] continuing happiness" of the young quartet.[74]

FIGURE 24.2 The "Loveland" sequence in *Follies* (1971).

That irony is highlighted in the next song, when the older Buddy descends into slapstick comedy. Dressed in "plaid baggy pants, bright blue jacket, and a shiny derby hat," with "a plywood model car" suspended from his waist, Buddy sings his hymn to discontent, "Buddy's Blues" (no. 19-3). The alternative title, "The-God-Why-Don't-You-Love-Me-Oh-You-Do-I'll-See-You-Later Blues," suggest a Gershwin song from *Lady, Be Good!* (1924), while the motorized encounters with Sally and Margie draw on Ira Gershwin's comic thespian rendition of a Blues lament: "I've got the You-Don't-Know-the Half-of-It-Dearie Blues. / The trouble is you have so many from whom to choose."[75] The contrast with Sally's song, "Losing My Mind" (no. 19-4) is striking. If Buddy's "folly" is the fear of commitment, Sally's is her addiction to the idea of love. It is expressed in a torch song reminiscent, according to Sondheim, of Gershwin's "The Man I Love." Other candidates are those songs that explore the masochistic underbelly of love: "Mon Homme" by Maurice Yvain (1916, recorded in English by Fanny Brice in 1921); "Ich bin von Kopf bis Fuss auf Liebe eingestellt" by Friedrich Hollaender, introduced by Marlene Dietrich in the film *Der blaue Engel* (1930) and then becoming her trademark song in the anglophone world as "Falling in Love Again (Can't Help It)"; the Rodgers–Hart, "Falling in Love with Love" (1938); or "I Got It Bad And That Ain't Good" by Duke Ellington and Ben Webster (1941).[76]

The counterpoint of "folly" songs continues. Phyllis's song, "Lucy and Jessie" (no. 19-5), is a story "about two unhappy dames," reflecting a personality problem that tips, near its noisy close, toward schizophrenia. The theme of the song recalls *Lady in the Dark*, the lyrics demonstrate a verbal felicity equal to Noël Coward or Cole Porter, and the music resembles Porter's "It's Alright with Me" (1953).[77] Ben, too, has a personality disorder, expressed in his song "Live, Laugh, Love" (no. 19-6), its triad reflecting the title of the 1869 Strauss waltz *Wine, Women and Song*. He confesses that his many achievements mean nothing to him, and the revelation causes him to break down under the pressure of the relentless music. Stephen Banfield suggested that the number recalls the Gershwins' "Fascinating Rhythm," again from *Lady, Be Good!*, and, certainly, its "little rhythm" is driving Ben "insane."[78]

Ben's frightening breakdown precipitates another reversal. The Follies backdrops are raised, and the cacophony brings us back to the ruined Weismann Theater, where the party is in its final drunken stages. The younger quartet watch as Buddy and Sally, Ben and Phyllis prepare to go home. A furious Phyllis shouts the moral of the evening, symbolized by the songs of the old troupers: "hope doesn't grow on trees; we make our own and I am here to tell you it's the hardest thing we'll ever do." But the Curtain (no. 19-8) does not reinforce her angry optimism. It is, rather, a reprise of "Waiting for the Girls Upstairs," with the five-note figure on the oboe introducing the call of Young Ben and Young Buddy: "Hey, up there! / Way up there!" It suggests that the four still have much to learn from the Walpurgisnacht that was Weismann's reunion.

The structure of *Follies*, maintaining a delicate balance between the celebration and critique of earlier American music theater, is derived from Sondheim's understanding of the art of Ravel. That structure is well represented by the image on the cover of the vocal score, LP, and CD of the 1971 production. It is based on the caryatid, the female sculpture that acted as a column on classical Greek buildings. Caryatids, revived by neoclassical architects, are to be found in many environments. For instance, they surround the auditorium of the Goldener Saal of the Musikverein in Vienna, built in 1870. Unlike the caryatids of the Goldener Saal, their *Follies* sister will not survive the burden placed upon her, for there is a fissure running down from the entablature and across her face. This was certainly the case with the 1985 *Follies in Concert*, semistaged in the Lincoln Center. There were of course a number of positive moments. Sondheim's music deserved the virtuosity of the New York Philharmonic. Lee Remick carried a pink feather boa even longer than Gloria Swanson's. Elaine Stritch performed "Broadway Baby" with her customary verve. But the ironic structure of *Follies* was lost with the dramaturgy. It is frequently said that nostalgia isn't what it used to be, but the audience at Avery Fisher Hall forgot that timely joke. As Mark Steyn put it, *Follies in Concert*, "packed with ageing stars to whom we accord standing ovations for merely standing," suffocated the cool self-examination that characterized the 1971 production.[79] A similar fate swamped the 1987 London production, although it was fully staged. Any of the songs sung out of context will lose their ironic potency. In July 2010 a Promenade Concert at London's Royal Albert Hall celebrated "Sondheim at 80." "Too Many Mornings," beautifully sung and played, lost its bite and became merely a lovely love song. The place to start a fresh-air approach to *Follies* is the recording of the 1998 Paper Mill Playhouse production. The denizens of Broadway are frequently contemptuous of New Jersey, but that production at Milburn, NJ, captured much of the spirit of *Follies*. The songs in the recording are sometimes poorly sung, but poor singing can be an essential part of Sondheim's lovingly ironical, antimusical musical.

Notes

The author gratefully acknowledges the award of a Leverhulme Emeritus Fellowship, and the musical advice of Jenny Wigram; both have been invaluable in the preparation of this chapter.

1. Stephen Sondheim, *Follies* (vocal score) (Milwaukee, WI: Hal Leonard, 1971), 5. The numbers in brackets refer to the numbering of the 1971 vocal score. To date there have been five CD recordings of *Follies* productions. The (heavily cut) "Original Broadway cast recording" of 1971 is on Angel ZDM7 64666-2. The 1985 New York Philharmonic *Follies in Concert* is available on videotape and DVD, and the audio recording is on 2CD RCA RCD2-7128. The 1987 "Original London cast recording" is on 2CD First Night/Encore CD3. The recording of the 1998 Paper Mill Playhouse production is the most complete, with the entire score and an appendix of rejected songs; it is on 2CD TVT Soundtrax TVT 1030-2. The latest two-CD recording on PS Classics, PS-1105, is the 2011 Kennedy Center revival, which played on Broadway later that year with Bernadette Peters as Sally, and includes a fair amount of dialogue.

2. Matthew F. Jordan, *Le Jazz: Jazz and French Cultural Identity* (Urbana: University of Illinois Press, 2010), 49–53.

3. Sondheim, London *Guardian* Lecture, quoted in Meryle Secrest, *Stephen Sondheim: A Life* (New York: Alfred A. Knopf, 1998), 72.

4. On Sondheim's interest in Ravel, see Stephen Banfield, *Sondheim's Broadway Musicals* (Ann Arbor: University of Michigan Press, 1993), 12, 400–401; and Steve Swayne, *How Sondheim Found His Sound* (Ann Arbor: University of Michigan Press, 2005), 10–20.

5. Ravel, 1928 comments published posthumously in "Une Esquisse autobiographique," *La Revue Musicale* (December 1938), 22. There is a translation in Arbie Orenstein, ed., *A Ravel Reader* (New York: Columbia University Press, 1990), 32.

6. Ravel, interviews in *De Telegraaf* (Amsterdam), 1922, and *ABC de Madrid*, 1924, translated in Orenstein, *Ravel Reader*, 423, 433–4.

7. Ibid.

8. Ibid.

9. See, for instance, Madelaine Goss, *Bolero: The Life of Maurice Ravel* (New York: Henry Holt, 1940), 187–9; and Gerald Larner, *Maurice Ravel* (London: Phaidon, 1996), 173–4. Deborah Mawer, *The Ballets of Maurice Ravel: Creation and Interpretation* (Aldershot, UK: Ashgate, 2006), 149–56, suggests a Symbolist analysis in addition to the aesthetic and sociocultural ones.

10. Ravel, letter 4 April 1916 to Jean Marnold, translated in Orenstein, *Ravel Reader*, 162–3.

11. Jessica Duchen, *Erich Wolfgang Korngold* (London: Phaidon, 1996), 87–8.

12. Rosenthal, in Roger Nichols, *Ravel Remembered* (London: Faber, 1987), 62–3.

13. Rosenthal, in Nichols, *Ravel Remembered*, 62–3.

14. See Swayne, *How Sondheim*.

15. Mark Eden Horowitz, *Sondheim on Music: Minor Details and Major Decisions* (Lanham, MD: Scarecrow, 2003), 49.

16. Larner, *Ravel*, 149.

17. For a thoughtful analysis of the complex relation of Ravel's life and work, see Steven Huebner, "Maurice Ravel: Private Life, Public Works," *Musical Biography: Towards New Paradigms*, ed. Jolanta T. Pekacz, 69–87 (Aldershot, UK: Ashgate, 2006). Although Huebner never mentions Sondheim, there are many parallels to be drawn between the two composers.

18. Horowitz, *Sondheim on Music*, 40.

19. Theodor Adorno, *Quasi una Fantasia: Essays on Modern Music*, trans. Rodney Livingstone (London: Verso, 1992), 10.

20. Adorno, "On Popular Music [1941]," in *Essays on Music*, ed. Richard Leppert (Berkeley: University of California Press, 2002), 462. On negative attitudes to Ravel, see Swayne, *How Sondheim*, 15–16.

21. Margaret Rose, *Parody: Ancient, Modern, and Postmodern* (Cambridge: Cambridge University Press, 1993), 72–7, 221–42; Simon Dentith, *Parody* (London: Routledge, 2000), 155–6, 194.

22. Sondheim, in "The Once and Future Follies," *Time*, 3 May 1971, 35.

23. Sondheim, "The Musical Theater," in *Broadway Song and Story: Playwrights, Lyricists, Composers Discuss their Hits*, ed. Otis L. Guernsey Jr. and Terrence McNally (New York: Dodd, Mead, 1985), 234.

24. Sondheim, quoted in Craig Zadan, *Sondheim & Co.*, 2nd ed. (New York: Harper & Row, 1989), 136.

25. Sondheim, "Theater Lyrics," in *Playwrights, Lyricists, Composers on Theater*, ed. Otis L. Guernsey Jr. (New York: Dodd, Mead, 1974), 91. For a thorough sociopolitical analysis of *Follies*, see James Fisher, "Nixon's America and *Follies*: Reappraising a Musical Theater Classic," in *Stephen Sondheim: A Casebook*, ed. Joanne Gordon (New York: Garland, 1997), 69–85.

26. James Goldman and Stephen Sondheim, *Follies: A Musical* (New York: Random House, 1971), 3.

27. Sondheim, "Musical Theater," 238.

28. See, for instance, Peter Brook's minimalist definition of "an act of theatre," in Brook, *The Empty Space* (London: MacGibbon and Kee, 1968), 9.

29. Hal Prince, *Contradictions: Notes on Twenty-six Years in the Theatre* (New York: Dodd, Mead, 1974), 158–70; and Sondheim, "Musical Theater," 231–2. Federico Fellini, Director, *8½*, 1963. For an overview of Prince's career, see Foster Hirsch, *Harold Prince and the American Musical Theatre*, rev. and expanded ed. (New York: Applause, 2005).

30. Jean-Paul Sartre, *Literary and Philosophical Essays* (1955), quoted in *Faulkner: A Collection of Critical Essays*, ed. Robert Penn Warren (Englewood Cliffs, NJ: Prentice-Hall, 1966), 93. Dorothy Hart, *Thou Swell, Thou Witty: The Life and Lyrics of Lorenz Hart* (1976; reprint, London: Elm Tree, 1978), 135–6, 240.

31. Busby Berkeley, director, *Babes in Arms*, 1939. Gene Kelly and Stanley Donen, directors, *Singin' in the Rain*, 1952. Stanley Green, *Broadway Musicals: Show by Show* 6th ed. (London and Boston: Applause, 2010), 98. Stanley Green, *Encyclopaedia of the Musical Film* (New York: Oxford University Press, 1981), 18–19. For an analysis of the swing vs. opera sequence in *Babes in Arms*, see Jane Feuer, *The Hollywood Musical*, 2nd ed. (London: Macmillan, 1993), 58–9.

32. Billy Wilder, director, *Sunset Boulevard*, 1950. On Swanson, see Ted Chapin, *Everything Was Possible: The Birth of the Musical "Follies"* (New York: Applause, 2003), 7–8. The photograph of Swanson is opposite p. 144.

33. F. Scott Fitzgerald, *The Great Gatsby* (1926; reprint, Harmondsworth: Penguin, 1990), 106, 171.

34. Goldman and Sondheim, *Follies*, 7.

35. Doris Eaton, quoted in Ann Ommen van der Merwe, *The Ziegfeld Follies: A History in Song* (Lanham, MD: Scarecrow, 2009), 133, 52. Irving Berlin, *A Pretty Girl is Like a Melody* (London: Herman Darewski, 1919).

36. Sondheim, "Beautiful Girls," *Follies*, 1971.

37. Prince, *Contradictions*, 158. In her excellent discussion in *Art Isn't Easy: The Theater of Stephen Sondheim* (New York: Da Capo, 1992), 81, Joanne Gordon suggests that George White—originally Weitz—could also be the original of Weismann.

38. Charles Castle, *The Folies Bergère* (London: Methuen, 1982), 104–105.

39. Howard Hawks, director, *Gentlemen Prefer Blondes*, 1953. On Hawks and the Hays Code, see Robin Wood, *Howard Hawks* (London: BFI, 1981), 174–7.

40. Lewis A. Erenberg, *Steppin' Out: New York Nightlife and the Transformation of American Culture, 1890–1930* (Chicago: University of Chicago Press, 1981), 218–24. Robert C. Allen, *Horrible Prettyness: Burlesque and American Culture* (Chapel Hill: University of North Carolina Press, 1991), 245–6. Linda Mizejewski, *Ziegfeld Girl: Image and Icon in Culture and Cinema* (Durham, NC: Duke University Press, 1999), 92–103.

41. Eddie Cantor and David Freeman, *Ziegfeld: The Great Glorifier* (New York: Alfred H. King, 1934), 9.

42. Mizejewski, *Ziegfeld Girl*, 159–68.

43. Green, *Encyclopaedia of the Musical Film*, 114.

44. Robert Z. Leonard, director, *The Great Ziegfeld*, 1936.

45. Robert Z. Leonard, director, *Ziegfeld Girl*, 1941.

46. Vincente Minnelli, director, *Ziegfeld Follies*, 1946.

47. Prince, *Contradictions*, 160.

48. Sondheim, "The Musical Theater," 229, 231, 238, 242.

49. Minnelli, *Ziegfeld Follies*.

50. Sondheim, "The Musical Theater," 229. Sondheim, interview with Sheridan Morley, "Sondheim by Sondheim," *The Listener*, 1 May 1986, 21. *In their Own Words: Contemporary American Playwrights*, ed. David Savran (New York: Theatre Communications Group, 1988), 227. An analysis of the 1971 Broadway production in Brechtian and postmodernist terms can be found in Ann Marie McEntee, "The Funeral of *Follies*," in *Reading Stephen Sondheim: A Collection of Critical Essays*, ed. Sandor Goodhart, 89–99 (New York: Garland, 2000).

51. Jerome Kern and Oscar Hammerstein II, "Make-Believe," *Show Boat* (New York: T. B. Harms, 1927). James Whale, director, *Showboat*, 1936. George Sidney, director, *Showboat*, 1951.

52. Richard Rodgers and Oscar Hammerstein II, *Carousel* (vocal score) (London: Williamson, 1945), 41–42. Henry King, director, *Carousel*, 1956.

53. Sondheim, quoted in Zadan, *Sondheim & Co.*, 135.

54. Mark Steyn, "Seventies Sondheim on Broadway: *Follies*," broadcast on BBC Radio 3, 28 July 1990.

55. Goldman and Sondheim, *Follies*, 72, 17–18. Victor Herbert and Henry Blossom, *Mlle. Modiste* (New York: Witmark, 1905). Neil Gould, *Victor Herbert: A Theatrical Life* (New York: Fordham University Press, 2008), 343–61.

56. Banfield, *Sondheim's Broadway Musicals*, 43; Secrest, *Sondheim*, 240–43, 267–8.

57. Banfield, *Sondheim's Broadway Musicals*, 198. Mark Sandrich, director, *Top Hat*, 1935.
58. Ira Gershwin, *Lyrics on Several Occasions* (1959; reprinted, London: Elm Tree, 1977), 177–8. Bruce D. McClung, *Lady in the Dark: Biography of a Musical* (New York: Oxford University Press, 2007), 66.
59. Rouben Mamoulian, director, *Love Me Tonight*, 1932.
60. Goldman and Sondheim, *Follies*, 32–6, 57–60; Zadan, *Sondheim & Co.*, 147; Gordon, *Art Isn't Easy*, 88–9, 91–2.
61. Goldman and Sondheim, *Follies*, 19–20, 24–31.
62. "Ain't We Got Fun" (1921), words by Gus Kahn and Raymond B. Egan, music by Richard Whiting. Fitzgerald, *The Great Gatsby*, 92–3.
63. Goldman and Sondheim, *Follies*, 37–40. Sondheim, "Theater Lyrics," 71.
64. Goldman and Sondheim, *Follies*, 41–6, 17; "Doris E. Travis, Last of the Ziegfeld Girls, Dies at 106," *New York Times*, 12 May 2010.
65. Goldman and Sondheim, *Follies*, 48–52.
66. Goldman and Sondheim, *Follies*, 62–70. Gordon, *Art Isn't Easy*, 100–105. A photograph of the staging of "Too Many Mornings" is in Chapin, *Everything Was Possible*, 178.
67. Gershwin, *Lyrics*, 287. Mark Sandrich, director, *Shall We Dance?*, 1937
68. Walter Lang, director, *The King and I*, 1956.
69. Goldman and Sondheim, *Follies*, 75–7.
70. Sandor Goodhart, "Reading Sondheim: The End of Ever After," in *Reading Stephen Sondheim: A Collection of Critical Essays*, ed. Sandor Goodhart (New York City: Garland, 2000), 24–6.
71. Millard Webb, John Harkrider, directors, *Glorifying the American Girl*, 1929. See Mizejewski, *Ziegfeld Girl*, 148–9.
72. Goldman and Sondheim, *Follies*, 77–83. Victor Herbert and Glen MacDonough, *Babes in Toyland* (New York: Witmark, 1903-4).
73. Prince, *Contradictions*, 161.
74. Zadan, *Sondheim & Co.*, 147. Goldman and Sondheim, *Follies*, 87–94. Gordon, *Art Isn't Easy*, 111. Busby Berkeley, director, *Babes on Broadway*, 1941.
75. Goldman and Sondheim, *Follies*, 95–100; Gershwin, *Lyrics*, 32.
76. Goldman and Sondheim, *Follies*, 100–101; Horowitz, *Sondheim on Music*, 48.
77. Goldman and Sondheim, *Follies*, 101–103; Swayne, *How Sondheim*, 59; Chapin, *Everything Was Possible*, 242.
78. Goldman and Sondheim, *Follies*, 103–8; Banfield, *Sondheim's Broadway Musicals*, 199–200; Gershwin, *Lyrics*, 172–4.
79. Mark Steyn, "Seventies Sondheim."

CHAPTER 25

NARRATIVES OF PROGRESS
AND TRAGEDY IN *PACIFIC*
OVERTURES

....

PAUL FILMER

PROGRESS AND TRAGEDY IN THE MOMENT
OF *PACIFIC OVERTURES*

....

THE mixed critical reception that greeted *Pacific Overtures* prefigured a continuing con-troversy about its difficulty as a work of musical theater.[1] Apart from the exoticism and unfamiliarity to its early audiences of its oriental setting, it marks the realization of an incipient tendency toward exploring tragedy as a cultural phenomenon of modernity that can be found in Sondheim's work as early as the murder or suicide dream sequence in *All that Glitters* (1949). The dramatic structure of *West Side Story* (1957) as a specifi-cally American tragedy provided a site for its consolidation. The "Sharks" and the "Jets" represent the structural clash between migrant and indigenous communities in urban and metropolitan American society, which the individual attempts of Tony and Maria to transcend through their love cannot so simply resolve. The progressive ideal of the "melting pot" of large-scale immigration as assimilative Americanization, central to the political cultural identity of the United States as an industrial democracy, is exposed as generating in reality a discriminatory societal and economic hierarchy of irreconcilable otherness. In individual and subcultural terms, this both causes and is reflected in the inevitable tragedy of the death of the two lovers.

In *Pacific Overtures*, the principal characters themselves are involved or implicated in murder: of Kayama, the erstwhile samurai, by his friend, the former fisherman, Manjiro; of the Shogun by his mother, from whom we learn, almost incidentally, that he has earlier killed his own father. These homicidal acts explicate and develop the narrative—a fea-ture which may be seen as prefiguring Sondheim's later, more detailed exploration of it as the actions of psychopaths and sociopaths in *Sweeney Todd* (1979) and *Assassins* (1991). Murder is unavoidably tragic, the antithesis of comedy and perhaps, therefore, at least implicitly, one of the grounds on which some critics (e.g., Lahr[2]) have accused Sondheim of betraying the vernacular tradition[3] of entertainment in American musical theater.

THE PROGRESSIVE NARRATIVE
OF MODERNITY

Accidental deaths as minor tragedies can feature in musical theatrical plots as necessary conditions for a successful resolution, the proverbial happy ending (the death of Jud Fry engineered by Sondheim's mentor, Hammerstein, in *Oklahoma!* for example). But as a serious dramatist of late modernity, Sondheim has to confront the tragic interruptions to the continuing and unfinished project of modernity, as well as its dark side, that have come to constitute for some critical theorists the threatening specter of its failure. Late modernity is premised on the ambitious, Western Enlightenment vision of increasingly secular, humanist rationalism replacing the theologies, myths, and superstitions of (often non-Western) traditional societies. The federal republic of United States of America was the first society to formulate itself in these terms by creating from scratch the institutions through which the political philosophies in which its constitution was rooted could be put in to practice. As a consequence, it became the first postcolonial society, having to defend its integrity against a series of attempted reincursions by the original, colonizing European powers. The wealth and scale of its subcontinental resources enabled it initially to turn, under the isolationist foreign policies of the Monroe doctrine during the first half of the nineteenth century, away from Europe toward its own internal development.[4] By the mid-nineteenth century, however, its burgeoning industrialization and mercantile wealth led to the development of its own form of orientalism.[5] And this is the moment of the historical narrative at which the action of *Pacific Overtures* begins. Sondheim formulates this quite specifically in setting out what he terms "The Notion" of the work:

> A chronicle of Japanese history, beginning with the 1853 incursion of American warships…into Japanese waters in order to open up trade with a nation that had been closed to foreigners for centuries.[6]

The text thus has a dual character: it is about both Japanese society and the American incursion into it. This duality generates a reflexive interrelation between the two societies, concerned with the confrontation of tradition by modernity and the historical and cultural consequences for both of them in the immediate and longer term. For both societies, the encounter is a traumatic event that changes irrevocably the existing orders of each of them in ways that may not immediately be apparent and which, thus, have continuing consequences that are yet to be experienced or understood. For the Japanese, the consequences of the incursion are immediately apparent and potentially tragic, precipitating strenuous attempts to contain them in order to sustain their exist-ing cultural traditions. For the Americans, the encounter is an event in the inevitable progress of modernity's surmounting of tradition. From a cultural sociological perspec-tive,[7] the structures of both cultures are altered irrevocably and require new represen-tations of the meanings of the changes to those experiencing them—in effect, a new chronicling of the historicity of the events. It is from this necessity that the tragic narra-tive of *Pacific Overtures* emerges, since there can no longer be any "sense that something else could have been done, and no belief that the future could, or can, necessarily be changed.... [In both cultures] the protagonists are tragic...because...they are in the grip of forces larger than themselves".[8]

The problem of historicity is a constant and unavoidably ambiguous presence in Sondheim's work, as it must be for any serious modernist. Modernism ties itself to the existential immediacy of the present, insisting on both a necessary break with the past, and a refusal to predicate a future, as the dual conditions of its distinctive real-ity. Sondheim explores recurrently the contingent relativization of history that follows from this for contemporary Americans in different ways and between different struc-tural levels of social relations. In both *Company* (1970) and *Merrily We Roll Along* (1981) he examines the emotional effects that the biographies of individuals have on their rela-tions with others. He moves beyond the distinctive individualism of American culture to examine the constraining structural effects of social status on personal relationships in the Swedish setting of *A Little Night Music* (1973). The continuing influence of tra-dition on modernity is exposed through the permeation of cultural consciousness by myth in *Into the Woods* (1987), and in *Follies* (1971) he engages reflexively with the tradi-tion of musical theater itself. The distinctiveness of *Pacific Overtures*, however, is that it moves the site for this historiographic aspect of Sondheim's work from the individual and intrasocietal to the intersocietal relations between America and Japan, and thus, implicitly, onto a global scale and the attendant grand narratives that doing so entails.

STRUCTURING THE TRAGIC NARRATIVE OF MODERNIZATION

The structural abstractions required to accomplish this are embedded in the text of *Pacific Overtures* from the outset, though they draw on conventions characteristic of Sondheim's work. Despite Sondheim's own dislike of the term,[9] it is not inappropriate to consider *Pacific Overtures* as a concept musical, but in a reflexive sense. He has said that he wants it to induce in its audience a sense both of exhilaration and thoughtfulness:

> I want them to consider what's happened in the world, how time is catching us at the throat, how we are being rushed into careless and thoughtless decisions, as a govern-ment and as a people. We Americans have a special tendency to ignore history. We remember only what is pleasant. We must have a sense of the past. Without it the present is meaningless and stupid.[10]

The concept at the core of *Pacific Overtures* is history itself, and the elegance of the organization of its narrative on several homologous levels invites structural analysis. The work's presentational form is located in the semiotic conventions of Japanese kabuki theater, complemented by the narrator and chorus of classical tragedy, while its lyrics and music recurrently use, respectively, the minimalist conventions of the haiku and the dissonant harmonies of the Japanese minor pentatonic scale.[11] Sondheim elaborated these conventions to provide several representations of global cultural otherness. While the primary other, for this presentational form of Japan, is America, Sondheim also evokes, through pastiches on earlier musical theatrical and vaudeville genres (with the song "Please Hello" in the second act), Britain, Holland, Russia, and France, as the cultural invaders that followed, two of which (Britain and France) had attempted postcolonial reincursions into the United States during the half-century prior to the moment of *Pacific Overtures*. Sondheim and Prince initially drew the logic of the conventions from an engaging reflexive conceit. As Sondheim puts it:

> What we actually did was to create a mythical Japanese playwright in our heads, who has come to New York, seen a couple of Broadway shows, and then goes back home and writes a musical about Commodore Perry's visit to Japan. It's this premise that helped to give tone and style for the show.[12] (Figure 25.1) This "myth" is itself an inversion of what actually happened in Sondheim and Prince's own preparations. The sense of "tone and style" that Sondheim sought stemmed at least in part from

FIGURE **25.1** Commodore Perry's ship in *Pacific Overtures* (1976).

his dismissal of the exoticism of Rodgers and Hammerstein's orientalist incursions in *South Pacific* and *The King and I*, both of which, he suggested, could as well have taken place in Brooklyn,[13] which led him to make a short visit to Japan with Prince, but one long enough for them to be able to attend Noh and kabuki theater, as well as gain some knowledge of both music and visual art.

Also characteristic of Sondheim's work is the exploration of history through the effects of social changes on individual experience. He teases out the reflexive structural features of personal relationships in their social contexts as a basis for the typifications required for all cultural representations—not least in the chronicling of history. This is at the core of "The Notion" of *Pacific Overtures*:

> In particular, it concerns the relationship during the next fifteen years between Kayama, a minor samurai relegated to order the ships to leave, and Manjiro, a Japanese fisherman recently returned from the United States.[14]

Throughout act 1, alongside the other characters, Kayama and Manjiro consciously embody and enact, in and as their living present, the historical changes that it chronicles. In each number, the characters represent and explore their experiences of changing events, concluding with "Someone in a Tree," the song which Sondheim says "comes closest to the heart of *Pacific Overtures*."[15] Act 2, by contrast, opens and continues with a series of typifications, stereotypes for the most part, of individuals and groups as cultural representations. These senses of Western and non-Western otherness, and their inversions, mark the overarching outer dimensions of the entire narrative structure of the work. The reciter opens the narrative thus:

> Nippon. The Floating Kingdom. An island empire which for centuries has lived in perfect peace, undisturbed by intruders from across the sea. There was a time when foreigners were welcome here, but they took advantage of our friendship. Two hundred and fifty years ago we drove them out…and ordered them never again to set foot on our ancestral soil. From then until this day…there has been nothing to threaten the serene and changeless cycle of our days.[16]

And closes it: "Nippon. The Floating Kingdom. There was a time when foreigners were not welcome here. But that was long ago. One hundred and fifty years. Welcome to Japan."[17]

The inversion inherent in Weidman and Sondheim's conceit is here embedded as the narrative's historiography of sociocultural change. Time has suffered the postmodern compression: centuries of serene and changeless isolation have been condensed into a "long ago" of a century and a half, during which Japanese society has undergone an almost complete change from being grounded in tradition to a condition of modernity—indeed, it has become the exemplar of postindustrial economic inversion of universal consumerism as the motor of economic production.

The opening is followed and the closing is preceded by nondiegetic songs, that as Sondheim himself puts it, tell "a story which occurs over a period of time and which contains actual incident, but in song form, as opposed to *recitative*."[18] Most of the songs in act 1 use such nondiegetic form to set out the narrative historical sequence, a function which Sondheim further develops by deploying what Banfield terms "musically and lyrically, a matter of additive structure. The picture of what happened is built up by a complex concatenation of statements, including contradictions and corrections,"[19] which are expanded by the music and described in the lyrics.

Thus, following the opening, "The Advantages of Floating in the Middle of the Sea" elaborates with a quiet, rhythmic languor the structuring routines of the "changeless cycle" of days in which the simple binary opposition of here/not here (somewhere) organizes what does happen in Nippon to sustain its feudal agrarian and mercantile social order (planting, blessing, and selling rice) and what might threaten it (kings burning, trains being run, wars won, gods crumbling, machines rumbling) and therefore goes on somewhere else, but not here. This incantation is inverted in the fast, jazzy, staccato urgency of "Next!" the final song, which, as Sondheim summarizes it, "deals with the apocalyptic effect of western cultures…blasting open a serene, self-contained society that had existed snugly and smugly for centuries…an onomatopoeic blast…which sums up the violence of the intrusion sonically."[20] In stark contrast to the calm, slow metapoetics of the opening number, it nevertheless uses the same additive technique in its lyrical construction, in which kings *are* burning, machines *are* rumbling, and so on. As well as being punctuated by the cry of "Next!" itself, this is further interrupted with authoritative voices announcing snippets of quantitative statistical information about the utter modernity of Japan's industrial productivity and concluded with the triumphant cry:

> Who's the stronger, who's the faster?
> Let the pupil show the master
> Next!
> …
> Brilliant Notions
> Still improving
> …
> Make the motions
> Keep it moving—
> Next!
> Next!
> Next![21]

The seemingly endless *process* of cyclical time in traditional society has been both ruptured into discrete episodes of the divided labor essential to industrial production, and transformed into the urgent *progress* of material industrial technology, with its accelerating, self-reinforcing cycle of economic production and consumption. The superior power of the Americans, which enabled them to initiate the economic invasion of Japan, is inverted into an emulatory Japanese imperialism. The reciter, now embodying the "puppet" emperor-made-flesh, in human form, announces angrily:

> We will organize an army and a navy, equipped with the most modern weapons.
> And when the time is right, we shall send forth expeditions to visit with our less

enlightened neighbours. We will open up Formosa, Manchuria, Korea and China. We will do for the rest of Asia what America has done for us![22]

The reciter prefigures here the tragic consequences of the invasion as they will continue into the future. He is, Sondheim observes,

> outraged at what happened to the country.... This is a man who is telling us with-out ever saying it: "We were raped." And they were, though it was highly controlled and ritualised. When Meiji becomes the emperor, at the penultimate moment...he becomes a real emperor and he says: "We will do to the West what they have done to us." That's anger. And they did it. And they were right. They were *wrong*, but they were right.[23]

The ominous irony of the reciter's announcement is reinforced by one of the statistical interjections in "Next!" when an anonymous voice reports: "Over fifty per cent of the radar equipment currently installed at the US Naval Base of Pearl Harbor was made in Japan!"[24] Within the overall structural framework of *Pacific Overtures*, numerous binary oppositions occur within and between characters and events, all of which are sustained by inversions comparable to that of the process of time in the opening and closing num-bers and the balance of power between Japan and America throughout the first act. The most important, in terms of developing character through inversion, is the relation between Manjiro and Kayama. Each reverses his representational position on the rela-tive importance of tradition and modernity. The evolving narrative of their developing relationship is the microcosmic key to the meanings and consequences of the macrocos-mic social and cultural changes described in *Pacific Overtures*. Their individual actions and experiences reflexively constitute the larger sociocultural structures and processes in which they take place, and which they reinforce and contribute to. They embody not only changing representations of the progressions of modernization, but the corollaries of this in tradition's inevitably tragic resistance to progress. The turmoil following the arrival of the Americans brings the traditionalist samurai Kayama into contact with the shipwrecked and imprisoned fisherman Manjiro, who has recently returned from the United States, enthused by what he has seen there. Kayama is promoted to Prefect of Uraga police and charged with repelling the invasion. His failure to do so leads to col-laboration with Manjiro in a plan to erect a treaty house in which the Americans can be received without allowing them to contaminate the sacred ground of Japan, by flooring the hut with tatami mats, which can be destroyed after the meeting. Such a joint project would have been impossible in ordinary, stable times. The rigid divisions of a feudal social structure would have prevented such interaction completely. As they enact their plan together, a friendship grows. Each insists the other has saved his life through their partnership, Manjiro with the idea for the subterfuge of the mats, Kayama by secur-ing the former's release from imprisonment. Over the ensuing fifteen years, however, each inverts his own to the other's perspective on the consequences of the incursion. Kayama embraces Western progress as Governor of Uraga, while Manjiro becomes a traditional samurai, reacting with hostility to the changes of modernization. The rela-tional processes involved in this reversal of beliefs and attitudes provides the narrative link between acts 1 and 2, until its tragic but historically necessary conclusion in the final scene of the play, when Manjiro kills Kayama in a hopeless attempt to reassert the force of tradition over progress.

One song in particular, "Someone in a Tree," which Sondheim later announced as "my favorite song of anything I have ever written,"[25] is both central to the process of the narrative and constitutes an encapsulation of the work's core concept of history itself. As well as liking "the swing and relentlessness of the music and the poetic orientalism of the lyric," Sondheim is especially taken with the song's "ambition, its attempt to collapse past, present and future into one packaged song form . . . this song comes closest to the heart of *Pacific Overtures*: historical narrative as written by a Japanese who's seen a lot of American musicals."[26]

The someone who is in the tree is crucial to a sense of historical evidence, since s/he claims to have witnessed what took place in the treaty house as Perry's officers force the representatives of the Shogun to sign a trade agreement which will end the isolation of "the floating kingdom." All physical evidence of the meeting was destroyed, so there is no record of what transpired during it. The history of it is dependent, therefore, on the recollections of those who have witnessed it. In attempting to recover a coherent account from these characters, Sondheim teases out the complex processes of historiographic inquiry in what is his most detailed consideration of the core focus of the work.

Initially the someone in the tree is an old man, who has difficulty in climbing the tree, and in remembering just where the Treaty House was and quite what he saw and heard, saying "I was younger . . . I saw everything . . . I was hidden all the time . . . It was easier to climb." A boy appears, representing his younger self, who can climb the tree, but rather than revealing the empirical details, he is afflicted by the recollected immaturity of the old man at the time of the events they seek to recall: "I was only ten . . . I'm a fragment of the day." They conclude together: "Without someone in a tree / Nothing happened here."[27] Then a warrior is introduced, who was hiding beneath the Treaty House, ready to intervene if the negotiations should become violent. He exclaims:

> Pardon me, I am here—
> If you please, I am also here
> . . . in the treaty house
> . . . or very near
> . . . I'm below.[28]

Swayne notes wryly that: "The characters' locations are . . . difficult to establish. It would have been impossible to see the Warrior at the time the Treaty House was in place; hence, we 'see' him 'under' an invisible Treaty House."[29]

Similarly, the old man and the boy cannot be at the Treaty House simultaneously since each is the other at different historical times—a problem in the reconstruction of historical record that is compounded by the warrior's contemporary presence at the Treaty House with the boy, and the third, atemporal dimension in which are located the comments of the Reciter. Moreover, none of the characters, when asked, can tell the Reciter quite where the Treaty House was anyway, and nor can any of them do more than describe the activities of those inside the Treaty House: they report that the participants talk, argue, shuffle papers, drink tea, light candles, but they can neither recollect nor record anything of the substance of the talk or argument or the contents of the papers. Finally, the warrior echoes the old man and the boy, saying:

> I'm a fragment of the day
> If I weren't, who's to say
> Things would happen here the way
> That they're happening?

And all three conclude:

> It's the fragment, not the day
> . . .
> That is happening
> Not the building, but the beam
> Not the garden, but the stone
> Only cups of tea
> And history
> And someone in a tree.[30]

Time and place, two of the key coordinates of historical fact, are here relativized by the fragmentations and distortions of perspective and memory. But this seems, for Sondheim, to be the essence of historical process, the result of the existential choices of the boy and the warrior, the old man's memory and the interrogation of all three by the Reciter. As Marx has pointed out, all history consists of accounts of conflict and struggle between competing power groups—in this case, the American imperialists and the Nippon Shogunate—and the histories are constantly being rewritten in the interests of whichever groups are in the ascendancy. The reality of history, of "what happened," here or anywhere, is represented as contingent on the vicissitudes of the memory of "someone in a tree" or "underneath a floor." Sondheim deconstructs history itself here into the constitutive, remembered fragments of place, presence and activity, rather than substantive actions: contingencies made still more fragile by the erection of the Treaty House as somewhere which was "not here" (or there) then, as a way of sustaining "the sacred decree of the great Shogun Tokugawa" 250 years earlier, which forbade foreigners from setting foot on the ancestral soil of Nippon. Sondheim's implicit historiography here not only follows Marx's formulations but also endorses the much pithier, apochryphal and appositely American contention of Henry Ford, that "History is bunk!"

The search for clear, empirically sustainable causal historical explanation is doomed by the chaos of different, apparently irreconcilable accounts of events of those who have been involved as participants or observers. As if to reinforce this, Commodore Perry concludes the first act by bursting onto the stage for the first time to perform the Lion Dance, the traditional kabuki dance of victory, in a costume which is a pastiche of kabuki and Americana. This potential inversion of binaries (the American victor performing a Japanese dance in mixed costume but according to kabuki convention) is reinforced through the pastiche of the songs and dance of the foreign admirals, preceded by the appearance of an American marching band, at the beginning of act 2.

PROGRESS, TRAGEDY, AND CONTEMPORARY NARRATIVE

Pacific Overtures describes and explores the traumatic experiences that constitute the nineteenth-century American incursion into Japan, and reflects on their tragic consequences. The gradual revelation of their implications for the social and cultural structures of both societies transforms the narratives of progress carried by the dominant consensual ideologies, mythologies, and historiographies that sustain the collective identities of modern societies into tragic narratives. The difference between tragic and progressive narratives is that the former bring the latter to a halt. Reinterpreting as traumatic, historical events—like those of modernization—routinely treated as progressive, challenges the logic of their underlying historicism. As Alexander notes: the implication of the tragic narrative is not that progress has become impossible... [but] rather... that progress is much more difficult to achieve than moderns once believed."[31]

The myth of the American Dream of progressive post-Enlightenment rational humanism is at the core of the continuing vernacular tradition of American musical theater. Like the project of modernity itself and the populist ideologization to which it has contributed so successfully, the American Dream has a dark side. Secular humanism has been shown to carry not only the civility and altruism of the common weal anticipated by Locke, but also to retain elements of a Hobbesian state of nature, characterized by "a war... as is of every man, against every man," and where human life is characterized so graphically as "poor, nasty, brutish and short."[32] Sondheim's works have continuously exposed this at all levels of human relations, from the interpersonal to the intersocietal and global or international. The blatant military power with which Commodore Perry opens Japan to international capitalist imperialism as the means of its enforced modernization can be seen as the first in a series of subsequent expeditions and interventions in power-based international diplomacy. The consequences of these have been good (consider the significance of US intervention in both twentieth-century world wars), but they have never been unproblematic in their longer-term effects. Notwithstanding his ironization of the search for historical causes in *Pacific Overtures*, it cannot possibly be a matter of coincidence, given the endemically reflexive character of Sondheim's work, that the show was first produced in 1976, the 200th anniversary of the declaration of American independence. It is not unreasonable to infer that Perry's economic invasion can be seen as the first in a series of events that led to the American entry into the Second World War with the Japanese bombing of Pearl Harbor; to the American decision to take a postimperial stand against Communism in South-east Asia by dispatching heavily armed and proactively aggressive military advisers to Vietnam;

to recurrent, usually covert confrontations with radical political and social liberation movements in South America. Indeed, the tiny Ryukyu island kingdom of Okinawa, where Perry first dropped anchor at Naha in 1853, continues to be a focus of tension in Japanese–American relations. Since 2004, the bay at Henoko has been the site of a sit-in, where Okinawans are protesting at a proposed new American military base, estimated to cost $16 billion, which is seen as essential to Japanese foreign policy and to sustaining American influence in East Asia.[33] However unintended and unforeseen some of their consequences, the complex sequence of loosely interlinked, international political events and processes—both retrospectively and prospectively (consider current US involvement in the Middle East and Afghanistan)—can be constructed interpretatively as constituting a cultural trauma, the consequences of which are to require critical review and reevaluation of the sustainability of the post-Enlightenment myth of the American Dream.

It is no longer necessary to argue the sociological case for the serious critical study of musical theater, whether or not it is in what is regarded as the authentic vernacular tradition. Whether or not Sondheim's work is closer to opera than the musical is, from both sociological and political perspectives, far less important than the significance of its articulation of critical engagement with the coherence and integrity of American culture and society and, especially in *Pacific Overtures*, of their global influence and consequences. This is a large claim to make on behalf of contemporary musical theater, and the mark of Sondheim's genius is that it can be both made and sustained as a further, contemporary elaboration of the tradition from which he is charged as having strayed. It is in this sense, surely, that with Sondheim's work above all, as Gordon has argued, the musical has come of age.[34]

Notes

1. Craig Zadan, *Sondheim & Co.*, 2nd rev. ed. (New York: Harper and Row, 1989), 218–27; Joanne Gordon, *Art Isn't Easy: The Theatre of Stephen Sondheim*, updated ed. (New York: Da Capo Press, 1992), 204–6.

2. John Lahr, "Sondheim's Little Deaths," *Harpers* (April 1979), 71–8.

3. Geoffrey Block, *Enchanted Evenings: Broadway Musicals from "Show Boat" to Sondheim* (New York, Oxford University Press, 1997); Paul Filmer, Val Rimmer, and Dave Walsh, "*Oklahoma!* Ideology and Politics in the Vernacular Tradition of the American Musical," *Popular Music* 18, no. 3 (1999), 381–6.

4. H. Brogan, *The Pelican History of the United States of America* (London: Penguin, 1986), 450–52.

5. Edward Said, *Orientalism* (New York: Pantheon, 1978).

6. Stephen Sondheim, *Finishing the Hat: Collected Lyrics (1954–1981)* (New York and London: Virgin, 2010), 303.

7. Jeffrey C. Alexander, *The Meanings of Social life: A Cultural Sociology* (New York: Oxford University Press, 2003), 3–26; Roger Friedland and John Mohr, "The Cultural Turn in American Sociology," in *Matters of Culture: Cultural Sociology in Practice*, ed. Roger Friedland and John Mohr (Cambridge, UK: Cambridge University Press, 2004), 47–50.

8. Alexander, *Meanings of Social Life*, 53.
9. Gordon, *Art Isn't Easy*, 7; Steve Swayne, *How Sondheim Found his Sound* (Ann Arbor, University of Michigan Press, 2005), 258.
10. Gordon, *Art Isn't Easy*, 203.
11. Mark Eden Horowitz, *Sondheim on Music: Minor Details and Major Decisions* (Lanham, MD, and Oxford: Scarecrow, 2003), 157–161.
12. Zadan, *Sondheim & Co.*, 210.
13. Gordon, *Art Isn't Easy*, 176.
14. Sondheim, *Finishing the Hat*, 303.
15. Ibid., 323.
16. Stephen Sondheim and John Weidman, *Pacific Overtures* (New York: Dodd, Mead, 1976), 9.
17. Sondheim and Weidman, 127–8.
18. Sondheim, *Finishing the Hat*, 311.
19. Stephen Banfield, *Sondheim's Broadway Musicals* (Ann Arbor: University of Michigan Press, 1993), 262.
20. Ibid., 329.
21. Sondheim and Weidman, 127–8.
22. Ibid., 123.
23. Horowitz, *Sondheim on Music*, 164.
24. Ibid.
25. Meryle Secrest, *Stephen Sondheim: A Life* (London: Bloomsbury, 1998), 43.
26. Sondheim, *Finishing the Hat*, 323.
27. Sondheim and Weidman, 74.
28. Ibid., 75.
29. Swayne, *How Sondheim Found*, 173.
30. Sondheim and Weidman, 75–79.
31. Horowitz, *Sondheim on Music*, 55.
32. Thomas Hobbes, *Leviathan*, ed. J. C. A. Gaskin (Oxford: Oxford University Press, 1996), 84. Originally published in 1651.
33. Gavan McCormack, "Obama vs Okinawa," *New Left Review* 64 (July–August 2010), 14–26.
34. Gordon, *Art Isn't Easy*, 1–18.

CHAPTER 26

··

QUEER SONDHEIM

··

SCOTT F. STODDART

With the arrival of *Road Show* in 2009, Stephen Sondheim gave his gay fan-base some-thing they had craved during his fifty-year reign as America's preeminent Broadway lyricist and composer—a homosexual couple in Addison Mizner and Hollis Bessemer. Not only do the men represent the one functional relationship in the show, but the lovers sing "The Best Thing that Ever Has Happened" —the show's one duet. While *Road Show* met with some negative criticism, reviewers agreed that when the pair sang this complex song, the show soared.

Road Show was an important moment for Sondheim's queer aficionados because it marked an acknowledgement of gay sensibility in his work—something that many queer spectators and critics have desired since his career began in 1957. Sondheim him-self did not come out publicly until 1998, when Meryle Secrest released her authorized biography. Having given Secrest his full cooperation, Sondheim used this moment to state the reasons he had remained silent about his sexuality for so long:

> I was never easy with being homosexual, which complicated things.... I don't think
> I knew more than maybe four homosexuals in the fifties and sixties who were openly
> so. I'm guessing four. I'm actually thinking of one couple who were quite effeminate,
> so there was very little to conceal. I knew a lot of homosexuals who did not want it to
> be known. Everybody knew the theatre was full of homosexuals, but nobody admit-
> ted to being so.[1]

Sondheim admitted that his first gay sexual experience occurred in college, but he never admitted to fully developed same-sex attraction until much later, during the writing of *Do I Hear A Waltz?* (1965). However, the composer never kept his sexuality a secret among his close friends, especially actress Lee Remick and composer Mary Rodgers, both of whom claimed to have had a romantic relationship with Sondheim. Secrest discusses Sondheim's continued male relationships throughout the biography—most specifically his relationship with Peter Jones. Regardless, Sondheim believed his homo-sexuality was a very small aspect of his larger life. In discussing therapy, he sums up his dismissal: "I'm just another ordinary neurotic fellow ... it included homosexuality, but you know, it was not being open to let somebody else into my life. I had thought it was all about homosexuality, but when homosexuality became the lingua franca it didn't affect me at all."[2]

Sondheim's relationship to "Queer Sondheim" is complex. Regardless of his silence on queer issues, within and without his work, there is a mighty queer fan-base that sees his work as speaking directly to them. Critic John Clum states this in his chapter on Sondheim:

> Sondheim is the kind of gay wit my generation of queens aspired to being in the fifties and sixties... Sondheim also is the bard of terror and anguished self-loathing some of us—many of us—had been taught to feel and that in many ways we triumphed over.[3]

Clum's assertions are correct if one reads Sondheim only to a point. Choosing to see Sondheim as a closeted writer for closeted men, one would have a tendency to focus on the uncomfortable questions regarding relationships extolled in many of his works: from the Bobby's chosen isolation in *Company*, through Sweeney's villainous rampage in *Sweeney Todd: The Demon Barber of Fleet Street* (1979), to Fosca's destructive behavior patterns in *Passion* (1994). Though he is not an outspoken champion for gay issues, Sondheim is a beloved gay icon among the queer theater set. What is it about his work (and his long silence) that fascinates gay men? How do the queer instances that do permeate his work resonate for gay men? Do these sporadic instances explain his popularity with gay men?

Sondheim's decision to remain quiet on the subject of his personal life did not cause him to remain entirely mum on the issue in his work. Its first manifestation is a song composed for *The Mad Show* (1964), an Off-Broadway revue. "The Boy from...," introduced by Linda Lavin, is a parody of bossa nova–influenced songs of the early 1960s, such as "The Girl from Ipanema." While the lyric mirrors "Ipanema" in its unrequited desire of the title character, "The Boy from..." is noteworthy because the female speaker sings of a man who is unabashedly homosexual. In the version recorded by Millicent Martin for *Side by Side by Sondheim* (1976), her breathy delivery as the tempo quickens makes for a comic tour de force. The unwitting speaker's questions offer clues to the audience that the subject is not remotely heterosexual:

> Why are his trousers vermillion?
> Why does his claim he's Castilian?
> Why do his friends call him Lillian?
> And I hear at the end of the week
> He's leaving to start a boutique.[4]

While the speaker sings of a rather stereotypical homosexual—flamboyantly effeminate—the song does not make fun of queerness; the laughter from its performance focuses on the clueless inamorata who desires more than what "The Boy" cares to offer.

Queerness remains a haunting question in regard to Sondheim's *Company* (1970), though Sondheim has dismissed critics who suggest that Robert, the protagonist, might be gay because of his inability to commit to a woman. As Paul M. Puccio writes, "In the final version of the play, there are no available single women, so Robert cannot suddenly marry. Both the play and Robert are strenuously heterosexual, so his coming out as gay (as some have conjectured he might be) would sacrifice narrative coherence."[5] Given that commitment is the subject of the musical, marriage in essence is Robert's antagonist, as the married couples who comprise his social network do not appear happy. At the end of the play, Robert appears more willing to take a chance on commitment, and his singing of "Being Alive" attests to Sondheim's notion that *Company* "says that to be emotionally committed to somebody is very difficult, but to be alone is impossible; to commit is to live; to not commit is to be dead"[6]

A queer angle does exist in a newer version of *Company*, first performed at the Donmar Warehouse and directed by Sam Mendes in 1995. Included in George Furth's original book, this conversation was cut from the script right before the play opened in 1970; however, Sondheim permitted its reintroduction when Mendes requested it be part of his production (and it has remained a part in subsequent revivals, most notably the 2006 Broadway revival starring Raul Esparza). In act 2 scene 3, Peter engages Robert in this particular discussion about homosexuality:

PETER: Robert, did you ever have a homosexual experience?
ROBERT: I beg your pardon?
PETER: Oh, I don't mean as a kid. I mean, since you've been adult. Have you ever?
ROBERT: Well, yes, actually, yes, I have.
PETER: You're not gay, are you?
ROBERT: No, no. Are you?
PETER: No, no, for crissake. But I've done it more than once though.
ROBERT: Is that a fact?
PETER: Oh, I think sometimes you meet somebody and you just love the crap out of them. Y'know?
ROBERT: Oh, absolutely, I'm sure that's true.
PETER: And sometimes you just want to manifest that love, that's all.
ROBERT: Yes, I understand. Absolutely.
PETER: I think that sometimes you can ever know someone for, oh, a long time and then suddenly, out of nowhere, you just want to have them—I mean, even an old friend. You just, all of a sudden, desire that intimacy. That closeness.
ROBERT: Probably.
PETER: Oh, I'm convinced that two men really would, if it wasn't for society and all the conventions and all that crap, just go off and ball and be better off for it, closer, deeper, don't you think?
ROBERT: Well, I—I don't know.[7]

It is a curious conversation, as it underscores the fragility of the masculine mystique—something not ready to be questioned in 1970, but quite pertinent to the budding metrosexuals of the 1990s. Homosexual panic frames many discussions of male pampering now, and Robert's inability to engage is characteristic—men over thirty who have not married, who take pride in their appearance, and who live grandly and without "real" responsibility, must be queer. The exchange is well placed between Robert's half-baked plea to April to forego her flight to "Barcelona" and Joanne's singing of "The Ladies Who Lunch," which ends in her unsuccessful attempt to seduce Robert. With its addition, Peter's come-on adds to the musical's questioning of marital mores in the twentieth century. Robert is still undecided about commitment at the show's end, but adding Peter to the mix of potential seducers makes the ending of the show, in which Robert hides in the shadows of his apartment and avoids his friends, much more cynical. After his friends leave, Robert "sits on the sofa and takes a moment. Then, he smiles…" —the smile becoming a signal to the audience that while togetherness may result in "Being Alive," Robert will commit to someone on his own terms—and not out of desperation.

Sondheim wrote only one screenplay, *The Last of Sheila* (1973), coauthored with friend and famed *Psycho* actor Anthony Perkins. The film uses queerness in a very bold way for the early 1970s. Sondheim's love of games and puzzles provides the background for the film's elaborate murder mystery, its star-studded cast and snappy dialogue reminiscent of Rene Clair's *And then There Were None* (1945), based on the novel *Ten Little Indians* by Agatha Christie (1939). Through the late 1960s, Sondheim became famous in his social circle for throwing elaborate mystery parties; one such party, attended by director Herbert Ross, was a "Halloween treasure hunt…which sent several teams of celebrities searching thirteen locations all over New York" for clues for an unspecified prize.[8] Perkins, who assisted Sondheim in these clever fetes, decided to help his friend to move from book and lyrics to full-fledged screenplay. They collaborated via the mail for three months before finishing this complex mystery. They sent it to Herbert Ross, who agreed to finance the project, which was filmed on location in the south of France.

The film opens with a coda: while rock music whines in the background, a fight breaks out between Clinton (James Coburn), a wily, mean-spirited film producer, and his younger wife Sheila Green (Yvonne Romaine), a powerful gossip columnist. As Sheila breaks away from the drunken soirée to escape Clinton's tirade, a speeding car, obviously driven by a drunken driver, plows through a pile of garbage cans and "bounces" Sheila "through the hedges," killing her instantly. A year later, as the credits role, Clinton sits at a typewriter addressing invitations to a group of friends, who, it turns out, were all at the party that fatal night. We see each guest receiving his or her invitation: Tom (Richard Benjamin), a rewrite man, and his wealthy wife, Lee (Joan Hackett); Christine (Dyan Canon), a boisterous Hollywood agent; Philip (James Mason), a mild-mannered director of commercials; and film star Alice (Raquel Welch) and her obstreperous husband Anthony (Ian McShane). This clever sequence becomes more so on a second viewing, as each introduction reveals a facet of character that becomes instrumental to Clinton's game. As the group comes together on Clinton's yacht for the first time since that night, each one remains suspicious as to the real motive behind the vacation (Figure 26.1).

Clinton soon reveals the ground rules of "The Sheila Green Memorial Gossip Game," an elaborate mystery game based on a secret that each character continues to hide:

> The idea is to discover everybody's secret—without peeking, of course—and prevent the other players from discovering yours…every day we will park in a different port where you can discover the proof of one person's secret. I'll announce what secret it

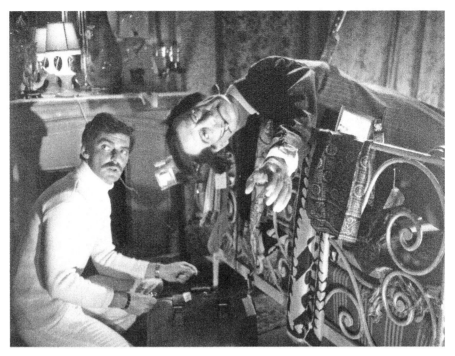

FIGURE **26.1** Richard Benjamin in *The Last of Sheila* (1974).

is to look for and give you a clue, which will tell you what to do and where to go on shore. Now, if you solve the clue properly, it will lead you to where the proof is.[9]

The secrets that Clinton has stored away reveal the back stories of each character: One is a "shoplifter," another is an "informer," still another is an "ex-con," and another is a "little child molester." The clue for the second night, which proves fateful for the scheming Clinton, reveals that one player is "a homosexual."

Seeing the film a second time reveals how Ross cagily screens homosexuality. As Tom and Lee receive their invitations, Lee begins to sulk while Tom seems to leap to life, bounding over to his bookcase to retrieve a screenplay that he once wrote for Clinton. Tom returns to his desk and a close-up reveals a framed photo of Tom with Clinton, playing croquet, both men attired in crisp summer whites, Clinton standing behind Tom seeming to display the proper way to hold a mallet (coding Clinton as a top?), Tom looking into the camera with an unabashed grin. After Clinton is found murdered, Tom admits to an affair with him.

Homosexuality is one of several naughty secrets in Clinton's game—more so, it seems, than who ran down Sheila Green. After Clinton himself is found murdered, Tom and Philip emerge as the master sleuths, and they seek to reveal the identities connected to the secrets. Tom readily admits to the "homosexual card," explaining to his drunken wife, Lee, "It just happened." As critic Vito Russo contends, "Nobody is ever really homosexual in Hollywood on Hollywood; it is always something that people 'tried once' when they were nobody."[10] Lee's distraught reaction to this news leads to her later admission that she was the "Hit and Run Killer" who ran Sheila down. When she later ends up in a tub with her wrists slashed, the film suggests that Lee cannot live with the shame of the truth, as it relates to both Sheila and her husband. We ultimately witness through flash edits that Tom is not only queer at heart, but the murderer—guilty of stabbing the sadistic Clinton with an ice pick, and guilty of drugging his drunken wife and slashing her wrists with a pair of scissors. In this regard, *The Last of Sheila* mirrors the murder mysteries of the 1940s and 1950s, where the villain is often a closeted queer. Tom's fairly fastidious nature—well-dressed and groomed—and cagey demeanor code him as homosexual.

The film opened to mixed reviews. *Variety* designated it "a major disappointment...far from the bloody *All about Eve* predicted.... [It] is simply a confused and cluttered demi-*Sleuth*, grossly overwritten and underplayed."[11] In the *Sunday News*, Rex Reed believed that, "The crowning disaster of the [Cannes] film festival was *The Last of Sheila*...Sondheim['s] first movie script requires a post-graduate degree in hieroglyphics to figure out. The film is so full of impossible situations, demented logic and clues that are indecipherable even while they are being explained, that the end result is one of total pretentiousness."[12] The film did, however, have some champions. Roger Ebert found it a "devilishly complicated thriller of superior class....It's the kind of movie that wraps you up in itself, and absorbs you at the very time you're being impressed by its cleverness."[13] Stephen Farber, writing for the *New York Times*, found that the film asked some serious questions regarding humanity:

> The murders in *The Last of Sheila* are committed for mundane rewards—money and sex—but the diabolical cunning of the murderer takes us beyond the mundane into a darker, more frightening realm. The evil in this story isn't banal; the murderer is truly fiendish, and although we may find the plot implausible, the idea of evil teases the imagination. Modern psychology and sociology offer explanations for murder, but can the act of murder be fully explained or understood? The paradox of *The Last of Sheila*, and of all good mysteries, is that while it celebrates the triumph of reason, it also hints at the existence of hellish, irrational forces. The murder itself can be "solved," but the deeper mystery of human behavior is not easily so.[14]

Reading Farber's thoughtful review against a queer grain, however, reveals that *The Last of Sheila* is rather quaint in its depiction of queerness. It is certainly an oddity in the Sondheim canon. While the film is a carefully constructed mystery that has overtones of camp in its sparkling dialogue, it is decidedly old-fashioned in its use of a queer villain.

Merrily We Roll Along (1981) has proven to be a difficult musical for Sondheim enthusiasts. While it famously played for only sixteen performances when it opened, the show has been characterized as Sondheim and George Furth's "most winning" accomplishment, its score thought to be of "intellectual depth and emotional passion." Its successful revival at the Donmar Warehouse in 2000 and a subsequent run during the Kennedy Center's Sondheim celebration in 2002 attests to its ability to transcend its experiment in form to be enjoyed as a central contribution to the Sondheim canon.

The show is a musical adaptation of a Kaufman and Hart fable concerning a Broadway songwriting team; the story is told backwards, the show starting with the end of the narrative and ending with its start. In their adaptation, Sondheim and Furth maintained the original backward narrative, but *Merrily* underwent serious revisions from its initial conception—these revisions elucidate the plot's complex relationships, forming a more coherent narrative that focuses on the rise and fall of the partnership between Franklin Shepard and Charley Kringas. Franklin Shepard's initial vision of the duo's future—together—becomes revised in his personal decision to sell his artistic promise for the materialistic American Dream. Franklin's greed destroys the partnership, leaving Charley alone, yet true to his craft. The pair never composes the songs they desire to as young men, songs that would criticize the very American ideology that creates the monstrous "Franklin Shepard, Inc."; Frank, alone, only regurgitates his one hit—a song that he wrote with Charley when they were both idealistic, hungry artists. The backward trajectory of the piece self-reflexively criticizes the materialistic aspect of the American ideal and its corrupting effect on the young artist; consequently, the play criticizes the very Broadway tradition that staged it—and ultimately condemned it.

While neither Frank nor Charley is ever labeled "gay," their relationship is the core of the show, a homoerotic relationship that is the centralizing experience—particularly as it presents their partnership of artistic creativity as a marriage, the moral center of the text. The monetary success they register with their one hit song forms a phallic power in the ideological sense of America; the money it brings becomes the one "mistress" who succeeds in wooing Frank away from his more virtuous partner.

Since its initial Broadway opening, Sondheim revised the score significantly, complicating any discussion of *Merrily* and making the partnership of Frank and Charley even more central. The first noticeable deletion is "The Hills of Tomorrow," a mood piece that opened and closed the original show. The song positioned the forty-two-year-old Franklin Shepard as the commencement speaker at the same high school he and Charley had attended twenty years before. Originally, the song not only introduced the "Merrily We Roll Along" vamp, but it created a metaphor for the musical—the play represented the mental breakdown of Frank—the musical being a mental depiction of all that transpired in his head during the speech. This move, in essence, created sympathy for Franklin's altered character. Ending the play with a reprise of his graduation speech and this song of celebration revealed that Frank acknowledged his artistic corruption, paving the way for him to change during this mid-life crisis. Replacing this scene, the musical now opens with a raucous party celebrating Franklin Shepard's compromise of his artistic ideals for the American movie scene. The overture is more frantic than before, becoming cacophonous as it raises the curtain on a scene similar to Kaufman and Hart's original: while the superficial guests swill champagne, Frank placates his second wife, Gussie Carnegie, a washed-up Broadway singer, while wooing a young starlet, who is later blinded when Gussie dashes a vial of iodine in her eyes. The new song "That Frank" presents a passive Frank who lets others extol his virtues—the guests singing of Frank's success. The idea that Frank becomes more likeable is central to the revised plot because the play becomes a personal drama, rather than the social drama that Kaufman and Hart wrote originally.

Charley's manic memory song "Franklin Shepard, Inc." captures his desire to bring "That Frank" back to the artistic fold:

> And the telephones blink
> And the stocks get sold
> And the rest of us he keeps on hold,
> And he's gonna start producing.
> And now he's a corporation,
> Right?
> And I play at home
> With my wife and kids
> And I wait to hear the movie bids,
> And I've got a little sailboat.
> And I'm into meditation,
> Right.
> He flies off to California.
> I discuss him with my shrink.
> That's the story of the way we work,
> Me and Franklin Shepard, Inc.[15]

The song's faster tempo intensifies Charley's mania as he pleads for a return to the simplicity of the past, making the song resonate as a frantic patter-song detailing Frank's dehumanized decent. The lyric, however, points to more than simple jealousy—Charley is obsessed to the point of having to "discuss" Frank's desertion to the dark side with his psychiatrist. The catalog of phrases beginning with "And..." helps the song build to a frenzy that reveals Charley's obsession with his former partner, and even though Charley's life allows him the luxury to remain to "play at home / With my wife and kids," it is obviously Frank he desires: "a friendship is like a garden. You have to water it and tend it and care about it. And you know what? I want it back." The frantic desire of this song allows us to draw a more obvious parallel between it and act 2's "Opening Doors," a second frenzied song, this time celebrating the glories of artistic integrity and material poverty—a life that generated happiness because the youthful Frank and Charley were in artistic and personal harmony.

Making the drama personal places the relationship between Charley and Frank center stage. The conscious use of vamps, beginning with the many "Transitions" that now punctuate the musical, helps to highlight the ironies in the "Old Friends" number, first sung by a drunken Mary—the third friend in Frank and Charley's relationship—and later sung by a naïve Frank. Vamps, in this sense, create a symbolic matrix for the play. Frederic Jameson states in his reading of Georg Lukács that when a writer applies a symbolic touch, that writer is consciously distancing the plot to be read moralistically, and somewhat more universally.[16] In this musical, the vamp takes the place of narration or description, working on the spectator's mind in a subconscious manner, instilling an interpretation of the moment. When Mary originally sings "Old Friends" in her inebriated present: ("Friends this long / Has to mean something's strong, / So if your old friend's wrong, / Shouldn't an old friend come through?"[17]), she ironically suggests that *the idea* of friendship is really the only bond left between the friends—and that each is impotent to restore what they once had. This gesture conditions Frank's version later in the act, sung ten years earlier, to resonate with the irony of Mary's later version: "Most friends fade / Or they don't make the grade. / New ones are quickly made / And in a pinch, sure, they'll do. / But us, old friend, / What's to discuss, old friend?"[18] Even though the younger Franklin sings of a genuine love for his friends, the repetition of the music ironically stirs something in the audience who have in fact already heard the tune. Now, we never believe Frank the way that Charley and Mary once did, because we have seen what he will become.

The revisions to the second act, beginning with Gussie's bravado performance of Frank and Charley's one "hit," creates a sadder effect, showing more fully where Franklin goes wrong. It is in this act where we realize that the American Dream itself, complete with its promises of material wealth, thwarts the musical marriage of Franklin and Charley. Gussie's interpretation of their one hit, from Franklin and Charley's fictional Broadway smash *Musical Husbands* heard before experiencing the "original" version, is loud, brassy, obnoxious. The second version, representing the song's initial unveiling as a part of *Take a Left*, Charley and Franklin's politically idealistic show, is sung first by Charley, then as a duet with Frank—the one significant moment that Sondheim never touched in his three major revisions.

> It started out like a song.
> We started quiet and slow,
> With no surprise.
> And then one morning I woke
> To realize
> We had a good thing going.
> It's not that nothing went wrong:
> Some angry moments, of course,
> But just a few.
> And only moments, no more,
> Because we knew
> We had this good thing going.[19]

The simile that starts the song helps us to focus on the real core of Franklin and Charley's relationship—not just that they write songs, but that they are, in essence, a song—and a love song at that. The ballad, while foretelling the tragedy of their eventual "going," also spells out the depth of their spiritual connection, the "singer" speaking as if to a lover, recognizing the fragility of a relationship. However, by adding Gussie's brassy version, and hearing it first, the lyrics underscore the lengths that Franklin goes to in compromising his artistic integrity for wealth. Her version, now only a "standard," has lost the poignancy of the original. The "song" comes from the youthful passion of Frank and Charley, and their duet here captures the tragedy of their inevitable separation.

While Sondheim has always had his gay fan base, *Merrily We Roll Along* appears to be the show that separates the mere fans from the die-hard Sondheimites—and that has much to do with the homoerotics of Frank and Charley's friendship. Gay men understand losing friends because of differences in sexual orientation, and Charley's manic meltdown early in the show, articulating his rage over Frank's decision to turn his back on them, speaks clearly to men who have lost a friendship as a consequence of their sexuality.

Sondheim's shows since *Merrily* steered clear of any overt queerness, but that does not mean that his work has not been at the forefront of queer uses in popular culture. The Pet Shop Boys produced an electro-punk album for Liza Minnelli called *Results* (1989) that featured a dance version of "Losing My Mind" from *Follies*. The recording features a techno-beat that turns the song into a manic plea rather than the sad lament of the show. The video that helped the song become a dance hit featured Minnelli gradually losing her grounding, ending up in a strait jacket as the refrain turns to a haunting echo. Gay icon Madonna famously performed Sondheim's Oscar-winning song "Sooner or Later" in Warren Beatty's gorgeously empty *Dick Tracy* (1990) and at the Academy Awards. Terry Gilliam's *The Fisher King* (1991) employs two songs from *Gypsy* in a wildly comic moment when Michael Jeter, playing a homeless cabaret singer, dons a strapless brocade and a crown made of a Frederick's of Hollywood "nightie" and belts "Rose's Turn" and "Some People" to the embarrassment of the mousey Lydia (Amanda Plummer). Drag performer Albert/Starina (Nathan Lane) performs a repertoire of Sondheim songs in *The Birdcage* (1996), Mike Nichols's rescreening of *La Cage aux Folles*[20] that takes place in the tacky splendor of Miami Beach. The film cuts away just as Starina begins "Can that Boy Foxtrot" but lingers for a comic meltdown as she rehearses "Little Dream" (cut from *A Funny Thing Happened on the Way to the Forum*) with a gum-chewing boy-toy. Sondheim also made an appearance at the annual *Broadway Backwards* series, where male singers sing songs written for women, and women sing songs for men. In its fifth series, sponsored to raise money for New York City's Gay, Lesbian, Bisexual, and Transgender Center, Whoopi Goldberg led a gang of female toughs in a lesbian version of "Gee, Officer Krupke" from *West Side Story*, and Michael Urie performed "Getting Married Today" from *Company*. Both pieces revealed political overtones: Goldberg's piece heightened awareness of girl gangs and Urie's performance became a plea to support gay marriage just after the passage of Proposition 8 in California. Sondheim's songs written for overtly heterosexual storylines have the potential to become queer political statements regardless of the venue.

Sondheim is a deity in writer and director Todd Graff's *Camp* (2003), an independent film based on Graff's experience as a counselor at Stagedoor Camp in the Catskills. The film captures on- and offstage dramas of a group of talented high school misfits who have remarkable performance abilities. Camp Ovation, the fictional show camp, helps the students to perfect their talents by staging a variety of shows during the summer; Graff punctuates his film with musical showcases that help the teens articulate their feelings, showing that Broadway warhorses still have resonance for young stage enthusiasts.

Sondheim figures in the plot, literally and figuratively. The film's opening joke shows the students getting on the bus bound for Camp Ovation. Instead of singing traditional camp songs, such as "Michael, Row Your Boat Ashore," or "100 Bottles of Beer on the Wall," the fey boys and determined girls sing "Losing My Mind" from *Follies*. Spitzer (Vince Rimoldi), a very out gay boy, keeps an 8×10 framed photograph of Sondheim on the dorm room dresser. When Vlad (Daniel Letterle), the lone straight boy, asks Michael (Robin de Jesus), "Is that your father?" Michael replies, with a note of disdain, "That's Stephen Sondheim—the greatest songwriter in musical theater!" Vlad simply shrugs, not yet clued into the Sondheim mania that fuels the camp.

Two of the shows produced during the summer provide back stories to the relationships between the young girls at the camp. The auditions for the first show, *Follies*, are screened as a montage to show a group of hopeful, eager young women belting out "I'm Still Here." Graff is careful to stage the humor of this sequence so the variety of adolescent types singing the song is not what makes one laugh—it is the fact that young girls (some with incredible vocal ranges) are singing this paean to age, experience, and showbiz survival with such conviction. In another story set with lesbian overtones, Fritzi (Anna Kendrick) becomes the compulsive handmaiden of Jill (Alana Allen), the camp's blonde bombshell. When Jill "fires" Fritzi—after catching her washing her underwear—Fritzi chooses the opening night of the second Sondheim show of the summer, *Company*, to exact revenge. Jill begins her performance as Joanne singing "The Ladies Who Lunch" when the laundry detergent Fritzi placed in her Snapple kicks into gear. While Jill vomits onstage in front of a full house, Fritzi appears dressed in a variation of Joanne/Jill's costume; the director Bert Hanley (Don Dixon) sees her immediately as "a scheming little bitch." Fritzi's retort, "She's fucked, I'm ready, and the goddamn show must go on!" allows her to go on stage and terrify the audience with her bravado, bringing them all to their feet as she mandates them to "Rise!"

Sondheim himself makes a cameo at the end of the film when the camp stages its annual benefit. All of the minidramas are put aside as Ovation comes together to stage the affair. Just as it is to begin, a limo pulls onto the gravel drive, and it halts as the license plate fills the screen: "4-UM." The soundtrack ominously accompanies a close-up of the driver opening the backdoor; a close tracking shot moves up from a pair of brown suede shoes, to travel up the khaki-clad legs and a smart blue blazer to focus on the face of the master himself. A quick cut to all of the eager students registers their gasps until Spitzer yells, "It's Stephen Sondheim!" and all of the actors encircle the songwriter in celebration. The sequence helps to make sense of the in-jokes regarding the songwriter made throughout the film, allowing Sondheim to be seen as the real life-force behind the camp's efforts to help young queer actors find their voices.

Road Show (2009) is the first show Sondheim wrote with a complex gay man at its center. In real life, Addison and Wilson Mizner were brothers who infamously lived during Gilded Age America. The pair tried their luck in the Klondike after the death of their father in 1897, where their only success was in bilking unsuspecting miners of their claims at cards. However, Addison, the younger brother, did have a talent for architecture, and his building of palazzi for the wealthy during the Florida land boom in the 1920s helped to establish the city of Boca Raton as an emerging artists' colony. The brothers split between 1910 and 1920, when Addison travelled to Florida to perfect his talent; after hearing of his brother's addiction to morphine, Addison brought Wilson to Florida as a partner in the housing venture and together, the brothers sold their "Palm Beach Style" homes to such luminaries as the Wanamaker family and Paris Singer. Wilson would purchase the land and Addison would design the home to suit the personality of the client. With the end of the land boom in 1926, the pair became destitute; Addison remained in Florida to settle the brothers' debts and died in 1933. Wilson absconded to Hollywood where, with backing provided by Gloria Swanson, he opened The Brown Derby restaurant. Some twenty-nine of Addison's homes still stand in the old section of Boca Raton.

The musical play written by Sondheim and John Weidman uses the metaphor of the road to relate the crimes and misdemeanors of the brothers, following them from their father's death in California, to their exploits in the Klondike, to their success and failure in Florida. As Papa dies at the start of the show, his dying words set the boys on "a road straight ahead, / There's a century beginning, / There's a land of opportunity and more."[21] The image of the road appears through this song and others as the brothers ponder their methods, and *Road Show*, its set "an eclectic pyramid of trunks, old furniture and packing crates"[22], becomes a vaudeville staging of the Mizners' nomadic lives.

On the train to Florida, in an effort to escape his brother's latest scheme, Addison meets Hollis Bessemer, a wealthy young man who is traveling to relatives in the south. Descended from the man who invented the Bessemer coal furnace, Hollis is on his way to Florida to live with his aunt after being disowned by his father for wanting a career as an artist—a feminine profession according to his father—rather than as a titan of industry. The problem is he has money, but no talent, so he sings "Talent," which expresses the plight of a homosexual man who desires acceptance, but does not have the talent or confidence to excel on his own:

> When I was a tyke,
> I said, "What I like
> Is art.
> I know I'm a boy
> But what I enjoy
> Is art.
> Looking at paintings, going to plays,
> Music and books informing my days,
> Filling my mind,
> Flooding my heart
> With art!"[23]

The song not only expresses Hollis's deep desire to do something aesthetic with his life, but it speaks to Addison's own complicated relationship with his brother—another man who does not have an artistic temperament. In essence, "Talent" is a seduction song; Hollis woos Addison with the sad realization that he does not have what it takes to be artistic: "Just enough talent to know/ That I hadn't the talent."[24] Through the rest of the song, Hollis explains his vision for a new Palm Beach: "I had this dream of a city of artists, / Versailles by the Florida sea,"[25] and Addison sees Hollis's vision become his own. The song on the train brings the men together as they realize that they need each other to fulfill their artistic dreams.

After they successfully begin their cul-de-sac venture, with the assistance of Hollis' wealthy aunt, the men openly and joyfully celebrate their relationship with the duet "The Best Thing that Ever Has Happened." As mentioned earlier, it is the one real love song in the show, and the men sing it to one another as the action of their immediate success with their wealthy patrons plays out in a montage. The song unfolds as Hollis unveils the new homes that Addison has built for their wealthy patrons.

> ADDISON: You... You're the answer to my prayers... You... You're one in a million. You...
> HOLLIS: You...
> ADDISON and HOLLIS: Where have you been all my life?....
> HOLLIS: We—
> ADDISON: We—
> ADDISON and HOLLIS: Both have a dream.
> HOLLIS: Me, I'd say we're a team.
> ADDISON: Me, too.
> ADDISON and HOLLIS: Who knew that you'd come into my life? Where have you been?[26]

The song mixes the desire for artistic and financial achievement with the design process that both men understand is the commodity they sell to the wealthy. The catalogs of architectural detail float among the longings each man expresses for the other, making the duet a complicated articulation of queer desire. As the song builds to a climax, Addison and Hollis each extol how this new-found love has made them whole:

> ADDISON: You are the best thing that ever has happened to me,
> You are.
> Okay, then,
> One of the best things that's happened to me,
> You are.
> They say we all find love—
> I never bought it.
> I never thought it
> Would happen to me...
> HOLLIS: What do you say we just go
> Out on the boat and get smashed
> And make love on the beach
> And stare up at the moon?
> You might just be the best thing that has happened to me,
> So far.
> Of course not much ever really happened to me...

FIGURE **26.2** Michael Jibson as Addison Mizner and Jon Robyns as Hollis Bessemer in *Road Show*, London (2010).

ADDISON: Give us a kiss.
ADDISON AND HOLLIS: We may just be the best thing that has happened to us—[27]

In a standard love duet, each singer is given equal time to speak of his desire for the other, the mutual goal of the song articulating how their partnership has manifested into love. Even though Hollis's and Addison's relationship does not survive the intrusion of Wilson's return (and subsequent drug addiction), the song is a landmark in Sondheim's oeuvre: the first time two men stand center stage to sing a love duet to one another.

In its annual "150 Reasons to Have Pride in 2010" Pride issue, *The Advocate*'s Reason 3 states the following:

Because We Made Broadway What It Is Today.
   Stephen Sondheim, the most Tony-winning composer, turned 80 in the spring and is being feted throughout the year for his body of work. I'll drink to that (We'll be toasting with a vodka stinger!)[28]

Despite Stephen Sondheim's long silences and his veiled references to queerness throughout his work, the gay community embraces him as an artist who challenges the conventions of the Broadway musical, ensuring that the form still resonates with the youth of today. In dismantling the heteronormative structure of the traditional musical,

Sondheim has "queered" the form, whether there are openly gay characters or not. In examining the trajectory of Sondheim's work, I believe we can see that his complexity provides a more positive political note; reading him as an outsider to the heterosexual love that forms the foundation of Broadway's dream factory and dissecting it with his verbal and musical scalpel allows Sondheim to expose how humans interact with one another. In that light, Sondheim's work appears more open to queer appropriation and deconstruction than ever before.

NOTES

1. Secrest, *Stephen Sondheim: A Life* (New York: Alfred A. Knopf, 1998), 180.
2. Secrest, *Sondheim*, 230.
3. John Clum, *Something for the Boys: Musical Theatre and Gay Culture* (New York: St. Martin's, 1999), 243.
4. Millicent Martin, "Can that Boy Foxtrot." by Stephen Sondheim. *Side by Side by Sondheim* (London, 1976).
5. Paul M. Puccio and Scott F. Stoddart, "Ever After? Marriage in *Company* and *Into the Woods*," *Sondheim Review* 2, no. 2 (1995): 20.
6. Secrest, *Sondheim*, 189
7. Stephen Sondheim and George Furth, *Company* (New York: Theatre Communications Group, 1998),
8. Craig Zadan, *Sondheim & Co.*, 2nd updated ed. (New York: Da Capo, 1994), 167.
9. *The Last of Sheila*, director Herbert Ross; starring James Coburn, Richard Benjamin, Joan Hackett, Dyan Cannon, James Mason, Raquel Welch, and Ian McShane. Warner Bros., 1973.
10. Vito Russo, *The Celluloid Closet: Homosexuality in the Movies* (New York: Harper and Row, 1987), 191.
11. Zadan, *Sondheim & Co.*, 170.
12. Ibid.
13. Roger Ebert, "*The Last of Sheila*" *Chicago Sun-Times*, July 19, 1973.
14. Stephen Farber, "Who Murdered Sheila? It's Worth Finding Out." *New York Times*, July 29, 1973.
15. Stephen Sondheim and George Furth, *Merrily We Roll Along* (New York: Music Theatre International, 1981).
16. Frederic Jameson, "The Case for Georg Lukács," in *Marxism and Form* (Princeton: Princeton University Press, 1971), 160–205.
17. Stephen Sondheim and George Furth, *Merrily We Roll Along*, 14.
18. Ibid., 17.
19. Ibid., 118.
20. Original directed by Edouard Molinaro, 1978.
21. Stephen Sondheim and John Weidman, *Road Show* (New York: Theatre Communications Group, 2009), 16.
22. Ibid., 9.
23. Ibid., 58.
24. Ibid., 58.

25. Ibid., 59.
26. Ibid., 64– 5.
27. Ibid., 71–2.
28. Ibid., 44.

CHAPTER 27

SONDHEIM'S AMERICA; AMERICA'S SONDHEIM

RAYMOND KNAPP

SONGS originally written for the musical stage constitute the most abundant repository for expressions of personal and collective affirmation in America. While there is no single group that American musicals single out for affirmation, ranging freely among the local, the regional, the national, or just the human, most such groups are capable of standing in, allegorically, for either an aspect of America or America *tout court*. As well, the optimistic personal affirmations prevalent in American musicals derive implicitly, and sometimes explicitly, from the personal freedoms and opportunities understood to accrue to Americans.

Stephen Sondheim is without a doubt the leading writer of American show songs of his generation. But given this repertory's legacy of specifically American affirmation and Sondheim's more querulous engagement with America—encompassing both its actual histories and its mythologies, both its realities and its espoused values—his place at the forefront of Broadway composers over the final decades of the twentieth century has proven troubling to some. Further complicating the project of trying to map "Sondheim" onto "America" is the fact that his own level of received affirmation, in terms of first-run box-office success, has consistently fallen well short of the high esteem accorded him by critics, academics, practitioners, and devotees. Moreover, his seeming disconnect with the country at large in favor of a more narrowly cultured elite has been reinforced by his evident distaste for uncritical, rah-rah Americanism.

This situation might usefully be compared with that of Gilbert and Sullivan, even if Sondheim has rarely generated anything approaching their enthusiastic reception with the larger public. With Gilbert and Sullivan, there can be no doubt of either their fervent love of England or their myriad dissatisfactions with it. Both are amply in evidence in their operettas, and often simultaneously, even if American audiences have been quicker to appreciate the playfully critical dimension of their satires. Building fairly directly on this foundation, American musicals have nearly always found room for political critique without seeming to require vouchsafing for either their basic loyalty or their capacity to celebrate American institutions and values.[1] Indeed, political critique, on Broadway as elsewhere, has generally been understood as an exercise of American freedoms, thus bringing the celebratory dimension of those musicals that indulge such freedoms squarely into alignment with what is understood to be "American."

That Sondheim is often viewed apart from this paradigm is puzzling. Perhaps this has to do with the way Broadway began to splinter into irreconcilable opponents shortly after Sondheim first emerged as a major Broadway composer with *A Funny Thing Happened on the Way to the Forum* (1962); from this perspective, the battlefield (if not the stake) narrows from America to Broadway. Perhaps also it has to do with the simultaneous heightening of generational differences, and the perceived brokenness of the "America dream" as an ideal among youth in the 1960s, developments that had nearly as direct an impact on Broadway as on other forms of commercial artistic expression, which were increasingly available to (and controlled by) youth, whether as artists, producers, or consumers. Against this generational divide, Sondheim sometimes has appeared, from either side, as belonging more to the other. Thus, whereas traditionalists found in his critical engagements with America something akin to what they thought to be the destructive impulses of youth, "youth" just as often found either his liberal politics outdated or his devotion to craft beside the point within a new expressive environment that prized "authenticity" over craft. Craft itself, from this perspective, became politically suspect, as a vestige of a hidebound past.

Yet, detailing these circumstances does not address the fundamental differences between Sondheim's reception, as a composer for Broadway, and that of other songwriters, who may be more easily understood to offer direct expression of their own values and beliefs, in line with the emerging cult of authenticity that has overtaken much of the aesthetic and political dimension of popular musics.[2] In this, Sondheim represents the extreme version of Broadway's alternative aesthetic: his show songs are more resolutely directed to their dramatic contexts, and grounded within the characters in the drama, than is generally true even of Broadway. Complicating the situation even further, his characters and dramatic situations are largely predetermined by his principal collaborators. Thus, my opening description of Broadway songs, though true and obviously relevant to the central question of this chapter, might seem misleading, or at least irrelevant to Sondheim himself. While the traditionally affirmational ethos of Broadway sets the terms for the reception of any Broadway composer, Sondheim songs tend to be more about contributing to their dramatic situations than about adding to any generalized repository of song. Moreover, this tendency has shaped the reception of his shows, leading generally to his being seen as their primary author, despite the obviously fundamental contributions of his collaborators, simply because so much of the drama is persuasively embodied within his musical numbers. Because of this dramatic centrality—but not only this—"a Sondheim show" is a more obviously distinctive category than, for example, "a Hal Prince show," "a John Weidman show," or "a Hugh Wheeler show."

It is the caveat to the previous sentence that establishes the premises and constitutes the central problem for this chapter: *but not only this*. In the present context, the dramatic profiles of Sondheim's songs, however distinctive and central to what we think of as a "Sondheim show" —will seem initially less to the point than his fairly consistent manner of engagement with topics relatable in some sense to "America." In the following, I will first address this "manner of engagement" within the context of his heritage, which in both a narrow and a general sense comprises the major works of his mentor, Oscar Hammerstein II. Contextual comparison of these two figures will allow a crucial difference between their manners of engagement to emerge in high relief, regarding not only "America" but also their American audiences. I will then consider a pivotal but somewhat neglected show, *Anyone Can Whistle* (1964),[3] with a specific eye to the dynamic between Arthur Laurents's book and Sondheim's musical numbers, in order to argue that this dynamic, as it develops and takes different forms in later collaborations with other creators, lies behind both Sondheim's embrace of America and his apparent alienation from it. Finally, I will more briefly consider his own developing legacy, heralded by the extraordinary success of the 2002 Kennedy Center series.

Hammerstein's America

Oscar Hammerstein's most successful musicals are strikingly consistent in being both deeply political and severely compromised in their presentation of political issues. The earliest of these, *Show Boat* (with Jerome Kern, 1927), broke new ground by prominently presenting African Americans and European Americans on the same stage, while giving sympathy and an important musical presence to both groups. Yet, the show's blacks are dramatically secondary except at two pivotal moments, when Julie is first "outed" in the first act as a mixed-race woman attempting to pass as white, and when she is called upon late in the second act to perform a redemptive and ritualistic sacrifice for the show's white heroine. The two moments combine to constitute a familiar trope of the tragic mulatta, through which we are presumably meant to understand more fully the humanity of individuals scorned by mainstream society, both for what they are and for their attempts to pretend otherwise. However salutary this familiar trope might have been in many respects—endowing such victims with considerable sympathy, and often Christ-like attributes—it nevertheless represents a compromise, and as such has tended not to wear well. In *Show Boat*, Julie's sacrifice remains a "sore spot," running much deeper than the show's discomfiting use of racial epithets and dialect.[4]

Similar compromises undermine the basically liberal politics of Hammerstein's collaborations with Richard Rodgers. *South Pacific* (1949), *The King and I* (1951), and *Flower Drum Song* (1958), while centering on poignant and even (in their time) controversial engagements with racial or ethnic differences, also indulge a pandering taste for racial and ethnic stereotypes, in the service of comedy and spectacle. Even if we understand this dimension of these shows as stemming from Hammerstein's roots in operetta, with its distinctive predilection for exotic settings and peoples, it nevertheless severely compromises each show's central political statement. Moreover, the egregious historical misrepresentations in many of their shows—of a savage King Mongkut in *The King and I*, of a seemingly Indian-free Claremore in *Oklahoma!* (1943), of a victimized Austria with no hint of anti-Semitism in *The Sound of Music* (1959)—offer an odd counterpoint to their pointed situational conflicts.[5] To be sure, the depiction of King Mongkut as a primitive, like the equally obnoxious paternal slap in *Carousel* (1945), delivered in anger but nevertheless feeling "like a kiss," stems from the materials with which Hammerstein worked. But it was Hammerstein himself who, in adapting Lynn Riggs's *Green Grow the Lilacs* (1931) for *Oklahoma!*, purged it of all references to Indians, and who (with Howard Lindsay and Russell Crouse) shaped Maria von Trapp's memoir into *The Sound of Music*, leaving aside all traces of the former's frank engagement with anti-Semitism.[6]

All that said, and with all that might be said along these lines, there can be no doubt that Hammerstein's liberal messages registered strongly with American audiences. *Show Boat* and *South Pacific*, in particular, are much venerated as breakthrough shows, and each has been seen to have played a significant part in helping to chip away at America's grievous history of racism. Nor should there be much doubt that Hammerstein's sometimes awkward mixture of elements contributed to his shows' success in furthering their liberal agendas. Without the orientalism of either "Bali Ha'i" in *South Pacific* or the King in *The King and I*, for example, neither show would have achieved sufficient success with the public to bear its political freight, neither the former's literal embrace of racial otherness nor the latter's sharp reminders that the barbarous persistence of slavery in the supposedly primitive "Orient" directly paralleled that of the American South at precisely the same historical moment.[7] For Hammerstein, the pragmatic compromise, in which political progress is charted across and within shows that celebrate the privileged perspective they also challenge and problematize, was a key element in his characteristic dramatic profile, ensuring that his liberal political messages could never jeopardize his standing as an archetypical *American*.

Such compromises are rare for Sondheim, whose liberal politics are seldom undermined by traditional dramatic or musical tropes. Rather, when those more conservatively tinged elements of his musico-theatrical heritage do seem inescapable, they acquire in Sondheim's treatment a layer of complexity that also calls them into question, and demands that we do the same. For example, *Pacific Overtures* (1976) is on one level as Orientalist as *South Pacific* or *The King and I*, indulging our fascination for musical spectacle based on a culture not our own, yet it queries that perspective in so many ways that it can seem not to be Orientalist at all.[8] More generally, Sondheim fine-tuned, among other techniques, the prism of pastiche, through which too familiar or no longer viable song types could be refracted—sometimes gently, sometimes violently, but either way adding a touch of stylized artificiality to the theatrical mask any show song puts on. Sondheim thus invites us to acknowledge the critical distance between us and the stylistic pastiche while enjoying the type itself, often with a new appreciation for its possibilities.

The Hammerstein compromise—perhaps deriving from the inherently conservative nature of any strongly affirmative gesture or genre—was decidedly *not* one of the lessons Sondheim learned from his mentor; indeed, it provided a fulcrum for articulating generational difference, becoming the locus of Sondheim's own desire to "let the pupil show the Master."[9] While it may not be fair to describe the Hammerstein compromise as a kind of pandering (since pleasing audiences is after all the central project of commercial theatre), Sondheim's aversion to anything that might be taken as such—or, more positively, his commitment to challenging his audiences—has inevitably shrunk his audience in proportion, undermining his ability to engage America with anything like the immediacy and scale of his mentor. This aversion seemed well in place early on in his career, dating perhaps to the lesson he learned from the too-easy wit of *West Side Story*'s "I Feel Pretty" (1957),[10] but his characteristic means for dealing with his consequent estrangement from traditional "America" took shape mainly within his subsequent collaborations with Arthur Laurents, particularly *Anyone Can Whistle*, their only major collaboration for which Sondheim also composed the score.

SONDHEIM'S AMERICA: *ANYONE CAN WHISTLE*

> But this is a free town in a free county in a
> free state in a free country and I am a
> free woman with a free mouth.[11]

West Side Story lost out to *The Music Man* at the 1958 Tony Awards in three of the four categories for which both were nominated, the latter winning for Best Musical, Featured Actress, and Conductor/Musical Director, the former only for Choreographer.[12] While *West Side Story* was the first Broadway musical for both librettist Laurents and lyricist Sondheim, losing in the Tony competition to fellow Broadway newcomer Meredith Willson (who wrote book, music, and lyrics for *The Music Man*) would have been especially painful for Laurents, who had worked intermittently for eight years on *West Side Story* and had a particularly strong investment in its material (which originally was to pit Catholics against Jews).[13] The competition and outcome of that year's Tony Awards could have been read in only one way from Laurents's and Sondheim's perspective: on Broadway, in a competition pitting the gritty truth about America against sentimental myth-making, truth lost.

In their next collaboration, Laurents and Sondheim returned to this particular battlefield with fierce determination. *Gypsy* (1959) presents a version of the American dream that leads, as if inevitably, to striptease, the ultimate act of pandering—a seemingly bleak outcome that is turned on its head when, against all odds, stripping becomes the engine of personal triumph for one character and indirectly offers a kind of redemption for another. Despite *Gypsy*'s dramatic power, however, when it came to the Tonys, its hard truths, like those of *West Side Story*, competed unsuccessfully against sentimental myth-making, this time courtesy of Rodgers and Hammerstein in their final collaboration. *Gypsy* lost in all eight of the categories for which it was nominated, five of which went to *The Sound of Music* (Best Musical, Actress, Featured Actress, Conductor/Musical Director, and Scenic Design).[14]

With *West Side Story* and *Gypsy*, Laurents and Sondheim helped create breakthrough musicals that stood apart from the Hammerstein compromise, squarely facing unpleasant realities of America and struggling within that bleak landscape to lay a claim to some space of personal fulfillment. Though these shows were both successful, they came in second at the Tonys and in general box-office popularity to shows that celebrated mythologies of America's innocent roots and infinite promise, whether stemming from small-town virtues or salvaged from a decadent Europe on the brink of World War II.[15] With *Anyone Can Whistle*, their third and final full collaboration (undertaken after Sondheim separately achieved unqualified success at the Tonys with *A Funny Thing Happened on the Way to the Forum*, which won six awards including Best Musical),[16] Laurents and Sondheim tried to continue along the route they had helped chart in *West Side Story* and *Gypsy*, but ran unceremoniously aground, closing after only nine performances. Despite the show's failure, Columbia Records recorded a cast album for *Anyone Can Whistle* after it closed, which then achieved a kind of cult following; over time, a few of its songs emerged as staples for covers, revues, and compilations. Between the short life of the musical itself and the extended life of its musical numbers lies the core dynamic that has shaped Sondheim's ambiguous status as a specifically *American* composer of musicals.

Laurents's book for *Anyone Can Whistle* addresses the trajectory of his and Sondheim's earlier head-to-head losses at the Tony Awards with some specificity, especially regarding *The Music Man*, whose setting, characters, and situations are reimagined in a much harsher light for *Anyone Can Whistle*.[17] Thus:

1. The small town in "Trouble" (River City in *The Music Man*) now actually *is* in terrible trouble—with a *Das Kapital* "T." The unnamed small town in *Anyone Can Whistle* is economically devastated, with no immediate prospects for reopening its factory, since it "manufactured a product that never wore out" (3).[18] To make the town's devastation more complete, it is also in the midst of a drought.
2. The "Mayoress" (Cora Hoover Hooper, the owner of the factory), like River City's Mayor Shinn, is comically ineffectual, but she is also considerably more cynical in her conniving, and hated by everyone.
3. River City's bickering school board is reborn in *Anyone Can Whistle* as the scheming town council: Treasurer Cooley, Chief Magruder, and Comptroller Schub.
4. Marian Paroo, the professionally responsible but sexually repressed librarian and piano teacher of River City, who early on seeks to expose Harold Hill as a fraud but then uses the famous Habanera from Bizet's *Carmen* to help her seduce Charlie Cowell (the anvil salesman with "the goods" on Hill), becomes the even more severely repressed Nurse Fay Apple in *Anyone Can Whistle*, who assumes earnest responsibility for the "cookies" from the "Cookie Jar" (the town's mental institution, its only thriving concern). Nurse Apple seeks to expose the town's

fake miracle, and becomes sexually awakened only when assuming the costume, accent, and manner of a French soubrette.

5. Baby Joan Shroeder, who specializes in "trances," displaces the relatively innocent children of *The Music Man* (Winthrop and Amaryllis—perhaps displacing as well the Captain's children in *The Sound of Music*, given the near coincidence of names with the latter's cynical Baroness). Baby Joan's "innocence" is as phony as Baby June's in *Gypsy*—from which world *Anyone Can Whistle* also borrows the Mayoress's backup group ("the Boys").[19]

6. Several plot elements from *The Music Man* are reconfigured for *Anyone Can Whistle*, including:

   a. a nonexistent "product" that promises to get the town out of its trouble (miracle water from a rock, in parallel to music from the "think system");

   b. the arrival by train of a charismatic "expert"—J. Bowden Hapgood, in parallel to Harold Hill—a trickster who mesmerizes most, but not all, of the town's citizens, who in turn later feel betrayed and turn on him;

   c. the transmutation of the practices of *Luftgeschäfte* (literally, "air business") into something genuine, when Hill's band actually performs Beethoven's Minuet in G (if haplessly), and when Hapgood's pop psychology offers release to the repressed Nurse Apple, with the couple then becoming the locus of hope within a world gone mad from a combination of cynicism, religious gullibility, and unfeeling logic; and

   d. the metaphoric importance of whistling as natural and effortless, forming the basis of Hill's "think system" in *The Music Man*, and serving as the emblem of Nurse Apple's repression, as articulated in the title song of *Anyone Can Whistle*.

7. The central parallel between the two shows—Hapgood's derivation from Harold Hill—is reinforced in many ways beyond those already mentioned; most significantly, each character is a "natural" musician who does not read music, and whose success at group persuasion rests not only on a skilled, patter-based manipulation of clichéd "watch cries," but also on an innate idealism, which redeems not only him, but also the woman who sees through his façade to that idealist core.[20] Moreover, for both male characters, redemptive love cuts off the possibility of escape, since Hapgood, like Hill, finds his "foot caught in the door."

To be sure, many of these parallels derive from the common ancestor of both shows, *The Pied Piper of Hamelin*, a centuries-old story that traditionally includes many of these elements in some form: a town in trouble, with corrupt community elders; the promise of delivery through magic and/or music; a mysterious stranger/trickster who initially beguiles the populace but is later denounced by them; and a particular focus on children, most prominently in *The Music Man*, which (like most versions of the Pied Piper story) features a disadvantaged child whose fate is held in the balance.[21] But the connection between the shows is considerably stronger than this common ancestry, since neither musical even hints at the tragic outcome of *The Pied Piper*, focusing instead, in each case, on the redemption of the Piper himself, achieved through the actual good that he accomplishes, inadvertently, through his innate idealism.[22]

Given these (surely conscious) parallels, then, and given the overt patriotism of *The Music Man*, it is hard *not* to see *Anyone Can Whistle*'s troubled town as a much bleaker version of America itself, an America of dysfunctional capitalism, with a corrupt government and a gullible populace easily taken in by religious and psychological quackery. Yet *Anyone Can Whistle*, like *West Side Story* and *Gypsy*, also holds out the possibility and hope of redemption, and—unlike its two predecessors—grounds that hope, as an enduring possibility, within its romantic couple. By offering a traditionally grounded redemption to its central couple, if not to the community at large (as would also have been traditional), *Anyone Can Whistle* establishes a dramatic situation that would become the prototype for Sondheim, in which characters seek redemption within a hostile environment, an environment that may or may not stand in for "America" in some sense.

Sondheim's musical numbers for *Anyone Can Whistle* fall fairly neatly into two categories: those establishing and developing the setting and larger context (the town and its leadership; and the Cookie Jar), which are largely inhospitable to personal redemption, and those songs that establish a space within that setting and context that might nevertheless support redemption, with the first-act finale and two later numbers serving as a sort of pivot between the two categories, opening up a potential shared space between them (see Table 27.1).[23]

Table 27.1 Deployment of Songs in *Anyone Can Whistle*

	Setting and context (Cora, Cookies, etc.)		Toward personal redemption (Hapgood and Nurse Fay Apple)
Act 1			
1.	I'm Like the Bluebird		
2.	Me and My Town		
3.	Miracle Song		
4.			There Won't Be Trumpets*
5.		Simple	
Act 2			
6.		A-1 March	
7.			Come Play with (wiz) Me
8.			Anyone Can Whistle
9.	A Parade in Town		
10.			Everybody Says Don't
Act 3			
11.	I've Got You to Lean on		
12.			See What It Gets You
13.		The Cookie Chase	
14.			With So Little to Be Sure Of

* Dropped from the original production. Although "Trumpets" is not included in the song list at the beginning of the published libretto, it is included in the libretto itself (38–9).

As may be seen from this deployment of songs, it is the friction between the two main storylines that generates the three-act structure, quite unusual for a Broadway musical. Act 1 is mainly about establishing Cora's crowd and their plot to manufacture a "miracle." Hapgood appears only at the end of the act ("Simple"), seemingly integrated into the ongoing drama about the town itself. But the crisis Fay and Hapgood create at the end of act 1 becomes the background in act 2 for their revealed potential to find something of their own amid the chaos. The only song given over to Cora and her crowd in act 2 ("A Parade in Town") documents that the dramatic focus has been wrested away from her,[24] as foretold by Fay in her song from act 1 ("There Won't Be Trumpets"; dropped from the original production as noted in Table 27.1). Two of the songs that have been particularly successful outside the show come from act 2: "Anyone Can Whistle" and "Everybody Says Don't" —these songs, along with "Trumpets" from act 1 and "With So Little to Be Sure Of" from act 3, provide a core trajectory for the "personal redemption" dimension of the show. Although act 3 ends with a measure of hope, however, it is mainly about Cora and her crowd reestablishing control and manipulating a disillusioned Nurse Apple to cooperate (Figure 27.1).

The three-act structure of *Anyone Can Whistle* is important not only because it sets the show apart from typical Broadway musicals, but also because the structure reinforces the dominant, cynical sensibility of the show, and makes personal redemption

FIGURE **27.1** Angela Lansbury as Cora Hoover Hooper with her henchmen in *Anyone Can Whistle* (1964).

all the more precarious. Thus, within this dramatic arch, the mere fact that the latter dimension emerges so powerfully in act 2 ensures that it will be put down in act 3, and so it is. Moreover, the three-act structure allows Hapgood opportunities to function more powerfully as a pivot figure, colluding with Cora in act 1 (albeit with an independent spirit), bringing Fay out of her shell in act 2 while enhancing his level of audience sympathy, and opposing himself to Cora in act 3, so that he can, in the end, redeem himself and provide an anchor of sorts for Fay.

In principle, this structure ought to work, and yet it doesn't, because by act 3, we have simply lost our bearings. Granted, disorientation is a perfect setup for "With So Little to Be Sure Of," but we have been lifted up too far in act 2 to be let down so abruptly and with such seeming finality in act 3, at least within the world of a Broadway musical. Again, this reversal is an effective setup for Fay's song of disillusionment ("See What It Gets You"), but it is hard, even in the name of realism, for an audience to cede this slice of America to the cynical manipulators and their gullible minions. Compounding the show's difficulty with fully engaging its audience, that slice is painted in distinctly "pink" colors, not only critiquing American capitalism (as already mentioned), but also sprinkling a fair number of other references throughout the show that either point to Communism or "fellow travelers," or can otherwise seem un-American (this list does not include the show's more direct assault on religion, which compounds the problem even further):

1. Cora's Czar-like references to her "poor! starving! miserable! dirty! dreary! depressing! Peasants" ("Me and My Town," 10)
2. Hapgood's satirical response during "Simple" to the direct accusation by Schub that he is "Communist!": "The opposite of Left is right, / The opposite of right is wrong, / So anyone who's Left is wrong, right?" (71); this follows several allusions to familiar anti-Communist rhetoric from Schub, such as "He's taking over!" (69) and "He's boring from within!" (71)
3. Hapgood's later logical progression, in the same song (in a side-conversation with Comptroller Schub):

   "Where does most of your money go?"...
   "In taxes."...
   "What do you think of someone who makes a product and doesn't use it?"
   "He's crazy."...
   "Most of your money goes to the government in taxes. What does the government do with most of the money? Makes bombs.... But you say to make a product and not to use it is crazy.... doesn't that make you crazy for letting them waste your money?... But perhaps the government is making bombs because it means to use the product. Which means that everyone will be killed.... Including you... Which means you are paying most of your money to have yourself killed.... Which means,... you are the maddest of all!" (77–8).

4 Hapgood's exchange in act 2 with Fay, who is disguised as "the Lady from Lourdes":

> *"Pardon: parlez-vous français?"*
> *"Un peu."*
> *"Anglais?"*
> *"Parfaitement."*
> *"Et puit, vous êtes Américaine."*
> *"Qui n'est pas?"* (89–90)[25]

5. Hapgood's adaptation of a phrase familiar from the McCarthy era when Fay refuses to believe he is not a doctor: "I am not now, nor have I ever been, a member of the medical profession" (124).

6. The names of the "cookies," which include allusions to prominent figures associated with either Communism or strongly leftist ideals, beginning with "Engels, David J." (127, repeated 129 and 130); later identified "cookies" include Susie B. Anthony, Herman Brecht, Rodney Chaplin, and Salvatore Gandhi (171–2).

7. The list of negative epithets hurled by the crowd, headed by "Communist" and also including "Red," "Pink," "Foreigner," and "Egghead" (171).

To be sure, the idealism espoused in *Anyone Can Whistle* is that of nonconformity, which was not only trendy in the 1960s, but also characteristically American in its fostering of individualism. Indeed, the show's most pointed barb aimed at *The Music Man* is that the latter's enforced conformity, symbolized by the band, is opposed to the human and creates environments in which chaos and madness are the only appropriate alternatives. It would thus be easy enough to read *The Music Man*, from the perspective of *Anyone Can Whistle*'s satirically presented parades, as anti-American, and that circumstance alone suggests why *Anyone Can Whistle* was probably doomed from the start. How probable is it that an audience, after having their core sensibilities mocked by the scattershot barrage of *Anyone Can Whistle* and watching the ridiculed conformity of "A-1 March" —which provokes Schub to observe, "the rabble worships anyone who tells 'em they belong to anything" (112)—will feel sufficiently validated to go out humming any of its (actually quite hummable) tunes? Given that Broadway trades fundamentally on its audience's desire to join in, to become part of the group through shared song, throwing that back at them as insultingly as does *Anyone Can Whistle* seems a sure recipe for the disaster that ensued. In "challenging" their audience, Laurents and Sondheim had gone too far.[26]

Anyone Can Whistle stands apart from *The Music Man*, and the Broadway attitude it exemplifies, in creating a situation in which redemption can happen, not *through* community, but only by opposing or standing apart from community. All of the Laurents–Sondheim shows involve this kind of necessary estrangement, and it thereafter became a pattern for Sondheim, often experienced as alienation. Notably, this situational dynamic is *not* true of *A Funny Thing Happened on the Way to the Forum*, which, like most mainstream Broadway shows, successfully reconstitutes its community in the end, with its romantic couple front and center. But Sondheim's later shows mainly follow the lead of *Anyone Can Whistle. Company* (1970), for example, barely rescues its alienated protagonist through its odd semblance of community. Moreover, while this resolution was virtually demanded by preview audiences, Sondheim himself regarded it as a "copout," even though having to rewrite the caustic "Happily Ever After" gave him the opportunity to revisit (and reinterpret) a key claim made by *Anyone Can Whistle*'s charismatic Hapgood, that there is but one genuine miracle, "Being Alive" (107).[27]

Most of Sondheim's shows involve even less hospitable worlds. *Sweeney Todd* (1979) unfolds within a version of Industrial Revolution–era London that directly mirrors the distorted perspective of Todd himself.[28] In the fairytale world of *Into the Woods* (1986), the kingdom is laid waste, the princes are useless womanizers, their brides are justifiably ambivalent, and many sympathetic characters die. Both *Follies* (1971) and *Merrily We Roll Along* (1981), in resurrecting the promises of youth, invite the bitter conviction that the inevitable complement of such promises is disillusionment, and that there are two fundamental choices (for Americans, implicitly): to sell out or to fail. That is *not* the situation in act 1 of *Sunday in the Park with George* (1984), where George's inhospitable choice is between art and conventional romance, but it *becomes* the choice, as if by default, in act 2 when the scene shifts to twentieth-century America (whose citizens are as susceptible to trendy art as *Anyone Can Whistle*'s are to trendy psychology). *Pacific Overtures* (1976) overtly presents America as the principal villain in the "opening up" of Japan; more fundamentally, it too sees promise (Manjiro's infatuation with America) as doomed to disappointment and bitterness. Indeed, a strong sense of alienation, with at least some edge of bitterness, drives the plots of most of Sondheim's post-Laurents musicals, including *Company, Follies, A Little Night Music* (even though, in the end, all are redeemed), *Pacific Overtures, Sweeney Todd* (even though, in the end, some are rescued), *Merrily We Roll Along, Sunday in the Park with George* (even given its transgenerational redemption, courtesy of the temporal transcendence of art), *Assassins* (Off-Broadway 1990, Broadway 2004), and *Passion* (1994). In some, such as *Passion*, the choice between redemption and community is as stark as in *Anyone Can Whistle*.

But the fullest culmination of the contradictions that bedevil *Anyone Can Whistle* may be found in *Assassins* (though the latter's emergence as a repertory staple has demonstrated that it is far more viable as theater). The most direct assault on the audience in *Anyone Can Whistle* occurs with the close of act 1, when Hapgood, suddenly alone on a quieted and darkened stage, turns to the audience to say, "You are all mad" —whereupon, after a blackout, the rest of the cast reappears in onstage theater seats to applaud and laugh at the actual audience (80). This invitation for the audience suddenly to see *themselves* as escapees from the Cookie Jar directly anticipates the final curtain of *Assassins*, when the assembled assassins turn to the audience, aim their guns, and fire.[29] There are, however, several key differences between the parallel dramatic gestures. Hapgood is a sympathetic character, whose own madness has yet to be either revealed or beatified (as will happen across the subsequent two acts), whereas the assassins, although rendered understandably human, pitiable if not sympathetic, are established psychopaths who have proven themselves to be our enemies. John Wilkes Booth, in particular—*Assassins*' Pied Piper—though suave and persuasive, is also rendered unsympathetic in key ways, not least by his climactic accusation against Lincoln as "nigger-lovin'" in "Ballad of Booth." The end of *Assassins*, then, reminds us that we are all the victims of the assassins, that whatever sympathy we may have felt for them, they are *our* enemies, *America's* enemies.[30]

That *Assassins* is, still today, sometimes read as anti-American—whereas there has never been a more fiercely pro-American show on Broadway—probably comes down to a confusion of types and gestures, through which the refracted edge of pastiche might pass unnoticed (e.g., seeing "Another National Anthem" as celebratory), the delivery of effective theater translates into sympathy irrespective of content (e.g., seeing Booth's verbal mastery over Lee Harvey Oswald as triumphant), and prior assumptions allow subject matter to eclipse its treatment. Thus, *Anyone Can Whistle*, simply by raising the issues of Communism and anti-Communism, provokes assumptions that are hard to dislodge, even if the individualism actually advocated by the show is neither Communist nor capitalist (or anti-Communist), but necessarily opposed to all of the above. It is these tendencies that have made it necessary for Sondheim, repeatedly, to dissociate himself from the ghost of Bertolt Brecht, however much he may owe to him, both because Sondheim insists on more nuance than Brecht typically provides, and because Brecht's established leftist profile, however it might seem to line up with Sondheim's liberal bent, is actually quite incompatible with it, given Sondheim's concern, both dramatically and politically, for safeguarding the essential individual liberties through which happiness might be pursued.

AMERICA'S SONDHEIM: THE KENNEDY CENTER SERIES

In summer 2002, the Kennedy Center mounted an ambitious "Sondheim Celebration," a retrospective miniseason of six Sondheim shows, including *Sweeney Todd, Company, Sunday in the Park with George, Merrily We Roll Along, Passion*, and *A Little Night Music*. The choices were interesting, providing a daring mix of popular and less popular shows, but avoiding the more controversially political shows, *Anyone Can Whistle, Pacific Overtures*, and *Assassins*. This latter-day version of the Hammerstein compromise (if that's what it is) may be understandable, given the setting in the nation's capital—although a Japanese-language version of *Pacific Overtures* was staged at the Kennedy Center shortly after, following its transplantation from Tokyo to New York. But even if the setting did not play a role in the selection of shows, it nevertheless had political significance, for it wrested the importance of Sondheim away from Broadway and—with the Kennedy Center acting as a kind of national cultural custodian—literally placed his work on a national stage.[31] It was, moreover, a huge success, on all levels, not only delivering versions of each show that were received well by both critics and audiences, but also removing Sondheim from the stigma of generating "poor box office," since, on the day tickets went on sale, the event broke the single-day sales record for the Kennedy Center.

It is probably too easy, if also compelling, simply to see this event as part of a Sondheimian scenario, in which he in the end finds "redemption" in the form of deserved recognition, thus triumphing over a harsh commercial environment. Certainly there are many signs that the embrace of Sondheim's musicals as a national treasure will be a lasting one. It has become increasingly hard to tabulate (or even categorize) the array of tributes, compilations, and revues based on his work that have accumulated over the decades since *Sondheim: A Musical Tribute* (1973) and *Side by Side by Sondheim* (1976 in London, 1977 on Broadway). Many of his shows have become staples of regional and local repertory, often representing the year's "stretch" show for the company involved. Professional revivals, often with deliberately limited runs (emulating the strategy of the Kennedy Center Celebration) have done exceptionally well, and have often allowed additional honing of shows whose problems were not fully resolved in their initial Broadway runs. Thus, the Kennedy Center Celebration gave *Merrily We Roll Along*, *Sunday in the Park with George*, and *Passion* a chance to be reconsidered both in their staging and by audiences, and the limited run of *Assassins* on Broadway (2004) presented a deftly reimagined and (by most accounts) more effective staging of the show than its original Off-Broadway run. Sondheim's work for Broadway has survived both scaling down and scaling up, generating renewed respect not only as viable theater even in low-budget regional and local productions, in John Doyle's cast-as-orchestra versions for Broadway of *Sweeney Todd* (2005) and *Company* (2006), and in the scaled-back orchestrations of *Sunday in the Park with George* (2008) and *A Little Night Music* (2009),[32] but also as first-rate music on a grand scale, with well-received "concert versions," especially of *Follies* (1985, 2007) and *Sweeney Todd* (1999, 2000, 2001). It is a gratifying, affirmative story, worthy of both Golden Age Broadway and of Sondheim's reconsideration of that legacy.

SONDHEIM'S AMERICA; AMERICA'S SONDHEIM

Nevertheless, this strong telling of the story requires some additional nuance, if it is to remain true to the standard of honesty Sondheim strives for in his shows. First, while the Kennedy Center Celebration and other limited runs of his musicals have indeed mitigated the pressure of making money on a new Broadway show, it is short-sighted to suggest, as many have, that it makes better sense to think of Sondheim's work in the context of operatic traditions, where limited runs are the expectation, and where no one aims for full houses for eight performances a week across a multiyear span. For better or worse, it is the latter environment—commercial Broadway—and the tradition of collective affirmation that flows from that environment, that provide the foundation and context for the body of work we now prize.

However we may want to spin things as historians and critics, the fact remains that Sondheim created his shows through his continued and only rarely successful attempts to meet the challenge of producing commercially viable musical theatre. Furthermore, it is highly doubtful that America would now be claiming him as theirs with the same passion had he not first tried to meet that challenge by, in turn (and at nearly every turn), directly challenging audiences in Broadway theaters. Broadway may not fully or adequately represent "America," but it is considerably more "American" than opera and its attendant sensibilities and pretensions could ever be, and it has served as the default—and, arguably, requisite—venue for Sondheim's America. And we care a great deal more about Sondheim because of his Broadway setting—his struggles, his failures, his triumphs—than if his way had been made easier by a less demanding commercial environment.

It is in the end too tempting to forgo noting that the ambivalences and situation of Hapgood in *Anyone Can Whistle* parallel Sondheim's to a considerable extent. Whatever we think of Hapgood as a character, he would have been considerably less dramatically viable without Cora and her henchmen to struggle against, and without Fay to fight for. If we might imagine a Hapgood and Fay in later years having come into their own, still living in the town of *Anyone Can Whistle* (inevitably become a better place through their continued opposition to its less admirable tendencies), we could never imagine them in those later years at all if they had somehow bypassed the traumas they undergo in *Anyone Can Whistle*. So, too, with Sondheim's America—which, along with its Broadway setting, ultimately determines everything about America's Sondheim.

If, as I've suggested, *Anyone Can Whistle*'s unnamed town may serve as a stand-in for Broadway (and thus, for America)—replete with cynical establishment and gullible populace—the show may seem prophetic for the short term in showing that town unable to take the full measure of its glib yet earnest new arrival, who seems initially willing to play his part but in the end is compelled by his own ambivalent nature not only to seek his own path, but also to remain in town, unable to leave. In the longer term, Sondheim matters to America because he, like Hapgood and Harold Hill, got his foot caught in the door.

NOTES

1. There are occasional exceptions, generally owing to a perceived "Communist" content, most notoriously with Marc Blitzstein's pro-union *The Cradle Will Rock* (1937), whose funding by the Federal Theatre Project was withdrawn due to budget cuts the day before the show was to open. But the list of shows that critique America while remaining central to the tradition is substantial, including among others (through the so-called "golden age" and choosing one representative per decade): *Show Boat* (1927), *Of Thee I Sing* (1931), *South Pacific* (1949), *West Side Story* (1957), and *How to Succeed in Business without Really Trying* (1961).

2. I discuss the issue of "authenticity" as a criterion of value, detailing its roots and its negative effect on the cultural standing of musicals, in "Performance, Authenticity, and the Reflexive Idealism of the American Musical," in *The Oxford Handbook of the American Musical*, ed. Raymond Knapp, Mitchell Morris, and Stacy Wolf, 408–21 (New York: Oxford University Press, 2011).

3. The important exceptions to this relative neglect are Michael C. Adams, "The Lyrics of Stephen Sondheim: Form and Function" (PhD diss., Northwestern University, 1980), 75–124; Stephen Banfield, *Sondheim's Broadway Musicals* (Ann Arbor: University of Michigan Press, 1993), 123–45; and Scott Miller, *Rebels with Applause: Broadway's Groundbreaking Musicals* (Portsmouth, NH: Heinemann, 2001), 48–65. My discussion is indebted, in different ways, to all three, as well as to Craig Zadan's and Meryle Secrest's discussions of the show in their biographies (Zadan, *Sondheim & Co.*, 2nd ed., New York: Harper and Row, 1986; and Secrest, *Stephen Sondheim; A Life*, New York: Alfred A. Knopf, 1998).

4. For more on the mixed-race aspect of *Show Boat*, see Knapp, *The American Musical and the Formation of National Identity* (Princeton: Princeton University Press, 2005), 185–94; Todd Decker, "Black/White Encounters on the American Musical Stage and Screen (1924–2005)," PhD diss., University of Michigan, 2007; and Decker, "'Do You Want to Hear a Mammy Song?' A Historiography of Show Boat," *Contemporary Theatre Review* 19, no. 1 (2009): 8–21. Regarding the tragic mulatta figure, see Sterling Brown, *Negro Poetry and Drama and the Negro in American Fiction* (New York: Atheneum, 1969); Donald Bogle, *Toms, Coons, Mulattoes, Mammies, & Bucks* (New York: Continuum, 1973; 3rd ed. 1994); and Teresa C. Zackodnik, *The Mulatta and the Politics of Race* (Jackson: University Press of Mississippi, 2004). Especially as used in *Show Boat*, the "tragic mulatta" is akin also to pre-Stonewall films (and a distressing number of post-Stonewall films) that treat outed homosexuals sympathetically but end with their quasiritualistic sacrifices; regarding this trope, see Vito Ruso, *The Celluloid Closet: Homosexuality in the Movies*, rev. ed. (New York: Harper and Row, 1987).

5. I discuss the historical distortions or omissions of several of these shows in Knapp, *American Musical and National Identity*, 122–34, 230–39, and 261–8. For related discussions of the political contexts—and political consequences—of Rodgers and Hammerstein's shows, see also Bruce A. McConachie, "The 'Oriental' Musicals of Rodgers and Hammerstein and the U.S. War in Southeast Asia," *Theatre Journal* 46, no. 3 (1994): 385–98; Andrea Most, "'You've Got to Be Carefully Taught': The Politics of Race in Rodgers and Hammerstein's *South Pacific*," *Theatre Journal* 52, no. 3 (2000): 307–37, and *Making Americans: Jews and the Broadway Musical* (Cambridge, MA: Harvard University Press, 2004), which includes her essay on *South Pacific*; and Christina Klein, *Cold War Orientalism: Asia in the Middlebrow Imagination, 1945–1961* (Berkeley, Los Angeles, and London: University of California Press, 2003).

6. For all the shows discussed, Hammerstein wrote both books and lyrics, except for *The Sound of Music* (book by Lindsey and Crouse), for which he was credited as coproducer and lyricist.

7. For a detailed and nuanced account of how these compromises operate in *South Pacific*, see Most, "'You've Got to Be Carefully Taught.'"

8. See Knapp, *American Musical and National Identity*, 268–280, and Knapp, "Marking Time in *Pacific Overtures*: Reconciling East, West, and History within the Theatrical Now of a Broadway Musical," in *Musicological Identities: Essays in Honor of Susan McClary*, ed. Steven Baur, Raymond Knapp, and Jacqueline Warwick, 163–76 (Aldershot, UK: Ashgate, 2008).

9. This quoted line from "Next" in *Pacific Overtures* may refer obliquely to a lyric from "Getting to Know You" in *The King and I*—"By your pupils you'll be taught" —which Sondheim understood to be the point of reference for Hammerstein's inscription to him on a family portrait shortly before he died: "For Stevie, my Friend and Teacher" (Secrest, *Sondheim*, 142–3). The connection between these lines is also indicated by the title and

first epigraph of Andrew Milner's "'Let the Pupil Show the Master': Stephen Sondheim and Oscar Hammerstein II," in *Stephen Sondheim: A Casebook*, ed. Joanne Gordon, 153–69 (New York and London: Garland, 1997), an essay that deftly traces a number of other significant connections—and disconnects—between this particular master and pupil.

10. See Zadan, *Sondheim & Co.*, 21–2, for Sondheim's familiar critique of his lyric for "I Feel Pretty." (Sondheim reports with obviously lasting chagrin how his pride in the song's witty lyric was burst when the plausibility that an unsophisticated immigrant girl would express herself this way was questioned.)

11. Fay Apple, in Arthur Laurents and Stephen Sondheim, *Anyone Can Whistle: A Musical Fable* (New York: Random House, 1965), 36. All subsequent references to this source will be given in parentheses in the text.

12. In categories where the other show was not in competition, *West Side Story* won one additional Tony (Best Scenic Designer), and *The Music Man* two (Best Actor, Best Featured Actor).

13. To be sure, much the same could also be said of Willson, who had developed *The Music Man* over the same period, and had a similar personal investment in its material and setting. Reflecting its original focus, Laurents's earlier draft was entitled *East Side Story*.

14. Two of the other three categories (Director, Featured Actor) went to *Fiorello!* (which tied with *The Sound of Music* for Best Musical); the third (Costume Designer) went to *Saratoga*.

15. Regarding the implicit presence of America in *The Sound of Music*, see Knapp, "History, *The Sound of Music*, and Us," *American Music* 22 (2004), 133–44; see also Knapp, *American Musical and National Identity*, 228–39.

16. Laurents and Sondheim also collaborated on *Do I Hear a Waltz?* (1965), with Sondheim contributing lyrics to a score by Richard Rodgers, who also produced. While their unhappiness with the collaboration and disappointment with the show stemmed mainly from frictions between Rodgers and the two of them, it was in fact the successful *Do I Hear a Waltz?*, rather than the unsuccessful *Anyone Can Whistle*, that effectively ended their Broadway partnership, although their friendship endured.

17. Ironically, *Anyone Can Whistle*'s primary producer was Kermit Bloomgarden, who had also produced *The Music Man*.

18. The quoted phrase refers obliquely to the idea of "planned obsolescence," which maintains that capitalism requires that its consumer products be built to wear out, or become outmoded or simply unstylish, so that there will be a continuing need for more, similarly temporary products. The term originated during the Great Depression (Bernard London, *Ending the Depression through Planned Obsolescence*, published as a pamphlet in 1932), a context directly evoked by *Anyone Can Whistle*'s "terrible depression all over the town" (10). The phrase was reintroduced by Brooks Stevens in 1954, and its ideas formed the basis for pop sociologist Vance Packard's *The Waste Makers* (New York: McKay, 1959), an influential "exposé " of American capitalism allied in spirit to his earlier *The Hidden Persuaders* (New York: Pocket Books, 1957), which accused the advertising industry of using "subliminal suggestion" and other nefarious means to manipulate the buying habits (and voting practices) of consumers.

19. *Anyone Can Whistle* also seems specifically responsive to the world of *West Side Story*, with the concluding song, "With So Little to Be Sure Of," rejecting the postponed paradise of "Somewhere" in favor of pragmatic accommodation to real-world possibilities for happiness. Thus, the lyric of "With So Little to Be Sure of " may be read as an overt rejection of "Someday! / Somewhere, / We'll find a new way of living" in favor of "Everything that's here and now and us together."

20. See Banfield, *Sondheim's Broadway Musicals*, 143–4 for another discussion of Hapgood's relationship to Hill; in particular, Banfield notes with telling detail *Anyone Can Whistle*'s inversion of the "metaphor of music and its instruments standing for the motivating conditions of life."

21. Traditionally, the aggrieved Pied Piper, after the town refuses to pay him for solving their rat problem, uses his music to lure all the town's children to a mysterious fate, save one who is lame and unable to follow (in some tellings, other children with infirmities also escape, including a deaf child and/or a blind child). *The Music Man* at one point had two "infirm" children, a spastic boy and a lisping boy, who were then conflated into Winthrop, with the spastic element eliminated; see Meredith Willson's account of this transformation in *"But He Doesn't Know the Territory"* (New York: Putnam's, 1959). It is at least possible that Baby Joan's trances derive from the "spastic" element eliminated from *The Music Man*. *Anyone Can Whistle*, in which music is *not* the agent of the town's delivery, refers explicitly to the Pied Piper, when Hapgood tells Fay about his trumpet ("I thought it was loud enough to waken the dying. Turns out I'm only the Pied Piper for lunatics," 127). *The Music Man* also alludes to the Pied Piper, but more obliquely, when in the opening number ("Rock Island") Harold Hill's success as a "music man" is summed up with the repeated phrase, "When the man dances, certainly boys, what else? The piper pays him!"

22. The situational parallels between these shows find at least a faint echo in *The Sound of Music*, which like *The Music Man* has as its main character a Pied Piper figure, a stranger who rescues a community (household) through music, with a focus on its at-risk children, and with—veering toward *Anyone Can Whistle*—a romantic attachment to this stranger offering emotional rescue to the stern character responsible for its most at-risk population, who has previously erred in achieving an effective balance between empathy and discipline. In both *The Music Man* and *The Sound of Music*, the backdrop is, implicitly, a rosy (but definitely not pink!) snapshot of America: River City as small-town America in a more innocent time, and the America that would welcome the Family von Trapp as refugees.

23. Adams, Banfield, and Miller all note this division, with somewhat differing bases. Banfield's distinction between pastiche-based divertissement numbers and original "symphonic" numbers (see his chart, *Sondheim's Broadway Musicals*, 136) provides a particularly useful mapping of the show's disparate sensibilities, although his distinction is not always easy to enforce. "Come Play with [wiz] Me," for example, is clearly Cole Porter pastiche, yet so sympathetically rendered that it becomes indistinguishable from the type itself, and functions more like an homage. Thus, for example, the song seems to delight in extending the bilingual verbal play of the final four words of Fay's part of the song ("*Mais oui!* / We may") into the melodic setting, reversing direction while replicating the notes and rhythm of "*Mais oui*" for "We may" (A–C/A–C; cf. Banfield, *Sondheim's Broadway Musicals*, 145). Here, the wit of the type itself merges easily with the wit of extending the type and—most importantly—with the flirtatious frisson between Fay and Hapgood. Moreover, this merger of type, sensibility, and dramatic moment makes this song, despite its archness, seem both genuine and distinctively theirs, contributing to the redemptive (Banfield's "symphonic") side of the score. This kind of alignment—deriving from homage rather than pastiche—becomes the mainstay of *A Little Night Music* (1973).

24. Banfield sees Cora's song as the "trio" in the act's recurring "A-1 March" (*Sondheim's Broadway Musicals*, 138), which reinforces her marginalization in musical terms. A similar formal hierarchy ultimately works to her advantage and against Fay and Hapgood, since the couple's emergence in act 2 functions as the "trio" for the musical as a whole, as discussed below.

25. During this segment, English translations are provided to the audience as subtitles, as "in an old French sex film" (87): "Excuse me: do you speak French? / A little. / English? / Perfectly. / Then you're an American. / Who isn't?"

26. For similar arguments regarding the problems with *Anyone Can Whistle*, see Scott Miller, *Rebels with Applause*. Zadan and Secrest recount the many professional and interpersonal factors that also contributed to its failure.

27. See my related discussions of this song in Knapp, *The American Musical and the Performance of Personal Identity* (Princeton: Princeton University Press, 2006), 300–303; "'How great thy charm, thy sway how excellent!': Tracing Gilbert and Sullivan's Legacy in the American Musical," in *The Cambridge Companion to Gilbert and Sullivan*, ed. David Eden and Meinhard Saremba, 201–215 (Cambridge, UK: Cambridge University Press, 2009); and "Temporality and Control in Sondheim's Middle Period: From *Company* to *Sunday in the Park with George*," in *Time: Sense, Space and Structure*, ed. Nancy van Deusen and Lenny Koff (Leiden: Brill, forthcoming). Regarding Sondheim's "copout" comment, see Zadan, *Sondheim & Co.*, 125.

28. See related discussions in Knapp, *American Musical and Personal Identity*, 335–7, and "Temporality and Control."

29. The ending is played differently in different productions, sometimes having the assassins turning back away from the audience to fire at presidential targets at the back of the stage; either way, it is clear that the assassins' assault is directed *against* the audience. *Anyone Can Whistle*'s strategy of encouraging identification is also recalled, chillingly, in the final scene of the film version of *Cabaret* (1972), with its images of audience members in Nazi uniforms reflected in distorted mirrors.

30. For related arguments, see Knapp, "*Assassins, Oklahoma!* and the 'Shifting Fringe of Dark Around the Campfire,'" *Cambridge Opera Journal* 16 (2004): 77–101.

31. The significance of this move is astutely noted in John Rockwell's overview of the event in the *New York Times*, "Sondheim Has His Shrine, and It's Not on Broadway," *New York Times*, August 18, 2002. http://www.nytimes.com/2002/08/18/theater/music-sondheim-has-his-shrine-and-it-s-not-on-broadway.html?pagewanted=all&src=pm.

32. Regarding the latter, and for insightful reflections on the resilience of Sondheim's shows, see Patrick Healy, "Making His Entrance Again, Intimately," *New York Times*, January 4, 2010, C1.1 and 5.

Bibliography

Adams, Michael C. 1980. "The Lyrics of Stephen Sondheim: Form and Function." PhD diss., Northwestern University, Evanston, IL.

Adler, Thomas P. 1979. "The Musical Dramas of Stephen Sondheim: Some Critical Approaches." *Journal of Popular Culture* 12 (3): 513–525.

Anon. 1974. "Stephen (Joshua) Sondheim." In *Current Biography Yearbook 1973*, ed. Charles Moritz, 386–389. New York: H. W. Wilson.

Banfield, Stephen. 1993. *Sondheim's Broadway Musicals.* Ann Arbor: University of Michigan Press.

——. 1996. "Sondheim and the Art that Has No Name." In *Approaches to the American Musical*, ed. Robert Lawson-Peebles, 137–160. Exeter: University of Exeter Press.

Bell, Arthur. 1973. "The Best and Worst of Sondheim." *Village Voice*, March 15, 60.

Bell, Marty. 1994. *Backstage on Broadway: Musicals and Their Makers.* London: Nick Hern.

Berkowitz, Gerald M. 1982. *New Broadway: Theatre across America, 1950–1980.* Totowa, NJ: Rowman and Littlefield.

Billington, Michael. 1987. "*Follies* Is a Show around which Legends Cluster." In *Follies. A Broadway Legend. The First Complete Recording.* Original London cast 1987 (First Nights Records Encore 3), liner notes, not paginated.

Block, Geoffrey. 1993. "Stephen Sondheim's *Assassins*." *American Music* 11 (4): 507–509.

——. 1997. *Enchanted Evenings: The Broadway Musical from "Show Boat" to Sondheim.* New York: Oxford University Press.

Blyton, Carey. 1984. "Sondheim's *Sweeney Todd*—The Case for the Defence." *Tempo* 149: 19–26.

Bordman, Gerald. 1981. *American Operetta: From* H.M.S. Pinafore *to* Sweeney Todd. New York: Oxford University Press.

——. 1992. *American Musical Comedy: From* Adonis *to* Dreamgirls. New York: Oxford University Press.

——. 1992. *American Musical Theatre: A Chronicle.* 2nd ed. New York: Oxford University Press.

Brubaker, Gary. 1985. "Thematic Unity in Steven [*sic*] Sondheim's *Merrily We Roll Along*." PhD diss., Northern Illinois University.

Brylawski, Samuel S. 1986. "Sondheim, Stephen (Joshua)." In *The New Grove Dictionary of American Music*, ed. H. Wiley Hitchcock and Stanley Sadie, vol. 4: R–Z. New York: Oxford University Press.

Cartmell, Dan J. 1983. "Stephen Sondheim and the Concept Musical." PhD diss., University of Santa Barbara. Ann Arbor: University Microfilms International.

Chapin, Ted. 2003. *Everything Was Possible: The Birth of the Musical "Follies".* New York: Applause.

Citron, Stephen. 1991. *The Musical: From the Inside Out*, London: Hodder and Stoughton.

——. 2001. *Sondheim and Lloyd-Webber: The New Musical.* New York: Oxford University Press.

Cohen, Matthew Isaac, and Phyllis M. Cohen. 2006. "Psychopathic Characters on the Stage of Stephen Sondheim." *Psychoanalytic Study of the Child* 61: 308–319.

Conrad, Jon Alan. 1986. "Taking Stock of Sondheim." *Opus* 2 (4): 30–35.

Dickar, Mary Lynn. 1980. "An Analysis of the Adaptation of *Sweeney Todd* into a Musical." PhD diss., University of Illinois, Chicago.

Dorgan, Charity Anne. 1982. "Stephen (Joshua) Sondheim." *Contemporary Authors* 103: 479–485.

Draper, Natalie. 2010. "Concept meets Narrative in Sondheim's *Company*: Metadrama as a Method of Analysis." *Studies in Musical Theatre* 4 (2): 171–183.

Druxman, Michael B. 1980. *The Musical: From Broadway to Hollywood*. London: Yoseloff.

Engel, Lehman. 1977. *The Making of a Musical*. New York: Macmillan.

——. 1979. *The American Musical Theater*. 2nd, rev. ed. New York: Macmillan.

——. 1981. *Words with Music: The Broadway Musical Libretto*. 2nd ed. New York: Macmillan.

——. 1984. "The Condition of the American Musical Today." In *Musical Theatre in America: Papers and Proceedings of the Conference on the Musical Theatre in America*, ed. Glenn Loney, 13–20. Westport: Greenwood (Contributions in Drama and Theatre Studies 8).

Everett, William A., and Paul R. Laird, eds. 2002. *The Cambridge Companion to the Musical*. Cambridge, UK: Cambridge University Press.

Ewen, David. 1970. *New Complete Book of the American Musical Theater*. New York: Henry Holt.

Finkle, David. 1976. "Stephen Sondheim. Send in the Heart, Where Is the Heart?" *Village Voice*, January 12, 93–94.

Flinn, Denny Martin. 1997. *Musical! A Grand Tour: The Rise, Glory, and Fall of an American Institution*. New York: Schirmer.

Freedman, Samuel G. 1984. "The Words and Music of Stephen Sondheim." *New York Times Magazine*, April 1, 22–32, 60.

Gänzl, Kurt. 1997. *The Musical: A Concise History*. Boston: Northeastern University Press.

Given, John. 2011. "Creating the Outsider's Political Identity: Nathan Lane's Dionysus." *Helios* 38 (2): 221–236.

Goodhart, Sandor, ed. 2000. *Reading Stephen Sondheim: A Collection of Critical Essays*. New York: Garland.

Gordon, Joanne. 1992. *Art Isn't Easy: The Theater of Stephen Sondheim*. New York: Da Capo.

——, ed. 1997. *Stephen Sondheim: A Casebook*. New York: Garland.

Gottfried, Martin. 1984. *Broadway Musicals*. 2nd ed. New York: Harry N. Abrams.

——. 1991. *More Broadway Musicals since 1980*. New York: Harry N. Abrams.

——. 1993. *Sondheim*. New York: Harry N. Abrams.

Grant, Annette. 1994. "Line by Line by Sondheim. One Song, Start to Finish: a Music Lesson." *New York Times Magazine*, March 20, 42–45.

Green, Stanley. 1984. *The World of Musical Comedy: The Story of the American Musical Stage as Told through the Careers of Its Foremost Composers and Lyricists*. 4th rev. ed. New York: Da Capo.

——. 1984. *Encyclopedia of the Musical Theatre*. 2nd ed. New York: Da Capo.

——. 2010. *Broadway Musicals: Show by Show*. 6th ed. London and Boston: Applause.

Grinenko, Aleksei. 2012. "*Follies* Embodied: A Kleinian Perspective." *Studies in Musical Theatre* 6 (3): 317–324.

Hattersley, Roy. 1995. "Send Him the Crown." *Times Magazine*, October 14, 27.

Henry III., William. 1986. "More than Song and Dance: With Each Show, Stephen Sondheim Redefines the Musical." *Time Magazine* (US ed.), June 16, 59.

Herbert, Trevor. 1989. "Sondheim's Technique." *Contemporary Music Review* 5 (1): 199–214.

Herrera, Brian Eugenio. 2012. "Compiling *West Side Story's* Parahistories, 1949–2009." *Theatre Journal* 64 (2): 231–247.

Hirsch, Foster. 2005. *Harold Prince and the American Musical Theatre*. Rev. and expanded ed. New York: Applause.

Hirst, David. 1985. "The American Musical and the American Dream: from *Show Boat* to Sondheim." *New Theatre Quarterly* 1 (1): 24–38.

Hischak, Thomas S. 1991. *Word Crazy: Broadway Lyricists from Cohan to Sondheim*. New York: Praeger.

Holden, Stephen. 1984. "The Passion of Stephen Sondheim." *Atlantic Monthly* 254 (6): 121–123.

Horowitz, Mark Eden. 2003. *Sondheim on Music: Minor Details and Major Decisions*. Lanham, MD, and Oxford: Scarecrow.

Huber, Eugene Robert. 1990. "Stephen Sondheim and Harold Prince: Collaborative Contributions to the Development of the Modern Concept Musical, 1970–1981." PhD diss., New York University.

Ilson, Carol. 1992. *Harold Prince*. New York: Limelight.

Jackson, Arthur. 1977. *The Best Musicals: From "Show Boat" to "A Chorus Line."* Broadway, Off-Broadway, London. New York: Crown.

Jones, John Bush. 2003. *Our Musicals Ourselves: A Social History of the American Musical Theater*. Waltham, MA: Brandeis University Press.

Jubin, Olaf. 2010. "Experts without Expertise? Findings of a Comparative Study of American, British and German-Language Reviews of Musicals by Stephen Sondheim and Andrew Lloyd Webber." *Studies in Musical Theatre* 4 (2): 185–197.

——. 2012. "There's No Escaping Nostalgia: The 1987 London Version of *Follies*." *Studies in Musical Theatre* 6 (2): 199–212.

Kasha, Al, and Joel Hirschhorn. 1985. *Notes on Broadway: Intimate Conversations with the Great Songwriters*. Chicago: Simon and Schuster.

Kimmel, Bruce. 1997. "Sondheim at the Movies?" *Sondheim at the Movies* (Varèse Sarabande Records VSD-5805), liner notes, not paginated.

Kislan, Richard. 1995. *The Musical: A Look at the American Musical Theater*. 2nd, rev. and expanded ed. New York: Applause.

Knapp, Raymond. 2005. *The American Musical and the Formation of National Identity*. Princeton: Princeton University Press.

——. 2006. *The American Musical and the Performance of Personal Identity*. Princeton: Princeton University Press.

Knapp, Raymond, Mitchell Morris, and Stacy Wolf, eds. 2011. *The Oxford Handbook of the American Musical*. New York: Oxford University Press.

Konas, Gary Paul. 1993. "From Gershwin to Sondheim: The Pulitzer Prize-winning Musicals." PhD diss., University of California, Davis.

Lahr, John. 1979. "Sondheim's Little Deaths: the Ironic Mode and Its Discontents." *Harper's* 258 (1547): 71–78.

Laufe, Abe. 1977. *Broadway's Greatest Musicals*. 4th ed. London: Funk and Wagnalls.

Leer, David van. 1987. "Putting It Together: Sondheim and the Broadway Musical." *Raritan* 7 (2): 113–128.

Lewine, Richard, Betty Comden, Sheldon Harnick, Stephen Sondheim, and Jule Styne. 1985. "The Anatomy of the Theater Song." In *Broadway Song and Story: Playwrights, Lyricists, Composers Discuss their Hits*, ed. Otis L. Guernsey Jr. and Terrence McNally, 320–330. New York: Dodd, Mead.

Mandelbaum, Ken. 1991. *Not since Carrie: 40 Years of Broadway Musical Flops*. New York: St. Martin's Griffin.

Mankin, Nina. 1988. "The *PAJ* Casebook #2 *Into the Woods*." *Performing Arts Journal* 11 (1): 46–66.

Martin, George. 1989. "On the Verge of Opera: Stephen Sondheim." *Opera Quarterly* 6 (3): 76–85.

Mast, Gerald. 1987. *Can't Help Singin': The American Musical on Stage and Screen*. Woodstock, NY: Overlook.

Mates, Julian. 1985. *America's Musical Stage: Two Hundred Years of Musical Theatre*. London: Praeger (Contributions in Drama and Theatre Studies 18).

McGill, Craig M. 2012. "Sondheim's Use of the 'Herrmann Chord' in *Sweeney Todd*." *Studies in Musical Theatre* 6 (3): 291–312.

McMillin, Scott. 2006. *The Musical as Drama: A Study of the Principles and Conventions behind Musical Shows from Kern to Sondheim*. Princeton: Princeton University Press.

McNally, Terrence, Leonard Bernstein, Arthur Laurents, Jerome Robbins, and Stephen Sondheim. 1985. "*West Side Story*." In *Broadway Song and Story: Playwrights, Lyricists, Composers Discuss their Hits*, ed. Otis L. Guernsey Jr. and Terrence McNally, 40–54. New York: Dodd, Mead.

McNally, Terrence, Arthur Laurents, Stephen Sondheim, and Jule Styne. 1985. "*Gypsy*." In *Broadway Song and Story: Playwrights, Lyricists, Composers Discuss their Hits*, Otis L. Guernsey Jr. and Terrence McNally, 55–74. New York: Dodd, Mead.

Michener, Charles. 1973. "Words and Music—by Sondheim." *Newsweek* (US ed.), April 23, 54–64.

Miller, D. A. 1998 *Place for Us: Essay on the Broadway Musical*. Cambridge, MA: Harvard University Press.

Milnes, Rodney. 1987. "*Follies*." *Opera* 38 (9): 1094–1096.

——. 1987. "*Pacific Overtures*." *Opera* 38 (11): 1317–1321.

Mollin, Alfred. 1991. "Mayhem and Morality in *Sweeney Todd*." *American Music* 9 (4): 405–417.

Mordden, Ethan. 1976. *Better Foot Forward: The History of American Musical Theatre*. New York: Viking.

——. 1981. *The American Theatre*. New York: Oxford University Press.

——. 1983. *Broadway Babies: The People Who Made the American Musical*. New York: Oxford University Press.

——. 1998. *Coming Up Roses: The Broadway Musical in the 1950s*. New York: Oxford University Press.

——. 2001. *Open a New Window: The Broadway Musical in the 1960s*. New York: Palgrave Macmillan.

——. 2003. *One Last Kiss: The Broadway Musical in the 1970s*. New York: Palgrave Macmillan.

——. 2004. *The Happiest Corpse I've Ever Seen. The Last 25 Years of the Broadway Musical*. New York: Palgrave Macmillan.

Morley, Sheridan. 1990. "Side by Side with the Sondheim Art." *Sunday Times Magazine*, March 4, 66–70.

——, ed. 1979. *The Stephen Sondheim Songbook: Words and Music by Stephen Sondheim [and others]*. London: Elm Tree.

Morley, Sheridan, and Ruth Leon. 1998. *Hey, Mr Producer! The Musical World of Cameron Mackintosh*. New York: Back Stage.

Most, Andrea. 2004. *Making Americans. Jews and the Broadway Musical*. Cambridge, MA: Harvard University Press.

Orchard, Lee Frederick. 1988. "Stephen Sondheim and the Disintegration of the American Dream: A Study of the Work of Stephen Sondheim from *Company* to *Sunday in the Park with George*." PhD diss., University of Oregon. Ann Arbor: University Microfilms International.

Peyser, Marc. 1998. "Send in the Fanatics. Who Needs a Hit? Stephen Sondheim's Got a Kult." *Newsweek*, May 25, Vol. 131, Issue 21, 73.

Prince, Hal. 1974. *Contradictions: Notes on Twenty-six Years in the Theatre*. New York: Dodd, Mead.

Prince, Harold, and Stephen Sondheim. 1985. "Author and Director: Musicals." In *Broadway Song and Story: Playwrights, Lyricists, Composers Discuss their Hits*, ed. Otis L. Guernsey Jr. and Terrence McNally, 355–370. New York: Dodd, Mead.

Ratcliffe, Michael. 1996. "Knock, Knock! Is Anybody There?" In *Company: Theatre Programme* [not paginated]. London: Dewynters PCL,.

Rich, Frank. 1984. "A Musical Theater Breakthrough: With *Sunday in the Park with George*, Stephen Sondheim Has Transcended Four Decades of Broadway History." *New York Times Magazine*, October 21, 52–66, 71.

——. 2000. "Conversations with Sondheim." *New York Times Magazine*, March 12. http://www.nytimes.com/library/magazine/home/20000312mag-sondheim.html.

Riley, Brian Patrick. 2010. "'It's Man Devouring Man, My Dear': Adapting *Sweeney Todd* for the Screen." *Literature Film Quarterly* 38 (3): 205–216.

Rockwell, John. 1983. "Urban Popular Song, the Broadway Musical, the Cabaret Revival and the Birth Pangs of American Opera: Stephen Sondheim." In *All American Music: Composition in the Late Twentieth Century*, ed. John Rockwell, 209–220. New York: Alfred A. Knopf.

Sams, Jeremy. 1987. "Sondheim's Operatic Overtures." *Opera* 38 (9): 1002–1007.

Savran, David. 1988. "Stephen Sondheim," In *In Their Own Words: Contemporary American Playwrights*, ed. David Savran, 223–239. New York: Theatre Communications Group.

——. 2012. "'You've Got That Thing': Cole Porter, Stephen Sondheim, and the Erotics of the List Song." *Theatre Journal* 64 (4): 533–548.

Schiff, Stephen. 1993. "Deconstructing Sondheim." *New Yorker*, March 8, 76–87.

Secrest, Meryle. 1998. *Stephen Sondheim: A Life*. New York: Alfred A. Knopf.

Sennett, Ted. 1998. *Song and Dance: The Musicals of Broadway*. New York: Metro.

Singer, Barry. 1993. *Unsung Sondheim* (Varèse Sarabande Records VSD-5433), liner notes, not paginated.

Smith, Cecil, and Glenn Litton. 1981. *Musical Comedy in America: From "The Black Crook" to "South Pacific," from "The King and I" to "Sweeney Todd"*. New York: Routledge.

Sondheim, Stephen. 1974. "Theater Lyrics." In *Playwrights, Lyricists, Composers on Theater: The Inside Story of a Decade of Theater in Articles and Comments by its Authors, Selected from their Own Publication*, ed. Otis L. Guernsey Jr., 61–97. *Dramatist's Guild Quarterly*. New York: Dodd, Mead.

——. 1980. "Larger than Life: Reflections on Melodrama and *Sweeney Todd*." In *Melodrama*, vol. 7, ed. Daniel Gerould, 3–14. New York: New York Literary Forum (New York Literary Forum 7).

——. 1981. "Composer's Note." In *Merrily We Roll Along*. Original Broadway cast recording (RCA Records CBL 1–4197), liner notes, not paginated.

——. 1985. "The Musical Theater." In *Broadway Song and Story: Playwrights, Lyricists, Composers Discuss their Hits*, ed. Otis L. Guernsey Jr. and Terrence McNally, 228–250. New York: Dodd, Mead.

——. 1999. "A Musical Isn't Built in a Day, but This Took 47 Years." *New York Times*, September 12. http://www.nytimes.com/archives.

——. 2010. *Finishing the Hat: Collected Lyrics (1954–1981) with Attendant Comments, Principles, Heresies, Grudges, Whines, and Anecdotes*. New York: Virgin.

——. 2011. *Look, I Made a Hat: Collected Lyrics (1981–2011) with Attendant Comments, Amplifications, Dogmas, Harangues, Digressions, Anecdotes and Miscellany*. New York: Virgin.

The Sondheim Review. 1994–2014.

Stempel, Larry. 2010. *Showtime: A History of the Broadway Musical Theater*. New York and London: W. W. Norton.

Steyn, Mark. 1997. *Broadway Babies Say Goodnight: Musicals Then and Now*. London: Faber.

Sullivan, Kathleen. 1989. "Stephen Sondheim.," In *American Playwrights since 1945: A Guide to Scholarship, Criticism, and Performance*, ed. Philip C. Kolin, 437–446. New York, Westport, and London: Greenwood.

Suskin, Steven. 2010. *Show Tunes 1905–1985: The Songs, Shows and Careers of Broadway's Major Composers*. 4th ed. New York: Oxford University Press.

——. 1990. *Opening Night on Broadway: A Critical Quotebook of the Golden Era of the Musical Theatre, "Oklahoma!" (1943) to "Fiddler on the Roof" (1964)*. New York: Schirmer.

——. 1997. *More Opening Nights on Broadway: A Critical Quotebook of the Musical Theatre 1965 through 1981*. New York: Schirmer.

Sutcliffe, Tom. 1973. "Coming up Rose's." *The Guardian*, May 29, 12.

Swain, Joseph P. 1990. *The Broadway Musical: A Critical and Musical Survey*. New York: Oxford University Press.

Swayne, Steve. 2004. "So Much 'More': The Music of *Dick Tracy*." *American Music* 22 (1): 50–63.

——. 2005. *How Sondheim Found his Sound*. Ann Arbor: University of Michigan Press.

——. 2007. "Remembering and Re-membering: Sondheim, the Waltz and *A Little Night Music*." *Studies in Musical Theatre* 1 (3): 259–273.

Symonds, Dominic. 2009. "Putting It Together and Finishing the Hat? Deconstructing the Art of Making Art." *Contemporary Theatre Review* 19 (1): 101–112.

Taylor, Millie. 2009. "Integration and Distance in Musical Theatre: the Case of *Sweeney Todd*." *Contemporary Theatre Review* 19 (1): 74–86.

Whitfield, Sarah. 2011. "Two Different Roads to New Musicals in 2011 London: *London Road* and *Road Show*." *Studies in Musical Theatre* 5 (3): 305–314.

Winer, Linda. 1985. "Sondheim in His Own Words." *American Theatre* 2 (2): 10–15, 42.

Wittke, Paul. 1980. "Review of *Sweeney Todd*." *Musical Quarterly* 66 (2): 309–314.

Wolf, Stacy. 2012. *Changed for Good: A Feminist History of the Broadway Musical*. New York: Oxford University Press.

Zadan, Craig. 1989. *Sondheim & Co*. 2nd rev. ed. New York: Harper and Row.

Zinsser, William K. 1961. "On Stage: Stephen Sondheim." *Horizon* 3 (7): 98–99.

INDEX

Page numbers in *italics* indicate illustrations. Numbers followed by "n" or *t* indicate notes or tables.

Lightning Source UK Ltd.
Milton Keynes UK
UKOW05f0654210816

281005UK00001B/10/P